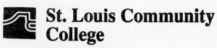

THE MYTHS OF THE OPOSSUM

THE
MYTHS
OF THE
OPOSSUM

University of New Mexico Press

Albuquerque

Pathways of
Mesoamerican
Mythology

ALFREDO LOPEZ AUSTIN

Translated by
Bernard R. Ortiz de Montellano
Thelma Ortiz de Montellano

To Martha Rosario

Opossum stamp motifs from *Design Motifs of Ancient Mexico*, Jorge Enciso, Dover Publications, Inc.

Library of Congress Cataloging-in-Publication Data
López Austin, Alfredo.
   [Mitos del tlacuache. English]
   The myths of the opossum: pathways of Mesoamerican mythology /
Alfredo López Austin; translated by Bernard R. Ortiz de Montellano,
Thelma Ortiz de Montellano.
      p.   cm.
   Includes bibliographical references and index.
   ISBN 0–8263–1394–9
   1. Indians of Mexico—Religion and mythology.   2. Indians of Cen-
tral America—Religion and mythology.   3. Indians of Mexico—Folklore.
4. Indians of Central America—Folklore.   5. Opossums—Folklore.
F1219.3.R38L713   1993
299'.72–dc20
92-27258
CIP

CONTENTS

ILLUSTRATIONS

Figures

Tables

PREFACE

Nothing is easier than blaming the gods for our acts, and I use that excuse. I have followed many different paths looking for the origin, order, and the significance of the Mesoamerican gods. This essay is the result of one stage of that search. A large part of the wanderings of my journey and of the diversity of my paths are reflected in it. There will be smooth chapters, stretching out like a plain; some will be winding, and others will seem far from the goal. But in spite of such appearances, all of them are directed at elucidating a religious thought, thousands of years old, and the presence in it of an enchanting protagonist in the myths—the opossum. The reader will find that—as in detective stories—the strands will come together. But in contrast to detective stories, they will meet at various places and not only at the end of the book. There are at least three groups of chapters whose presence is based on arguments from previous chapters. In the first group are the chapters entitled "The Nature of the Gods" I, II, and III. In these I offer an overall evaluation of some of the chief religious principles governing the Mesoamerican tradition. The second group is that of the chapters entitled "The Character" I and II. In them I explain the life and miracles of the hero. The final chapters bring the essay to a close with the promise of further works on the subject.

The reader may ask two questions from the beginning. First, why was it necessary to follow such devious paths to reach the goal? And second, why, at times, does the reader have to follow closely the progress of the work?

As to the first question, I go from one subject to the other in a certain order, for reasons which only the end of the book will fully explain. The areas to be investigated are *extremely* heterogeneous. The central one is the ancient Mesoamerican religion, because it contains the problem that interests me. I want to understand the religious thought of the past as a product of the societies that gave it birth. But that subject is too large, and I had to choose only one of its aspects as the principal topic. I chose myth as the theme for this essay. Not satisfied with the limitations of documental and archeological sources, I wanted recourse to ethnological research, to look for more abundant information. Then the panorama changed. I entered a more recent reality, and into a field of study traditionally different from those of history and archeology.

But the change in time frame also made it necessary to enter into the field of epistemology.

How accurate are our specific examples of the Mesoamerican tradition, or our abstract inferences drawn from analogy? The matter of inference took me to another theoretical field, in which I not only had to question inference through analogy, but also to study problems basic to the theory of myth. It could not be otherwise, since studies of myth today must be founded on sound theoretical bases, and also due to the fact that we Mesoamericanists have not been careful enough in this theoretical aspect. On the other hand, I had to focus on some particular aspect of the investigation. The study of myth in the Mesoamerican tradition cannot be done without limiting a field that is extremely extensive. One myth must be chosen, or at least a myth cycle. I chose the myth cycle of the opossum.

What was the result of the need to resolve this entire group of problems? This essay goes from a zoological presentation to posing the central problem, from this to theory, from theory to the ancient Mesoamerican religion, from that to contemporary traditions, or to the nature of the elements, or to myths of the Mesoamerican tradition, or to our character the opossum, who occasionally seems to evade us—everything that the ebb and flow of reciprocal inference makes necessary.

Mesoamericanists do not usually deal with matters of mythology in this way. Too often we prefer a strict limitation of the topics, so restricted that instead of opening the forum to a scientific discussion of myth, we have created with our thematic, geographic, temporal, or methodological specialization small strongholds where we engage in the dialogue of the deaf. Someone had to undertake the comprehensive and complex problem, and it was my chronic temptation to unveil the mysteries of the ancient Mesoamerican religion that forced me to undertake the task. I acknowledge it was not a simple matter, since I had to adjust each argument like the stones of an arch, the solidity of which depends on the support of all the adjoining stones. Here I give an account of the results, and I propose some methodological bases for the study of religion to my Mesoamericanist colleagues.

The second question is why the reader must follow the debate so closely. Some readers will acuse me of not having given the results of the investigation in their briefest form. The topics for debate are so controversial it is necessary to air them publicly. This is the reason why, in each chapter, I invite the reader, specialist or not, to participate in the discussion, to become familiar with the multiple problems that Mesoamericanists have not dealt with opportunely enough when researching the religious tradition. For example I deny that a mytho-poet is necessary for the birth of a myth. Is it possible for this proposal to be accepted today without debate, when in academic circles there is still a strong belief that the poet and the philosopher are the creators of religions? Some colleagues will accept the idea readily; others will not. But for all of them it would merely have the weight of an opinion. Conclusions need more solid foundations.

Many friends and colleagues helped me write this book, so many it is impossible to name them all. I thank those who contributed to the work with their interesting comments and suggestions, for the loan of hard-to-find texts, for their patience in hearing me tell stories of the opossum. Among them I must mention Marina Anguiano, Ramón Arzápalo Marín, Artuto Azuela, Fernando Botas Vera, Victor M. Castillo F., Bárbara Dahlgren, Jacques Galinier, Renato González Mello, Javier González Vásquez, Salvador Guil'liem, Roberto Heredia, Marie-Areti Hers, Carlos Incháustegui, Antonio Lazcano Araujo, Xavier Lozoya, Carlos Martínez Marín, Jorge Martínez Stack, Andrés Medina, María Montoliú Villar, Guido Münch Galindo, Carlos Navarrete Cáceres, Federico Navarrete Linares, Francisco Noriega, Lorenzo Ochoa Salas, Tomás Pérez Suárez, Antonio Pompa y Pompa, Elisa Ramírez Castañeda, Jesús Rentería, Ingrid Rosenblueth, Otto Schumann Gálvez, Francisco Soberón Mobarak, Yoko Sugiura, Raúl Valadés Azúa, and Paola Vianello. I especially thank those who patiently read the text and volunteered their valuable commentaries: Pablo Escalante Gonzalbo, Leonardo López Luján, and José Rubén Romero.

ALFREDO LÓPEZ AUSTIN
Ciudad Universitaria, Mexico
December 1988

Preface to the English Edition

The work of Thelma and Bernard R. Ortiz de Montellano in this edition is outstanding. Their translation is, as usual, of very high quality and to the benefit of both the readers and the author. In addition to a personal interest in this book, they have a profound professional knowledge of the material—and aside from that, an old friendship—for which I have always felt honored and grateful.

ALFREDO LÓPEZ AUSTIN
Ciudad Universitaria, Mexico

Translators' Note

In an attempt to shorten this long work without unduly affecting the content, we have eliminated a number of things: the appendixes, several citations in Nahuatl for which translations were provided elsewhere, parenthetical expressions, and most identifications of myths to particular groups. Citations were changed from the original format to a briefer, anthropological style.

To avoid difficulties in pluralizing, names of cultures and native groups have been treated as collective nouns. Nahuatl words are all accented on the next to last syllable; therefore accents, which are used to indicate stress in Spanish, have all been omitted on Nahuatl words.

To avoid the errors involved in double translations, in many cases we introduce passages from the original English version or from English translations from the original language, rather than retranslating López Austin's Spanish quotations.

THE MYTHS OF THE OPOSSUM

1 THE COMINGS AND GOINGS OF A MARSUPIAL

He stole what is yours, fire, the flower of your wealth,
the source of all art, to give it to mortal man!
He must pay this forfeit to the gods.
He must learn to submit to the rulership of Zeus
and cease to play the lover of mankind.

Aeschylus, *Prometheus Bound*

Reader, this is an essay. I am convinced that the greater part of the tasks to which we enthusiastically devote ourselves in life are essays. But sometimes we have to formally clarify their nature. In classifying my work as an essay, I do not follow the criteria that guided Locke and Malthus in their profound and systematic treatises. I choose another definition. I wish to avoid, as far as possible, the rigidity of the forms of discourse usually used in developing mythological subjects. I am looking for a more flexible way that will allow me to freely develop and discuss myth. I hope the reader will agree with that decision.

While working on this investigation, I have kept in mind a parallel field—iconography. Mythology and iconography as subjects of study are not as different as they might at first seem, especially if one follows closely Voloshinov's ideas about language (1976:120).[1] Myth and image, as symbols, can be studied from the viewpoint of ideology. Their particular qualities as forms of expression lose their distinctiveness in a social context in which their respective aesthetic, logical, and historical values complement each other.

A considerable part of the pictorial and sculptured works of Mesoamerica directly depict mythology. The scenes on the sides of vases, the deeds told on the walls of buildings, the dialogues that seem to emerge from lintels of zapote wood or limestone, the personages clad in complicated robes painted on pages of hide or paper reveal episodes in the world of the gods. The images of clay and stone lead us to believe that behind each detail there is a series of actions attributed to invisible beings. How does one separate myth from image?

Any approach to myth—or image—makes one return to old questions. Was there a significant degree of unity among the different regional concepts of the world in Mesoamerica? If there was a common basis underlying Meso-american thought, how long did it last, and how did it change in general and regionally across the centuries? What was the geographic extent of these similar concepts, and in what particular respects were these similarities weakened or preserved? These are old questions that will be around for a long time; but with the progress of investigations, they are questions that are being answered gradually. The questions will reappear constantly throughout this study.

The precision of our interpretation of iconography depends to a great extent on the mythological resources available, not only because of possible mechanical correspondences that might be established between myths and images, but above all because of the possibility of reconstructing a mythological order that can be compared, in a reciprocal process of elucidation, to the iconographical one. There is a sizable collection of myths recorded in early colonial times. However, they are not enough to provide a satisfactory comparison. An attractive possibility is to complement them with native tales produced from the time of the Conquest to the present day. Beliefs, myths, and rites derived from the ancient ones exist today, and we cannot overlook them in researching Mesoamerican thought. No doubt they have been altered by a history plagued by oppression, ideological penetration, exploitation, and plunder, but they still belong to a strong tradition, used as an instrument of resistance. Beliefs, myths, and rites cannot be understood without referring to their remote origin, nor is it wise to study the ideology of preconquest societies without taking into account their legacy.

The above places before us two undeniable realities of an opposing nature. If we cannot deny the importance of indigenous thought during colonial times as a focus for the study of ancient Mesoamerican societies, neither can we ignore the fact of a radical transformation of such thought beginning with the Conquest and, above all, under the tremendous impact of a capitalist society. What is to be done about these facts? Historians and anthropologists have long based their studies on the traditional sequence from start to finish, and that has produced great advances in understanding both ancient societies and those of today. We must recognize, however, that our conclusions have not always been free of inaccuracies, and that the method has not been sufficiently discussed. We must continue the debate on this resource. It is necessary to find more solid, more scientific ways to handle this information, with which both history and ideology are enriched. The debate must be intensified and deepened.

In my quest to understand myths and images, I now state one of the central concerns of this work: how to use present-day information as a complementary source for studying the Mesoamerican past in such a way that the major dangers in processing the data are made clear, the most serious perils of utilizing the material revealed, and the ways to use methodological resources with an acceptable degree of confidence are agreed upon. All of this will hinge on the tie existing between ancient and present-day myth, and with repeated reference to an important mythical being, the *tlacuache* (opossum).

The Opossum

If any creature can pride itself on being native to American territory, it is the opossum. The descendants of pre-Cenozoic marsupials widely distributed over the globe, the ancestors of the opossum became isolated in South America when that continent, separated from Africa, became an enormous island. Didelphids continued to exist in Europe during the Tertiary; but when they disappeared, the only near relatives left were the South American didelphids. Millions of years after the separation, during the Pliocene, the Isthmus of Panama formed a bridge between North and South America. This union allowed enormous migrations of animals in both directions. Thus the opossums journeyed to other lands, ranging from the Argentinian pampa to the northern coasts of the Pacific in North America. Little by little, they made America their domain from southern Canada to the southland, from where they had begun their expansion. Opossums occupied the neoartic as well as the neotropical regions, with the exception of the extremely cold lands and the desert region, which did not suit them. They adapted so well that their appearance changed very little. Evolution appears to have come to a halt in them. No mammals resemble so closely their remote ancestors as the didelphids. It is as if at some time in the distant past—and may biologists forgive the heresy—they had installed themselves in their optimal phylogeny, from which they could face the catastrophes of the Pleistocene and the dominating presence of modern mammals. The didelphids were spread over a territory that later, detached, adrift, would become in its insularity the beginning of what is now known as America. Here, well adapted to their environment, they have remained faithful to their genetic inheritance through millions of years, and armed with this, they have spread across the two great regions populated by American fauna. Compared with the opossum, the rest of us are newcomers to these continents.

How have they survived in the life struggle with the placental mammals? One of the factors in their survival is the wide variety of their diet and the fact that insects play a large part in it. This reduces considerably the competition with more highly developed animals. Opossums eat small mammals, birds, eggs, amphibians, snakes, fruit, roots, corn, and even carrion when necessary.

The yapok [*Chironectes minimus*] is the exception, since it is the only opossum that is entirely carnivorous.[2] It feeds on mollusks and crustaceans. It is a poor trapper of fish but a voracious consumer of their roe. It is well adapted to its limited environment. It has the anatomical features of a good swimmer: inter-digital membranes on its back paws; short, fine, dense fur; a fusiform body; and a pouch provided with a sphincter that closes over it when, with her young inside, the mother plunges into the water in search of aquatic prey (Walker et al. 1975, 1:25).

The didelphids have other weapons that have contributed to their survival. Several of the species are accustomed to "play possum": they fall down apparently lifeless before their enemies, tongue hanging out, eyes glazed, in a fake death that protects them from all but carrion-eating predators. A strong garlic-like odor emitted from their bodies when they are frightened also deters attackers. They intimidate their pursuers by opening wide their immense snouts, exposing long rows of teeth. During periods of drought, cold, or hunger, they go into a state of lethargy similar to the hibernation of placental mammals (Gewalt and Grzimek 1968:60–63). Finally they have the advantage when they live near humans. People hunt them for food, but the meat is fat and unappetizing (Leopold 1982:373–74).[3] On the other hand, the opossum—cunning, an agile climber, and accustomed to overcoming obstacles—takes advantage of that proximity to steal corn from fields and granaries. When a Mexican farmer carves a hollow in the center of the maguey plant [*Agave sp.*] to gather the sap, the opossum will get there first, remove the plug of the vessel, and drink the sweet juice (Ceballos González and Galindo Leal 1984:47). Besides being thieves, they are bloody ones, beheading domestic fowl and terrorizing chicken coops. This has earned them the incorrect appellation of weasel, although they have no resemblance to the mustelids (Santamaría 1974: see *comadreja*), nor to *zorro*[4] or *zorra*[5] [fox], names also applied to him.

There are 12 genera, 76 species, and 163 subspecies of the animal disseminated over the continent (Gewalt and Grzimek 1968:57). There is a well-developed pouch in the *Didelphis, Chironectes,* and *Philander* genera; in the others there are only rudiments, two folds of skin that protect the young (Hall and Nelson 1959). As in many other marsupials, the female opossum has two uteri and two vaginas (Heinemann and Thenius 1968:50)—hence the derivation of the term didelphids—and the male has a forked penis (Hartmann 1921:322). The females are very prolific. They have two or three litters a year, numbering from eight to eighteen. After a brief gestation period of thirteen to fourteen days, the young come out and, climbing blindly with their still incomplete limbs, follow a path of maternal saliva leading them to the pouch. Firmly attached to the teats for two months, they complete their growth in a warm and fetid atmosphere. Afterwards they emerge, little by little, to discover the world. After about three months of coming and going from foliage to pouch, the little opossums are abandoned by the mother. Then they begin their nomadic, twilight and nocturnal life, alone except during the mating season, armed for their subsistence with a long prehensile tail, usually hairless and scaly, opposable toes, and a strong, solid body.

These are the *tlacuaches, churchas*, opossums, *filandros, zarigüeyas, cuicas, catitas, zorras mochileras, llacas, coyopollines* or *cayopollines, comadrejas overas, mucurás, carachupas, micures {mbicuré}, mucamucas, picazas, runchos, paricatas, guaquis, chuchas* . . . that live so near to people. And throughout the American continent, we have vigorously incorporated them, with their real or imaginary characteristics, into our traditions. It is unnecessary to stress the importance of the animal's presence in the myths of the continent. Lévi-Strauss, in his studies, recognized the opossum as one of their most important figures, when he wrote the "Opossum's Cantata" (Lévi-Strauss 1968b: ch. 11).

Of course the same holds for Mexico, where there are five genera of opossums (*Chironectes, Didelphis, Marmosa, Philander,* and *Caluromys*), and where one of the species, *Marmosa canenscens*, is endemic (Ramírez Pulido and Müdespacher 1987:52–58). Their differences are expressed in native terms such as little flower possum, mountain possum, *totol*, and spiny and mouse possum (*Uejkauitl nauaueuejtlatoli* 1982:28–32). Since ancient time their importance is expressed in many myths and legends. The opossum is and has been a popular character for centuries. An interesting article by Munn (1984) portrays the opossum's role in Mexican and Mesoamerican mythology. Munn attempts to clarify the ties between the pre-Hispanic past and our own time.

The archeological traces left by the opossum provide excellent testimony to its lasting fame. There are some very simple primitive representations. The date of a small clay figure found in Tlapacoya is calculated to be about 1000 B.C. [6] Over time the figure of the opossum accumulated various symbols. [7] The images in such important codices as the *Fejérváry Mayer, Vindobonensis, Vaticanus B, Dresden,* and *Nuttall* link it to a traditional ball game, crossroads, decapitation, to the New Year ceremonies, to the moon, and to *pulque* [fermented *Agave* sap]. It wears multicolored mantles, rich headgear, rattle staffs, and it is seated upon stools covered with jaguar skins. Its dwelling can be identified in the pictographic documents. Its emblem is its long tail covered with bristling hairs, an image used repeatedly as an architectural element on the upper part of an edifice (Munn 1984:47). An order of warriors among the northern Maya was named for it. According to the *Chilam Balam of Tizimín*, two military groups supported a usurping government in Mérida, the *Balam Ochil*, or "jaguar-opossums," and the *Balam Ch'amacil*, or "jaguar-foxes" (*The Ancient Future of the Itza* 1982:64n).[8] In ancient ceramics there are images that allow us to identify this animal by the wealth of its associated symbolism: round ear spools, complicated headdresses, breastplates with glyphs, ears of corn tied around its neck, and what has been described as "a kind of braid across its nose," which is one of the most notable characteristics of the Mexican rain gods (Ramón 1972:12–13).[9] The image of the marsupial is present among the Mixtec gold jewels found in Tomb 7 at Monte Albán. Among them are three small pieces that depict the rain god, the jaguar, and the opossum (Caso 1969:94–95 and pl. 3). In Mayan texts, even in the *Popol Vuh* and the *Chilam Balam of Tizimín*, the opossum appears as lord of the half-light preceding dawn, or as a representation of the gods who hold up the sky at each of the four corners of the world.

These complex ties to the invisible world are centuries old. Although it is not possible to know exactly when people began to associate the opossum with mythological deeds, it is known that by the Classical period there were enough representations in the Zapotec region to confirm the deification of the marsupial (Caso and Bernal 1952:265–66; Baus de Czitrom in press:10–11). In Teotihuacan, in a workshop located to the north of the Ciudadela, molds were found for casting small opossum figures, possibly to be stuck to cult vessels (Carlos Muñera, pers. com., in Baus de Czitrom in press:11), and its important presence has lasted. One of the twenty-day "months" of the Tzotzil year is named for it (Guiteras Holmes 1965:35–36). At the beginning of the twentieth century, the Nahua of San Pedro Jícora, Durango, believed that the opossum was the *nahual* [animal alter ego] of the goddess Tonantzi (Ziehm, "Introducción," in Preuss 1982:49). Villa Rojas (1978:49) wrote that the Maya believed that the cottonlike debris from opossum dens could be mixed with gunpowder to kill a legendary deer of "pure air" that belonged to Saint George. Its effigy hung in temples and huts (Zingg 1982, 1:332, 2:227n15; Lumholtz 1970, 2:148), its remains used as medicine, its recurring presence in stories and myths, all of these point to a tradition in which the opossum holds a prestigious place. He is the chief of the world, the one who resists blows, the shattered one who reconstitutes himself, the shrewd character who faces the mighty jaguars, the leader of the wise old counselors, civilizer and benefactor, the respected wise grandfather, the bold one. In the folk concept of morality, these attributes did not conflict with his being sly, a thief, a drunkard, a party lover, high on the hog and lascivious.

The most important myth about the opossum, widespread and rich in its variants, is the one that recounts the deeds of the marsupial as a kind of New World Prometheus. A synthesis of the different versions takes us back to the era before humans possessed fire. In some cases fire was owned by celestial beings, in others, by inhabitants of the underworld. One of the most commonly cited owners is an old miserly woman; in another beautiful version, found among the Chatino by Bartolomé and Barabas (1982:111–12), demons are the possessors of fire, festivals, *mescal,* and tobacco. The opossum, either commissioned to do so or on its own, craftily approaches the flame and steals fire by setting its tail ablaze, a tail that henceforth is hairless (Incháustegui 1977:67–68). In another version, it hides live coals in its pouch.[10] As a great benefactor, the opossum gives its treasure to people. However, the myth does not always end with the gift of fire. Among the Cora, the world is set afire by the gift, and the Earth extinguishes it with its own milk (Preuss 1912, 1:169–81). According to the Huichol, the civilizing hero is dashed into bits, but he reunites his parts and is reborn (Zingg 1982, 1:358n13, 2:187; P. T. Furst 1972a:9–11).

The myth of the theft of fire has merged with the Christian tradition, and some versions[11] link it to the birth of Christ; the Virgin and Child suffer from cold, and the opossum steals fire to warm them. It is rewarded by the gift of resurrection or with the pouch in which young are reared.

The opossum as a manipulator (although a clumsy one) of fire appears in other myths. In a Zoque-Popoluca tale of the spirit of maize, the opossum is the ally of the hero, who tries to set fires around the tree where his enemy is hiding. He fails and sets fire to his own tail, which thereafter is hairless (Técnicos bilingües 1985:135–136). Other versions of the myth substitute another animal for the opossum: the fox (135–36), the skunk,[12] the monkey,[13] the dog,[14] the mouse,[15] or the toad (Giddings 1959:13). The myth of the opossum (or its substitutes) is today the most important of those dealing with the gift of fire, but not the only one. Other very different mythical heroes are Quanamoa or Hatsikan among the Cora (Dahlgren 1961:63), the lightning bolt among the Mocho (Petrich 1986), and, among the Tzotzil, the youth who became the sun (Rubel 1985:789).

The Mazatec say that one day the animals discussed the course a river should take. Their opinion was that it should run in a straight line to allow fishing. Not sure about the efficiency of their solution, they sought the advice of the opossum. They went from tavern to tavern looking for him, until at last they found the old sage in a small one where he was getting drunk, merrily singing and playing his guitar with friends. When the old man was consulted, he answered that it was absolutely necessary for the river to have curves and small eddies so that all the animals could fish and sleep in their boats. The group applauded him, and thus rivers acquired their definitive form (Incháustegui 1977:53–56).

Two Trique myths touch upon characteristics of the opossum: the first on the position of its testicles, the second on its legendary capacity for returning from the dead. In the first one, the opossum, on his son's wedding day, climbs on his daughter-in-law's back and dances in this position. His testicles shift and remain in a strange position relative to the penis. In the second, the opossum invites a friend to eat at his house. He asks his guest to wait for him while he bathes in the river. From there he orders his wife to take his own flesh to prepare a dish for his companion. The opossum kills himself in the river and his wife prepares the meal, being careful to leave the nerves attached to her husband's bones. The opossum reconstructs himself on this skeleton in the water, revives, and like a good host, returns to chat with his friend (Hollenbach 1980:458–59).[16]

The opossum is also the principal actor in many folktales. He and the jaguar are the regional equivalents of another pair, the rabbit and the coyote.[17] In these stories it is always the weak but astute character who mocks the might of his powerful, cruel adversary. These stories have ancient origins and have born fruit on our soil. They are similar to the famous Uncle Remus stories. Some of the adventures have more than an accidental resemblance to tales throughout the world. The opossum reminds us of Delilah the Sly, the evil, but clever, blue-eyed old woman who cunningly induces an unsuspecting Bedouin to take her place at the place of punishment. He also reminds us of Renard, who tricks Isengrin by making him believe he is seeing cheese in the moon's reflection on the water. Such tales have made him an international animal. The choruses of Indian children are revitalized echoes of African, Asiatic, and European voices.

The hyper-American opossum sailed to the Old World early. He was the first marsupial known to Europeans, and his existence amazed the Spanish sovereigns, King Ferdinand and Queen Isabella. In Europe, however, his fame spread through books, and the original imaginings of his character are reflected in engravings and drawings. For instance the female is pictured in a pose with an upraised tail, like a perch, to which her young cling—a pose unknown to opossums (Gewalt and Grzimek 1968:67), but one that served as inspiration for illustrations and the reconstruction of dissected opossum corpses in old museums.

Our hero, then, is almost a household animal, a domestic thief but also the master of marvelous secrets. He is the wise but stinking old one who can put himself together again and survive death. He will be a companion on this journey to investigate how Mesoamerican tradition has survived historically. The opossum will be the guide in the home of the gods.

2 HOME OF THE GODS

I believe that few sciences are obliged [as history is] to use simultaneously so many different tools. This is because human deeds are so complex, and man himself is located on the borderline of history.

Marc Bloch, *Apologie pour l'Histoire*

Where is the home of the gods? Where one wishes to deceive Zeus. There where "With both hands he took up the white fat, and spiteful anger rushed through his mind and heart when he saw the white bones of the ox laid out in deceit" (Hesiod 1983:27). It is the site of Prometheus's trickery when he wished to deceive the father of the gods with a diminished portion of the sacrifice. It is the place of the altars, the meadows, and the planted fields, the wooded mountains, the market place, the village, the open paths of the sea and of the desert. The gods live where people live, and their dealings with the gods are only aspects of the dealings they have with each other. Because of this, stories of the gods are human history, with all the complexity that entails.

Today myths are being reevaluated. The attitude that labeled them primitive, absurd, dreamlike, infantile, or as infirmities of the language is laid aside. They have been taken seriously again, though with the seriousness of the scientist, not the believer. Today myths are approached from an interdisciplinary perspective. Folklorists dissect motifs and plots, pursuing them across centuries; linguists concern themselves with the language and the interplay of linguistic structures; psychologists search for the intimate mental origins of the tales; and specialists, with highly varied methods and techniques, unveil different mysteries—perhaps too different—by viewing myth from the many angles of epistemology, sociology, ethnology, comparative history of religion, and semiotics.

No one can deny the rigor and the extent of contemporary study of myth. However, I believe that in this methodological multiplicity it is necessary to have a single unifying vision, capable of locating in the same scientific context the fundamentals of analysis as well as the results obtained from each of the perspectives used in the research. The essential vision is a historical vision, and I mean history in its most ample sense, history that includes ideology and myth.[1] Myth is a social product, emerging from innumerable sources, loaded with functions, ever present in time but not immune to it. Like every human product, it acquires its true dimensions in relation to society as a whole. For this reason it must be studied primarily and definitively through the science of history—history in its most exact sense—which has as its subject the dynamic of human societies (Vilar 1981:43). The central obligatory focus of studying myth is not merely its analysis, but that which leads to the discovery of its forms of integration into the processes of the societies that produce it. Specific independent methods and techniques should be subject to the all-encompassing vision of scientific history, which, faced with the heterogeneous problems of human events, will make use of many methodological and technical resources. The historian will utilize—justifiably and not as borrowings from other disciplines—the investigative techniques needed to understand matters as complex as social processes. The distinctive unity of that insight renders unnecessary the recent proliferation of hybrid disciplines. Above all of them (and with no need for titles made by the joining of the names of simple disciplines, of forced combinations, or barriers that limit the fields of study) is social science, the science of history. Braudel (1974:107) completes the definition: "It is a science, but a complex one."

With this historical science, let us go to the home of the gods, the time and space in which a common history made a common tradition.

Starting with the idea that many of today's indigenous myths of Mexico and Central America show evidence of ties with Mesoamerican myths, it is essential to identify the fundamental problems that affect recognition of these ties and to propose bases for their solution. The problems, broadly speaking, are the following:

1. What is Mesoamerica?

2. Was there a common religion and mythology in Mesoamerica?

3. Is it possible to speak of a Mesoamerican tradition that extends to the present?

4. How should one understand Mesoamerican religious and mythical unity when taken as a point of departure for studying contemporary indigenous traditions?

Let us consider these problems in detail.

The Boundaries of Mesoamerica

We owe a debt to whoever coined the term *Mesoamerica* and established its limits. In 1943 Paul Kirchhoff, aware of the scientific value of a debate on this subject, started the controversy when he published "Mesoamerica, its geographical limits, ethnic composition and cultural characteristics." Years afterward, in a revised edition (1960), Kirchhoff complained:

> I conceived this study as the first of a series of investigations that would success-
> fully deal with these questions, expecting that others would take charge of the
> greater part of the work. I was disappointed in that expectation because, while
> many have accepted the concept of "Mesoamerica," no one, as far as I know, has
> made it the subject of a constructive criticism or has systematically applied or
> developed it.

The same complaint appeared in the third revision, published in 1972. Kirchhoff died in 1967 without having the dialogue he expected. By that time the term *Mesoamerica* had been universally accepted for decades.

Today when the bases for Kirchhoff's definition have aged to point of falling apart, and the name "Mesoamerica" has acquired the solidity of rock, a debate over the nature of Mesoamerica has become more and more necessary. This is not the right place for the debate, but research on the subject of myth requires that we set forth, at least, a few definitions.

1. What we call Mesoamerica was a historical reality. It was a sequence, spanning a thousand years, of strongly linked societies.

2. Obviously the complexity of the interrelated societies was heteroge-neous, as much in the succession of events across a thousand years as in the simultaneous existence of societies developing in different ways.

3. The ties established among these societies were diverse and changeable. The social relationships that gave rise to Mesoamerica are not limited to one, permanent, universal type.

4. Although during certain epochs and some regions of Mesoamerica some kinds of relationships prevailed over others, the essence of Mesoamerica derives from the whole complex of relationships, their combinations, relative strengths, and not merely from the dominant type.

5. Therefore what is Mesoamerican cannot be discovered by the presence of characteristic relationships or traits at all times and places. The totality of relationships is not an average of constants, but a historical succession.

6. The dominance of some relationships over others was not a matter of chance. It obeyed the above-mentioned common course of history.

7. Relationships among the various Mesoamerican societies gave rise not only to similarities among them, but also to differences and limitations due to asymmetrical interdependencies.

8. There was no obligatory coincidence in the extent or duration of the common elements in different areas of social behavior. For instance similarities in the field of politics that might have existed among various Mesoamerican peoples in a given epoch did not necessarily imply that there were similarities in the artistic field over the same period. Nor did political relationships last the same length of time as artistic ones. If we block out on maps of Mesoamerica the various common elements, the colors for the different elements would not overlap in a uniform way. This would also be true if we drew them on chronological scales. This is due to the fact that between one social area and another there was no mandatory reciprocal correspondence, because this coordination, although firm, could involve multiple, rich variables.

These are some of the understandings necessary for the study of Meso-american myth and its continuity. Let us take up briefly some of the points mentioned. In the age-old history of Mesoamerica, the ties among the various peoples living there are particularly noticeable from the beginning of the sedentary period. This enables us to identify the origin of Mesoamerica with sedentary agriculture, even though the connections began in even remoter times. The decisive step in the formation of Mesoamerica was the domestication of corn between 6000 and 5000 B.C. The slow process of settling down would come later and, with it, the development of agricultural techniques, which made advanced farmers of the Mesoamericans.

Relations among the ethnic groups who occupied the area between 25° and 10° north latitude had to be varied and changeable. Through history the Mesoamericans formed societies differing widely in complexity, from primitive farming villages to populations of high density made possible by intensive agricultural technology; from simply structured groups to stratified societies forming centralized states. Their ties were economic, political, religious, and cultural in the broadest sense of the word. Geographical diversity and specialization in production originally brought about a simple exchange of goods, foreshadowing later commercial routes and, later still, the establishment of markets and even suprastatal organizations for production. Politically Mesoamerican ethnic groups associated through alliances, often strengthened by kinship or marriage, and also through wars, conquest, and consolidation (in epochs of major development) of tributary systems. Political complexity reached its peak with the founding of governments based not exclusively on blood ties but on territorial domination over populations differing in ethnicity and language. From the conflicts arising among neighboring nations resulted regulatory norms that culminated in tribunals formed by several dominant nations. Ethnic and linguistic ties were important in all of these alliances, sometimes as conditions favorable to harmonious relationships, at other times to justify political consolidations through hidden or outright conquests.

The intensity of links of either kind created a joint cultural creation in which ideology in its widest forms of expression served to defend interests in agreement or in conflict. In this way a common Mesoamerican culture was built, of which the Olmec, Teotihuacan, Maya, Zapotec, Mixtec, Toltec, Mexica, Huaxtec, Totonac, Tarasca, and many other cultures are merely variants created by particular traditions in different regions and historical periods. A common history and local histories interacted dialectically to form a Mesoamerican world vision in which the variants acquired extraordinary individual peculiarities.

Institutions such as markets, war, or courts produced and were regulated by norms, traditions, and organizations, including societies at various stages of development. In time these norms and institutions crossed state boundaries. Institutions overlapped in multiple, reciprocal dependencies and mingled to form several complexes. Among the functions of some political organizations was the regulation of internal and external exchange; others permitted the existence of organized merchants; others placed them under their aegis. Conquests could be justified as means of guaranteeing the existence of politico-legal institutions. At times tribute was disguised as offerings to the gods of allied peoples. Trade routes served as paths for military penetration.

It is not possible to conceive of Mesoamerica as the product of a uniform and permanent type of cohesive structures. Within its territory the influence of different relationships varied, sometimes simultaneous, sometimes successive, the profound dominating ones, as well as the more apparent ones that overlaid them. The shifting existence of one and another made Mesoamerica an area of evanescent horizons, above all in the northern regions. What is "Mesoamerican" vanishes, evaporates, along the northern and southern boundaries, and what might be considered typical in some regions is lacking in others, in which different cultural elements mark the "Mesoamericanism." They do not spread like colors of continuous and uniform intensity, nor characterized by the same hues. Mesoamerica was a continuum of a historical character which neither in time nor in space owed its unity to the same factors.

Neither can what is Mesoamerican be characterized by the mere similarity of cultural elements. Often the intensifying of many relationships resulted in cultural withdrawal rather than in a drawing together. As an example political domination resulted not only in the exaltation of the dominant group, but in the inhibition of the development of the dominated. This applies to metropolis-village relationships as well as to interregional economic dependency. External direction of the production of a region could limit its free participation in the life-style we call Mesoamerican. However, their "marginality" linked them to the hegemonic states so that their prospects for independence and economic autonomy were slighter than those of many groups in Mesoamerica proper. Therefore the inclusion of a dependent zone in Mesoamerica should not be determined by the number of common cultural elements; the complexity of the ties must be found and, through them, likenesses and differences explained. Thereby the degree of participation of the different groups in greater Mesoamerican dynamics can be established.

Religion and Myth in Mesoamerican Context

The common history and the particular history of each Mesoamerican culture function dialectically to form a Mesoamerican world vision rich in regional and local expression. The history of Mesoamerican religion can be found, above all, in artistic representations that developed in many forms through the centuries. Here myth is predominant. We find it abundant in written records; further testimony comes from more remote epochs. There are sculptured scenes from the Late Formative period that have been identified with representations of myths of a much later date. Rivera Dorado, referring to the Izapa-style stelae, carved around 400 B.C. along the border region of Mexico and Guatemala, was amazed at how material from the Classic period and from colonial documents could throw light on figures from the Formative.

> For example, we see depicted there the concept of the sacred tree, a metaphor for resurrection and life, which sinks its roots into the earth dragon linking the levels of the cosmos. Also depicted are the celestial serpents, symbols of monarchy and a significant image of native cosmovision in the lowland of the North (Rivera Dorado 1985:50).

The same occurs with respect to space. A common concept of what is sacred links rituals, gods, calendars, and other artistic manifestations associated with religion across the length and breadth of Mesoamerica. The Quetzalcoatl myth appears with all its political force supporting governmental systems in northern Tollan Xicocotitlan, among the Mixtec, in the northern Mayan region, and in the valleys and lakes of the Guatemalan high plateau. Religion and myth are part of a shared language of the Mesoamerican Babel. Through them those who wished to carry on commerce, become relatives, form alliances, or justify conquests understood each other.

Did a common religion and mythology exist in Mesoamerica? I shall uphold that idea for now, with the proviso that I will refine and explain it in this and in later chapters.

Is There a Mesoamerican Tradition That Extends to Our Own Time?

Yes, although in stating this we must recognize the great difference between Mesoamerican religion and contemporary indigenous religions. In fact there is an important and unquestionable religious tradition with roots in Mesoamerica. It is necessary to say this, despite obvious evidence, because it is denied by some, at least so far as myth was concerned, and the all-encompassing denials continue. At the beginning of the century a dispute took place that, because of the importance of the participants, must be mentioned.[2] Based on materials from Mexico and New Mexico, the highly esteemed Franz Boas concluded in 1912 that most of Hispanic-American folkloric narrative, and much of that of North American blacks, derived from Spanish sources (Boas 1912: 247).

Boas's opinion seemed to be fully confirmed with the 1917 publication of tales collected by Radin in *El folklore de Oaxaca*. A milestone in the study of indigenous oral tradition because of its extent and novelty, the work is, nevertheless, defective. The texts, gathered without rigor and most of them reworked, are inauthentic. Espinosa supported Boas's opinion when he said, in the introduction to the book, that it was surprising how the Mexican Indians had absorbed the traditional elements of their European conquerors; he believed that native tradition was at the point of disappearing and found that it was replaced by the traditions of Spanish narration (Radin and Espinosa 1917:i–iii). Radin himself did not agree. Bothered by these statements and other views expressed in the book, he disassociated himself from the opinion given in the introduction (Radin 1943–44:14–15).

Beals also insisted on the European origin of native Mexican folklore. He barely excluded a determining European influence among the Huichol, and possibly the Cora, but stated that other ethnic groups, among them the Tarasca, had predominantly European culture (Beals 1943:8–10). Radin, to the contrary, affirmed the presence of the old indigenous tradition along with the European, although he acknowledged the difficulty of determining the extent of the former (Radin 1943–44, 1944).

Foster ended this long polemic when, in 1945, he concluded in Solomon-like fashion that, despite much that is European in native folklore, a significant part is rooted in Mesoamerican traditions (Foster 1945a, 1945b). This settled a question that, with the perspective of years, can be seen as a mere disturbance stirred up in academic circles by Boas's prestige, rather than a viable controversy. As Moedano Navarro (1975) says, the work of researchers with better knowledge of pre-Hispanic culture was enough to reveal abundant material with authentic indigenous roots.

The persistence of myths from the remote past to our day will be a constant theme in this book. Examples of this important continuity abound. Among these we can easily see the relationship between two versions, separated by four centuries, of the myth about the discovery of corn. One is a Nahuatl story written in the second half of the sixteenth century; the other was found among the Chol Indians of Chiapas. There is no doubt about their concordance. In both, the black ant, the red ant, and the rain gods, characterized by their colors, extract the grain from its stony enclosure, and afterwards break up the mountain in which the vegetable treasure was stored (*Leyenda de los soles* 1945:121; Morález Bermúdez 1984). The continuity of the legend takes other forms; the connection, in various forms, appears in numerous stories. Even in the dialogue between characters there are interesting relics. When Tama-kastsiin, the modern spirit of corn in the south of Veracruz, asks the turtle to carry him, swimming, to the place where his dead father rests, the turtle replies, "But don't you see that I am clean and that you are very dirty?" (Campos 1982:167–68). This corresponds to Sahagún's report (1956, 1:296) of ancient Nahua beliefs about the journey to the underworld. The deceased had to cross the river of the world of the dead, and he asked a ruddy-colored dog for help.

> Moreover, they said that dogs with white and black hair could not swim and cross the river [of the underworld], because the dog with the white coat said, "I washed myself"; and the dog with the black coat said, "I have stained my coat black and, because of that, I cannot take you across."

Even today, according to many writers, it is possible to clarify the meaning of many contemporary myths by referring to ancient songs dedicated to the gods (Garcia de León 1969).

The range of the myths is also impressive. Brinton (1970:vii–viii) has already pointed out that one of the distinctions between myth and legend is that myth can exist among groups widely separated by language and place. Many myths cross the traditional boundaries of Mesoamerica, which simply demonstrates that the spread of myth covers one of the widest areas—not, however, a homogenous area.[3] There are myths, among them the ones studied by Brinton, that can be considered Panamerican. One, very important in Mexico, is about the twins who are changed into the sun and the moon. Others, such as the myth of the flood, which ends in the descent of humanity from the native Noah and a dog, are found with great variations among different American groups; it is still possible to perceive their kinship.[4] In others there are passages that are remarkably similar. One tells of the weaver who is visited by a small bird, and who miraculously becomes pregnant.[5] Far from Mesoamerica, in the Andean world, Cuniyara Viracocha, transformed into a bird, lights on a *lucuma* tree under which the maiden Cavicalla was weaving, and leaves her pregnant (*Dioses y hombres de Huarochirí* 1975:26–27). In their entirety Mesoamerican myths form a coherent nucleus, a particular order, that served as an ideological framework for societies that existed before the European conquest.

The Religious and Mythical Unity of Mesoamerica as a Starting Point for the Study of Present-Day Indigenous Traditions

The mythology and religion of Mesoamerican people are the products of that common history to which we have referred. Temporal and regional differences cannot be denied (Rivera Dorado 1986a), but given the fact that ties of a very different type, chiefly economic and political, were managed under the cloak of religious interest, or on the basis of an order established by the gods, both mythology and religion served as common denominators that permitted a normal development of diverse relationships among Mesoamerican groups.

As a matter of fact, religious conflicts were not caused by antagonistic religious creeds. Historically they usually appeared as a form of resistance to the imposition on a people of the patron god of another group, but this is the flimsy disguise of a struggle for power, the real cause of the conflicts. Records also indicate religious conflicts as causes of what in reality were political struggles, when the tyranny of despots found no better ploy at hand. They are a pretext for plunder. A clear example of this is the capture and death of the Chichimec who refused to perform certain rites in Colhua territory; the Mexica intervened to execute the guilty—and appropriate their lands (*Anales de Cuauhtitlán* 1945:31).

The unity of the basic nucleus of the predominant deities, the calendar, cyclic rituals, symbolism and the myths of origin has been supported.[6] It is also imperative to point out that this religion emerged as a whole, not just an aggregate of pieces gathered from all the corners of Mesoamerica. Several factors have contributed to the erroneous idea of a religious mosaic. First, documental sources repeatedly state that a god originated with or "belongs to" a certain people. Such statements have been taken too literally, interpreted as referring to the invention of a god rather than to its patronage. The proper meaning, the tutelage of a group recognized in a god, has been neglected. Second, the multitude of names given to Mesoamerican gods is confusing. There is frequent mention of the introduction of gods foreign to Mesoamerica by recently arrived groups; in most cases, these are either existing gods, presented under new names, or hitherto minor avatars of the Mesoamerican pantheon, rather than foreign gods bursting upon the scene with the arrival of the newcomers. Furthermore the introduction of regional iconographic elements can likewise be confused with the presentation of a new god, as can intensification in the cult of an already present but little-known god. Lastly, the fact that conquerors collected the idols of conquered people is misinterpreted as evidence of syncretism rather than as a means of political control.

Misunderstanding of this matter has led to faulty judgments, such as that of Ricard (1947:102) concerning the Mexica: "Their religion was a polytheism of extraordinary richness, due largely to the Aztecs' custom of adopting the pantheon of gods of the conquered tribes." Ricard's opinion dates to 1932, but similar ones are still around. A role has been attributed to certain groups, among them the Mexica, of concentrating diverse elements, of integrating and diffusing a syncretic cult through their conquests. This image is false. The possible incorporation of foreign deities into a well-structured, stable cult of long tradition would have been, in any case, of minor importance. Davies (1979: 22) correctly states, "In general terms, I find in the Mesoamerican pantheon more restored gods than new ones."

What is true of religion can also be said of mythology, of the interpretations of myth, narration, and iconography. Regional independent creation is overreported, because not enough attention is paid to the constant and vigorous interrelationships of the Mesoamerican peoples, nor to the rich heritage of indigenous traditions today. It is essential to assess correctly the extent of cultural processes. For that reason J. M. Martinez (1985) denies that a narrative from Yucatan can be called Yucatecan if the material therein cannot be clearly perceived to be from that area. There is no reason to classify tales as Yucatecan if the same ones are found abundantly outside the peninsula. Even more commonly a mistaken origin is attributed to a myth. A myth need only have been recorded in one place in early colonial times for that place to be designated as its supposed and only source. Today if ever a myth is found bearing a resemblance to some passage from *La leyenda de los soles*, an attempt will be made to explain its presence by saying that in the pre-Hispanic past the group was dominated by the Mexica and that the myth is proof of ideological imposition. There is no assumption that such a group may have participated in the Mesoamerican tradition as much as, or perhaps more than, the Mexica themselves, and that to explain their possession of a myth it is not necessary to resort to a reconstruction in which the Mexica played a role. We may because of the limitations of our knowledge or for practical reasons, continue to call a narrative Nahua, Mayan, Mazatec, or Totonac. We need the indications of geography and time, but our designations will only be helpful if we realize that they do not imply creation or exclusive possession.

Taking Stock

Once we have identified the four fundamental problems in determining the links between Mesoamerican myths and indigenous myths in contemporary Mexico and Central America, we need a term to refer to religious continuity. In chapter 10 I will return to the problem of the singularity or plurality of Mesoamerican religion and the continuity of Mesoamerican religious thought to our own time. I will not give the arguments in advance. I will simply propose two assumptions: that indigenous religions in Mexico are not contemporary versions of the religion of Mesoamerica and that, nevertheless, they derive in a large part from it. Today's native religions originate as much from Mesoamerican religion as from Christianity, though colonial history has distanced them considerably from both, and are as different from each other. I shall therefore distinguish between the *Mesoamerican religion* (which came to an end as an institution with Spanish domination) and the *colonial religion* (which emerged from Mesoamerican religion and Christianity and continues until the present time), and I will include both as the product of a long and eventful development in what I will call *Mesoamerican religious tradition* (see chapter 24).

Finally, after posing the four problems and a plan for their solution, and proposing a term I believe to be suitable, I can enumerate the four central propositions of this book.

1.   I propose a more intensive debate on Mesoamerican myth. The study of Mesoamerican myth has a long history but insufficient results. Publication of ancient myths, more or less adhering to texts from the primary sources, has been scarce, as have in-depth studies. The works of Brinton and Spence can be cited,[7] Krickeberg's work ([1928] 1985), or the recently published collection of the National Institute of Anthropology and History (*Mitos cosmogónicos del México Indígena* 1987), which includes both ancient and modern myths. There are studies of particular myths, mythical personages, or sources (Moreno de los Arcos 1967; Montoliu Villar 1981; Alcina Franch 1984; Garza 1983; Rivera Dorado 1987), among them several that offer very interesting theoretical problems (Graulich 1981); but works that focus principally on ancient Mesoamerican myth are lacking. An exception is Graulich's recent book, *Mythes et rituels du Mexique ancien préhispanique* (1987b), a profound and erudite study. A major examination of theories, as well as methods and techniques, is essential.

2.   This work is a search for bases precise enough to improve ethnographic information as it serves to enrich our understanding of ancient Mesoamerican societies. The mass of myths gathered in the first years of colonization is significant (Krickeberg 1985:9). However, research on myth and, in general, on ideology, requires a considerable amount of material. It is necessary to gather information that can be turned into reliable data. One criterion used in the past is persistence through the long trajectory of Mesoamerican religious tradition.

Incidentally this persistence can be useful in evaluating the first colonial collections of myths and legends. Sometimes seriously (Lévi-Strauss 1968b: 178n6) and sometimes lightly, a lack of confidence has been expressed regarding colonial texts, because their content or their recording have been thought to be defective. The degree of coherence between today's texts and those of early colonial times could be a measure of the trustworthiness of both.

In general all comparative studies of cultural processes (J. Thompson 1965– 67; Gossen 1978; Bruce 1978) will help refine theoretical discourses and investigative methods and techniques proposed for parallel study in other fields of scientific research (e.g., in archeology; see Hodder 1982).

3.   On the same model, an attempt will be made to strengthen the research on present-day indigenous myths. Nowadays the real need is not so much for quantity of recorded tales as for specialized studies.[8] Moedano Navarro (1975) and J. M. Martínez (1985) complain about the lack of theoretical statements

Mesoamerican Religion

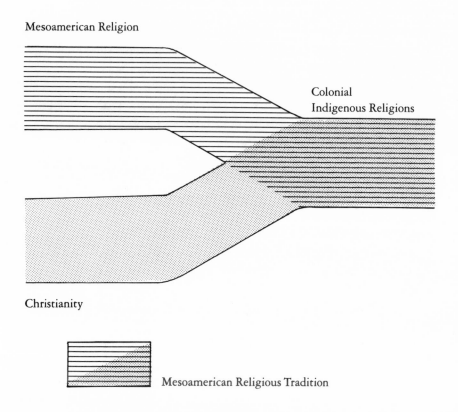

Figure 1. The Mesoamerican religious tradition

and of overall insight in the study of native Mexican narrative.[9] They are right, although studies based on theory and the rigorous comparison of the past and the present are not entirely absent (Hunt 1977).

One should be aware that these persistences, those of present-day myths directed toward the Mesoamerican past as well as those in the reverse direction, are frequently questioned. There are two fundamental problems. The first is of a historical nature: the explanation for the persistence of religious content in the diverse beliefs and practices across the centuries and, above all, through the radical changes in socioeconomic organizations. This problem, present throughout the book, will be addressed in detail in chapter 24. The other problem is a problem of logic: the value of analogical inferences in general and, in particular, their value in the field of myth. This question will be examined in chapter 28.

4.   Finally, this work seeks less to analyze myths than to explore the analyzable nature of myth. It does not pretend to formulate complex formulas to be applied mathematically to particular texts. To the contrary the desire is to stimulate readers to understand myth in all its complexity, not simply as a text, nor as something fortuitous and superfluous, an exotic toy, but as a social institution, such as Mauss (1971:147–48) proposed—an institution, one must add, that can speak for and explain the society that created it.

3 THE POINT OF DEPARTURE

How could you say that you know half of all the sciences,
when you know nothing about them?
   Because Aristotle said, "Anyone who answers,
'I don't know,' has revealed half of wisdom."

Yosef ben Meir ben Zabarra,
Libro de los entretenimientos

Myth, according to Mauss, is a social institution. If through myth we wish to
understand the social relationships of the peoples who have produced it, we
must begin by analyzing and defining it. Following the advice of handbooks
on logic, we should use the method of Porphyry's Logical Tree: indicate the
genus most similar to the myth and then point out specific differences—as
simple as that. But what we find is a jungle. In the study of mythology, a common complaint is that every researcher has a different concept of what myth
is (S. Thompson 1965). The problem is not simple diversity but the extreme
heterogeneity of the concepts. In this respect myth is similar to religion and
magic. The enormous gamut of defining criteria, in the best of cases, and the
absence of clear criteria in the rest, cause what some researchers call a real
hodgepodge. This hinders adequate communication among the specialists.
The definitions should be made explicit, not with the utopian idea of ulti-
mately reaching the true definition of myth, an accord on what myth is, but in
order that a clear understanding of the points of departure may facilitate a scientific discussion. Everything must start from an adequate framework of reference: history, as I have proposed, or the religious ethnology of Lévi-Strauss
for anyone not convinced of the need for a history that is an all-encompassing
social science. Otherwise myth will retain its character as a free-fire zone where
everyone can set up their own rules for the game. In Lévi-Strauss's words
(1968a), the study of myth will continue "to indulge itself in chaos."

It is impossible to arrive at a single, simple definition of myth. Definitions
are elements of conceptual bodies, of theoretical structures. Their relativity,
however, does not diminish their value. They are the indispensable instruments in research. But the one who defines, when trying to determine limits,
may face, as I do now, the problem of knowing where to start. Much of what
I will propose in the following chapters will form part of my concept of myth,

for which I must give convincing proof there. So from the beginning I would have to state as fact that which I will try to demonstrate later. To avoid this problem—and since I do not believe in a cartesian departure from zero, but in the creation of judgments deriving from prior knowledge—I will take a tentative definition as a starting point.[1] I will then use it as a basis for discussion, to contradict it, correct it, or add to it, depending upon how the discussion develops. At the end of the book I will offer a different concept that, in turn, will serve as a point of departure for the reader to shred and transform creatively, as I intend to do with this first one. I will begin, then, by crystallizing my prejudgments.

Although I cherish my preconceptions, they are not entirely my own. If they were I would make a nominal definition like those of mathematicians, simply saying that to me *definiendum myth* corresponds to *definiens x*. I cannot do it. If I did so I would be ignoring a reality. What kind of reality would I pretend not to recognize? Is there something called myth to which a definition of myth should correspond? No. Let us say it simply in historical terms: realities have existed that deserved to be called myths. Certain societies perceived in particular complexes of realities a conjunction of similarities, and tied the representations of them to the term *myth* (or its equivalents). Lacking complete harmony, the complex of realities marched along on one side, the representations on another, and the term myth (or its equivalents) on another. The complex of realities was diversified and transformed; the representations also changed; and the term, *myth,* was stretched to include other representations of similar realities. In conclusion, although historically the reality-image-term formula could be reconstructed, some of the social realities included today under the term *myth* are too diverse, or their links are not exactly based on the most important characteristics of the realities referred to. Any attempt to embrace all of them under a single concept would risk stretching the defining limits so far as to lose the content. This is what happens, in spite of an author's precautions, to definitions like those of Count (1973:318–19), when he affirms that mythic narrative is everything that expresses in explicit terms a vision of the world.

What can be done in this complicated situation? First, it is necessary to discover in the wide range of specific complexes of realities the one that possesses the most typical features attributed to myth. They will not necessarily be characteristics held in common, because of the scope of realities now included in the term.[2] Second, it is necessary to analyze this complex enough to formulate a concept of myth. Third, call it myth, but after specifying the content of the term.

We could go from there to the next stage of the problem of defining myth. Are we capable of understanding the social realities of traditions foreign to us? In the field of myth the question arises when the researcher faces classifications not compatible with those in his own culture. Gossen (1974:248–49), to whom we owe a profound study of the oral tradition of the Chamula, recommends explaining indigenous narrations in terms of the Chamulas' own categories. Gossen's proposal considerably expands the possibility of understanding Indian thought. However, there is no reason why an investigator should not principally use categories from his own culture. The two ways are not mutually exclusive, but complement each other. A scientist cannot renounce the formation of his own concepts. This is not to deny that in studying myth it is very useful to take into consideration the concepts of the creators themselves. For example consider the clearness of definition Boas (1968:454–55) derived from the indigenous distinction between myth and story. This is a fundamental part of the investigation, but it cannot be carried to the extreme of believing that a social reality cannot be investigated except by using the categories—scientific or not—from the group under study. What would happen in the case of groups that have not formed categories or have not made them explicit? To go even further, can social realities be studied that were not even given a single name by the people who created them? Oliver Bloch (1976) gives us a clear example of this when referring to Greco-Roman antiquity. He says that Greece had no word corresponding to the modern term *religion*.[3]

In this study I begin with the idea that the historic complexity of our present reality allows us to scientifically understand the social realities of less complex societies.[4] Does this mean that a concept applicable to a reality at one historic stage can necessarily be applied to the reality of another? Not at all, since social realities are transformed during the course of history.[5]

This brings us to another serious problem in defining myth. Can we create a concept that is applicable to all societies, regardless of the stage of history at which they are found? In other words can we assume that our idea of myth has the characteristics of a closed concept, useful in the interpretation of social realities in any part of the world in any epoch? Kirk, one of the most penetrating critics of the theory of myth, attacks the persistent and distorting effect of treating myth as a closed category that attributes the same characteristics to the myths of different cultures (1973:42). The criticism is accurate and must be taken into account throughout this book. It is only reasonable to assume that myth relates to the total social reality in different ways and under different historical conditions, and that this affects its characteristics considerably. It would seem then, that the concept of myth ought to be an open concept.

The next problem is perhaps the most important in defining myth. We are speaking of myth as if its nature were a given, but what kind of thing is a myth? The first answer that comes to mind is that myth is a story; but it is also seen as a complex of beliefs, as a way of capturing and expressing a specific kind of reality, as a system of logic or a form of discourse. These are some, not all, of the forms of mythic expression.[6] However, it is pertinent to review, although briefly, the different ways of understanding myth.

Many writers—most of them—refer to myth as an account, as a narration. Its usual form is oral, anonymous text, although one cannot overlook the monumental contributions of a Homer or a Hesiod. Myth, in any case, is a work, a product, a crystallization of thought, a discernible object, a unit, subject to analysis and comparison.

For others myth is a complex of beliefs. Watts (1954:7) defines it as a collection of tales that reveal an inner sense of the universe and of human life. These beliefs, he tells us, are embodied in narrations, images, rituals, ceremonies, and symbols. Myth has also been seen as a specific way to capture, feel, and express a type of reality. For symbolists, mythic thought, starting from an intuitive, primordial, and religious experience, is directed not only to knowledge but to fantasy and sensibility, expressing itself tautologically in a language rich in images and symbols that cannot be converted to the arbitrary signs of ordinary language (García Gual 1984). Cassirer, one of the most outstanding spokesman for symbolism, refers to myth as "a unitary energy of the human spirit; . . . [a] kind of idea which asserts itself amid all the diversity of the objective material it presents" (1955, 2:235).

Special mention should be made of the concept developed by Lévi-Strauss of the myth as a system of symbolic logic. For this anthropologist there exists a universal system of logic that operates through binary opposites and through transformation, which is expressed in the internal structures of specific narrations that deal with the fundamental enigmas of mankind and of the world.

Myth can also be interpreted as a form of discourse in which the message itself is not transcendent. Barthes finds the essence of myth in a second-order relationship between signifier, signified, and sign. If in the first statement the integration of the signifier and the signified becomes the sign, in myth this primary sign goes on to be a signifier that, united to a second signified, makes up the sign of the myth:

> In myth, we find again the tri-dimensional pattern . . . the signifier, the signi-
> fied, and the sign. But myth is a peculiar system, in that it is constructed from
> a semiological chain which existed before it: it is a second-order semiological

system. That which is a sign (namely the associative total of a concept and an image) in the first system, becomes a mere signifier in the second. (1972:114)

Barthes concludes that "Myth hides nothing and flaunts nothing: it distorts; myth is neither a lie nor a confession: it is an inflection" (ibid.:129).

Lotman and Uspenkij hold a semiotic view in which the relationships among the textual components are also fundamental. These writers specifically state that they are not concerned with myth as a specific narrative text, and that they make a distinction between phrases of a descriptive character ("the world is matter") and phrases of a mythological nature ("the world is a horse"). In both sentences the copula is the same (is), but it indicates totally different logical operations. The mythological form implies a recognition or identification, while the descriptive form is linked to a translation. In mythology a transformation of objects occurs and, consequently, understanding the texts requires understanding the processes of transformation. According to these authors, the mythological text is not exclusive to societies with mythological sensibilities, but extends to modern times. Minds not oriented toward mythology prefer to give a metaphor its literal meaning, which annuls the very metaphor in the text. That is how Lotman and Uspenkij (1979) explain surrealism.

Let us move on to the subject matter of myth. Since many writers regard the nature of myth—or at least part of the thing-myth—to be identified with a text, it is not unusual that another problem of definition is the character of the subject matter. It is often said that a myth should deal with gods or heroes, with no need to distinguish between them, since no insurmountable barrier separates them (Bastide 1947:50). Thus myth becomes a sacred account—a characteristic also defended by some writers. Supernatural beings perform their deeds in sacred history. Through the presence of gods in primordial time, the supernatural emerges in the world to establish its existence. Myths reveal the creative activity and develop the sacred nature of the work (Eliade 1968:18–19, 32). The emergence of gods is present in the repetition of the myth. Repetition is linked to the essence of sacred actions, and in repetition myth and ritual become mutually credible. Myth becomes a reality, it is "the repetitive expression of a powerful event"; time is suspended; myth is beyond temporality (Leew 1964:398–403). According to Berger and Luckmann (1979:142), the concept of the emergence of what is sacred implies a high degree of continuity between the social and cosmic orders and between their respective processes of legitimization, since all reality seems to be made of the same material.

It is also held that myths summarize concepts that always accompany human life: the I and the other, bravery, space, time, nature as power and as a numinous being, the sacred, the universe, the permanent and the transcendent, continuity, tradition, the regulation of world phenomena, the person, ethics . . . (Count 1973:341–432).

This survey of the problems of defining myth cannot end without addressing its functions. Cohen (1969) divides theories about myth into seven principal classes. Although he does not uniformly establish function as a characterizing criterion in all classes, he does concede prime importance to function, as he distinguishes between:

1. Theories that deal with myth as a kind of explanation;

2. Those that make it a symbolic affirmation that has the function of mytho-poetic expression;

3. Those that define it as an expression of the subconscious;

4. Those that give it the function of creating and maintaining social solidarity and cohesion;

5. Those that give myth the function of legitimizing institutions and social practices;

6. Those that consider it a form of symbolic establishment of social structure, possibly linked to ritual; and

7. Structuralist theory.

Cohen's principal criteria for the classification of myth, then, address its functions: the explanatory myth, a category stressing the interpretation of natural phenomena; the expressive myth, sometimes of the ineffable in the world, sometimes of the depths of the mind—myths are "the secular dreams of a youthful humanity (Rank n.d.)"—at times of the great enigmas of the world and of society; and the myth that gives society solidarity, cohesion, legitimacy, and structural regulation by means of the symbol.

Those who have pointed out the importance of function in myth emphasize its profoundly social character:

> Myth fulfills in primitive culture an indispensable function: it expresses, enhances, and codifies belief; it safeguards and enforces morality; it vouches for the efficiency of ritual and contains practical rules for the guidance of man. Myth is thus a vital ingredient of human civilization; it is not an idle tale, but a hard-worked active force; it is not an intellectual explanation or an artis-

tic imagery, but a pragmatic charter of primitive faith and moral wisdom. (Malinowski 1954)

Dumézil affirms the imperative need for myth when he writes that "the people with no myths would now be dead," and adds:

> The function of that particular class of legends known as myths is to express dramatically the ideology under which a society lives; not only to hold out to its conscience the values it recognizes and the ideals it pursues from generation to generation, but above all to express its very being and structure, the elements, the connections, the balances, the tensions that constitute it; to justify the rules and traditional practices without which everything within a society would disintegrate. (1969:3)

This is the concept of myth as a justification of values. Its logic corresponds to the sad judgment of Jung, faced with the modern abandonment of ancestral symbols on the altar of rationalism. "[Man's] spiritual and moral traditions disintegrated, and now he is paying the price of that collapse in the disorientation and dissociation extending throughout the world" (1977:91). This recalls an earlier concept of myth as a weapon in the fight against oppression, the image of an undetermined future in time, capable of guiding the proletariat to triumph (Sorel n.d.:125–29).

Finally, it must be mentioned that there are theories that reduce myths, outside all historical bounds, to a genesis and a function. Girard (1983:100, 101, 319) maintains that myth had its origin in the pristine mechanism of the propitiatory victim. Not only myth but everything religious—rituals themselves—the essential rules for cultural order, political power, judicial power, festivals, games, incest taboos, the art of theater, and philosophy had the same origin. The roots of myth, according to Girard, are found in the institution of the propitiatory victim used to channel uncontrolled violence.

A Provisional Definition

After reviewing problems of definition, there remains the problem of elaborating a provisional definition of myth that will serve as a point of departure for subsequent discussions in this book. I cannot consider function as one of its elements; in order to do that, it would be necessary to delineate the other characteristics of myth clearly enough to place it in particular social contexts.

It is preferable to determine whether or not the provisional definition corresponds to an open or to a closed concept. Prudence indicates the first. This definition-in-progress cannot lay claim to universality, either in its origin or when it corresponds to a more elaborated concept. Afterwards it will be possible to determine if some of its elements apply to other times and other places. The reader will judge.

> From all these points of view it is essential to have a clear idea of what myths are and what they are not, and, so far as possible, of the ways in which they are likely to operate. The ways, in the plural—for I regard it as axiomatic that myths do not have a single form, or act according to one simple set of rules, either from epoch to epoch or from culture to culture. (Kirk 1970:2)

Kirk does not deny, however, the possibility of finding many resemblances:

> There is no single type of myth . . . and unitary theories of mythical function are largely a waste of time; but that does not mean that there may not be a primary mode of mythical imagination or expression which is then applied in different ways and to different ends. (1970:252)

I share Kirk's idea, because the concept sought can be applied to the Mesoamerican religious tradition. However, two clarifications are in order. First, the possibility of similarities allows reference to many diverse traditions, not necessarily because of the identity of human nature, but through the similarity of the forms that are produced in the parallel development of societies. Second, to the contrary, that the historical distance between Mesoamerican myth and indigenous myth today does not permit an easy general conceptualization, and that this applies fundamentally to the functions of myth.

The following definitory note derives, then, from a pragmatic purpose, hence its provisional character. I consider, for the present, that myth is a story. Its means of expression is the word. Its autonomy and its ending make it a text (Ducrot and Todorov 1974:337). Every myth is a unit, subject to analysis and comparison. Having taken this practical position, I must define the text, and I shall do so according to the theme of the narration. The themes of gods and heroes, or of sacred subjects, do not exclude or include enough. I have chosen as the determining theme that emergence from the other time into human time, which brought about the origin of the world or the origin of something in the world: origin as foundation and origin as a beginning (Kerenyi 1972:14).

Figure 2. Common opossum, *Didelphis marsupialis*

Does this limit me to the myth of origins? Yes. Perhaps it does not do justice to Oedipus or Asdiwal, mythical heroes par excellence, but I see no alternative at this stage of the discussion. I define myth, tentatively, as a text that relates the emergence of the other time into human time, causing the origin—beginning and creation—of something.

Therefore, let us continue. What is the other time? Let us look for the answer in the narrations that speak of our hero, the opossum.

4 THE OTHER TIME

The palms of your hands from the life-giving forces
   of the firmament
will certainly be yours.
A small nose from the life-giving forces of the firmament
will certainly be yours.
Little eyes from the life-giving forces of the firmament
will certainly be yours.
A little strip from the life-giving forces of the firmament
will certainly be yours.
A bristling mane from the life-giving forces of the firmament
will certainly be yours,
since, nearby, he slumbers peacefully!

> "Words that we send to follow the anteater,"
> a chant of the Pai-Kaiova Guarani

The Mazahua say that when the opossum had hair on his tail, he ruled over the other animals (Castro 1963:653). The Mazatec affirm that, when the earth was formed, when it was not yet solid, the opossum was king of the world (Portal 1986:45). There was a time, another time, when animals talked and things were acquiring the forms they have now.

According to Lévi-Strauss, the Indians of British Columbia and Alaska distinguished story from myth by saying that myth developed at a time when the distinction between animals and men had not yet been established (1979b:2). The idea of this primary time of the first ancestors, when mythical deeds were unfolding, is prevalent throughout Mexico and Central America. The traditions take us back to a time so dark (Hollenbach 1977) and so impressionable that the feet of ancient beings left their imprint on the still-damp rocks (Lumholtz 1970, 1:293). According to the Huichol,

The first creatures in the world were not Huichols, but héwi and nanáwata, who were people and animals at the same time. The nanáwata lived near the boundary of the world at the four cardinal points, while the héwi set up their residence near the central hole from which they had emerged and where they settled after wandering through the four regions in search of an appropriate place. In those times, nobody knew anything about peyote. Moreover, there was total darkness, since the Sun had not yet appeared. (Anguiano and Furst 1987:28–29)

There is constant mention of the imprecise distinction between humans and animals, but it is not just a blurring of a boundary. One of the characteristics of beings at that time was language, a quintessential human attribute. The creatures spoke *as humans do*. Their human nature was also implied in calling them Christians, assuming that *to be Christian* is synonymous with *being a person* (Ichon 1973:67). But animals were not the only ones who could speak. The Mixe affirm that "all things—the deer, the *temazate* [*Mazama americanal*], the boar, rocks, sticks, water—everything talked" (W. Miller 1956:90). The Sun and the Moon were people who walked about the world (Bartolomé and Barabas 1982:108), and Mother Earth strode among the cliffs "and devoured the people who passed that way, our animal ancestors" (*Wirrarika irratsikayari* 1982:55). Finally it must be noted that at that time, mythic time, people as such did not exist. We are speaking of the ancestors, the ones who gave origin to the beings who exist today: humans, animals, plants, stones, water, the Sun, the Moon, the Earth. They were the beings that, before the beginning of the human world and time, had other characteristics, which resembled those of human beings. They were *similar* to people, they spoke *like* people, they had thoughts and passions, because they were persons. They were distinguishable by their ancient nature and by the germ of the existence they would later have on earth. The Huichol say that the wisest of those who awaited the birth of the Sun was the person-quail; but there were other person-animals in the gathering, among them the field people-ants [*Atta sexdens*] (*Wirrarika irratsikayari* 1982:31–35). All this was true until the moment of the great transformation, at which time all superior faculties were lost, and all acquired the conditions that would endure into human time.

Ichon (1973:66–67), in his study of current Totonac religion, says that the arrival of the Sun brought strange events. All persons were turned into animals, into birds, etc., or all the "Christian" animals turned into savages, who fled toward the mountains. The Trique say, "God made their voices descend to their stomachs, and then they were convinced that they were indeed animals, and they went to the mountains to live" (Hollenbach 1980). The Mixe relate, "Everything talked. Then, when Jesus Christ was born, all became mute" (W. Miller 1956:90). According to the Zapotec, "Then the Sun and the Moon came out and all the ancestors were afraid and hid themselves under the ground" (Parsons 1966:327), which explains the presence of images of gods beneath the soil. Old Mazatecs still hold that "when Christ was performing miracles, if a tree was wounded, it would cry out, and the earth also did this when it was about to be planted. At Christ's coming everything changed and became what it is today" (Incháustegui 1977:108). They also say that "In the time of darkness, Lord Opossum was the chief of the old ones who gave advice; the boar was his pig. Animals were domesticated, but once the light and the universe came, they changed into wild animals" (Boege 1988:100).

There are several ways of describing the creative moment. It is commonly called the first dawn, the first rising of the sun [1]—ideas resembling those of the ancient Mesoamerican myths. The religion superimposed by the Europeans resulted in the fusion of the figure of the Sun and of Christ. Thus the first creative light appears also in the tales of the birth of Christ and of his ascent into heaven after the crucifixion. The moment is also marked by the crowing of a rooster, which in some accounts is involved in a miraculous sequence of events:

When Jesus saw [that men believed he was a demon and that Jews could not carry the cross], he offered to bear it and he placed it inside the Larrainzar church. At 12 P.M. he climbed upon the cross and they nailed him to it. He threw a paper at the Virgin, who turned into a white rooster that began to crow, and all the Jews died. Then Christ came down from the cross and, three days later, ascended into Heaven with the Virgin. Jesus became the Sun, and the Virgin the Moon. Previously only a faint light had existed. Thus were the Sun and the Moon born. (Holland 1963:76)[2]

The Kanholabal of Guatemala tell a similar tale, in which the Jews take Jesus prisoner and crucify him, but Jesus orders a ladder to appear above the cross and climbs into Heaven. The cock crows and the world is illuminated (J. Thompson 1975:404). The moment of creation is often marked by a benediction (Taggart 1983:102).

The ancestors were caught in one particular action that became the beginning of a pattern. The original *tepescuintle* [spotted cavie, *Cuniculus paca*], for example, was a bandit that had been imprisoned. When Jesus Christ appeared, there was general confusion. The captive tepescuintle took advantage of this to escape from prison and hide in a cave. Since then the tepescuintle has made caves his refuge (Incháustegui 1984:69).

Creation gave rise both to beings and to names; at the moment of transformation a new name is given. Tonantzi was riding horseback when a boy frightened the animal. The mare reared on its hind legs and threw the goddess.

The goddess transformed the boy, naming him "crocodile." She also punished her mount, taking away her ability to conceive, and giving her the name of "mule" (Preuss 1982:173). Moreover those who were enlightened received their names at the moment of transformation. There was a group of ancestors who awaited the miracle and who had to receive the Sun by saying his name. In a previously mentioned Huichol myth, person-quail could name the dawn and person-turkey could pronounce the name of the Sun, while the other ancestors could not (*Wirrarika irratsikayari* 1982:31–35). The Mixe, using Christian nomenclature, say that at the birth of Christ, the rooster called out, loud and clear, "Jesus is here—here—here!" The donkey, who was not awake at the precise moment of creation, could only give sad cries, and since then has been limited to his "Ou-ou-ou-ou!" (W. Miller 1956:207).

The first of these two myths recalls the old solar legend about Nanahua-tzin, the "pimply one." [3] Nanahuatzin cast himself into the fire, changing into the Sun. The ancestors waited for his appearance, looking for signs of him in every corner of the earth. In the old Nahua versions of the myth, their failure was due to not having opportunely prepared an offering, or of not as-certaining the place from which the Sun would emerge. One of the ancestors himself had eaten the offering for the Sun and could not find another in time for the Sun's arising. His punishment was to be changed into the nocturnal *huinaxcatl:* timid, always hungry, pursuing shadows when he looked for food (Ruiz de Alarcón 1953:59). In another version, quails, locusts, butterflies, and snakes could not verify at what place the Sun would appear and, since then and because of it, they were condemned to be sacrificed to the gods.

Summing up, it is seen that in the other time the ancestors, with capabili-ties similar to those of humans, were caught up in their own particular stories. At the terrible moment of transformation, they were hurled into human time with diminished attributes, destined to initiate a new class. [4] Their distinguish-ing characteristics appear from the moment of the amazing transformation. From that time on they were given names with which they would be known in human time.

Let us look at this process from another point of view, that of people who live in societies in which it is difficult to perceive the development of tech-niques of production, of institutions, or of values or rules of behavior; a point of view in which the ideas of evolution, transformation, or progress are weak or nonexistent. It is the somewhat static perspective of people who perceive time to be a constant repetition of the same processes. The point of departure can be the ordinary act of common people. Why ordinary actions and actors? My explanation falls back on that simplicity so esteemed by natural-science researchers, making it clear, however, that this use is not due to the mere attraction of a purely mechanical transference from one science to another. On the contrary it is not justifiable to force simple solutions onto processes as complex as those involved in society.[5] But this is only the beginning of formulating an explanation, for simplicity will avoid an answer that is dependent upon an unnecessarily complex and possibly gratuitous process. So long as it is not necessary to formulate a highly detailed hypothesis, we will seek a solution in the simplicity of the statement of the problem. If we can do without the unexplainable—beings terrorized or ecstatic before the magnitude of natural phenomena, primitive philosophers tormented by the great mysteries of the universe, people searching for their place in the order of the universe and in history, poets haunted by the muses, creating myths, the dreams of a child-like humanity, and with protologics or different logics—if none of these are necessary, let us try to understand how common people, carrying out ordinary actions, perceived their time and the other time. We speak of those who worked in the world, for whom the absence of or the excess of rain was to be feared because they knew the effect of drought or deluge on their crops. They were born, grew, and died knowing their exact—sometimes too precise—place in society and nature, burdened with problems and fundamental mysteries found in the course of their daily lives.

People who conceive their reality to be static rely upon the regularity of processes, on the existence of classes of beings, realizing that if something were not as it is, it would affect the existence of everything related to it. These are basic principles, the precepts indispensable to living as human beings. Why is a class as it is, regardless of the appearance or destruction of its individual members? Because there is a characterizing link that binds each individual to the class. Where does this link come from? If the world is perceived as static, from a characterizing principle. There is some transcendent essence, a force, an independent element in each of the individuals; this element exists from the time of origin. Why are the multiple classes different from each other? Because the different forces, essences, and virtues are not alike. Each one characterizes the individuals that comprise a class. Why are these forces, essences, or elements not alike? Because something different happened to each one at a precise, determining moment. Because they had their own processes, lives, happenings, histories. Such as what? Such as the histories of humankind.

Men build images of the world in which they live, not of just any world. Even when they visualize other worlds in their fantasies, they construct them out of the experience their existence gives them. (Cardoso 1977:71)

And that time, why is it the *other time*? Why must it harken back to an origin and leave its mold behind? Because if that time were now, one would see different marvelous beings emerge daily. One would live in the chaos of creation, but this is not so. One lives in the order of what is established, not in the terrible ordaining, establishing process.

These general, fundamental questions about daily life are enough to explain the need to construct an image such as that of another time. The hypothetical answers are enough to formulate a model by which humans could formulate the diverse causative chains that gave birth to beings and the circumstances surrounding them. So it has not been necessary to go beyond the hypothesis of the common person.

The *other time* is not homogeneous. Previously I have identified three different times: first, that of the intranscendental existence of the gods; second, truly mythic time, that of creation; third, the time of humans (López Austin 1975). Thus, we can presume that the *other* time has been conceived to have a dual nature; a first part, amorphous, similar to the idea of eternity, seems to withdraw from the mythological background, like Borges's sea (1983:17):

> Before the dream (or terror) wove
> mythologies and cosmologies,
> before the time when days were coined,
> the sea, the forever sea, existed and was there . . .

It is the time of negation of the world as well as of the creative work of the gods. There is no creation yet. Therefore there are no histories of the gods. The stories about the gods also have to have a beginning, and this beginning makes one aware of a former reality. The time before creation, however, should be described, and the description must start from a specific reality that is negated: the reality of human time, over which a negative sign is superimposed. In antiquity, an old Cholulteca said:

> In the beginning before light or the Sun were created, earth was in darkness and shadow and devoid of any created thing. Everything flat, without hill or hollow, surrounded on all sides by water, without a tree or any created thing. (Durán 1984, 2:16–17)

The ancient Mixtec described that time in a similar way:

> Before there were days or years, the earth being in great darkness, everything was in chaos and confusion, the earth was covered by water; there was only slime and mud on the face of the earth. (Garcia 1981:327)[6]

The ancient Quiche were more explicit in their *Popol Vuh* (1950:81):

> This is the account of how all was in suspense, all calm, in silence; all motion-less, still, and the expanse of the sky was empty.
>
> This is the first account, the first narrative. There was neither man, nor animal, birds, fishes, crabs, trees, stones, caves, ravines, grasses, nor forests. There was only the sky.
>
> The surface of the earth had not appeared. There was only the calm sea and the great expanse of the sky.
>
> There was nothing brought together, nothing which could make a noise, nor anything which might move, or tremble, or could make noise in the sky.
>
> There was nothing standing; only the calm water, the placid sea, alone and tranquil. Nothing existed.
>
> There was only immobility and silence in the darkness, in the night. Only the Creator, the Maker, Tepeu, Gucumatz, the Forefathers, were in the water surrounded with light. They were hidden under green and blue feathers, and were therefore called Gucumatz.

Like an echo of those distant words, today's Huichol say that in the first time, "there was not a village on all the earth. Wolves, snakes and other animals lived in darkness, because at that time neither Sun, Our Creator, nor Fire, Our Grandfather, existed" (*Wirrarika irratsikayari* 1982:21). A scarcely defined time, perhaps created in response to the need to conceive of the originating forces as breaking away from the undifferentiated.

Isolated they would acquire individual traits, dance, fight, play, copulate, or destroy themselves in the following time, the time of creation. The vague time of intranscendence remains in the shadows, indefinitely open to the past. Its past disappears. On the other hand, the passage of forces toward the time of myth is precise. At times it is indicated by the appearance of giants, and with a previous appearance of the Sun (Durán 1984, 2:17), perhaps a projection of human time. Thus just as the time of myth is distinguished from human time by the appearance of the Sun, one can imagine the separation of intranscendent time and the time of myth by a protodawn.

The existence of the ancestors began with continuous prayer, retreats, labors, and penitence. These activities correspond to the period of intranscendence before the period of creation, and are interrupted by the beginning of mythic accounts.

Since the beings that will be inanimate have no links with the laws of human time, in the intranscendent period they are soft and formless, or they act recklessly and aggressively. The ancestors had to intervene or the transformations had to occur in order to achieve today's conditions. The soil and rocks were originally soft; the ancestors searched for wood that would give off smoke capable of drying the great surface. The opossum, the most intelligent of the ancestors, found the right tree, the copal (Portal 1986:45). There is also the tale about the Lord of Corn, who, when traveling, sat down to rest upon a stone. The stone bit him and Tamakastsiin, outraged, killed it with his knife. Since then stones have been immobile (González Cruz and Anguiano 1984). The Nahua of Tepoztlan say today that "in another time, order had still not been established on earth. They say the hills moved about; but afterwards, when order was established, they no longer moved, but remained where they were" (Nahuatl text from Dakin 1977).[7]

The order we know today did not exist, but there were laws and a supreme ruler. At least that is what the ancient Nahua believed. In the time of myth, a god of the ancestors ruled. His name was Centeotl Icnopiltzintli (Ruiz de Alarcón 1953:56–57; Serna 1953:198), which translates as the "unique god, the orphan," or as Ruiz de Alarcón puts it, "the only god, the god without a father." Today's Mazatec, not following this tradition, say that in the time of darkness Pontius Pilate governed (Boege 1988:100). And these same Mazatec attributed the foundation of everything, the combining of all forces, to the beginning of the world:

> Things as they are today, such as the plants that restore strength to the ill, all
> come from the beginning, from the birth of the universe, when nature was
> created. When day appeared, everything was already prepared, everything
> was ready before there was life as we have it today. Everything had its place,
> everything was arranged for the moment light came, when illumination began.
> Everything had been thought out when the sky appeared, the earth. . . . That
> plant leaves must be medicine, that they must help the ill to recover their spirit.
> (Boege 1988:90–91)

For the ancient Nahua, who would be that unique god: the combination of all the forces, the god "without a father," who governs the human world? Perhaps he does not deserve all the credit. One of the most important gods of the pantheon of the Nahua was the Old God, the God of Fire. It is possible that he was the one charged with bringing about the transformations at the moment of creation. Soustelle sees sacrifice by fire as a requirement for resurrection to be one of the common ideas of ancient Nahua thought (Soustelle 1982:108–9), and the process of transformation as a true process of resurrection. This was apparent in the solar myth: Nanahuatzin threw himself into the fire to be changed into the Sun and, after him, Tecuciztecatl, who became the

Moon. When Ruiz de Alarcón (1984:70) refers explicitly to the two worlds and two kinds of people (those of the time of the ancestors and those of human time), he seems to generalize the rite by fire:

The first [world was one] in which the kind of men that it had were transformed into animals, and into the sun and the moon [in the second one], and thus they attribute a rational soul to the sun and moon and animals, speaking to them for the purpose of their witchcraft as if they understood, calling to them and invoking them with other names for the purpose of their incantations, as will be told in more detail later. And in order to establish a basis for the adoration of the sun they tell a fable after the manner of Ovid's *Metamorphoses*, which they relate briefly. They say that, since the transformation had to be according to the merits of each one, in order for those of that [first] age to transform themselves into the things that they were to be in the second [age], a very big bonfire was ordered to be made, so that, after it was burning strongly, by testing themselves in it, they might acquire merits for the said transformation, with the understanding that by means of the fire they would gain honor and excellence and would remain lords of what was superior in the second age.

It is probable that at some time in the past fire was considered to be the implicit transforming element of the gods in the process of creation. However, it is not and was not explicitly mentioned in all the myths as the means by which ancestors were changed into beings in human time. Mythic accounts are quite varied. It is possible to outline a pattern marking the transition from a peaceful, prolonged existence that often suggests the former intranscendent time, to a complicated adventure, often violent, to the culminating moment of the transformation (sometimes death), and finally the presence of a new being, a recently created one, in human time. It is the process from which come future distinguishing traits. Death determines the nature and rebirth of the ancestor, its resurrection in the world as an earthly species. This model of events can be useful in identifying the individual steps. However not all of them are present in the various accounts, and some are so faint they are barely mentioned in the mythological episodes, for example, when the ancestor is depicted as very similar to that of the species in human time, and the transformation consists merely of the acquisition of a trait that supposedly the ancestor did not possess.

In myths about antiquity, the first step may describe a happy, leisurely, often palatial life in a courtly atmosphere, protected by safeguards that prevent the hero from entering the adventure stage. It was said of the Tlaxcalans:

These nations had a goddess they called the goddess of love, just as the ancient [Romans] had the goddess Venus. In a similar fashion the natives of this land had a goddess, called Xochiquetzal, who, they said, lived above the air and the nine heavens, who dwelt in delightful places with many amusements, accompanied by and guarded by many people, served by other goddess-like women in great luxury amid pleasures of fountains and rivers and beautiful groves, with wonderful recreation, lacking nothing. And she was in such a secret and well-guarded place that men could not see her. In her service she had a great number of dwarfs and hunchbacks, buffoons and jesters, who entertained her with exquisite music, dancing, and dance performances. She trusted these people and they were her secretaries to take messages to the gods she coveted, and her entertainment was to spin and weave beautiful, unusual things. They described her as so beautiful and lovely that there was no match for her among human beings. The heaven where this goddess resided was called Tamohuan Ichan, Xochitl Icacan, Chicunauhnepaniuhcan,[8] Itzehecayan. (Muñoz Camargo 1981: fols. 152v–153r)

The old Mixtec also placed their two primogenitive gods in the midst of what was, in reality, only an exaggeration of the Mixtec rulers' luxurious life style:

The Indians claim that two gods became visible, one named One Deer, with the surname of Lion Serpent, and a lovely, beautiful goddess, named One Deer, with the surname of Tiger Serpent. These gods were said to have given birth to the other gods of the Indians. After the two gods appeared in the world with human figures, according to the stories of these people, with their omnipotence and great wisdom the gods created and founded a great cliff, upon which they built sumptuous palaces, made with marvelous craftsmanship, where they settled down and dwelt on earth. This was the first place the gods had as their residence on earth, where they remained for many centuries in peace and comfort, at an elegant, delightful place, while at that time the earth was in darkness and shadow. (García 1981:327–28)

The second step in the myth is the great adventure, the core of the time of creation. The action can begin with a desire to be worshipped, an abduction, an aggressive attack ending in bloodshed, the mutilation or the death of a victim, a robbery, a hoax, a seduction, a violation, an unchastity—anything, finally, that upsets the easy peace of the former age. This violence has led to a characterization of the myth as a process of transgression.[9] The element of transgression is important, but it is not always present. The intranscendent continuity may also be broken by the process of divine thought planning a change, by a mere defect, guile, a simple adventure, or mere circumstance.

The third step is the transformation, which in its astral prototype includes death by fire, descent into the world of the dead, and rebirth in human time, with a new nature. It is the type of inchoative death that characterizes the *dema* deities of New Guinea (Jensen 1963:109–11).[10] Outstanding among these gods are the ones who, dismembered or not, produce various beings from different parts of their bodies. According to the Nahua, the goddess Tlaltecuhtli produced trees, flowers, and herbs with her hair; with her skin, small plants and little flowers; with her eyes, wells, fountains, and caves; with her mouth, rivers and great caverns; with her nose, valleys and mountains. Centeotl also produced different species: cotton from his hair, edible seeds from his ear, sage from his nose, sweet potatoes from his toes, and corn from his nails (*Historia de México* 1965:108, 110). The Tzeltzal tell us that, after the fight between the brothers Blue-Sun and the Youngest-in-the-Family, Blue-Sun died and produced from the great pieces of his body the deer, the spotted cavie, and the peccary; with the small pieces, the birds in the sky; with his blood, a domestic fowl (Slocum 1965). The fourth step takes place in human time.

Two questions relating to the other time remain: the time of creation and the creation of time. A subsistence life-style (for both hunter-gatherers and sedentary peoples) is feasible only to the degree that labor is assigned on the basis of an adequate knowledge of seasonal changes. The time for gathering berries, grubs, or sweet sap, the time for the explosive appearance of flowers and edible seeds, the time for cultivating the ground before the first rains, the routes for gathering, all are part of this essential knowledge. Resources appear in definite cycles. Watching the succession of seasons, formulating them into a calendar, and adapting it to the daily struggle was a task without which social survival would have been impossible. The calendar did not originate from leisure, but from work. Its origin is in the management of time itself, social time, adjusted to the time of the other beings in this world.

Each animal, each fruit used by humans inspires an independent myth, a tale that, above all else, has its own value. The idea of the rising sun is deceptive. In principle, every being with a mythic origin has its solar beginning. It has its own cycle and an origin for that cycle. The independent production of myth continues, as with many myths in our own time. References to an origin may be made, often taking the story away from the main body of the myth. Obviously it is not a total withdrawal. It is limited to the lack of connection between the times of the different myths, and between the "historical" correlation among its events. We will return to this interesting theme later. What matters here is that, along with the simple, independent, individualized myth, a more complex myth emerges by agglutination, in which one single

Table 1. The Times and Transitions of the Creation

The Other Time			Human Time
Divine Intranscendence	Divine Transcendence		
		Birth of the Sun	
Divine leisure			
1. The happy life of the gods			
	2. Mythic adventure		
	3. Death of the gods (beginning of their transformation)		
		4. Resurrection of the gods (end of their transformation by the inchoation of beings in human time)	
			Existence of beings of human time

narration includes two, three, or many creations in the overall creation of the world. A simultaneous supercreation is described in the following myth from Soconusco, in which the transformation occurs with the terrible eruption of the Tacaná volcano at the beginning of the world:

> Then God spoke. But he did not do it with words, with the voice of men. He did it through fire and stones and earthquakes. Everything caught on fire, everything was dying.
> Men who entered the cool water to escape the fire were turned into fish. Those who climbed trees to escape from the seething ground were turned into monkeys. Those who jumped to the high rocks flew away as birds, and the

ones who dragged themselves, crouched, or crawled to enter caves or to hide, became snakes, opossums, pocket gophers, and all the animals of creation.

Those who repented in their hearts remained as they were. (Navarrete 1966: 423)[11]

A process of multiple creation similar to the above is found in the Colima Indians' legend about the flood, according to a sixteenth-century source. From the mists arising from the flood came not only the various animals, but the original instruments people would use: farming tools, weapons, and rattle-sticks (Suárez de Cepeda 1983:18). Nevertheless the simultaneous creation is the exception. The idea of cyclic pluralism still remains in the complexity of the myth, taking form principally in four different ways of dealing with time:

1.   The creative process can take a long time. This may be expressed vaguely as "many centuries," or it may be a fixed period of time, like the interruption for 600 years of all divine action after the creator couple gave birth to their first four sons (*Historia de los mexicanos por sus pinturas* 1965:24). The myth of the five suns, which comes, like the preceding one, from ancient Nahuatl tradition on the high central plateau, tells of a very prolonged creation that began with the ascendancy of the first sun, overthrown by a cataclysm and followed successively by four others, with chaotic periods that link each domination to the others. The different versions give the duration of the years of each of the suns. One source says, for example, that the sun called Nahui Oce-lotl lasted 676 years (*Leyenda de los soles* 1945:119), but there are numerous discrepancies among the different documents.

2.   Creations succeeded each other throughout time. One of the clearest examples is that of the five suns mentioned above. Each one of the five stages is centered on the creation of important beings, called humans. In reality they are the ancestors, all forming part of a narrative calculated to show how the human being of the Fifth Sun, the true, the definitive one, emerged from a succession of divine experiments. In particular cases they are demas changed into beings of human time: turkeys, birds, fish, monkeys. . . . Their transformations occur in turn, during transit, at the final, chaotic moment of the sun under which each one lived.

3.   Among the creation myths one of the fundamental principles is the division of time and the calendaric succession. This is not a strictly Mesoamerican question. The creation of what exists presupposes the creation of measurable time. I will cite here only two of the great philosophers who dealt with the connection between the creation of time and the creation of the world. Saint Augustine wrote (1907: bk. 12, ch. 8, p. 283):

Yea, neither is this very formlessness of the *earth invisible and without form,* num-
bered among the days. For where no figure nor order is, there does nothing
come or go; and where this is not, there plainly are no days, nor any vicissitude
of space and time.

Many centuries later the sage Maimonides explained (1956:144–46):

The universe has not been created out of an element that preceded it in time,
since time itself formed a part of the creation. . . . [Time] was created; for it
depends on the motion of the sphere, and the sphere has been created.

Among the obscure colonial writings of the Maya of Yucatan, there is a
tale of how the twenty days of the month were created and from what. The
document (*The Book of Chilam Balam of Chumayel* 1967:116–17) first shows the
combination of two series, that of the twenty names of the days and the thirteen numerals that accompany them. Both series joined their footprints on the
same path before the twenty successive creations appeared:

Thus it was recorded {by} the first sage, Melchise[dek], the first prophet,
Napuc Tun, the priest, the first priest. This is a song of how the *uinal* {twenty-
day month} came to be created before the creation of the world. Then he began
to march by his own effort alone. Then said his maternal grandmother, then
said his maternal aunt, then said his paternal grandmother, then said his sister-
in-law: "What shall we say when we see man on the road?" These were their
words as they marched along, when there was no man (as yet). Then they arrived there in the east and began to speak. "Who has passed here? Here are the
footprints. Measure it off with your foot." So spoke the mistress of the world.
Then he measured the footstep of our Lord, God the Father. This was the reason
it was called counting off the whole earth, *lahca* {12} Oc {*xoc lah cab oc* which
means counting off the whole world by footsteps}. This was the count, after it
had been created by {the day} 13 Oc, after his feet were joined evenly, after they
had departed there in the east. Then he spoke its name when the day had no
name, after he had marched along with his maternal grandmother, his maternal
aunt, his paternal grandmother and his sister-in-law. The uinal was created, the
day, as it was called, was created, heaven and earth were created, the stairway
of water, the earth, rocks and trees; the things of the sea and the things of the
land were created.
  On 1 Chuen he raised himself to his divinity, after he made heaven and earth.
  On 2 Eb he made the first stairway. It descended from the midst of the
heavens, in the midst of the water, when there were neither earth, rocks
nor trees.

On 3 Ben he made all things, as many as there are, the things of the heavens,
the things of the sea and the things of the earth.
On 4 Ix sky and earth were tilted.
On 5 Men he made everything.
On 6 Cib the first candle was made; it became light when there was neither
sun nor moon.

The text continues until the list of twenty days is complete. Esoteric, like
many writings that have come down to us, it guards secrets to be discovered
by future investigators.

The Nahua also spoke of the creation of measured time. The Mexica said
that Quetzalcoatl and Huitzilopochtli "made the days and divided them into
months, giving each one twenty days; and so there were eighteen [months]
and three hundred sixty days in the year" (*Historia de los mexicanos por sus pinturas* 1965:25). This belief persists today. The Mazatec affirm that it was the
opossum who was charged with the measurement and the succession of time,
establishing a boundary line between his era and the one dominated by his
rival: "It was Lord Tlacuache who gave names to the days. The Tiger said
only day after tomorrow, but the Opossum gave the dates" (Boege 1988:100).
The above explains why the Maya called the creation of the world *kalac kin,*
"the closing of time" (Alvarez 1980–84, 1:43). The name is appropriate if one
believes that the end of creation coincides with the conclusion of the establishment of one or all of the time cycles. There is a figure on plate 52 of the
Códice Vindobonensis in which, at the initiation of the world, a figure seems to be
waiting, with twenty stellar eyes, while another arranges, in five rows of four
units each, twenty spherical objects. Jansen (1982, 1:128) says of the drawing:

> The exact activity of the two men in regard to the days and nights cannot be
> precisely determined, because we lack knowledge about the meaning of the ges-
> tures. We see only that the nights are arranged around the first man, while the
> days are put in order. Perhaps the meaning of the scene is that in the primordial
> epoch nights were given to the sky and days were arranged in twenties.

This concept appears in several world traditions. According to the Iranians,
Ormuz created the universe in a year, giving a basis for the religious celebrations. The Biblical cycle was closed with the creation of the seventh day, after
six days of labor and one of rest. All of this takes us to a difficult question of
logic. If the measurement and division of time is not produced fully until the
closing of creation, how can the former mythic time be accurately determined?

How can one measure, for example, the 600 years of divine idleness of the creator couple and their four children? It is possible that the stories imply still greater cycles that came to an end with these events, as part of a great period of creation.[12] But it is also possible that the informants for the *Historia de los mexicanos por sus pinturas* (the source that speaks of the idleness of 600 years, before narrating how Quetzalcoatl and Huitzilopochtli divided time) became aware of the contradiction, since later on the document says, "all the above was done and created without giving it a year date, but it was all together and without a time difference" (*Historia de los mexicanos por sus pinturas* 1965:27).

4.   The beings created throughout the cycle were marked by the day of their creation. In the language used by Nahua magicians and priests, there were names belonging to a cycle of creation made up of 260 days. The earth was called Ce Tochtli (One Rabbit); trees and all objects made of wood, Ce Atl (One Water); earthy substances, Ce Miquiztli (One Death); stones, Ce Tecpatl (One Flint); structural fibers and all objects made with them, Ce Malinalli (One Twisted Grass); sharp objects, Ce Ocelotl (One Jaguar); fire, Nahui Acatl (Four Reed); deer, Chicome Xochitl (Seven Flower); agaves, Chicuei Tecpatl (Eight Flint); corn, Chicome Coatl (Seven Serpent); the gods could also be named for their calendaric signs.[13] These terms form part of the secret lexicon of the magic formulas. The calendaric cycle of 260 days was a pattern and a ritual and indicated opportunities for establishing contact with the different beings of the world.

Mythic time, the creation of the cycles, and the return of forces lead us to other interesting questions: the *other* space and the death of the gods.

5   THE OTHER SPACE

These things [in myth] never happened,
but they always are.

Salustio,
De los dioses y del mundo

Sallust "the Neoplatonic," allied with Emperor Flavius Claudius Julian, did not accept myth as real history. "If the gods are good," he asked himself, "why does evil exist in the world?" He found the answer in the idea that there is no positive evil, since evil derives from the absence of good, just as there is no darkness except as the absence of light. "If the gods are good, why do myths contain stories of adultery, robbery, imprisonment of a father, and all the other absurdities?" Sallust sees the answer in a highly allegorical concept of myth. If Kronus appears devouring his sons, that means that God is an intellect, and that every intellect turns inward upon itself. If the mother of the gods crowns her beloved Atis with her crown of stars, that means that the principle that engenders all life gave to the creator of all things that are born and die a portion of its celestial powers, because the primary gods refine the secondary ones. Myth refers to the essences of the gods; but the essences of gods never came to be, because what always is does not come into existence. For this reason Sallust, confronted with the problem of mythical events, concludes, "These things never happened, but they always are" (Salustio 1956:204, 205, 208, 217).

Sallust's thesis, in the fourth century A.D., shows the tremendous effort of classical thought to develop a philosophical religion. Myth is intellectualized and transformed into an allegory far removed from the ancient Greek or Latin believer. Myth is no longer true, it ceases to be real history because it is incompatible with the unchangeable God, the Primary Cause, the One, unengendered, eternal, incorporeal, who does not exist in space (Salustio 1956: 204). Up to what point does the philosopher's myth coincide with that of the people who create or believe in myth? There is almost no coincidence. For the believer myth has time and space, though a particular time and space.

One of the most persistent characteristics of the religions we examine here is the constant contact of believers with divine forces. This is accomplished in various ways, among them the ecstasy produced by pain, hemorrhage, and prolonged vigil (Ruiz de Alarcón 1953:40; Serna 1953:244). P. Furst (1976:11) compares self-mutilation to ingesting hallucinogens:

> Self-mutilation is depicted in the ritual art of different pre-Hispanic cultures and periods, from 1300 B.C. to the Conquest, and bloodletting rites that must have inflicted severe pain (including perforation of the penis, tongue, and other organs with cactus thorns, stingray barbs, and other sharp instruments) are described in early ethnohistoric literature about Maya and central Mexican customs.[1]

Psychoactive products, chiefly those of vegetable origin, held and still hold a very important place among the means of communicating with the divine. Specialists have been amazed at the abundance of plants used in rituals for their effectiveness in altering consciousness, in all more than four hundred, belonging to fifteen botanical families. In northern Mexico and southern Texas there are ten-thousand-year-old archeological remains that contain seeds of *Sophora secundiflora,* much used today in soothsaying (Wasson 1980; Diaz 1984).

We also note the belief in the possibility of contact with divinity through accidents, dreams, miracles, possessions, or visions. Frequent mention of these is found in sources describing Mesoamerican customs, as well as in current ethnographic studies.

Such communication may take place in a small dwelling as the normal vision in a dream, or in an accident that causes the absent-minded hunter to fall down in a place charged with divine energy, an "enchanted place" (Garcia de León 1969). But there are also transitions to another space, voyages beyond the limits of the world. This other space, which does not belong to humans, is the space of myth, as we shall see.

Another noteworthy characteristic of Mesoamerican religion was its preoccupation with the onset of time. It seems to be one of its great obsessions. It was the origin of complex calendric systems that permitted the flow of destinies and the institution of rituals to be calculated, and which gave life to a powerful and costly religious hierarchy. The preoccupation has lasted, but to a much smaller degree. The religious and divinatory institutions were supported by and were a part of the ideological base for the governmental apparatus. The Conquest severely damaged these calendric concepts when it dethroned the ancient ruling class which, until then, had almost completely monopolized the knowledge of time and the management of propitiation of the gods. It destroyed the political organizations whose computations of time provided one of the ruling class's most powerful supports. However, there still remain traces in the calendric cycles of a perceived return of the forces, and a perception, in the passage of time over the earth, of a conflict between gods who take turns dominating it with their transitory presence.[2] The term used by the ancient Nahua for festival, *ilhuitl,* contains the syllable *il-,* "return" (López Austin 1988, 1:191). A rite, a festival, is the return of another time, the return of the forces that give life to the world. Today this philological approach is still in effect. The Mocho Maya begin any mythic speech with an introduction that takes one back to ancestral times, *č-ak-len-ta ty ʔpo.* The same elements, *č-* and *ʔak,* are also found in the terms *č-ak-i-len* and *č-ak-len,* which mean festival (Petrich 1985:152–57). Myth is the reference to another time: the ritual, its new presence. Fiesta days, therefore, are dangerous, "delicate." Nowadays it is said that the magical danger of "fright" is greatest on Holy Thursday (García de León 1969:89). It is also said that during Holy Week the enchanted hills open up (Sánchez Azuará 1985). It is dangerous because the gods are there. The ancient Nahua spoke explicitly about the celebration of Teotleco. The gods (in this festival, all of them) came to the world. Other visits were those the celestial gods made to their own festivals, five times in each cycle of 260 days. In fact the calendars gave the gods the daily opportunity to act on the surface of the earth.

Where do the gods come from? From the celestial levels and those of the underworld, according to the constant repetition in the sources that refer to Mesoamerican traditions. These are the places where the gods await their turn to act, as indicated by the calendric order. According to ancient Nahua myth, those places are the two huge halves of the body of the original, gigantic, aquatic monster (*Historia de los mexicanos por sus pinturas* 1965:25–26; *Historia de México/Histoire du Mechique* 1965:105, 108). Cipactli, the feminine, primogenitive fish or crocodile, was split into halves by Quetzalcoatl and Tezcatlipoca. After their separation, four gods served as columns to prevent their coming together again. From this arrangement came the three cosmic levels: the nine heavens, the nine levels of the underworld, and the central section, composed of four levels and formed by the empty space in the separation of the two halves of Cipactli. The middle space was human habitat.

Magicians believed they could move outside the earth to influence the invisible forces. Their destination was sometimes the upper levels, sometimes the lower. In his conjuration, the prospective traveler of the seventeenth century said, *"niani Mictlan niani Topan"* (Ruiz de Alarcón 1953:163), "I am the one who goes to the Land of the Dead. I am the one who goes to the levels above us." There are nine levels in the heaven above, the true heaven. For this reason the Quiche, influenced by the Biblical concept, designated Mon-

day as the second day of creation, and said that on that day "the nine levels of
heaven received the life of God the Lord. The nine gyrate above the earth, and
gyrated every day; there they moved in the first level" (*El titulo de Totonicapan*
1983:168). On the central plateau of Mexico, when Motecuhzoma Xocoyotzin was chosen *tlatoani* of Tenochtitlan, the lord of Tetzcoco greeted him
saying, "Who can doubt that a lord and prince, who, before reigning, was able
to investigate the nine folds of heaven . . . will master earthly things and come
to the aid of his people?" (*Códice Ramirez* 1944:94). Thus there are eighteen
levels, half of them above the human abode, the remaining nine below it. The
traveling Nahua sorcerers acted upon the body of Cipactli. Time comes from
the eighteen levels, and there are eighteen months in the cycle of 365 days.[3]

   In previous works I have written about the composition of the cosmos, and
particularly of the currents that constitute time (López Austin 1988, 1:52–
68). I have pointed out that the ancient Nahua thought that divine forces came
down from the four trees or posts at the outer edges of the world—where the
four gods were charged with keeping the two halves of Cipactli separated—
revolving constantly in a counterclockwise movement above the surface of the
earth. The hot forces that descended from heaven combined with the cold ones
coming up from Mictlan. These are the Nahua traditions of the central plateau
of Mexico, but this basic cosmovision was held in common among the Mesoamerican peoples. Let us look at some examples. The concept of nine upper
heavens appears in an important Mixtec pictographic document. The divine
pair and Quetzalcoatl are depicted in the highest sky, above eight other celestial bands dotted with stellar eyes (*Códice Selden II* 1964–67: upper part). As
to the Maya, Rivera Dorado says that "the great levels superimposed over the
tri-dimensional space are, at the same time, the stage where the forces locked
in the twenty-day periods of the sacred cycles of 260 days manifested themselves." Of the cosmic tree, he states that "the aggregate gives a clear image
of the vertical concept of the universe, with emphasis on the relationship or
communication among the various levels." He also refers to the persistence of
a belief among some native communities "that the gods and the souls of the
dead ascend or descend the tree" (Rivera Dorado 1986b:59–60).

   The forces are the acts of the gods, and they move through the cosmic
trees, coming from the *other* space which is not human space. Why identify
Cipactli's body with the *other* space? When the Nicarao were asked where
their gods came from, they replied that they came from where "plants and all
edible things come from" (Fernández de Oviedo y Valdés 1944–45, 11:75).
The gods, thus, were located in the place of the ancestors. If this were so, we
must conclude that on the eighteen levels of Cipactli's body all the possibili-

ties for existence are found. The forces that constitute time are found on the levels of heaven and the underworld, but the movement of time begins only at the moment when the forces combine in the cosmic trees, before spreading out to cover the surface of the earth. Sallust said that myth always is, but Sallust accorded it essence, not existence. Contradicting Sallust's statement, myth, for the believer, is located in space.

This explains why the healer, in order to cure a fracture, using magic, traveled to the *other* time-space, precisely at the point where a mythical fracture took place. This episode corresponds to the myth of the creation of human beings. Quetzalcoatl descended to Mictlan to obtain a bone from the beings who lived before the Fifth Sun. Mictlantecuhtli gave him the bone he sought, but, regretting his gift, Mictlantecuhtli ordered the quail to intercept Quetzalcoatl. The quail frightened Quetzalcoatl and the bone fell down and was broken into pieces. From the fragments, human beings were formed. For this reason they are not giants, and also, since they are formed from fragments of bone, some are tall, others short, some fat, and others slim. Myth *occupies* a place in the other time. At that point in the *other* space-time, "the fracture of bone" is located. It is an instant of creation—soft, weak, and pliant. A healer locating himself at "the fracturing of bone" place fights against the quail, as his conjuration indicates, and he expects the result to be the healing of the sick person.[4]

I return here to a premise from previous works: the simultaneous existence of the totality of time in the *other* space (López Austin 1988, 1:57–61). It must be presumed that the sorcerers who believed that they were transferring themselves to another space must also have believed they would find there the presence of those who were on earth, their own present, past, and future. Time must be total and devoid of sequences. On this point there are also irrefutable affirmations. Serna explains how a *tlachixqui*, or soothsayer, in the seventeenth century, after becoming intoxicated on *ololiuhqui (Rivea corymbosa)*, revealed to his client how and under what circumstances he would find his runaway wife. The client went to the town indicated, and what the soothsayer had said happened. He was able to find his wife. The unfortunate woman was returned to her home, where she hanged herself (Serna 1953:236). Francisco Hernández (1959, 1:105), the royal physician of Philip II, referring to one of the plants named *poyomatli* [uncertain identification], said that upon drinking it, "through some strange madness, the Indians believe that hidden and future things are revealed to them."

The ancient Nahua of the central plateau were not the only ones who believed in the simultaneity of total time in the *other* space. As with all basic concepts of the structure and dynamics of the universe, the ideas were shared by the different Mesoamerican peoples. Rivera Dorado (1986b:194), in his study of the ancient Maya, agrees with what I have attributed to the Nahua. He states that according to the Maya:

> while activity over the earth is ordered in continuing sequences, the chronology that obtains in the "other world" is cyclic and repetitive to the degree that past, present, and future co-exist simultaneously. . . . Events do not occur little by little, but are always present in the aggregate, awaiting their opportunity to occur, following the rhythm of the sacred calendars.

Belief in the possibility of perceiving the entirety of time during the journey to the other space persists. The Mazatec affirm today that "What one tries to do with the mushroom [several species of *Psilocybe*] is to go back to the beginning and forward to the future. By means of the mushroom, one can see Adam and Eve." Moreover one can see the inhabitants of the original time: "formerly there were only flies" (Boege 1988:90). In another chapter we will speak of the important role of insects.

To the space in which all the processes of myth occur the Aztecs gave the name of Tamoanchan. The same name applied to several stages. The initial stage, which was not transcendent (see chapter 4), was called Tamoan-chan, as well as Where-the-Flowers-Grow, At-the-Confluence-of-the-Nine, and Where-the-Obsidian-Wind-Blows (Muñoz Camargo 1981: fol. 152v–153r). It is also the site of the transgression, because breaking the flowering branches of the sacred tree was a terrible sin. It was the place of punishment, which in this case was the expulsion from Tamoanchan:

> This place, called Tamoanchan and Xuchitl Icacan, is the place where their gods were created. That is the same as saying that it is an earthly paradise. They say that those gods, being in that place, transgressed when they cut flowers and branches from the trees, and that, because of it, Tonacateuctli and the woman Tonacacihuatl became angry and they cast them out of the place. Some of them came to earth and others went to hell. (*Códice Telleriano-Remensis* 1964–67: pt. 2, pl. 23; *Códice Vaticano Latino, 3738* 1964–67: pl. 43–44)

Finally the earth as the birthplace of the human species is also Tamoan-chan, the place where the forces of the underworld (the winds) and those of the heavens (the flowers) not only produce time, but also mock humans:

> No one is free in Tamohuanchan, the place of the winds, the place where the winds break. Here remain the inhabitants of the place of wind, the inhabitants

of the place of the flowers, who mock people on earth. They delight in people's misfortune; they laugh at people; they make fun of people on earth. Nothing is true; nothing they say is truth, what they express, what they manifest to people; they are only mocking them.[5]

We will now look at the final phase of the drama of the gods, the culmination of the adventure with death, and the beginning of an earthly existence after resurrection. In the astral prototype, it was said, metamorphosis implies death. For the believer the process of destruction is one more myth, a beginning in which is seen the origin of archaic ritual practices; the death of the gods is the model for human sacrifices on earth and a way for the sacrificed to obtain eternal life. In 1579 Gabriel de Chávez (1985–86:62), in Metztitlan, recorded this explanation:

> And it is said of those four demons named Itzcuin, Hueitecpatl, Tentetemic, and Nanacatl Tzatzi, that they killed the Great Mother, beginning the way sacrifices would be carried out in the future, by taking out her heart and offering it to the Sun. They also said that the idol Tezcatlipuca killed the God of Wine (Ome Tochtli) with his consent and conformity, declaring that in that way he would become eternal and that, if he did not die, all those who drank wine would perish.

The death of the gods occurs not only in individual victims, but as the great destruction of the ancestors. Today's Tzotzil believe that all the Jews, gods opposed to Christ, and stellar ancestors, perished when the white rooster began to crow at the moment of the crucifixion (Holland 1963:76). If the miraculous dawn repeats the coming of creation, what is sacred becomes stone. Ancestors, in whom the distinction between human and animal is fragile, are converted to images.

> The light of dawn fell upon all the tribes at the same time. Instantly the surface of the earth was dried by the Sun. Like a man was the Sun when it showed itself, and its face glowed when it dried the surface of the earth.
> Before the Sun rose the surface of the earth was damp and muddy, before the Sun came up; but then the Sun rose, and came up like a man. . . . Immediately afterward Tohil, Avilix, and Hacavitz were turned to stone, together with the deified beings, the puma, the jaguar, the snake, the *cantil*, [6] as well as the hobgoblin. Their arms became fastened to the trees when the Sun, the moon, and the stars appeared. All were changed into stone. Perhaps we should not be living today because of the voracious animals, the puma, the jaguar, the snake, the *cantil*, as well as the goblin. Perhaps our power would not exist if these first animals had not been turned into stone by the Sun. (*Popol Vuh* 1950:187–88)

This same concept is expressed by the Zapotec at the beginning of the twentieth century, in terms that reveal the profound influence of Christianity. The images of the gods are the *moctezumas*, the remains of time gone by, like the glory of Motecuhzoma Xocoyotzin, after the arrival of the Europeans. The Spanish Conquest was, for the convert, the real beginning of the world, the birth of the Sun and the Moon. With the dawn—the arrival of the Spanards—the old gods fled to where they are found today, under the earth (Parsons 1966:137).[7]

The confusion caused by the death of the gods or by the birth of the Sun results in various situations. In the most typical cases, the gods die and are transformed into beings in human time. Zipacna kills the four hundred youths, who, at the moment when the Sun and Moon ascend to the sky for the first time, accompany them, transformed into stars (*Popol vuh* 1964:39, 102). In other myths the gods who inhabit the unstable, original world abandoned what will become the human abode to go to their dwelling in the sky. A third case is just the opposite. After the Sun's appearance, the powerful beings come down to populate the earth: "Afterwards, Holy Mary descended to where we are created, and then she sent us here to earth. Then all the saints came down, those who are in each town. The saints came down and with them the customs that we, the Indians, now observe" (Preuss 1982:181).

Is there a contradiction in all of this? Perhaps it is only an apparent contradiction. These are the features of the process of creation:

1.   The gods have two kinds of names. Their calendric names locate them in the process of creation. When Gregorio Garcia (1981:327) tells us that the ancient Mixtec believed in the visible apparition of two creative gods, the male named One Deer Lion Serpent, and the female One Deer Tiger Serpent, we should understand that both of them, Lion Serpent and Tiger Serpent, were born on the day called One Deer of the transforming cycle. The differing names correspond to two different kinds of divine action, while the identical names refer to the same time of divine action.

2.   The process of creation may appear to be the extermination of the gods. Some mythical accounts tell of an earlier state of unrest, of general conflict among the protagonists. In the adventures of the opossum, the ancestors fall into a turmoil that disturbs the order, without our hero, the one charged with maintaining order, intervening adequately:

> Opossum commanded the rest of the animals. . . . And one day they came
> to him to complain. "Lord Ntlacuach," they said to him, "the Fox and the
> Raccoon fought each other and you didn't impose peace. Were you aware of

that?" . . . Then the Rabbit and the Deer fought and the Opossum again did not settle it. Another time, it was the Deer and the Fox; the next time, the Fox and the Rabbit. And Lord Opossum [behaved] as if nothing had happened! . . . The animals were greatly displeased. There were even deaths, because they did not respect each other. It was as if they had no master. (Castro 1963)

In other mythic accounts the destruction of the gods is terribly clear. The changing of Nanahuatzin into the Sun and of Tecuciztecatl into the Moon forced all the gods to give up their lives so the astral bodies could cross the sky.

After they had both ascended above the earth they remained fixed; neither the Sun nor the Moon moved. And the other gods spoke and said, "How can we live? Doesn't the sun move? Must we live among inferiors? Let us all die and revive him with our death."

And then the Air took on the task of killing all the Gods, and he slew them. And it is said that one of them, called Xolotl, refused to die, and he said to the gods, "Oh gods, let me not die!"

He cried in such a way that his eyes were swollen with his weeping. And when the one who was killing came toward him, he ran away and hid himself among the cornfields and turned himself into a corn plant that had two stalks, which farmers call *xolotl*. When he was discovered among the stalks of corn, he fled again and hid himself among the maguey plants, changing himself into a plant that has two bodies, now called *mexolotl*. Again he was seen, and he ran away, entered the water, and made himself into a fish called *axolotl;* and they captured him there and killed him. (Sahagún 1956, 2:261–62)

Some sources (Mendieta 1954, 1:83–86; *Historia de México (Histoire du Mechique)* 1965:109; *Códice Telleriano-Remensis* 1964–67: pt. 2, pl. 22) say that the number of gods that died was 1,600—the number formed when the creators, Citlalicue and Citlallatonac, hurled a flint from heaven that fragmented into that many smaller pieces.[8] The gods who died in Teotihuacan were patrons. They carried out the functions attributed to patron saints today, whom, according to the Nahua of Durango, the Virgin sent to protect the towns.

3.   There are signs of diminished power in the beings that remained in the human world. In the Huichol myth, while the Sun was waiting to be given a name, some of the ancestors prepared to attack the newborn, and their punishment was their transformation into snakes, coyotes, foxes, mice, and badgers. But before changing into their definitive state as animals, they were stricken with blindness (*Wirrarika irratsikayari* 1982:35). It is interesting to compare this myth with the one concerning the ancestors of the Quiche. The gods had

made people so like themselves that it was feared that beings with so much knowledge would not worship their creators and would not reproduce. The remedy was to cast a mist over the creatures' eyes, limiting their ability to see (*Popol vuh* 1964:104–7).[9]

4.   A breaking up and a reconstruction of the ancestors took place. The power to break up into parts and to undergo divine restoration appears often in Mesoamerican religious tradition (see chapter 12). The mythical prototype of this power seems to have been the opossum himself. Again it is the Huichol who tell how, after stealing fire, the opossum is destroyed and puts herself together again:

They ran after her. They climbed and overtook her. They broke her into a thousand pieces, one part here, another part there. They shattered her into small bits. They took what she had in her hands. They took it away from her. They descended, leaving her there. There she lay, dead. They had destroyed her life, taken the fire from her hand. They had taken everything away. She was dead.

Well, after a while, she regains consciousness. She begins to think about it. She begins to get up, to gather up her pieces: skin, hair, heart, all; sandals, hands, the top of her head, what is called the crown. Brains, everything. She put everything in its place again. Once revived, she felt better. Everything was all right again. She was very happy and said, "Oh, perhaps they took that little piece I hid in my pouch. That piece that flowered from Tatewari. Did they take it?" She looked for it. She found the little piece there. She took it out and began to blow on it—wiwiwiwiwiwiwi (P. Furst 1972a:9–10).

5.   The beings of human time are transformed ancestors. That is what is understood today. Rocks, trees, animals are the ancient people transformed (see Kelly 1966:396).

6.   The gods also go to dwell in the other space, but they maintain links with their terrestrial images and, from the other space, they send their influences. Muñoz Camargo refers to the beliefs of the Tlaxcaltecan Nahua:

But these bundles we serve and worship are images, figures and likenesses of the gods who on earth were men, and who, because of their heroic deeds, rose into heaven, where they dwell in eternal peace. . . . Their statues remain among us. They went to live in their places and dwellings of joy, where they reside peacefully and send to us on earth their divine influence, seeing that their shapes and figures are worshipped by the people. (Muñoz Camargo 1981: fol. 191)

7.   There is also a link—or better, an identity—between the beings of the other space-time and their specific creations. Among today's Totonac, whoever kills a snake risks encountering the Lord of Water at night in a dream. The god complains about the offense as if it had been done to him: "Why did you kill me? I was not going to hurt you. I was only passing by" (Kelly 1966: 401).

From the above facts, as though from the dismembered body of the opossum, a concept of the dramatic end of the gods and their resurrection can be reconstructed. The process of creation is the passage through time and space. The transition is destruction and reintegration. The beings of human time-space are the very forces of the gods, tempered at the crossing of the boundary. The divine, emanating forces do not die, but continue in their own time and space. There and then the gods continue in their permanent adventure. Their emanations are the ones who die in the passage and are transformed into the beings and forces that people this world. The calendric flow is a renewal. It proceeds selectively, invigorating all the beings on the earth's surface and in the lower heavens. The gods have opportunities to be present in the human world through the time cycles of different dimensions; that presence is shown by the strengthening of what partakes of their own qualities. This flow is concentrated in the receptacles of images and relics, and these are the ways by which the faithful can make contact with the distant gods.

This is Tamoanchan's last link, the place where the winds break. How long will this be the world? Until the Fifth Sun is destroyed, because then the latent souls of the inanimate beings will be awakened. It will be the *butic,* the end of the world foretold by the ancient Guatemalans (Las Casas 1967, 2:507). Then the stones, the pitchers, the jars will rise up against the people (López Austin 1988, 1:243–47). Time will be one, and space will be one. There will be no succession of days, nor years, nor centuries.

Meanwhile the terrible inhabitants of the sky and of the underworld—the flowers and the winds—come to mock us. The gods are cruel and silently spy on our vanity. Woe to those who take themselves too seriously!

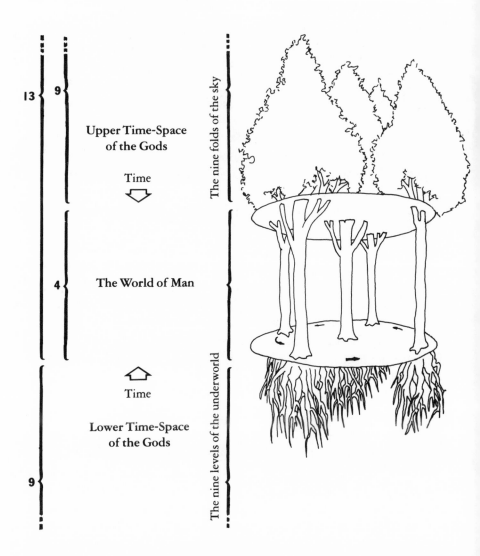

Figure 3. The five trees and the human world

6 THE PASSAGE

Gods within, gods without,
gods above, gods below,
gods toward the ocean, fleshless gods,
gods who punish sins, gods who pardon sins
gods who devour men,
gods who slay warriors, gods who save warriors,
gods of darkness, gods of light,
gods of the heavens.
It is possible to count all the gods?
The gods are uncountable.

Tahitian invocation

The gods are innumerable. They occupy places in the sky and in the underworld; they argue within the trunks of the cosmic trees; they circle in the astral paths above the surface of the earth and under it; in time they come forth to expand and to penetrate all that exists, and they remain concentrated, hidden, guardians in the "difficult places," in the "enchanted zones." They exist in long-buried images and in the ones that now enhance churches. When canonical law indicates their turn for domination, they are active, strong, and aggressive. They slumber in their stone images for centuries when the reigning sun orders them immobile. At night they wish to change themselves into jaguars, but the sun's archers, the stars, shoot them into submission to wait again. They are everywhere: in springs, in the currents of water, in the wind. They are clouds, the lords of overturned water jugs, and in lightning flashes. From inside the corn stalks they push the juice toward the sky. They have been patrons of kingdoms and of cities, and they still are of villages, communities, and families. They are insidious, slipping into every crack and cranny. Mountains shelter them. Their sparks are kept in plants, in animals, and even in manufactured jars and metates. Humanity itself possesses divine fire.

Gods flow, irradiate, struggle, become concentrated, or vanish.[1] Their forces circulate throughout the universe, and the order of their course is set by time.

Among the Maya the days themselves were divine, and still are in remote villages of the highlands of Guatemala in which the old Maya calendar still survives. Each day is not merely influenced by some god; it is a god, or, rather a pair of gods, for each day is a combination of number and name—1 Ik, 5 Imix, 13 Ahau, and so on—and both parts are gods. The Maya still speak of a day as "he" and often prefix the masculine ah to the name to emphasize that the day is a living god.[2] (J. Thompson 1963:163)

Belief in this flux is based on the possibility of communication between *this* time-space and the *other*. The transition is difficult and, as we have seen, it produces serious modifications in the sojourners. The passageways for the gods are the cosmic trees. They rise and descend inside the trees in a spiral pattern. That is the way the gods move, forming with their paths—one warm and descending, the other cold and ascending—a pattern that the ancient Nahuas called *mallinalli*. This process, as mentioned above, is an aspect of the mythical Tamoanchan.

I could certainly be accused of tending to view Mesoamerican thought through the traditions of the central plateau, especially through that of the Nahua. There is justification for this. As it happens the concept of Tamoanchan appears in the very sources that describe the traditions of the Nahua people of the central plateau. It is widely assumed that fundamental concepts of Mesoamerican beliefs are held in common, so that independently of the details of the idea and the name of Tamoanchan, which belong to the Nahua peoples,[3] the nucleus of the idea must have been present in a wide geographical area. Furthermore I believe that in the study of myths it is of prime importance to reconstruct the context of mythological beliefs. This reconstruction should begin with the most explicit sources, and today those are precisely the documental sources that refer to the Nahua peoples of the central highland. The above is a fact, although one should not claim exclusivity for these sources, and one must be careful not to use them as Procrustean beds.[4]

Tamoanchan expresses the broad mythical process that begins with the pleasant and leisurely life of the gods, describes their adventures and their punishments, and initiates human time-space with the formation of new beings. This process can be interpreted in two different ways: as an origin myth, an account of the beginning of the world, and as a continuing generation of the flux of forces. In fact any mythological process must be evaluated from both perspectives. One is a conservative concept that sees in the continuity of classes the cyclic stability of the human sphere. It imagines the other world with an aura of eternity because the lack of a distinction between time present, time past, and time future is the essence of eternity. The confluence of the eternal with the finite world of the Fifth Sun is its origin and its permanence. The creation was and is; the contact was and is; the forerunners were and are. The passage from one space to the other keeps occurring without interruption, marked by cycles of ample dimensions. The only interruption will be when the sun, which marked the beginning of the era, fails to appear in the east—when Cipactli is reconstituted.

Tamoanchan the mythical place and the place of myth has myths of its own. In the version of the *Códice Telleriano-Remensis* previously cited, the gods went out of bounds by cutting the flowers and breaking the branches of the tree of Tamoanchan. The creators, the couple Tonacatecuhtli and Tonacacihuatl, punished their abusive children and cast them to earth and to the underworld. Let us understand what the text tells us simply and directly. As a creation myth it speaks to us of a serious transgression that led to the presence of the gods on earth and in the underworld. In other words the gods produced by the creator couple descended from the heavens to be dispersed throughout the universe. The transition of the creation, the passage to the human world, is caused by the breaking of the tree.

According to other sources, the gods do more serious damage than only breaking the branches. In the illustration in the *Códice Telleriano-Remensis* and in illustrations in other sources, the tree itself is split. From inside flows a stream of blood, ending in what appear to be beads of green stone. This liquid is the divine effluvium that constitutes time. The myth reveals itself to us, then, as a myth of origin, of the distribution of the gods throughout the cosmos; but it is also a myth that refers to the daily flux of time, of the way in which the gods constantly descend to the earth's surface to revitalize what was originally created. The hypothesis that the stream of blood is of divine origin comes from the depiction of the Tamoanchan tree on page 15 of the *Códice Borbónico*. The synthesis of the four cosmic trees that, at the ends of the earth, separate the two halves of Cipactli's body is shown there. We will see why.

Each of the four cosmic trees has different characteristics. In the *Códice Tudela o Códice del Museo de América*, the tree of the east is the precious mesquite; the one of the north is the precious silk-cotton tree [*ceiba*]; to the west, the precious bald cypress; and to the south, the precious willow.[5] They can be accompanied by different birds (*Códice Fejérváry Mayer* 1964–67: pl. 1-44; *Códice Borgia* 1963: pl. 49–52); they can also be characterized by the colors of the directions to which they belong. This occurs with the Maya, who imagined a red ceiba to the east, a white ceiba to the north, a black one to the west, and a yellow one to the south.[6] The Tamoanchan tree in plate 15 of the *Códice Borbónico* has alternate stripes of four colors,[7] an indication that it is a synthesis of the four trees that hold up the sky.[8] At the same time, the stripes are diagonal, consistent with the idea of a spiral movement in the trunk. This symbolism is also found on the skirt of the goddess Itzpapalotl, seated beside the tree.

It is interesting to compare these symbols with those of the festival. In the *Códice Telleriano-Remensis*, in the month of *huei tecuhilhuitl,* "great feast of the lords," the festive element is indicated by a disk placed in the hands of the main figure. The disk has a small circle in the center and four others, of different colors, symmetrically placed on the exterior. Attached to each of the small circles is a small branch of a different color that, if they indicate direction of movement, would suggest a counterclockwise spin. The feast therefore represents the time that flows from the four external circles in what may be an image of the earth's surface, with a cross section of the four trunks and the navel of the world.[9]

Tamoanchan is mentioned in poetry as the site of the creation of humanity.

> The Flowering Tree arises in Tamoanchan:
> There you were created, the law given to us:
> With regal words he made us spin.
> That god, our god, for whom all live.
> Whatever gold I melt, what ever jade I carve,
> Our beautiful song:
> Like a turquoise he makes us whirl four times,
> Four times in Tamoanchan,
> Tamoanchan is the home of the giver of life.
> (Garibay 1964–68, 2:139)

The emanation from the Tamoanchan tree, its jeweled blood, is the daily descent of divine forces to earth. Sources of Mesoamerican history relate that there were critical moments when the link between a people and its patron god had to be renewed. This new tie, which could be interpreted as the rebirth of the great cycle in the life of a people, was produced by a miracle. For some time I have been fascinated by the motif of the miraculous breaking of a branch from a robust tree. It appears, for example, when the Mexica seek the promised land. I have interpreted it to mean the rupture of the tree of Tamoanchan, the liberation of the divine force and the establishment—a return to original conditions—of the alliance between a god and his people (López Austin 1973:93–95). The breaking of the tree is preceded, or followed, by the message from Huitzilopochtli, commanding the Mexica to travel alone henceforth, abandoning the other peoples who accompany them (Alvarado

Tezozómoc 1949:19–20; Chimalpahin 1965:67; *Códice Aubin* 1979:13). In the drawing of the *Tira de la peregrinación,* the trunk is severed and the lower half has arms, indicating the divine nature of the tree (*Códice Boturini, o Tira de la peregrinación* 1964–67: pl. 2).[10] The passage of the gods to earth is indicated by the rupture of the tree.

The passage of the gods to the underworld and to the human world is marked by sorrow. Previous mention was made of death and transformation by fire, which changes divine forces into beings who will inhabit human time-space. We will now see how this conversion in time, and in their occupation of the underworld, were associated with disgrace, sexual sin, excrement, and blindness.

I am speaking of celestial joy, of sin—sexual sin in particular—and of the disgrace of the gods through their fall into the underworld. Here I must make clear a pertinent point. Graulich (1983a) wrote an article about the myth of the expulsion from Tamoanchan, and based his study on the concepts of sexual sin and the opposition between heaven and the underworld, one being a place of pleasure and the other a place of sorrow. I cannot say I entirely agree with Graulich's thesis, though I recognize that his study is serious, balanced, thought provoking, and well documented. However, some of the specialists who commented on the article criticize the author for failing, in their judg-ment, adequately to take into account the Christian influence on the docu-ments he uses. It is true that this influence exists, particularly in the writing of Fray Pedro de los Ríos, whose opinions and interpretations led to the glosses of the *Vaticano Latino 3738* and *Telleriano-Remensis* codices. Christians in general, not only de los Ríos, viewed Tamoanchan as the Earthly Paradise of their own tradition. This is a great misconception. It cannot be denied that a similarity exists, as there often does between myths produced in different societies; but the similarity can be exaggerated, if the commentators believe that a common origin exists. The interpretations of the Spaniards were based on the belief that the native accounts were derived from an ill-remembered Biblical history or, even worse, ·that a demonic intervention had deformed the truth. Thus they believed indigenous gods took the place of Adam and Eve, and the flower-ing tree from which flowers and branches were broken was confused with the plundered tree in the Garden of Eden. However, all this was duly noted by Graulich. Some critics write that Graulich should not have given a strong context of sexuality to the terms *transgression* and *sin,* because this meaning is derived from Christian influence, and that Mesoamericans did not distinguish between a place exempt from sin and sex (heaven) and another where sin and sex did exist (the underworld).

There is no need for me to defend Graulich; he defended himself adequately in his reply to his critics. However, I will deal with an anticipated similar criticism, because it constantly reappears. The word *sin* is often avoided in Mesoamerican historical studies, with the claim that it is a Christian concept. I see no reason for this, since the wrongdoings in Mesoamerican myth fit perfectly the definition of *sin* (*pecado*) in the *Diccionario de la Real Academia Española*, which has often been criticized for its conservatism in religious matters. Furthermore, the close association of the generic idea of *sin* and the specific idea of *sexual sin*—the epitome of sin—is not unique to Christianity.[11] It is enough to note here that the metaphor *in teuhtli in tlazolli* ("dust, garbage") meant carnal sex in its generic and specific aspects to the ancient Nahua; note as well the tremendous importance of sexuality and sexual transgression in the symbolism of all the Mesoamericans and especially in the Mayan texts. Remember also the admonitions to children, premarital virginity, the chastity of priests, the periods of sexual abstinence for all people during religious festivals, the punishment of adulterers, the violent prosecution of homosexuality among many of the Mesoamericans, even the story of Quetzalcoatl, who had to abandon Tollan because he had broken his vow of chastity. Lastly there is certainly a direct association between the underworld and sex (more on this below).

Let us return to the tree of Tamoanchan. The connection between the birth of time and falling into disgrace is obvious. The gods, before covering the earth, lived in a place of wealth, delights, and amenities; after their sin, they fell into disgrace. This association is implicit in the *Códice Borbónico*. Of the aforementioned thirteen-day period that begins with the day One House, where the Tamoanchan tree and the goddess Itzpapalotl appear, the gloss states that persons born on these days "would be rich men, but afterwards would be poor" (*Códice Borbónico* 1979: pl. 15).

Garbage, excrement, sexual sin, and death were closely associated in the concepts of the ancient Nahua, where we find all these ideas linked to the idea of punishment and the blindness of the gods caused by their expulsion from Tamoanchan. I agree that the glosses to the *Telleriano-Remensis* and *Vaticano Latino 3738* codices are distorted by Judeo-Christian influence, but it is possible to identify there concepts deriving from an ancient Mesoamerican religion. The latter presents Ixcuina as the consort of Mictlantecuhtli, lord of the world of the dead: "It was said that this Ixcuina, a word which means shameless goddess, defended adulterers. She was the lady of salt, of excrement, of shamelessness, and the cause of all sins. . . . She was the wife of Miquitlan-teutle, god of hell. She was the goddess of evil women" (*Códice Vaticano Latino*

3738 1964–67: pl. 39). The *Códice Telleriano-Remensis* calls this goddess "the woman who sinned before the flood," "goddess of trash and shamelessness" (1964–67: pt. 2, pl. 20). Another goddess is portrayed among those who tore away the flowers in Tamoanchan-Ixnextli. The codex says of her, "They portray her the same as Eve, always crying and looking at her husband Adam. Her name is Ixnextli, which means eyes blinded by ashes, a name given to her after she sinned by plucking the flowers; and they say she can no longer look at the sky" (ibid.: pt. 2, pl. 8). The same codex says of Itztlacoliuhqui, "He was a lord of sin and blindness. He sinned in Paradise; therefore he is depicted with his eyes covered. . . . Under this sign adulterers are slain. . . . Those born on this day would be sinners and adulterers" (ibid.: pt. 2, pl. 18).

The gods, upon abandoning heaven, became contaminated. Their expulsion meant the diminishing of their sight—as in the myth about the forebears of the Quiche when they entered the world—or complete blindness (Itztlacoliuhqui has no eyes), given as punishment to the ancestors of the Huichol when they attacked the rising Sun (see chapter 5). The beings who originate time on the earth's surface (the forces transformed into time) remain diminished and, after the powerful transition, can no longer see heaven, their former home.

The Tamoanchan myth, then, is also the myth of the origin of sexual pleasure, with emphasis on its sinful aspect. This aspect is magnified by the patronage of the expelled gods, who instigate, punish, or pardon sexual transgressions. In classical Nahuatl, one of the terms for sex was *tlalticpaccayotl,* "what belongs to the surface of the earth." The underworld is death and it is sex. The broken branch gives rise to sex in the underworld, and from there it goes to earth in the very passage of the gods. The beginning of sexual pleasure and of time coincide, coming from the mythical adventure in Tamoanchan, the breaking of the tree. This identity is also clear. On the plates where the image of Tlazolteotl, the goddess of sexual sin, appears, the glosses of the *Vaticano Latino 3738* and *Telleriano-Remensis* codices state, "They say that this head signifies the commencement of sin that began with time, that there has been sin since the beginning (*Códice Vaticano Latino 3738* 1964–67: pl. 24)," and "then, when time began, sin began, and all of the things that follow from that" (*Códice Telleriano-Remensis* 1964–67: pt. 2, pl. 9).

Even today there are gods who lose their sight upon giving birth to their creatures. According to present-day myth, Nanahuatl, creator of the Nahua of the Huasteca, created people by chewing on grains of corn. The people formed from the dough also received the gift of corn as food. The ears of corn hung from their jaws and they did not have to work for them. But they lost the ears of corn, and their creator was furious. They were then thrown into the world and condemned to obtain their corn through their own work. The god also threw his eyes upon the world. One divine eye fell on the Huasteca and dancers retain it in the form of a mirror; the other one was lost between the Papaloapan and the Coatzacoalcos rivers. However, Nanahuatl's lost eye will reappear when the human world finally ends (Stiles, Maya, and Castillo 1985:18–19). When the beings of the world recover all of their diminished nature, when the body of Cipactli is reunited, when everything returns to a seamless time, then Nanahuatl will have eyes again.

There is no need to go into more detail about the coming of the gods. In describing the forebears of the people, it would be necessary to cite their drunkenness or their stupor at the moment of their departure, their passage through the Pánuco River,[12] their initial hunger, even the crossing of the waters that withdrew at the passing of the migrants, an episode that was declared—prematurely—to have a Biblical origin.[13] It is a difficult era, in which the misfortunes of the ancestors contrast with the treasures enclosed in vaults, as in indigenous myths of today.[14] We will return to these topics later.

Belief in the possibility of passing from one world to another has endured. The gods are not the only ones to cross over between worlds. Humans can cross over in dreams,[15] by ingesting psychotropic mushrooms, through ecstasy, carried by the gods, or by accidentally falling into the spaces of communication. The ancient Nahua, for example, believed they could see the gods in the other time-space during a dream, and in these visions they could see the future. Upon returning their recollection was not always clear, because the passage changed the order of the images. It was necessary to consult the priests, who read the *temicamatl*, or books of dreams, of which hardly a trace remains.[16] Durán, the Dominican (1984, 1:132), tells us:

> I asked an elderly man . . . the reason for having an agave god, and why they painted an agave with his face and hands surrounded by stalks. He answered that one of the dignitaries and leaders of the ancient law had dreamed that he saw an agave with face and hands. Astonished by such a dream, he announced that the agave god had appeared to him. He ordered him to be painted just as he had seen him in the dream, and had him worshipped, inventing rites and ceremonies befitting his worship as a god. . . .
>
> And when these people are accused of believing in dreams, the father confessors should know that the Indians in olden times took dreams to be divine revelation: if they dreamed that their teeth fell out, then children in their family would die; if they dreamed they were eating meat, they feared for the death of a husband or a wife; if they dreamed they were being swept away by water, they feared that they would be robbed; and if they dreamed about flying that they would die.

It is interesting to compare the dreams of the ancient Nahua of the lake region of the central high plateau, as told by Diego Durán, with those of present day Otomi in the southern part of the Huasteca, as told to Jacques Galinier (1987:485): "The imminent death of a child is foretold by a father's dream about losing a tooth or in the impulse to eat mushrooms. A violent death is foreseen in images of food (peas), in an airplane landing, or in a hog having its throat cut."

One point needs clarification. It is necessary to distinguish between the possibility of transcending natural human limitations of perception in order to encounter the supernatural that forms the imperceptible part of the human world, and the possibility of transcending the limits of this world to find oneself in the world that belongs exclusively to the gods. Within the human world, those with heightened perception can verify that some beings have a real, invisible supernatural aspect. The tales, although they do not refer to actual events, give us information about this concept of the world. One Chol story tells about a magical transformation. A man, related to a jaguar (often called a tiger in stories), covers himself with a jaguar skin that the feline gives him and is changed into an animal. His new form allows him to see what a jaguar sees; that is, with the transformation, the barriers of human perception are broken, and he sees in wild animals much more than others perceive. The animals appear in forms familiar from other tales, as they appear when they are caught by beings from the underworld and spend the night in their subterranean dwelling next to the Master of the Game:

> The man put on a tiger's skin, and, transformed into a tiger, set forth for the mountain in search of animals.
>
> His first encounter was with armadillos, but he saw them as a multitude of people bearing cudgels, and he was so frightened he had to run away. The same thing happened with the spotted cavies, whom he saw as an enormous crowd of old people coming toward him screaming. Deer also appeared to be Bachajontecos armed with lances. In the same way, his encounter with wild boars terrorized him and made him flee, since he saw them as a ferocious people who made their machetes resound, cutting the undergrowth of weeds in their path.[17]

Caves are the direct paths to the underworld.[18] Ancient history tells us that the *tlatoani* (ruler) of Chalco shut a hunchback up in the cave of a volcano. Since he had nothing to eat, he went deeper into the cave and found the palace of the Water God. Soon afterward the emissaries of the Lord of Chalco went to see if the hunchback had died. They found him alive, and he recounted his extraordinary experience to them (*Historia de los mexicanos por sus pinturas*

1965:26). Even more surprising is an old Yucatecan Maya tale. In the absence of caves in hills, the Yucatecan paths to the underworld are the grottos and *cenotes,* enormous wells which open to subterranean rivers. The Maya used to throw sacrificial victims into the cenotes, to carry messages to the gods. Hunac Ceel Cauich submerged himself of his own free will in the cenote in Chichen Itza, looking for communication. He did not die. He returned to the surface to announce that he had received the word of the gods. After leaving the water, he said that they had told him that he would be the governor of Chichen Itza. And so he was, from that time on, even though he did not belong to the reigning lineage (J. Thompson 1964:141–43).

What are the principal effects of passing to the other world? According to modern native accounts, there are two. One often hears of the change in the subjective time of the traveler. Occasionally upon returning through the mouth of a cave, the traveler discovers that time in the human world has been running on a different scale than time as experienced in the cave. On other occasions the traveler cannot calculate how much time has gone by in the other world. A Popoluca example is that of a young man who went to the sky:

> Afterwards, the Lord Santiago asked [the youth], "How many years do you think it took to get to sky?" The young man replied, "A year." He felt that only a short time had gone by. But Lord Santiago informed him, "You were gone thirty years." He plucked a hair from his head and said, "Look at this hair. You are an old man now." (Técnicos bilingues 1985:33)

In a Pipil myth, a hunter wounds a deer with his shotgun, and it turns into a girl. The girl leads him to the other world, to her father, who demands that the hunter marry one of his daughters, so that she can give new life to the deer he has killed. The hunter believes he has been in the other world ten days, but when he comes out, he finds that he has been there for ten years (Schultze Jena 1977:30–31).

The second effect of the passage is inversion. This often happens with food. The land of the dead is the reverse of the human world. It is the place of excrement. The ancient Quiche recount the battle of Ixbalanque against the Lord of the Underworld. When the latter was defeated, he begged Ixbalanque not to take him out into the light of day. The victor kicked him and said, "Return and may all that is garbage, and rotten and stinking be yours" (Las Casas 1967, 1:650). Thus the foods of the underworld are things that are loathsome to eat. The ancient Nahua saw it this way:

> Mictlantecuhtli, Mictecacihuatl, there in Mictlan, eat feet, hands, and their main dish is the black beetle, their atole [a thin corn gruel], pus. This is how

they drink it, out of a skull. They eat many fart tamales; they eat them there in Mictlan. Their tamales are beetle farts.

The one who on earth used to eat stews with sauce, there in Mictlan eats the seeds of fruit and all of the above. There, thorny plants are their food and all who go to Mictlan must eat thistles. Everything that is not eaten on earth is eaten there in Mictlan. (*Primeros memoriales* 1905: fol. 84r, 111; author's trans. from the Nahuatl)

Nowadays the Lacandon also attribute loathsome food to Kisin, Lord of the Underworld. "Kisin's food is not good. . . . [T]ree fungus is food for Kisin. He doesn't eat beans . . . but [human] corpses. . . . It has a horrible smell!" (Bruce 1974:244).

Food, gold, garbage, and excrement most frequently change as a result of the passage. According to a Cuicatec story, meat brought over from the region of the dead becomes rotten wood, tortillas become oak leaves, and tepache [fermented pineapple juice] muddy water (Davis 1963:202–3). A Chinantec account is quite similar. In a cave a man received a tortilla with some meat. Upon leaving the other world, he wanted to eat it. The tortilla turned into a big leaf and the meat into a rotten stick (*Relatos, mitos, y leyendas de la Chinantla* 1981:121). Yellow beans obtained inside a cave turn into gold dust when they reach the earth's surface (Madsen 1960:137). The Otomi believe that *pingos,* beings of the underworld, can swallow gold and transform it into excrement (Galinier 1987:451). According to a myth in the Soconusco, dwarfs who live underground gathered the Sun's gold from the earth's surface, took it to the center, and placed it on some roots. The roots grew upward, and the corn sprang forth on the earth's surface with kernels the color of gold (Navarrete 1966:426). The Chontal of Oaxaca refer to two transformations resulting from passage to the land of lightning. A man was fishing on a beach when an enormous crocodile arrived. The animal swallowed the man and took him far away to a mountain with beautiful houses, where he deposited him safe and sound. The traveler found tortillas and ears of corn everywhere and he wished to eat, but another man prevented him from doing so, telling him that what seemed to be food in reality was only the refuse from lightning. Afterwards the Chontal discovered another secret. When farmers burn offerings in their fields, the smoke goes to the land of lightning, and there it is converted into tortillas, another food eaten by the gods (P. Carrasco 1960).

In the mountains of Puebla they say that "in Mexico City there are skyscrapers forty stories high that also have forty stories underground." Based on this, Lok (1987) states that their image of the underworld is not merely a duplicate, but an inversion of the human world. It is an inversion not only in

form. It is a subterranean world full of freshness, gold, honey, perpetual vegetation, fish, wild animals, with dwarf inhabitants, towns, and roads similar
to those on the outside. What is savage becomes domestic: "It is populated
by families of Chanecos who use armadillos as seats. Their domestic animals
(pigs, hens, dogs, and cats) are the wild boars, pheasants, coyotes, and tigers.
Their boats are big crocodiles, and deer are their cattle" (García de León 1969).
It is a picture of the time when our hero performed his deeds: "In the time of
darkness, the Lord Tlacuache was the chief of the old men who gave advice.
The wild boar was their pig. All animals were domesticated then; but with
the arrival of light and the universes, they changed into wild animals" (Boege
1988:100).

It is an inverted world with its own laws. People cannot imagine a reality
without laws, even though that reality may exist beyond their own time and
space. Chaos, true chaos is faceless. Events in the myths have mythic causes,
but causes nonetheless.

The gods have their own laws, and in the myth of creation and throughout
the events by which the gods gain life, throughout the adventure that fills with
realities the broad actuality of valleys, mountains, lakes, and deserts, there
is order. Here is the truth of Tamoanchan, the steps in which time is born.
First, two complementary elements exist separately, one above and one below;
second, both of them are united in a tree trunk where they swirl around each
other; third, from their friction, a new being is born; fourth, the being is freed
and extends over the face of the earth. The liberated one is a flower, a flame.
Is this not the image of the two sticks rubbed together to produce a spark and
light the fire? The fire is a flower.

7 HOW DO YOU MEASURE A MYTH?

I am going to chop you down and carve you up.
Do not allow harm to come to me.

Conciliatory words
of an Ashanti artisan
to a tree he is about to cut down

Buddhist tradition attributes the *Milindapañha* to the dialogue of the sage Nagasena and the Greek king Menander (Milinda), who ruled over the Bactrians in the second century B.C. The king was faced with one of the great philosophical problems of reincarnation—the retention of individuality—and he asked the Old One:

"Does one who is born remain the same one, or is he transformed into another?"

The Old One answered, "Neither one nor the other."

Milinda begged the monk for a clearer explanation and Nagasena replied,
"You were a child at one time, a small, tender thing, flat on your back. Are you the same one, now that you are grown?"

"No, I am another," answered Milinda.

"If you are not that child, it would follow that you have had neither mother nor father."

The king implored the Old One to give other examples and Nagasena continued.

"Suppose, oh king, that a man lights a lamp which will continue burning throughout the night."

"Yes, that is possible."

"Now, is that flame that burns in the first night watch the same as that of the second?"

"No."

"Or is that of the second night watch the same as that of the third."

"No."

"Then there is one lamp in the first watch, another in the second, and yet another in the third?"

"No. The light proceeds from the same lamp throughout the night."

"Precisely. In that way, oh king, the continuity of a person or of a thing is maintained. One is born and the other extinguished, and the rebirth, so to

speak, is simultaneous. Thus a man, neither as himself nor as another, goes to
the last stage of self-consciousness."

"Give me another example."

"It is like milk, which, once it is taken from the cow, becomes clabber; from
clabber, it becomes butter, and from butter, *ghee* [oil derived from butter]. Is it
correct to say that milk is the same thing as clabber, butter, or *ghee?*"

"Certainly not. But they derive from it."

"Exactly, oh king. That is the way the continuity of a person or a thing
occurs. One is born and the other extinguished; and the rebirth, we can say, is
simultaneous. Thus neither as himself nor as another, does man enter the last
phase of his self-knowledge." (*The Questions of King Milinda* 1963: vol. 1, 63–65)

How is a myth measured? If it is defined as a text, it is measurable, since
its precise limits are the beginning and the end. Pragmatically I suggested, as
a provisional definition, the myth as a text. But is a myth not more like the
process of Buddhist continuity, as Nagasena explained it to King Milinda?

The problem should be restated, taking into account that the interesting
part of myth is its ideological nature, capable of producing any one of the many
links that tie the present to the remote Mesoamerican past. Is it necessary to
consider the origin of myth from this point of view? Yes, because the purpose
is to see it as a social product immersed in the current of history. Since we
are dealing with an ideological fact, we must take into account its genesis as
well as its capacity for generating and altering other processes. Does it modify
peoples' concept of the world? Does it change social conduct? Does it change
cosmovision even among the people who have heard the same account many
times? Is it taken as truth and is it a model for believers? Is it an unchangeable representation? Each telling of it is a new creation. The tale changes as
it goes along, moved by its dynamics and the circumstances. Is it an autonomous crystallization? Because of its relationships in the social totality—reciprocal relationships—with the processes of cohesion, with social structure,
with political domination, with religion, literature, beliefs, and art, myth is
a complex, multilinked institution. Is it a permanent reality? The reality of
myth changes in a similar fashion to Nagasena's lamp. We call "myth" what
we afterwards transcribe and publish in the cold medium of the printed word,
and we believe it is the same myth we heard from the lips of a native narrator.
But it is not the same myth, nor is it different. It passes from one tradition to
another, and is profoundly modified, because a myth is not composed of words
alone. In the transition it is tainted with the asymmetry of relationships that
transcend linguistics, because that transition is part of a greater one, the actual

transformation of indigenous societies. This is a subjugating, irreversible step in which the narrator, the listeners, and their traditions and life situations are involved.

> In spite of the ancestral existence of the oral tradition, the strength and prestige of the written word—unquestioned, powerful, exact, dominant—threatens the purpose and the voice of the old one, and the attention and the ears of youth, the relationship between them, the concept itself of what must be remembered. . . .
>
> In a way writing operates in a countersense to the word: from the multiple to the single; from the adaptable to new conditions, to the frozen, the fixed, the given. (Ramírez Castañeda 1985:14–15)

It is evident from the above that a myth is much more than its text. The beginning and end of a narrative are not enough to hold it. My provisional definition fails because the inherent complexity of social realities was not included in it.

Then what must myth as an object of knowledge be? We will start from the idea that the object of knowledge is not merely a reality in and of itself, external, studied by a person. Neither is it an abstraction of the person's thought. The object of knowledge is the product of real human activity, sensory, objective, and practical (Marx 1966:404). Let us propose new foundations for the object of knowledge. Myth is a social reality and, as such, a complex reality. Its limits disappear in the complex of relationships that exist in the social totality.[1] Its complexity is due in part to the fact that it is crossed by so many causal chains. Thus it can be classified as an ideological object, as a text, as a particular means of cultural transmission, as a way of preserving collective memory, etc. In each particular case, it will be seen to obey particular laws of cause and effect, which may be interdependent. Its identification as a social object depends on the particular mode of knowing, which includes the purpose of the people doing the thinking. Clearly the possibilities for determining its limits are many. Myth can make up diverse study units, differing in quality as well as in quantity. However, the relativity of the units does not imply that they are merely subjective. They are realities based on the different kinds of causes that determine myth. One's understanding will be greater according to how clearly the real limits of myth fit one's mode of thinking and specific purposes in knowing. Finally, consider the objective character of its representations and concepts. When they are totally or partially crystallized, they form a part of the transforming stream, the social reality they represent or conceive. The social conception of a myth can modify it or affect its nature.

While admitting that myth can be perceived in many ways, from different points of view, with diverse qualitative as well as quantitative units, we must remember that our purpose is to find a concept that can identify myth as an ideological reality. We seek a point of departure broad enough to allow us to develop specific foci. In this we follow Voloshinov, who faced a similar problem in trying to identify the object of study in the philosophy of language. His purpose, too, was to define the object of study so that it would be clearly understandable.

> The task of identifying the real object of study in the philosophy of language is not easy. With each attempt to find the boundaries of the object of the investigation, to reduce it to a compact and complex topic with defined and perceived dimensions, we lose the true essence of what we are studying, its semiotic and ideological nature. If we accept sound as a purely *acoustical phenomenon,* we will not have language as our specific object. Sound belongs completely to the field of physics. If we add the *physiological process in the production of sound* and the *process of reception of sound,* we still do not approach our goal. If we add to this the *experience* (internal signs) of the speaker and the listener, we get two different psychophysiological entities and a physical sound process whose natural manifestations are governed by the laws of physics. Language as a specific object of study continues to escape us. We already encompassed three spheres of reality, physics, physiology, and psychology and got a quite elaborate mixed complex. What is missing in this complex is a "soul." Its component parts are a collection of separate entities that cannot form a unity based on an internal power, which would turn this complex into the phenomenon of language.
>
> What then should be added to our complex? Above all, this complex must be included in a broader and more comprehensive one, in the unified sphere of organized social interchange. (1976:62)

As a result, Voloshinov opposed a methodological approach that would result in a divided study of the subject. He argued against the separation of the actual act of speaking from the linguistic system. Saussure (1982:40), in proposing a separation of language (*langue*) and of speaking (*parole*) had, at the same time, separated what is social from what is individual. Voloshinov (1976:76ff.) rejected Saussure's proposal. He argued that, dialectically speaking, language and speech are inseparable. One cannot be understood without relating it to the other.

How does this apply to myths? Let us consider the aspect of oral narration of myth. This is a human social relationship established through the medium of the word. There is no doubt that speech is the bond par excellence. But in each of the participants (narrators and listeners) there is a complex of common, normative systems that allows and establishes this relationship.

We have then a real act, the specific narration of a myth. We also have a norm that regulates it. However, in the case of myth, we cannot guarantee the existence of a single regulating norm. There is no grandiose code, no general system of mythology, carried on by all the participants, which governs exclusively the production of the text of the myth. It is something more complicated, a confluence of regulating systems. No doubt linguistics is a fundamental part of that complex, but the norms that regulate myths are also basic. In three preceding chapters we have dealt with part of that normative system, a group of basic beliefs from which the origin myths evolved. But there are also systems unrelated to linguistics or mythology that form an important part of the full process.

The narrator and the audience share value systems. It is never a total sharing, because the social position of an individual determines the internal integration of these systems. But this same difference, which in communication produces contradictions, misunderstandings, confrontation of opinions, even jests, is part of the interesting interplay that gives rise to myth.

It is not necessary that the normative systems of all those who are present be identical. It is neither necessary nor possible. In spite of that, there is communication; the similarity in the group of systems makes it possible. The range of systems is broad, sufficiently wide to allow the inclusion of strangers. There is enough communication that even we outsiders who occasionally enjoy the native tales can participate. Our relative capability for understanding is low. We do not take part in the kind of social relationships that rule the circle of listeners. Nevertheless the myth attracts us and holds our attention, making us listeners.

We believe, however, that we have a fuller participation. We have deified the text. We forget that the same words heard by various listeners have different meanings, and that communication is a relationship, deriving from a set of social interchanges. Some listen as believers, others do not—this single difference makes a great distinction. For us the myth may be beautiful, but it is not true. Carpentier tells the myth of the sorcerer, his wife, and the three *obones*. It was a time when the number three reigned and, therefore, there were three dignitaries (obones), in the Ñañigo ritual. The sorcerer's wife, the beautiful Sicanecua, caught a roaring fish [unidentified]. With it she made an *ecue*-caller, the ritual instrument used in initiations. This instrument gave power to the sorcerer. However, the triangle was broken, since from that day on there were not three obones but four, and a new institution was born. The secret was in the *ecue*-caller and, since no woman can keep a secret, the four obones beheaded the beautiful Sicanecua. This is the end of our myth, which all of Carpentier's readers can enjoy. But what a different effect the myth would have on any royal Menegildo Cue. How real it would be when, at the moment of his Ñañigo initiation, he heard the harsh roar of the *ecue*-caller! (Carpentier 1980:158–65).

The creation of the mythic narrative and the normative systems that rule it are inseparable. They cannot be understood if they are studied separately. Joined they establish communication, greater or lesser depending on their mutual concordance.

How have the different systems that make a myth possible entered the consciousness of people? By many previous performances, not all of a mythic nature. The internal integration of these normative systems does not have to be explicit. Formal transmission, as in teaching-apprenticeship, is very important, but the greater part of an individual's grasping and structuring of systems is informal. In social interaction, people communicate norms without being aware of it, without a need for formally explaining them, without necessarily having to make the system abstract. The road is formed by walking it. When the myth is told, all those social elements that work on the narration and upon the people upon whom the narration works, trigger memories, prompt deductions, justify themselves, prepare future realizations of the mythic text, and make it live as it is, not merely as a sequence of sounds, words, or concepts, but as a unified whole of social interactions. Because even if a myth is not told, all those elements are still present. Mythic relationships persist. That is why a myth cannot be limited to just a text.

Myth is a belief. When the artisan confronts the tree and begs it to understand why he has to carve it, the possibility of dialogue stems from that time in creation when the first trees were born and a divine substance resided in them, which was not only capable of hurting the woodcutter but was also able to have compassion on the pleas of whoever needed to cut them. The artisan's prayer is not, properly speaking, a mythic narration; its expression, however, is a mythic act.

Beyond the narrative, the thief of fire regulates conduct. The Huichol teach their children that no matter how hungry they may be, they must never eat opossum meat, the flesh of the hero who gave them fire. In the next life, the soul of the disobedient Huichol would face the underworld opossum, and it would crush him in its stone trap.[2] The myth's influence extends further than its presence as a narrative; it regulates eating habits and enriches the wealth of beliefs. How can one discern, then, the reality that is myth? It exists in multiple varieties with diffuse, changeable, often imperceptible boundaries. Those varieties are what give it life. They are the myth.

Let us recognize, then, this primary characteristic of our object of study: its limits are too broad and always blurred, as is all social reality. We will always have to keep the social totality as a frame of reference. But it is necessary to make distinctions. Limits do not exist of and for themselves. The setting of limits is part of the construction of the object of knowledge. Here we may recall what L. White (1949:7) said in relating the whole to its parts:

> "Whole and parts" means relationships. "Relationship," too, is another conceptual device, a symbolic instrument, with the aid of which we render experience intelligible to a degree, and by means of which we effect our adjustments to our environment.

Dialectically speaking, the specification of a myth should rest on the identification of sets of similar realities in that indiscernible social totality. These sets can be identified phenomenologically.[3] But the scientific focus, based on the regularity of the phenomena and the orders of regularity that group them, can discover in them specific laws that serve as bases for the formation of a concept.

Here we encounter one of the serious difficulties in constructing the object of knowledge, the fact that the dimensions of myth should be based on rules of order. Myth, like all social reality, is crossed by several rules. One must choose the optimum dimension of the aggregate of realities, making one or several of its identifying rules of order suit the specific purposes of knowledge. Too much breadth excludes important specific laws that may not cover all of the aggregate of realities; and too much reduction excludes social realities that are regulated, in their totality, by important specific rules of order. In the same way, a reduction or an expansion unsuitable to the purpose of knowledge can lead to a caricature of the specific problem. If in provisionally defining myth I had included all the tales in which heroes and gods took part, the conglomeration would have been too loose. There would be so many differences among the various tales that finding specific points that would lead to understanding would be difficult. On the other hand, the selection of the thematic range I chose—the inchoative eruption of the *other* time-space—allows the discovery of other regularities that are peculiar and important to explain the aggregate of realities. One of the most important steps in the creation of a concept is the one that leads to its optimal boundaries.

The dimensions of myth in order to construct an object of knowledge are determined from different aspects: historical depth, geographic extent, the origin of narrative elements, extent of functions, etc. The point of departure must be the one that places the myth within its fullest social context. In understanding, the whole will not be the sum of its parts. The sum of partial studies with different methodological perspectives does not lead to this holistic vision. A regional study that does not take into account the real, geographic extent of myth can lead to an explanation based upon limited natural, social, or historical conditions. This happens too frequently. Distinguishing between the local, the regional, and the general is important to a myth's interpretation.

Studying a myth from too specific a focus, without taking into account its various versions or the mythological systems producing the myth, will yield easy but mistaken ideas of the meanings of its elements. Any specialized view, any specific method, no matter how serious or well founded, can fail if it does not deal with the correct dimensions.

Another problem of setting limits is that we cannot always reach a fixed, static concept. Myth is not the same set of regularities permanently. Myth as a social custom has a history. Social acts are affected by two kinds of history: that of their transformation as a class, and that of their transformation as specific processes. In Haeckelian terms, in a way not entirely appropriate to the field of social sciences, it could be said that there exists a phylogeny and an ontogeny of myth. Phylogenetics would study the characteristics of the mythic complex of a particular tradition. Ontogenetics would deal with the process of creation of myth X or of myth Y. Both kinds of history raise disturbing questions. At what moment is a myth born and at what moment does it cease to exist? What constant elements in a long chain allow it to be identified as the same process? Do these permanent elements have an essential character? "Neither the one nor the other," said Nagasena. Myth is crystallization, and it is process.

The search for what is specific to a myth yields a very complex picture. A large collection of differing social relationships may surround the two nuclei. These nuclei are: an accumulation of beliefs and a mythic narration. Dissimilar social relationships are not merely deeds influenced by myth: they form a part of the myth as it is practiced, as it is exercised, with the carrying out of its beliefs. These acts, along with the two nuclei, make up the sets that are characterized and linked among themselves by their orders of common or complementary rules. A mythic belief is produced in those relationships, because it is not merely a formal and structured thought, a psychic act independent of social practices. It is in them, as a generating element of feeling, as a communicator of congruency. Mythic belief is widespread, it is present in ritual acts, in power, in the ingestion of food, in work, in copulation, in the formation of the family. The act of narration is its most finished expression, but not the only one, and perhaps not the most important.

Mythic expression occurs in two very different forms. One is the text, a formalized, structured, complete act. It is the face of myth. The other is a scattered, omnipresent, often diffuse expression, comprised of words, gestures, attitudes, and visual images, often scarcely perceptible; but it is this form of mythic expression that, refined as social communication, creates the systems of congruency and rules that regulate a good part of social behavior. Myth is the product of the harmonic, collective action of believers speaking and acting in varied social areas.[4] Without this expression spread throughout the most diverse human practices, the nucleus of mythic beliefs would not only be impoverished, it would not exist. It is in this kind of communication that it has its most vivid social existence. Individual psychological myth, belief as thought, is created in the process of communication. Belief exists in multiple and heterogeneous social practices, and in these also are found the reason, formation, meaning, congruency, transformation, conservation, and death of mythic belief.

Myth, then, is not only a text; neither can it be reduced to the two nuclei of narration and belief. It is a reality made up of many social relationships grouped around both nuclei. Myth is not a performance on one hand, nor a set of rules on the other. It is the dialectical union of different rules of order with multiple, heterogeneous, omnipresent realizations. Myth is formed by crystallizations and by diverse historical sequences.

Figure 4. Mouse opossum, *Marmosa mexicana*

8   BELIEFS AND NARRATIONS

If each day falls
within each night,
there must be a well
that encloses the light.
One must sit at the rim
of the cistern of shade
and patiently fish
for the fallen light.

Pablo Neruda,
El mar y las campanas

The construction of an object of knowledge, of a concept of myth, continues. It began by taking it apart, looking at differences and separating them, in order to find in the complexity of its nucleus—a truly essential process, which reveals rules of law sufficiently valid to explain the nature and dynamics of the specific. So far there has been not just one set of processes but two principal nuclei, which we could designate as *myth-belief* and *myth-narration*. We can see several characteristics of their coexistence: the two nuclei are quite different from each other; they are mutually interdependent; their ties are asymmetrical; and their rules of law are different. This duality has divided researchers from the moment myth was defined. Some of them, including Cohen (1969), claim that the narrative nature of myth distinguishes it from a general idea or a group of ideas, such as cosmology. Others, like Count (1976), consider narration to be just one of several forms of expressing mythic content. Instead of enclosing one in the other or examining each in depth—to the degree of separating both nuclei—it is advisable to understand their differences, their ties and oppositions as mutually dependent entities. Myth-narration is not just the spoken part of myth-belief, nor does it have complete autonomy with respect to it. Let us regard myth as a reality that possesses two (or more) integrating nuclei, and let us begin with the nucleus of belief.

In dealing with myth as belief I do not wish to restrict myself to its ideas. It is true that belief is formed by ideas, but it is also formed by convictions, tendencies, habits, purposes, and preferences, which lead us to confront nature and society—including ourselves as individuals—in an inner examination that can define our place in society and in nature. Beliefs "place us before what to us is reality itself," according to Ortega y Gasset (1964:24, 1984:38), and he also states, "Rather than us having beliefs, they are us."

Among all beliefs let us identify the ones with a mythic aspect. They are the ones that relate the inchoative activity of the gods in human time-space (at the moment of origin or in the daily repetition of the original deeds) to their presence as a flow of forces that emerge in the world to create its movement. In spite of its limits, this is not a small set.

The magnitude and the wide dissemination of myth-belief make it difficult to study. Myth-belief is spread throughout society, often in very small units. Even today, when many of us consider ourselves to be free of mythic beliefs, we should remember, as Wittgestein (1985:29) does, that "an entire mythology is built into our language." In daily life language spreads and reinforces belief. Thus it can be said of mythic belief what Lucien Febvre (1971:160) said of geography: "Geography is *everywhere* and *nowhere;* just like art history; just like law; just like ethics." What the outside observer sees most clearly is not always the key part of mythic belief. From the outside we clearly see the origin of the sun and the moon, the development of people, the struggle among the forces of nature, and the destruction of previous eras. But for the believer there are in myth processes and patterns that predict and guide daily life. The nature and the classification of all things are determined by their origins. Mythic beliefs speak of the tiredness of muscles, the evaporation of water, the specific attributes of stones, of good or bad luck in hunting, of the consequences of not dancing on the festival day of a patron saint, of the fight against plagues and hail, of children's character, of the obligations of an uncle to his nephew, or of the visit of phantoms. Belief is lived intensely in every sense, in the truly important acts—many of them small ones—of daily life. This makes it possible to discover mythic structures in different areas of social life. Durkheim and Mauss (1971:41), based on Powell and Cushing's studies on the Zuni, called "mythosociological" those social organizations in which categories of the human order and those of the universe were intermingled and blended. But the mythic is also mixed and blended in a doctor's garden or a cook's pantry.

Because of this, there can be no total compilation of myth-belief. However, limited compilations of some key areas exist or have existed. Sources mention a book of the Toltecs, the *teamoxtli,* which included the history of the tribe and its lords; its forms of government; ancient penalties; exemplary deeds; descriptions of temples, idols, sacrifices, rites, and ceremonies; prophecies; and the secrets of architecture and other arts (Alva Ixtlilxochitl 1975–77c:270, 277–78). A similar list is found among the peninsular Maya, in the so-called books of Chilam Balam, and the calendrical codices of the different Meso-american peoples are a wealth of information. These and similar documents, which record partial visions, can be compared and the complementarities used to reconstruct the foundations of the beliefs.

One of the researchers most concerned about the order derived from myth-belief and implicit in these documents was Paul Kirchhoff. Assuming that there was parallelism, Kirchhoff looked into the order of the lists (lists of gods, rites, priests, sections of towns, of eras, of populations) for the keys that would apply to orders in different areas (Kirchhoff 1971, 1985; Rojas Rabiela 1983). Others have followed the same path in their search for matching elements: P. Carrasco (1978), Reyes Garcia (1978), Zantwijk (1985), Matos Moctezuma (1987), and I myself (López Austin 1986). Important works by Maya scholars include those of Coe (1965), Barthel (1968), and Marcus (1976). The latter studied the four-part organization of the state in the Maya lowland during a good part of *baktún* 9. Vogt (1966b) investigated similar questions among the contemporary Maya.

We have all encountered similar problems in this difficult undertaking: his-torical facts that violate rules of structure, errors in the sources, rules misinter-preted by researchers, undetected differences between beliefs under study, mistaken leads pursued, or exaggeration in the application of rules. All of us are prone to error due to the emotion of discovery. At times conclusions derive from forced corrections, and they are weakened by conjectures, gaps, and long arguments about the place some element should have, or over the justification for some irregularity. Some of the conclusions are convincing, others less so. Nevertheless this laborious and not always fruitful task has undeniably dem-onstrated the existence of a mythological belief that permeates and bestows order upon social situations and the actions carried out in them. Kirchhoff's (1985) criticism of Seler and of Krickeberg serves its purpose, when he says of their works:

> They remain completely within their unilateral focus of religious-ideological research. . . . However, the organization of the Toltec capital, of its inhabitants, and of the empire in its entirety built on the same principles escapes them. . . . The Mexican man, like any other from a high archaic culture of the world, pat-terned all his social life in the image of the religious world, with the same basic principles applying to the real world and to the imaginary world.

The total order is broken up in its uses and expressions, but it lacks an ex-plicit, unifying form. Its congruence is due to the social communication of its believers, in their heterogeneous environments, in a two-way transfer—conscious or not—from one group to another. It is an order that usually is produced outside of any regulating will.

Reference is frequently made to a collective memory, to the transmitting and preserving function of social communication; but the collective creative activity—the great organizer that filters the participation of many, thus creating the nuclei of social thought—is often forgotten.[1] This activity produces the mythic set of beliefs. It must be made clear that this purification leads to a unity and a congruence that are never total. Mythic beliefs are the result of social relationships, and likewise reflect, in their differences, the contradictions of society. General mythic belief exists as a complex system, but not as a unitary, homogeneous, or static one. It is made up of movable pieces with changing relationships. Myth-belief is social knowledge, an interrelationship of separate beliefs acted out in the context of different practices. The congruent nuclei are not discrete entities. They are simultaneous, changeable, quite a few of them contradictory, and often interdependent, in spite of—or due to—their contradiction. The shifting totality of coincidences and oppositions constitutes the totality of mythic belief.

Since myth-belief occurs in many different spheres of social life, it has very different forms of expression. Semiautonomous spheres are produced, of which myth-narration is a good example, but not the only example. The definition of myth as a group of social relationships cemented together by two great nuclei (myth-belief and myth-narration) does not preclude the existence of systems and subsystems of practices and beliefs that have lives and manifestations of their own and, at the same time, form part of the whole. Some of these maintain a strict dependence on the nucleus of myth-belief; others achieve—or achieved—a greater degree of autonomy. In Mesoamerica the most outstanding example was perhaps the calendrical system, rooted in the concept of the emergence (the original as well as the daily) of gods into human time-space. Even this system broke up into subsystems that operated in specific areas, but which were still closely linked to each other. Thus among the ancient Maya, the three time cycles called *haab* (365 days), *tun* (360 days), and *tzolkin* (260 days) had specific uses: the first one, in the monthly rituals related to agriculture, hunting, fishing, and food gathering; the second, in historical-prophetic recording; the third, in divination and soothsaying.[2] These were subsystems with their own strong characteristics, whose interrelationships—interacting with still other cycles—composed the extremely complex Mayan calendaric system.

Other secondary systems can be named—secondary, that is, from the viewpoint of the study of myth, which having that declared object of knowledge, gives prime importance to the nuclei of myth-belief and myth-narration. Magic means the handling of time and the mastery of the transition from one time-space to the other; its origin in mythic narration can be heard in its spells. Religious ritual, sometimes as action (chants, offerings, dance . . .), sometimes as an attempt to invoke divine, calendrical forces, is closely tied to mythic belief and narration. Narration includes the production of myth-narrative; and many of its forms, which cannot be correctly called myths, are nourished by mythic creation. The plastic arts offer rich images of a world not accessible to the senses. Finally, history is conceived on the mythic archetype, and in turn records the miracles that reaffirm faith. The mythic message invades even the most remote corners of social life. A researcher can find it in the most unexpected places: the opposition of two phrases, a metaphor, a courteous act, a geometric design. A counterpoint of flutes and drums conveys, half hidden, the message of some primogenital time. A Chenalhó *huipil* (shift), is embroidered with designs whose names—Saint, Great Saint, Crown, Head of Our Lord Esquipulas, On the Holy Cross, Serpent's Path, Blood Path, Giant, Scorpion, Great Serpent, Tiger—beg for investigation (Turok 1976).

These areas are not merely derivations from the conception of and the crystallization of myths. Their processes are not unidirectional; a strong, mutual influence enriches both ends of the chain. It does not merely pass from one social sphere to another, for each system has developed its own peculiarities of function, materials, laws, and specific media. A visual image, for example, is not a servile description of a myth, but an appropriation of the myth; in art, mythic symbolism has its own set of values, independent of myth-narration. The image may be an explanation from which the clever believer can extract knowledge not accessible through analysis of the myth.

One of the old questions is the nature of the dependence between myth and ritual. The long and hard-fought polemic, first introduced by Edward Burnett Tylor, has featured mythologists with widely divergent positions.[3] Some specialists consider ritual to be the dramatic representation of a preexisting myth, while others maintain that the function of myths is to explain or to sanction preexisting rituals. Some insist that neither derives from the other, but that both are closely and necessarily associated. There are mythologists who say that myth is the counterpart of ritual: myth states what rituals enact. By contrast some researchers find little evidence in the particular cultures they investigate of any strong connection between myth and ritual.

The relationship does not simply connect the narrative and the ritual act. It is necessary to take into account the entire complex from which the myth

comes: the accumulation of social relations gathered around the two principal nuclei and the secondary ones, in a context based on the idea of an initial
creative emergence of the gods. The entire complex must be considered because the relationships are established between at least three, and not two,
of the nuclei mentioned. Myth-belief forms the principal vertex of the triangle, as the source of a knowledge that is expressed both in myth-narration
and in ritual. However, there are other direct and indirect links, the most important being those stemming from ritual and from myth-narration. On the
other hand, ritual and myth-narration are not merely the simple expression of
myth-belief, but semiautonomous systems with functions, structures, laws,
and even their own history. Ritual does not merely record fundamental definitions of the cosmos, nor merely reproduce symbolically the significant acts of
the beginning of time. Ritual has an important value as a calendrical action, a
means of propitiation of the gods who erupt into the human world every day;
it assists the gods present in the world; it is an act of participation with which
people believe they can guarantee order in the cosmic processes. Significantly
it is also an efficient means of defense against such erupting forces. Ritual
provides an opportunity to act precisely at the proper moment for accomplish-
ing precise ends. The cyclic succession of time makes it possible, through the
management of ritual, to propitiate the forces, to be forewarned against them,
to correct one's own offenses and omissions, to strengthen one's body, to avoid
danger, and to enact in daily life the process of transformation.

Believers do not themselves often interpret their ritual acts. However, interpretations appear sporadically in the documents, as valuable guides. The
Códice Tudela records why people who fell ill on a date ruled by Piltzinteotl
(one of the nine lords of night) went to the ball-game court to give offerings to
win the goodwill of the god in whose time domain the illness had begun. The
reason for selecting that site was the myth in which the god died. The court
was the place of his transformation.

> The third day was called *yei calli,* which means three houses. The ruling demon
> they had for that day was called Pilzintecutli [*sic*], which means Lord Young
> Child, and the augury was called *cocotzin,* which means turtledove. And those
> who became ill on that day went to sacrifice themselves or to offer paper be-
> fore the edifice they had erected for a ball-game called *tlachco.* When they were
> going to offer the sacrifice, they wore a net on their bodies and they offered
> feathers from the roosters of this land. The elders said that they had to go there
> to sacrifice and to take offerings before the ball-game. So that Piltzinteotl, the
> ruling demon of that day who had died while playing ball, would be favorable
> to them. (*Códice Tudela* 1980: fol. 91)

Other practices, though not interpreted by the believers themselves, give clues that link myth and ritual. There are types of gods who, when dying, created human food from the different parts of their bodies. In a ritual to the gods of rain, worshipers tore to bits an image made of seeds, and the seeds were used for the next crop (Serna 1953:191–92). The rite recreates the mythical emergence of domesticated plants from the bodies of the gods. A religious prohibition implies that marriage did not exist until the moment when the mythic adventure of an archetypical matrimony ended. In the month that commemorated the union of the god Mixcoatl and the goddess Chimalma, married couples abstained from sex until the last day of the festival (Serna 1953:181, 189). In both cases something deeper that a mere expression of mythic narrations can be seen. These and many other examples suggest research that will clarify the evolution of ritual and the ties between myth-belief and myth-narration.

Of course the simple mention of rituals in myths does not necessarily refer to their real origin. Raglan (1965), studying the Biblical tradition, went too far in his interpretation. Upon finding in *Leviticus* two references to a ritual, he thought this sufficient to show that the myth was a simple narration associated with the ritual.[4] Likewise in indigenous Mexican myths rituals are mentioned and there are references to their origin.[5] But at least in the case of the Mexica, this is because the believer attributes to ritual, like every other institution, an origin in the first times. These references do not imply a deeper, more generalized relationship between myth and ritual.

The links between myth and magical spells are very strong. Magicians use the names thought to belong to beings at the moment of their creation, and they place themselves at that first moment—by mentioning it or going to it across the barrier—to reach the situation and the path they seek.[6] This procedure is based on the profound belief in primogenital time. Narration is a source in some of the magical spells. Ruiz de Alarcón (1953:176), in the seventeenth century, was aware of this when, speaking of the cure for a scorpion's poison, he gave the mythic text only, and justified it by saying, "To understand this chapter, it is necessary to refer to a fable and an ancient legend fully accepted by these barbarians, and so well established that I believe few escape believing it." The passage he quotes makes both the spell and the curing process clear to the reader: The doctor plays the role of the goddess Xochiquetzal and, as in the myth, conquers the patient, who becomes another character (Yappan) because he has been invaded by the scorpion's poison.

Myth speaks forcefully in the plastic arts. Vases from Uaxactun, Ratinlinxul, Chama, Nebaj, Altar de Sacrificios, Huehuetenango, and other sites of the Classic Mayan period graphically depict scenes from the lives of humans and gods. The constrained position of a deer's hooves reveals an anthropomorphic being inside; the presence of hummingbirds in a picture indicates the participation of the Sun in the episode (J. Thompson 1975:441–42). We can imagine complex stories in these pictures where heroes are captured or a captive is beheaded. We know nothing else, because the narrative was fixed on clay walls more permanently than in the memory of the people. Today we do not know what tales of divine adventure led the painter to create those works. We wish to divine the episodes of the narratives that were enjoyed from the seventh to the ninth century; but today we barely participate, feeling merely compassion for a captive about to be executed with an ax, or ridicule for the scene of the lustful old God L, among five of his young wives and with his rabbit scribe at the foot of his dais. We see the gods of the underworld dancing, among them the plump infantile Jaguar God, lying on his back on the head of the Cauac Monster,[7] but nothing more. The Maya of the Late Classic period no doubt joined two complementary forms of expression into a single tale. In Mesoamerica, in India, and in Greece, the creation of the visual image is another way of expressing mythic belief: "Myth occupies the ball courts, the metopes, the friezes, the products of different arts. Their purpose is no different from that of literary myth" (Rodriguez Adrados 1984:65). The phenomenon occurs throughout the world.

However, an image goes beyond the story-telling possibilities of mythic narration. There are details of dress, elements of construction loaded with symbolism, environments usually not described in myth-narration, colors and instruments that refer to the other nucleus, to myth-belief as a source of knowledge. This source is less emotional but richer in details, in relationships, and correspondences, than the formal relationships of myth-narrative. Such as when the opossum appears leading the decapitated woman, both with hands lifted on high or carrying vessels filled with flintstones (*Códice Vindobonenesis* 1964–67: pl. 33-20, 40-13; and see fig. 11 of this book); or seated on a throne covered with a spotted skin, with his fan of green feathers, his luxurious headgear, and his multicolored, checkered mantle; or with a feather headdress and wings, capturing a wounded person, while brandishing an ax; or being grasped by a warrior with bristling hair, and perhaps defending himself with a white disk; or devouring a disarmed enemy; or sharing—apparently eating—with a disembodied head, a necklace made of a bone and fine beads; or incorporated into a crossroads (*Códice Fejérváry Mayer* 1964–67: pl. 30-15, 38-7, 39-6, 40-5, 42-3, 43-2; and see fig. 10 of this book)—these images show us an opossum never completely described in mythic narration. Here is a great deal of information not included in the words of the narrator. Perhaps the knowledge came from other forms of oral transmission: poems, prayers, songs, magical spells, descriptions of the gods, lists of ritual objects, even informal chats with no pretensions to the beauty of formal discourse, such as conversations a mother and her daughter might have had beside the three hearthstones. Painting, and sculpture as well, do not depend solely upon myth-narration. Their foundation is richer and more varied.

Four mythical opossums are pictured in the *Dresden Codex* (J. Thompson 1972: pl. 25–28; see fig. 9 of this book), one carrying a god of corn on his shoulder, another the God of Rain,[8] another the God of Death, and another the figure of a jaguar, each one bearing a scepter terminating in a hand. They are the *bacaboob,* the four gods who hold up the sky, the "opossum actors" associated with the New Year festivals celebrated among the Maya of the north on the last "five unfortunate days" of each year and the first day of the following year (J. Thompson 1970b; 1972:90). The importance of these four characters—the four gods who hold up the world, in cosmic geometry—in the arrival of time, as bearers of an annual destiny for the four year signs, extends further than a mythic narrative explaining their presence—if, in fact, such a narrative existed. The image—their finery of spiral shells, their jewels, their bonnets, their fans, the glyphs on the cenote above which two of them stand—indicates a myth-belief complex, difficult to transmit by myth-narration.

Neither is myth-narration a handmaid to myth-belief. Myth-narration develops in the context of an entire literary tradition (Christiansen 1965), in such a way that mythical heroes are changed by literary patterns to meet the demands of popular taste. More details about the formation of mythic narration will be given in later chapters, but here it is maintained that literary and linguistic modes, and the oral form itself, have an influence on myth-narration beyond its merely linguistic and literary aspects. For example the need to memorize requires rhythm.[9] Listeners expect adventures. The vivacity of the narrator colors the story; the place and time encourage or inhibit inserting, here or there, a certain event. The story told must be governed by the circumstances attending the telling; the relevance of the tale may ritualize it, reconnecting it to myth-belief; even the incidental situation itself, the appropriateness of the message, all affect the tale (Leach 1965:276). Mythic narration has its own laws, and these go to the very core of the adventures of the gods. These adventures, accepted and repeated, are incorporated into myth-belief, enriching it, coloring it, turning themselves into the source of the beliefs that provided their origin.

We find ourselves in the false dilemma of the chicken and the egg. Which came first, myth-belief or myth-narration? Assuming—hypothetically, of course—that we could go back in time to trace the birth of a certain myth, we would find between the birth and the narration in question a much greater distance than there is between milk and ghee in Nagasena's teaching. What concerns us is not the impossible search for an origin, but a coexistence in which both principal nuclei (and the others) are reciprocally transformed. One depends upon the other and changes the relationship in the following stage. However, does one of the nuclei dominate the others? Yes, though not necessarily due to its origin. First, myth-belief has stronger social functions than those of myth-narration; for instance, its value in the organization of government, where it serves as a structural model. Its changes will be based largely on the interplay of social relationships and, at the same time, will determine the most important changes in myth-narration. Second, in the multiple interrelations between both principal and secondary nuclei, myth-belief will hold the central position. The most important currents will flow from it or toward it. It is the focal point in the confluence.

Boas (1968:406, 429–30, 433) stressed the possible unlinking of beliefs from mythic narrations. This is much more noticeable when there is a borrowing of narratives between two societies that have different visions of the cosmos, or where there is minimal correspondence. The fact that the beliefs are different, as Boas points out, does not prevent the exchange. This is true, but we must not exaggerate the importance of the separation between narration and belief, nor of borrowing, with respect to Mesoamerican religious cosmovision. In Mesoamerican religious tradition there is a considerable affinity of cosmovisions, so that borrowing should be viewed rather as a mutual participation in a common cultural creation. On the other hand, acceptance of a mythic narration produces an immediate transformation in it, which tends to assimilate the story on the basis of beliefs already current in the receiving society. Examples of this process abound in the indigenous mythology of Mexico and Central America. This process is even more noticeable when it occurs with narratives of Christian origin. Thus stories about the life of Christ have been changed into solar myths, in a trajectory that is obviously not limited to adapting myths.[10] The relative congruency produced in the transference not only produces concordant elements but reduces the outside elements.

The history of the myth is the history of withdrawals and approaches of the component nuclei, which modify their rhythms to overtake, exceed, or trail behind each other. The four bacaboob, the opossum actors with their luxurious headdress, bearers of the four destinies of the years, were left behind, in remote history. Nevertheless the story of the iguana that took fire from

Figure 5. Wooly opossum, *Caluromys lanatus*

heaven; of the failure of the crow; of the hummingbird; of the other birds that wanted to recover it; and of the success the old ones had when they at last, called upon the opossum to take charge of the mission in which the other animals had failed . . . the tale of the ascent of our hero, his crossing through the waterfall, his presentation to the old guardian of fire, and of the wiles of the crafty opossum, is still told today:

> Then the opossum sat down. The old one remained there and went to sleep. While he [the old one] was sleeping, the opossum took the fire with his tail. Little by little he withdrew it, but the old one awoke.
>
> "You are taking away the fire, my nephew."
>
> "No, I am blowing on it."
>
> The old one went to sleep again. This time he slumbered deeply. While he was snoring, the opossum raised himself slowly, took the fire and slid along with it gradually. Soon he was near the cornice.
>
> At this instant, the old one awoke and saw him. Immediately, the opossum took the fire near the parapet. The old one got up at once and pursued him. He overtook him at the cornice and the fire slipped and fell over it.

His grandfather came running toward him. In the race he struck him repeatedly with a stick. He grabbed him and beat him down to the ground many times with his cane. Opossum caught on fire, was broken to bits and slid down below. When this happened, the old one backed off, saying, "You are not going to take fire from me, opossum." (Preuss 1912, 1:180–81; Spanish trans. from the German by R. Arzápalo Marin)

9 TO THINK THAT WAY

The stone they call crystal is from the first phase
of the sign of Cancer, which in this book we named
the fifth degree of the sign of Scorpion.
  It is endowed with such power that anyone who
carries it will travel over the sea safely, and will always
escape any danger from it. And if they put it in a place
where there is little rain, it will rain forthwith:
but this will be accomplished better when the moon is full,
ascending, in its turn and safe from sinister influences.
[It works better] when the power of a man with a
twisted head and fingers, who is shaded by fig leaves
falls on it.

Alfonso el Sabio,
El Lapidario

"You are not going to take fire away from me, Opossum."

The ones [who were waiting] looked up at the fire; a little later it came falling down. They were waiting for it with their blankets. It fell, not there, but on the ground. They picked it up from there, but the earth had already caught on fire.

While they were putting it out, the opossum came running. They saw him arrive and fall down dead on the ground. Then they covered him with one of the blankets. A moment after he was covered, he began to move. He was alive; he got up heavily and sat down. Little by little he regained consciousness, and when he had recovered he stood up and asked them.

"Did the fire arrive? I threw it down here. My own grandfather killed me. He set me on fire."

They said to him. "The fire fell here, but no one caught it. It fell to earth and is spreading fire. How are we going to put it out? It is impossible for us to extinguish it."

Then they called on our mother (the goddess of the earth) and she put it out with her milk. That is how she quenched the blaze. Then they recovered the fire and it remained here. (Preuss 1912, 1:181, Spanish trans. from the German by R. Arzápalo Marin)

The hero is a small mammal who hurls fire from the edge of the sky. He dies and is reborn. The earth is the great mother who puts out the fire on the burning surface with her own milk. Preceding the deed were the failed attempts of the crow, the hummingbird, and other birds. An elderly man hoarded the fire far from the reach of others. Why were tales told with episodes so far from the reality of daily life? Why did animals speak? Why did they believe the earth to be the great mother? Does the personification correspond to the letter or spirit of a particular way of thinking? Is there an elusive, inarticulate thought we can designate as primitive and which escapes our understanding? Is there a whole substructure of myth underlying this thought? Is there a concept of causality unique to myth? These deeply disturbing and still unresolved questions continue to confront this investigation. At the termini of the tradition studied here are two kinds of very different societies, the Mesoamerican and those of contemporary Indians. Their forms of thinking are hardly homologous, even if they are both labeled "mythic thought." This is not the place to point out even the central aspects of this problem, which is fundamentally epistemological and psychological. All we can do here is to question, explain, and suggest from a historical point of view what might affect the work of ethnologists, psychologists, and philosophers who undertake comparative studies of the modes of thought in different stages of social development.

Hallpike (1986:8–9) is one of the contemporary writers who has tried to deal with the problem. Based on the psychology of development and particularly on Piaget's ideas, he proposes that ethnologists base their investigations on theories of apprenticeship (perhaps based on cognitive development) and on the application of psychological techniques.

His view is valid since the material is so complex that it needs to be viewed from multiple perspectives, each firmly articulated, and handled with the dexterity that specialization and complex techniques afford. Simply adding multiple disciplines, however, does not guarantee a solution. The task requires an intricate methodology. The problem is not limited to the ways in which thought develops. It includes another important problem: the concept that modern societies have of the societies to which mythic thought is attributed.

The history of mutual evaluation of different societies is long. Appraisal has been characterized more by ideology than by actual knowledge. History usually reflects the point of view of the colonizers. Throughout the centuries the question has been posed as a distinction between *us* and *them;* and underlying it, consciously or unconsciously, is an entire group of judgments, based on relationships of conquest, exploitation, oppression, plunder, demagoguery, nationalistic appropriation of native cultural values, self-judgment, and self-esteem, that have marred the possibility of a scientific approach. Prejudices and ideological judgments have been elevated to the status of principles for studying alien cultures. If this is not taken into account, and if the prejudices and the ideology of colonizers remain in the methodology, research may deteriorate into the semiscientific illusion of quantification, of questionnaires, of comparisons that accept procedures without questioning their theoretical foundations.

Many centuries ago in the Mediterranean region, rationalism dealt with classic myth by calling it sheer fantasy; and this disdain for the tales of the gods of antiquity fostered the self-affirmation of Christianity, which faced the persistence of pagan cults. What had originally been an opposition of reason to myth became for many Christians an opposition between revealed truth and belief in false gods. Once the source of the fallacious narrations was identified, the myths, attributed to the devil's inspiration, were literally satanized.

This idea lasted for centuries. It came to America with the Conquest. The Spaniards believed they had found the devil on this continent, and that assumption proved to be one of the most effective justifications for their destruction and subjugation of the conquered peoples. Behind the American gods they wanted to see a real, malicious, cruel demon, a perverter of the sacraments, who had subjected the unfortunate Indians to the slavery of false belief. According to this calculated viewpoint, the devil many centuries ago took control of the natives, and now the Christians had appeared as their liberators. For this benefit to their souls, they could collect from their bodies. Native myths were transformed into the self-evident proof of the devil's presence.

Now after four and a half centuries, myth is still used to demonstrate the backwardness of Indians whenever an effort is made to turn them into more efficient producers for the good of the nation. Even today, when new dominating forces attempt to destroy Native American communities and abolish their myths and rituals, the satanic justification is still at hand: "Satan has had a free hand among the Macunas for hundreds of years. . . . We pray we will not be easily discouraged, that we can demonstrate Christ's love to those whom Satan will try to use to frustrate this work." [1] The frail bodies of the natives continue to support that desire to dominate, in exchange for the glass beads of salvation or progress.

The persistence of mythic belief is still a pretext for aggression. Powerful political or economic interests are behind the evangelical and civilizing efforts. Can we pretend that the scientific study of mythic thought is free from these influences? One could argue that scientific thought rejects the ideas of fanatics who see devils with horns and tails behind the tellers of myths, and detect the smell of sulphur in the offerings of copal. But consider the hidden presence of certain ideas in the theoretical totality, the real ties between scientific creation

and political practice; consider the aggression that—in the name of science—
tries to put an end to what is considered the unjustified continuation of an
anachronistic world view. Social science is neither produced, fostered, nor put
to use in the aseptic isolation of the laboratory.

The opposition *mythic thought/non-mythic thought* can be defined on three
levels, each posing very interesting particular problems. At the first level,
scholarship would seek criteria for identifying the historical development of
human societies. It would then define stages of development, some characterized by a predominance of mythic thought, others by scientific thought.
One of the culminating moments in this debate was the position taken by
positivism; the other was Frazer's concept of the evolutionary development of
thought.[2]

At the second level, we would establish the differences among individuals
belonging to the same society—some more deeply engaged than others in the
production of myth and its belief; or, in certain societies, some immersed in
myth and others free from it. This would apply to societies classified as belonging to a stage of mythic thought, as well as contemporary industrial and urban
societies, in which key traces of a mythic concept of the world still exist. But
problems involving these different kinds of societies will be radically different.

On the third level, examining the differences between kinds of thought
would involve reference to the kinds of intellectual activities produced under
particular circumstances and in different fields of human endeavor. These, for
an individual, may range daily from free imagination to the rigidity of a logical
derivation, from perceptive vagueness to deep concentration, from aesthetic
emotion to the pragmatism of running a business. It is at this level that the
concepts of myth make it possible to capture and express a part of that reality
that—according to some theoreticians—cannot be obtained through rational
thought: the concepts that give myth its ability to present several contrasting
meanings.

Let us return to the first level of opposition, the comparison of two types
of societies: some developed, some archaic. Lévy-Bruhl's work on this topic is
a classic. According to him the primitive mentality is essentially mystical and
prelogical, and thus difficult for an outside investigator to comprehend. The
attention that a primitive mentality gives to causes in the invisible world makes
a person indifferent to causes that are real and immediate. Such a person does
not investigate necessary and sufficient conditions for the regularity of natural
phenomena (Lévy-Bruhl 1975:369–82). Lévy-Bruhl's exaggerations, in particular his denial of logic to primitive thought, have been justly criticized by
different schools of anthropological thought, among them structuralism (Lévi-

Strauss 1964:388); yet it must be acknowledged that social development is also tied to the development of knowledge, both quantitative and qualitative. The fundamental problem is assessing the differences that emerge in the process of development accurately enough to establish a more objective and precise division of the stages of thought.

The great number of criteria that have been used to define the problem over the years makes it difficult to summarize. Let us abandon the old Christian/non-Christian opposition, forget about the current distinctions between botany and ethnobotany, medicine and ethnomedicine, astronomy and ethnoastronomy. Let us put aside the powerful and simplistic occidental/nonoccidental dichotomy. One must still cross the swampy, shaky terrain of the archaic against the modern, of scientific against prescientific. At what stage in human history did science begin? And—even supposing that we adopt a definition of science congruent with our theoretical position, establishing the historical limits of two opposing kinds of thought—would a reductionist, dichotomous division be useful in understanding the evolution of human thought? Lévy-Bruhl has been criticized for proposing too broad a definition of primitive mentalities, which included cultures as refined as those of India and China (Lowie 1974:268). This mistake must not continue.

If we try to differentiate the forms of thought, starting from the dichotomy of mythic/non-mythic thought (if one chooses opposition through contradiction) or mythic/scientific thought (if one chooses opposition of opposites), two problems must be solved: first, the looseness of the categories formed by establishing only two opposable stages in the development of thought; and second, the lack of precision in the definitions of said categories.

Considering the first of these problems, the characterization of mythic thought is useless for the purpose of studying historical development, because as a class it includes such widely differing societies. Mythic thought would be common to societies that evolved over thousands of years, from the beginning of the human species up to the eve of the appearance of science. Some societies with scientific thought have endured from the appearance of science to the present. If we took as our dividing point the disappearance of feudalism due to the appearance of the bourgeoisie, we would create two enormous contrastable epochs, but each would be composed of such tremendously heterogeneous societies that it would be impossible to understand them by the same historical measuring rod.

Homologation simply cannot be applied to all those societies to which mythic thought is attributed. We repeat the objection to Lévy-Bruhl. If we start from a conclusion that, a priori, equates the cognitive styles of our most remote ancestors, of the urban Chinese of the Sung Dynasties, the last Tasmanians, the Trobriand Islanders, the farmers of the Roman Empire, the Dobu magicians, and Zapotec merchants of the Classic period, our psychological conclusions will be pitifully weak. The exaggerated abstraction of the cognitive processes leads to the loss of elements essential for understanding them.

The second problem stems from the extreme diversity of opinion concerning what is mythic, which in turn is due to the vagueness of myth. Regardless of the precision and erudition of the authors, most studies of myth focus on its most finished form: the narrative. Few researchers take into consideration the conceptual framework in which it is produced. That and its manifestation in the diverse fields of human activity are ignored. This leads to a definition so narrow that it seeks to find in mythic narrative the most important bases for a generalized type of thought—mythic, primitive, or archaic. In short myth is seen as a type of narrative, rather than narrative being seen as one expression of myth. Myth is understood as a fantastic narrative, as a tale of deeds that violate the laws of nature. Furthermore a belief is identified, and then the violation is no longer just the mere exercise of story-telling freedom, but a violation of logic itself. Mythic thought becomes synonymous with absurd thinking. A foreign myth scandalizes. For an observer coming from a complex, industrial, urban society, the tale of a hero who at one time put the Sun, the Moon, and the stars in a box—perceived as a belief—is an attack on the laws of logic and the principles of cause and effect. The believer's capacity for thought is then judged from the standpoint of the observer's own astonishment. Then, depending on the observer's self-esteem, several options will emerge: condemnation, disdain, tolerant sympathy, or even nostalgia for a reality supposedly lost through the predominance of scientific thought. Myth then has been seen fundamentally as a story, and sometimes only as a story. It is not surprising that judgments about myth from this limited point of view are varied and even contradictory. Some specialists will say that myth is the ideal epistemological and existential way to face and solve the great contradictions. Others, diametrically opposed, will say that myth is a profound emptiness and that the so-called primitive person did not act on the basis of opinions (Wittgenstein 1985:31).

Conceptual precision is a very different matter when the problem is the definition of the nature of science and of scientific thinking—a subject of prime importance in contemporary thought. Science and the scientific method are at the heart of today's philosophical polemics. The very intensity of the controversy demands deep penetration into the social, logical, and philosophical aspects of the problem.

One of the chief obstacles to the definition of science is its variability over time. J. D. Bernal (1969, 1:30) refuses to attempt a definition, noting the transformations in its relationship to society throughout history:

> My experience and knowledge have convinced me of the futility and empti-
> ness of such a course. Science is so old, it has undergone so many changes in
> its history, it is so linked at every point with other social activities, that any
> attempted definition, and there have been many, can only express more or less
> inadequately one of the aspects, often a minor one, that it has had at some
> period of its growth.

Bernal's real difficulty is his awareness that the position and relationships of a subject within the social whole need to be reflected in its definition. Many interpretations of myth are debatable precisely because its significant relations with other areas of the societies that created it are ignored by the researchers, and because these relationships of myth are much more difficult to understand than those of science, with which we are more familiar. Forms of thought cannot be explored with philosophical techniques based on external judgment of the rationality of a belief, nor by a simple questionnaire. (Imagine the enormous gamut of interpretations that might result if an urban middle-class European explained the Trinity to an observer who was alien to and unfamiliar with the history of Christianity.)

In many approaches, mythic thought has been characterized (and thereby contrasted with scientific thought) by the presence of fantasy, the importance of subconscious forces in it, its subjectivity, its origin in dreams, its rejection of objective reality, and, particularly, by its dependence on faith. Here we will neither accept nor reject these attributes or their relevance to the tradition under study. Having called for a broader and more detailed investigation, we must hope that solutions will emerge from explorations of the production of myth, its background of beliefs, its functions, and the kind of truth attributed to it. However, it is appropriate to make some brief comments on this characterization of myth, and to cite Lévi-Strauss's (1966:16) opportune criticism of it:

> Myths and rites are far from being, as has often been held, the product of man's
> "myth-making faculty," turning its back on reality. Their principal value is in
> deed to preserve until the present time the remains of methods of observation
> and reflection which were (and no doubt still are) precisely adapted to discover
> ies of a certain type: those which nature authorized from the starting point of
> a speculative organization and exploitation of the sensible world in sensible

terms. This science of the concrete was necessarily restricted by its essence to results other than those destined to be achieved by the exact natural sciences but it was no less scientific and its results no less genuine. They were secured ten thousand years earlier and still remain at the basis of our own civilization.

Let us begin with the role that dreams play in producing myth. The broad movement called symbolism (including Freud, Jung, Cassirer, van der Leeuw, and many others) deprives myth of logical status, stressing instead the importance of its exegesis in a search for a profound way of understanding the world. It postulates that the subconscious generates mythic images, and that dreams play a key role. This focus is not applicable here. In the tradition we are studying, dreaming is considered a valuable path to knowledge, especially when one hopes to establish communication with the invisible beings through it. Dream images have given rise to chants, narratives, and therapeutic procedures. However, it must be stressed that in this tradition, the dreamer has made only the first step in conscious social acceptance; as a social resource, dreaming is only one of several ways to carry on a dialogue with divinity. It is not a unique or exclusive approach, nor is its language the principal one.

In the study of alien religions, a prejudice exaggerates the dominance of faith in them. The strict requirement of faith in religion began only with the influence in Christianity of such authorities as the Africans Tertullian (*credo quia absurdum,* "I believe though it is absurd") and Arnobius the Elder. Kerényi (1972:81) says that faith was not a fundamental concept in classical Greco-Roman religion, but that it was in Christianity. Therefore faith and religious or mythic belief cannot be connected arbitrarily. In every case it is necessary to seek in each culture the links between truth and myth, acceptance and faith. We can agree with Bronowski (1978:142) that "No truth exists, even religious truth, that does not require the sanction of empirical facts"—though even this statement must be qualified, recalling that only science makes it a deliberate policy to "expose its cognitive claims to the repeated challenge of critically probative observational data, procured under carefully controlled conditions" (Nagel 1961:12).

A number of schools of thought coincide in attributing a different logic to myth. Mauss (1971:148) states that myth is a special logical apparatus, with its own procedures for analysis and particular ways of associating images. Eliade (1972:55), drawing on the attempts of Hellenic speculation, feels that the management of symbols is carried out according to a logic that employs a style of thinking completely different from the modern one. Turner (1967:50) develops his theory based on the notion of the polysemy (multiple meanings) of symbols, which also leads to a special logic. These are only a few examples.

The problem can be divided into two parts. On the one hand, it is undeniable that social development produces stages in which forms of thought change. Hallpike (1986:124–32; see also Greenfield and Bruner 1986) gives as an example the effects of formal education and reading on cognitive development. On the other hand, it is quite possible that some of the peculiarities of the formal aspect of mythic thinking come from its content, that is, from a particular view of the world. An explanation of mythic thought based on a specific form of logic yields formulas that are attractive because of their neatness. Trias (1970:58), utilizing Frazer's principles of magical thought, compares the fundamental categories of magic (similarity and contagion) to those of scientific thought (identity and difference). But it would be wise to compare these neat theoretical schemes more often with the complexities of cosmovisions in their historical settings. It might be possible to find in them a causality that will perhaps seem strange to the investigator; but a causality, nevertheless, for which there is no need to consider a unique logic.

From the above, two (perhaps too obvious) conclusions can be reached. First, that for a comparative study of the stages of development of thought, correct period identification must be deduced from a parallel study of myth and science. Second, that the characterization of thought in a society is not possible without considering such topics as the concept of the invisible world, the formation of myth, and the relationship between truth and myth in that particular society.

The first conclusion goes much further than myth. In order to understand the different stages of development of mythic thought it is indispensable to contrast it with the development of science, not because myth and science are simply opposite forms of thought, but because they are simultaneous forms and have complemented each other during a good part of human existence. Likewise the history and nature of science cannot be understood without better understanding—prejudices aside—mythic thought, common sense, and poetic intuition as complementary parallels.

The second conclusion should not be taken as an exaggeration of the uniqueness of the study of indigenous thought in Mexico and Central America. On the contrary the possibility is suggested of great similarities among other societies at the same stage of development. But this must be verified by specific studies, capable of appreciating the position and the relationships of myth to the very diverse environments of the social aggregate. I do not deny the value of comparisons. The real flaw in comparative studies of religions has been their tendency to restrict these comparisons to strictly religious matters.

Gaia now first gave birth to starry Ouranus,
her match in size, to encompass all of her,
and be the firm seat of all the blessed gods.

Hesiod, *Theogony*

The Mesoamerican world was filled with gods and invisible beings. Their presence reverberated over fields, springs, homes, and mountains. Astral bodies crossed the sky, and the heavens were crowded with small water carriers, winds, lightning bolts, and hail. The hills were hollow and filled with water; they were, therefore, the source of rain. Hills were also the abodes of the patron gods of the towns, and so were named after them. From the hills, patron gods drove away illnesses. The forces of the ancestors protected family honor. The vitality of the home was distributed among its dwellers and the plants they sowed. The nights were filled with phantoms. Sickness invaded bodies and took possession of the centers of vitality. Human souls communicated with the forces of destiny and went forth to dream. In Mesoamerica as in many other polytheistic societies, social development multiplied the areas of dominance and the number of gods in charge of each. Pomar (1985–86:54) tells us, "almost everything had one."

The complex, varied pantheons acquired different aspects as the links among societies intensified and as social groups subdivided. "These gods had many names, a name was given to them according to what was understood about or attributed to them. They had many names because each group gave different names to them due to differences in language" (*Historia de los mexicanos por sus pinturas* 1965:24). In this broad field the researcher must try to detect sponsorships and to understand equivalencies, functions, types, and hierarchies of gods. At the same time we must look for the order, the play of imaginary causes that would change a pantheon into a systematic complex governed by principles and rules. We must have an overall understanding of the ancient concepts of the divine and know that the order of legitimacy was distributed throughout the cosmos. To understand the rules of the pantheons is to understand the principles of Mesoamerican cosmovisions. The discovery of rules and their application to the ordering of information are two processes of mutual clarification.

Indigenous societies began to be evangelized more than four and a half centuries ago in accidental and widely differing ways. Obviously the degree and form of Christianization differed widely among the various groups, but even where conversion seemed to be more nominal than real, there were profound changes in religious concepts. On the other hand, even groups that were more completely Christianized still retain beliefs that can in no way be attributed to the sermons of the missionaries or to the dominion of the Christian Church.[1] Fields, springs, mountains, and homes are still inhabited by invisible beings similar to ancient ones; the etiology of diseases, the cyclic recurrence of cosmis forces, and the hierarchy of supernatural beings have Mesoamerican origins. It is also common to find indigenous divine beings, products of a unique colonial history, that are as far removed from Mesoamerican forms as they are from the European. Thus, among some Tarasca, rain is personified as Tatá Hanikua, a horseman with a carbine, a shining sword that is a lightning bolt, and a black steed whose hooves cause celestial thunder (P. Carrasco 1971). Of course neither horses, swords, nor rifles come from pre-Hispanic times. Under the influence of the conqueror, the figure of the god has been completely transformed, but it does not derive from the dominating European religious tradition.

Then why turn to ethnography for an understanding of ancient concepts? Because in spite of the changes, since present-day native religions are part of a Mesoamerican tradition, they convey unique ways of looking at the world. These ways cannot automatically interpret the remote past, but they can shed light where the historians of the early colonial period are obscure. Those Spaniards thought the proper way to understand polytheism was to relate it to classical Greek antiquity. In one of the most authentic sources we read, "Huitzilopochtli was another Hercules," "Tezcatlipoca . . . is another Jupiter," "Chicomecoatl is another goddess Ceres," "Chalchiuhtlicue is another Juno," "Tlazolteotl is another Venus," "Xiuhtecuhtli is another Vulcan" (Sahagún 1956: book 1, vol. 1, 43–56). These sources do not even refer to a recent historical reality; they are the vague, bookish, completely ideological appraisals based on Christian ideas of a remote classical world, anathemized for centuries. The anathema was repeated here. Neither the present indigenous world nor the historical records of the sixteenth century offer an easy path to a deep understanding. However, seen as two alternative routes, they offer orientation and reciprocal clarification.

Let us return to the old (but not finished) polemic on the unity or diversity of Mesoamerican religions. More than a century ago, Seler's scholarship brought about a considerable development in studies of ancient Mexico and

Central America. One of the learned German's greatest achievements was to demonstrate the essential unity of the advanced cultures of the area.[2] His conviction served as the basis for extensive comparative investigations (see Seler 1904). Since then the unity among Mesoamerican religions, and their strong influence on contemporary religions, have been taken for granted.

There was at least one prestigious dissenting voice. In 1922 an article by Hermann Beyer appeared in the monumental work edited by Manuel Gamio, *La población del Valle de Teotihuacán*. This German archeologist objected to the interpretation of Teotihuacan material using data concerning the Mexica.

> Almost all modern Mexicanists recognize that the culture the conquerors found in the Valley of Mexico is different from the one represented by the grandiose monuments in Teotihuacan. Nevertheless, some of them make the methodological mistake of interpreting details of Teotihuacan antiquities by customs and beliefs current among the Aztecs and people similar to them in the sixteenth century. . . .
>
> In general, the Teotihuacan culture should be approached with the same methods science uses for European prehistory. Conclusions must be drawn from the material itself, beginning with typological classification and comparison of the aggregate of cultural products with civilizations at a similar stage of evolution or those having similar physical conditions, etc. Only elements whose identity or near affinity can be proven should be explained by the things known about Aztec culture. (Beyer 1979)

Beyer did not criticize the making of comparisons, but rather their extent and lack of precision. With this in mind, he continued:

> First we have to determine whether, among the ruins of ancient Teotihuacan, there are objects that through their form, decoration, composition, purpose or other qualities are so similar to Aztec objects that their affinity is undeniable.
>
> . . . each characteristic cultural element that the Aztec or the Valley civilizations have in common with Teotihuacan must have been derived from it. (Beyer 1979)

Thompson offered an authoritative opinion in an article published in 1934 comparing the religious thought of the Maya and the Nahua. He says, "The elements of Mexican and Maya mythology cannot be put together like the pieces in a jigsaw puzzle, but they can be integrated in intertwined aggregates that cannot be completely separated" (J. Thompson 1934).

Years later in a symposium on Mesoamerican religions at the 1968 International Congress of Americanists, Alfonso Caso and Paul Kirchhoff strongly asserted the unity of the religions. According to Caso (1971), the compari-

son of cosmological and mythic principles, of the attributes and symbolism
of the gods, of rituals, of the calendar, and of the organization of the priest-
hood evinced an undeniable unity, at least after the Classic period. Kirchhoff
(1971), more specific, compared the eighteen annual festivals included in the
various ancient calendars and concluded that historically they belonged to the
same religion. Jiménez Moreno's (1971b) position was less categorical and more
critical. He pointed out the existence of deep ruptures in Mesoamerican history, breaks that resulted in considerable transformations in religious thought.
New concepts of the world were introduced when groups from the west and
northwest penetrated into Mesoamerica. One of the most notable changes was
in the character of the Mexica religion, whose symbols and values, in Jiménez
Moreno's opinion, were very poorly integrated at the time of the Spaniards'
arrival.

Four years later, Kubler (1972; see also 1984) maintained that the argument
was largely semantic, and that the application of ethnological analogy to the
study of ancient and modern religions produced dubious results because it did
not take into account historic breaks. Kubler went so far as to deny the possibility of comparison, especially between the past and the present, suggesting
that contemporaneous indigenous societies are nearer to their rural European
counterparts than to their pre-Columbian ones. Kubler's thesis, partly derived from Panofsky's principle of separation, is mainly aimed at the study of
figurative representation. Nicholson (1976), replying from the field of iconography, questioned the legitimacy of applying Panofsky's principles to cultural
histories so different from those of western Europe.[3] Nicholson's reasoning is
accurate and well founded, since Mesoamerican history is not characterized by
the existence of deep cultural separations parallel to the well-documented ones
of Western Europe, which are the foundation for Panofsky's iconographical
studies.[4]

The brief mention of a few debaters and summaries of their positions does
not do justice to the subject or to the debate, but it does provide a sampling
of opinions on Mesoamerican gods. I agree with Kubler that there are some
semantic aspects to the debate, where the object is a simple position for or
against cultural breaks. But the problem is much more complex, and should
be approached in all its magnitude. It is not a question of stating that there
was one single Mesoamerican religion or that today's indigenous religions are a
prolongation of it, or, on the other hand, that ancient regional variations were
considerable, and that Christianity replaced old cults, beliefs and institutions.
Both positions have a certain degree of truth. It is not a question of taking sides;
it is a question of solving the problem. A tradition undoubtedly exists that, like
all historical reality, is transformed over time and space. The object for study is
this changing reality. The problem cannot be simplified. It is necessary to see
what the religions include, what their most important variations and constants

are, what the causes were for transformation or stability, and how religious action and thought are reconstituted in different, changing social contexts.

What constitutes religion is very heterogeneous, not only in terms of the diversity of elements, but also in terms of the kinds of resistance of said elements to social changes. An example of little resistance to the impact of the Conquest is the calendric system. One of the most noteworthy differences between Mesoamerican religious thought and that of natives today is its relationship to the calendar, a fundamental system in the past that is almost absent today. The calendar was one of the most solid and elaborate creations of Mesoamerica, but it was rooted in politics. In fact its history was tied to those of writing and of power. As Joyce Marcus (1979) says, "When writing emerged in the Middle Formative period, it took the form of political information presented in a calendric structure." During the Mayan Classic period, one of its principal functions was to legitimize the ruler's power. In Oaxaca it had a similar function, at least at the end of the Classic and the beginning of the Postclassic period (Marcus 1979, 1980). With the collapse of the Classic period, the Mayan calendar was greatly simplified, but nevertheless it still held a privileged position in the most important areas of social life, including government. This was the case in all of Mesoamerica during the Postclassic period, until the arrival of Europeans. According to documental sources of very detailed information about the Postclassic period, the calendar strongly permeated all aspects of human existence; it was one of the obsessions of Mesoamerican thought, and was, of course, associated with power. And yet, after two thousand years as one of the most stable pillars of the religious tradition, the Spanish Conquest overthrew its preeminence. Sustained and controlled by the centers of political power, the calendric system fell along with the indigenous states. Today derivations of it can be found here and there—in Guatemala, Chiapas, Oaxaca—helping people to face the forces of destiny, but these are mere shadows of the robust pre-Hispanic omnipresence.[5] If a judgment on the survival of ancient thought rested only on the preservation of the calendar, we would have scanty remnants to go by.

On the other hand, where religious observance did not require outward forms that might betray the faithful to colonial authorities; when it did not depend on the apparatus of government; when belief dictated the use of working tools, dealings with the body, or family relationships; in these areas the religious traditions remained under domestic protection and were passed along at the warmth of the hearth. They remained by the fire in the sacred family bundles (Gruzinski 1988:198–99). In these safe, family settings it is still possible to find information revealing an ancient concept, scarcely mentioned in the old testimonial documents; or, more significantly, a concept of the organization of the world, a way of understanding and working in it. Signorini and Lupo have found that people of the Sierra Norte of Puebla believe in the dual nature of one of the animistic forces, the *tonalli*. The discovery helps clarify concepts of the soul held in ancient Mexico:

Finally, an examination of the ideological patrimony of the Nahua of the Sierra about the spiritual components of mankind reveals its richness, dynamics, and stratification. The relationship of the pre-Columbian conceptual system is evident, the inner logic of which has governed and continues to govern the transformations that time and the processes of acculturation keep on producing. (Signorini and Lupo 1988)

Besides recording presences and absences of specific features, we must view current native religions as complexes that differ considerably from Meso-american ones. We are speaking of marginal, dominated, rural religions. Indigenous societies are often frankly dependent on the preservation of be-liefs, practices, and institutions. These are invaded religions, over which the Catholic and Protestant churches wield control; from those external powers flow authority, dogmas and principles, customs and prohibitions, competing with or opposing innate beliefs, which then the natives must reinterpret, re-assemble, and assign new functions. The new evangelism intrudes and disturbs these communities. They have few resources to combat these assaults. Out-side political and economic forces support the domination of the missionaries. Faced with this situation, the natives accept and incorporate the alien element, though it does not lose its feeling of strangeness, its quality of imposition. The adaptation leaves its mark. The alien patch, the incongruency remains.

Indigenous religions are colonial religions, and they conform to the colo-nial situation. After the destruction of their ancient institutions, their own heritage, Mesoamerican religion was burdensome to the people. In their new situation, the legacy of their ancestors was inadequate. Their ancestors' reli-gious concepts belonged to a departed world. Their universe had been over-turned. This is why the forging of new indigenous religions—difficult for laypersons—never became part of the struggle in defense of the Mesoamerican tradition against the imposition of Christianity. It has instead been a part of a fight against total oppression; as a religious process, it is a fight on two fronts, against two apparently irreconcilable traditions, under the worst possible con-ditions. The creation of colonial religions led to such adjustment problems that the internal congruence of each one of the original traditions has in several cases called for categorization of the gods based upon their areas of power—that is, by function rather than by origin. The following is an example from the peninsular Maya, cited by Villa Rojas (1978:302–3).

The natives recognize the difference between pagan and Christian deities, not in terms of their different historical origins, but in terms of the various and special powers belonging to each group and according to the diverse occasions appropriate to invoke them. Thus the natives call on one or the other, or both at the same time, according to the occasion and the ends that motivate them. This gives rise to two kinds of ritual in the religious complex: the Catholic kind and the ritual of pagan nature.

Let us look for Mesoamerican gods in this complicated and heterogeneous field. We will not find the gods today as fossilized, mummified, and anachronistic. The gods are gods created in the remote past, but they are also gods today, recreated day by day. The calendric framework for the gods no longer exists. The abscissas and the ordinates that ruled their presence no longer exist, but they retain their character as beings that were formed in a consciousness of time's regularity. The dates were their names; in the painted codices they were associated with the twenty signs of the days, the nine of night, the series of thirteen, the years, their multiples and submultiples. The precise sequences marched in order; they calculated and were used to calculate.

The nature of the gods was understood as a play of dialectical oppositions. It was conceived in the characterization of predictable time; and the gods turned out as different from one another as the time differences attributed to each one. The gods brought about order, sequence, periods. At the same time, the intrusion of anomalies in the order implied divine volition, the capricious acts of invisible beings whose arbitrary deeds provoked the event and the disorder. But humans wanted to understand more; they wanted to scrutinize the mysteries of the cosmos. They looked for the cause of the capricious acts, and thought that they could distinguish another, more profound order, the discovery of which promised them control over what was apparently random. Thus the gods were subjected to fatalism. The sequence was: order, disorder, more complete order; law, willfulness, a more rigorous law. The gods were created out of opposing concepts, which ruled simultaneously.

Indigenous religions today retain a rich polytheism in which the diversity and changes in the world are explained by many and varied gods. The gods favor or do damage to humans with the power of regularity and with the surprising appearance of the unexpected. Gods cannot be absolutely good nor absolutely bad. They have free will, and today, when the calendar has lost its preeminence, their capricious nature stands out. The gods decide. Because of this, humans had better maintain an enduring relationship with them. Referring to the inhabitants of the Sierra Madre Oriental, Montoya Briones (1987) says that the Nahua, Otomi, Totonaca, and Tepehua

consider it natural that if the earth gives them food and, in exchange, it is polluted daily with refuse and filth, men must "pay" through diverse rituals, prayers, food, drink, and ceremonial objects. If corn is the principal mainstay of existence or is the "owner of our flesh," as the Totonac say, it is equally necessary to render it tribute, offering it music, dance, and even food.

To characterize the gods we must enter their proper environment, the supernatural. But like other basic terms in the history of religions, the term *supernatural* refers to different concepts, resulting in a lack of definition. Durkheim denied that the supernatural could be treated as a characteristic of what is religious. He refused to define religion as a "kind of speculation about everything that is not science and, in a more general sense, a distinct kind of thought." Nor did he accept the idea that the supernatural—meaning the world of the unknowable and incomprehensible—constituted the territory of religion. He rejected Spencer's and Max Mullers's definitions, which speak of the mystery, the inconceivable, the inexpressible, and the infinite. For primitive people, in Durkheim's (1968: ch. 1, 30–32) own words, the forces in question are not mysterious, for they are no more puzzling than gravity or electricity are for the physicist.

Durkheim prefers to start with the idea that religious beliefs divide the world into two opposing domains: the profane and the sacred. The sacred includes not only beings (gods, spirits), but everything (objects, words, rituals, gestures, formulas), to which one cannot yield with impunity, which requires a delicate operation in order to make contact. "Sacred things are the ones that are protected and isolated by interdictions; profane things are those to which these prohibitions apply and which must be kept at a distance from the former" (Durkheim 1968: ch. 3, 41–43).

This strict division has not convinced all specialists. Evans-Pritchard (1965: 65) says, in regard to Durkheim's dichotomy of the sacred and profane:

> I doubt it. Surely what he calls "sacred" and "profane" are on the same level
> of experience, and, far from being cut off from one another, they are so closely
> intermingled as to be inseparable. They cannot therefore, either for the indi-
> vidual or for the social activities, be put in closed compartments which negate
> each other, one of which is left on entering the other.

Leach (1965: 12–13) is also opposed to the total separation of the two fields.

> For my part I find Durkheim's emphasis on the absolute dichotomy between
> the sacred and the profane to be untenable. Rather it is that actions fall into
> place on a continuous scale. At one extreme we have actions which are entirely
> profane, entirely functional, technique pure and simple; at the other we have

actions which are entirely sacred, strictly aesthetic, technically non-functional. Between these two extremes we have the great majority of social actions which partake partly of one sphere and partly of the other.

From this point of view, technique and ritual, profane and sacred, do not denote *types* of action but *aspects* of almost any kind of action.

Is there, or was there ever, a distinction between the natural and the supernatural in Mesoamerican religion or in the modern religions of Mexico and Central America? Let us start out by acknowledging that, in addition to those beings strictly known as gods, others were envisaged who shared some of their characteristics. There is a great difference between the supreme, ubiquitous god, lord of all existence, often called the Only God, and the minor gods, dwarf guardians of springs or carriers of water jugs among the clouds; and between these and human souls, or the parts of human souls associated with animal companions; and between human souls and those of rocks; between these and the forces circulating throughout the universe; between these powers and the power of merchandise to be sold—a quality lost when a sinner approached. But it is difficult to parcel out the entire field, and even more difficult to determine precise limits. It was necessary to go fishing, deer hunting, or honey collecting with a peaceful spirit, without grief or hatred, anger or quarrels, because the hunters' feelings had to combine harmoniously with the beings that were to benefit them. Hunting, fishing, and gathering honey were practical activities, but not exempt from ritual or conjuration in which the participation of divinity in the animals was acknowledged. Ruiz de Alarcón (1953:76) was told that one must collect honey in a peaceful state of mind, "because [the bees] feel like gods; because they provide men with what is necessary, and they do not like tribulations."

Forces, souls, and gods have one prime characteristic in common: they cannot be perceived by human beings. Like the wind, like night, they are invisible and impalpable. Or rather, almost imperceptible, since a gust of wind, a flash, a voice, a shadow, a creaking, or a slight touch can betray their presence. Death's arrival can be detected by a whiff of stench (Incháustegui 1984:78). Villa Rojas (1978:435), speaking of the beliefs of contemporary Maya, says, "The jungle is peopled by sounds that make the existence of these beings real." They are not immaterial beings, but it is difficult for beings of this world to perceive their substance. Under normal conditions, a person goes about knowing that they are all around, but unable to locate them. They are invisible to people and to animals, although it is said that on the Day of the Dead, when the deceased return to their villages to partake with their relatives, dogs and poultry can see them.[6] They are invisible under the usual conditions of wakefulness, but in dreams, in coma, in ecstasy, or under the effects of a drug, humans see them clearly. A person may also see them when accidentally trespassing on sites that belong exclusively to them. They also have the power to make themselves visible in order to challenge mortals to fight, or in order to transmit messages to them (López de Gómara 1954, 2:409–10). Ordinarily it is the specially designated penitent who summons them to dialogue, but sometimes an inner disequilibrium will cause an individual to discover them by unhappy accident. The Nahua of Veracruz say today that *chaneque*, beings with childlike bodies, are like winds that play through the treetops, and that travelers who bear evil in their souls, or who travel fearfully, are aware of their presence (Sedeño and Becerril 1985:169).

Supernatural beings—let us call them that, for the moment—are not like all other beings. They are hard to perceive, but this is partly due to the limited capacity of mortals. One myth tells us that the gods diminished the perceptive powers of the first Quiche from the very moment of their creation (see chapter 5). The gods predicted that humans, made in their image, would resemble them so closely that they would see no point in continuing the worship owed to them. Therefore they cast a mist over the eyes of the humans, which tarnished their surface like mirror glass, so that the ancestors of the Quiche could see only a little of the earth's surface. According to other myths, humans originally had the ability to see the gods, but lost it (Fernández de Oviedo y Valdés 1944–45, 11:75). In Soconusco it is said that God, after coming to earth and having created people,

> went back confidently, and did not return to earth to hear what men were saying, nor did he want to see them again because he was sure that his work had been perfect.
>
> But one day he returned to see how his children were doing and to see if they knew how to worship him. And he wept, and he became sad when he witnessed the condition of the fields. The young people paid no attention to their elders; no one missed his presence. For that reason they no longer worshipped him.
>
> He spoke to them and they did not listen. He made his presence known and they did not know how to perceive him. He changed himself into a whisper and they thought it was the river. He turned himself into feathers and they could not feel him. (Navarrete 1966)

Did humans lose the power to see the divine after they were created? No. A careful reading of the Soconusco text shows that the perceptive limitation is inborn in the human species. Myopia occurs at the moment of creation.

Those with total vision were not yet truly human; they lived before the gods left earth. In the Soconusco tale, those who confronted the divine anger (in the form of the Tacaná volcano) fled into the water and turned into fish. Others turned into monkeys in the treetops; others into birds among the high cliffs. The ones who fled by crawling were changed into serpents, opossums, and moles. These were not true humans; they were dema deities. Only the heart-felt repentant ones remained as human (Navarrete 1966), but for them, the true ones, God had been a murmur of the river and impalpable feathers.

Invisibility implies the ability to intervene in perceptible processes. If managing the world were possible through mastering known causes, then all mysterious effects indicated something hidden. Mesoamericans surmised that imperceptible causes existed, and they tried to manipulate them, as they did the perceptible ones, for maximum control of the environment. Imperceptible causes included forces, gods, and souls, which gave meaning to processes difficult to grasp with the senses. In this way the invisible completed the causality of the cosmos, since human certainty or assumptions about existence ruled out the possibility of causelessness. The concept of the invisible was part of the attempt to control the world: The world could be controlled by different methods of moving the invisible, conciliating beneficial processes and thwarting the harmful ones.

Attributing invisibility to the harmful forces made them terrifying, because even a small, weak, human-fearing force had the advantage of a treacherous, surprise attack. Jest is often the motif in texts referring to the relations between men and gods. The invisible ones mock mortals, hiding in order to offend and taunt them. *Tetzahuitl* is a Nahuatl term that indicates the power of the invisible. It was also the name of an important god, Huitzilopochtli. It refers to prognostication, the extraordinary, the portentous, but also to what causes scandal and fright, the heroic, the hazardous, either marvelous or terrible. *Mahuiztic* is another word describing the gods, which often appears in invocations. It refers to grandeur, fear, dignity, ostentation, marvels, authority, prowess, and esteem. Fear is the quality they have in common. Invisible beings cause fear.

The invisible ones are everywhere. They infiltrate the beings of the world, making themselves a part of them. According to the Mixtec, the sun, moon, morning star, corn, lima beans, string beans, peas, and the black bean all have a supernatural element (Jansen 1982, 1:134–35, 298–99). Modern Nahua say, "God gave souls to animals, trees, stones, mountains, rivers and also to creeks. Everything God made has a spiritual soul, because nothing can exist without a spirit" (Madsen 1960:126). The Mam (Wagley 1957:2, 25) say that the hands and feet of the god Paxil are made of corn, and according to the Otomi of the Sierra Madre Oriental:

> [corn] like all cultivated plants, possesses a "soul," that of a very highly respected deity. It sometimes appears in its masculine guise as an old man. The attribute of age is given to the most important divinities. . . . In its feminine aspect, corn takes the form of a woman with long blond hair, and she is called "the mother of corn," the source of life constantly renewed. (Galinier 1987:358)

Galinier also says that the Otomi pick up any grain of corn fallen on the path, following a Mesoamerican custom. The ancient Nahua gathered up corn scattered on the ground and, according to Sahagún's informants, said, "Our poor sustenance! It is crying! If we don't pick it up it will accuse us before our Lord. It will say, 'Our Lord, this man did not pick me up when I lay scattered on the ground. Punish him, or perhaps make him suffer hunger.'" And women, before cooking corn, warmed it with their breath, saying that if they did so it would not fear the heart (*Augurios y abusiones* 1969:66–69, 189–90; P. Carrasco 1976a:144–45). Today the Tzeltal say that the corn in their fields has a soul, that the soul can leave the plant, and that corn should be treated with respect because it is the Virgin's body (J. Nash 1970:43–44).

Other old documents refer to the souls of plants. In the first half of the seventeenth century, Jacinto de la Serna, parish priest of Xalatlaco (an important agricultural center in a zone where the Nahuatl and Otomi languages were spoken) accused the Indians of worshipping plants, of attributing to them a vegetative soul as well as free will. He added that trees were believed to have souls because they were considered to be men of the "other century" (other time). Therefore the Indians imagined their having the use of reason, and before cutting them down, they placated them and they interpreted their creaking as complaints (Serna 1953:231).[7] Invocations directed at plants are common. Today prayers are offered to plants, just as in the seventeenth century. The following Tlapanec invocation comes from Malinaltepec, Guerrero, and it was used to propitiate the agave plant before cutting open a hollow to collect its sap. The faithful approach the plant holding a brazier filled with copal in one hand and a machete in the other, and say to it,

> Forgive me if at this moment I am going to cut and perforate your breast. I do not want you to suffer because I am going to wound you. I do not want you to inflict on me such illnesses as itching, swelling, fever, and other sickness that come from you.
> Therefore, eternal maguey, mistress of itchings, before wounding you, I im-

plore you, and I make offerings to you in the name of the Father, Son, and Holy
Ghost. Amen. (Loo 1987:183)

From the first half of the seventeenth century, we have information about
belief in mineral souls, specifically a soul capable of causing a traveler's weari-
ness. Sánchez de Aguilar (1953:276) says that among the Maya of Yucatan,
"If a traveler encounters a big rock, of the many that are moved to open the
roads, he worships it, placing a branch on top of it and shaking another across
his knees in order to ward off tiredness."

The customs of the ancient Nahua of the central high plateau, including
that of the New Fire Festival, reveal that cut stone fashioned into a *metate*
(grinding stone) or roller, or baked clay made into a vessel, retained a soul
that could free itself and harm nearby humans. This was especially dangerous
when the sun reached its critical moment every fifty-two years. Carved wood
also sang and predicted misfortune, and some wooden beams could generate
illnesses, unless they were buried with offerings of pulque and tamales (Serna
1953:232–33).

Vogt (1976:17) says that present-day Zinacantec "believe that many natural phenomena, all the animals, and even some manufactured objects have
innate souls," and adds,

Virtually everything important and valuable to Zinancantecos also possesses
a *ch'ulel:* domesticated animals and plants, salt, houses and household fires,
crosses, the saints, musical instruments, maize, and all the other deities in the
pantheon. The most important interaction in the universe is not between persons, nor between persons and objects, but among the innate souls of persons
and material objects. (Vogt 1976:18–19)

From the pre-Hispanic past to our own days, humans have attributed several different kinds of souls to themselves. Some vivifying forces are so connected to life that they cannot be separated from the body while a person
exists. Others can enter and leave the human being, wandering the earth, as
well as the regions of the gods and of the dead. Some are so external to the
individuals that they are bound to them in destiny but reside in companion
animals. There are also souls without bodies, that return to merge with the
energy of the universe or inhabit the heavens or the underworld, working as
small divine servants of vegetation, rain, the sun, the mountains, and springs.
There are divine elements in humans as well as in objects, minerals, plants,
and animals. They make people think, feel, live, act passionately, and move

their joints. They are forces of exaltation or of madness, virtue or crime, of heroic life or of obscure tranquil daily existence.

Let us remember that divine forces became a part of every species in this world, stamping their characteristics upon them. They also operate when the nature and the fate of individual beings are determined in the heavens and in the underworld. They emerge in the form of time, saturating and transforming reality like an avalanche of invisible power. Everything that exists in the world has its portion of the invisible material. A Chuj narrative tells us:

> Also there are the *ora* (day-gods) who are with us. There are twenty day-gods who see us (take care of us) each day. One day-god sees us each day. There-fore we feed those day-gods. If we don't feed them, they will become angry with us. Those day-gods have exactly the same power as the sun, which is our god. Therefore we must appease them. . . . All those things are companions together—all are gods. The wood things, the crosses, they are really our gods, because that is where the day-gods live. (Shaw 1971:99–100)

Time is the invisible and personified matter. Time is introduced into trees, crosses, and things to give them a divine quality. Matter is not inert. The dif-ferent kinds of forces pass from some beings to others, break away from the abodes of the gods or return to them. Opposing forces fight here on the earth's surface, constantly changing its face. The Popoloca say that "The Earth de-vours men's bodies so that corn can grow. The Sun devours men's hearts so that it can shine. The heart of the Earth is live men. The heart of the Sun is the hearts of men" (Jäcklein 1970:286).

For several decades Mayanists have insisted that for the Maya time was divine and that it permeated everything. They also insist that the order of the passage of time was at the core of Mayan thought. "The Maya conceived of the divisions of time as burdens which were carried through all eternity by relays of bearers," according to J. Thompson (1978:59, 69), evoking a time of supernaturals alternating in a cyclic pattern. He continues, "The days are alive; they are personified powers, to whom the Maya address their devotions, and their influences pervade every activity and every walk of life; in truth, they are gods."

Time was gods in succession, and the power of the gods over the earth was influenced by time. Landa (1982:104) explained the sequences of the gods' authority as follows:

> If it had not been for the Spaniards, they [the Maya] would have worshipped the idol Buluc-Ahau until the year 51 [1551], a period of ten years, and on the

tenth year they would have raised another idol, Bolon-Ahau, and worshipped it; following the omens of Bolon-Ahau until the year 61. Then would they have removed it from the temple and replaced it with the idol Uuc-Ahau, and followed it with the omens of Bolon-Ahau[8] for another ten years; and so each would be given its turn.

Pursuing his studies on the Maya, León-Portilla (1968) devoted his book, *Tiempo y realidad en el pensamiento maya*, to showing the conceptual complex surrounding the word *kihn,* including ideas of sun, day, time, and divinity. Vogt (1971) says that today the preoccupation with time continues even in towns where the old calendar is no longer in use, and Bricker (1966) has studied the analogy that the Zinacantec make between the divine time bearers and the burdens people bear, as well as the rotating *cargos* (ritual offices) of native officials.

Not only the Maya had an obsession with time. It is true that no other Mesoamerican culture carried the precision of calculations and the articulation of so many different cycles to such extremes, but the concept of time-gods and their alternating influence in the modification of the world is one of the fundamental characteristics of Mesoamerican thought. This is also true of the conception of time-force-god-destiny as a burden. It was believed that the sun bore destiny as energy and distributed it daily over the world. That was why the ancient Nahua said that at the moment of creation, before the Sun existed, "All the gods met together and debated, 'Who will carry things? Who will carry everything on his back? Who will be the Sun?" And at the beginning of the same solar myth, they ask, "Who will carry things? Who will carry things on his back? [Who] will irradiate? [Who] will make the dawn?" The correlation between human work and that of the gods is also Mesoamerican, the gods taking turns in power, and the people in the payment of tribute, at collective labor, or in rotating official duties. P. Carrasco (1976b) says that for the Mexica:

> Each sign, each number, each day, each unit of thirteen days, etc., is associated with a deity who governs the events that happen during its time. It was as if the gods took turns in governing the world in the same way human groups took turns in carrying out public functions.

He also says:

> These gods, or groups of gods, can also be associated with the cardinal directions and calendrical periods. In this way they rule different parts of the

world at different time periods. Thus, [among the Mexica] the principles of the division of work are replicated, as we have seen teams of officials who govern together or who rotate the exercise of their functions in successive periods. (P. Carrasco 1976b)

The gods, in turn, order what happens in the world. Each one has its time to dominate. "The great Tlaloc speaks," says an ancient source (Castillo 1966: 75), during his particular calendric period. The mandate, the word, comes from the sky and the underworld. "It has been said, it has been done unto us, in the sky, in Mictlan."[9] Once determined, the command crosses the borders of the gods' world and arrives in the human world. For the ancient Nahua as well, "the word has now crossed the bridge" (Garcia Quintana 1980). These are gods-forces-times and destinies—though perhaps it would be better to say that destiny was an interaction between all these forces, the new ones arriving and the remnants of the departing ones, with each one in each of earth's beings. In fact it is a struggle, resembling the hieroglyphic symbol for war of the old Aztecs, which unites a stream of water (from the underworld) and a stream of fire (from the sky).[10] Destiny in its strictest sense is the result of this conflict, it is the final combination. The gods-forces-times ascend and descend in a spiral motion along the route of the *malinalli,* a double helix that unites heaven, earth, and the underworld (López Austin 1988, 1:60–61, 210). It is the kind of movement the Pipil of El Salvador remember: "They tell about a kingdom inside a mountain, from which beings descend and ascend as a spiral" (Schultze Jena 1946:74, 1977:35, 38).[11] Each being arrives, in turn, from one of the four trees of the four different colors, from each of the four directions:

The red flint is the sacred stone of the Ah Chac Mucen Cab. The Mother Red Ceiba [silk cotton] tree, its Hidden Center, is in the East. The *chacalpucté* [*Bucida buceros*] is their tree. The red zapote and the red reed belongs to them. Red turkeys with a yellow crest are their turkeys. The toasted red corn is their corn.

White flint is the sacred stone of the North. The Mother White Ceiba is the Invisible Center of the Sac Mucen Cab. White turkeys are their turkeys. White lima beans are their beans. White corn is their corn.

Black flint is the stone of the West. Mother Black Ceiba is their Hidden Center. Black speckled corn is their corn. The black-tipped sweet potato is their sweet potato. Black turkeys are their turkeys. Black night is their house. The black bean is their bean. The black lima bean is their lima bean.

The Yellow flint is the stone of the South. Mother [Yellow] Ceiba is their Hidden Center. The yellow *pucté* is their tree. Yellow is their sweet potato. Yellow their turkeys. The yellow-backed bean is their bean. (*Libro de Chilam Balam de Chumayel* 1973:3–4)

Figure 6. Four-eyed opossum, *Philander opossum*

Because of the rotation of power, it was not always possible to act according to plan. Groups of merchants could not leave on any given day for far-off
lands, nor could magicians work their spells on people on any day (Sahagún
1956, 1:340–41, 357). Nowadays the Mazatec say a magician must gather
his hallucinating mushrooms on Friday, "because it is the day our Lord died.
Good is weakened. It is the day all the sorcerers seize to go to the mountain"
(Boege 1988:213). Among the Quiche a healer explains the timing of a cure
for a particular patient: "We beg a favor of that Lord, day 'seven *ix'*, the day
divinity returned to earth" (Schultze Jena 1946:40).

To sum up, the gods travel by turns in a spiral, from their dwellings in the sky or the underworld. They emerge on earth as transforming forces through each of four trees; the four trees also cast their emanations by turns. On earth they battle to impose their own characteristics, and through this divine war change and destiny are produced. Their time for dominance is limited, because new invisible forces arrive constantly on earth.

Time and god are one. Because of this, they usually bear the same name. For example, Mol' Uch (Grandfather Uch) is one of the terrible gods, an ancient, voracious, crafty actor. He is the ruling force during the twenty-day period from the tenth to the twenty-ninth of June: the dangerous "month" called *'uch* or *mol 'uch*.

The earth is not an arid plateau of health and, comfort,
but a great sprawling female with velvet torso
that swells and heaves with ocean billows;
she squirms beneath a diadem of sweat and anguish.
Naked and sexed she rolls among the clouds in the violet
light of the stars. All of her, from her generous breasts
to her gleaming thighs, blazes with furious ardor.
She moves among the seasons and the years with
a grand whoopla that seizes the torso with paroxysmal fury,
that shakes the cobwebs out of the sky; she subsides
on her pivotal orbits with volcanic tremors.

Henry Miller, *Tropic of Cancer*

The opossum is a thief. How could he be otherwise, since his "hands are almost human-like!" (Castro 1963). With them he opens lids, slides bolts, and removes the stones that cover the cavity of the maguey plant to look for juice. He traps hens to suck their blood and brains. At the birth of the world, he climbed to the top of a steep hill to steal the fire guarded there by seven jaguars. He stirred the embers with his tail and the sparks fell on the eyes of the animals, blinding them. He fled with the fire and gave it to humans, making four pyres (Loo 1987:157–58). Then he climbed the slopes covered with thorns and drank the pulque of an old woman who had the secret for making it. He returned with his belly full and gave the beverage to humans, pouring it into four great jars (ibid.:180–81). In those first days, there was a festival of the devils. Pretending to be drunk, he filled his pouch with mezcal and cigars and ran away with them, taking fire with him at the same time. Since then animals have enjoyed fire, liquor, and tobacco at their celebrations (Bartolomé and Barabas 1982:111–12).

The opossum is a thief, and because of that, the arrival of the "month" *mol 'uch* is dreaded. At the beginning of the twenty-day period of mol 'uch, the Tzotzil place an offering at the entrance to each home, consisting of a small ear of corn, a tiny tortilla, a few beans, a cigar, salt, and a small bowl of pozole (fermented dough), all in small packages wrapped in corn leaves. The Tzotzil believe that if they do not set out such an offering to Grandfather Opossum, the harvest will be meager and hunger will prevail (Guiteras Holmes 1965: 281).

The meaning of *'uch* is manifold. Grandfather 'Uch is a period of time, a twenty-day "month." He is also a god, whose anger may be appeased with offerings so that he will not devour the crops. And he is a force that, in its turn, circles the world. He has his own individual peculiarities. He steals the fruit from plants. He is a corn-thieving god, who acts like an opossum because he has an opossum's nature.[1] Therefore, for the believer, opossums must have been charged with an essential opossum quality ever since the beginning of the world, because the creator implanted his own characteristics in the original opossum. The god is a kind of force. The name 'uch belongs to the opossum and to the twenty-day period, but it is said there is also an unidentified insect called 'uch, which devours the power of food (Guiteras Holmes 1965:281). There are insects that function as a host for invisible forces. One might conclude that in this case the devouring force 'uch enters the insect's body in order to consume another force, the nutritious value of the food. The Popoloca say that the "shadow" (one of the kinds of human soul) can take the form of small insects (Foster 1951). The Mixe claim that there are fireflies in June, the month of Lightning, because Lightning brings them there, and that they abound in cemeteries because they are the souls of the dead (pers. com., Münch Galindo 1988). In Zacapaxtla the Nahua say that the "shadow" that left the body can return to it in the form of a small moth (Robinson 1961). In Pajapan it is believed that a "shadow" that has strayed returns to its owner in the form of a grasshopper, which falls dead at the moment of retrieval (García de León 1969). A large fly with a white head,[2] or one that is entirely white, can contain the souls of the dead (Zingg 1982, 1:297, 299, 306–7). In the Guatemalan highlands, the Quiche believe that the souls of the dead float in the air as the tiny *us* fly, as the *natúp,* and—although this rarely happens—as the *ameló,* a larger fly than the other two (Schultze Jena 1946:22).[3] In the original time, the world was full of flies. The Mazatec can see the past, the future of the world, and Adam and Eve by using hallucinatory mushrooms, and they assure us that "formerly there were only flies" (Boege 1988:92). The insects can shelter and protect the forces with their bodies, and the forces are qualities. The opossum quality comes and goes throughout the world, inside the insect named 'uch. Through it the 'uch insect devours the force of grain.

Thus each god resembles creations. The *Códice Telleriano-Remensis* (1964–67: part 2, pl. 11) states that Quetzalcoatl made the first people and that only he, and no other gods, had a "human body." If each god is an individual type of force that characterized a species at the beginning of the world, that continues to form part of today's individuals, and that circulates in the form of time over the earth, then there must be an essential participation between the gods and their influences, their creations and infiltrations, their surroundings and garments, their possessions and powers, their field of operation, and their victims. This is the case, and there are many examples of it. Among the ancient Nahua, a male born under the sign of *ce mazatl* (one deer)[4] was "timid, weak-spirited and faint-hearted," and "could not hear thunder or see lightning without being terrified." A male born under the sign of *ce cuetzpalin* (one lizard) could survive a fall, as lizards do. If it were under the sign *ome tochtli* (two rabbit), one would be a drunkard, like the rabbit gods of pulque. Males born under *ce cozcacuauhtli* (one vulture), would live to old age, like that bald bird (Sahagún 1956, 1:322–23, 350, 355–56). The god and the individual shared characteristics because the person's force was a portion of the god's force. Males born on the day *ce miquiztli* (one death) were given the name Miquiz or another of the proper names of the powerful god Tezcatlipoca (Yaotl, Cenyaotl, Necoc Yaotl, etc.), and would possess a force so great no one could desire their death, since the death would befall whoever had wished it (Sahagún 1956, 1:331–32). The god of fire could burn, but he could also liberate from fire. If a person communed with the fire god at his annual festival, by eating a piece of god's image made from amaranth seed, that person's body and property would be protected from fire during the following year (Serna 1953:187).

Women who died in childbirth became divinities. As goddesses, their domain of power was childbirth. Women who were about to give birth prayed to them for good luck (ibid.:174). The domain of the rain god, his motives for causing death, his weapons, the fate of those wounded by them, and the power of Tlaloc's priests all demonstrate an essential unity:

> And he who was placed beneath the water died there. And when a few days later, the water cast forth the body of the drowned person . . . No one dared to take it out. They told the idol's priests, and only they took it out, because they said that the others were not worthy of touching it. . . . If any layman wanted to take that body from the water, he would also be drowned or would be stricken with gout.
>
> They said that whoever died that way did so because of one of two causes: either because he was so good that the tlaloque gods wanted him to accompany them to their earthly paradise, or because, by some chance, he had precious stones in his possession, a circumstance which angered the tlaloque gods, because they did not want men to have precious stones. This is the reason they killed him. They took him also to their earthly paradise. . . .
>
> They also had another superstition, one concerning the relatives of those

drowned people. They said that, at the request of the one who had been carried off to the earthly paradise and wanted a relative to join him, one of them would suffer that death or be struck by lightning. Because of this, great care was taken to avoid bathing. (Sahagún 1956, 3:264–65)

The transmission of a god's power extends beyond the observable effects of willful acts. That power is a unique substance that takes possession of whatever it impregnates. Tlaloc has his green stones, his priests, and his way of acting; his victims are the drowned and whoever touches them, those who treasure green jewels, and the relatives of those killed by his acts, in his domain. People who have been in contact with the power are at risk and they transmit its influence. Only Tlaloc's priests, who usually control that power, are free from threat—and only provisionally.

The forces have their spheres, their times, their ways and reasons to act or to mitigate the results. All of this comes together when a body is possessed. The possessor and the possessed share the essence; the transfer itself is a form of possession. Mexica sacrificial rituals clearly demonstrate that unity (P. Carrasco 1976b:255). The victim was often dressed like the god receiving the sacrifice. Death on the altar of the god made the victim a part of that god, and in the extraterrestrial life, the sacrificial victim was assimilated into that specific source of power.

Although gods are commonly identified with meteors, elements, or astral bodies, it is important to look for the special qualities of the gods, their functions and processes, rather than looking for one-to-one correspondences with natural beings, real or imaginary. Everything that exists seems to have been branded at the moment of creation, which implies the existence of a common force behind what is similar, even in minor things. For example, today's Tzotzil avoid eating river snails during corn-planting season; they say the snails' shells resemble the corn seed without roots (Vogt 1976:56),[5] and eating them would be like eating the sown kernels. Pleasure and lust were identified with the god Huehuecoyotl (Old Coyote), characteristics that were attributed to coyotes (Nicholson 1971). Huehuecoyotl accounts for one of the realities of the world, eroticism. All of this makes it necessary to identify the essential attributes of each god.

Other gods will be only vaguely present, but they too enable people to account for various aspects of the human condition. There is little use in viewing the gods as clusters of symbols; it is necessary to find the common threads in their attributes. For example one of the most important gods is Quetzalcoatl, god of dawn, of knowledge, of the wind, of fertility (among other attributes), author of the names of things on the earth's surface (López Austin 1979). At first sight the attributes of different gods seem to merge in his person. But the theme of *beginning,* or of *extraction,* unifies this apparent conglomerate of attributes: the emergence of light before sunrise; the emergence of earthly things beneath that light; the emergence of rain after the wind that sweeps a path for it;[6] the beginning of human life. Within this unifying idea, particular qualities call forth different names: Quetzalcoatl becomes Ehecatl with the specific qualities of wind, or Tlahuizcalpantecuhtli, with those of dawn.

We see cosmic processes and astral movements in the gods. Believers see similar processes on earth, in their homes, their surroundings, inside their own bodies, in their cornfields. All these processes can be seen as a single process, expressing the essence of a particular god whose function is to move various parts of the world with the motion that characterizes him.

Every being on earth has its share of forces. The invisible forces (the innate as well as those acquired or bestowed) make up the hidden depths of its history. Each being participates in the cosmic energy, but each has a unique, particular, and ever-changing combination, bathed day after day as the Sun sheds time over the surface of the earth. Gods are not excluded from transformation in the total circulation of divine forces in the world. They themselves are combinations of forces acquired during their passage in this world—processes formed by lesser processes, and forming in turn part of larger processes. Their qualities may be complementary, opposites, or at odds. The gods are dynamic beings, and their changing phases can be recognized by the garments and emblems that appear in their different avatars (López Austin 1979, 1983). The garments and emblems constitute a code. Gods do not always wear the same emblems and garments, because their position, acts, and circumstances in this world change constantly. Their temporal history on earth is guided by the combination of ritual festivals (P. Carrasco 1978). Garments and emblems are shared among the gods because each of them must occupy the same position and perform similar acts at some point in their existence.

Time is matter, and "it participates in the decline of the universal movement" (Duverger 1983:37). Ritual killing prevents the total decline of the divine forces that are present in the world. There are several kinds of ritual killing, and their effects are very different; the two main forms serve to strengthen the divine forces. Certain ritual killings nourish the gods with the blood of the victims, in order to renew and maintain the cyclic succession of forces. In a second type of killing, the victims are people who have been possessed by the gods; the gods that have possessed them die with them, diminishing a portion of the force in the world in order to make possible an immediate vigorous

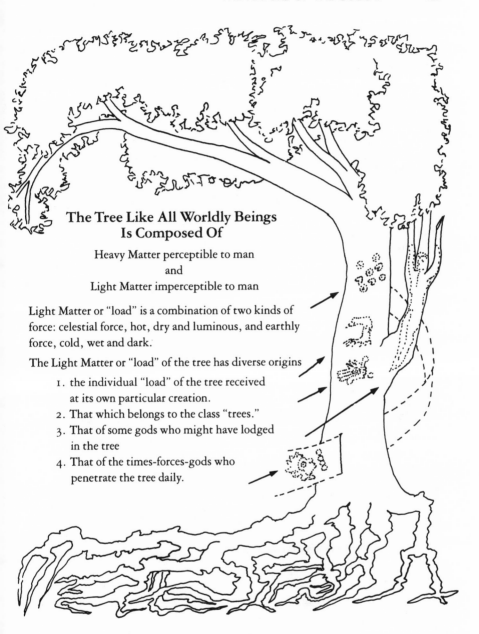

The Tree Like All Worldly Beings
Is Composed Of

Heavy Matter perceptible to man
and
Light Matter imperceptible to man

Light Matter or "load" is a combination of two kinds of force: celestial force, hot, dry and luminous, and earthly force, cold, wet and dark.

The Light Matter or "load" of the tree has diverse origins

1. the individual "load" of the tree received at its own particular creation.
2. That which belongs to the class "trees."
3. That of some gods who might have lodged in the tree
4. That of the times-forces-gods who penetrate the tree daily.

Figure 7. The composition of beings in the human world

rebirth.[7] The person who dies as a god, with the force of the god within its body, will return as such into the dwelling of the gods. The loss of this force completes an entire cycle in the world. Now fully integrated into the divine time-space, this force can fully return to the world at its next opportunity in a new cycle, reconstituted by the killing. The ease of transition is one of the great differences between the gods and people. The gods circulate, renew themselves; in short, they are immortal. Humans "cannot move freely to other states of time and space as the supernatural beings, the gods, can" (A. Miller 1974); they are mortal.

People kill plants and animals to feed themselves. They become contaminated with death (with the earth) by ingesting both the visible and the invisible. By contrast the gods eat only the invisible parts of things (Holland 1963:74; Knab 1979). The invisible is matter, but a light kind of matter that can move easily across the barriers of time and space in the cosmos. The food mortals eat creates their obstacles. Motecuhzoma Ilhuicamina's magicians crossed the barrier and reached Coatepec, where the gods live, but there their bodies sank to their waists in sand. Their guide, an old man from the other time-space, came to their aid. "What has happened, Mexicas? What has made you so heavy? What do you eat there in your land?" Motecuhzoma's envoys answered, "Lord, we eat the food we grow there, and we drink chocolate." The old man responded, "Children, those meals and beverages make you ponderous and heavy and they will not allow you to see the places where your forefathers existed, and they have brought you to death . . ." (Durán 1984, 2:221).

Saint Lucia became heavy because she ate heavy food (animal remains), so she remained in the world as a buzzard. The Nahua of Veracruz say:

> Here is where poor Saint Lucia lost her sanctity, lost it through greediness and disobedience of God's commandments.
> When she wanted to fly to Heaven, she could not, because her body weighed her down. Because of that, they now say that buzzards are our brothers, are our offspring since the beginning of the world. Now, they are going to remain here on earth forever, and now we know that the buzzard was God's messenger, and because of his gluttony, he can now fly no higher. Because of his disobedience, he came to remain on earth forever. Now he is nothing, having lost all because of his gluttony. (*Seis versiones del diluvio* 1983:14)

The invisible is a combination of forces. There are two kinds of forces that unite in different proportions, opposing forces that make every being a dynamic being. One, the celestial force, comes from above and is luminous, masculine, dry, and hot; the other one, coming from the underworld, is dark, feminine, wet, and cold. Both emanate from the cosmic trees in the form of time.

As mentioned in the preceding chapter, Signorini and Lupo found in the mountains of Puebla a belief in the dual nature of the human soul. The soul is half luminous and half dark. This belief is thought provoking, in light of some still obscure pairs of terms from old magical texts, terms that indicate a light/dark opposition in the composition of the invisible. Among the pairs are *yayauhqui tonalli*/*iztac tonalli* in Nahua invocations,[8] or *ch'ab*/*akab* in Maya invocations.[9] Contemporary Chontal in Oaxaca (P. Carrasco 1960) also divide the spirits of things into two, although, perhaps owing to Christian influence, the distinction is made in terms of the opposition of good and evil:

> According to the informant everything has two different spirits, one good and
> the other evil. Thus, there are both kinds of spirits in springs, mountains,
> among thunderbolts, and so forth. In regard to the earth, for instance, the good
> spirit is a young woman and the evil one is an old woman. There is also a good
> and a bad spirit of the rainbow, a good and a bad guardian of the deer, etc.

The composite nature of the gods explains their heterogeneity, this heterogeneity explains their oppositions, and all this explains why, on earth, things seem to be in conflict, and sometimes achieve a temporary dominance over one another. Good and evil are caused by nature and the will of the gods. There is no movement on earth without divine cause.

> Lord Hunabku is the one who distributes good and evil
> among the good and the bad people.
> because he spreads light over the earth;
> because he is the Master of all things under his hand;
> the Same for the Sun as for the Moon;
> the same for the smoking star
> which is like a luminous flower in heaven;
> the same for the clouds and the rain;
> the same for the lightning as for the smallest fly;
> the same for the birds and the other animals;
> the same.
>   (*El libro de los cantares de Dzitbalché* 1965:58).

Some gods are kind. Others are terrible, such as Hun-Camé and Vucub-Camé, Xiquiripat and Cuchumaquic, Ahalpuh and Ahalganá, Chamiabac and Chamiaholom, Ahalmez and Ahaltocob, Xic and Patán (*Popol Vuh* 1950:50–

51), whose names are linked to the most terrifying diseases. But it is not likely that any god is totally good or totally evil. The gods, as changeable as the elements that comprise them, operate for or against humans with an irregularity that leaves no doubt about their free will. Their composition also explains their aggressiveness. The predominance of one kind of force in them provokes an appetite for its opposite. Thus the water gods (who are also the gods of cold, the terrestrial, and of death) try to trap the forces of movement (hot, celestial, vital forces) that reside in the human organism. Women who die in their first childbirth, having become divine, horrible, fleshless dwellers of the solar sky, will descend to earth to snatch away the beauty of children. In the invocations the magicians used to defend themselves against the attacks of powerful enemies, and to control the dangerous, allied forces, there are many terms that suggest that the invisible forces are full of anger, fury, a wish to mock, to offend or to damage, or a desire to cause harm. The main reasons for their attacks are their hunger and thirst, their need and envy.[10] In short the composition of the invisible ones makes them subject to desires, which govern their relations with people.

The nature of the gods explains the processes of this world. Composition is converted into causation, both specifically and globally. Humans try to imagine the gods—consciously or not—in order to understand their behavior. Possessing their secrets, they hope to control the invisible part of the world, finding the great regularity underlying divine whims. The supernatural in Mesoamerica cannot be characterized by its evasion of the laws, least of all those that apply specifically to the invisible. As Ovid said, "The gods have their laws" (Ovidio 1985: vol. 2, 78–79, bk. 9, 499). They are particular, distinctive laws, but norms nevertheless, and sometimes, as among humans, a transgression leads to punishment.

> Near the large image of [patron saint] Santiago on the church altar stands a small image of Santa Ana. Diego Martin explained that she is the wife of Santiago, and, according to a well-known story, she once had an illicit affair with San Sebastian, the patron saint of the *municipio* of that name. Santiago discovered her infidelity, beat her soundly, and threw her in jail. Since then he watches her closely. (Wagley 1949:53)

The gods are subject to law. Therefore they are not all-powerful. Their laws, though specific to their own unique situations, are extensions of the laws believed to exist on earth. Causality extends over the entire universe. Will we be able to claim for myth the pandeterminism that Todorov (1981:87) claims for fantasy?

Light and Heavy

Distinctions such as *sacred/profane* and *natural/supernatural* carry with them such powerful European traditional connotations that the very terms may obscure the meaning and power of the Mesoamerican concepts they purport to describe. Distinguishing the perceptible from the imperceptible implies a necessary relationship to human faculties. New terms are needed, if not for greater accuracy in approximating indigenous categories, then at least to avoid premature equivalence with Christian categories. I propose, without pretending to approximate indigenous categories, a distinction between *light* and *heavy,* at least until other characteristics are shown. With these categories in mind, let us recapitulate the natural and the supernatural, the sacred and the profane, in the religious tradition we are studying. It is a long road. Here are some of the steps:

1.   The cosmos is made up of two kinds of matter. The limits of human perception allow people to detect only one of the two types, under normal circumstances.

2.   Everything that belongs to the human world partakes of both kinds of matter, the light and the heavy. At the beginning of the world, light matter characterized all things, and is a characteristic of every individual before birth. As an essence, it underlies all that is heavy and, as waves of time, it influences everything that is heavy.

3.   Invisible beings—those composed of light matter—are combinations of contrary elements that produce their dynamics, their traits, and the peculiarities with which they are endowed and with which they endow heavy beings. This elemental opposition is marked by contrasting features, such as *luminosity/darkness*.

4.   The light and the heavy, emanating into the world in cyclic patterns in the form of time, give rise to an ordered world that includes in its order even catastrophes, plagues, and famines.

5.   Despite their limited perception, humans are able to understand the laws governing light matter, by working hard on the double paths of recorded experience (studying nature) and mathematical operation (the art of combining the different cycles of influences). The purpose is not mere speculation, but mastery of what is earthly in both its heavy and light aspects. This is possible because the supernatural is material, governable, and understandable.

6.   That which is light circulates through this world, sometimes as a part of all beings, sometimes briefly traveling in utter freedom. There are indications that it cannot move without the cover of the other kind of matter, the

heavy. Such cover may be as delicate as a shadow, a breath, a creaking, the dust raised by a whirlwind, or as insignificant as an insect. Divine forces are contaminated as they move through the world this way, but their passage from one time-space to another is easy.

7.   Humans, like all beings on earth, are composed of both light and heavy matter. It therefore follows that the limits to human perception pertain to the heavy part. We have seen how "heavy" matter (including "heavy" foods) results in the loss of movement in the zones inhabited by the gods. The light part of peole has a greater perceptive capacity. Some of the light components can leave the body temporarily in dreams, in mystic trances, or under the influence of drugs, freeing the perceptive capability so that one may make contact with the gods and the dead. Ecstasy is nothing but temporary liberation from an obstacle. The supernatural forms part of all beings, but in some it is restricted by a thicker covering of heavy matter.

8.   That which is heavy emerges as part of the world. It is created by the progression of time. Divine forces, which are light, by contrast, are able to pass out of time sequences into the eternal present, freeing themselves from the eschatological process.

9.   Because of all this, the nature of all things in this world has a beginning and an end. For the gods, death is just a stage in their cycle. But for humans, composed of both heavy and light matter, death and decomposition cannot be reversed.

In our search for criteria to distinguish nature from supernature and the sacred from the profane, new questions arise. Humanity and the human world are perishable. But what about that intermediate creation, between the existence of the gods and the creation of the world? What about the sequence of time, the frame of creation? Does the calendar end with the world?

Such questions clearly worried the ancient sages. The enormous calculations of the Mayan priests to measure time suggest that the time cycles of all dimensions would someday coincide. This idea separates the concept of an immense (but not eternal) period of time from the concept of an eternal, absolute cycle.[11] The end of this world—meaning the completion of the cycle of forces that made its existence possible—and the end of other intermediate worlds, whose causes are also cyclic, are parts of the absolute cycle (see Farriss 1987).

It is probable that the ancient sages arrived at conflicting conclusions, or remained troubled by doubts. Let us leave the sages to their problems and return to the worldly actions of the gods, in which their divinity is completely manifested. The gods are immortal, they are creators, both in their linear time and in the absolute cycle. Humans and other earthly beings, and the world itself, are created, are perishable. Their light part (the supernatural in them) returns to the supernatural. I have found no information about the fate of the heavy matter when this world is destroyed.

The existing data suggest that pairs of contrasting terms are useful tools for analyzing the two types of matter conceived in this religious tradition. I have used the terms *heavy* and *light* provisionally, and other pairs have been suggested, but I consider it most appropriate to continue using the contrasting terms *natural/supernatural*. I reject some meanings derived from their etymology (e.g., the idea that the *supernatural* is not bound by laws), which also bothered Durkheim, and stand by my previous comments on their meaning. Nevertheless their use facilitates dialogue with other specialists who are familiar with the terms. When necessary, we can distinguish these concepts from those of Durkheim by using his terms, *sacred* and *profane,* when discussing Durkheim's categories.

By *sacred* is meant that which is dangerous because of the damage it can cause through the supernatural. As Durkheim said, this includes not only the gods, but objects, words, rites, or formulas. Here are grouped heroic and prodigious deeds, the horrendous, the sinful, the scandalous. However, it is not possible to set up a dichotomy. Just as nothing on earth lacks a portion of nature and the supernatural, everything supernatural (in all earthly beings) has some potential for danger. Moreover sacredness is relative. It depends on the quantity and quality of the force. It also depends on the nature of the intended victim. What is safe for a man may be harmful to a woman, or vice versa. The power of an invocation is not the same for one illness as for another. Certain forces represent a different kind of danger for a pregnant woman, a menstruating woman, or one who is neither. Supernatural forces threaten children, old people, and adults in different ways. A priest can control the objects of the god he serves, but not those of another. Some beings are especially weak before particular invisible forces; for instance, young turkeys drop dead if emanations from adulterers reach them.[12]

In this tradition, what name was given to that which is *sacred* in Durkheim's sense? Natives today often use the Spanish word *delicado,* "delicate," in reference to such things as festival time, a sacred site, archeological ruins, or the entrances to the other world. A circumstance by which the supernatural can produce strong effects is "delicate."[13]

With this understanding of the meaning of the terms *supernatural* and *sacred,* let us continue to study the characteristics of the gods. It is necessary to emphasize the time dimension of the gods in this world. On the day when a particular force arrives on the earth's surface, everything on earth that has the same type of force is strengthened. It is the day of the festival, the saint's day. Corresponding supernatural forces are increased and reinforced. Thus even the days for offerings must be set by calendrical order (*Augurios y abusiones* 1969: 20–21). In the seventeenth century, Balsalobre (1953:354–55) observed that the Zapotecs in Oaxaca determined the good and the bad days for offering alms to the church based on the advice of an expert on the ancient calendar.

A god's strength diminishes with the passage of time. One of the books of the Chilam Balam makes this clear when it speaks of the cult of the god of the five fateful days at the end of the year. On the first day, people performed the ceremonies enthusiastically; by the fourth day the festivals were in sharp decline and the image was taken to the door of the believer's house; on the fifth day the god was banished, because the next day the New Year would begin (*Códice Pérez* 1949:179, 327). Nowadays the dangerous gods are kept ignorant of the arrival of their day. In the Veracruzan Huasteca region (Williams Garcia 1972:77) the same care is taken with Sini, or Saint John, who, because of a blow to the head, never is aware of the date. It is said that when he asks from the sea about his festival day, they lie to him and say that it is still a long way off, because if he knew that his time was coming, he would send floods, as he used to do. Similarly, in Guatemala:

> The *mayordomos,* who are responsible for the care of the saints, usually take a
> drink to Santiago a few days before his fiesta so that he will be drunk during
> the noise and bustle of the three days, because "if Santiago knows the day of the
> fiesta, he will send a *juicio* (punishment) on the pueblo." The day of his fiesta
> is very "delicate"; people shout, sing, and make considerable noise. So when
> the *mayordomos* offer him *aguardiente,* they say "here is a drink for the Fiesta
> of Magdalena," which is a saint's day not celebrated in Chimaltenango. San-
> tiago, like any good Chimalteco, is fooled and drinks. He never knows that the
> villagers have celebrated his own fiesta. Only when the people from San Juan
> Atitán bring their patron saint to bid him goodbye after the fiesta is over does
> he realize that he has been drunk throughout his own fiesta day. (Wagley 1949:
> 53–54)

The opportunities of the gods are governed by space as well as time. From the same Guatemalans who make Santiago drunk comes a tale about the spatial power of the gods. A woman and her daughter went to the peak of the mountain Tui-pich-jap to gather herbs. The girl, ignorant of the sacredness of the place, cut a "delicate" flower she found at the top of the mountain. This was enough for the two women to suddenly find themselves surrounded by rock walls. Both of them began to cry and pray for several hours to Father Tui-pich-jap, guardian of the mountain, until finally the path reappeared and they could return home (ibid.:57–58).

In fact the world is divided into two territories. Humans live in one, with their houses, their plants, their domestic animals. The Mazatec call it *qui he'al* (Portal 1986:82). The other area belongs to the *dueños* (owners), to the Lord of the Earth, who governs and cares for wild animals, or to the lords of the hills, or to the lords of the springs, dangerous places that must be approached with special care because of the power of the gods who perpetually inhabit them. Before entering the dominions of the dueños, hunters, fisherman, and wood-cutters must spend long periods in preparation ("diets" or "abstinences"), in which sexual abstinence plays an important part. While they are on the mountain, hunting, fishing, or chopping wood, they must protect themselves with rituals to keep from falling into "enchanted places" where the forces are highly concentrated. Such accidents often occur because of the involuntary commission of some prohibited act; for instance, killing one of the beasts that are the exclusive property of the dueño, or destroying one of his plants, as in the case of the girl who cut the flower at the top of the mountain Tui-pich-jap. And there are other sites even more strictly off limits, entirely forbidden to humans. Some are entrances to the other space-time. They are protected by guardian monsters or by barriers that obstruct both view and passage—great briar thickets, rough terrain, sandbanks and lagoons, thick swamps of reeds, or rocky places with sharp stones (Durán 1984, 2:215–16).

It is necessary to invade the forest to prepare the soil for farming. This appropriation, which transforms the nature of the land, is achieved by means of propitiatory rituals addressed to Mother Earth, and she is also paid for the crop received (Boege 1988:152–53).[14] New gods will occupy the domesticated space, gods who are charged with the care of the diverse human groups. But even human territory does not belong equally to all people. Patron gods—or saints—legitimize only the tenure of their own devotees, and only within the radius of their authority.

The alliance between patron gods—or saints—and their protégés reveals other important characteristics of the invisible forces. Like the social groups they guard, the gods have friendships and enmities, affinities and dissimilarities. They are grouped by families, and their relationships are as changeable as the regional history. Good or bad relations among the inhabitants are projected onto the divine order of the region.

Since ancient times there has persisted an interesting belief in the individuality of the patrons. The same Tezcatlipoca was not the patron of two villages; each had *a particular* Tezcatlipoca. The same is true today of Saint John, Saint

Peter, and Mary Magdalene. The invisible forces are divided. Their fundamental characteristics are the same everywhere, but each portion has its own life and a particular story, played out among a specific group of people. In the extensive literature, gods and patron saints are found to be more closely connected with this earth than with their remote origins. Though periodically reinforced by the waves of kindred time, they seem to have been born with an original pact with their town and with the mountains that surround it. This does not mean that they are humans who have been raised to a divine position. No—they are "gods in origin" (see below), from the other space-time. But from the moment of their arrival, their involvement with their particular people individualizes them as patron gods and makes them belong to those they protect.

This makes the gods on earth divisible forces. Each image, each avatar, forms part of an individualized complex that has distributed its segments over the world. The segments collectively form a god, but each individual segment is also a god with its own attributes and history. Contemporary Cora give a description of this concept:

> There is a rule for the distribution of what is sacred and a tendency to constitute families or groups of saints. The figure of Christ who, for Catholics, represents a unity, an inseparable whole, for the Cora represents a succession of often isolated sacred moments. The Child Jesus is, above all else, the patron and protector of children . . . ; the Nazarene, the prisoner who carried the cross; the Great Christ of the Bones, the bearer, the guardian of the church; the Small Christ, Tamatú Kurujetsé, the one charged with receiving the stroke of the lance; the Holy Burial, the other Dead Christ, synthesizes the divine, the polarity of the sacred. . . . The Child, no matter how divine he is supposed to be, is not, in the strictest sense, the Christ of Calvary, nor of the Crucifixion, nor the Dead Christ. All carry a vision, fulfill a need, serve for something clearly defined.
>
> Divinity, if one may say so, can be taken apart and put together again. (Benítez 1985:141–42)

This is a concept that has emerged in many traditions throughout history. Fustel de Coulanges (1984:165), writing about religious thought among the Greeks, noted that "there was an Athena in Athens and another in Sparta, and they were two goddesses." And, "In the Trojan war we see a Pallas who fights with the Greeks, and the Trojans have another Pallas whom they worship and who protects her worshippers."

The gods have the power to reintegrate themselves with their source, but while they fulfill their mission here, separated into images, sacred bundles, or as the fire of vigor and reproductive power in each one of their men, in each one of the seeds that germinate in the fields, they belong here. They are just the opposite of Catholic saints. They have moved from divinity to humanity. Because of this native concept, Catholic saints are often (erroneously) referred to as gods of origin, preceding the human race.

The gods are divisible in their divine dwellings, as they are on earth. There are many examples of multiple, simultaneous locations of the gods in the other time-space. Mictlantecuhtli was the Lord of the Dead of the underworld, but he could also be, according to one source, in the sixth heaven (*Historia de México* 1965:102). This same idea is found in other parts of Mesoamerica, among the Maya (Rivera Dorado 1986b:70–71). Forces and gods—which are, in fact, the same—have similar divisibility in both kinds of space-time.

The divine forces contained in images and relics are also divisible. Protégés of a certain patron could form alliances based on that commonality. Sometimes an image was broken, or a relic separated into pieces, each of the allies retaining a portion of the image and of the cohesive force.[15] In such cases the parts remained connected. There is no contradiction between the independence of the parts and the permanent unity of the essence. The force of the image continues to be one, and what happens to each portion affects the whole in some way. This means that humans can manipulate their gods through the images. The images can be compelled, even by the most violent means, to the action desired from the gods.[16] This also means that forces of a similar nature "communicate" with each other. The Mixtec say that when someone goes to bathe in the *temascal* sweat-bath, the fire in the house tells the oven in the bath, and the latter informs the Grandmother spirit who resides in the bath (Jansen 1982, 1:302).

Images are vessels. The ancient Nahua used to refer to the images of the gods as *teixiptla* and *toptli*. *Teixiptla* derives from *xip*, meaning "skin, rind, or covering" (López Austin 1973:119). *Toptli* means "covering or wrapping" (Molina 1944: fol. 60v, 150r). The gods and their images recognize each other. Like naturally goes to like, so portions of divine forces are poured into their visible receptacles. In this way the gods fill natural formations as well, and humans detect the presence of the gods in the rocks that resemble them (Ruiz de Alarcón 1953:30). Because of such a resemblance, the Tarascans discovered the sacred place where they were to erect Pátzcuaro, their capital:

Since they had their site in the district of Pátzcuaro, called Tarichúndaro, they found the site for their temples, called *petatzequa*, which were some cliffs on high, on top of which they built their temples. These people said that the god of hell sent them those sites for their temples to their principal gods. . . . Walking upward through the water, they said to each other, "Come here. Here is the place our gods say is called Tzacapu-hamúcutin-pátzcuaro. Let us see what place it is," and, following the water—there was no path; it was completely closed off by trees and very large oak trees, and all was dark and mountainous . . . — they walked around, staring at the water in the place, and, after looking at all of them, they said, "Here it is, no doubt—Pátzcuaro. Let us look at the sites we have found for our temples." And they went to that place and they found the aforesaid cliffs called *petatzequa,* which means place of the temple. There is a mountain there, and they climbed up to it and arrived at the place. There were some stones standing up there like idols waiting to be carved, and they said, "Certainly this is it. Here is where the gods say. Those are the gods of the Chichimecs, and this site where it is located is called Pátzcuaro. Observe that this stone is the one that must be called Zirita-cherengue, and this one Uacúsecha, and that is her older brother, and this is Tingárata and this one Miequa-axeua. Notice that there are four of these gods." And they went to another place, where there were other rocks, and they recognized it as the place the gods had said, and they stated, "Let us clear this place," and they cut down the oaks and other trees that were there, saying they had found the place the gods had indicated. (*Relación de las ceremonias y ritos* . . . 1977:34–35)

There is such a resemblance between image and god that some visible forms charged with sacred power are considered to be gods themselves. Mesoamerican images are identified with the "ancient saints" who hid themselves when the Christians arrived.[17]

The belief in the eruption of divine force into an image explains the precautions ancient sculptors took to avoid a sudden contact with the god. The Maya of Yucatan, fearing contact with the divine, fasted, painted their bodies with soot, abstained from sex, and, during their work period, went to some specially constructed huts, burned incense, and daubed the figures with their own blood continually, in order to protect themselves and their families from death or serious illness. The finished figures were placed in tubs, where they were kept under cover (Landa 1982:72, 101–2).[18]

Communication between the image and the distant god is maintained among the parts of the same divided force. In the jungles of Chiapas, the Lacandon deposit offerings in clay braziers that are effigies of the gods. Here vehicle, force, and image are confused. The hunter, putting a piece of meat in the receptacle, directs a prayer to the brazier:

> I am returning my offering of meat
> so you may return it to the father,

so you may carry it to the father.
I am giving you an offering for your own well-being;
my offering of meat is for you.
(Tozzer 1982:204; see also 106–13, 125–66)

And in the jungles of Chiapas, the Lacandon believer can become a vehicle for the god, actually becoming the "hand" of celestial thought. This is the "Divination of the name of the god whose presence is desired":

That your name might be spoken in heaven,
That your name might be spoken in my hand,
don't allow the name in my hand to be false.
Take possession of me so I may receive your name;
don't allow the name in my hand to be false;
so it may say your name in heaven,
in the home of the gods,
say your name in heaven.
Don't permit my hand to lie.
Let it give the word in the home of the gods.
Let the message be received in the home of the gods.
Take possession of me. . . .
(Tozzer 1982:195–96; see also 120–21)

The use of the human body as a vessel to transmit the divine recalls the practice of the Atitecos, who accept the food and drink given at the festival—are in fact forbidden to refuse it—as a gift to the gods (Mendelson 1967).

The forces—the gods—live in their images, their relics, etc. They are the forces that determine characteristics. Surely everything has characteristics. Can anything exist without having qualities? Must not the gods therefore inhabit everything that exists on earth? This being so, sacredness is really a question of intensity. This world is the ball court where the struggle between the different, the opposite, the complementary is played out.

They come from over there.

Listen! Brown Person!
You and I have just come to live with Them.
You and I are Great Wizards.
You and I cannot fail in anything.
None of the Seven Clan Districts shall climb over You and me!
Listen! Brown Place of the Whirlwind!
You and I have just come to live with Them.
You and I are Great Wizards.
You and I cannot fail in anything.
None of the Seven Clan Districts shall climb over You and me!

Ade:lagh (a) dhí:ya Ga:n(i)sgawi
("To prepare tobacco when They are doing harm somewhere,"!
a Cherokee curing chant)

The hymn to Teteoinnan, mother of the gods, says, "Your point of departure is Tamoanchan!" Every eight years they sang to Centeotl, the god of corn, in the *atamalcualiztli* festival, "He was born in Tamoanchan, where the flowers bloom!" In another hymn the goddess Xochiquetzal clearly states her origin: "House on the banks of Tamoanchan." Macuilxochitl says, "I have come from where the flowers lift their heads" (*Veinte himnos sacros de los nahuas* 1958:68, 109, 152, 219). But once here on earth, what is the fate of the immortals?

The presence of the gods on the earth takes various forms. Some have characterized everything that exists on earth since the days of creation. A portion of their being has remained in each species, guaranteeing its nature. They came to earth to form part of earthly beings, and they remain there as the souls of people, animals, plants, and things, and as processes. The divine forces grow and diminish with the passage of time, because every being born brings to earth a new portion of divine substance, generated by the whirling of the four trees that hold up the world. The forces can concentrate dangerously within sacred things and take possession of human beings. Patron gods travel and settle near or within their protégés. But there are also diminutions. Parts of the divine force are scattered over the earth or return to the dwelling of the gods upon the demise of the individuals containing them.

Not all the forces that created earth's beings are distributed among them. A significant number took refuge in wild places and retained their divine individuality. These are the ancestors. The Mocho say that this was the fate of the "kings" of the dark era. When the sun rose—and Adam and Eve made their appearance—God banished all of them. The "kings" retired to the highlands and each one made himself dueño of a parcel of land (Petrich 1985:162). Today the highland Maya believe their ancestors are lords of the heights, each one the protector of one of the lineages. The power of the dueños dominates the hills, each containing a replica of the human world. The wilderness and the town have parallel lives, since they are activated by the same forces of destiny. The mountain is a mirror in which wild animals are a reflection of their corresponding human beings. Specific animals lead lives in the hills parallel to those of the humans of the town with whom they share a soul. The fierce wild animal is the chief; the shy rabbits bear part of the soul of the town's most timid inhabitants. The death of the animal or of the person produces that of the companion.[1] Movements in human abodes are similar to the movements occuring in the corresponding hill, filled with divine forces and home to animals.

The hills are sanctuaries for the gods in their retreat from the world. The hills are filled with dangerous invisible forces. As the ancient Nahua said, the forest is

> a sinkhole, the cause of misery, the place of sorrow, where one weeps, place of sadness, site of affliction, site where misery is spread . . . place of unhappiness, place of fear, place of terror. (*Códice Florentino* 1979: bk. 11, fol. 109v–110r)

Today a Tzotzil contrasts a cultivated field with the forest: "In the cornfields there is no shadow or darkness; it is open country and we are not afraid. In the mountain there are darkness, snakes, sink-holes, caves" (Guiteras Holmes 1965:236).

As a refuge for the gods, the mountains are also a depository for future creations, a storehouse for incipient towns awaiting a patron to arrange their birth and to lead them into light and history.[2] From Chicomoztoc, the mountain of seven wombs, ancient Nahua towns would emerge in their historical turn and the patron would lead them to the promised land. Reciprocally the towns would replicate the sacred hills, and pyramids would be erected in them, artificial hills, whose tops the gods would inhabit. The name of the great pyramid at Tenochtitlan was Coatepetl, "serpent hill."

The presence of the gods make sacred sites of these wild places.[3] The hills are hollow. Under their coating of stone and dirt are the dwellings of the gods and the dead, cool and fertile places, forbidden to humankind. But the broken surface, carved into ravines, springs, and the mouths of caves, makes ambiguity possible on both sides. The perceptible and the imperceptible mingle there. Wild beasts take cover in the caves and are known to the gods. Deer can go inside the mountain to rest, and there the gods repair the skin of animals wounded by the hunter's weapon. The gods and the dead—who have become minor gods—go forth to take care of their appointed areas. They are beings of night and death. They produce food and vegetation and the heavy matter that makes those who ingest it heavy. They are filled with moisture, and are found sometimes in the veins of the earth, sometimes on the surface as inhabitants of rivers and streams, and in the skies as wind, clouds, and lightning, released from the mountains. Because of this, in the Isthmus of Veracruz they say that lightning bolts are *totahuan*, "our fathers" (Münch Galindo 1983:169). The Cora say you have to ask permission from the "old ones," who live in a cave on Huaco mountain, in order to succeed in any undertaking (Dahlgren 1961:48). The great dueño (today's Nahua call him Chane) is master of the underworld of vegetation and rain.

> The Saint of the Mountain, Saint of the Forest, Saint of the Trees, Saint of the Rain, Saint of Lightning, Saint of Everything, is a very old man. . . .
> "I command the Lightning, I command the Marsh, I command the River, I command the Mountain, I command Trees, I command Everything. . . ."
> Oh, Saint of the Mountain, Saint of the Place, Saint of the Rain! (Bartolomé 1979:27)

The gods are also present on earth in the transitory form of time, washing over the earth's surface. These forces struggle, weaken, and fade away, ebbing and flowing as they gradually lose their presence. These temporary forces strengthen the corresponding permanent ones, which is how the gods become revitalized on their calendrical days.

Gods disintegrate and reconstitute themselves during their brief or prolonged circulations on earth. Their divisibility allows them to dwell in two kinds of time-space and to journey to the human world while still inhabiting their heavenly or underword dwellings, from whence, according to the Tlaxcalteca, "they send to earth all that we need through their divine influence" (Muñoz Camargo 1981: fol. 191v). One day, however, all the gods will return to the earth together and then the world will end. Meanwhile the gods operate like *naguales,* magicians who can take possession of bodies. The term *nagual* also refers to the one who undergoes such an invasion.[4] Diverse earthly forms can serve as cover for these forces. "They say that Tezcatlipoca often became a nagual in the form of a coyote." Or the cover may border on the imperceptible:

"Tezcatlipoca and Huitzilopochtli became naguales only as wind, as night," and "it was said that Titlacahuan was invisible, like night, like wind. When he called to someone, he spoke like a shadow" (Muñoz Camargo 1981: fol 178).

In a thought system where all beings have a share of divinity, nagualism was only one more form of possession. Ordinary behavior was explained by the hidden movement of forces within an organism. The average, peaceful, tranquil person carried within the fire of a protector god. This circumstance could sometimes limit the capabilities of the individual. For example violation of the rule of endogamy resulted in children with divided loyalties, rights, and powers. Two or more gods could coexist in some human beings, although not always without conflict. Tariacuri, the Tarasca chief, had political problems and difficulties in communicating with the divinity because he possessed only a part of the force of the god Curicaueri and belonged as well to his mother's god.[5]

In the ordinary course of events, a person's forces of origin would combine with those of destiny, the latter forces arriving daily in the form of time, and the combination favoring or harming the individual depending on their compatibility. It is easy to see how vulnerable a person would be when faced with something extraordinary. Anything unusual (sin, artistic inspiration, glory, madness) was attributed to momentary or permanent possession by the gods. Death was another form of possession, which converted most human beings being into slaves of the possessor (López de Gómara 1954, 2:387–88); certain other individuals, strongly possessed, became living images of the gods (López Austin 1973). "People said that when Cuerauaperi took possession of a person, she entered the person and drank the blood" (*Relación de las ceremonias y ritos . . .* 1977:234–35). Tarascans would feed the possessed person the precious fluid [blood] in order to satisfy the divine hunger. Possession was also a source of power for rulers, a divine connection. Mayan inscriptions link their rulers with the gods, dating the legitimacy of their power to a very remote past (Kubler 1974). Mexica rulers had divine names and were responsible for the stability and functioning of the world (Reyes García 1978; García Quintana 1980; Sullivan 1980). Their bodies sheltered the forces of various gods, manifested in the alternating or combined use of characteristic godly apparel and divine insignia (see Obregón Rodríguez 1985).

So far the words *force* and *god* have been used as synonyms, *force* conveying the idea of an invisible, galvanizing, strongly characterized substance that gives its nature to perceptible beings, and which struggles, is complemented, or combined with other similar substances; and *god* connoting a powerful, invisible, and personal creator.[6] The divisibility of forces, their emanations, and their power to augment and recompose themselves serve to complement and illuminate these same characteristics in the gods. Moreover the comparison makes understandable the simultaneous presence of the gods in many places and the possibility that the death of mythic characters (the creative beings) does not preclude their later existence.

All the gods are forces, but are forces gods? According to Hume (1957: 29–30), the answer lies in the personal character of the gods.

> There is a universal tendency among mankind to conceive all beings like them-
> selves, and to transfer to every object, those qualities, with which we are famil-
> iarly acquainted, and of which they are intimately conscious. We find human
> faces in the moon, armies in the clouds; and by a natural propensity, if not cor-
> rected by experience and reflection, ascribe malice or good-will to everything
> that hurts or pleases us. Hence the frequency and beauty of the *prosopopoeia* in
> poetry; where trees, mountains and streams are personified, and the inanimate
> parts of nature acquire sentiment and passion. . . . Nay, philosophers cannot
> entirely exempt themselves from this natural frailty; but have oft ascribed it
> to inanimate matter the horror of a *vacuum,* sympathies, antipathies, and other
> affections of human nature.

Mesoamericans attributed human behavior to the gods. They believed that the force of divine will entered people and became part of human will. Lust, for example, did not originate solely in one's sexual impulses; gods possessed the individual and inflamed those passions. Later, when the sinner repented, only the forces that incited the acts were able to retrieve the invading forces; the gods of sexual sin devoured their own lasciviousness. The force returned to its source.

The gods incited positive and negative passions in humans, and, like all passionate beings, they themselves had needs. They were powerful, but lim-ited, incomplete, swayed by passions and desires. The Mesoamericans saw these struggles of divine passions and needs as the movements of the cosmos. Although one source (*Códice Telleriano-Remensis* 1964–67: part 2, pl. 2) says that only Quetzalcoatl had a "human body," Mesoamerican gods were clearly anthropomorphic.

Throughout the history of the world, divinities with human similarities have ranged from the god credited with human perfection—inhuman and inexplicable precisely because of that perfection—to the extreme of the one Milan Kundera (1986:251–52) visualized as a child, complete with functional bowels, of which a human being is the image and the likeness. To say that

Mesoamerican gods were anthropomorphic leaves questions: How much so? How human were they?

The Mesoamerican gods were human enough to have idiosyncracies, individual peculiarities that made their behavior and actions predictable, limited spatially to their own territories and limited temporally to intervene in the world in their appointed turns. Human enough to love, to willfully violate human expectations, and to show by their desires that the world was not a tediously exact machine. Human enough to listen to human speech and alter their plans because of what they heard. Human enough to need gifts, worship, and suplication—and human enough to betray the giver, accepting the offering without repaying it. Human enough to be deeply loved or profoundly hated, to be loving parents or terrible parents. Human enough to be closer or more distant from human beings, depending on the degree of their kinship.

They had human shapes. According to some texts, their faces were beautiful. In one source (*Relación de las ceremonias y ritos . . .* 1977:232–33), a Tarascan woman was carried on a white eagle to the Xanoato-hucatzio mountain, where the gods of the province were meeting. She found them richly dressed, their faces blackened, "all very handsome." But other sources tell of the ugliness of the gods. The Mexica magicians sent by Motecuhzoma Ilhuicamina to the world of the gods described Huitzilopochtli's mother as an old woman with a dirty black face, the ugliest person one could portray or imagine (Durán 1984, 2:220). The first leader of the Mexica also went to the world of the gods, mounted on an eagle, and found all of them awful, frightening, resembling huge fiends, poisonous serpents, and bats (Castillo 1966:68–69, 91). It is possible that the difference has to do with the location of the encounter. The Tarascan woman traveled to an earthly site, while the Mexica chief and the magicians traveled to Culhuacan or Hueiculhuacan, also identified as Ximohuayan, the place of the dead. The mountain of the ancestors is a door of communication with the world of the fleshless, of death and darkness, which could explain the ugliness and terror of the gods in that place. Yet there may also be an inherent relationship between darkness and divinity, perhaps linked to the gods' invisibility. The Nahuatl word *teutl*, which means "god," also seems to signify "blackness" in some compound words.[7]

At any rate, the gods are usually human in form, or human in some features, even in the many instances where they are pictured in animal form. The opossum is often portrayed in a human posture (*Codice Fejérváry Mayer* 1964–67: pl. 38-7, 39-6, 40-5, 42-3, and 43-2; see fig. 10 in this work). Does this betray the presence of a nearly human god within the animal?

There are humanized gods with precise characteristics, with will, passions, names, many with a personal mythic history. But are all divinities like that? Do the forces found in trees and rivers, in fish and in stones, in herbs and in ants, also have volition and the ability to listen to humans? Sorcerers talk to water, medicine, tobacco, and fire, addressing them as persons, threatening and bargaining with them, asking for their help. The Maya physician invoked illnesses, saying to one, "It will be I who destroys your spell, younger brother of madness," and to another, "First-one-ahau, will I have to stand up to catch you, licentious spirit of birth? Have you been whirling for four days?" (*El ritual de los Bacabes* 1987:342, 363). The Nahua magician did something similar, calling water "our venerable deity of precious green stone" and addressing fire as "mother of the gods, father of the gods," fish hooks as "curved divinities," peccaries as "my uncles the priests adorned with black feathers"; fish were "people sprinkled with rubber," and tobacco was "the priest of the dark green color" (Ruiz de Alarcón 1953). These are no mere rhetorical flourishes. The magicians' words are the essence of their power over the invisible aspect of the world. The gods are inside the earthly creatures, forming their characters, their wills, their souls, causing their very motion.

Still the gods always retain their divine unity, their own character, when they guide the astral bodies as well as when they are lodged in the minuscule body of an ant. The god Huitzilopochtli sings, "Not in vain did I take the clothing of yellow feathers, because I am the one who made the Sun rise" (*Veinte himnos sacros de los nahuas* 1958:31). Even today the fiery red predawn of May and June is lit by the hand of the gods, that of Okin'ajwal, that of 'Uch (Guiteras Holmes 1965:236). This is the fire contained in the mountains, in the earth, and in the sky; this is the fire stolen by the opossum in myth. Fire is still called 'Uch, like the month, like the thief.

These are individual gods with strong personalities, but their individuality was not permanent. There is no contradiction in that. The gods merged or divided themselves, and in each union, or in each one of the divided parts, they acquire a new personality. Morley and Brainerd (1965:203) cited these examples:

> The ancient Maya conceived of some of their deities not only as single entities but as composite or multiple in character. Chac, as we have seen, was considered as a single god and at the same time as four gods. Similarly the Oxlahuntiku, or Thirteen Gods of the Upper World, although regarded collectively as a single deity, were considered as thirteen separate gods; the Bolontiku, or Nine Gods of the Lower World, were also regarded in this dual capacity.

In certain myths preserved in the Book of Chilam Balam of Chumayel, this unity and composite character of the Oxlahuntiku are clearly set forth, while in the inscriptions of the Classic stage the dual conception of the Bolontiku is repeatedly emphasized. Each of the nine Bolontiku was, in turn, the patron of a day in the Maya calendar, and it was believed that these nine gods followed each other in endless succession throughout time. Thus, if God x were patron of the first day, he would again be patron of the tenth day, the nineteenth day, etc.; and if God y were patron of the second day, he would again be patron of the eleventh, the twentieth, etc.

Other examples are closer at hand. Each day, at the most basic level, is a combination of at least two different forces, that of a numeral and that of its name. Thus the day 9-*cauac* will have the attributes of the number nine on the one hand, and of rain and thunder on the other. Together these refer to the installation of the underworld (*Libro de Chilam Balam de Chumayel* 1973:99), the nine levels of the humid region of the dead, where rain originates. P. Carrasco (1976b) says that each sign in the ancient Nahua calendar had a specific characteristic, related to its namesake; numerals also had corresponding qualities, seven being related to vegetable foods, nine to sorcerers, and one to favorable beginnings. The force of a day is not merely a god, but a compound god, as students of the Maya have insisted.

There is also explicit reference to the fusion of the quadruple gods distributed to the four corners of the world and often considered to be a single deity (J. Thompson 1975:248).[8] In Durán's description of the festival of the month of Tlacaxipehualiztli, four men were clad in the skins of sacrificial victims, each representing a god, one for each of the four directions. Each of the four was tied to the other dancers, and pulled them toward the part of the world corresponding to him. After this dance,

> in order to point out that all was one force and one union, all these gods joined each other as one, and they tied the right foot of one to the left foot of the other, binding their legs up to the knee, and, each one bound to the other in that way, they walked around all day, supporting each other. With this, as I have said, they gave to understand their equality and their conformity and indicated their power and unity. (Durán 1984, 1:97)

The ultimate fusion occurs in the supreme god. It is more appropriate to call him the only god, the union of all the gods. There was a definite trend in Mesoamerica toward the idea of a being in whom all the divine faculties and powers met. This is the Hunab Ku of the Maya, described by López Cogolludo (1957, 1:204).

> The Indians of Yucatan believed that there was a single, living, and true god, who was said to be the greatest of all the gods, who had no face nor figure because he was incorporeal. They called him Hunab Ku. . . . All things were said to come from him, and, since he was incorporeal, they worshipped no image of him, nor did they have one.

Morley and Brainerd (1965:188) analyzed the name Hunab Ku as *hun*, "one"; *ab*, "to exist"; and *ku*, "god." Perhaps this was the great creator of the sky and the earth to which the accounts of the city of Merida refer (*Relaciones histórico-geográficas* . . . 1983, 1:72). This is the Coqui Zee or Coquixilla of the Zapotec, the one "without beginning or end," also called Pijetao, "the great time," or Pixe Xoo, "the fountain of time" (Whitecotton 1985:189).[9] Among the ancient Nahua names of this creator were Tloque Nahuaque, Icnopiltzin, Moche, Moquequeloatzin, Titlacahuan, Ometeotl, and Moyocoyani. In this being, the Arbitrary One,[10] all limited individual divine volitions meet, free of conditions and limitations.

The supreme god is the ultimate concentration of power. Concentration of power was also the concept underlying the Mesoamerican process of expansion and centralization, which may have provided the model for the idea of the concentration of divine force (López Austin 1983).[11] The unification and subdivision of the domains of the gods (López Austin 1979) may have been caused by an increasing social complexity. The subdivision of the groups in society produced the division of the patron god into different aspects, each becoming in itself a patron god. Quetzalcoatl among other attributes was Lord of the Wind and Lord of the Dawn. The tendency to subdivide and multiply the gods is not incompatible with the concept of one comprehensive god. They are complementary features of a society which is experiencing, at the same time, increasing societal complexity and the concentration of power.

Forces and processes can present different aspects, and each aspect is the source of a personality. Take the case of the four gods of the horizontal plane. In Yucatan each one of the four columns of the world was called a *bacab* as one who held up the sky, a *chaac* as lord of rain, a *pauauhtun* as wind god, and a *balam* as protector of the cornfield. López Cogolludo (1957, 1:187) tells us, "They imagined other gods supporting the sky. Their names were Zacal Bacab, Canal Bacab, Chacal Bacab and Ekel Bacab, and they said that these were also gods of the winds." In an invocation recorded by Ruiz de Alarcón (1953:80), it is clear that the four pillars of the world and the four rain gods are the same. "You the priests, you the *tlaloque,* who were placed on the four sides, who are positioned on the four sides: you who hold up the world." Other sources refering to this common identity include the history of Alvarado Tezozómoc (1944:59, 260), which says that the *tzitzimime* are the supports of the sky and also the gods of the air, rain, and lightning.

In the sources these supporting gods are portrayed both collectively and individually. As a unit they sometimes acquire a particular set of attributes, or its opposite. One must remember that they have within them contrary forces, from both heaven and the underworld, either of which can characterize them from different standpoints. As gods of the cold forces, as lords of rain, the four are integrated into the god Nappatecuhtli, "Lord of the four places" (Sahagún 1956, 1:70), but the cold forces must alternate with the hot ones, within the four columns, to begin the flow of time. As a fusion of the four gods of a hot nature they show another face, that of Nauhyotecatl, "He of the four places," or Nauhyotecuhtli, "Lord of the Union of the Four" (Sahagún 1956, 3:23; Serna 1953:65).[12] Any of these three very similar names can designate the god who is a combination of the four columns. Nappatecuhtli refers particularly to the cold nature and Nauhyotecuhtli and Nauhyotecatl to the hot one.

The gods can be dissected because they are composites. The lunar deities, for example, are water, femininity, earth, sky, light, pulque, etc., and the same is true of the supreme god who, as such, could be called by the names of various aspects, such as Moche (lord of all that exists) or Titlacahuan (lord of human beings). Prayers to the supreme god could be addressed to the divine offspring, among them the divine sons Tezcatlipoca, the Lord of Fate, or Quetzalcoatl, the Creator, because these were considered facets of the comprehensive supreme power. "A theist religion is not necessarily monotheistic or polytheistic. It can be both" (Evans-Pritchard 1974:316).

The Mesoamerican gods were not thought to be static beings. They were considered to be dynamic, engaged in cyclic processes in which time and space generated their diverse personifications and traits (López Austin 1979). J. Thompson (1970a:199) says that Mayan gods

were indiscriminately marshaled in large categories so that a god could belong to two diametrically opposed groups. The sun god, for instance, was primarily a sky god, but because he passes at night through the underworld on his eastward journey from point of sunset to point of sunrise he became one of the nine lords of the night and underworld.

The ancient Nahua imagined similar divine cyclic fusions. The name of Tlahuizcalpantecuhtli, belonging to Quetzalcoatl as god of dawn (*Anales de*

Cuauhtitlán 1945:11), was also given to Xiuhtecuhtli, lord of fire (Ruiz de Alarcón 1953:127). The Lord of Dawn was a temporary fusion of both gods; both the day represented by Quetzalcoatl and the fire represented by Xiuhtecuhtli were symbolized by the light of dawn. Quetzalcoatl was changed into fire when it was dawn; Xiuhtecuhtli was converted into dawn in the east. Cuezalin was one name of the Fire God (*Códice Florentino* 1979: bk. 1, fol. 10v), but the God of the Dead was also called Cuezalin (*Códice Florentino* 1979: bk. 6, fol. 15v). The explanation is that the fire in the underworld consumed the dead astral gods so that they could surge forth anew in the east, wrapped in fire. Cuezalin is the God of Fire who descends in his cycles to the underworld. Tonatiuh, the Sun God, has the face of Tlaloc when he disappears in the west (*Códice Borbonico* 1979: pl. 16; *Tonalámatl de Aubin* 1981: pl. 16; and *Códice Telleriano-Remensis* 1964–67: pl. 25), because at the same time that he is the sun, he is already dead. He is, like Tlaloc, on the verge of being an inhabitant of the underworld. In both cases the transformation is clearly set forth in the source. Tezcatlipoca became Mixcoatl to make the fire for the festival of the gods (*Historia de los mexicanos por sus pinturas* 1965:33). In short the gods are not only transformed along their cyclic paths, they also merge with other gods along the way.

This interplay of changes, attributes, fusions, and separations does have its own codes. One is iconographic. Specific garments and attributes in the portraits place the gods at a given moment of power, at one point on their path (López Austin 1979). Rivera Dorado (1985:176–77), referring to the Mayan gods, says,

> We perceive the Mayan gods as kaleidoscopic, in perpetual mutation. Hundreds of names, faces and attributes produce various diffuse images and an inevitable sense of pantheism. But all the particular appearances of the gods, their different icons and functions, are the result of a closely woven web of associations, where real essential disparities are to be found. In other words, a few gods, subject to cosmic influences and to the predestined transformations, are in charge of a multitude of tasks and, for each one of them, they have different forms, apparel, titles and special names. . . . In pictographic representations, any detail can have meaning. This is true of the position of the body or its members, a gesture, facial features, ornaments, and colors. In general such details portray the psychological character of the personage. They place him in the structure of the universe and express the details of things related to his nature and activities.

Very diverse kinds of actions were and are attributed to these strong, specific forces, which can merge or separate to form their own personalities. The gods are multifunctional, and therefore can be classified as ancestors, dueños, patrons, celestial gods, creators, forces concealed in earthly beings, powers of nature, times, rulers of the dead.[13] But we must not be misled into thinking that these special functions imply the separation of divine persons. The gods cross levels, characterizing the different regions of the cosmos in a myriad of functions; but they are still the same gods.

Gods are forms of being, perceived in multiple manifestations. For example Tlaloc created the Moon (*Historia de los mexicanos por sus pinturas* 1965:35), water, and rain (*Historia de México* 1965:105). He was also one of the four cosmogonic suns that preceded the present one, and he participated in the creation of the Sun and the Moon in Teotihuacan, ordering Naui Tecpatl to cast himself into the fire in which he and Nanahuatl were transformed (*Leyenda de los soles* 1945:121–22). In the structure of the universe, he appears as a column separating the earth from the heavens. He was the giver of rain, the god of vegetation. He was the invisible part of illnesses that the sorcerer attacked with his invocations (Ruiz de Alarcón 1953:113). Based on the rite in which Tlaloc's image, which was made of seeds, was crumbled, the squash teeth and large bean eyes being saved for the next year's sowing, we can infer the existence of a myth in which Tlaloc was a dema divinity (Serna 1953:191–92). Tlaloc came to earth as a time force on the days called *quiahuitl* "rain." He was the celestial god, lord of the eighth heaven (*Historia de México* 1965:103), and he was the eighth of the thirteen gods of the days (Paso y Troncoso 1979:66). He was also one of the nine lords of the night. He was the god of the underworld (*Historia de los mexicanos por sus pinturas* 1965:30), and he has kept that office right up to the present, in his image of Chane, lord of the mountain, chief of the dead, owner of subterranean riches and of wild animals. In ancient times he was Tlaloctepetl, the god of the mountain, where he appeared to his worshippers (Relaciones de Xonotla y Tetela 1985). Sources name him as guardian of the cornfields (Ponce 1953:375). He was the patron god of the inhabitants of the Yopico district in Tenochtitlan (Monzón 1949:50). He was supposed to have been a man, a governor (made divine) of the giants, or *quinametin* (Alva Ixtlilxóchitl 1975–77a:273).[14] The list of his functions could be lengthened. To summarize, Tlaloc has participated in nearly every kind of activity attributed to the gods, and in this he is not unique. A similar list of attributes could be developed for other ancient and contemporary gods.

The attitudes and behavior of believers toward the gods also vary, according to the intensity of the force, opportunity, or circumstance. The faithful believe themselves to be burdened with invisible souls in an environment filled with the supernatural. Their usual behavior is appropriate to those who count upon and are accustomed to the presence of the gods. They must be acquainted with the gods in order to operate in this world, because everything that is perceptible obtains its characteristics from the imperceptible. They must not forget that the gods are terrible, neither must they forget their obligations. They are accustomed to living amidst the terrible, with the confidence that compliance with their precepts gives them. They know that the gods are perpetually hungry, and that humans are obliged to feed them. Tepeu and Gucumatz, the Progenitors, the Creators and Builders, said, "The time for dawn has arrived, the time for ending the task and for the appearance of those who must sustain and nourish us, the enlightened sons, the civilized vassals. Let mankind appear, let humanity appear on the face of the earth" (*Popol vuh* 1964:103). When Toscano (1952:6–8) was studying Mesoamerican art, alongside the categories of the *sublime,* the *beautiful,* and the *baroque,* he identified the *terrible.* Perhaps after more than four decades his categories need revision, but there is an echo when we examine the powerful indigenous gods. They are terrible, but one may try to avoid the strong concentration of the divine, to evade the dangers, to ingratiate the gods, to bribe them, and even to fool them. Above all one must learn about the forces found in each earthly being, because dominance of the world depends upon knowledge of the invisible. If the concentration is harmless, human action upon the perceptible aspect of beings is sufficient. If the concentration increases and danger is present, it may yet be possible to make a personal deal—to negotiate with the invisible. Those whose knowledge or courage are not sufficient may go to the specialist who is so strong, so pure, so wise, and so fearless as to be able to establish the dangerous dialogue.

Exchange characterizes relationships with the gods. They are paid for harvests, health, and rain. People also pay them for the damage done by sullying them with trash and debris.[15] The repayment is made with ritual, with offerings, with recognition. "When Our Father still walked the earth," the Tzotzil say, "he talked to the earth gods. He told them they could not make it rain without talking to him first, so that he could punish the people if they did not 'want' the rain enough" (Gossen 1974:330).[16] So it is today. Just as the mention of *paga* is common nowadays, so it was in the past. Among the Mexica, many of the individuals destined for sacrifice were called *nextlahualtin,* "payments."

Ritual is the proper way to receive the gods in their own time and circumstance. A festival is not merely a remembrance of the origin of time, nor is it merely a commemoration. The action is needed to accommodate the impending divine arrival. People collaborate with the god, the ritual harmonizing with the patterned action of the god. The action of the god is also regulated, and that is known. The believer must await the festival under the specific conditions required by the force that is arriving. Sexual abstinence and fasting can be the sources of animistic strength. At some festivals people ate only once a day, using no chili or salt. At others it was forbidden to bathe, or the faithful kept a vigil, bled themselves, or sang and danced for the gods, with the gods, or as the gods themselves.

Payment is made with the ritual, and requests are made. Ritual aids and feeds the every-hungry gods. Omission is an offense that will be avenged. Incomplete preparation for a ritual places believers in a weak position, where they risk dangerous contact with the forces that they may not have the strength to face. The festival is the culmination of the dialogue or the interchange.

Ritual requires a knowledge of the regularity of the gods. That regularity permits humans to investigate the supernatural. Since ancient times the Mesoamerican has attempted to penetrate the mystery of the cycles, and has followed two complementary paths in order to predict divine behavior: the first, mathematical and astronomical; and the second, the recording of historical experience. On the latter path, the Maya of the Postclassic period composed their records of the "Wars of the Katuns." Then came the search for concrete examples. Evidence may be found that things that are analogous move under the same influences: the position of kernels of grain on a cloth or under water resembles the location of the souls of the patient inside the body; the contortions of a decapitated quail, while agonizing, indicate the location of the invisible ones. Evidence may also come as a vision seen during a journey, a message brought by someone transcending the limits of this world to arrive at the place of ever-present time.

Today the gift of a penetrating vision is attributed to those who hold high office, or to those near to the deities (Gossen 1974:38). These individuals can operate upon the invisible on behalf of the rest of the people. The vision acquired through power and knowledge enable the specialist to act on the terrain of the imperceptible. Magical action is not a symbolic act. Sorcerers work on the invisible substances of things using their invisible and well-developed animistic bodies (*tonalli*, their own forces or "movable souls"). The substance to be transformed can be taken from its surroundings, since there is a communion between a substance and all its scattered parts. Whoever works on one part can influence—to a greater or lesser degree—the totality, even if the totality is distributed in an unequal way around the world and beyond. Everything depends on the suitability, the intensity, and the direction of the magical action.

Magic is a dual game, played on two parallel levels, those of the perceptible and of the imperceptible. On the second level there is a dialogue with persons, because imperceptible persons operate within every perceptible thing. In the seventeenth century, a Nahuatl midwife would invoke the tobacco used to combat illnesses, calling it "the one beaten against the stones in the nine places." [17] The midwife would also speak to the divinities of birth (Cuaton and Caxxoch), [18] and to the fingers of her own hands, which in the magical process would be independent from her, beings capable of autonomous movement ("masters of the five destinies and of a single patio"). The midwife was looking for the supernatural person who was causing the pangs of childbirth, and she asked for help from her bowl ("precious jar") and water ("my mother of the jade skirt") to bathe the newborn. Here is the invocation:

> Oh! Come, you who are beaten against the stones of the
>   nine places,
> you who are whipped at the nine places.
> Yes! Come to open the canal,
> you, Cuaton, you Caxxoch.
> Yes! Allow yourselves to come, priests,
> lords of the five destinies,
> lords of a single patio.
> Let us discover who is the person
> that here harms the son of the gods.
> Deign to come my precious bowl
> [and] my mother, she of the jade skirt.
> Here you will bathe, here you will cleanse
> the one who was born in your hand,
> the one who lived in your hand. [19]

And if the birth was difficult, and the midwife had to use the opossum's tail to hasten it, she acted in a parallel fashion on two levels. She used the opossum's tail as a powerful medicine, but she spoke of its curative power as a person, as the "black priest," and uttered this variation on the preceding invocation:

> Oh! deign to come,
> black priest,
> Please come to draw out the infant.
> The creature of the gods now needs your help.
>   (López Austin 1972)

13 ORDER

That horn of plenty, with its three syllables,
with its accented **e** that sounds like a cock or a trumpet
proclaiming dawn, that sonorous word *Me-xi-co*
does not ring out for ordinary folk. It has been remodeled.
It does not include workers, who are its enemies,
the Huichilobos in overalls who threaten
the Quetzalcoatl-like opulence of its domes.

José Joaquín Blanco,
Función de media noche

Alexis de Tocqueville, with his gift of theodicy, reflected on the great defect of human thought, which sees a need to postulate general ideas about beings who differ so much that they cannot be measured by the same yardstick, and he made this comparison:

> The Deity does not regard the human race collectively. He surveys at one glance and severally all the beings of whom mankind is composed; and he discerns in each man the resemblances that assimilate him to all his fellows, and the differences that distinguish him from them. God, therefore, stands in no need of general ideas; that is to say, he never feels the necessity of collecting a considerable number of analogous objects under the same form for greater convenience of thinking. (1945, 2:13)

Here the problems will be limited to human thinking. Even so, there is much to be discussed. Humanity, that complicated producer of classes, fills the universe with compartments so it can extend its arms and legs over the surface of the earth it inhabits. It has done so, with the aid of myth, for thousands of years. Durkheim and Mauss (1971) pointed out that, "Basically every mythology is a classification which draws its principles from religious beliefs and not from scientific notions." Both writers also attribute a global organization to mythology: "Well-organized pantheons divide up all of nature." Durkheim and Mauss found their examples in India, where things are divided, along with the gods, among heaven, atmosphere, and earth; and in China, where everything is distributed according to the fundamental principles of yang and yin. If mythology and the basic principles of classifying the world are united in this way, then we would have to accept, along with Tylor, that behind the animation of all natural beings there is more than just freedom of the imagination. Tylor (1977:271) tells us that, "the basis upon which such ideas are erected cannot be ascribed to mere poetic fancy transformed into metaphor. Such ideas rest on an ample philosophy of nature, primitive and elemental, of course, but also reflexive, consistent, and endowed with a completely real and serious meaning."

The study of myth leads us to the ordering of the world. For this work we need to find the broadest taxonomic principles of the Mesoamericans and compare them with those that exist in today's indigenous groups. Important taxonomic themes of this tradition have been studied. In 1886 Paso y Troncoso's incomplete "Estudios sobre la historia de la medicina en México" appeared. A small part of it was devoted to Mexica names and the taxonomy of plants in general. In spite of its brevity, this important work has been fundamental to research efforts in our own time. Among these are two excellent works by Ortiz de Montellano (1976, 1984) based on that nomenclature, which include the classification of plants as well as of animals. In the Maya area, the now classic works of Roys (1931); Berlin, Breedlove and Raven (1974); and of Barrera Marín, Barrera Vásquez, and López Franco (1976) are outstanding.[1] Along with these specialized studies on taxonomy, there have been a number of more general ethnographic studies dealing with the subject of universal classification; and some basic principles for the divisions have been discovered.[2] Among the works on native medicine of ancient as well as modern times, there is an old controversy about the division of medicines into hot and cold; some writers attribute it to the European conquerors, while another contingent considers it to have preceded the arrival of white people on this continent.[3] However, there is still no work that includes the entire panorama of Mesoamerican taxonomy, its continuity, and the transformation of its principles. Such a work would not be simple, but an overall review of the classifications would lead to a considerable advance in the study of indigenous thought, and no doubt our concepts of myth would be enriched. While waiting for someone to undertake such a work, let us look at some aspects of the link between order and mythology in this tradition.

It should be understood that by classification we mean the operation by which humans logically consolidate groups of beings in which they think they perceive some affinity. Each class, or group, is defined according to the function of some characteristic attributed to members of that group. The criteria for the classification vary, making it possible for a being to be a member of different classes, according to the different canons of classification.

Grouping is one of the bases of human thinking (weak and inept in Tocqueville's opinion). An individualized perception of every detail around us would drown us in a chaos of detail. It is not even conceivable, because perception itself is an interpretation and classification.[4] Mentally we cannot act any other way; by mental grouping we organize the world. No act of volition is possible without ordering the relationships that exist in society or nature, even though it may be an order founded upon fictitious bases. As Lévi-Strauss tells us (1966:15), "Any classification is superior to chaos and even a classification at the level of sensible properties is a step towards a rational ordering." Classification leads to economy of thought and allows us to act in society and in nature. This includes the nonscientific forms of classification that mix both nature and society. According to Leach (1970:34), one of the merits of Lévi-Strauss is his popularization of the subject of totemism as a form of classification of social phenomena by means of categories derived from a nonsocial field. Not only is order imposed on the outside world and information accumulated through this classification, but order is imposed on the society of the classifiers themselves. Verbal classifications efficiently impose order on human society and on natural surroundings alike, using the same regulating principle (Leach 1970:37–39). This principle of efficiency in symbolic classifications is emphasized by Needham (1979:60), who maintains that in each particular culture a great number of symbolically classified beings are subsumed in a very restricted number of symbolic categories. However, these categories are flexible enough to permit people to dialectically produce and transform their reality. As Godelier (1984: 21) says, they form the basis of that ideal point where the three functions of thought are exercised and combined: presenting, organizing, and legitimizing the relationships among people themselves and between them and nature. They are mental realities that society changes and interprets through the course of its history. Their firmness channels action, and their flexibility and frequent ambiguity guarantee their survival. Between concrete action and the ideal basis of classification lies a wide range of interrelations.

One of the great benefits of order is that it leads to the discovery of the mysteries of the cosmos. The principle is simple: if A, B, C, and D have the characteristic X in common and through it form a class; and if A, B, and C, moreover, share the characteristic Y, it is quite probable that D also possesses characteristic Y. This does not mean that it is a necessary inference, but it is a plausible one. This is true whether it be the periodic table of elements, the anatomical features of marine birds, or the actions of people at a subway station. Based on this assumption, humans discover a great deal that is real and construct what is imaginary, giving to their nonreal creations a significant amount of order, agreement, regularity, and congruency. The importance of this guide to daily life makes one doubt the relevance of the frequent debate on the practical or speculative purposes of classifications. Is the opposition between the practical and the speculative valid in this field? If the order of the cosmos includes all that the cosmos is for humankind, and if global knowledge provides the bases for action upon matter, what can be considered superfluous in knowledge?

When classifications are not scientific, they leave a wide margin for speculation and adjustment. This is partly due to the freedom that allows the same object to be placed in different classes, and to the fact that each class allows a wide range of possible inferences by analogy, easily reached when there is insufficient control. Classifiers can find the characteristics they believe advantageous to their conjectures, or even to their hidden desires, thus ordering and making their surroundings congruent, even though this may be far from reality. They will also be in a position to tie in parallelisms in society and in nature, in order to achieve a global synthesis. This procedure not only splits nature into compartments, but causes each one to reflect the pyramids of hierarchical organization.

Hierarchy is one of the principles of mythological classification. In the Mesoamerican tradition we often find one individual raised above others of its species, or one group among similar groups that is considered to be superior. Recall the Tzeltal belief of a person's having several animal companions but only one "true" one, whose demise will cause the person's death (Hermitte 1970:44–45). The highland Nahua have a similar belief. A person has more than one *tonal;* but the person's strength and personality depend on the ruling tonal, the *teyacanque,* and the other souls only "follow along" (Signorini and Lupo 1988). This is very similar to the hierarchy of daily destinies in the ancient tables of thirteen days. Each period of thirteen was composed of thirteen compound gods, one for each day, but the first one had influence over all the others. The ancient Nahua believed that one species predominated over all the others of its class (the pelican, for example, over all lake birds; the jaguar over other wild animals), and they were given the titles used for political dignitaries: *tecpilli, tlazopilli, pilli, tlatoani, achcauhtli* . . . (*Códice Florentino* 1979: bk. 11, fol. 1v, 28v). Or an individual is considered to be the chief, the father. It can be a deer among deer (Lumholtz 1970, 1:302), a fish crowned among fish (P. Carrasco 1976a:122), an eagle among eagles, or Takawiru among the buzzards (Giddings 1959:68). It can be the most beloved of (the closest to) the God of the Mountain and the Lord of the Animals. Was this hierarchical order a projection of a system of kinship or of government, in which an individual stood out whose lineage was taken to be the closest to, the most like that of the divine ancestor? We find strong parallels between the social and natural classifications. It is significant that animals were given titles from the political arena.

The classes in nature and in society are filled, are organized, and are reciprocally ranked by a process that is affected by aesthetics. In all comparisons there is a hidden and mysterious harmony, originating in a play of metaphor. In some cases there are two groups that concur in a parallel, open way, as the number of pairs increases through the intent to accumulate similarities. In other cases, by contrast, the membership in at least one group is circumscribed from the beginning, and a total correspondence is attempted with the kindred group. What is important here is to close and to complete both complementary groups in an exact correlation. The Arabs give us a beautiful example of the first case. The different parts of the horse, created by Allah from a handful of wind, have the names of birds: red owl is the top of the skull; eagle, the cleft in the hoof; ostrich, the skin on the head; pigeon, the brain; magpies, the two veins under the tongue; sparrow, the bony structure at the base of the forelock; rooster, the bones standing out behind the ear . . . and the list goes on (Hudayl 1977:45, 79–81, 161). For the second case, one can cite the story about poor Sisinia, a young Castilian girl who was murdered while defending her virginity from a stranger. Each spring neighbors in the town brought flowers from the fields to the site of the murder, and soon the priest found a meaning for each one of the flowers: white daisies represented Sisinia's purity; red poppies, her cruel sacrifice; mallows, the young girl's death. But when he came to the yellow lantana, he was stymied until he found that the yellow color signified the gold Sisinia had rejected rather than be defiled. Delibes (1980:55–56) says, however, that "the townspeople greatly doubted that the rustic from Avila had offered gold to Sisinia. They were convinced he was a poverty-stricken, mentally disturbed youth who didn't have a place to lay his head." At any rate a little poetic license allowed the metaphoric analogy to be completed.

Comparisons vary considerably in the Mesoamerican tradition. There are cases where the members that form a group are enriched by a wide array of images. Among the Zoque the human body becomes a jocular, heterogeneous collection. The skull is a bowl; dimples in the cheeks are snail shells; the shoulder joints are wings; the penis is a bird; and the testicles, eggs. The vaginal canal is a path; the bile sac is green chili; the liver is a pad of the prickly pear cactus; the heart is a red tomato; the lungs are a forge; kneecaps are two chocolate balls; the head of the femur contains two onions; the nerve branches are hammocks; etc. (Reyes Gómez 1988). A comparison can also be made between two groups. In such a case the gasoline motor of a corn mill will have the air filter as its nose; the carburetor as its heart; its stomach is in the tank; gasoline, oil, water, and air will be its food; the gasoline pump will be its lungs; and the fan belt will be its intestines (Jäcklein 1970:288).

The comparisons often have a festive air, especially when the subject of sex is involved. The Mocho (Petrich 1985:196) say, "The penis is a chili, because either one warms the body." But researchers must be cautious about accepting the apparent simplicity or keenness of the play on words; they may be facing one facet of an important complex in the intellectual perception of the universe. In the south of the Huaxteca, as in the rest of the country, chili is a synonym for penis. Galinier (1987:361) tells us that among the Otomi of that region, "Chili stands for strength, virility, the masculine element, dryness, and warmth." In antiquity, heat, masculinity, and dryness were attributed to Heaven, as opposed to the coldness, femininity, and humidity of the Earth. The Otomi pair off chili with the *chayote* [*Sechium edule*], as a feminine fruit. No doubt the comparison is due to its cleft, spherical shape and its covering of long, soft bristles, but for the Otomi the chayote is also *samu,* "the cool, fresh fruit," and the name reminds them of its soft, damp flesh. Galinier (1987:361) sums up the meaning given to chili and chayote in the following: "Their union symbolized cosmic fertility."

This is only one aspect of a distant, total concept, in which the complementary distinction between masculine work under the open sky and feminine work under the shelter of the hut was also possible. Nowadays as in ancient times, a farmer plunges the planting stick (as if it were a phallus) into the soil of the cornfield, imagined to be the earth's great vulva, adorned with the hairy fuzz of the grass that covers it (Taggart 1983:59).

Thus the metaphors can refer to a more profound order, whose existence is reflected in the strength of the image:

> Here is Mani, the base of the land. Campeche is the tip of the wing of the country. Calkini is the base of the wing of the land. Itzmal is the middle of the wing of the land. Zaci is the tip of the wing of the land. Conkal is the head of the land. In the middle of it is the city of Hoó, the cathedral, the house of everybody, the house of good, the house of night, which belongs to God the Father, God the Son, and God the Holy Ghost. (*Libro de Chilam Balam de Chumayel* 1973:114)

Some apparently simple comparisons reveal, in their constant repetition, links that perhaps someday will be explained by myth. In ancient times there was an omen bird whose calls *huac, huac!* or *yeccan, yeccan!* were taken to mean, respectively, "dry, dry!" or "good weather, good weather!" (Sahagún

1956, 2:16–18, 3:251; *Augurios y abusiones* 1969:22–27, 174–76). It has been identified by Martín del Campo (1940) as the laughing falcon [*Herpetotheres cachinnans*], well known for its propensity to feed on snakes. According to F. Hernández (1959, 2:330), its bones were used as a remedy for the pain caused in any part of the body by torn flesh; and the fumes from its burned feathers restored sanity to persons deranged by severe illness. The nature of its healing powers encourages a search for the deeper meanings of myth. In fact the pair falcon/serpent appears in a present-day myth among the Mazatec, where the *vaquero* ("cowboy") was created to free the world from snakes:

> At that time [of darkness], the snake was not poisonous. Everyone teased [humiliated] it. Then Saint George and Saint Ignace, who is the snake's patron saint, complained to the Holy Father, and the Holy Father gave saliva to the snake, so that it would be respected. The saliva became poison. Snakes became dangerous to human beings. Then the cowboy [a falcon] appeared, which kills snakes and cries out as he kills. If it were not for this kind of falcon, there would be all kinds of snakes. And this is the reason snakes come out only at night. (Boege 1988:102)

Nahua texts of the seventeenth century also mention the pair and speak of their healing magic. The name of *huactli* was given to the needle used for curative punctures, and its opposite, the serpent, was intestinal pain (Ruiz de Alarcón 1953:54, Serna 1953:88, 219–20). Puncture and exorcism mimic the struggle between the falcon and the serpent. Today the Huichol repeat the play of the falcon and the serpent in a different context. Tobacco (*yé*) was a falcon in the other time, while the serpent was a gourd [*Lagenaria leucantha*] receptacle (*kwé*) (P. Furst 1972c). The union of tobacco with its receptacle (*yekwé*) brings both elements together in battle. This image may provide an interesting link if we recall that tobacco and its container had an important symbolic meaning among the ancient Nahua. Merchants in their feasts gave their guests the tobacco pipe with their right hand and the tobacco container with their left hand, and they were received in the same order, because the tobacco pipe represented a spear-thrower, while the vessel symbolized the shield (*Códice Florentino* 1979: bk. 11, fol. 28). All of this suggests the following opposed groups: on the one hand, *falcon–needle against pain–tobacco–spear-thrower,* and on the other, the complements, *serpent–stomachache–tobacco container–shield.* And one detects as a superior pair in this play of opposites that of *dry season/ rainy season.*

Today the following stand out as comparable groups: the human body, the house, the corn plant, the temple, the town, the cornfield, the face of the earth, and the cosmos.[5] One of the groups provides names and images from its component elements; with these the elements of the receiver take on new meaning. There is a sustaining group and a group sustained. The characteristics of sustaining and sustained are interchangeable, although some groups predominate as donors. The structure of the earth's surface, for example, is the basis for the cornfield, the house, the town, and the temple, through which the four corners and the center acquire particular values (Münch Galindo 1983: 229).[6] The house, on the other hand, is a receiver that, enriched with meanings, fills daily life with sanctity. It can be a vaginal canal, a chapel, a grotto, or the sky (Galinier 1987:103–5). A house can be a microcosm of the universe and connect the names of constellations to different constituent features of the roof (Ichon 1973:116–17, 293). It can repeat the processes of the machinery of the universe, at whose center will be the surface of the earth like a *comal* (a ceramic griddle). The south projects upward and the north downward (toward the fire that cooks). The production of corn under the sun is paired with that of the tortillas made of its dough over the fire of the comal. The comal will be supported by three stones, the *tenamas,* which are God the Father, God the Son, and God the Holy Ghost (Lok 1987).

The pairs of comparisons are not limited to static mappings. Resemblance is also sought among processes, or occasionally it arises through imitation or ritual. The growth cycle of corn is reflected in a person's life. The Mocho "sow" people or "make them take root" in a sacred cornfield, the "sowing place," or *poomibal* (García-Ruiz 1982).[7] In this field a cross is planted for every member of the family. Petrich (1985:139–40) tells us that when a child is barely six or seven months old, its cross is planted in the cornfield, on a Thursday, so that its existence on earth may be established among its own kin, and that it may be accepted and protected by Mother Earth.

In every comparison there is a group that receives from another a basis that enriches its meaning and reorders its parts. But we must remember that the characteristics of sustaining group and sustained group can be interchangeable. If the principal beam in the roof of a house is the "Serpent Above" constellation, the universe, like a house, has four supporting columns. In the first case, the concepts of universal order are the sustainers; in the second, they are supported by the concepts of a dwelling. If a man has a gray beard like *ixtle* fiber, the maguey plant from which it comes has arms and a rump. The Zoque call the human body *ye'n gujy,* "top of the tree"; but in exchange, the Zoque call the whiteness of the tree, "muscles," and the thorns, "eyelashes" (Reyes Gómez 1988:207–8). People called their heads "heaven,"[8] but also called the center of the world its navel. There was a generalized isomorphism by which people discovered the secrets of the universe. Isomorphism implies reciprocity.

The possibility of the exchange of characteristics between the sustainer and the sustained does not indicate, however, that the two groups are equal. Because of this the question of superior levels of classification must be raised. Is there a level that organizes things in an exclusive way, or one approaching exclusiveness? What is this ordaining level? Durkheim and Mauss (1971:72) placed the center of the first systems of nature in society and spoke of the centrality of society. They were very clear about eliminating the individual as the center, in accordance with the Durkheimian postulate that "the determining cause of a social fact must be sought in antecedent social facts and not in states of individual consciousness" (Durkheim 1973:89). For these writers the prototypes of the classifications were phratries, clans, and lineages; in short, the basic types of social organization. Boas (1968:451–90) asked why animals, astral bodies, and natural phenomena appeared as characters and the central motifs of stories and myths. As heroes of popular narrations, animals and astral bodies are converted into prototypes, by which groups in nature, and especially in the animal kingdom, acquired important organizing characteristics. Lévi-Strauss (1965, 1970:47–50), while recognizing his debt to the thesis proposed by Radcliffe-Brown,[9] considered totemism to be a code that allowed for the expression of the isomorphic elements between nature and culture, through which the "logical properties" of vegetable and animal species are revealed; that is, their symbolic potential. But there is a fundamental difference between Lévi-Strauss's concept and those of his predecessors. He does not believe in a superior level of classification.

> The mistake which the upholders of totemism made was arbitrarily to isolate one level of classification, namely that constituted by reference to natural species, and to give it the status of an institution, when like all levels of classification it is in fact only one among others and there is no reason to regard it as more important than, say, the level operating by means of abstract categories or that using nominal classes. What is significant is not so much the presence— or absence—of this or that level of classification as the existence of a classification with, as it were, an adjustable thread which gives the group adopting it the means of 'focusing' on all planes, from the most abstract to the most concrete, the most cultural to the most natural, without changing its intellectual instrument. (Lévy-Strauss 1966:135–36)

All of the above allows the formulation of four conclusions regarding the different values, as sustainers and sustained, that the different levels and groups of classification have in our mythological tradition:

1.   Prototypes have existed in this tradition that imply a hierarchy, at the

top of which was placed the individual or the class nearest to the creator, a true archetype.

2.   Neither the historical nor the ethnographic material reveals a superior group (that is, a nearly exclusive one) as a sustainer of the classifications, with its structure, its nomenclature, or the characterization of its members. There have been important classification groups serving as sustainers of others. P. Carrasco (1976b) notes that Seler and his students used astral symbolism as a key to understanding the pantheon, the myths, and the beliefs in Meso-american cultures. His opinion is that although Seler exaggerated, there is no doubt that such astral ideas were an essential part of the ancient religious mentality. The cosmic mechanism was one of the most important sustaining groups, and in spite of changes in indigenous concepts of heavenly bodies, the astral level retains considerable influence. This does not, however, make it a privileged level.

3.   The importance of sustaining groups changes over the course of history. One sustaining group of outstanding importance in antiquity was the calendric system. Classes of divine and earthly beings were formed from its combinations. Now the native calendar is disappearing; there is no system to replace it. Today, given the heterogeneity of the indigenous world, one can speak of structuring patterns only in general terms, such as the quincunx of the surface of the earth as related to the concept of the house, temple, cornfield, and village.

4.   Durkheim and Mauss identified the value of the social in its capacity as a sustainer of the bases for classifying. Historically the process can also be the reverse. The importance of an area of relationships does not necessarily turn its conceptual groups into great sustainers. To the contrary, it can make them great receivers of support, since there is a reason to keep and strengthen them. Take, for example, a very asymmetrical institution. Its basic concepts will receive, as ideological support, a considerable metaphoric influx tending to demonstrate its natural or divine necessity. Among the ancient Nahua, the supreme ruler was the Sun, the one who carried the heavy weight (the people), the father, the massive tree, or the nesting bird. The difference between nobles and plebeians was maintained by the abundant conceptual correlations that crystallized into rhetorical phrases, sayings, or prophesies.

Affinities are easily found among certain conceptual groups. These frequent correlations are often reciprocal. There are many possibilities for combination, which permit a convenient flexibility in establishing an ideal order. This brings to mind a complaint by Chesterton (1952:148):

The real trouble with this world of ours is not that it is an unreasonable world, nor even that it is a reasonable one. The commonest kind of trouble is that it is nearly reasonable, but not quite. Life is not an illogicality; yet it is a trap for logicians. It looks just a little more mathematical and regular than it is; its exactitude is obvious, but its inexactitude is hidden; its wildness lies in wait.

Will this really be the greatest source of our errors? To the contrary, from incomplete rationality comes the possibility for the development of knowledge and, what is more important, the flexibility of our relationships with society and with nature. Fortunately cosmovisions are not perfect. They have contradictions, lapses, exceptions, absurdities, duplicates, and patches. Fortunately they are not the same for all members of society. They are constructions with which human beings try to adjust themselves dialectically to the present. "Culture," says Baynes (1976:10), "is more like a tool than a static collection of treasures. It is something men make, use, and continue to utilize until it is worn out." A perfect, firm, unchangeable classification would tie us down forever.

The classifications we are examining and the comparisons that have given rise to them are flexible enough to have allowed the incorporation, often unconsciously, of knowledge acquired by the societies that created them. Their flexibility has been present at times in the criteria for classification, at times in the lack of precision or the polysemy of the defining symbols. The comparisons and classifications are guides to knowledge. When a helpful experience, conscious or not, reveals something to people, these guides endow the discovery with a meaning that permits them to assimilate the new knowledge. They guide and allow for feelings, opinions, justifications, and they recompose themselves to integrate the order and regularity of society and of nature.

Figure 8. Yapok, *Chironectes minimus*

What adheres is fire, is the Sun, is lightning,
is the daughter of the center.
　It stands for armor and helmets, for lances
and weapons.
　Among mankind it signifies men with big bellies.
　It is the sign of drought. It stands for the turtle,
the crab, the snail, the cockle, and the tortoise.
　Among trees, it signifies desiccation at the top
of the trunk.

I Ching, book 2,
"Discussion of the trigrams"

According to the Nahua of Tecospa, the opossum, like the owl, has a cold nature, because both of them are nocturnal animals. The Nahua justify their classification by saying that neither of them receives the warmth of the sun. On the other hand, the coyote, the puma, and the skunk are hot. Their nature is revealed in their thick, warm fur. The Nahua say that in their classification everything in the world has a counterpart, even though the opposite of everything has not yet been discovered. For example they admit that they do not know the counterpart of paper (Madsen 1955).

　Binary classification is a contemporary subject that presents difficult but interesting questions in the fields of anthropology, psychology, and epistemology. Of course the subject is not new. In 1909 the French investigator Robert Hertz (1973) posed the problem of polarity in regard to the preeminence of the right hand over the left; of the hand that receives honors and prerogatives and which acts, orders, and takes, as opposed to the hand that helps, supports, and guards. Interest in the subject continues. Many studies have been done to demonstrate the ways of separating the world into two great divisions, following classifications that appear across the length and breadth of our planet, and which are founded on such oppositional pairs as *central/peripheral, male/female, right/left,* or *young/old.*[1] The kinds of societies in which these forms of classification can be documented and the levels of development of the classifications are not only numerous, but very different from each other. Examples emerge everywhere and in every epoch. Consider the distinction between male and female that evolved into a separation of *robust/tender* for food and clothing and for air and water among the medieval Persians (Tylor 1977, 1:286); or, also in the Middle Ages, the distinction alchemists drew between the spirit as a masculine principle and the soul as a feminine one (Taylor 1957: 24). The conjugal mystique can be found in Isaiah (26.19), "For the dew is a dew of light, and the land of shadows gives birth" (Schökel 1984). In Galicia the opposites *man/woman* are associated with *right/left*, and both are at the center of a number of different classifications (Lisón Tolosana 1971:326–27). Among all the innumerable classifications in which *male/female* is one of the fundamental pairs, the Chinese system of *yin/yang* is by far the best known.

The extent of binary opposites poses serious problems: first, whether these oppositions are intrinsic to human thought; and second, what the causes are for their universal, or almost universal, presence. In 1936 Hocart (1970:289–90) asked whether this dichotomy was merely traditional or whether it was innate in humans; whether it corresponded to an old habit that had persisted across time, or whether it originated, like a law, from the depths of human nature. He concluded that considering it to be the result of natural law was not enough to explain specific social conduct. Leach (1967), to the contrary, says that binary opposites are "intrinsic to the process of human thought," and that "any description of the world must distinguish categories in the form of 'p is what not-p is not.'"

Lévi-Strauss (1979a:9–14, 36–47) says that from the viewpoint of structural materialism, the formation of classifying systems should be sought in the conjunction of the social and biological in humankind: on the one hand, what is social, such as the constant compromise between historical developments and specific conditions of the environment; and on the other hand, what is biological, such as fundamental psychological needs. His study of systems of dual social organizations is firmly tied to this principle. In these systems the halves are associated with a dual division of beings and things in the universe. Lévi-Strauss (1985, 1:109–10, 124) believes that the origin of this dualism is none other than one modality of the social principle of reciprocity. These proposals are suggestive, but it is likely that we are still far from a solution to the central problems of binary classification.

The study of binary classification in Mesoamerican thought has strong antecedents in the investigations of divine duality. Among the researchers should be mentioned Seler, Spence, Soustelle, Vaillant, Thompson, Caso, Garibay K., León-Portilla, and Burland. The early opinion of Gamio (1960: 43–44) regarding the antithetical symbolism of *water/war*, present in the two major gods of the Central Highlands of Mexico, an idea Gamio derives from both physical and social factors, is also relevant. Seler (1963, 1:65)[2] points out that according to the ancient Nahua, the gods Ometecuhtli and Omecihuatl were procreative gods. Spence (1923:150–52, 1977:103–4, 118–19, 169) says the duality of the supreme pair is the opposition of contrary forces in the universe, and, with regard to the Maya, he emphasizes the polarity of their gods: darkness and light, happiness and death. Vaillant (1960:161– 62, 165–66) refers not only to the supreme divine duality, but emphasizes the generalized duality in Mexica religious thought, represented by a symbolic war between light and darkness, hot and cold, the rising and setting sun, the eastern and western stars. J. Thompson (1964:270, 277) points out the duality formed by the divine Mayan pairs in the oppositions of *masculine/ feminine, young/old,* and *good/bad.* Garibay K. (1953–54, 1:129) sees in Ometeotl (the fusion of Ometecuhtli and Omecihuatl) "the maximum duality in which the world is conceived," and he finds in the god's oppositions those corresponding to a cosmic duality (*night/day*), as well as those that belong to the humanization of the gods (*male/female*). León-Portilla (1959:146–76) looks for the attributes of duality in a philological analysis of the names of the supreme god. Burland (1967:130) insists on the equilibrium of opposing powers: the sun's rising and setting, light and darkness, male and female, which he also relates to contending human passions.

Some of these investigators (Spence, Vaillant, Garibay K., and Burland) address themselves to a wide system of classifications, not only to the pantheon. Others consider the concept of duality to be the result of philosophical speculations, not of a basic and generalized thought process. Caso (1953:19) says that the idea of divine duality corresponds to "a very ancient philosophical school," which held that the origin of everything was based on a dual masculine and feminine principle. León-Portilla carries this idea even further.

Other precedents in the search for binary classification can be found in studies on political organization. A reflection of the cosmic couple *Sky/Earth,* with symbolic implications (among them *male/female* and *light/darkness*), can be found in the two supreme rulers of some Nahua states: the *tlatoani* and *cihuacoatl* among the Mexica, the *tlaquiach* and *tlalchiac* among the Cholulteca.[3] The rulers are not only related to the Sky and the Earth, but also to the masculine and feminine aspects of the supreme god. Muñoz Camargo (1981: fol. 72v) points out that the names of the two Cholultecan governors were the same as those of the divinity; "here in this city and province [Cholula] they were known to have a god whom they called *Tlaquiach, Tlachiach,* governor of the sky, governor of the earth . . ."

Contemporary studies on the polarity of Mesoamerican dual classification have increased notably. In ethnographic literature the duality of the gods corresponds to that of earthly beings. Schultze Jena (1946:23, 31–32) cites a Quiche belief in the dual personality of the Earth God (*mountain/plain*) as a *male/female* opposition, and demonstrates that this sexual polarity is so profound that the soothsayer himself declares himself subject to the divine duality, attributing a double nature to himself, since in his prayer he says, "I am your daughter, I am your son." Carmack (1979:384) also addresses this polarity of the earth, making it clear that the pair *mountain/plain* refers to the masculinity of the mountain, which controls the rain, and the femininity of the plain, corresponding to agricultural production and water. The relationship of the farmer to the mountain is clear, because it has masculine authority. P. Carrasco (1971) tells us that the Tarasca address Catholic saints as mother and father (*naná, tatá*); but that they also address elements of nature in a similar fashion, and even objects they consider dangerous (*tatá troka, tatá reló;* "father truck, father clock"). Vogt (1976:31–34) gives a detailed list of binary opposites observed among the Tzotzil. They are *rising sun/setting sun, right/ left, greater/lesser* and *hot/cold.* Among present-day Nahua, the opposites *hot/ cold, light/dark,* and *poverty/wealth* have been noted. Heat, light, and poverty belong to God; cold, dark, and wealth, to the devil (Taggart 1983:64, 76). By extension from the dichotomy *God/devil,* the Tarahumara distinguish other beings: for instance, sheep (which give wool, have good meat, and do not cry out when they are killed) belong to God, while goats (poor wool, bad meat, and very noisy when they are killed) belong to the devil (Lumholtz 1970, 1:304). Among the Cora (Lumholtz 1970, 1:500), the opposition *masculine/ feminine* presupposes a dual origin. Men came from the east; women, from the west. Petrich (1985:90) discovered a neutral space between them. Between the cultivated field (masculine space) and the kitchen (feminine space) there is the granary, a true intermediary between the agricultural and the culinary. One of the most complete works on the subject is the investigation conducted by William Madsen (1955) in San Francisco Tecospa. His article is completely devoted to the opposition *cold/hot,* and demonstrates that according to the Nahua, everything has its counterpart. This law precedes God, and He Himself had to obey it and create his opposite, the devil.

These are a few examples of a widespread belief; together with other information on Mesoamerica, they reveal the existence of a concept by which the entire universe was divided, beginning with the face of the earth. In a previous work (López Austin 1988, 1:52–68), I referred to some of these oppositional pairs: *mother/father, female/male, cold/hot, below/above, ocelot/eagle, 9/13, underworld/sky, wet/drought, darkness/light, weakness/strength, night/day, water/fire, ascending influence/descending influence, death/life, flint/flower, wind/fire, sharp pain/irritation, smaller/bigger, nocturnal stream/stream of blood,* and *stench/ perfume.*

Many other pairs could be added. Sexuality is one (*abundance of sex/little sexu-*

ality). Sexual value belongs to the feminine sphere. The Nahua believed that sexuality was controlled by a soul located in the liver, that is, in the lower part of the body; possibly opposed to personal fame and glory, which emanated from the upper soul, situated in the head. The high and low in the body are paired with the high and low in the universe. Thus digestive functions, including excretion and the repository for food, occupy the lower part of the body, corresponding to the feminine sphere. In a reciprocal mapping, the subterranean world encloses vegetable, animal, and mineral wealth and, at the same time, is death, sex, and excrement. Because of this it is said that when the god Ixbalanque conquered the god of the underworld, the vanquished god begged him not to expose him to the light. Ixbalanque kicked him and said, "Go back there, and everything that is rotten, withered, and evil-smelling will be yours" (Las Casas 1967, 1:650). As Rivera Dorado (1986b:102) explains, this is why the god of the underworld and of death has, among other names, that of Kisin, derived from the Maya word *kis* (fart). It also explains why the dog, an animal associated with the underworld and the north, was linked in the calendric sign *oc* to adultery (*El libro de los libros de Chilam Balam* 1949:193). Today's Lacandon (Bruce 1974:103) say that Kisin has a hat, "Kisin's hat is the *tuxikin* flower, the 'stinking ear.'" Schultze Jena (1946:21) found a belief still present among the Quiche that anyone born on a "dog" day would be predisposed to sexual excess, his sexuality difficult to control; but he would be immune to the dangerous consequences of such excesses. With the coming of Christianity, Satan replaced the God of Death and of the Underworld. In the middle of the eighteenth century, the Tarahumara, far removed from the Maya world, called the Devil Huitaru, "the one-who-is-shit."[4]

Two mappings of the cosmic opposition of *above/below* are seen in ancient Nahua belief. Both divide the sky in halves, one with a *north/south* axis, the other with an *east/west* axis. The characteristics of the *above/below* dichotomy are selectively divided between the two. North and south remain, respectively, as *below and above,* with death toward the north and life toward the south, since the sun's course runs chiefly to the south. In the division of east and west, east is masculine and west is feminine; but also implied is a division into what is weakly sexual and what is strongly sexual. The ancient Nahua believed that the eastern half of the sky belonged to warriors slain in combat, some of them cherished by the Sun because they were youths who had not indulged in sexual pleasure.[5] In the western half of the sky were the women who had died in childbirth, the culminating moment of the sexual process.

For anyone unfamiliar with the anthropological literature, understanding binary polarities may be difficult. It is likely that the casual reader, when examining opposites in the various traditions of the world, will associate the *male/*

female opposition with the grammatical division by gender, or believe that the *hot/cold* polarity indicates a thermal condition. However, these categories do not coincide.[6] A more precise definition is required.

1.   Beings acquire their particular nature as destiny, as the hidden, divine, invisible forces that penetrate everything. To say *hot/cold* is to refer to the supernatural aspect of beings. The Maya of Quintana Roo (Villa Rojas 1978: 307) still speak of what has a "hot load" (*chocó cuch*) and what has a "cold load" (*ziz u cuch*). *Cuch* in Maya means, among other things, the relationship between gods who, when they unite, form a time unit. One of the gods is the bearer; the other is the load he carries on his back. Between them they form a "time-god." *Cuch* is "load," but it is also "fate" and "task," in its oral as well as in its glyphic form (J. Thompson 1962:225–26, glyph 601).

2.   There are no entirely pure earthly beings. They are a mixture, and their nature is determined by the dominant factor.

3.   Classification is based on a pair of basic opposites, revealed through multiple facets of reality. We can surmise the existence of an essential quality X and an essential quality Y. The first can reveal itself (depending on the beings it characterizes or the relationships between them) as masculine, hot, higher, luminous, southern, etc., while the second, reciprocally, can be feminine, cold, inferior, dark, or northerly.

4.   Nevertheless the category used as a basis for definition does not necessarily allude to characteristics simply and directly perceived. Food of a hot nature can have a very low temperature, occasionally or always, or a human of a feminine essence can be a man, and even virile, as in the case of the *cihuacoatl* among the Mexica, who was an outstanding warrior and at the same time a representative of the feminine aspect of the divinity on earth. Another example is ice cream, which modern Nahua consider to be a hot food, despite its temperature (Lewis 1968:61).[7]

5.   Classifications function in absolute as well as in relative terms. An obsidian object, for example, is classified as hot, due to the nature of the material; no comparison is necessary to recognize this quality. But beings are also classified by their relative positions. A man with a fair skin is warm in relation to a woman, but cold in relation to a dark-skinned man (Madsen 1955).

6.   In classification not only is the nature of an object important, but also its intensity. This is particularly important in the field of medicine, in which intermediate categories can exist, such as *fresh* with regard to food (Ryesky 1976:34).

7.   The formation of oppositional pairs can be of various kinds: contradictory (explained by Leach as *p/not-p*), which can produce pairs such as *edible/*

inedible; oppositional, such as *cold/hot;* complementary, as in the relation *male/ female;* associational, as *sun/moon;* symmetrical, as in *right/left;* asymmetrical, as *head/feet,* etc.[8]

These different kinds of oppositions are expressed linguistically in a unitary way. In sixteenth-century Nahuatl there is a morpheme that includes some of the varieties of opposition. It is the morpheme *namic,* used to form numerous compounds, such as the verbs *namiqui, namictia, namictilia* and *nanamiqui.* The verbs are translated as: to marry, to contend, to help, to favor, to harmonize, to unite, to find, to sorrow, to receive, to pay, to join, to equal, to be successful, to accomplish, to succeed, to barter, to explain dreams, to reward, to make friends, to make enemies, to rival, to be a neighbor, to support oneself, to be happy, etc. (Molina 1944: fol. 62r; Siméon 1977:300–301; Campbell 1985:197–98). It would be hard to explain this wide gamut of meanings without taking into account the plurality of oppositional forms contained in the morpheme. It would also be difficult to explain why the noun *namictli* is used in the field of medicine to indicate the relationship between the medicine and the illness,[9] and in culinary combinations to indicate that one food was appropriate to accompany another (*Primeros memoriales* 1905:120–21). *Tenamic* meant conjugal mate, companion, enemy, and opponent in a game.

8.   The criteria for classification vary greatly. In medicine for example, the pair *hot/cold* predominates, although this characterization is not exclusive. In the Mayan language the morpheme *ah* is placed before a noun to indicate masculine, and *ix* denotes feminine; but they are not limited to categorizing what is sexual. *Ah* implies superiority; *ix,* inferiority. Therefore *ix* applies to a man or woman of an inferior group; *ah,* to those of superior rank. A young single woman is *ix;* a married, respectable woman is *ah.* Felines are *ix;* insects are *ah.* This also occurs in the naming of sexual organs: *ix on* designates the masculine organ; *ix nicte,* the feminine. Both terms contain *ix* because, as sexual organs, they are both referred to in a disparaging way (Rámon Arzápalo Marín, pers. commun., August 10, 1987). Among contemporary Zinacantec, the *b'ankilal* and the *ʔits'nal* predominate as organizing principles, dividing beings into "older brothers" and "younger brothers." Vogt (1966a:94) says:

There are *b'ankilal* or *ʔits'nal* mountains, caves, *kalvarios* [ancestral sanctuaries], *hʔiloletik* [prophets, soothsayers], rockets, drums, and even two men who represent jaguars in the ceremonies in honor of Saint Sebastian in January. Perhaps our greatest surprise came when, at Christmas, we found that in the Nativity scene at the cathedral, Mary and Joseph had not one Christ child, but two, lying in the manger. One of these children was *b'ankilal,* and the other *ʔits'nal.*

9.   Aside from the essential nature that predominates in a being, the proportion and distribution of qualities in its composition can vary, giving it a special character and appearance. In human beings there are states of disequilibrium that arise either by the admission or through the liberation of forces. This causes illness in those who release, as well as those who receive, the emanations. Anger is considered to be a state of imbalance, where heat goes to the outside of the organism while the inside remains cold. In contrast shame sends cold toward the outside of the body (López Austin 1988, 1:258–64). Because of this, beings can change their nature, or at least their degree of belonging to a particular classification, throughout their existence.

In order to understand this system of binary opposites, we should relate classification to myth. All beings of this world have been formed by two kinds of supernatural forces, which can be identified, on the one hand, as celestial, hot, masculine, luminous, and dry; and on the other, as earthly, cold, feminine, dark, and humid. They are the forces that were united in Tamoanchan. Earthly beings are a mixture. Their generic and individual origins and their particular history place them on one side or the other of the universal division of everything that exists.

This classification can also separate entire classes into halves, as in the case of birds, divided into those belonging to the masculine aspect of divinity and those belonging to the feminine:

> You sing there, little dove, on the branches of the silk-cotton tree. There also are the cuckoo, the *charretero,* the little *kukum* and the mocking bird. They are all happy, these birds of the Lord God.
>   The Lady also has her birds: the little turtledove, the little cardinal, the *chichin-bacal,* as well as the hummingbird. They are the birds of the Beautiful Mistress and Lady (*El libro de los cantares de Dzitbalché* 1965:80).

The same happens to the stars, which Totonac today divide into northern and southern. Those belonging to the northern celestial half belong to the Great Thunder; those to the south belong to his enemy, the Sun (Kelly 1966). The division of those under the humid control of the Great Thunder and those under the dry dominion of the Sun indicates the rainy and dry seasons. This also corresponds to the ancient division the Nahua made in separating the *centzon mimixcoah,* the stellar gods of the north, from the *centzon huitznahuah,* the stellar gods of the south.[10]

Binary opposition creates a holistic classification that owes its explanation to myth in all its breadth, as a set of beliefs concerning the origin of the world and the permanent course of divine influence over the earth. But dual classification, although it is basic to Mesoamerican thought, is only a point of departure. Castiglioni (1972:122) attributed a definite inclination toward numerical and geometrical systematization to Mesoamerican concepts. According to Zantwijk (1985:22), there are three basic numerical organizing principles in Mesoamerica: the *masculine/feminine* duality; the triple structure of underworld, earth, and sky;[11] and the quadruple sectors on the horizontal earth. This quadruplicity divides stars, winds, rains, lightning, plants, animals, illnesses, times (Montoliu Villar 1980). Vogt (1976:6) also indicates the plurality of classificatory bases:

> Not only is each plant classified as wild or domesticated and highland and lowland but each also possesses an innate soul, defined as "hot or cold," and "active or quiet." Further, each soul has a color which, not surprisingly, comes from one of the five basic Zinancanteco colors of red, black, white, yellow, and blue-green. Ordinarily, the innate soul color does not correspond to the color of the blossom, leaves, or needles . . . These five colors are generally the most salient in all Maya cultures, and often have directional associations.

The world acquires an impressive appearance of order by combining basic principles, made more complex by adding other, geometrical bases of classification.

Mythical geometry is not merely a combination of planes with coordinates. Daily experience is imbedded in the imagined arrangement of the cosmos. Throughout thousands of years there has been a continuous relationship of reciprocal attributions and corrections between schema and praxis. Societies rely on an imaginary order for their understanding of the world, use it to validate the acts they accomplish, and plan their future acts by its rules. At the same time they gradually convert schema and praxis into the course of history.

There is an intimate relationship between myth and daily life. Zingg (1982, 2:173–74) says that "Huichol mythology is, not only a reflection of Huichol life, but also a rational explanation for the most surprising, most interesting, and for the most part, the most meaningful behavior of each individual in the tribe." The believer also looks for help in this mythical geometry, this knowledge of the nature of things, indispensable to any kind of management or transformation. Ordering the world is not the result of simple intellectual need. It is the basis for all rational action and proceeds from that action. "Ideological production, the production and communication of ideas," says Feuchtwang (1977:86–87), "is not only the practice of ideas, just as economic production is not just material production." The congruency of behavior reciprocally interacting with the congruency of the ordering of the world supports a permanent process of opposition and adjustment.

Classifications in the mythical context that produces them not only illustrate, they explain, warn, guide, normalize, order, impel, prohibit. Whoever is learned in matters concerning the gods and the movements of the universe can judiciously direct the acts of daily life. For any action one must count on harmonious interaction with the invisible. Because of this Hesiod (1983:77, 85, 87; lines 413–22, 727–32, 735–46, 794–97) advised cutting down a forest at the beginning of the autumnal showers, when the sun's force is diminished, at the time when the star Sirius travels little by day and reigns for the greater part of the night. He warns against standing and facing the sun to urinate, and advises prudent people that if they should do it at night, they should do so seated or against the wall of an enclosed courtyard. A man should sire offspring, according to Hesiod, when he returns from a banquet to the gods, but never when he returns from a funeral. He names the fourteenth day as the best one on which to tame sheep, oxen, dogs, and mules. Similar advice is found in Mesoamerican religious tradition. The modern opposition between *our own space/alien space* guides the Mazatec farmer, showing him the right way to face the world; myth revitalizes his wisdom (Portal 1986:82). Classifications orient and regulate conduct. Gossen (1974:37) says about the Chamula:

> men [in this patrifocal society] always sit on tiny chairs, which raise them above the cold, feminine ground, and wear sandals, which separate them from the ground and complement their masculine heat. Women, in contrast, customarily sit on the ground and always go barefooted, which symbolically gives them direct contact with the cold, feminine earth. Coldness, femininity, and lowness were prior to heat, masculinity, and height in the mythological account of the coming of order. The male sun was born from the womb of the female moon and was then killed by the forces of evil and darkness [the demons and Jews].

The sacred and the political are homologous. "In the so-called archaic societies, worldly elements and the diverse social categories are subject to the same modes of classification" (Balandier 1969:125). In Mesoamerican states the structure of the cosmos provided their power and distributed their functions among the rulers, allocated conquered territory, was projected onto the arrangement of cities, and gave order to administrative procedures (Zantwijk 1985:61–62; Reyes García 1978). Impressive power structures grew this way, and anyone who opposed them was tarred with sacrilege.

Religion and myth have precise functions in the area of power, but these are not their chief functions. It is in the daily struggle of the common man's life that religion is most fully revealed as "the general theory of this world, its encyclopedic compendium, its popular logic" (Marx 1967). What is most valued and what is most feared acquire specific dimensions in the mirror of mythical classification. This can be verified by a farmer's intense interaction with the plants he cultivates. According to the Totonac (Ichon 1973:125–27), domestic plants come from one of two opposite poles: either from the blood-flower of the Sun that fell on the earth or from the saliva of the woman who spit into the holes in the fields. Thus two domains are created: that of the Sun (a divinity confused with the God of Corn), which includes everything that grows in the free air, thanks to the warmth and blood of that astral body; and that of St. John (Lord of the Animals), which includes everything that, thanks to rain, grows under the earth, the place of tubers. The peninsular Maya (Villa Rojas 1978:181) confer or remove sanctity from corn according to the way it is used. Corn that keeps its name of pure "grace," the gift of God profoundly linked to the subsistence of a farmer and his family and to his religious life, is not the same when it is used for commercial purposes. The Otomi, like many other groups, follow the patterns they think they find in the harmony of the sky. They do not sow their seed at the time of the new moon, to avoid the plants being invaded by worms, a danger that comes to an end with the first quarter of the moon (Galinier 1987:366). In Santa Ana Tlacotenco (González Torres 1975:150, pl. 45), the sowing of grain varies according to its color.

> The furrows of the cornfield always follow an east-west direction. Sowing is begun in a predetermined direction and the point of the corn is laid in a certain direction according to its color. Red corn is sown from the west to the east side of the cornfield, with the point toward the east. If they want blue corn, they sow it east to west, with the point toward the west. White corn is sown north to south, with the point toward the north. With yellow corn the reverse is true, that is, beginning in the south with the grain pointing that way and ending in the north.

The sexual division of work and the sexual life of the couple is related to the success of the harvest. Among the Mam in Guatemala (Wagley 1957:26n9), a wife may fast during the agricultural rites, but she cannot work in the fields except during the harvest. She cannot touch the seeds or sleep with her husband on the eve of the sowing. They believe a violation of the rules would bring a strong, destructive wind to the cornfield or prevent the growth of the corn.

A complete and intricate mechanism is based on the order of opposites. In the opposition *cold/hot* lies the ability or inability of human beings to contract a successful marriage, prepare food, raise domestic animals, light a fire, or participate in certain religious festivals (R. Redfield and Villa Rojas 1934:163; Villa Rojas 1978:350–51; R. Redfield 1942:307, 311). But on a primary level, the explanation for illnesses, their origins, their prevention, and their treatment, is found in the *cold/hot* polarity. Among the Mocho in Chiapas, the protector takes his patient's ritual cross and "plants" it in a sacred field. If he suspects a "cold" illness, he chooses the dry field, well-exposed to the sun's rays, where the hog plum [*Spondias purpureae*] is grown. If he suspects a "hot" disease, he chooses the other field, irrigated by a river or a spring, shadowed by leafy trees, where the white *zapote* [*Casimiroa edulis*] grows. Not every corporeal object is subject to these opposites. Other knowledge can come from celestial phenomena. The Tzotzil (Holland 1963:78–79) believe that when there is a new moon, wounds bleed copiously and the healing of scars is slow. When it is full, there is little bleeding and healing is easy.

Rights and obligations also derive from religious organization. Karremans (1987) studied the distribution of water for irrigation in Izúcar de Matamoros, a mestizo town in the southeastern part of the state of Puebla. The inhabitants of the seven eastern districts and those of the seven western ones take turns in the ritual *cargos* (administrative positions for religious affairs), and they follow a similar order in the right to water usage. The position of *mayordomo* is not obligatory, but anyone who refuses it loses his right to irrigation. The explanation for this is not based on the lack of community solidarity, but on mutual obligations between the world and the supernatural. In the interchange, both follow the same rhythms. "Water is from the saint. He supplies the district, and we must serve him in payment."

These are only a few samples of the strong presence of cosmic order in every phase of daily life. Human action must be subject to the total order. Order itself is attributed to myth. Beginning with the creation of the cosmos, "the surface of the earth was converted into sacred space divided into parts ruled by divine powers, colors and symbols that inject a transcendent meaning into every space and place" (Florescano 1987:26). Humans, who in their belief in the gods endow them with their own actions, thoughts, and passions, believe themselves to be an extension of the supernatural. As Berger (1971:39) says, "the *nomos* [law] emerges as a microcosmic reflection of, and the world of men as an expression of, the meanings inherent in the universe itself." The correspondence presumed to exist on earth between earthly and divine planes brings to mind the emerald table, the secret words that in the Old World were attributed to Hermes Trismegistus, "What is below is like what is above, and what is above is like what is below, representing the wonders of the unique thing." There are still people today who believe that the division of the world of the gods explains social classes. The Mazatec (Portal 1986:85, 92) say that the sky is divided into thirteen spaces, that a saint lives in each space, and that each saint is the patron of a certain class of beings in this world.

In the other time-space, archetypes are not static. Their characteristics include passions, tendencies, and patterns of behavior. There is a life there that individualizes each one of the gods. There are histories. There are processes, and these processes are also archetypical. Processes that are similar can be grouped together. Comparisons among the diverse beings of the world also apply to their processes. If the planting stick of the Nahua farmer sinks like a phallus into the great terrestrial vulva of the cornfield, it is also true that the seed deposited in the hollow will give birth to the child-corn. The multiple fields of action and knowledge, with their own practices and laws, tend to combine in a system that approaches universality, without attaining it. Nevertheless the believer is confident that the laws that govern the cycle of the corn plant are the same as those of the sun's course and of human gestation. The orders interlace, planes correspond to each other, and the universe is simplified by the reduction of levels. Thus organizing principles evolve, projections of models of thought and behavior such as those studied by Vogt (1966b) under the name of *réplicas* (responses) among the Zinacantec. Total order is never attained; but believers struggle for it and believe in it, ignoring the exceptions. Belief crystallizes into great organizing principles such as the Mesoamerican calendar, the general explanation of the cosmic mechanism, a guide for conduct, and the synthesis of the classifications and their myths.

Belief can be synthesized. There is a single order for everything. Only through order and by discovering the mysteries of the classifications can humans understand the kinds of beings in this world and their processes. The efficacy of human action depends on that understanding.

Figure 9. *Bacaboob* from the *Dresden Codex*
    a. plate 25   b. plate 26
    c. plate 27   c. plate 28

15 THE GODS ACQUIRE HISTORY

Suddenly I see the answer, and I write with confidence:
"In the beginning was action."

Johann Wolfgang Goethe, *Faust*

Finding the secret nature of things in their birth is a beautiful illusion. The so-called primitive societies are not alone in this tendency. Atavism accompanies us and makes us seek more causal explanations in foundations, etymologies, and constitutional congresses than is reasonable to expect of them. Although institutions are changeable, we attribute to them a permanent illuminating character, capable of showing us the essentials.[1] The sources in our investigation are often exhausted because they lack the historical depth we require of them. Facing failure, we fall back on the old, trite expression, "The origin of X is lost in the mists of time." This addiction of historians, which Bloch called the "embryonic obsession," has been justly criticized:

> Explaining what is nearest by what is farthest, which obviously appeals to men who primarily study the past, has dominated our studies to the point of hypnosis. In its most characteristic form, this ideal of the tribe of historians has a name: an obsession with origins. (M. Bloch 1965:27)

The search for the origin of religion has been rejected as unscientific for a long time.[2] Any attempt at an investigation of such an origin does not go further than elaborate guesswork. If we accept that rejection, we will also have to reject, as a part of the problem, the search for the origin of mythical thought. At what point in history did the fabrication of divine adventures begin? We cannot even begin to imagine on a solid basis what the first mythical adventures were, or how people conceived of gods then. The embryonic obsession, in this case, is a vain illusion. However, it is necessary to distinguish between the origin of mythical thought itself and the origin of specific myths. While the first is "lost in the mists of time," the second comes to the present, through information preserved in historical sources or as a living process, even though it is hard to perceive. Therefore it seems feasible to investigate the manner in which myths are constructed and transformed. A study of their construction is likely to contribute to an understanding of the logic, the meaning, and the truth (attributed to it by the believer) of the history of the gods.

One should not look for the original myth, then, but for myth born in a mythical setting. It is a matter of discovering a process in which the characteristics attributed to the gods become their impulses, the impulses become deeds, the latter are arranged as episodic sequences, and are finally integrated into a divine history. And it is also a matter of observing the transformation of myths, the ways the stories unfold or are simplified, become enriched with certain elements or lose them, interchange adventures or adapt to new circumstances or needs. It is not easy to determine what processes come together to kindle the imagining of an incident, nor how incidents are linked to make an adventure. It is not easy to determine when and where an adventure is expressed. It is not easy to evaluate whether a narrative, upon being collectively created, is accepted and integrated into the whole of the concepts accepted by society.[3] Nevertheless, these are processes that leave traces. They are recorded in the sources.

The creation of myths has not ceased. Their production and transformation continue. We become aware of this when we listen to native mythical narrations that apply to their present situations, comparing them to those of Mexican mestizos or to those of North Americans, tracing the course of their conditions to the time of origin. We notice that some of the native pantheons include real persons from recent history or imaginary ones from motion pictures or television. Not only this. Recent ecological changes lead to the creation of invisible beings. The jungle and its rich fauna have disappeared around Hidalgotitlán. Industrial waste and the exploitation of petroleum and sulfur have poisoned the water of the Coatzacoalcos River and laid waste to the farmland. It is a fate that extends like a cloak of present and future misery over vast areas of the country. In Hidalgotitlán there is a new being, who is the invisible lord of the land:

> The king of sulfur lives in the sulfur mine. The men who die there are only food for the king. He needs them in order to keep on living. The peasants say that this king makes the sulfur suck the vitamins from the earth, and that is why the land cannot produce now. They know that fertilizers are made from sulfur, but only the well-to-do can buy them. And they add, "It gets worse and worse for us because of the damned sulfur" (Pérez Castro 1978: fol. 14–15).

Sometimes the destructive forces that invade the land that belonged to their ancestors are personified as gods. In Tabasco the Chontal (Incháustegui 1987: 307) say that

the land is weak and it doesn't rain, because the protective spirit of the earth
is annoyed by the extraction of petroleum. They say that he requests a pair of
boys. This week they told me that he had given that notice. He wants them this
color [brown], brown they say, true natives, they say. In order for him to give
them petroleum—they say.

We must be careful not to project our observations of the present onto the
Mesoamerican past. The creation and evolution of myths occur under greatly
varying circumstances. Today as in ancient time there is a dominant ideology[4];
but it is an ideology not understood by indigenous societies. It is a truth that
does not collate with their vision of the world. The dialogue is established with
few codes in common, and this distance between concepts is reflected in the
mythical production. The pressure of rapidly changing and hard-to-assimilate
outside elements distorts cosmovision at the present time. In spite of this,
however, studying contemporary myths is invaluable.

The sources of *myth-belief* and *myth-narration* are different. We will first study
the origin of *myth-belief* and leave the problems of the composition of mythical
narration to later chapters. Beginning with the study of *myth-belief* will help
to distance us from the old and limited image of the mytho-poet, who, inspired by the muses, became, through that inspiration, the undisputed source
of narration, which began a belief. The idea is an old one, begun by Herodotus
(1987:154–55), who claimed that Homer and Hesiod created the gods:

> But whence each of these gods came into existence, or whether they were for-
> ever, and what kind of shape they had were not known until the day before
> yesterday, if I may use the expression; for I believe that Homer and Hesiod were
> four hundred years before my time—and no more than that. It is they who cre-
> ated for the Greeks their theogony; it is they who gave to the gods the special
> names for their descent from their ancestors and divided among them their hon-
> ors, their arts, and their shapes. Those who are spoken of as poets before Homer
> and Hesiod were, in my opinion, later born.

But the poets who actually should have credit for creating with their songs
the infinite wealth of the pantheons were either further away from or nearer to
Herodotus's time.

Along with the exceptional presence of the mytho-poet, there are other
problems. What room is there, in the birth of myth, for dream images, which
according to Freud (Rank n.d.) are the product of the hidden disguises of
subconscious fantasies, or which emerge in dreams as the mature product of

a youthful humanity (Jung 1956:24)? Do fantasy and dreams dominate and thus limit the importance of speculative development (Frankfort and Frankfort 1954)? In today's theories of myth we find Jung's (1977) proposals of the collective unconscious (the innate archetype of historic content, tendencies as strong as the instinct of birds to build nests, symbolic manifestations of physiological needs); and Lévi-Strauss's (1968a:184) subconscious (always devoid of content and as removed from the images as the stomach is from the food that passes through it, an organ of a specific function that is limited to imposing structural laws on inarticulated elements). Is myth born, as Freud (1953:24–27, 30, 41) surmised for religion, not as an experience, but as an illusion deriving from human beings' inner and urgent desires to free themselves from the overwhelming power of nature and the imperfections of civilization? Does the impossibility of controlling the invisible forces of nature and society contribute to the creation of myth, as Godelier (1974:378–79) thought? Or is it the natural outcome of the control human beings have over society and nature? At any rate, a study of the birth and transformation of mythical beliefs should confer on the following oppositional pairs: intentional or unintentional, rational or emotional, gradual or sudden, individual or collective, popular or elitist, holistic or fragmented. To pose these problems, investigate them fully, and reach a conclusion is beyond the scope of this essay. My proposals and arguments are thus only a starting point.

Let us begin with the idea, set forth in chapter 8, that the histories of the gods constitute a very important part of myth-belief, but do not exhaust it. Myth-belief is present in every area of social life, diluted, scattered, but doubtless having an enormous capacity to explain and guide. It is found in maxims, images, omens, rules for the most diverse techniques, governmental structures and actions, family relationships, invocations, rites, insults and curses, classifications, and jests. It has many faces in multiple areas and performs multiple functions. Not everything is divine history; but there is often agreement between scattered myth-belief and divine histories. Many concrete instances refer to these histories. Others seem to have preceded them as episodic beginnings, as personifications, as explanations for classifications.

The general picture shown by a tradition at a given historical moment is like a sampling of the different stages of development of mythical history: here an object to which a will is attributed, there a relationship underlying kinship, further on an episodic explanation of a natural cyclic phenomenon, all of them social acts that are parts of processes potentially forming mythical narratives. Sometimes they run on parallel courses, sometimes they merge.

Up to this point the mytho-poet seems superfluous, but myth—the story of the gods—begins to take form. In a given tradition we can perceive various processes as potential ways to construct the deeds of imaginary personages. They are slow, collective processes, in which a gradual accumulation of images fixes the action of the gods. Some of the processes, of course, are strongly interrelated:

1. The primary personification (prosopopoeia)

2. The explanation of regularities in the world by means of a single group of rules including both social and natural ones.

3. The association of all that is not human with social criteria for belonging, distribution, and hierarchy.

4. The concept of a great, imperceptible (or nearly imperceptible) sector of the universe.

5. The inclusion in this sector of a part of all earthly beings, so that their characteristics acquire meaning with an imprint from the original time.

1.   Primary personification (prosopopoeia). One of the processes that is a potential path to mythical adventure is the personification of nonhuman beings. Believing that myths are based on a mental process that projects human characteristics onto animals or the inanimate is not new.[5] From the earliest Mesoamerican times up to the present, the personification of all that exists is the normal course of people's relationship to everything around them: animals, vegetables, minerals, astral bodies, manufactured objects. In daily work, magical or not, a great deal of the logic for an action is guided by the personification of the raw material, instruments, and whatever is beyond the operator's control that may contribute to or oppose the transformation.

Often a reference to divine history can be found in the name given to an object or in a trait attributed to it. In the seventeenth century, when planting sweet potatoes, the farmer invoked the sun's rays with the name Nanahua-tzin (Ruiz de Alarcón 1953:106), an obvious allusion to the birth of the Sun in Teotihuacan. But in the majority of acts and expressions, personification seems to be free from any reference to mythical history. It is the product of a concept of the world in which giving human attributes to everything does not need to be based on previous adventures. To the contrary, personifications independent of such adventures are often found, which may, however, be the possible points of departure for adventures.

Even geography becomes human; people distribute their vices and virtues throughout the environment. This includes the personification of both mythical and real places. Tulán Siwán, the place of origin for the Quiche, appears as a god whom the ancestors thanked for the existence of humankind.

> Two times thanks, three times thanks, to you Ts'akol, to you Bitol, you the Center of the Sky and of the Earth, you the Four Sides, the Four Corners. Thanks for the dawn we just saw, the daybreak, the Sun and the Star. Thank you, our mountain of Tulán Siwán, intensely yellow and green mountain. (*El título de Totonicapán* 1983:185)

Carmack (*El título de Totonicapán* 1983:233*n*189) notes that Tulán Siwán was considered to be a part of the god Unic'ajal Ulew, Upam Ulew, Uc'ux Uleu, the fertile and productive part of the mountain. Today the Chinantec say that there are envious, avaricious places on the mountain where hunting is impossible unless the hunter draws a cross on each bullet and covers the rifle with flowers that have been blessed (Weitlaner and Castro 1973:51).

People become brothers and sisters to nature. In the process of projecting their traits, they give part of themselves. Something of the farmers themselves is transferred to the cultivated plants. Some Mixtec say that anyone who plants a maguey cannot cut the hollow that receives the sap, because cutting the center of the plant is the same as wounding oneself. Another person must do it (Mak 1977).

The attribution of human traits includes language, even though the language of gods, animals, plants, and things may be incomprehensible to many. Animals know how to pronounce human words, and plants can listen to the message. In the following example (Hollenbach 1980), the dialogue of animals reveals a rivalry in the opposition of wet and dry. A farmer cultivating his field encounters two opposing characters: the lizard, a friend of the god of thunder; and the *gulo* (a lizard with smooth scales). The first, allied to humans and to farming, stands erect in the branches of a tree and urges the corn to grow. The gulo, to the contrary, incites weeds to invade the fields and warns them when the farmer is approaching with his tools: "Here comes the sharp head [the machete], the round head [the farmer], and the broad head [the shovel]."

A wise person can participate in the secret dialogue. In order to extract sap from the maguey, a farmer must know the hidden names—*nahualtocaitl*—and use them when speaking to the plant and its children, to the farm tools, to the tobacco that helps people control the invisible, and to the copper spoon used to scrape the hollow (Serna 1953:304–5).

The plots of land are peopled by small, invisible beings whose acts explain the progress or failure of the crop. In Quintana Roo the *arush* attract people in order to beg food from them. If they do not get it, their mischief harms the corn, and the winds they send make the farmers ill. An opportune offering, however, will make the arush a guardian of the cornfield, capable of capturing any of the small gods of rain and forcing them to water it (Villa Rojas 1978: 297).

Not only do supernatural beings act, but their action is almost an adventure. The character of natural phenomena, the order human beings give to the cosmos, and the imaginary attributes of the invisible reconcile themselves in a complex procedure described by Tylor (1977, 1:286):

> However difficult it may be to determine to what degree objects and ideas were classified in the language as male and female because of having been personified, and to what degree they were personified because of having been classified as male and female, it is evident that the two processes adapt to each other and mutually stimulate each other.

Prosopopoeia gives human members and garments to things. New meanings cover each part of the personified being. The corn plant is "our mother corn": her breasts are in the knots where the fruit is born; her clothing consists of the husks that enclose the ears; her ornaments are the large leaves; and her grain is the milk that nourishes people (Carmack 1979:384).

There are a few times when the historical causes behind the characterizations are within our reach. Sugarcane, brought during colonial times, cultivated by black slaves, and today exploited by mestizos, is as alien to the Otomi as corn is familiar. Sugarcane is "the old man's bone," a diabolical plant that brings evil and death. In San Pablito they say that when Christ was born, the Otomi went to help him. A devil tried to lead them astray by offering them rum. That demon was the Lord of Sugarcane (Galinier 1987:362).

When the environment is humanized, social relationships are distributed in it. Personification is, at one and the same time, the product and the producer of the forms with which people daily manage everything that surrounds them. Records from early colonial times speak of the permission that had to be asked of the land before breaking it for sowing; of burning incense when the plant sprouted; of offerings at weeding time; of the respect shown to the corn plant until it produced grain; of the gift to the granary; the sprinkling of pulque or the supplicant's own blood on the first ears of corn before they were roasted; in short, of the personal treatment given by the laborer to the visible and the invisible (Ponce 1953:375–77). In our time traditionalists from Guatemala were opposed to the use of chemical fertilizers, claiming that they burned the earth and made it suffer. They also claimed that the live, sensitive earth should not be cut nor pierced too much, nor impoverished, sold, or rented (Carmack 1979:383). Today the Tzeltal know that not all kinds of grain can be sown in any soil whatsoever, because acid soil "does not want" to be sown with the kind of grain that grows rapidly (J. Nash 1970:36). Techniques become a dialogue.

2.   The fusion of social and natural regularities. Durkheim's proposals lead to a second potential way to form mythical episodes. Durkheim (1968: 34, 233) says that "the object of religious concepts is, above all, to express and explain, not what is exceptional and abnormal in things, but what is constant and regular," and he criticizes the formula *primus in orbe deos fecit timor* ("fear made the gods foremost in the world"), contending that it is the feeling of confidence in primitive people, and not fear, that brings them closer to the gods. The observation of the regularity in processes and the parallelism—real or apparent—found in these regularities leads to a belief in causes identified with the hidden character of things. Similar things and processes seem to have a common nature, and this leads people, in a broad generalization, to endeavor to manage the similar visible and invisible realms with similar techniques.

> No less important is the industry these natives have of transporting wood, sell-
> ing it themselves and cutting it for sale to those who buy it on the mountain.
> Here, as in everything else, they make use of invocations. All the branches
> of industry related to wood can be included: beams, planks, shingles, and
> others, according to where they live. After having understood the invocation
> to the tree, it is easy to locate the other superstitions associated with kindred
> industries. (Serna 1953:329)

Regularities extend to every area. The world is completely bathed by the same ebbs and flows. The wet and dry periods attributed to lunar phases are also seen in the child lodged in its mother's womb, in the harvests, in grain, in the trees marked for cutting or the domestic animals to be castrated or sac- rificed. If the moon is humid as it grows and declines, dry when it is full, and tender when it is new, then it is best for children to be born in the growing or declining period, because they will be softer. Sowing should be done when the moon is humid (or tender); corn and trees should be cut by the dry (solid) moon, so they will not rot, because otherwise they would be full of water; hogs are slaughtered when there is a full moon and castrated when it is tender (Petrich 1985:220).

In this analogy there are no barriers between what is social and what is natural, and the same yardstick is used for different things. If what is masculine has ritual primacy and what is feminine is its complement, the paths of the masculine sun and the feminine moon are explained in ritual terms, the latter dependent on the former, the former the principal one, and a human tie is established between the two, possibly the kinship between mother and child (Gossen 1974:40–43).

The techniques of humankind, understood as lessons received from the gods, accommodate themselves to the great natural rhythms. The distribution of work in time and space, the sequence of the cultivation of diverse plants, the waiting for the arrival of migratory species are all kinds of behavior based on seasonal changes.

The gods follow each other, ordering their coming by the regularity of agricultural work. Rivera Dorado (1985:182) says that in the hieroglyphic texts of the ancient Maya, Tak is present, with his sonorous name like the stroke of an ax, at the first stage of the cornfield's preparation. Following him is Mox, the god of fire, who leaves the field clean and ready for seed. Afterwards the rains come with Kaxix, Xanom, and Tit Sot; and the plentiful harvest is gathered through the intervention of Yum Uil, the god of corn. The course of nature and that of human procedure form part of the same type of endeavor, and the occurrence of natural phenomena is filled with meanings. All that is constant and regular, all—human or natural—that seems to respond to the same regularities, is conceived of as the effect of the same cause, and this cause is more intelligible if it is explained in human terms. Any adage that links an agricultural operation to the calendar may contain the germ of a mythical episode.

3.   Things are tied together by the social criteria of belonging, distribution, and hierarchy. A potential third way to mythical adventure is closely tied to the above. It is the ties between beings that people discover, sometimes in society, sometimes in nature, expressed in terms of kinship, hierarchy, or any kind of personifying correspondence. In many of the numerous cases, the bond may be a mere metaphor. Among the Otomi, for example, the main cylinder of a sugar mill is the mother, the dependent cylinders are the children (Galinier 1987:387). Occasionally the relationship seems to have a deeper but unclear meaning, as when the arrow is thought to be the flesh of the bow (Ruiz de Alarcón 1953:85).

The most interesting part of the process is when a bond leads to humanlike conduct. In the Chamula tale in which the Sun acquires the character of son of the Moon, the latter must leave a bowl of *atole* (corn gruel) on the eastern horizon each morning for her son's breakfast (Gossen 1974:43). Such a maternal custom, explained or added to other human procedures of the astral bodies, can contribute to the creation of an episode.

Often a relationship is established between animals and meterological changes or the beginning of seasonal periods. It can be strong enough to appear in the name of an animal. The *cenotzqui {Falco columbarius}*, or "ice caller," was a bird that, according to the Nahua began, to sing when it felt the arrival of frost in the wind (*Códice Florentino* 1979: bk. 11, ch. 2, fol. 49r). Certain animals "belong" to a particular natural process and should, therefore, be respected, since they are the property of certain forces or certain gods. The Mocho (Petrich 1985:130) forbid eating crabs, saying that their consumption will result in a drought, and to the east of Mocho territory, in Honduras, the Jicaqui explain even more clearly that one must not crush crabs because they are the companions of water (Chapman 1978:102).

Higher up the hierarchical scale are the messengers or war captains of the gods, the owl, for example, or the weasel, whose mission was to relay to humankind the ominous messages of the Lady or Lord of the Dead (*Códice Florentino* 1979: bk. 5, fol. 7v–8v).[6] They also relayed messages to the *nahuales* (shaman sorcerers) or to the god images, earthly containers of divine forces; among them, according to the ancient Nahua (*Códice Florentino* 1979: bk. 5, ch. 9, fol. 9v; ch. 15, fol. 14r), were the fox and the coyote and, according to modern Nahua, the donkey and the opossum (or fox), who belong to Tonantsi, the Mother Goddess (Ziehm in Preuss 1982:49). Traces of these primary relationships are often found in the pantheon of Mesoamerican people: Pahtecatl, Mayahuel's husband, is the god of the plant that begins the fermentation of maguey juice that becomes pulque. Mayahuel, she of the four hundred breasts, is the maguey plant (*Códice Vaticano-Latino* 3738 1964–67: pl. 35).

4.   The great sector of the imperceptible (or nearly imperceptible). Another of the processes that are potential paths to the formation of the history of the gods is the objectification of the attributes as invisible forms. Here there is a double inverse process. With regard to the "sympathy of all,"[7] the human characteristics of what is not human are conceived as being imperceptible. What human beings have in common with the nonhuman is also imperceptible. People are therefore filled with invisible, animistic forces, and the world is full of playful, mocking, often ill-intentioned beings, which deride men and fight, converse, or love each other. A creaking is taken to be their whispering or their cautious steps through a thicket. Nature acquires a will.

In the imaginary dealings with the invisible are born the episodes people claim to perceive. In the pictographic codices of the ancient Maya, "divine fights are frequent, death fights against abundance, drought against corn, moderate rain against devastating floods" (Rivera Dorado 1985:182).

5. Everything has an imperceptible part with characteristics impressed in the original time. The last of the processes proposed here is the remission of all that exists to the "first time." Through this process, the worth and the characteristics of beings are recognized. It is convenient for there to be a starting point in the time of creation for everything in the area of the invisible that must be manipulated. And in daily life, should not everything be manipulated in its visible aspect as well as its invisible aspect? Everything has a portion of the supernatural, and because of that, everything can be affected by procedures for managing the supernatural. It is not strange, then, that action directed toward the invisible is found in the most diverse practices. In the seventeenth century, Balsalobre (1953:351–52) encountered this situation among the Zapotec:

> Where, by sorcery, they get most of their magical answers and prognostications: for what kind of fishing, what kind of hunting, the harvesting of corn, chili, or cochineal; any illness and the superstitious medicine to cure it; the division of work and the avoidance of death in their homes; the success of pregnancy and of giving birth by their women; the success of their children; the songs of birds and animals that are auguries for them; dreams and their interpretation; the success they will have in their undertakings; and the reparation of damages forecast for them.
>
> And in particular, when the first ears of corn are gathered on the day specified by the director of said rites, there is the sacrifice of a native black hen [turkey], the sprinkling of thirteen pieces of copal with its blood, in memory of their thirteen gods. Then the copal is burned and the rest of the blood is sprinkled in the patio of their house. They offer this to the god of corn and of all their food, called Loçucuy, in thanks for the good harvest they have had. And, when they offer it, they repeat certain words in their language in a very low voice as if they were praying. They do the same thing when they reap the first chili peppers, offering a sacrifice to Lociyo, the god of lightning, in the same way as the preceding one. And when they plant the nopal cactus or harvest cochineal, they sacrifice white hens to the god they call Coqueelaa, said to be their advocate. And when they hunt deer or other animals, they sacrifice to Niyohua, god of hunters; but if in their hunting they fail to secure game through the intervention of said god, they sacrifice a second time, and observe a three-day penitence and a twenty-four-hour fast. For the same reason, they sacrifice to the god Noçana, one of their ancestors. At the time of their women's pregnancy and giving birth, they appeal to the goddess Nohuichana. And to her also at

the time of trout fishing, they burn copal and light wax candles on the banks by deep places of the river to insure success in the catch.

All these manifestations of myth-belief, germs of divine episodes, show a very slow genesis in the history of the gods. It is not an explosion in the imagination of the mytho-poet. It is the slowly paced accumulation of meanings that are refined in the communications of the users. Each step is repeated innumerable times and tested in social intercourse. Included in historical myth are people's thoughts about themselves, their work, their interrelations, and conditions, through the everyday action that is a form of knowledge. Historical changes (including technological ones) cause myth to transform itself, and the results of the conflicts that exist in social life remain imbedded in the myth.

Contrary to what is currently believed, there is little place for fantasy. The logic of classifications, the reality of work processes, the rigidity of natural processes, and the logic of projections of the social onto the natural or the imaginary, as well as of what is natural onto the social or the imaginary, are united in a mythical stream with characters that have previous attributes, with histories that have their own laws of formation.

The adventures of the gods are made up of episodes dictated by the sum of converging currents, and the formative events remain as one more piece of the harmonious "first time." A legitimate order is formed, that of the law that governs the invisible, an order that some investigators today try to find in order to explain the reason behind the ancient beliefs:

> obsidian is black and cold, just the opposite of white, hot flint. Itztlacoliuh-qui[8] was born from the earth, in the darkness, in the same way that Venus, the Morning Star "is born" from earth and night. The gods love him. Flint, to the contrary, appeared in the place of fire and of heat, the highest place in the heavens. The gods were horrified. One of them went to the sky; the other descended to earth. Flint precedes obsidian as the germ precedes the fruit . . . Flint is the grain of corn; obsidian is the new sprout. One is the celestial fire and the other may be domestic fire (Graulich 1987b:110).

For the believer there is an abyss between mythical history and real life. The faithful believe in two different orders—one visible, the other invisible—each with its own laws and its own ways of impinging on the unique and compound reality of the world of people. There can be a place for oneiric vision; but in the production of myths, dreams—which also derive from what is social—are socially adapted.

The history of the histories of the gods is social, not as a simultaneous creation, but as a play of relationships among individuals who think, act, and express themselves, having as a basis their daily experience and their own relative positions within society. The stories of the gods are a synthesis of the infinite forms of ordered thinking with which human beings face nature and society to transform them; a synthesis of the infinite forms of interrelations among human beings; a synthesis of new and old episodes. They are born in *daily life,* or as Agnes Heller (1985:39–40, 42) defines it, the life of *every person,* in which all aspects of individuality, of personality, participate; in which are put to work all the senses, passions, ideas, and ideologies; the heterogeneous life that has, as organic parts, the organization of work and of private life, entertainment, rest, or systematized social activity, trade, and purification, a life that is not outside history, but at the center of historical events, the true essence of social reality.

The adventures of the gods are, for the most part, the product of designs, but not an intentional product. The intentions are found in the management of the body, of the cornfield, of the workshop, of the kitchen; but the adventures integrate themselves beyond any creative volition, going beyond any consciousness that emerges from human thinking. Praxis has a dual face, as Sánchez Vásquez (1985:387) says:

> It is intentional inasmuch as the individual pursues a particular purpose with it; unintentional inasmuch as his individual conscious activity adopts a social form and is integrated into a collective praxis—production as a social activity—that leads to global results . . . the production and maintenance of a set of social relationships . . . that elude his consciousness and his will.

It is also a praxis in which the action of coherence is manifested in a dual fashion; on the one hand, in the occurrence of minor, daily actions; on the other, in the great and slow collectivization that ends by producing the history of the gods. The coherence of these histories—like that of cosmovision—does not require a·harmonizing consciousness of the universal order. Multiple normative systems end by producing harmony in the beliefs. But it is never a total harmony. It is always changing, never perfect, dispersed in social consciousness, but sufficient for incongruencies to pass unperceived in the eyes of the believer, who will always find in that harmony the hand of the gods.

Finally, divine adventures are the result of a daily life in which the rational and the emotional, the conscious and the unconscious, are mixed; but they are purified in the rationality of collective creation. They emerge finally from all

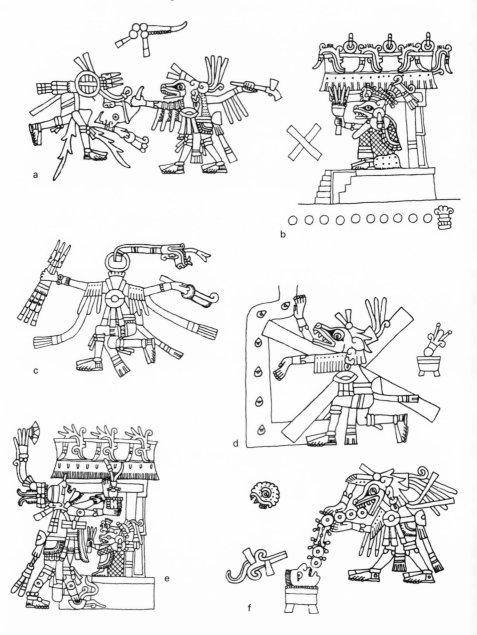

Figure 10. Opossums from *Fejérváry Mayer Codex*

    a. plate 37=7   b. plate 30=15
    c. plate 41=4   d. plate 43=2
    e. plate 33=12   f. plate 42=3

social levels and are shaped by the processes of ideological dominance, subordination, and marginalization. They are formed in the mold of the social order, but also under a parallel, different order, a law of the gods that is a distorted copy of the law of humanity. They are born integrated into the total concept of the universe, even though it is a concept that never achieves total harmony.

The Beginning of Art:
The song of the man who is sowing
the ricefields.

Matsuo Basho

In Huauhtla de Jiménez, Pablo Guerrero Contreras, a Mazatec, told Carlos Incháustegui (1977:67–68) the myth about the fire and the opossum:

They say there was an old woman who succeeded in capturing fire when it scarcely had fallen away from some stars and planets. She was not afraid, and she went to bring it from where the fire had fallen. She held it a long time until people thought the fire should belong to everyone and not just the old woman. They went to the old woman's house to ask for fire, but the old woman defied them and refused to give it to anyone. Word went around that the old woman had captured fire but did not want to give it away. Then the opossum came forth and said to the gathering:

"I, Opossum, promise to give you fire, and, if I don't you can eat me."

They they laughed at the poor animal, but he, quite serene, answered,

"Do not keep on laughing at me, because the joke will be on you. I will have the last laugh, because this very evening you will see how I keep my promise."

That afternoon, the Opossum went from house to house, saying he was going to the old woman's house to get the fire, but that the others were to gather up as much as they could. At last he came to the old woman's house, and he said to her,

"Good afternoon, Lady Fire, how cold it is! I would like to stand before your fire a while to get warm, because I am freezing to death."

The old woman believed the opossum was cold and let him come near the fire; but the crafty animal kept getting nearer and nearer until he could put his tail in the fire and carry it off. As soon as his tail was ablaze, he ran away, distributing the fire as far as it would go.

And that is why, even today, opossums' tails are hairless.

This tale is a crystallization of many different parts of myth-belief that go into the making of a divine history, the story of how fire was taken from Lady Fire by trickery. Listeners recognize old images in the tale, well-known truths that, through repetition, become even more precious. The story of the opossum thief, probably known to all Mazatec, is always entertaining. It is the best-developed expression of a belief (the origin of the use of fire by humans), because nothing surpasses language as a means for expressing thought. However, it cannot be said that myth-narration is merely a product or a part of myth-belief. Both have parallel existences, intimately linked in their mutual influence. Myth, when it becomes narration, comes under a particular set of rules, those of oral literature. The styles of oral narrative remodel it and subject it to patterns that narrator and audience integrate into a creative unity. After the myth-narration is formed, it adjusts beliefs to its own canon. It is true that it is created by mythic belief, but it also generates it, recreates it, sets the norm. Mythic belief and narration, in their most advanced forms, compose two overlapping, dynamic nuclei.

The story is not the only verbal form by which myth-belief can be expressed. Invocations, sayings, songs, jests, and riddles can also refer to the marsupial that stole fire from the gods. If a Trique woman carries coals borrowed from a neighbor to her house, her friends make fun of her, calling her "opossum" (Hollenbach 1977). By referring to the divine tale without actually telling it, a Huichol father can forbid his son to eat opossum meat. Many forms can be used to express the belief, but the mythical narration is the clear, complete, coherent verbal expression of it from beginning to end. Expression of myth-belief finds many forms—some are verbal, some are gesture, others iconographic; but myth-narration is mythical expression par excellence. Myth-belief is made up of dispersed, often contradictory, heterogeneous pieces. Myth-narrative, in its unity, possesses a great internal congruency.

Myth-narration, even though it is more easily defined than myth-belief, presents problems when ethnologists try to distinguish it from other kinds of popular narrative. In 1941 Boas (1968:454) complained about the confusion in collections of American indigenous narrative in which the terms myth and folktale were poorly defined. In order to make the necessary distinction, ethnologists apply the literary theory of genres. This theory is not devoid of problems, but they are interesting problems, some of which will be addressed here.

The debate about genres is intense, and it is sharpened by the inclusion of oral literature in the theory. Oral forms of expression have only recently been accepted as a subject for study in literary theory. Literature as a subject for study was delimited from the heights of the intellectual elite. Often prejudices were supported by weak etymological arguments. Literature was the art of the letters, its beauty transmitted through the written word. In Mexico these boundaries were maintained until very recently. Less than three decades ago, there were arguments about whether the pre-Hispanic Nahua had a literature. Those who argued against it claimed that the Nahua did not have a phonetic system accurate enough for use in an artistic presentation of the language. Garibay K. was the defender of pre-Hispanic literature. He fought to extend the concept of literature so that it would include any artistic manifestation of the language. He won the battle against strong opposition. In other countries the concept had been expanded years before to accommodate similar scientific needs. The criteria changed with the increased study of ancient or current popular texts, all of them oral. The forms of expression that literary theory could include were increased, and as a result, the problems of the theory of genres became more complex.

One of the fundamental problems of the theory of genres is precisely what their nature is. Tzvetan Todorov opposes Benedetto Croce's position, which gave to genres no more validity than that of abstractions useful in classification, and Maurice Blanchot's position, which denied any relevance to literary genres. Todorov (1981:10) argues that there is a need to recognize the properties that every literary text has in common with a like group of subtexts (or with a subgroup in literature) that receives the name of genre. It is undeniable that literary works fall into groups, and that they do this because of obvious attributes that presuppose the existence of fundamental, less-perceptible bonds that constitute a causal chain. This is the basis of the concept of genres. The attributes arise from literary practices, understood in the widest social sense. Any individual creation is to some degree innovative, but not completely new. It takes place within a framework of "norms" that cause the work to emerge in close affinity to a group of texts that have responded to similar social factors and have had similar purposes and uses. The reaffirmation of the attributes of kindred works is part of the path of "appropriate" expression, which allows authors to present their work to the public conveniently. Authors and their public follow a convention that often is not explicit and is never so in its minor details.

Seeing a cluster of literary attributes in kindred works leads to thinking in terms of genres. However, there have been and still are different concepts of what genres are. According to Wellek and Warren (1949:243–45):

> Anyone interested in genre theory must be careful not to confound the distinctive differences between "classical" and modern theory. Classical theory is regulative and prescriptive, though its "rules" are not the silly authoritarianism still often attributed to them. Classical theory not only believes that genre differs from genre, in nature and in glory, but also that they must be kept apart, not allowed to mix. . . .

Modern genre theory is, clearly, descriptive. It doesn't limit the number of possible kinds and doesn't prescribe rules to authors. It supposes that traditional kinds may be "mixed" and produce a new kind (like tragicomedy). It sees that genres can be built up on the basis of inclusiveness or "richness" as well as that of "purity" (genre by accretion as well as by reduction).

And so there is a genre from classical theory that is predominantly regulative and prescriptive. Also, according to these writers, there is an plainly descriptive genre, coming from the modern theory of genres. There is also a third meaning of genre, a genre that can be a theoretical tool, as a result of practical action of the subject on reality. In this third sense, the genre is not a mere abstraction of characteristics observed in the specific works, but a design to explain and describe scientifically a type of literature, based on observation and also—fundamentally—on a literary theory. Its purpose is to explain but also to take into account the distinguishing features, their causes, and their effects on the social use of the works; to understand their historical transformation; to define similarities and differences of creation in different traditions, which may or may not have communicated with each other; to find the processes that produce parallelisms or divergences in the comparison; and to predict hypothetically what characteristics literary works will have under certain circumstances. Such a genre is a valuable methodological tool for the identification, classification, and study of literary works in all societies.

The concept-genre, coming from specific reality, should be useful in learning about that specific reality. But it should also help to understand other realities that were not taken into account in the process of its construction. Can it be applied to literary works belonging to very different and distant cultural traditions? Concepts are tested by reality, are transformed by it, and should in theory have the ability to adapt to different objects of study. Concepts, then, are objects of knowledge that change with time and under different circumstances. Here is a double effect: There is one historical transformation produced in a literary creation, and another in the construction of the genres, whether these be considered predominantly prescriptive, descriptive, or theoretical.

Let us first look at literary creation. It is true that the attributes of literary works, as well as groupings derived from them, are subject to historical events, that they belong to a specific social reality; but it is also true that a coincidence in the factors of the composition and the social use of the literary product can produce attributes shared by differing literary realities. If a kind of verbal creation, for instance mythical narration, and a similar social use of said creation are the same in two or more groups of people in different cultural traditions, it is reasonable to assume that the similarity of their literary creations will be such that they can be brought together into one literary genre. In this particular case, our scientific object of knowledge would be the mythic genre. The existence of enough common characteristics to use the concept of a literary genre will be possible if there are coincidences in the nature of the characters, in the natural or supernatural laws that govern them, in the quality of the cosmic time in which the action unfolds, in the degree of verosimilitude accorded the tale by society, in the type and conditions of its expression, and in the social use made of the texts. It is obvious that such mutual characteristics would be more numerous in societies having a tradition, development, and historical period in common; but that does not exclude the possibility of a real, important coincidence in the products of different societies.

The reality of the attributes is perceived from different traditions and forms of knowledge. This results in the construction of literary genres from literary theory and from outside it, based on the literary works of the culture itself and those of different cultures. But it must be made clear that there can be great differences in the forms of perceiving and of constructing reality. We should not expect, for every society that creates mythical literature, that groups will be identified in the same way, that they will participate identically in the process of literary creation, or that they will have the same motivation for seeking common attributes in the works produced.

What should be done in the case of an indigenous literary reality that has its own characteristics? Some authors choose not to apply their own categories if these do not coincide with the native classification (Bricker 1981:5). Others strive to ascertain the existing genre differences, independently of whatever distinctions their creators make (P. Carrasco 1976a:98–99).

For the subject we are studying, it is indispensable to establish the distinction between two concepts of genre. 1. One that is predominantly normative and prescriptive, with a large descriptive component, which could be termed an indigenous literary genre, and which belongs to the native cultural tradition but is a foreign concept to the investigator. An indigenous literary genre, since it is normative and prescriptive, is characterized by the extent of its influence on the reality to which it refers. It not only characterizes that reality, it guides and regulates its production. 2. A concept coming from the investigator's own literary theory, which suffices to describe and explain groups of texts (whether they belong to the investigator's tradition or not), characterized by their literary attributes. This could be called a theoretical literary genre. Both concepts of genre come from a broad and abstract intellectual corpus, not just from the study of literary reality. Both are logical instruments used to perceive, order, and understand reality. Both concepts are mutable; but the theoretical literary genre changes through the will of the investigator, faced with the need to adjust the concepts to the objects under study.

Boas (1968:455) found that among American Indians there was often a clear distinction between myths and folk tales. According to the indigenous classification, myths deal with incidents at a time when the world did not yet have its present form and when humanity did not possess all the skills and customs that belong to our own era. Folk tales, on the contrary, are stories about our own times. How can ethnologists or historians use information about classifications made by a society with a tradition different from their own and from a different perspective of knowledge? We base our knowledge on our own theory. Our concepts are the basic tools we use to express our disciplines. Can we temporarily lay aside our concept of the world to accept, through empathy, past or alien concepts? Many thinkers have had this illusion, but the results have not gone beyond an expression of solidarity with a stranger, or, from another angle, a romanticism that looks to the past, reconstructing it from a present it cannot renounce. An Arabian proverb says, "Your knowledge is not like the clothing you wear. It is not possible to eliminate it when you submerge yourself in your bath." Accepting foreign categories as your own is just a beautiful illusion. We cannot believe, like a believer can, that the mythical story is the narration of real events of existing gods.

However, there may be great wisdom in the categories of the creators of myths, past or present. This wisdom can be used advantageously to construct or to reconstruct our own concepts. Indigenous classifications refer, in the case of literary expression of mythic belief, to a way of thinking with which we will never be sufficiently familiar and to a social life (collective or individual) that we will never fully share. However, it is knowledge reflected in native literary classification, which can be used to approach our object of knowledge. Classification is one of the most important factors in a concept of the world. How can we create an adequate literary concept of theoretical mythic genre without being well acquainted with the concepts of the society that produces the myth? The operative rationality of the indigenous mythic genre makes it a prime source of information.

The normative-prescriptive nature of native literary genre requires the existence of a specific terminology. Even though terminology is not indispensable, it is useful for regulation and direction. The required first step is thus a search for native classificatory terms. To this end it must be remembered that in some cases the investigators will seek to discover native classes and classifications; in others the investigators will create the classes and order them hierarchically, according to their own personal criteria.

As examples, let us see how two investigators of pre-Hispanic Nahuatl literature, Fernando Horcasitas and Miguel León-Portilla, have dealt with the problem of mythic narration. Horcasitas (1978, 1982) divided ancient Nahuatl prose into six classes: 1. myth; 2. epic, or the history of the deeds of heroes; 3. legend; 4. the etiological story; 5. the example; 6. *huehuetlatolli*, or speech. In spite of the fact that one of the classifying words is in Nahuatl, Horcasitas does not seek to discover the ancient classes. His division is not applicable to the criteria that I have given, since the mythic narration to which I refer would fall into the first, second, and fourth genres, according to the description and examples given by the author. Thus Horcasitas considered the birth of Huitzilopochtli to be an epic.

In a long article, León-Portilla (1983) divides the literary production of the ancient Nahua into classes and subclasses, including the mythic tale. León-Portilla begins with a genre, the *tlahtolli*, and divides it into three groups of subgenres: 1. those "found in the field of narrative," called *tlaquetzalli*; 2. "a kind of subgenre that includes among others the *huehuetlahtolli*, "ancient words," often containing didactic material or exhortations and the exposition of ancient religious or moral doctrines or those referring to modes of conduct under different circumstances"; and 3. another group of *tlahtolli*, among "those that describe (either for information or for normative purposes) different cultural institutions, such as the organization of trade and markets, the responsibilities of people in certain professions, knowledge about certain animals, plants, pharmacology, medicine, the calendar and destinies, etc."

The subgenre tlaquetzalli is subdivided into three groups: 1.1. *teotlahtolli*, or "divine words," which refer to the cosmos, the gods, culture heroes, and other personages; 1.2. those *in ye huecauh tlahtolli*, also called *itoloca* and *tlahtollotl*, which are "discourses or the relating of a subject, sometimes legendary or strictly historical"; and 1.3. the *tlamachiliz-tlahtol-zazanilli*, that is, "remembrances of real or imaginary events, transmitted by word of mouth, which could be compared to fables, advice, and even to certain kinds of stories." The teotlahtolli (1.1), among which mythical narrations can be found, are also subdivided into: 1.1.1. those that deal with cosmic and divine origins; 1.1.2. those that tell of culture heroes (for example, the story of the wise priest Quetzalcoatl); and 1.1.3. those that refer to "the doings of other gods and personages."[1]

The present critique will focus on the mythic tale, its classes, and nomenclature. León-Portilla does not make clear whether he is dealing with the classes and nomenclature of the ancient Nahua or those created by him. If the former, the citation of sources in which the nomenclature is linked to specific Nahua texts is lacking; if the latter, his reasons for creating the classes are missing. What is certain is that the nomenclature is disconcerting; some of its problems are as follows:

1.   The term *teotlahtolli* does not appear to be directly related to any mythic text of pre-Hispanic origin, in spite of its meaning "divine words." It is found in reference to the Bible (*Códice Florentino* 1979:bk. 1, appendix ch. 16, fol. 29r, 30r, 30v, 31v),[2] and in Molina's *Vocabulario*, among words formed during colonial times, such as *teotlatolcuepa*, "to be a heretic." The term could have been used in pre-Hispanic texts, but there is no proof of its use in them.

2.   Mythic texts written in Nahuatl refer to their own narration with different terms: *zazanilli, tlamachiliztlatolzazanilli, tlatlatollotl, nenonotzalli,* and *tlanonotzaliztli.*[3] León-Portilla mentions none of these in referring to myths, although he does use them for other subclasses, such as *tlahtollotl* (1.2), and *zazanilli* and *tlamachiliz-tlahtol-zazanilli* (1.3).

3.   León-Portilla classifies the story of the priest Quetzalcoatl as a *teotlahtolli* in subcategory 1.1.2. Nevertheless one of the versions of the story (*Códice Florentino* 1959: bk. 3, ch. 3, fol. 9r) begins with the words "inic ei capitulo, itechpa tlatoa in itoloca in Quetzalcoatl," and thus should be included among the *itoloca* (1.2).

Thus in spite of his use of Nahuatl nomenclature, the classification proposed by León-Portilla, at least that corresponding to mythical narration, differs considerably from the terminology used by the Nahua themselves.

What can be obtained from the names in the mythic texts written in the Nahuatl language? It is doubtful that there is a name for the myth genre in the texts. The terms *tlanonotzaliztli* and *nenonotzaliztli,* both derived from the verb *notza,* cannot refer specifically to myth. Their meaning of "relation," "exposition of something," is too general. The same is true of *tlallatollotl,* since it means "speech." The term *zazanilli,* however, does approach the sense of mythic narration. Molina (1944: Nahuatl-Spanish fol. 13v) and Siméon (1977: 55), respectively, give the meaning as "amusing tales" and "jokes," but the meaning is actually less specific. As Siméon (1977) and Campbell (1985:442) both point out, *zazanilli* is derived from *zazan* ("without a motive," "without importance"), from which it can be deduced that it refers to any speech for the purpose of amusement. It becomes more specific when greater precision is given to the term. Thus there are the *zazanilli mitoa zazan tleino* (*Códice Florention* 1979: bk. 6, ch. 41, fol. 183r), or riddles, literally "the amusing narrations that are called 'What is this?' " In our case the specific term for the myth genre would be *tlamachiliztlatolzazanilli,* a word Velásquez (*Leyenda de los soles* 1945:129) explains as follows:

> *Tlamachiliztli, tlatolli, çaçanilli.* The second and third are well known. According to Father Carochi, *tlamachiliztli* is "wisdom"; and *tlamachilizyotl* or *tlamachilizçotl* are derived from it. This meaning could be dubious, because *machilia,* applicable to both cases, forms *tlamachiliztli,* and Molina in his *Vocabulario* renders the regularly formed *tlamatiliztli* as "wisdom." However, Molina himself accepts the other meaning, as is seen in "ignorance, *amomachiliztli.*"

Velásquez (*Leyenda de los soles* 1945:119) translates *tlamachiliztlatolzazanilli* as "the tales of the wise." Literally it is "the amusing narrations of wise words." Was that word in common use to designate the myth genre? It appears only once in the texts. There really is no term to designate mythic narration that we can attribute to the ancient Nahua.

The distinction in terminology is not very precise in the records of the oral literatures of other peoples of the Mesoamerican tradition. In the *Título de Totonicapán,* the Quiche word *bixel* is used to designate the biblical myth of the Earthly Paradise. *Bixel* means "song"; Carmack (*Título de Totonicapán* 1983:167, 205n7) surmises that the word is related to the singing of the Mass. At the present time, the Spanish word *cuento* ("story") is used for mythic narrations among the Tepehua, the Trique, the Tzotzil, and the Nahua, for example (Williams García 1972:61, Hollenbach 1977, Gossen 1980, González Cruz and Anguiano 1984). In other regions, however, the term *sasanilli* is still used among the Nahua (Barlow and Ramírez 1962).

The lack of precision in terms does not imply a lack of distinction between myth and story. The Mazatec (Boege 1988:90–91), for instance, distinguish between tales to "pass the time" and those "that are not lies," the ones that tell "how life was before." Speaking of the second kind, they explain that "we live in accordance with the stories because that is the way life is." The Huichol (Furst and Myerhoff 1972), when speaking of their myths, point out the same characteristics:

> This is how it was. We must know it well. We must know it all. Because the symbols tell all that is sacred to us, and the tales I tell you are our legends, our history. What they say, what they bring in their wisdom, that is our history, that is what has to be fully understood. I tell you these things, how it was for us in ancient times, how it is now.

The imprecision in terminology and classification cannot be generalized. There have been valuable investigations into native classification of the forms of expression that have revealed a well-developed taxonomical system. Only two of these investigations will be examined here, and only as they deal with classifying narratives about the time of creation. Gossen (1974:47, 50–51, 140–43) found that the Chamulas in their oral expression have what they call "open words," belonging to ordinary language, and the "closed or tied ones," "pure" words that refer to the creation of the world. The "pure" words can only be uttered under certain circumstances. "Authentic ancient narrative," characterized by its redundancy and its multiplicity of terms, is, according to the Chamula, a language that has stored the warmth of the creations from which it came. Ordinary unrestricted language, on the other hand, is cold. The Mocho, another Maya-speaking group, also distinguish their forms of expression based on the polarity of cold/hot, but they place the sacred account on the cool side. Petrich (1985:41–45, 65) says that the Mocho think words exist autonomously, as forces, after they have been spoken. They glide "like an arrow through the air" and enter the body to which they are directed; through the ears when they are beneficial and tranquil, and through the joints when they are harmful and filled with bad intentions. Hot words are the ones used with evil, disturbing intent. The sorcerer has a "mouth of fire." The *qamán* (the "defender"), on the other hand, pronounces cool words. The words the gods address to men are also cool, as are the ones used in the histories of the ancestors. Those stories are divided into free narrations about "deceitful animals" and "true histories of the ancient people," or sacred stories. These divisions of the Chamula and the Mocho clarify some expressions that appear in the texts of other indigenous groups. In Quintana Roo, when the presiding official defines the words used in the prayer accompanying his offering, he says they are "cold virgin words," *zuhuy zizolan than* (Villa Rojas 1978:456).

Indigenous peoples' conception of their own literature offers a rich field for investigation. It is invaluable, of course, for historians and ethnologists to construct the required concepts, which cannot be done without taking the indigenous viewpoint into account. Nor can it be done by focusing only on what is strictly literary. Of what use would the Chamula and Mocho categories be to us if we had no idea of the importance of the cold/hot polarity in the general taxonomy of the cosmos? Lévi-Strauss has been criticized (Leach 1970: 27) for his tendency to deal with myths for their own sake, without referring to their social content; and for his idea that their meaning can come only through a study of the oppositions. The study of myths, and even the literary study of mythic texts, cannot ignore the rich social reality that produces them. Malinowski (1954) said that myth "is not only a story told, but a reality lived," and he concluded that "limitation of the study of myth to the mere examination of texts has been fatal to a proper understanding of its nature."

How can we construct the proposed theoretical myth genre? I believe we are still far from an adequate formula; fieldwork still needs to be done on its complex problems. Here we will examine some of the traits that have been attributed to the genre.

What kind of discourse is a myth? The nature of its text was discussed in chapter 3, in order to emphasize its autonomy and its limits. One of its most important linguistic aspects is that it is oral. This oral character allows myth to be produced in its proper environment. The text is disfigured when it is separated from its customary way of expression and its expectant and partici- pating audience, the public who receives the discourse in its native tongue and is familiar with the motives and themes of the characters, the style and repu- tation of the narrator, and usually with the story being told. The word, the finest vehicle for thought, is not the only one by which myth is carried. There are also gestures, the surroundings, the occasion for the narration, everything that a specific, emotional state transmits, given life both by narrator and audi- ence. There are the onomatopoeias, the exclamations of admiration, questions (pertinent or not), pauses, voice modulations—all of these condition the word and limit it, enrich it, dictate the rhythms, the grammatical structures, the resonances.

An oral myth transcribed can be a beautiful imitation. But a myth dictated to an investigator, our most precious resource, is incomplete. It lacks the force of expression that goes beyond the word, the force that modifies the word. The myth that the informant writes down, convinced that it is in the "cultured language" and that writing is the best recipient of popular wisdom, is at best an exercise in a different literary field.

> On the road she came face to face with mister chameleon, who, because of his
> ashen color, she would do anything to avoid stepping on. Puffing himself up
> in an indignant fashion and straightening his "little horns," he said to her,
> "through a reliable source in the forest I have been informed that you ate the
> barbecued flesh of your husband. Aren't you ashamed of yourself? You're a can-
> nibal!" But the lady, because of her distress and her continuous weeping, paid
> no attention to what the Saurian reptile was saying and continued on her way.
> (Domínguez Martínez 1970)

By its syntax the mythic text is characterized as a narration. Time and logic define its nature.[4] As Bremond (1985) says:

> Every narration consists of a discourse that integrates a sequence of events of
> human interest in the unity of a single action. Where there is no succession,

there is no story but perhaps a description (if all the objects in the discourse are associated in a spatial contiguity), a deduction (if one implies the other), a lyric effusion (if metaphor or metonymy is used), etc. Where there is no integration in the unity of a single action, there is no story but only chronology, the presentation of a series of uncoordinated happenings. Finally, where there is no implied human interest (where the events told are not produced by agents nor suffered by passive anthropomorphic subjects), there can be no story, because it is only in relation to a human enterprise that happenings acquire a meaning and can be organized into a structured temporal series.

The mythic tale has its laws of syntax, its particular interplay of agents and conditions, its own sequences. Other texts may share characters, acts of power, and references to the world of the gods and their order; but they will not be myths if they lack mythic syntax. Agents must perform in a certain determined order the kind of actions that will have as a corollary certain kinds of consequences. Moreover the relations among the textual units will form a story, an adventure. Therefore the interesting text (Díaz Hernández 1945:64) about the god of rain from the Nahua along the Gulf of Mexico is not a myth:

> Nanahuatzin, the God of Rain, is in the sea. All the towns that are near, say a six-day walk to reach the seashore, will say, they will tell you, that when Nanahuatzin is angry, he makes the ocean tremble, and that is what is heard in these places: Altotonga, Ver[acruz]; Jalacingo, Ver.; Tlapacoyan, Ver.; Teziutlan, Pue[bla]; Zacapoaxtla, Pue.; Tetela de Ocampo, Pue.; Zacatlan, Pue.; Huachinango, Pue. When one listens early, the rain always falls hard, about eight or nine o'clock (in the morning). Then nobody can go outside, sheep and goats cannot go to the pastures to graze . . . Nanahuatzin is not heard always, only in June, July, August, and September. They say he sleeps in the depths of the sea during the other months.

The citation above is the verbal expression of a mythic belief. It has the same degree of truth as a myth. There is the telling of an action that accounts for the seasonal presence or absence of rain. A god acts as the agent. However, it lacks the particular sequence of textual units that makes the narration an adventure.

References to beginnings are essential to the semantic aspect of the myth. Moreover that theme is the link between different types of time and space. As Lévi-Strauss (1979b) says, "The first characteristic of a myth is that of operating on time as a totalizing action, one that folds—like an accordion—the present over the past and the future over the present." Before discussing the truth of a myth, it can be said that a mythical theme is, as the natives declare, a real event. There is an agreement between narrator and audience that the subject deals with an actual happening. Thus a narration with a theme of beginnings, even if it has the syntaxical form of a myth, will not be mythic if it does not refer to passage between divine time-space and human time-space. Today there are stories in Mexico that have the appearance of myths; but here I would like to tell an Arabian story recorded in the fourteenth century. It is a beautiful tale that Ibn Batutta (1981:355) tells about the origin of the coconut. The story does not go back to an original time:

> They say that formerly there was a doctor in India, who was very close to that country's king, who esteemed him greatly. This king also had a vizier, who was the doctor's enemy. The feeling was mutual. One day the doctor said to the king, "If you cut off the vizier's head and bury it, a palm tree will spring forth bearing extraordinary dates that would be an advantage to all the people of India and to the other parts of the world." The king answered, "And if what you say doesn't spring forth from the vizier's head?" The doctor replied, "In that case, you will do to my head what you have done to his." The king then ordered the vizier to be beheaded. The doctor took the head and planted a date seed in the brain and cultivated it until it became a tree and produced coconuts as fruit.

The theoretical myth genre awaits its construction. Will the day come when literary theory can create a concept applicable to the tales of Mesoamerica and the Arabian Peninsula, applicable to the mythic texts produced everywhere around the world? I think it would be possible only in the most general terms.

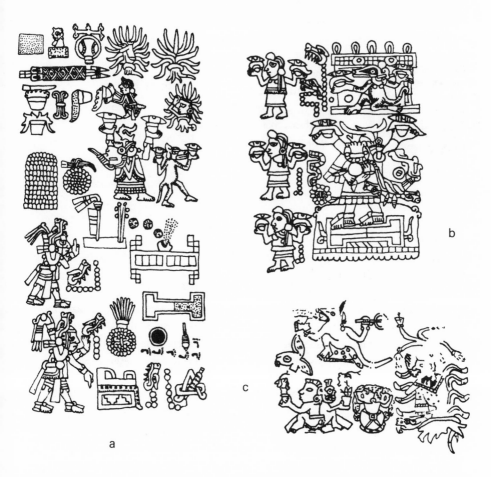

Figure 11. The opossum associated with beheading, the maguey, pulque, the ball game, and the cradle

    a. *Vindobonensis Codex,* plate 40 = 13

    b. *Nuttall Codex,* plate 5

    c. *Codex Vaticanus 3738,* plate 31

17 INVENTION

The name of the author is unknown.
The Hindus attribute his works to the divinity,
to a sect, to a character in a fable, or simply to Time,
a hypothesis that seems plausible to me,
but which alarms the erudite.

Jorge Luis Borges,
Prologue to the *Bhagavad-Gita*

Jesús Rentería, a Huichol, told me and a group of friends the myth of fire and the opossum:

Far off, at a gravelly place, on a rocky cliff, a small light is seen. At that time there was no such thing. Fire did not exist. "Well," they said, "What can that be? Let's go nearer to see what it is." They went there as best they could. Struggling, they got to the place. And there it was. There was something there like a little star. And then, "I believe that this—that this can be put to use. It can eat something. We must eat. We must search." Then they looked for the *palo bobo* tree and they began to throw in pieces of the wood. It began to smoke, small flames began to come out, and they began to blow on it. Then it caught fire.

All the people were amazed. "It is going . . . I think it is fire. With this . . . We are going to have this now." They thought that it could be used to cook something . . . Then all the people came around to get warm, and it felt good. They were very pleased, very happy to get warm. Then the others began to be vigilant. "We are going to keep watch over this so no one can steal it, because this is going to be for us alone."

And with that, at that time many other people arrived. "We too are going to take it." Seeing that they would not let them, they waited until the guards were sleeping, and one of them carried off a live coal to start a fire away from there. When the watchmen awoke, they couldn't find it. They went right away to recover it, and they overtook them on the road to take it away. They grabbed the firebrand and ran, but they overtook them and beat them. And so they kept their fire until the opossum came and said to them, "I am going to warm myself here by the fire because I am very cold." [They responded] "No, they are trying to steal it. Perhaps you too want to steal it." "No, I did not come for that. I just want to get warm." And now the plan to steal it was taking form. When the guards went to sleep, the opossum put the fire in her pouch. There is an open-

ing, there, where the female raises her infants, and she put the fire there. The
next day she said, "Well thank you very much, I am warm now, I am leaving."
   They searched her all over to make sure she was carrying nothing away. "Be
sure there is nothing in her mouth or anywhere else." And they examined her
all over, but, no, she was carrying nothing. They didn't see the pouch that has a
hollow in it.
   And the following night, they saw the fire far away. And when they got
there, no deal. When they wanted to recover it, there was fire at several places.
They knew it was, indeed, fire. They tired of their attempts to recover it, and
now that it was all over the world, well, definitely no one could recover it, and
so it remained.

   Jesús Rentería told us the myth in Spanish one night in Cohamiata in August
1972. Minutes before, he had told it in Huichol, also at our request, and each
time we taped the myth. Both natives and visitors enjoyed the myth, especially the Huichol children during the first narration; but I could not help
feeling—I have never been able to get over it—that I was a stranger interfering
in that event.
   Let us compare the narrations of Pablo Guerrero Contreras and Jesús Rentería. Both are interesting accounts of the fire thief's adventure, but which
is closer to the true myth? Did the male opossum carry off fire with his tail,
or did the female hide it in her pouch? The two tales are quite similar. If we
add a Cora account, then the opossum dies while carrying out the theft and
resuscitates shortly afterwards. If we add to these a Huichol version different
from Renteria's, we find that death and resurrection are not secondary parts of
the adventure, since the cutting up and restoration of the hero are emphasized
dramatically. The following questions arise now. Are death and resurrection
present in the true myth? Was this part lost in the first two versions? Or was
it a later addition? If we continue to add accounts, we find those that make
the hero not an opossum but a fox, a monkey, a dog, perhaps even a toad.
Is it essential for the main character of the adventure to be an opossum? Was
it so in the beginning? We are again faced with the "embryonic obsession."
The mystery of the mythic tale again recalls Munz's (1986:82–83) discouraging phrase, "historical origins are lost in the mists of time." Although the
invention of this mythic tale is recent, by its very nature it seems to escape
our understanding. The problem is not just an epistemological one. Was there
some time when an original myth of the opossum thief of fire existed? Was
there a primitive, inspired singer who invented the adventure of the appealing
marsupial thief who transformed the human world by escaping with a flower

lighted by the gods? Was that the way mythical narration began? Or was there a slow development, with multiple byways? Lévi-Strauss (1981:644–45) feels that

> there is never any original [text]: every myth is by its very nature a translation, and derives from another myth belonging to a neighboring, but foreign, community, or from a previous myth belonging to the same community or from a contemporaneous one belonging to a different social sub-division—clan, sub-clan, descent group, family or brotherhood—that some listener tries to plagiarize by translating it in his fashion into his personal or tribal language, sometimes to appropriate it and sometimes to refute it, and therefore invariably distorting it.

His opinion carries some weight, but it is not enough to dispel doubts about an unknown that is difficult to grasp. In the problem of the invention of myth, some basic topics for discussion are: 1. The grouping of the versions of the myth; 2. The myth's permanence and transformation; 3. The various sources of the myth; 4. The problems of the original myth, of the prototypic myth, of the mytho-poet; 5. The meaning of "beginning" in the invention of myth.

1.   The grouping of the versions of the myth. Which elements indicate kinship among different versions of the myth? Myths share characters and places; the same motifs and themes occur; there is a similar sequence in the adventures; the same coming-into-being brings the tale to its climax; in some versions there may be similar phrases, onomatopoeia, riddles that lead one of the characters to receive a terrible answer. This does not mean that the aggregate of elements revealing the kinship of the versions constitutes a common denominator. Important as some of the elements are, not all of them are essential. In some versions some of them may be completely absent; in others, equivalent elements appear, such as adventures that lead characters to similar results. There are primary equivalents that lead to secondary ones derived from the principal variable, and which lead to the same, or equivalent, results. This makes the aggregate of versions a large family, whose members have different degrees of kinship and where there are some branches that depart from and others that reaffirm their kinship. In all these aggregates there is a subgroup that has such a large number of common elements or equivalents that they can be called typical, those that preserve the "family look" to the highest degree. There are also some families so extensive that they form two or more kindred groups.

2.   The permanence and the transformation of myth. Not all the important elements are indispensable. Are some of them? At least two of them are,

and here some ideas will be presented that will be further developed in following chapters. The first is the theme of the myth, the link between the adventure and a particular creation at the beginning of time. The second is a plot that is highly resistant to modifications. It is not completely immune to changes, but it is the axis for ordering the elements and the bulwark of the myth's identification.

Therefore there are indispensable elements as well as others that, although they vary, are frequent, and important in the composition of the narration. The fact that it is oral gives the narration two apparently opposite characteristics. On the one hand, the verbal account adapts to any change of circumstance; on the other, it is an account that resists the passage of time, century after century. A paradox of the gods! Kirk (1970:74) speaks of variation in myths:

> If, then, myths are traditional tales, then their telling is subject to the rules of all traditional tales: they will be varied in some degree on virtually every occasion of telling and the variations will be determined by the whim, the ambition or the particular thematic repertoire of the individual teller, as well as by the receptivity and special requirements of the particular audience. Themes will be suppressed, added, transposed, or replaced by other apparently equivalent themes.

According to Vansina (1968:36), there are two kinds of traditions: some with fixed form, memorized and transmitted with strict adherence to the text; and a freer kind, not learned by heart, and repeated by each teller in his own way. As an example of the former, he gives the written text of a poem, and as the free form, the narration. While the words of a poem belong to a tradition, those of a narration belong to the narrator. Only the underlying canvas, he says, belongs to the tradition. No doubt there are societies where mythical texts are memorized literally and faithfully transmitted for generations, but as Hérskovits (1951:373) says, this kind of rigid legacy is the exception, not the rule. Then how is myth preserved?

In the invention of a myth, a distinction must be made between its permanence and its variability. Along elements indispensable to the myth, there is a group of elements that, although they may vary, set limits to the principal versions. The lability of the myth makes them vulnerable, and they can be transformed or disappear; but experience shows that they are very tenacious. What does this tenacity mean? Is it due to the myth having reached with them its optimal point? This is very likely. In the gamut of possible changes they sometimes persist as a unit that cannot be improved, at least during a given historical period. This study will be directed toward these "optimal," or least variable, elements. How does this limiting group of elements come about? Does a myth spring into being from a prototypical myth, or is it the product of an evolutionary process?

3.   The different sources of myth. Another problem in the invention of a myth is its sources. The general outline of the adventure is developed in the area of myth-belief, where a coherence in the understanding of the world sets rules for the dynamics of the invisible. From this same source come the character of the protagonists, their attributes, some of their names, and their hierarchies. The central themes come from daily work, its joys, sorrows, and revelations, its techniques perfected through practice and imagination. The relationships among the textual units, the logical sequence of the action, and the timing of the events are part of an established, accepted form of expression, with established precepts and norms. From this convention come the phrases, the pauses, the idioms, the onomatopoeias, and the audience's appetite that leads the narrator—mytho-poet?—to insert episodes that provoke laughter or fear. The adventures themselves can come from other mythical tales; myths interchange the comings and goings of the characters.[1] Or they may come from a nonmythic oral source (Christiansen 1965). Other verbal forms, nonnarrative and quasi-narrative, belong to mythical beliefs. They show the relationships among the characters at the beginning of their adventures.

Myth engenders myth. Sometimes a myth from another region will be inserted into a native one, enriching it with its adventures. This happened in an altered African myth, of which Frazer (1981:32–40) gave eleven versions.[2] A divine being sends the message of immortality to humankind, but the messengers, either through malice or stupidity, change the content and give a message that in the future will make humans mortal. The myth was widely accepted in the Americas among tribes along the Amazon, in Venezuela, and in Panama (Métraux 1948:29; Jiménez Núñez 1962:41–42). It appears in Mexico among the Zoque-Popoluca, as one more episode of the Spirit of Maize myth. The hero disinterred and revived his father. He sent the iguana to warn his mother not to look straight at her resurrected husband, and not to laugh or cry. The iguana passed the message on to the lizard, but the lizard changed it. When the husband came home to his wife, she looked straight at him and laughed and cried. Her husband turned into dust, and human immortality disappeared with him (*Técnicos bilingües* . . . 1985:19–26; among the Chontal, see P. Carrasco 1960:111).

At other times the foreign tradition is like a jar into which native elements are emptied. In different regions of Mexico one often finds the story of the flight of Mary, Joseph, and Jesus as the solar myth, in which the stars, powers of the night now personified as Jews, are defeated.

Sometimes the composition is not a good one; the myth is made up of remnants, and it is easier to trace their origin than to make sense of them. That is the case of a Tarahumara myth, found by Lumholtz (1970, 1:296–97), in which the deer, the toad, and the crow await the sunrise. The myth contains an episode, common in both ancient and contemporary versions, concerning a doubt as to where the sun would rise along the horizon. There is also a race in which the most astute of the competitors tricks his adversary, asking members of his own species to place themselves at different points between the starting line and the goal (a trick that occurs in a well-known tale from the Old World). There is also a mythic story about the deer and insects that punish with their bite, in this case horse flies, belonging to a myth in which the Sun and the Moon are orphans adopted by the deer's wife. The tale is such a mixture that it is a complete loss.

Finally, there are two cases where the fire myth is a part of myths that are completely different. In one of them, Homshuk, the God of Corn, is chased by the old woman Tsitsímat and asks the opossum to help him by setting fire to the grass when the old woman arrives. The opossum obeys, but with disastrous results. He says to Homshuk, "Uncle, my tail got burned." The god, displeased, answers, "Why did you offer to burn the grass if you were not capable of doing so?"; and he continues in his adventures (Elson 1947). In the second case, the opossum helps the Christ child by carrying the stolen fire to the cold manger. It was not Christ's name that gave origin to the common exclamation; it was the animal that first used it. The opossum, when he felt his tail burning, cried out "Oh Jesus! Oh Jesus!" thus creating the name at the beginning of time (Taggart 1983:103–4).

These are more than the simple transmission of one part of a mythic narration to another myth. In varying degrees they are adjusted to new narrative axes. If a myth is foreign, it has to be adjusted to the concepts of the receiver, even though part of the vision of the transmitter is incorporated in the process. Or it may give birth to ideas that are alien both to the original culture and to that of the receiver. This is the difficult mechanism of assimilation. The link is easier if there are many common elements, but these elements are not always clear. Christ's identification with the sun explains how his birth and death are tied to the origin of time; and the rooster that crowed to Saint Peter is made the herald of human time. Myth travels across immense areas, but there will always be an adjustment to be made between beliefs and the enjoyment of narrations. This is also part of the creation of mythic narration.

A myth crystallized in a narration is not free from its sources. Unless it is set down in writing, it is not fixed for the future. The flux between belief and mythic narration continues. Belief, with all its sources, will keep on revitalizing the narrative; and the narrative, having its own norms, changes the belief of the narrators and their audience as it is told. Just as Homer, as described by Apuleius (Apuleyo 1946:308), heard the warnings of heaven and the advice of his own wisdom at the same time, so the storytellers are guided by the sanctity of the history of the gods and by the voices of their own historic reality.

4. The problems of the original myth, the prototypical myth, and the mytho-poet. How acceptable is the existence of the mytho-poet who narrates a myth for the first time? In order to answer the question a distinction must be made between two very different ways of inventing myths: a slow, uninterrupted invention, in which each narrator of the myth is an author; and a swift, primordial one, in which the author is an exceptional mytho-poet. The first one is amply proven by every narration, because the myth is never repeated in the same terms; and it is also verified in the wealth of recorded versions, in their wide range of near and remote kinships. The second kind of myth creation is hypothetical.

We must distinguish between mythic type and prototype. A type is composed of a heterogeneous collection of unessential but important elements, which in different versions of a myth are the same, similar, or equivalent. In fact there is no typical myth, but a collection of versions of the same myth that approach or diverge from typicality. What is typical is a matter of degree. There may also exist one or more centers of typicality. On the other hand, the prototype is the original myth, or it is the most nearly perfected myth. Or it is, at the same time, the original and the most nearly perfected myth. Extant versions originate from it. Again we have to contrast the proven reality of typicality with the hypothetical nature of the prototypical myth.

What is meant by the "most perfected" myth? I have referred to an "optimal" type, possessing qualities that, because of their inherent nature, have persisted. Does this correspond to a unique version? No. Mythical narration is history. It is a product of historical reality, and as a human creation it responds to that historical reality, to governing mythic beliefs, to reigning ideologies, to specific social structures and dynamics, to the adjustment of native and alien, and to style, modes, and tastes. The excellence of a mythical narration is not absolute, but relative; relative to history and therefore as variable as history itself. If perfection is relative and changeable, at which points along the trajectory do we place the mytho-poet, the singer of the prototype? We would identify the great narrators and the innovators. But that leads us to consider a slow, uninterrupted kind of invention, not a sudden primordial one. There is no single optimal version possible, but various optimal versions across the changing course of history. Since there is no single optimal version of the myth, the prototypical myth cannot be defined as "optimal."

Then what is the prototype? Let us discard the terms "most perfected" and "optimal," and retain the terms "original" or "pristine" in the discussion of the possibility of its existence. It is necessary to think about the "birth" of a myth, to look for the moment of its consolidation, when it acquires both its fundamental elements and the optional ones that confer its limits. Again there are two kinds of consolidation, a gradual one and a sudden one. The first will be one where the mythic narration incorporates elements from narrative and nonnarrative areas, mythic and non-mythic, both native and foreign, in a nonordained succession, in which the "formative step" is one of many in a long chain in which some narratives are transformed into others. On the other hand, it is possible to conceive of an instantaneous synthesis, where with all the principal elements present (the sustaining mythic beliefs, the adventures borrowed from other mythical narrations, etc.), a moment may come in which the inspiration of a mytho-poet may give definite form to the myth.

5. The meaning of "beginning" in the invention of a myth. The gradual form of consolidation can be proven through the series of loans characteristic of mythical narrations. The other, sudden form is still hypothetical. Does an original, a "pristine myth," exist? Is myth born through mutation? Do those spectacular steps Hugo de Vries proposed for another area of reality actually exist? Many writers favor this version of the making of myths. I prefer the gradual transition of one mythic narration into another, or the transition from an almost narrative verbal form to a very simple mythic narration; a seed suspended in the current of a vigorous creative stream.

The beginning? It is difficult to know what the beginning was. The "initial" impulse might have come from a popular etymology, from a small mythic aggregate that, enriched, freed itself from the principal myth of which it was an original part, or from a farmer's chant that linked the season with an agricultural task and to the whims of the Sun and the rains. From one of these points the myth would be invented in gradual changes by the narrators, changes dictated by different kinds of norms, by diverse social requisites. The "sudden impulse," not to be confused with a mythic nucleus, could be lost in the twists and turns and disappear from the myth without leaving a trace.

This may true of simple, "emerging" myths. Some have very simple plots, barely the shadows of acts that, in spite of their simplicity, depict creative acts at the beginning of time. One of these myths of incipient adventure comes from Michoacan. Among the Tarasca, as among many other indigenous groups of Mexico, the meeting of the two currents of religious thought caused many conflicts that the faithful still had to resolve, with some leaning toward beliefs from Mesoamerican sources, others toward the Christian. The devil has fused with the beings of the cold, aquatic world, and his dwelling claims dead souls from different places. Those who favor Christian beliefs say that people who die in sin go to the underworld; those who favor the native tradition say that the people who drown or die drunk go there. No doubt the following myth came from the first group, in which the only action is the devil's request to God and its refusal:

> There (below) the Devil said he needed someone, and God said yes, that he would give someone to him. "What do you want?" And the Devil said that he wanted those who drown themselves in alcohol, those who die in sin, the ones who kill people, and the ones who drown in the lake. God said that so many die that way that he could not give them all, that none would be left for him, and that he would give him only those who committed a great sin . . . (P. Carrasco 1976a:108–14)

No adventure develops in the story; there is barely the indication of a conflict between the two divine characters. The only action is a dialogue in which the answer is unilateral.

Summarizing, then, there are two kinds of myth invention, one proven and the other hypothetical. Both are compatible. Slow, uninterrupted invention does not rule out the possibility that, through revealing dream, mystic trance, or poetic inspiration, a mytho-poet and audience may together create an original mythic narration. It is a seductive hypothesis, but is it necessary? Everything can be explained by the gradual process, but the image of the mytho-poet has been indispensable in many treatises on myth. I believe there is a large dose of ideology in this. The elitist view denies the great, anonymous, hard-to-trace production of ordinary people. It is still difficult for us historians to refute three issues: that creative thought comes exclusively from the ruling classes,[3] that in a transcendent creation an extraordinary individual act is indispensable,[4] and that all valuable transformation of thought is born from leisure. Creative leisure! What can leisure create? When I was very young I was attracted to an idea in a mathematics text: "Idleness can only give to men the opportunity to reflect on the changes brought about in the world by the work of these who cannot afford to be inactive (Hogben 1944:46)." However, the three topics are ideologically strong. They exact a measure of individual glory for those who do not soil their hands with the earth.[5]

Gradual creation is what most interests us, because here the suggestive processes characteristic of what is spoken are produced, processes found especially in oral tradition. In gradual creation there is the paradox of the narrative that changes each time it is retold, that adjusts itself to the performance requirements of each singer and audience, that meets the expectations of a changing society, transmits ideologies, imposes new images, responds to new fashions and styles, and is nevertheless the tale that endures through the centuries. There is no identical repetition in narration. Myth is one of the forms of social memory, and "in the case of groups as well as of individuals, memory does not record, it constructs" (Vilar 1981:29).

From this freedom, a flood—a chaos—of myths could be expected, an overflowing wealth in the production of narratives. Why should we not expect it, we who value novelty so much? Some consider the reality we find due to laziness. Always fewer myths than we want. Always—or nearly always—old myths, myths that are common to the plains, to the valleys, to the mountains, common to people who for generations have not seen each others' faces, generations spread over wide territories. Why do humans limit one of their best areas for the creation of beauty?

Creative limitation seems to be one of the ways myth is protected. A proliferation of tales would lead to chaos. Excessive production would do away with their important functions. Their durability is not due to a simple process, just as the process of transformation is neither simple nor unilateral.

The affiliation of narratives with a literary order makes them part of the historic dynamics of the genre and, in a broader sense, in the dynamics of oral literature. And this goes even further, since oral literature is not immune to other, different forms of expression. This has happened to the story "Macario," which has been transformed among the people. Derived from "Death the Godmother" by the Grimm brothers, "Macario" became a popular tale in Mexico. It was collected and written down by B. Traven, and later made into a movie. Today motion pictures and television, with their prestige, have modified the folk version, particularly among young people (Navarrete 1982:109, 112).

This process also goes beyond the forms of expression: "What is essential in myth is not based *in* language, but *on* language" (Pérez 1986:61). Change in mythic narration often comes from a change in mythic belief, and there are changes both mythic and nonmythic that, in their turn, modify mythic beliefs and ritual practices. Several examples of how a new social relationship changes mythic thought have been given. Here is another one. Formerly all Mazatec agricultural activity included agricultural rituals. Today the Mazatec retain them only for plots used for traditional crops, such as corn, beans, and chili peppers. The Mazatec farmer does not perform the ancient religious rites for the sugarcane fields belonging to the collective and excluded from the traditionally organized area (Portal 1986:90). This distinction penetrates deeply into mythic beliefs, since Mother Earth, formerly of a unitary nature, now receives two kinds of treatment during cultivation by the faithful, a distinction originating in different kinds of land ownership and relations of production. Thus a chain of transformations begins.

Since the ways of changing mythic narration are varied, open, and permanent, how is a myth sustained across the centuries? What makes narrators and their listeners act within the limits of what is permissible and what is permanent in the narration? Why is respect for the history of the gods rigid in some aspects and lax in others? Gradual invention is not the sum total of all contributions. Narrators propose a version when they tell the myth. Mythic narration is mostly aural, the form of expression that emotively transmits the encyclopedia of collective knowledge by mouth and by ear (Detienne 1985: 35). Detienne (1985:56) says that for a work to enter and hold a place in the aural tradition, it must be heard, that is, accepted by the community. It needs the "preventive censorship" of the group. Behind the narration there is an often invisible, silent test, in which beliefs in their most diverse expressions, the constantly contested social circumstance, and taste serve as judges. Acceptance or rejection are manifested in many ways, including those that may affect the prestige of the narrator. Inventions are open proposals. The life of the myth is fleeting if the variations are not approved. Myth has mechanisms for its preservation. Part of the myth's content, protected by tradition, is solid and serves as the axis around which the variations, limited in their possibilities, turn. It is an underlying plot overlaid by episodes arranged and transformed by rules of equivalencies. Do narrator and audience consciously respect this nucleus of truth? Yes, since there is a consciousness that the freedom of the narrator should not exceed certain bounds. This nucleus is also respected since it corresponds to an order expressed in the mythical narration and that transcends it. It is expressed in belief, but goes beyond it. It is the source of both narration and belief. It is an order present in a thousand sites of daily reality, a subject to which we will return later.

In the case of myth, narrating and inventing are one and the same thing, and invention is a joint task. Circumstances vary. Some commentators emphasize the ritualization of the act. Even the season and hour must be appropriate (Eliade 1968:22). But this is not always the case, and there are societies where a myth is told by both men and women, at any time, at any place—under a tree, by the family fireplace, in the planting fields, often as part of the educational task of parents (Giddings 1959:11). For others myth is adjusted to the circumstances of seasonal migratory labor. At night in the dormitories of the coffee estates, Chatinos from different regions renew their cultural ties in the sharing of myths (Bartolomé and Barabas 1982:106). Some see myth as words that every member of the group may speak. For others narration will be reserved to a limited number of narrators.[6] In all cases performance is produced jointly by narrator and audience. Myth, as narration, is part of the linguistic wealth of the people. Voloshinov (1976:118–19) says that the reality of language is in social interaction. Of course oral literature can be translated; but with the loss of the natural medium of the texts, of the social ambience, its verbal features, and its language of origin, it is impoverished. When Esteban Márquez, a Tarasca, was interviewed, he said,

> Stories in Purepecha, well, they are more tasty in Purepecha . . . When you hear a story in Spanish and want to tell it in Tarasca, in Purepecha, it's like it doesn't taste like much. This is also true of stories in Purepecha, what happened, what was done, some happening of the past, if you want to tell it in Spanish, it's no great deal. Every language has its own way of coming out well. (Ortiz 1985)

We who were present as visitors when Jesús Rentería told the myth in the Huichol language about the theft of fire participated in the creation of the myth. We will never know the changes our intervention caused there in Cohamiata. What variations has Jesús Rentería given after that night? Which ones will have passed on to other narrators, children then, but now adults? We strangers also formed part of the story, although a part that may help the traditions disappear. Which variations had a short existence in the life of the fire myth? Was that version a blind alley? Perhaps the innovation was only a single, insignificant turn. Sometimes we wish that the imprint of our passing by, even though it may be faint, could be washed away. Romanticism.

"The eagle is a decorative and servile creature," say I.
"There is more heraldry in its wings than flight."

León Felipe, "La gran aventura"

Characters or actors? That is, are the heroes of myth *discrete* beings or are they other characters playing a role? This is the question for debate. What are mythic beings? Are they important disguised gods? Are they gods who have fulfilled their primordial mission with the creation and afterwards lead a life of leisure? Are they symbols?

Our hero is not the best suited to solve the problem. He has a reputation as an actor. He has names that, although not clearly proven, tend to define him as a performer. J. Thompson (1970a:277) stated the problem clearly when he related the opossum to the four gods who hold up the sky. He points out that the Motul dictionary defines the word *bacab* as "performer, *zingles* (?)," and he tentatively interprets the strange word *zingles* as *zincalis* or *zingales,* meaning "gypsies" or "roving actors." Pursuing this idea Thompson says that this explains why in the books of *Chilam Balam* the Opossum is called Tolil Och or Ix Toloch, which can be translated as "opossum actor." He also uses this to explain why there is an actor with an opossum mask and a grasping tail on four pages of the Dresden Codex.

Thompson's opinion is interesting, although his arguments are not completely convincing. Plates 25–28 of the Dresden Codex (*Códice de Dresde* 1972; see fig. 9 of this work) do not actually show four men with masks and artificial, false tails, but rather four anthropomorphic beings with the opossum's head and tail. *Zingles* also has the meaning of "trickster" (Ramón Arzápalo Marín, pers. comm., April 19, 1988). Arzápalo Marín interprets the meaning of the manuscript more accurately, but by a strange coincidence attributes the same character to the animal as Thompson does and accepts the idea that the supporters of the world are actors.

It is also probable that the morpheme *tol* of the opossum's name refers to the long, whitish, bristling hairs mixed with the soft, short fur of the genus *Didelphis*.[1] The morpheme alludes to coarse weaving (Barrera Vásquez et al. 1980: 805), but this does not invalidate the buffoonish character of our actor. Ix Toloch can mean "opossum actor," "bristly opossum," or both, using the play on words of which the ancient Maya were so fond. Given the opinion of the specialists and the Maya propensity for homonyms, it must be acknowledged that the bacab, the opossum, or the bacab-opossum is an actor.

All of this is important for our opossum's biography, but it does not answer the general question as to whether mythical heroes are actors or characters. The fact that the opossum may be an actor is no solution, since his personality cannot be projected onto other mythical heroes, nor do we know to what his histrionics might be referring. Neither can we reject each bacab-opossum's being an actor-god and, as such, a real character for the believer, i.e., a character who can be portrayed as a hero.

Tentatively let us accept the heroes of myth as characters. This classification will be easier to accept if we contrast them with the characters in stories. The works of Propp on the marvelous Russian tales will give us some insight. Propp (1972:62–63; 1977:31–35) finds that despite the great variety of characters and particular actions, the functions and actions of characters are remarkably constant. Therefore the only important question in the tale is knowing what the characters do. Who does it, or how, is only incidental. The king, the grandfather, the sorcerer, Baba Yaga, the bear, or the woodland god are interchangeable pieces. The peculiarities of the character fade before the function—the definite action that gives a clue to the meaning of the plot's development.

Propp was criticized (Lévi-Strauss 1972) for attributing such extreme flexibility to the characters in tales, especially since it was assumed that such freedom implied arbitrary substitutions; but it is undeniable that one of the most notable differences between a character in a tale and in a myth is the ease with which characters can be substituted in the tale. The difference is not merely quantitative. If the character in a myth is more difficult to substitute, it is due to the fact that its place in the narration depends on reasons outside the text.

The character does not exist through the narrative or for the narrative. The believer understands the narration to be an evocation of the action of the character. Its personal attributes are linked to its actions in time and space. The presence of Huracán in his adventure must be understood that way. According to the Popoluca (Foster 1945a:194), the gopher cut the roots of the tree where Huracán was hanging, and he fell into the sea and became lame. The Popoluca continue the tale without pointing out the consequences of his lameness. In another version (P. Carrasco 1976a:125), the Tarasca say that the circular movement of whirlpools is due to Huracán's lameness. The characteristics of the gods are permanent. Because of this the pimples of old Nanahuatzin, who was changed into the Sun in Teotihuacan, continue in the contemporary myth of the Huichol child who receives the bow, the wheel, and arrows in order to become the Sun (*Wirrarika irratsikayari* 1982:26–30).[2] The characters' actions can be so much their own that they drag them from one myth to another as specialists in a particular procedure. Thus the opossum not only steals fire, but manages it. In other myths the gopher cuts loose the cords, the reeds, or the chains from which it or other characters hang (Hollenbach 1977). The hummingbird has sexual relations with the virgin weaver in the myth about the origin of the Sun and the Moon and also in the one about the origin of corn (Schumann 1988). It is so difficult to change characters in a myth that people will claim ignorance rather than invent a substitute. One of Rubel's Tzotzil informants said, "The Moon was the Sun's mother. She had male children. The youngest was the Sun. I don't know the name of the eldest brother" (Rubel 1985).

The rich personality of the opossum has roots in the remote past. The mythic ties of the opossum in ancient sources fall into four groups: the polarity of creation, the four columns that support the sky, lunar myths, and the theft of corn.

1.   The opossum in the polarity of creation. The *Popol Vuh* gives the names of the couple who created the Quiche: the Grandfather and the Grandmother, Ixpoyacoc and Ixmucané. They are also called Hunahpú-Utiú and Hunahpú-Vuch. The name *hunahpú* ("hunter with a blowgun") corresponds to the twenty-day sign *xochitl* ("flower") of the Nahua and to *ahau* ("lord") of the peninsular Maya (Caso 1967: pl. 9).[3] In the text the Grandfather is given the name of *utiú* ("coyote"), the Grandmother the name of *vuch* ("opossum"). This seems to place the animals in a binary opposition, in which the coyote is the night sky, the masculine force; and the opossum is the feminine force, the god of dawn (Seler 1961; *Popul vuh* 1964: Preface n. 3, 4, 164–65). Edmonson (1965:48) has given an explicit list of opposites: Ixpiyacoc is the masculine principle, the creator, father, grandfather, and great grandfather, associated with the coyote, the tapir, turquoise (?), carved sculpture, the sky, tinder, the sun, and corn. Ixmucané is the feminine aspect, the maker, mother, grandmother, and great grandmother, associated with the opossum, the peccary, jade, painting, earth, incense, the moon, and beans. Given the twilight and nocturnal habits of both animals, the question remains whether one represents the evening twilight and the other the half-light just before dawn. If this is so, the opossum would be the animal coming from the night and emerging into the morning light, while the coyote, coming from the day, announces the coming of darkness at sunset. The two animals would thus be intermediaries between solar light and night, but with opposite signs: the opossum born in

darkness, the bearer of light, and the coyote born in the day, the bearer of darkness.

2.   The opossum and the four pillars. In chapter 8 the four opossum-bacabs were said to be the gods who hold up the sky, and J. Thompson's works (1934, 1970b) were cited to support this. The bacabs have a large spiral shell they carry on their backs, as one of their distinguishing marks.[4] Adorned in this way, the bacabs are carved on posts and pillars in the form of plumed serpents, monsters whose heads form the bases, their bodies the shafts, and their plumed rattles the capitals (Kubler 1983). The bacabs are the four columns at the extremes of the earth, two-way streets that the gods follow, with descending and ascending strands that unite in a helix. For the ancient Nahua this helix was one of the symbols of the *tlaloque,* the gods of rain, who also personify the four pillars holding up the sky. The representations of the tlaloque's noses often have the form of a helix. This is also true of the opossum. Two Zapotec ceramic figures show a richly robed opossum and a man dressed as an opossum. In both, the marsupial's nose is a helix in the center of the face (Munn 1984: fig. 10, 11; see fig. 12, d and f of the present work).

3.   The opossum and the moon complex. In the Borgia and Mixtec codices, the opossum seems to be related to the moon complex, to the earth-lunar goddess, to beheading, to pulque, and the maguey plant. Seler (1961; 1963, 1:89–90, 92) finds him in the *Codex Nuttall* (1973: pl. 3) beside the headless earth-lunar goddess. He identifies the same animal, beheaded, in the *Códice Fejérváry-Mayer* (1964–67: pl. 61-4), and he points out a white mammal that drinks pulque and carries a circular fan, similar to the bacabs of the *Dresden Codex*, which is shown seated on a jaguar skin, in the *Codex Vaticanus 3773* (1964–67: pl. 31).[5] Krickeberg (1966:239–42) identifies the opossum in the *Códice Vindobonensis* (1964–67: pl. 13, 20, 22; see fig. 11 a of the present work) beside the decapitated goddess, a maguey, a cradle, and a ball game in flames, and thus associates the opossum with pulque, the moon, maternity, and childbirth. Caso (1977–79, 2:109, 135) referring to this interpretation and that of Seler in the case of the *Codex Nuttall*, says that the god 10 Lizard Black-Eagle Tiger-Mouth and his wife 11 Serpent Entwined-Serpent-Headdress are also shown. They are the founders of a place called (in clear binary opposition) "Ball game of Darkness and Flames."[6] The goddess appears in the fountain, celebrating the new-fire ceremony. Munn (1984) states that the red liquid shown in the vessels of the *Vindobonensis* is menstrual blood, which is related to the moon, and he maintains that a relationship exists between lunar decapitations and the dismembered goddess, Coyolxauhqui, of the Mexica.

The kinship of the opossum to the moon is even found in one of the marsupial's names, with the difference that the feminine form is used for the astral body. Among the Mame (O. Schumann Gálvez, pers. comm., May 9, 1988), the word *ajaw* means "opossum," and *xajaw,* "moon."

4. The opossum as the thief of corn. The connection of the opossum to corn is especially attractive to me, because of the relationship to meanings I have studied for a long time—those of corn, fire, the Sun, and the flower.[7] The opossum steals corn as well as fire. Munn (1984) identifies the figure of an opossum on the Zapotec urn, mentioned in paragraph 2, above, from the Etla Valley (now in the National Museum of Anthropology). His argument is valid. Ears of corn hang from the neck of the animal. Knowing the habits of the opossum, it is easy to realize what that means. He has a bad reputation as a thief from granaries and cornfields, confirmed in myths. The opossum was the author of a plan for the animals to steal corn from Lisibe and Lisiyá, its owners. After the theft, it was he who proposed painting the white grain yellow and black, so that Lisibe, "the mistress of fire," would not recognize it (Boege 1988:99–100). The flower symbol is another element that seems to be related to the theft of corn. The figure mentioned above, as well as a companion figure and a third from Monte Alban depicting a human being with an opossum-head helmet, all wear a breast plate with the flower symbol (Munn 1984). Spranz (1982:432; see fig. 10, b of the present work) refers to an opossum with a multicolored robe seated on a jaguar skin in plate 30-15 of the *Códice Fejérváry Mayer*, and notes that the day sign at the foot of the image is the day "flower." Recall that the name Hunahpú, given by the Quiche in the *Popol Vuh* to both the Grandfather and the Grandmother creators, corresponded to the last day of the twenty, which among the Nahua is equivalent to xochitl ("flower"). Fr. Francisco Ximénez (1985:291), in his vocabulary, says:

> hunahpú—a day of the week = flower or rose:[8] the name of one they say was the redeemer;
> *hunahpuvuch*—an opossum marksman = a name given in their paganism to their creator.

In ancient sources there is one characteristic of the opossum that is not strictly mythic but does show the marsupial's relationship to the Mother goddess, to maternity and birth. Its tail was one of the medicines most used by ancient Nahua doctors, and was recognized as such by the Spanish in the first years of the colony. The principal virtue attributed to the tail was the acceleration of birth, and it was also recommended for abortion (*Códice Florentino*

1979: bk. 11, ch. 1, par. 4, fol. 13r, ch. 7, par. 5, fol. 171r; Fr. Hernández 1959, 2:299; Cruz 1964: fol. 34r). This was not its only use. It functioned as a marvelous obstruction remover. It could open the urinary tract, extracting gallstones and anything obstructing the passage. It drew out retained menstrual blood. It softened the belly of the constipated. It eliminated the phlegm that caused constant coughing. It extracted thorns and other objects, even if they were imbedded in the bone. It aided the production of mother's milk and helped fertility (Fr. Hernández 1959, 1:127, 239, 2:5, 299; Cruz 1964: fol. 34r). Serna (1953:250) sums it up as "the opener of the passages." The *Códice Florentino* 1979: bk. 11, ch. 1, par. 4, fol. 13r) says, "It clears the passages, the tubes, it cleans and purifies." The extractive power of the opossum's tail and bones was so great, it was said, that eating an excessive amount of its bones could cause the intestines to emerge. The case was told of a dog that, after gnawing on such bones, suffered an expulsion of its bowels and was seen the next day dragging them on the ground behind him (*Códice Florentino* 1979: bk. 11, ch. 1, par. 4, fol. 12v–13r). There was even a tree called "opossum's tail" (*tlacuacuitlapilli*), which had an extraordinary power to unblock the urinary tract (*Códice Florentino* 1979: bk. 10, ch. 28, par. 4, fol. 109r).

In comparison to the power of the opossum's tail, that of his mythical companion pales. Fr. Hernández (1959, 2:303), referring to the coyote, says, "Toothache is diminished by cleaning the teeth with the tip of its tail." It has lost this reputation, but that of the opossum's tail continues.

Mythic deductions or the discovery of real active principles? They are not necessarily mutually exclusive. Experience has demonstrated that within a reputedly medicinal product attributes deriving from mythology can coexist with curative substances. In lay healing there is a mixing of information coming from beliefs about the invisible and the daily observation of the processes of illness and its cure. They are contiguous, complementary routes. The search for active principles in traditional medicine can reveal a considerable number of challenges in contemporary as well as older medical beliefs. If a mythic belief is not sufficient to guarantee the efficacy of a medical treatment, neither is it enough to deny its effectiveness for that reason alone. The reputation of the opossum's tail has brought about intense investigations of its effectiveness as an oxytocic. The Unit for Investigation of Herbal and Traditional Medicine of the Mexican Institute of Social Security investigated the opossum's tail in search of concentrations of prostaglandins, substances that mimic the activity of oxytocin in contracting the uterus during birth. These studies were suspended in 1986, because the instability of prostaglandins makes it hard to determine their presence with ordinary techniques. When better equipment becomes available here, it is hoped that the research will begin again (Xavier Lozoya, director of the Unit for Investigation of Traditional and Herbal Medicine, pers. comm., April 24, 1988).[9]

The list of characteristics is not complete, but with what we have already mentioned, our character is clad with a motley array of attributes and symbols. Can they be simplified? Is there any coherence in this array of elements? The answer is found in the theme of the theft. The opossum is the thief par excellence; and what he steals are the divine forces, which he carries to the surface of the earth. He is the character who carries the two polar forces of the cosmos to the site of their conjunction. The two forces, the heat of the sky and the cold of the underworld, are united in a gyration that produce smoke and fire. This union is a sacred marriage (hierogamy), the primal, total sexual act. The place of union is Tamoanchan, and the fire consists of flowers snatched from the great tree. Upon arriving at human time-space, the united forces are transformed. Here they are days, months, years, destinies, war, the souls of the newly born. Cipactli's uncontainable demand for recomposition is a sexual demand, and the flux of his two halves flows through the inside of the cosmic conduits to meet in violent union like the friction of the two kinds of wood to produce fire. Tamoanchan is the site of the union—not of the recomposition— of the two halves of Cipactli's body. The pillars that support the sky prevent the recomposition, but at the same time, they are the passages through which the fluids of the cloven body circulate, unite, and catch fire. The pillars are Tamoanchan. The thief goes to Tamoanchan to take away the force of the gods. The thief is the being who can enter the great tube—the four great tubes— as the lord of the blowgun. To do this he starts from primordial night and brings out primordial light, the dawn. The opossum is the being, born cold, who at the place of transformations becomes the burning being. He goes from the surface of the earth to the land of the gods and returns; from darkness to dawn; from the feminine nature to the masculine. He is the intermediary for primitive, changing sexuality. The thief is the founder of the helical path. His insignia are the spirals of the snail, the great helix, because the forces of the gods ascend and descend in spirals through the great tubes.[10] The thief takes fire but also the cold force, because Tamoanchan is Chalchimmichhuacan, "the place of those who have jade fish," as in the song that tells of the birth of the god Ear of Corn on the day 1 Flower (*Veinte himnos sacros de los nahuas* 1958:150–53):

> Centeotl was born in Tamoanchan:
> where the flowers arise: 1-Flower.

Centeotl was born in the region of rain and mist:
where the sons of men are made,
where the owners of emerald fish are found!

He is the thief of destinies, of the hot and the cold current. That is why the corn thief also steals pulque, the cold milk of Mother Earth, the refreshing lunar liquid.[11] The opossum is the great opener. He clears the tubes so that the universal fluids can flow to the outside.

The opossum has reached the twentieth century with many of his ancient attributes. He is still the hunter with his coyote companion, and both die poisoned for having stolen hens from the Morning Star in tales collected in 1907 among the Nahua of Durango by Preuss (1982:253–67). The animals continue in their taxonomical opposition. The opossum is cold because he never receives solar heat, while the coyote is warm because of his thick fur (Madsen 1955). There is also an interesting homonym, perhaps with an ancient mythological meaning, about the nature of the animal that goes from nocturnal cold to the heat of a firebearer: the Tojolabal call the opossum *ujchum,* and also give the same name to malaria, with its terrible bouts of intermittent fever and chills (Otto Schumann Gálvez, pers. comm., April 27, 1988).

The opossum continues to be the Owner of the Dawn. For the Tzotzil, *'uch* is both the opossum and the red light that in the month of 'uch (June 10–29) precedes the dawn (Guiteras Holmes 1965:236). The Quiche also give the opossum and the moment preceding daybreak the name 'uch (Edmonson 1965:2).

We have seen the opossum as a thief of fire, corn, maguey juice, pulque, tobacco, and mescal in contemporary myths; but we should examine other tales in which the opossum appears in a more explicit form as the creator of time, and where he steals the hot and cold fluids of the cosmos and carries them to the four pillars, from which they will flow to benefit humankind. An antecedent is found in another parallel myth, in which the hot and cold principles are distributed to the four rain gods. The Totonac say that the Child Lord of Corn went to the shore and cut four reeds with which he gathered the foam— the sweat—of the water. There he was attacked by a crocodile that tried to devour him, but when the beast opened its jaws, the child cut off its tongue. The child divided the tongue into four pieces, placed them on the reeds along with each part of the water's foam, and sent the four reeds to the four thunders, so that each one would release rain and lightning from the east, west, north, and south (Ichon 1973:75, 79–80). In another myth (Loo 1987:160–61), the Lord Fire rips out his sister's tongue, because she used it to set fire to everything she wanted. Fire cut the tongue into four pieces and distributed them among his four adopted sons, who, thus armed, flew to the four corners of the earth, from which they sent rain and lightning.[12]

The opossum is the Lord of Time because of his distribution of the fluids to the four posts. Mazatec myths about the theft of fire expressly state that it was our hero "whose tail caught on fire and who carried fire everywhere," and that it was he who gave the days their names. "The Tiger could only say, 'the day after tomorrow'; it was the Opossum who gave the dates" (Boege 1988: 99–100). Not only this, but he stole corn from the goddess Lisibé, "Owner of Fire." In the granary the stolen corn was white. It was the opossum who, after stealing it, changed the color to yellow and black so that the goddess would not recognize it. Corn, undefined in the granary, took on the colors of day and night.

It was the opossum who gave order to time, because the calendar marked the times of arrival on the earth of the fluids from the sky and the underworld. Two Tlapanec myths give a precise account. The first is about the theft of fire (Loo 1987:157–58). When the opossum returned to the dwelling of humans, four piles of wood were set up so that fire could be taken from them. The second tale is about the theft of pulque (Loo 1987:180–81). The opossum returned carrying the liquor and told the people to prepare four great jars to hold the liquid. Pulque is, according to the Tlapanec, the milk of Mother Earth. Thanks to the opossum, there is fire and pulque in the four pillars as alternating hot and cold forces.

The distribution of fire and pulque among the four posts and the spiral movement for their extraction were part of the housewarming celebration held by the ancient Nahua. The creative moment was repeated by pouring pulque and by taking a torch to the four corners of the new house. The ceremony was called *calmamalihua,* alluding to the movement of the malinalli (twisted grass; Durán 1984, 1:77–78).

Today the Cora also speak of a sequence of forces that balance happenings over the earth. The opossum fell with the stolen fire, causing the earth to catch on fire; but Our Mother put it out with her milk (Preuss 1912, 1:181).[13] This is the alternation of the divine forces on the earth's surface. In Honduras (Chapman 1985–86, 1:94), the Lenca say that in the beginning of the world, Jesus sprinkled his own blood over the first cultivated fields. Afterwards he asked his mother, the Virgin Mary, to sprinkle them with her own milk.

The Cora and Huichol tell of the death and resurrection of the opossum, of his shattered body and its recomposition (Preuss 1912, 1:180–81; Zingg 1982, 2:187; P. Furst 1972a). This is not the only myth about the opossum's recomposing himself after being torn to pieces. The Trique myth (Hollenbach 1980:458–59) about the opossum reconstituting his body after his bones had been thrown in the river was mentioned in chapter 1. A Mazatec myth (Portal 1986:56) recalls the decapitated Earth and Moon Goddess in the Nuttall and Vindobonensis codices. It is the myth about the origin of the Sun and Moon:

> Formerly there was no light. Only one woman had it. Then they called all the animals together. The woman had a party and the opossum went around to invite everyone, but the rabbit did not want to go. The woman ate people.
>
> The Moon, who was more foolish than the Sun, was eaten at the fiesta, and only the Sun remained. The bones were given to a little dog. The Moon's head was in the pot. The Sun asked the dog to steal the head. The dog complied and went to the mountain dragging the bones.
>
> The animals took the woman outside to dance, but she was reluctant because she was watching the head in the kettle and was afraid that if she left they were going to steal it.
>
> But the opossum, playing his little guitar, distracted the woman, who began to dance, and the dog carried off the kettle with the head.
>
> Then the opossum, because he can withstand many blows, went running through the patio where the fire was burning, set his tail on fire and distributed it. That is why his tail has a scorched appearance.
>
> The Moon and the Sun are brother and sister. The Sun put the Moon together again, but he lacked a piece of bone. That is why the Moon is so pale.

The myth continues with the capture and liberation of the Sun, the pursuit of the woman who devours people, and the finding of the sea.

In today's myths the opossum still has to do with the aquatic path (dark, humid, cold) that takes him to the place of fire, and with the spiral reconstruction of this watery way (Munn 1984). A necessary path for the transit of the gods, particularly so that the forces of the cold gods, the precious fish of Chalchimmichhuacan, can flow in spirals. A Mazatec myth, mentioned in chapter 1, tells the story of the opossum's reconstruction of the course of a river when the others wanted it to be straight:

> Sirs, gentlemen, if you want to know about this, you do well in asking me. I'll tell you the truth, all the truth, gentlemen. You are very mistaken. You have lost your heads. How can the river be straight? No, not that. The river should never be that way. No, never. The river must have another form, because if it is left this way, we will never be able to fish. We can never do anything, because the river's current will be too strong. Therefore, we must do this. We are going to reshape the river. We are going to give it curves and more curves with small

whirlpools where one can go fish and go to sleep in his boat, so that we can sleep peacefully and no one can bother us. That is my opinion, gentlemen. What do you say? I say this because I am poor. I only stay alive eating fish, more and more fish so my poor stomach will not protest . . . (Incháustegui 1977:53–56)

And the animals, following the wise counsel of the opossum, modified the river, giving it the curved form it has today.

When it is not the opossum but the frog who steals fire, his return is in the form of a helix. The Yaqui (Giddings 1959:63) say that the frog Bobok was the benefactor. Bobok, the crow, the roadrunner, and the dog were entrusted with the theft of fire. But only Bobok could enter the water and swim to the house of the God of Fire without drowning. He stole the fire by putting it in his mouth and swam back. The God of Fire threw lightning and thunder at him, as he had at all who had dared to do this, but Bobok saved himself by making whirlpools, filled with trash, in the water. With the help of his many children, frogs who swam beside him carrying fire in their mouths, he gave light to everything on earth and put fire inside the tree trunks and the stones, where it remains hidden to this day.

19 THE CHARACTER II

Monkeys certainly understand
much that is said to them by man.

Charles Darwin,
The Descent of Man

Do opossums—astute animals—understand human language? Opossums are nearly perfect; only speech is lacking. If they could talk, they themselves would spread their fame as mythical thieves across the globe. Neither Bobok nor his crafty tadpoles, nor foxes, skunks, dogs, monkeys, nor mice have half his talent for such a task. The fire-theft myth seems made for the opossum, or the opossum for the myth. The real or fictitious characteristics of the didel-phids coincide precisely with those of characters in divine narrations. In some cases biology seems to dictate the meaning of the adventure; in others, the adventure requires an attribute that points to all, some, or one of the mar-supial species. In still others a part of the myth deals with the reason the character has some particular trait. Fire burned his ears and tail, which after-wards remained hairless (among others, Bartolomé and Barabas 1982:112). The opossum danced on his nurse's back, and since then he has had inverted testicles (Hollenbach 1980). The Virgin rewarded the one who brought fire to the Child, and since then the female has given birth painlessly (Ichon 1973: 95–96), has a pouch and seven lives (Williams García and García Ramos 1980: 31). The animal's habits and customs will always fit the preconceived ideas of the observer, and it will be informal ethology that will inspire people when they think about nature and the origins of the laws of the world.

The opossum and his biological characteristics are evidently not one of the "zoemes," the clusters of minimally differentiating elements in the oppositions of mythic narration (Lévi-Strauss 1981:79). The opossum is not like Lévi-Strauss' loons, tanagers, meadowlarks, or butterflies. The opossum's peculiari-ties go further than mere symbolism. The marsupial is not simply "used" to express secrets of the world through myth. The marsupial and his attributes, revealed in the granary, the cornfield, the chicken roost, on the mountain, in the invalid's bed, or in the world of the gods, exist for the believer in the myth and through the myth. But these qualities do not exist only in the myth and through the myth.

A clever thief, his fame is justified because of his almost human hands, his cleverness in evading humans' locks, and his ability to climb. He specializes in his thefts. His fondness for corn is told in regions far from the one studied here (for example, the Apinayé myth in Lévi-Strauss 1968b:167). His taste for the juice and the sweet scrapings of the maguey are attested to in sixteenth-century documents (*Códice Florentino* 1979: bk. 11, ch. 1, par. 4, fol. 12v), and in the practice of today's farmers, who protect the hollows they open in the plant with large stones. His gluttony is well known. He is the enemy of chickens. He is said to suck their brains, behead them, and drink their blood. The historian Gonzalo Fernández de Oviedo y Valdés, (1944–45:165) complained early in the sixteenth century about the damage the beast did in his henhouse. The prehensile tail and the pouch are characteristics that have been assets in mythical thefts. It is no wonder that those who dream about an opossum feel they will be robbed:

> And once I dreamed about an opossum. To dream about an opossum is not good, because though an opossum is just a little animal, it is quite mischievous and crafty. . . . Once when I was carrying my money, it was stolen. The dream meant robbery. Robbers.
> The opossum steals money and it steals corn. It steals beans and it steals chickens. The opossum steals everything. And it steals women and fruit. This is the significance of dreaming about opossums. (Shaw 1971:230)

Some Huichol versions attribute the origin of the marsupial pouch to the theft of fire. The animal swallowed the live coal and kept it lighted in his heart. This burn was the beginning of the pouch (Zingg 1982, 1:358n13). The pouch also links the animal to the mother goddess and to the cradle drawn in the Mixtec codices. The opossum's twilight and nocturnal habits link him to the lunar world on one hand, and on the other, to daybreak. When he is seen stumbling along level paths due to his clumsy gait, it is easy to associate him with the rosy light that begins to light up the earth. During the day he disappears, hidden in slumber that may last up to eighteen hours (Zimmer 1985:36). He is the cold master of the night who brings the fire of morning. If one of his genera, in this case the *Chironectes*, does not share these habits, it is considered to be an exception. In fact the Kekchi distinguish the water opossum from other members of the family, saying that it has a "hot" nature, and they use its flesh as a "hot" medicine. The rationale is simple: It is so hot that it needs to enter the water to catch and consume fish (cold beings) in order to maintain its bodily balance (Otto Schuman Gálvez, pers. comm.,

April 27, 1988). Even so the water opossum acts in accordance with its mythic characteristics. It extracts fish from the river.

The opossum is a mediating character. He lives in caves under the earth as well as high in the trees. This reveals his familiarity with both the underworld and the sky (Munn 1984). If he lives in the woods and—as a thief—in the human domain, he unites nature and society (Taggart 1983:61). His transitions are marked by an aura of strange sexuality. His habitual celibacy is broken by active periods of sexual receptivity. To the physical makeup of the female (two uteri and two vaginas) and that of the male (a bifurcated penis and oddly placed testicles) can be added the mother's custom of licking a path to her pouch. This is the reason why people in the U.S. South believe that copulation occurs through the nasal opening of the female, and that she blows the embryo into her pouch through her nose (Hartman 1921). Lévi-Strauss (1968b:166–96, 1984:146–50) describes beliefs about the sexuality of the opossum in various parts of the continent: the female conceives without the intervention of the male; the latter is castrated; his erotic efforts are repulsive because of his smell. Moreover he is a repulsive suitor: old, bald, gray-haired, covered with dung, and evil-smelling. He is old and he is poor (Munn 1984).[1] "I am poor," Grandfather Opossum says, when he gives advice about the curves of the river. In one of the tales about the Opossum and the Tiger, his poverty is attributed to his abundant progeny. "The two opossums were married, and the next year they had a dozen children. Then the husband told his wife he didn't know how he was going to support a dozen children, the twelve children who were begging for food" (Bartolomé 1979:51–53). Add to its sexual peculiarities the traits linked to maternity: the marsupial's easy birth and the life of the young who have not been completely expelled and are not completely inside the mother's womb—the female opossum is a cradle. Her maternity is also involved in influencing birth by virtue of her tail, a marvelous medicine in cases of difficult childbirth. It can also increase fertility and the secretion of milk.

Finally, its enormous resistance to blows and pain and its strange ability to "play possum," feigning death to deceive its enemies, should be noted. The opossum is a resurrected being, and, if he has that power, why not believe he can reconstruct himself after being torn to pieces?

The close correspondence between myth and the biological traits of the opossum indicate concepts and observations spanning centuries. However, it is not simply the observation of the habits and nature of the animal that has resulted in mythic beliefs, nor is it those beliefs alone that shape perceptions of its biological attributes. All these concepts, reciprocally, have slowly come together in a structured thought that places the opossum—the mythical hero and the species—on a firm footing in the cosmovision of indigenous peoples in many different cultural circumstances. If the myth reveals unexpected traits in the animal—real or not—its conduct and physical peculiarities also reveal to believers mythic aspects that perhaps they had not suspected. Learning is not unidirectional. There is a single reality, composed of the visible and the invisible. The opossum is a mythic character; he is not just a pasteboard mask, not just a symbol.

All this reinforces previous statements about the nature of the gods; but it is also necessary to emphasize the aspects of possession, both in the contagion and in the reabsorbing of the invasive substance. The gods are forces with specific qualities. When they take possession of bodies, their forces rule, the characteristics are shared. The god Tetzauhteotl, patron of the Mexica, protected his children during their migration, entering an eagle, which flew above them. Castillo (1966:64) says that the god became the nagual of the eagle. He also made its plumage white. The god was the whiteness that possessed the body. Possession is transfer of a substance.

Elsewhere (López Austin 1985a) I have referred to the identity that is created when two beings come together violently. Death, which is a kind of possession, gives to the dead the characteristics of the god who has possessed them. When possession takes place, the one who absorbs, as well as the being absorbed, acquire the same nature. The invisible forces distribute or concentrate their own qualities, the dominating qualities in the participating body. The goddess of lust, for example, would enter human bodies and provoke strong sexual desire, but she also cured carnal appetite through forgiveness and cleansing. According to the ancient Nahua, she ate filth (sin), and she owes her name, Tlaelcuani, to that. Other gods were understood in similar terms. Gold was the Sun's excrement. But the sun was also the transformed, pustule-affected Nanahuatl. Speaking of gold, the *Códice Florentino* (1979: bk. 11, ch. 9, fol. 213v–214r) says:

> Those in the know took this excrement from the Sun, because they said it was a cure for pustules. It was said to be a medicine for pustules. Whoever doesn't have pustules eats it, in order not to get them; and it cures whoever already has them. They said they remembered the story about the Sun, who was said to be afflicted with pustules. They said, for this reason, his excrement is a medicine that sometimes appears here on earth.

The Nahua of Tecospa say that since dogs and coyotes are enemies, a man who eats a coyote will be attacked by dogs, while one who eats a dog will not be safe in an area inhabited by coyotes (Madsen 1955). Food and those who ingest it share qualities. For example, this also takes place in the flood myth of the ancient Indians of Colima (Suárez de Cepeda 1983:18):

> They say that the green corn they had sown at that time, as the water covered it, turned into green parrots, the black corn turned into black parrots; and that, because of this, now both are addicted to eating the corn from which they originated. When the corn is tender they come to eat it in the fields.

Our character is an eater par excellence. His Nahuatl name, *tlacuatzin* or *tlacuatl,* comes from the verb *cua,* "to eat." What he eats is that superior food, corn, whose nature he shares. Among the Maya this is made even clearer, since the word *och* means "opossum," but it also means "sustenance or food" (Barrera Vásquez et al. 1980:593). In other Mayan languages, the reference to corn is precise. In Kekchi, *och* means "tender ear of corn" (Sedat 1955). *Och,* therefore, is a quality. It is a quality shared by the opossum, corn, and the red light that, according to the Tzotzil, precedes dawn (Guiteras Holmes 1965:35, 236).

If we recognize that the characters in myths are manifestations of qualities that circulate as forces in the world, the transfer of information from the myths of the Mesoamerican past to those of the present is more plausible. The equating of some contemporary characters with ancient gods is very interesting. This is not a new idea, but it should be emphasized. Of course equating today's mythical characters with the ancient ones is not always possible, among other reasons because in the different versions of the myth (ancient or present), different characters can appear in the same positions. It is not common, but it can happen. A complex example is the character who during the deluge makes the tree, cut by a farmer the previous day, grow again, and who warns the man that he should build a vessel that will save him from the imminent flood. In the Huichol myth of the flood (Lumholtz 1970, 2:189–90), the person is the goddess Nacahué, Lady of the Earth and of the Vegetation, and Mother of the Gods. In the Totonac myth (Ichon 1973:52–53), however, the character is the Rabbit. This is no problem, since the ancient Nahua gave the calendric name 1 Rabbit to Mother Earth. But in other versions of the flood myth, the analogy is impossible. Among the Mixe-Popoluca, the one who makes the trees spring forth from the leveled field and orders the farmer to build the rescuing boat is Jesus Christ or the Sun (Münch Galindo 1983:160–61). Among the Mixe of Oaxaca, it is the Buzzard (*Seis versiones del diluvio* 1983:23). In the ancient Nahua version, the character is neither Mother Earth, the Sun, nor the Buzzard, but the god Titlacahuan (*Leyenda de los soles* 1945:120).

Neither is our character free from an important substitution. In the Maya region there is a version of the fire-theft myth in which it is the dog, not the opossum, who brings fire to humankind (told to María Montoliu in Chan Kom, Yucatan, 1973). It is probable that the myth is quite old. In the *Códice Madrid* (1985: pl. 26), there is a strange carnivorous animal with its back marked with grooves. It seems to be running and to have the end of its tail on fire. Some writers have identified the animal as the God of Lightning (Villa-corta and Villacorta 1976:296–97). In spite of such exceptions as these, how-ever, we should trust the information passed down to us as a rich source of knowledge about ancient and contemporary mythological thought.

The Grandmother of the Sun and Moon twins is one of the characters of contemporary myths that has been identified with the ancient Mesoamerican gods. She is Yohualticitl or Toci of the Nahua, protector of childbirth and in-ventor of the *temazcal* (steam bath). Today's myths, besides naming her as one of the principal characters of the solar myth, describe her death in a temazcal, where she remains enclosed in order to protect those who have recently given birth, as well as their children (Cicco and Horcasitas 1962). There is no such wealth of detail in ancient sources.

Like the myth above, contemporary myths can shed light on the ancient ones, not only by identifying characters, but by clarifying the meaning of the story. In the old Nahuatl myth of the origin of the Sun and the Moon at Teoti-huacan, the god Naui Tecpatl, changed into the Moon, came to the edge of the sky and was attacked by savage beings that left him clothed in rags (*Leyenda de los soles* 1945:122). Nothing in the ancient myth seems to justify such a violent attack. A myth found today in Soconusco clarifies the ancient text. The Sun, on fire, jumped to the sky, and in doing so, burned the Grandmother's hair. The other brother, the Moon, jumped over a ditch to escape the furious uncles, the Grandmother's sons. They tried to catch him and seized his garment, which fell apart. The Moon escaped, but the uncles held the luminous tatters in their hands and with that radiant splendor became the stars (Navarrete 1966).

It is possible to compare our hero's collection of attributes and symbols with those of another mythic character. This creates a wealth of perspectives in the field of interpretation. The traits that come together in the opossum can belong, wholly or in part, to another who, like him, was the archetypical manifestation of forces revealed in the world's reality. The fire thief seems to be very close to the old lord of dawn, Quetzalcoatl, but since Quetzalcoatl is a god extraordinarily rich in attributes, myths, and symbols, the identification will have to be based on some of the most outstanding features.

Quetzalcoatl is the preeminent initiator of things in the world, the traveler to the Region of the Dead and the one who extracts its secrets and wealth. The ancient Nahua considered him to be the forerunner of rain, the sweeper who opened roads (Sahagún 1956, 1:45). He was Ehecatl, the Lord of Wind, who was thought to be a substance of the underworld. Today among the Zinacantec, it is also he, as the Morning Star, who opens the path to the sun (Vogt 1973:13). In his guise of Tlahuizcalpantecuhtli, he was the Lord of Dawn, the one who brought to the surface of the earth the light that illuminates things before the sun rises. He was the traveler who went to Tlillan Tlapallan, the place of opposition between darkness and the colors of the world. He was, in short, the wise bearer of light.

Quetzalcoatl not only extracted light from the Region of the Dead, but also life, and specially human life. He stole the bones guarded by Mictlantecuhtli, took them to Tamoanchan to be reconstructed, and drew blood from his own penis and sprinkled it over the cold, inert matter. Thus the human body was formed (*Leyenda de los soles* 1945:120–21).

After giving birth to humankind, Quetzalcoatl was concerned about food for the new creature. He found the red ant that had taken grain from Tonacatepetl ["Hill of Sustenance"] and, changing himself into the black ant, he went to the subterranean store. With the help of the blue, white, yellow, and red rain gods, he broke into Tonacatepetl and took away white, black, yellow, and red maize, along with the bean, amaranth, *michhuauhtli,* and *chia {Salvia sp.}* (*Leyenda de los soles* 1945:21).[2]

His relationship to fire can be seen in his ornaments. "He wore feathers resembling flames on his back as an emblem" (Sahagún 1956, 1:46). Taking fire from the gods produced the same effect we have seen in the tales about the opossum. Bringing the force of the gods to the earth's surface brought an ordering of time; it created the calendar. The *Historia de los mexicanos por sus pinturas* (1965:25) says, "And they commanded both Quetzalcoatl and Huitzilopochtli to bring order, according to their judgment and command. They made the fire . . . Then they made the days, dividing them into months, giving each month twenty days, and so there were eighteen, and three hundred sixty days in a year." Quetzalcoatl, as lord of the first light, is fire, and therefore one of his names if "flower."[3] He is fire and he is wind, in an opposition of contrary forces, heat and cold, because he rules over malinalli, like the opossum who steals pulque and fire for humankind.

Quetzalcoatl works in Tamoanchan. He creates human beings. His actions make a sponsor of human fertility, and he is mentioned as such in ancient sources (Cervantes de Salazar 1914–36, 1:43).

As an extractor, as a being who changes things from one place to another, Quetzalcoatl is as much a thief as the opossum. He is the patron of thieves and also of merchants. As a merchant he is the patron of the city of Cholula and of the diligent and skillful Toltec (Sahagún 1956, 3:189). He was the patron of the worst thieves, of the sorcerers known as *temacpalitotique*, born on the day 1 Wind, a day ruled by Quetzalcoatl. The temacpalitotique put their victims to sleep by magic, carrying the image of the god Quetzalcoatl for this purpose (Sahagún 1956, 1:357–58, López Austin 1965).

Stresser-Pean (1952–53:229) says he has witnessed market celebrations under the great silk-cotton tree in Huaxtec towns. This ceiba (or *pochote*) tree was the principal symbol of the Nahua merchants, from which they got the name of *pochteca*. The ceibas were also trees that, according to the Maya, sank their roots into the underworld and raised their branches to support the sky.[4] Five ceibas, one in the center and the other four at the outer edges of the world, were for the Maya the channels of the gods. The ceiba is the generic image of the four columns of the bacabs (as well as the central one), conceived as the coverings for the helix. Does the word *necuiloa* have a double meaning— mercantile and spiral movement—in this complex concept of the cosmos? According to Molina (1944: fol. 65r), *necuiloa* means "to trade and to bargain," as well as "to twist something." Quetzalcoatl is the protector of trade; but also, like the opossum, he twists things.

The literal meaning of Quetzalcoatl is "plumed serpent." It is the figure represented on the columns upon which the western Maya of the Postclassic period engraved the images of the four bacabs. Myths about Quetzalcoatl include the activities of the god the other time and acts attributed to actual history, deeds of those who on earth were thought to be corporeal containers of the force of the god. These stories, extensions of the time of origins, often tell of miraculous deeds, or they relate the glory of the Toltec age ruled by Ce Acatl Topiltzin Quetzalcoatl. The *Anales de Cuauhtitlan* (1945:8) say that when the priest Quetzalcoatl lived in Tula, he began to build his temple, "where he placed columns in the form of a snake." As a god Quetzalcoatl is one of the divinities generically related to the four trees that hold up the sky. But in the myths he is also one of the sacred trees in particular. Collectively they are considered to be ceibas, each particular one a different species. Quetzalcoatl is the *quetzalhuexotl* [*Salix lasiopelis*], the column of the south (*Códice Tudela* 1980: fol. 118r). That is what the myth about the abduction of Mayahuel says, and it is also the way he appears in the *Historia de los mexicanos por sus pinturas* (1965: 32):

> The two gods made themselves into great trees. Tezcatlipoca is the tree they call *tezcacuahuitl*, which means "mirror tree," and Quetzalcoatl's tree is called *quetzalhuexotl*. Men and trees and gods raised the sky with its stars where they are now.

In the Vindobenensis codex there is a figure of the Lord 9 Wind, who supports the sky on his head. Several writers have called attention to the close
relationship between the Mixtec 9 Wind and the god Ehecatl-Quetzalcoatl
of the central highlands of Mexico (Nicholson 1978).[5] Jill Furst (1978:109)
says that the character carries out the mission of a sky bearer, as other pictographic documents corroborate. The figure is very similar to that of plate 51
of the Borgia codex, in which the god Quetzalcoatl is one of the bearers.
Quetzalcoatl's tie with the four cosmic pillars is confirmed by the symbol of
the cross, often a part of his vestments, as well as by one of his names, Nacxitl
("Four Feet"), resembling that of the quadruple god of chapter 11. Among his
symbols there are also those referring to helical movement, a cross-sectioned
snail shell that shows its spiral (the "wind necklace," or *ehecailacatzcuzcatl*) and
his twisted golden ear spools, *tzicoliuhqui teucuitlanacuchtli* (*Primeros Memoriales*
1905: fol. 261v, p. 24). The god's propensities can be summarized in a few
words: he forms the wind, he makes the whirlwinds, he blows, he is something
that moves in spirals (*Primeros Memoriales* 1905: fol. 270v, p. 42).[6]

He is a thing in circles and Owner of the Whirlwind. Just as the opossum
is creator of the river's curves and wears the spiral on his face, Quetzalcoatl
has the form of the malinalli. Lord 9 Wind appears in the *Códice Vindobonen-*
sis (1964–67: pl. 5-48; see fig. 16 e of the present work) with his whole body
in the form of a helix. There is an andesite sculpture, 195 centimeters high, in
the Rautenstrauch-Joest Museum in Cologne, in which Quetzalcoatl-Ehecatl's
body is depicted as a twisted rod.[7] When referring to this piece, I cannot avoid
the question of the antiquity of the Wind God in the highlands of Mexico,
at least to support an interesting theory proposed by Niederberger (1987,
2:466, fig. 280; see fig. 16, c and d of the present work). The archeologist
equated the profiles of the two small ceramic heads of the Preclassic with that
of the Mexica Ehecatl-ozomatli sculpture, found in the subway excavations in
Mexico City, thus suggesting a reconsideration of the supposedly late Huaxte-
can origin of the Wind God. I suggest another comparison: that of the andesite
figure of the Cologne museum to that of a similar ceramic figure published by
Niederberger (1987, 2: fig. 381).[8]

Quetzalcoatl is also closely tied to the lunar complex of pulque and dismemberment. He is the abductor of Mayahuel, the Goddess of the Maguey Plant:

> The gods said among themselves, "Man will be sad if we don't do something
> to cheer him up so that he will enjoy living on earth and will praise us and sing
> and dance." Hearing this, Ehecatl, god of air, thought deeply about where he
> could find a liquor to give to man to make him happy. While he was thinking,

he happened to remember the virgin goddess Mayahuel, and he went at once to see where they were, and he found them sleeping. He woke the virgin, who was guarded by her grandmother, a goddess called Cicimitl [Tzitzimitl], and said to her, "I have come to look for you to take you to the world." She agreed and he came down, with her on his shoulders.

As soon as they reached earth, they turned into a tree that had two branches, one called *quetzalhuexotl*, who was Ehecatl, and the other *xochicuahuitl*, who was the virgin. Meanwhile the grandmother was sleeping. When she awoke and didn't find her granddaughter, she immediately appealed to other goddesses, called *cicimime* [*tzitzimime*]. All of them descended to earth to look for Ehecatl. Then the branches broke apart. The virgin's was recognized by the old goddess, who took it, and breaking it, gave each of the goddesses a piece, which they ate.

They did not break the Ehecatl branch, but left it there. As soon as the goddesses had returned to the sky, Ehecatl returned to his original form. He collected the virgin's bones, buried them, and a tree sprang forth, which they call *metl*, from which the Indians make the wine they drink and with which they get drunk. (*Historia de México* 1965:106–7)

The priest Quetzalcoatl is a being who gets about on the surface of the earth as well as in the underworld. The history of Quetzalcoatl states that when he fled from Tula, "He built some houses under the earth, which are named Mictlancalco" (Sahagún 1956, 1:291). As a god he revives from death when (like the opossum) he falls with the booty from his robbery. Mictlantecuhtli ordered the gods to make a hole along his path so that Quetzalcoatl would fall into it. He fell into the trap and died of the blow, but he came alive again and arrived at Tamoanchan with the bones (*Leyenda de los soles* 1945:121). Quetzalcoatl is also a dismembered god. The ancient myth no longer exists, but there is an iconographic image: a sculptured Mexica monolithic cylinder has Quetzalcoatl's body parts and insignia carved on it (Solís Olguín 1976:35, fig. 79). Add to this the priest's abandoning Tula, after he had broken his abstinence, by becoming drunk on pulque and engaging in illicit sex. Add also the ritual practice of beheading quails for Quetzalcoatl, a custom that recalls the damage done by the opossum in the chicken coop.

Some other characteristics of the god tie him to the opossum. Quetzalcoatl, the priest of Tula, was an old man. As a god and as a human his rival is Tezcatlipoca, a god whose nagual is the coyote (*Códice Florentino* 1979: bk. 5, ch. 13, fol. 14r). He competes with him in the ball game (Torquemada 1969: bk. 6, ch. 14, vol. 2, 79). Seler (1963, 1:114) considers him to be in profound opposition to Tezcatlipoca, identifying Quetzalcoatl with the Heart of the Lake and Tezcatlipoca with the Heart of the Sky. Sexually the god—and the priest—is

without equal. He brings to copulation the frenzy of drunkenness and kidnap-
ping. He also undergoes sex changes. In the month Huei Tozoztli, the ancient
Nahua chose as the living image of their god Quetzalcoatl a beautiful virgin
slave, whom they dressed as the god. They cut her hair like that of the men
and threw the shorn locks into the fire. They painted her face red, and that
was the color used by all the women on that day of ritual killing ("Costumbres,
fiestas, enterramientos . . ." 1945).

There is a contemporary Huichol myth about the theft of fire in which the
hero—like Quetzalcoatl—is the Morning Star (*Wirrarika irratsikayari* 1982:
21–25). It is the first part of the opossum myth, but everything seems to indicate that it is a different myth, or perhaps a parallel one. At the beginning of
the world an extraordinarily luminous animal, resembling a bull, appeared in
the lake. The people shot arrows at it, but these caught on fire and did him no
harm. One of the ancestors asked the Morning Star for help. The latter jumped
on the beast and flayed it, while the people gathered up the skin that flew
from its body with tinder and wood. But the second part of the myth must be
connected. In the interweaving of both parts (or both myths) the receiving of
fire is limited to the inhabitants of one town. The people in other places would
have to rely on another theft, that of the opossum. The Morning Star and the
opossum are similar heroes. Or are they equivalent?

Recent archeological excavations in Tlatelolco have provided some valuable
information. As anticipated a statue of the God of Wind was found in a trench
dug in front of Edifice R, the circular construction dedicated to Quetzalcoatl-
Ehecatl. With it, however, were remains associated with maternity: twenty
female clay figures, some of them with children in their arms, a bride's trous-
seau, human bodies buried in a fetal position, and what archeologists have
interpreted to be wooden cradle. This would be meaningless, except that they
also found the ceramic figure of a mammal they at first believed to be a dog.
Afterwards, during the work of restoration, it was noticed that the figure had
over its eyes the classic triangular stain used to represent the opossum and, on
its back, over the fracture marks, a similar, smaller figure in the typical posture
in which opossum infants must have been placed (Matos Moctezuma 1988).[9]

Taking all this into consideration, could it be said that the opossum is
Quetzalcoatl? In this sea of mingled essences that form the gods, we may say
that he almost is. The list of attributes and comparisons could go on, but no
effort is made here to reveal all the mysteries of the god Quetzalcoatl and the
opossum. I am, however, trying to demonstrate that mythical characters can
share essences.

And what happens to the opossum as a character in stories? Often he occupies an uncommon place in tales that, although enhanced in Mexican territory, come from other traditions. In these tales the Rabbit/Coyote pair is changed to Opossum/Tiger. There are few opossum tales that do not belong to this opposition of characters (*Ap ayuuk* 1982:34–39; Ramírez Castañeda 1987:191–92). The pairs and their variations (Rabbit/Fox, Opossum/Coyote, Rabbit/Tiger, Opossum/Puma, etc.) from other lands and cultures are found throughout the country.

Examples of the struggle between the Rabbit and the Coyote, or their substitutes, the Opossum and the Tiger, are numerous (Radin 1943–44; Rendón 1970; González Casanova 1979; Dyk 1959:33–61; Boremanse 1986:384–87; W. Miller 1956:165–71; Trujillo Maldonado 1980; Lastra 1970), and the academic debate on the origin of the stories goes back to the beginning of the century (Boas 1912; Espinosa 1914a; Mason 1914; González Casanova 1946; Radin 1944). These stories form a series of confrontations between the two characters of the pair: the strong character (the Coyote, the Tiger) tries to take advantage of the weakness of its opponent (the Rabbit, the Opossum), but the astuteness of the weaker one prevails.[10] All the tales have a characteristic form, a sequence of independent pieces that vary in length according to the wishes of the narrator. The arbitrary chain and the indefinite length of the narrative are described by Martínez (1985) as follows:

> The plot, aside from the characters who carry it out, consists of a series of happenings that follow each other without any apparent logical connection, and without the deeds of one part of the series changing the development of the plot. Each one of the elements can be developed in a different way, and the narrator is entirely free to amplify a particular part, to complicate or prolong an action, choose the order in which the parts are presented, etc.; but he cannot exceed the particular limits of each event nor the form of the specific ordering of events imposed by the type.

Each link in the chain is barely connected to the one before it. They are parts that appear to be similar among the different indigenous groups. The astute character leaves the stronger one holding up a large stone in danger of falling; he makes him stick to a tar baby; he incites him to trap turkeys that are, in fact, buzzards; he throws him a piece of fruit that sticks in his throat; he makes him drink all the water in the lake, promising that at the bottom he will find cheese (the reflection of the moon); he asks him to discipline a classroom that has wasps instead of students; he induces him to crush his testicles; he covers him and urinates on him, saying it is rain. These are short tales told in many parts of the world.

The stories and myths about the opossum justify Boas's (1968:405) claim that there is a permanent interchange of material between stories and myths, with neither group having priority. There are transfers from myth to story. In one version of the fire theft, the thief throws an unpeeled prickly pear into the mouth of the small man he has just robbed (*Uejkauitl nauaueuejtlajtoli* 1982: 25–27). In another, about the theft of maize, the Opossum throws a hard, green *mamey* into the jaws of the Tiger that was the bodyguard of Lisibé, the owner of the granary (Portal 1986:38). There are also transfers from story to myth, as in the struggles of the Tiger against the Opossum, when the latter set fire to a cornfield and the Tiger's skin was left striped by the fire. Or the Tiger grasps the Opossum by the tail, pulls on it, and leaves it white and hairless (Weitlaner and Castro 1973:204–5). And in the struggles between the Rabbit and the Tiger, after leaving the stone that was about to fall, the tricked Tiger overtook the rabbit; but the Rabbit fled again and since then has sheltered in the moon (Incháustegui 1977:38). Transfers from myth to story and from story to myth are frequent. Are they important? The hybrid examples leave a strong taste of stories or myths poorly told.

Why does the Opossum substitute for the Rabbit? Perhaps because in the kinship of both with the moon, the Opossum has greater prestige. Perhaps in the myths there is an antecedent of rivalry as strong as that of the Rabbit and the Coyote, the rivalry of the Lord of Fire who defeats the Tiger in order to protect humanity forever (Bruce 1974:45–62). But the Rabbit also obtains some advantage and appears to be the wisest of animals, the one who can, better than all the other beasts, give a name to each of the days at the moment of the creation of time (Dyk 1959:62).

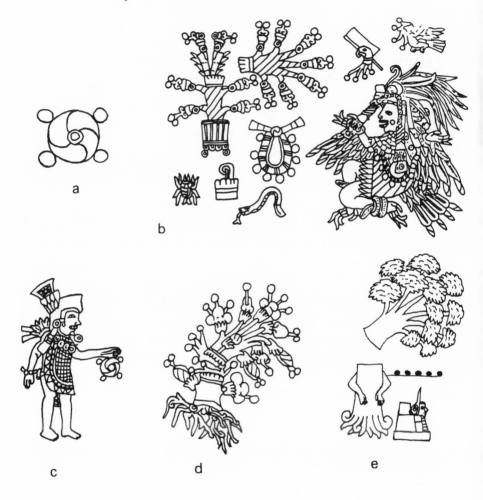

Figure 12. The Breaking of Sacred Trees
a. Symbol of the god Macuilxochitl, identical to the symbol for "festival" that the character for the month of *huei tecuhilhuitl* has in his hand, *Codex Maglia-bechiano*, plate 5v
b. The breaking of the tree and the goddess Itzpapalotl, *Codex Borbonicus*, plate 15
c. Character with the symbol for "festival" during the month of *huei tecuhilhuitl*, *Códice Telleriano-Remensis*, first part, plate 2
d. The breaking of the tree of *Tamoanchan*, *Códice Telleriano-Remensis*, plate 23
e. The breaking of the tree during the Mexica migration, *Códice Boturini*, plate 2

Hence, even the lover of myths is
in a way a lover of wisdom;
for myth is made up of wonders.

Aristotle,
Metaphysics

Gossip is the space where a subject of discussion rejoices. Where subjects of discussion rejoice, to be precise, because gossip carries a rich load. In gossip there is a large and complex assortment of heterogenous subjects, which run simultaneously along the same channel. Some are explicit subjects, some implicit. Some are clear, others obscure and diffuse. Some are conscious, some are less so. Some are emitted intentionally, some escape due to the liveliness of the medium. They are emotional or indifferent. There are subjects that are important and dominant, and there are secondary and ornamental ones. They may be joyful or serious; some, more worldly, and others nearer to the divine. Some are more concrete and others more abstract. Various subjects of discussion will have to be dealt with in articulating gossip. Different regulatory norms and various combinatory forms, all operate simultaneously to form a rumor.

The kinds of subjects, however, are not precise. They cannot be classified in a definite way. There are more gray hues than black and white. Gossip is made up of a sequence of components that support each other reciprocally. Gossip is not an aggregate of removable pieces. Characterizing the subjects of gossip would only be a methodological tool through which one would try to indicate some of the components, starting with the most outstanding.

A reproach, a picture, a dance, a sculpture, or a myth are groups, complexes of subjects, like gossip itself, because the subject matter is taken to be the object of the expression. It is assumed to be the expression of a thought in the communicative relationship, the expression of a sentiment or the means by which one of the participants tries to alter the thought or feelings of another. The subject matter is what the participants recognize, feel, or simply perceive as the material of their social interchange in the communication.

The nature of the subjects is not found just in the psychic interior, nor just in the crystallization of an expression. It is the link that is established between the expression and those who communicate through it. They are the ones who attribute meaning to an expression or to a topic. What does this mean? That to assume is to act mentally on an topic. This implies that any participants in the process of interchange identify the topic as a means of communication, attributing a particular content to the topic and assuming other participants, with mental ability similar enough to their own to understand the content. The content originates in the mind of a person, but is not necessarily what is uttered or what the receiver of the communication perceives through that content.

As a transmitter I can distinguish between what I wanted to express and what my actions actually expressed through clay, speech, or my own muscles. I can also know that I did not express what I really thought or felt because of what I hid, lied about, feigned, or was incompetent to express. As a receiver I can suspect lying, fiction, hiding, or incompetence in someone else's expression, or I can assume that I am incapable of complete understanding.

Assumptions are made at both ends of the communication process. Transmitters receive their own subjects. There is a reflexive effect in the process, since the expression instantaneously alters the thought of the one who emits it. A thought is changed during the expression itself, during the action that creates the topic and transforms a reality.

The content contains the messages, but it is not limited to what is created by a desire to express something. Profound subjects can be communicated that are barely understood by the communicator, that are received with only a slight understanding by the receiver, or that can be vaguely perceived by both parties; because perceptions can arise with varying degrees of awareness. There are subjects that I understand vividly, as soon as they are received, which together with a group of associations link my memories, putting them in place, enriching them, and immediately creating other thoughts and feelings. There are other subjects that I barely perceive at the time of their reception, grasping them by themselves without relating them intensely to other thoughts, placing them in my subconscious. Afterwards, however, my memory may recall them and place them among my interests and my means of perceiving reality, with abundant new relationships.

There are subjects that establish relationships between emitters and receivers who are separated by millennia. The expressions create a prolonged communicative process. Believers think they find an answer to their present trials and tribulations in the words of the sacred text. It is a language that extends further than a dialect, a culture, or an epoch.

In this sense there are complicated subjects even in inner language, which, though internal, is still social.[1] Inner language can be considered to be a segment of the process of communication, but the link that creates the subject exists entirely within it. This link is established between the expression and one (here, the only one) of the participants in the process, because language is a social process. Even if, mistakenly, I express myself believing that there is a listener before me, a subject is created. From the other side, isolated listeners can also produce a subject, as long as they pretend that there is a sender for the imagined message. I will find a subject from the gods in the sound of the wind in the shrubbery, as long as I believe in the gods, that the rustling is their voice, and that I can understand the divine words. The attribution of a message to an object is enough to produce a semiotic process.

Mythic narrations are tales about inchoative events at the time of creation. They have many subjects, of multiple types, and it is best to start from a clear classification in order to understand them. If myths are narrations of processes, their particular or general characteristics can be taken as a basis for determining types. It is possible to classify the topics of mythical narration into three broad types: 1. heroic subjects, vivid, colorful specific stories, almost impossible to repeat in the same way in every version of the myth, that tell how something came to be; 2. nodal subjects, which comprise the schematic sequence of steps in the creative process, an order present in different versions of the same myth; and 3. at a more abstract level, nomological subjects, the laws that underlie a group of different myths, the laws that govern different processes of creation or of existence.

Going from the particular to the general, mythical subjects are categorized by this simple division into those that narrate divine adventures, those that state the sequence of the creative processes, and those that refer to cosmic laws. They are not, however, independent levels in themselves, nor unrelated to each other. Neither are they sharply delimited topics. Their boundaries disappear along the continuum from the particular to the general.

Such a division is important, because there is insufficient clarity in the throng of subjects presented in a myth. It is necessary to separate the subjects to find the various correspondences in the tale. Moreover the type of subjects that form the axis of the mythic narration must be found. There is a central type. Without the control of a central theme, the narration would be chaotic, dispersed among the different rules that operate simultaneously in the expression.

Finding this axis is also methodologically important. An investigator should begin the study of the different subjects in the myth by starting from this central, predominant type.

Nodal subjects are the most important of the three types. The detailed narration of divine adventures, of heroic subjects, that amuse narrators and their audiences, is not the most important. In their versions the mythical background, the actions of the characters, and sometimes even the characters themselves change. The intensity of the tale and the extent and detail of the deeds are also changeable. However, when different versions of the myth are compared, it is evident that there is a limit to what is arbitrary. In actual narration there is an axis governing the motifs of the myth. Many events may be omitted, but there are fundamental ones that are interchangeable, omitted only when there are equivalent substitutions. Through this controlling axis the transformations are accomplished through the use of "synonyms." This axis is composed of nodal subjects, those that refer to the order of the creative processes; that is, to the schema of the inchoative action.

The third type, that of nomological subjects (cosmic laws), is usually presented through indirect references. The order of particular creative processes alludes to cosmic laws, in the same way that a dialogue between a father and a son may reflect a particular family arrangement, or a monument, the principles of an architectural school. The particular details of a myth are not found in these laws. However, the nodal subjects link the laws of the universe to the particular features of a creation.

The above is a compromise that proposes methodological bases that in turn can affect the results of a study of the meaning, the functions, and the amount of truth that a believer attributes to the myth. Some general points need to be clarified before giving examples of the three types.

1. Mythic narration is a composite of subjects, just as is a joke, a legend, a poem, a song, a story, a declaration of love, or a reproach. Communication is established through it. This statement would be a platitude, if in the past many writers had not taken mythic narration to be a radically different form of expression from any other. For some it has been an aberrant form, or the product of intractable thoughts, or an expression that evades socially imposed rules by its universality. For others it has been a depository of absolute wisdom. Here we propose it only and simply as a specific form of expression. Gossen (1974:248) supports this view:

> Recent considerations of myth may beg the question of explanation by assuming that "mythic thought" has a logic of its own and therefore belongs to a different order of translatability, comprehension, and meaning than do the infrastructures that make up the rest of the cultural content. The Chamula data, however, indicate that true ancient narrative (which some might gloss as "myth") has no special logical discreteness over any other genres. All of the genres respond ana-

lytically as different aspects of the same primordial time-space principle, which has different style and content associations at various levels.

2.   Those who participate in a process of communication define their topic by means of priority rules. These give different characteristics to each form of expression. The intent of mythic narration is to narrate divine deeds. Mary Douglas (1967), criticizing Lévi-Strauss's method, says that the participants are aware of the weight of this intent, and states that:

> The meaning of myth is partly the sense that the author intended it to convey, and the sense intended by each of its raconteurs. But every listener can find in it references to his own experience, so the myth can be enlightening, consoling, depressive, irrespective of the intentions of the tellers.

3.   This intent is basically manifested in the story, in the series of divine episodes that give order to the plot. Accepting the primary value of the story does not deny that mythic narration, like any other kind of text, has meanings beyond the concrete message that participants fully recognize as the topic of the communication. Relating the adventures of the gods is not the only significant realm of mythic narration. There is also meaning in the structural relations of the different elements of the narrative. The internal structure of mythic narrations plays an important part in the communicative process, but here we are focusing our attention on the open interchange of the user-creators of the myth, in their manifest intention, in their choice of codes, and in the forms they believe can best express this communication. The subjects that directly concern the actions of the gods form the core of the myth, forcing an emphasis on the relating of divine adventures. The adventures of the gods transcend their mythic narration; they do not depend essentially on the narrative structure. Mythic narration is not the sole channel for these fundamental topics. Besides the formal narration, the same divine actions, derived from belief, are manifested in other forms of expression, which are not exclusively texts, and which are influenced by different structures. There are codes in these structures, and it is possible to deduce the underlying messages that users perceive subconsciously; but the story has priority when it is a question of the meaning of mythic narration.

4.   Some subjects in the story are clear, some are not. The understanding of a subject can be kept to a superficial level, either intentionally or by a limited capability. A greater desire—or greater aptitude—transcends this level and leads to an understanding of the profound meanings. The reasoning of

the faithful, and also of the investigator, play a part in unravelling the message, because the knowledge it contains can be refined. Reason plays a part, because the predominant element in myth is thought. Mythic narration as an exposition of divine subjects, as a beautiful expression, has a highly emotive content; but thought predominates over emotion. This contradicts authors such as Cassirer (1951:126), who feel that the coherence of myth depends to a much higher degree on a unity of feeling than on rules of logic. Many investigators—among them those who see in it an expression of deep levels of consciousness, of dream processes—do not recognize the rational aspect of mythic narration and limit mythic narration to one of the types (that of heroic subjects), a type that is not sufficient to bring out the logical coherence of divine adventures.

5.   Mythic narration presents a tale of divine adventures because that is the wish of the tellers and their public. The central subjects of that expression are processes, aggregates of successive groups of causal processes, that lead to a marvelous result—the inchoation. This is what occurs in the categories of heroic subjects and nomological subjects. Are some of humanity's greatest concerns present in myth? Yes, frequently, as they are also in poems, stories, legends, and in many other manifestations of human thoughts and feelings. But this does not mean that mythic narration provides a solution to those great mysteries that is unattainable by other means. The stories narrate beliefs about the nature of the inchoative processes. Sometimes the subject matter is the inauguration of the complexity of the universe; at other times, the origin of the coat of a mammal or the plumage of a bird. They are not a "reflection" of the social structure, nor is there an automatic translation from the system that creates them. As Wittfogel and Goldfrank (1943) state:

> The realistic foundation of all myths cannot be questioned. But, at the same time, there can be no doubt that, except in a limited number of cases, their creators have been motivated by religious and artistic impulses rather than by a "mirror-like" autobiographical intent.

It is obvious that the aspirations, desires, problems, mysteries, and contradictions that emanate from all levels of consciousness come together in myth. Mythic narrations are structured by rules that strongly resemble those that govern society and nature. But the essential subject matter of mythic narration must not be confused with the complex origin of mythic narrations, these sources from which all kinds of expressions spring, nor with their deep tracks and solid presence in myth.

6.   There are many topics in each myth, but there is a central, predominant theme that organizes all the rest. An investigation of the subject matter of myth must begin with an examination of this theme. However, its meaning is not always obvious. Mythic adventures, with their wealth of characters and episodes, with their intense explicitness, cloak a more serious and profound subject. A layperson enjoys the details of the deeds, while a wiser, more questioning listener can perceive other messages that continue to reveal the creative impact of the invisible forces. The perception of believers is based on an ever-present interpretation of the innumerable manifestations of mythic beliefs, as well as their background in a particular, select tradition formed by experts on the sacred. An outside investigator finds the comparison of different myths to be useful. For everyone, however, there is always something more to be learned, because the understanding of nodal subjects is slow and additive. It is an issue for devotees, for the sagacious, and at times, for initiates.

Among all peoples there is a constant exegesis of the manifestations of their own beliefs. This exegesis produces a gradual development in the intellectual perception of the tale. In that "beyond" of mythic subjects there is no allegory. Myth is not a fiction that is believed only by the layperson. To think that allegory is the underpinning of myth would take us to the absurd conclusion that "instead of being a belief, it is a mere 'make-believe.' " [2]

7.   Does mythic narration explain? Yes, but for the present it is best to give the verb *explain* a wider meaning: to declare, to manifest. It is not convenient at present to define *explanation* as the elucidation of an obscure subject, or as the exposition of the reason for something. Neither is it convenient now to link the content of myth to definite functions or purposes. The functions of mythic narratives will be examined later, along with a more exact definition of the nature of what they explain.

More than an answer to the problems posed by human beings, myth should be seen as the product, as the synthesis of what people verify in their daily struggle. In this synthesis adjustments are made, similarities are assumed, and myth emerges from the consolidation. Myth summarizes the solution rather than solving the problem. Often it is a universal explanation, but there is no great conscious, corresponding universal question. It expounds knowledge, some inconsequential, some fundamental, because it is derived from thinking; and it captivates people who, consciously or unconsciously, discover, condensed in it, their own everyday answers to the heterogeneity of the world.

Mythic narrations often present inchoative processes very explicitly. The denouements—happy endings—are confirmations of what is created, of what is established, of what is characteristic: "we people were born from them," "since then it has had a spotted skin," "because of this, we have the custom," "buzzards have existed since the . . ." But not every explanation is that clear. Explanations are subjects of discussion, and nodal explanations do not necessarily coincide with those of heroic subjects nor share their clarity. The same myth can have explicit expositions of different subjects in different versions. A different development of a different subject can be found in each version of the myth of the origin of the Sun and the Moon: why the Sun is brighter than the Moon; why the Sun is golden and the Moon is silver; why they move separately; why the Sun is regular in his daily rounds and the Moon irregular in her nocturnal appearances; why the Sun is always full, while the Moon varies; why only the Sun shines radiantly and the Moon shares her light with the stars. However, myth does reveal overall knowledge, and this is revealed when attention is focused on the central, dominant nodal subject.

Some specific examples of our proposed tripartite classification of subjects follow. The divine adventure itself is the first kind, that of heroic subjects. It is rich in details, characters, and episodes, which differ in each version of the myth. Its meaning is explicit, unequivocal, and often the characters are fully identified at the moment of transformation. For example, the astral references in the *Popol vuh*:

> Zipacná immediately let the house fall on their heads and killed them all.
> Not even one, or two, were saved among the four hundred youths; they were killed by Zipacná, the son of Vucub-Caquix.
> Thus was the death of the four hundred youths, and it is said they became the group of stars they call Motz. (*Popol vuh* 1964:42)

> Then [Hunahpú and Ixbalanqué] arose in the midst of the light, and in an instant went up to the sky. One of them became the Sun and the other the Moon. Then they lighted the sky and the face of the earth. And they lived in the sky.
> Then the four hundred youths killed by Zipacná also arose and became their companions, and were converted into stars in the sky. (*Popol vuh* 1964:102)

This explicitness still exists in our myths today, to the point that the conclusion can be frankly explanatory. This is the case in the Chatino myth, in which two brothers prepare to go up to the sky. One of them is fond of sexual pleasures and plans to take his woman to the sky. The gopher, ordered by the other brother, cuts the cord by which the woman was going to climb, and only the two brothers reach the sky. The myth ends as follows:

> The Sun and the Moon do not work together. They do not work at the same time. This is because the Moon was delayed when he looked for his woman; the

Sun hastened, went on ahead, and the Moon fell behind. His brother did not catch up with him, and that is why, even today, the Moon comes later. They come and they go, and the Sun works every day while the Moon works sometimes all night and sometimes only a part of the time. He wants to return to his woman. (Cicco and Horcasitas 1962)

Let us go from the particular to the general, from heroic subjects to the nomological, those that deal with cosmic laws. These laws underlie the different myths, as they also underlie the great human preoccupations, their impulses, desires, aspirations. Why, then, is the study of the cosmic laws underlying narrations singled out and raised to the level of a type of subject matter? Because here the study of the subjects of mythic narration is focused on the most important aspect of their nature: they are descriptions of processes. As such, the most general aspect of processes is law, in this case laws so broad in their scope they are taken to be the ruling forces of all the universe.

Divine adventures are often transgressions: murders, the quartering of bodies, betrayals, violations, fornications, incest, theft, mockery; and frequently it is assumed that gods have special privileges. Nevertheless, antisocial behavior is an expression of the great conflict by which order is established. Cosmic laws are established by confrontation, in a struggle, because struggle brings about total dynamics. The confrontation takes place within the framework of cosmic laws. It generates them and tries to simplify them into absolute conformity.

What is sought is the submission of the different areas of the universe to general laws. This submission applies to the realms of kinship, social organization, economic relationships, and the interactions between different groups of people. But it also includes those of geography, the path of astral bodies across the sky and through the levels of the underworld, agricultural cycles, the changes of the seasons, and the body's health. For example, in the past the aging of the human body was compared to that of the earth, which was wet when created and dried out in order to house the beings of the world. It was believed that people were born tender, almost water, and attained the greatest dryness and hardness in old age. The correspondence of the greater and lesser spheres was the operating duality, thanks to these parallel processes.

Through parallelism the equilibrium between hot and cold in eating food is equivalent to the combination of the divine forces over the surface of the earth. The division of things into male and female is also due to parallelism. This is also the correspondence made between the cycle of the maternal womb and the cycle of life and death on earth. Similarly, the four gods of the cornfield, who guard and guarantee the crops, represent the four sustaining pillars at the corners of the world. Reality is stretched to make it comply with the uniformity of the laws, and myth is one of the tools. Mythic narration varies the rules to correspond to different levels of the cosmos. Myth is the crystallization of the "sympathy of everything" proposed by the Stoics. The challenge to the investigator is to discover the relationships that constitute "the ordering of the orders" (Lévi-Strauss 1968a:285).

The organization of the cosmos can also be a theme of myth; this is the interpretation given to the myth of the Fifth Sun (Florescano 1987:23, 31). This causes a significant simplification in mythic processes. The actions of the gods and the sequence of the episodes obey, in many cases, a limited general order of transformations. Graulich (1987b:268–69), referring to the ancient Nahua, says:

> Myth tells the story of an era, of a people. The plan, always the same, is as follows:
>
> 1. the union of opposites,
>
> 2. the separation of opposites,
>
> 3. the equilibrium of opposites, based on their alternation
>
> After a while, equilibrium brings about the union of opposites, establishing a cycle.

This universality of the laws allows mythic narration to be read in different ways. The message can also become a medium for widely different meanings. Thus myth can be a vehicle for transitory messages, more or less hidden, more or less intentional, that validate the position of a person, a family, or a group. In some cases all that is required is to emphasize on certain passages or to highlight particular characters. By this means history and myth are made to correspond. The faithful will find in the myth ancestral allusions to the present time. Myth applied to the present acquires the value of history and can preserve in its variants imprints of the events introduced by believers. Starting without didactic features, it is able to acquire them, and edifying elements occasionally appear in the narration (Rubel 1985).

The universal and the particular come together in nodal subjects. They also combine the core of literary creation and the heart of myth-belief. These subjects are not as clear as the heroic ones, but they are fundamental and dominant. They should not be just one more reading, but the one that should guide all other readings of the myth. In the preceding chapters, the existence of nodal subjects has been assumed without actually identifying them as such.

We said that the curves that the opossum recommended for the river were really the turning of malinalli, the spiral road of the divine forces. This was a transfer of an apparent feat (the explicit solution of an explicit problem, an intellectual feat of the wise opossum) to another level of understanding of the myth, in which the assembled animals are engaged in the building of the universe. The river becomes the channel through which time flows, and the old drunkard is more than just an opossum. There is something underlying the adventure, and that something must be the focus of the interpretation.

Perhaps the reader does not doubt the existence of these more important, but less explicit, subjects in mythical narration; but a justification of the proposal is worthwhile. There is something behind mere events, and sometimes it reveals itself in almost mathematical form. Graulich (1983a) cleverly points out, first, that in the myth of the flood in *Historia de los mexicanos por sus pinturas*, the earth was restored with the creation of four "men," who became pillars to raise the sky, and that four of the twenty-day names form part of their names: Itzcoatl (*coatl*, the fifth day), Itzcuintli (*itzcuintli*, the tenth day), Cuauhtemoc (*cuauhtli*, the fifteenth day), and Tenexxochitl (*xochitl*, the twentieth day). This might just be an interesting coincidence, but Graulich notes that these day names are all five positions away from each other in the calendar cycle. What can we conclude from this? That the geometry of the universe is involved in the creative process.

This underlying, ambiguous something often produces episodes that resemble "synonyms." An example are two the Popoluca versions of the origin of corn. In the one recorded by Foster (1945a:192–94), the hero Homshuk begins to beat his drum at the seashore. The noise bothers Huracán, who challenges him to a contest. The contest takes place, and Huracán tries to send the sea over his hammock; but the gopher eats the roots of the tree holding the hammock, and Huracán falls into the sea, breaking a leg. In the version found by the Técnicos bilingües (1985:23–25), the Saint of Corn comes to the edge of the sea and chops down cedar trees with an ax, making a noise that disturbs Centello (Lightning). The contest begins, the saint asks the gopher to make a hole in the center of the sea, and when Centello gets ready to run across it, he falls into the trap and remains there with his foot caught in the hole. Another example of an episode where a disturbing noise causes a confrontation between the hero and a powerful opponent belongs to the Nahua, neighbors of the Popoluca. The hero, Tamakastsiin, sat down under a leafy tree and played his little guitar to pass the time. His songs angered the king, who ordered him arrested (González Cruz and Anguiano 1984). Regardless of the meaning of the passages, such similar episodes prove the existence of interesting "synonymous" elements whose meaning transcends the heroic events but is not as clearly stated as they are.

Mythic narration can be regarded as a question and its solution. The question is why something exists; the solution is the explanation of the actions that produced such a result. This is a logical theory, but mythic narration is better understood if we focus on its nature as an instrument for revealing a process. It tells us about a group of successive phases of a phenomenon, and, more precisely, of a type of phenomena. Mythic narration places events at the origin of time, but the processes of creation are processes that persist in the human world. Creation was and continues to be. It flows through the pillars of time. What question about which beginning does the processual explanation of mythic narration answer? It answers innumerable questions about innumerable existences, those of the time of creation, of the present, and of the future. Process stands out, in nodal subjects, as an abstraction from those particular heroic events that are sung in differing versions of the myths.

The nodal subject often coincides with a divergence in the particular beginning expressed in the heroic subject. Why should the hairless tail of the opossum matter? The Mixe version (Miller 1956:103) says:

> The only thing lacking was fire. But it also happened that a fox was there, and the fox said, "I am going to bring fire." And then he went to where this raven had gone to bring earth, and the fox went there to get fire. Because fire was there. Then the fox arrived and asked permission to warm himself a little. The fox sat there a while, and as he was about to say good-by, he put his tail in the fire and ran away. This is the reason, they say, that half of the tail of the animal is black. That is how this gentleman found fire, and all the others became happy.

The opossum's hairless tail and the fox's scorched tail attest to what is really important: that fire (in its widest sense) belongs to the gods. That fire did not belong, in the beginning, to the human world (in the Mixe version, the Crow goes to hell to get earth), and that the transfer of fire from its place of origin to the surface of the earth takes place through violence.

The explanation of process in mythic narration refers to infinite existences in all areas of the cosmos. However, the explanation is restricted to particular fields, true models, used to illustrate the heterogeneity of all that exists. The principal fields are those that reveal the flow of forces in their grandest manifestations. One of them is cosmic geometry and its mechanics, where the points of reference are the heavens, the layers of the underworld, the four supports of the sky, the earthly surface quartered by two axes, the path of the sun from east to west, and the paths of the winds from north to south.[3] Within this framework are told the myths of the separation of the sky and the earth, the formation of opposing forces, the course of time, and the origin of fire. A second broad field is that of the order of the astral bodies, and here the myth of the origin of the Sun and the Moon predominates. The third field concerns the alternation of the wet and the dry seasons. There are few others of comparable importance. These fields are interconnected by an interchange of processes and a combination of adventures.

They are fields that concern the immensity of the universe, but human beings see in them an answer to their most urgent needs. They try to find the secret to the progression of time in the seasons because it is a secret that is vital to them. Ramón Medina, a wise Huichol, says:

Tender corn, the new squash, are sacred. They are purified by sprinkling them with deer's blood. We hunt deer because they are sacred, so that we can eat. During the rainy season, from May till June, till July, till August, even till September, until the last days of September, we go without food, without corn from the field, without squash, with nothing. Only old corn that we have stored away to make tortillas. Some of us don't even have that. It is a dangerous time for us, much hunger, much suffering. We are hungry. (Anguiano and Furst 1987:47)

On the other hand, his work was not just complacency.
It enclosed a message. It concealed a torrent
of lightless comets.

Miguel Angel Asturias,
"Leyenda de la máscara de cristal."

On the top of plate 19 of the *Códice Borgia*, the god covers his face with black paint and adorns it with five white circles: on his forehead, chin, nose, and cheeks. He swings an ax at a broken tree. Blood streams from its trunk and limbs, and a bird of prey rises in flight, carrying away the sacrificial cord. Behind the tree is a rabbit in the jaws of a serpent. The scene rests on a strip with the day-signs associated with the west: house, eagle, deer, rain, and monkey. The painter of this scene probably was a learned priest who, in painting the pages of the sacred book with his brushes, scrutinized the history of the gods and understood the reason for the feathers on the god's arms and the white and red stripes on his legs. He understood the reason for his attire, for the wide-open eyes on the tree, for the red serpent slithering among the branches, for the masked captive with his breast cut open by the sacrificial knife, as well as why the signs of the western days are shown. The priest would also know that the scene held many other secrets unknown to him at the time he painted it, and he would know that the path to that knowledge was exegesis, an explanation of a painting and a narration of the acts of the gods.

The believer's explanations and the interpretation of the historian or ethnologist, which differ in ends but run along parallel paths, do coincide with regard to their objects of study. All are looking for the nodal subjects that provide a framework for the adventures of the gods. The faithful see sacred history as a repository for messages that explain processes repeated in the universe since the beginning of time. Their goals range from finding a mystical guide to certainty in prognosticating births. Together with the signs of destiny in the paintings and the stories, divine actions take place, never to be perceived in their totality. Little by little the believer is immersed in myth. Historians and ethnologists also try to look beyond the simple adventure. In comparing the subjects—along with other knowledge—they look for uniform laws governing the principles that people believe or have believed in the tradition studied.

Historians and ethnologists lack many of the resources the faithful possess for explaining their myths, but they usually find it easier to assemble different versions of the myth, both contemporary versions from groups with similar cultural backgrounds and those from different epochs of the same tradition. Many writers have proclaimed the usefulness of comparison in studying myth, although they follow different methods and techniques, and in so doing make the comparative method a different instrument for each school. Lévi-Strauss (1968a:197, 199) has been one of the strongest defenders of the value of comparison, and he has also criticized, as an obstacle to mythological studies, the search for an authentic, original version of a myth. He opposes the idea of and the habit of some researchers of emphasizing certain versions instead of studying all of them. This refusal to accept one privileged version prevails in Mesoamerican studies (Horcasitas 1953).

My position is this: Comparison of different versions of myth is a heuristic procedure for historians and ethnologists. In this way one can find similarities in episodes, uncover the meaning of obscure passages, identify the characters, discover complementary data, or determine whether a myth is incomplete or a mixture of myths. It helps to clear up the meaning of the myth, and this leads to the next step, that of nodal subjects. Comparison is a task for outside investigators, not for believers. Believers generally hold to the version they think is correct and which is sufficient for their needs. Historians and ethnologists should take the position of the faithful into account, since their particular version of the myth has for them a thorough explanatory potential, and it should be studied from that point of view. As outsiders there are two principal evaluative perspectives: the social value of each of the versions, and the value of the aggregate of versions in the search for meanings.

Motifs as well as episodes and plots should be compared. There are interesting equivalencies in all three cases. Within the plots, parallel trends can be seen in which the presence of episodes will be as important to the study as their absence. The result may be a long "complete" chain that, even though it never corresponds to a real version, will be useful as a basis for ordering the different episodes and classifying the offshoots of the plot.

Historians and ethnologists, like believers, have recourse to other materials besides mythic narration to arrive at the nodal subjects. Mesoamericanists are well aware that myth is not limited to a narrative framework. For a long time, we have obtained good results using pictorial images, sculptures, and rituals, among other resources, to interpret mythic texts. Equivalents, substitutions, and additional elements arise from this kind of comparison, which allow us to go beyond the divine adventure to the node of the myth. The use of broad, heterogeneous sources within a given tradition and the search for the nodal subjects of a myth give a more secure basis to our research. They avoid the short, easy path of focusing on a particular phase or on a single version of the myth. They also avoid universalist and ahistorical positions. Unfortunately one too often sees a facile interpretation, a superficial association, a hurried judgment, a comparison of rules from disparate traditions, or drastic modifications that distort the facts. Focusing a study on nodal subjects can expose these deficiencies. But we should remember that the node can also change. It is very resistant to transformation, but it is not entirely invulnerable to historical change.

In fact profound nodal changes can occur in a single myth, which cause it to maintain opposite ideas in different versions. One example, although not Mesoamerican, is a classic in the history of religion. In the biblical story of the creation of man, the two versions are quite different messages (Frazer 1981:9–25). In the version given in the first chapter of Genesis, Jehovah created terrestrial animals on the sixth day (Gen. 1:24–25), and then made man and woman (Gen. 1:26–28), creating humans at the culminating moment of his work and placing woman on the same plane as man. In the second version, Jehovah formed man of clay (Gen. 2:7). Then He said, "It is not good that man should be alone; I will make a helpmate for him" (Gen. 2:18). He created all the animals of the earth and sky (Gen. 2:19), but there was still no helpmate similar to man, and Jehovah made woman from one of man's ribs (Gen. 2:21–22). According to Frazer the meaning is radically different in the two versions. It is enough to consider the relative position of woman with respect to man in each of the versions.

What else can be found in the search for nodal subjects? Comparisons can complement information from myths that are centuries apart. The clarification is often very limited, but it can contribute to the slow task of reconstructing myths whose recording has been flawed. One example is that of the Salt Goddess. The contact-period Nahua told Sahagún (1956, 1:171) a synthetic and incomplete version of the origin of salt:

> They call the seventh month *tecuilhuitontli*. In that month they offered festivals and sacrifices to the goddess of salt whom they call Huixtocihuatl. She was the goddess of the saltmakers. They said she was the sister of the rain gods, and, because of an unfortunate incident that took place between them and her, they

pursued and banished her to salty waters. There she invented salt, as it is made today, with large jars and mounds of salty earth.

They do not specify what the offense was, but four centuries later, a Oaxacan Mixe version tells of the sister's offending her brother and of the tragedy that gave origin to salt. The girl cut the biggest and most beautiful ears of corn from the family cornfield and offered them as a gift to her brother. He did not like her selection, and in a violent response took his machete and cut off the girl's hand. She bled into the river, and her blood gave rise to the salt mine of Zacatepec (P. Carrasco 1963). Is this enough to explain the older myth? Certainly not. But it can be a useful piece in the attempt at explanation.

Something similar can be expected from comparing contemporaneous myths. There are episodes that appear in very few versions of the plot sequences, but which are links with a high potential for clarification. A fair number of the versions of the myth about the Moon and Sun twins have only a brief unfolding before the birth of the pair. But a few episodes refer to the pregnancy of the mother and the birth of the children. One of these provides suggestive details. A Mixe version (Hoogshagen 1971) tells how the king vulture [*Sarcoramphus papa*] acquired its characteristic red wattles. The version tells the story of a young orphan girl who hated men; but one day she had sex with a stranger and became pregnant. When her grandmother heard about her pregnancy, she drove the orphan from her house. The girl met a squirrel that invited her to swing on a vine. The squirrel, pretending to secure the swinging vine, gnawed it apart, and the woman fell to her death. The king vulture flew down to the lifeless body and heard the voice of a baby boy begging to be released. The bird pecked at the dead woman's hard abdomen, and, in trying to open it, broke its beak. The baby boy, after being born, repaired the beak with a piece of leather, and the leather remained as the bird's red adornment ever after. Then the baby boy and girl, who would ascend to the sky, were born from the young woman's womb. This wealth of detail can be useful in analyzing other versions that lack these episodes.

Beliefs and rituals of contemporary groups related to the Mesoamerican tradition are also useful in the comparison of myths. There are Yaqui myths that tell how Yomuli, the mother of the different tribes, heard a sound like the buzzing of bees issuing from a pole that extended from the earth to the sky. Only she could understand the meaning of the sound, and she told human beings and animals how they should live and what would happen in the future. Giddings (1959:15), referring to this myth, says that the Papago also mention a talking tree. The episode is simplified if the Yaqui post and the Papago tree are seen as the paths by which the gods communicate with the earth. The confessions and dances some contemporary groups do before very large trees they consider to be sacred (such as the *guanacaste* [*Enterolobium cyclocarpum*] of the Zapotec Tehuano or the great pine of the Mixtec) support this view (pers. comm., Guido Münch Galindo, May 12, 1988).

Some examples of important nodal subjects in the Mesoamerican tradition follow. Together they illustrate the concept of nodal subjects and are given more as suggestions for research than as final conclusions.

1. Myths about the origin of the Sun and the Moon. Among the nodal subjects pertaining to the solar and lunar myths two stand out: the hierogamy that gives rise to the astral bodies, and the sequence in which they occupy the sky. Three of the myths in which these nodal subjects are clear are: the birth of Huitzilopochtli in Coatepec; the origin of the sun and the moon in Teotihuacan; and the origin of the twins. The ancient myth of the birth of Huitzilopochtli begins with a hierogamy; in the ancient myth about the transformation of Nanahuatzin and Tecuciztecatl into the Sun and the Moon, the problem is their sequence. In the modern myth of the twins both the hierogamy and the establishing of the order of the Sun and the Moon in the sky are problems. The latter myth, perhaps the most important in the Mesoamerican tradition today, has many differing versions. An in-depth study is needed, since all the details cannot be given here. Here (see chapter 18) we only point out the kinship of the Sun with corn and with Christ and the interesting extensions that this link affords today.

Let us begin with the hierogamy, as described in the myth about Huitzilopochtli's birth in the *Historia general de las cosas de Nueva España*:

> There is a mountain called Coatepec near the town of Tula, and a woman named Coatlicue lived there, who was the mother of some Indians who called themselves Centzonhuitznahuah [and] who had a sister called Coyolxauhqui. Coatlicue did penitence every day, sweeping the Coatepec mountain, and one day it happened that, as she was sweeping, a little ball of feathers, like a cluster of tangled thread, fell. She took it and put it in her bosom, next to her stomach under her skirt, and after having swept, she wanted to remove it. She didn't find it, and it made her pregnant. When the Centzonhuitznahuah Indians saw their mother was pregnant, they became very indignant, and said, "Who made her pregnant, who insulted and debased us?" (Sahagún 1956, 1:271)

The interpretation of this myth is well known. The goddess, Mother Earth, receives the semen of the Celestial God and becomes pregnant. Her star sons and her lunar daughter become angry and rise up against her, and her solar son,

Huitzilopochtli, is born to defend her. He does battle with his brothers and sister and defeats them. There is no doubt that the celestial father impregnates Coatlicue: the feather ball is a symbol of celestial light. The disappearance of the feather cluster is similar to that of the saliva in a well-known passage from the *Popol vuh*. The skull of Hun-Hunahpú, hanging like a fruit from the branch of a tree, speaks to the young girl Ixquic. He asks her to hold out her hand, and he spits on her palm. The girl looks at her palm, but the spittle disappears, and the skull informs her that she has just become pregnant (*Popul-vuh* 1964: 58–59).

Often today the maiden in the narration of the hierogamy is a young weaver. In some cases she is the mother of the twins; in others, of corn. Instead of the ball of feathers there is a bird, a multicolored one in some versions; in others, a hummingbird. The animal is dead, unconscious, or just maliciously faking, is revived by the warmth of the maiden's body, and frisks about in her clothing. The girl becomes pregnant. The maiden, called Mary in some versions, is a weaver, as the ancient Coatlicue was a sweeper. She is inaccessible because she detests men, because her father does not want to give her away in marriage, or because she aspires to become a celestial goddess, an impossibility if she marries and has children (Hollenbach 1977). She also appears as the mother of wild animals (in Guatemala, Colby and Colby 1986:196–98). The range, the importance, and the diversity of this myth today indicate its antiquity. Another indication of its age is an early Classic Mayan ceramic figure from the island of Jaina. The weaver is seated in front of her loom, and a small bird is perched on the upper beam (Piña Chan 1968: fig. 63). According to the modern Mixe, the small bird defecates on the threads, Mary strikes him, and then, compassionately, she places him under her blouse (W. Miller 1956:86).

It is not always a bird. In a Nahua tale, the maiden who did not want to marry picks a small white flower beside a brook and conceals it under her blouse. When she arrives home, the flower has disappeared. Through some strange twist, the story goes on to say that the girl had relations with a man who made her pregnant and then abandoned her. Their son would become the Crucified One (Preuss 1982:181–83). For the Totonac it is a flea, or rather a man who makes himself a flea in order to lie down with the maiden "Whom no one could approach" (Ichon 1973:73).[1]

Because of these changes, the miracle gradually disappears. The conception without a male, exalted in the myth of Huitzilopochtli, ends up, thanks to the comparisons, in the category of mere heroic subjects. The nodal subject is the union of Sky and Earth. The small bird is only a disguise for a man—or for a god. It is a small bird that knows how to talk (Law 1957), or it is the old God of

Hunting, mocked by her when he passed by her house carrying a deer,[2] or the god ʔOyew ʔAči, who used deceit to couple with the goddess Maria Markaao (Colby and Colby 1986:196–98). Some versions do not involve a transformation. According to the Mixe (Hoogshagen 1971), "Then it happened one day, that [the maiden who hated men] had relations with a stranger. She was not aware that he was deceiving her until she felt that she was pregnant." What is important is that the protagonists be the Sky and the Earth, and this is apparent in a Trique myth. When the suitor is rejected, the girl's father counsels him to go up to the sky:

> "Climb to the sky and stay there! There is no reason for you to remain on earth," the father said to the man who came to ask for the woman. And he ascended to the sky and he was there; and the woman thereupon lay down on the ground, and he was overhead in the sky. He let fall to earth only three drops of water. The woman conceived a boy, they say. Actually, she conceived two children, they say. And afterward the man went away (Hollenbach 1977).

Other nodal topics may appear in the first part of the solar myth. A good clue is the celibacy of the maiden, her separation from young men because of misandry, of her aspiration to deification, or because of her father's command. The Cora go to the extreme of calling the maiden, because of her withdrawal from men, the Savage Virgin (González Ramos 1972:148). There is a suspicious insistence on celibacy, not only because of its ubiquitousness, but because it is justified in various ways.

We will go on to the question of the celestial order of the astral bodies. In a Chinantec version, the Sun and the Moon kill the eagle with glowing eyes and take possession of them. The Moon took the right eye that shone like gold, and the Sun took the left one. Later, during a difficult journey, the moon became thirsty. The Sun promised to tell her where there was water if she would trade eyes. His sister agreed, but the Sun added another condition: that she would not drink the water until Priest Rabbit had blessed the well. The Moon disobeyed, and her brother struck her across the mouth with Priest Rabbit. That is why the Moon has a blotched face (Weitlaner and Castro 1973:197–202). This myth can be compared with the ancient one about the origin of the Sun and Moon in Teotihuacan. Tecuciztecatl, a wealthy god, offered himself to light the world. The gods convinced Nanahuatzin, the pimply god, to also attempt the trial by fire, which would allow the victor to go to the sky. Both gods made offerings according to their resources, those of Tecuciztecatl luxurious, those of Nanahuatzin poor. After their acts of penitence, the two prepared to cast themselves into the fire. Tecuciztecatl, the first to try, drew back four times. Nanahuatzin, by contrast, had enough courage to throw himself into the fire. Tecuciztecatl, humiliated, followed him, but this gave him second place in the sky, where Nanahuatzin was preeminent. The hierarchy of merit was denoted by brilliance. The gods struck the face of Tecuciztecatl with a rabbit, and his light was dimmed. One of the versions ends by saying, "Tecuciztecatl would have been the Sun if he had thrown himself into the fire first, because he was chosen to begin, and he offered precious things in his penitence" (Sahagún 1956, 2:262). What do both myths have in common? Much more than the blow that dimmed the Moon's splendor. This is shown in the brilliant explanation given by Gossen, referring to the Chamula myth of the origin of the Sun and Moon:

> Coldness, femininity, and lowness were prior to heat, masculinity, and height in the mythological account of the coming of order. The male sun was born from the womb of the female moon and was then killed by the forces of evil and darkness (the demons and Jews). . . .
>
> The relationship is analogous to that between the male and female principles in this patrifocal society. Maleness receives ritual primacy; the female principle complements it. In the beginning the moon bore the sun as her child, but soon afterward he asserted his authority over his mother in innumerable ways. Among other tricks, the sun blinded his mother with hot water while they were taking a sweat-bath together, which explains the moon's lesser radiance and her tendency (according to Chamula belief) to follow behind the sun in the sky at a point in her circular path on the second level of the sky that is nearly always just opposite the sun's position in his path on the third level. Furthermore, the moon has the responsibility of leaving a breakfast of maize gruel for the sun each morning at the eastern horizon. In sum, her relationship to her son is like that of the female principle to the male principle in Chamula life: submission within a larger sphere of economic interdependence (Gossen 1974:37, 40).

. This is the way a nodal subject appears. There is a situation, either preexistent or arising in the myth, in which wealth, maternal status, or first possession of the golden eye establishes supremacy. There is an episode in which the hierarchical order is inverted. A new order is established in the sky. Gossen emphasizes the feminine role, but it is only one aspect of that half of the world: that which is feminine, cold, nocturnal, below, the rainy season, and it is also the procreator, that which is rich, treasured, and gives rise to future benefits. Tecuciztecatl had enough wealth to dominate the sky, "he offered precious things in his penitence," but the order was changed, because courage was placed above the value of production. The initial hierarchical state, the overturning adventure, and the final order appear in many forms. In another one a mother and son go to a fair to amuse themselves on the mechanical rides. They climb on the Ferris wheel and are attacked by the people below them. The mother is struck on the face by a stone and, thus wounded, arrives with her son in the sky. The wound keeps her face from shining as much as his (Hermitte 1970:25). The old formula reads, "Formerly, the Moon was the elder brother, but the Sun took the light and became bigger" (Portal 1986:56). And that which goes from the heroic to the nodal can continue until reaching the nomological.

2. The Sun's musicians. The last part of chapter 20 addresses the mythic areas where the processes of the universe are manifested. The first were cosmic geometry and the cosmic mechanisms, including the establishment of the four pillars, their internal flow, and the outpouring of divine forces. There are sources that indisputably refer to this foundation. The manuscript of *Anales de Cuauhtitlán* (1945:3), its initial folios damaged, starts with what remains of a beautiful myth that emphatically states that "The four enumerators of the years had their beginning there: the first, *acatl* (reed); the second, *tecpatl* (flint); the third, *calli* (house); and the fourth, *tochtli* (rabbit)." In spite of its mutilation, the references to the colors that distinguish the pillars and their directions are clear. This suggests that the myth of the Sun's musicians—dressed in four colors—has as its principal nodal subject the extraction of the forces from the four posts in order to spread them all over the world, under the guise of obtaining music:

> They also say that this same god [Tezcatlipuca] created the air, which appeared as a black figure, with a great thorn covered with blood, the sign of sacrifice. And Tezcatlipuca said to the figure, "Wind, go across the sea to the house of the Sun, who has many musicians and trumpeters there, who serve him and sing. Among them is one with three feet, and the others have such big ears they cover the whole body. Once you have arrived at the shore, you will call my servants Acapachtli, that is 'turtle,' and Acihuatl, who is 'half woman, half fish,' and Atlicipactli, who is the 'whale,' and you will tell them to make a bridge so you can cross over, and you will bring the musicians with their instruments from the house of the Sun to do me honor." And saying this, he departed and was never seen again.
>
> Then the god of the air went to the seashore and called their names; and they came hastily and made a bridge, over which he crossed. The Sun, seeing him coming, said to the musicians, "Here is the miserable one. Let no one answer, because anyone who answers will go with him."

These musicians were dressed in the four colors: white, red, yellow, and green.

Then, the god of the air having arrived, he called them, singing. One of them answered immediately, and went with him and took the music, which is what they now use in their dances in honor of their gods (*Historia de México* 1965:111–12).

This myth expresses interchanges through various pairings: the pigmented musicians respond to the call of the black figure of the air; the warm solar beings answer the son of the cold Tezcatlipoca; music responds to song. Alternation is established in the world. Mendieta (1954, 1:86; copied by Torquemada 1969: bk. 6, ch. 43, vol. 2, 78) says, "Some of them, liking the mellifluous song, answered [the Wind], whom he attracted with the drum, which they call *huehuetl*, and with the *teponaztli* [wood drum]. And that is when they began to make fiestas and dances to their gods." Festivals were established. It is the beginning of the sequence of time. The forces arrive in order: cold, heat, cold . . .

This alternation initiated the calendar at the beginning of the world. The day of the first dawn, for the modern Mixtec, was that of the arrival of music. When the Sun was born, "a great deal of music was played, and there was much warmth" (Dyk 1959:3). For the Nahua of Durango, the day of the Sun's birth began the alternate succession of music and tobacco smoke. The gods, after giving the Sun the name of Juan Tonát, said to the majordomo:

"Now make a musical bow, get a *jícara* [gourd], make five small clay vessels, make a pipe for your tobacco, make your ceremonial arrow and fast for five days. Then call us. We are going to name someone to play music."

Later they went to the festival patio, lighted a fire, and said to the majordomo:

"Now place yourself before us, take your pipe and make a speech. Put tobacco in your pipe and light it. Also take two feathers. Now call us. We will come without delay. And now you are going to blow smoke over us." (Preuss 1982:167–69)[3]

The ancient myth speaks of pigmented musicians because they are the colors of the four pillars, and because destinies are colored fires. The forces that issue from the tubes are spread as colors. When Quetzalcoatl dies, the most beautiful birds take flight: the *tlauhquechol* [roseate spoonbill, *Ajaia ajaja*], with its reds and pinks; the *xiuhtototl* [lovely cotinga, *Cotinga amabilis*], a fiery blue; the green and black *tzinitzcan* [Mexican trogon, *Trogon mexicanus*]; the green and yellow *toznene* [yellow-headed parrot, *Amazona ochrocephala*]; the multicolored *alo* [scarlet macaw, *Ara macao*]; and the *cocho* [white-fronted parrot, *Amazona albifrons*] (*Anales de Cuauhtitlán* 1945:11). Another contemporary Nahua myth tells of the reception diverse melodious birds gave to the Sun with their songs, when the god emerged from the cave that was the mouth of a serpent (Croft 1957).

3.   The quartering of the opossum. When Quetzalcoatl, the procurer of light, dies, does he perhaps become colored feathers? Three characteristics of Quetzalcoatl stand out: his nature as the discoverer and lord of polychromy, his dismemberment into four parts, and his belonging to the four directions of earth. As Lord of the Dawn, Quetzalcoatl gives colors to humankind. With the light of dawn, he reveals the surfaces that, during the night were gray. In a story dominated by the myth, the man-god Quetzalcoatl discovers polychromy in Tula:

> In his time he also discovered the great richness in emeralds, fine turquoise, gold, silver, coral, snail shells, the quetzal bird, the green *xiuhtototl*, the *tlauhquechol*, the *zacuan* [troupial, *Gymnostinops montezuma*], the *tzinizcan*, and the *ayocuan*. He also discovered chocolate of various colors as well as striped cotton. (*Anales de Cuauhtitlán* 1945:8)

These are the precious minerals of various colors, shiny coral, the plumes of beautiful birds, and polychrome plants. As a skillful craftsman, he made tableware of rich hues, "The clay vessels from which he ate and drank were painted blue, green, white, yellow, and red . . ." (*Anales de Cuauhtitlán* 1945:8). Tollan and Quetzalcoatl are characterized by their colors, as pointed out in the *Historia general de las cosas de Nueva España*:

> And they also say that [Quetzalcoatl] was very rich and that he had all that was desirable and necessary to eat and drink, and that maize (under his reign) was abundant, and squash very large, a fathom in circumference, and the ears of corn so big that they carried them embraced in their arms, and the stalks of wild amaranth were so long and wide that they climbed them as if they were trees. They sowed and picked cotton of all colors, red, flesh-colored, yellow, purple, whitish, green and blue, brown, orange, and tawny; and these cotton colors were all natural. They grew that way. They also say that in the city of Tula, they bred many kinds of birds with rich plumage of different colors, such as the *xiuhtototl*, the *quetzal*, the *zacuan* and *tlauhquechol*, and other birds that sang sweetly and softly.
> And Quetzalcoatl had all the wealth of the world, gold and silver and the

green precious stones called *chalchihuites,* and other precious things, and a
multitude of cacao trees of different colors, which they call *xochicacahuatl* . . .
(Sahagún 1956, 1:279)

In the rich houses of the Toltec ruler, the four colors are also divided into
groups that characterize the four directions. According to the *Anales de Cuauhtitlán* (1945:4):

> In [the year] 2 acatl [reed], Topiltzin Ce Acatl Quetzalcoatl built his fasting
> houses, his places for penitence, for prayer. He built four houses: his house of
> round blue feathers; his house of corals; his house of snail shells; his house of
> green feathers . . . [4]

This text is clear. However, the version in Sahagún's (1956, 3:185) work is
much more meaningful:

> There was also a temple belonging to the priest called Quetzalcoatl, much more
> polished and magnificent than their houses [those of the Toltecs]. It had four
> rooms. The one facing the east was of gold and it was called the golden room,
> because instead of plaster it had cleverly placed sheets of gold. Another room
> faced the west and was called the emerald and turquoise room, because inside
> instead of plaster it had fine precious stones of all kinds, all marvelously placed
> and joined together like a mosaic. Another faced the south, and instead of plas-
> ter there was silver, and the shells that made up the walls were so subtly placed
> that their joining was not detectable. The fourth faced the north, and was made
> of red stone and jasper and ornamented shells.
>   There was another house with featherwork instead of plaster, and it, too,
> had four rooms. One faced the east and was made of rich yellow feathers instead
> of plaster, with all kinds of fine yellow feathers. Another, facing the west, was
> called the plumage room. Instead of plaster, it had the feathers called *xiuh-
> tototl,* fine blue feathers, and it was cleverly glued in mantles and nets like a
> tapestry, for which it was called *quetzalcalli,* meaning house of rich plumage.
> Another room faced the south and was called the house of white feathers, be-
> cause inside everything was of white feathers in the form of headdresses, with
> all kinds of rich, white plumage. And the other one faced the north and was
> called the house of red feathers, because inside there were tapestries of all kinds
> of precious birds.

There are two interesting facts here. On the one hand, there is a correspondence of colors with the four directions: yellow to the east, red to the north,
green or blue to the west, and white to the south. Second, there is a sepa-

ration of materials: cold ones from the underworld, that is, the metals, the stones, and the marine animals; and the celestial ones, the feathers. There are four pairs of opposites, one for each direction. We will not dwell here on the other attributes of Quetzalcoatl, such as his dismemberment, which tie him to the four directions and their pillars. In chapter 19 we spoke of the Mexica monolith referring to his dismemberment, upon which the different parts of Quetzalcoatl's body are clearly shown.

What nodal subject is implied in the quartering of the opossum, whom we see in a luxurious, multicolored mantle in the *Códice Fejérváry Mayer* (1964–67: pls. 30–40 and 33–12)? It is that of the distribution of the combined divine forces through each one of the four cosmic trees. Let us summarize the stories. The opossum is the godfather who tore himself apart in the river (Hollenbach 1980). Was it the river Chalchimmichhuacan?[5] The opossum distributes fire over the face of the earth. "He set his tail on fire and thus distributed fire everywhere" (Boege 1988:99). But as Lord of the Dawn he is auroral and as an extractor of fire he is igneous. The opossum is, at the same time, the robber and the stolen thing. The force that he steals from the world of the gods comes out through the four posts as fragments, as heterogeneous sparks of destinies. He himself, the fragmented opossum, must remain in pieces and be distributed to the four directions. There is a Huichol version of the myth in which the nodal subject is elucidated. The Lord of Fire, upon discovering the theft, pursues the opossum, cuts him into bits, and hangs them in the four directions over the steps of the five levels that lead to the Upper World (Anguiano and Furst 1987:29). There he remains dismembered and distributed on the four posts to give himself, as fire, to the world.

In the northern part of Yucatan, far from the land of the Huichol, there is another character who was said to be a wise and civilizing ruler, the founder of a people who knew all the arts and sciences. He gave names to earthly beings and was "the dew and sustenance of the clouds." He did not practice human sacrifice. He worshipped a phallus as the symbol of universal procreation, and like the opossum and Quetzalcoatl, clothed himself with the contours of each one of the colors of the four cosmic trees. It is Itzamná or Zamná, of whom today it is said:

> When he died they cut his body into four pieces. Afterwards they buried them
> at each of the four cardinal points. They said his head remained under the
> temple of the Sun to the north, his hands to the west, his legs to the south, and
> his penis to the east. (Montoliu Villar 1988)

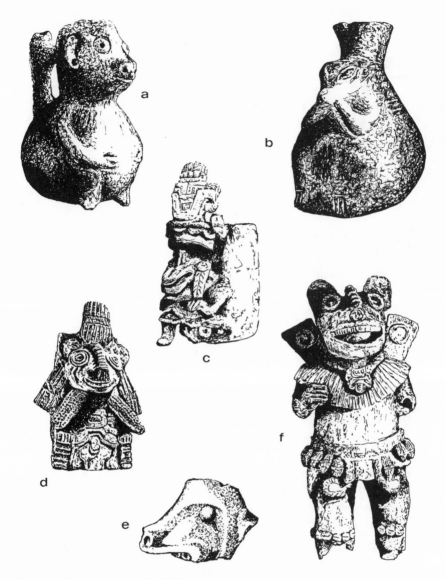

Figure 13. Opossum ceramics I
   a. Zapotec Opossum God, Miahuatlán (Monte Alban II), Frissell Zapotec Art
      Museum
   b. Zapotec vessel with opossum figure
   c. Vessel with Zapotec Opossum God
   d. Zapotec Opossum God with ears of corn around his neck and a helical nose,
      San Pedro Ixtlahuaca
   e. Small head of an opossum from Zohapilco, Basin of Mexico (Manan-
      tial Phase)
   f. Zapotec character in opossum costume. The mask has a helical nose.

Pax in terra hominibus. You don't know Latin;
what then do these words mean? *Pax in terra hominibus*
means that on this Christmas Eve you should have observed
the custom of bringing a young goat to your pastor.

Carlo Levi,
Christ Stopped at Eboli

In the winter of 1901–2, a stela of black diorite, broken in three pieces and inscribed with a message dictated by the great legislator Hammurabi 3,650 years ago, was found on the banks of the Karkeh River. The code was promulgated around 1753 B.C., and the monolith containing it was taken by the Elamite king Shutruknakhkhunte as war booty to Susa, in the twelfth century B.C. In the prologue, in the archaic hymn style that is very different from that of the legal part, is written:

> When the sublime Anum, king of the Annunaki [gods of the underworld], and
> Enlil, lord of heaven and earth, who determines the destiny of the Universe,
> chose Marduk, the first born of Enki, as the divine sovereign of all mankind,
> (when) they had exalted him among the Igigi [gods of the sky], (when) they
> had proclaimed the sublime name of Babylon (and) made it outstanding in
> all the world, (when) they had established an eternal kingdom in its midst for
> him (Marduk), the foundations of which are as firmly set as those of heaven
> and earth, then Anum and Enlil chose me, Hammurabi, a pious, god-fearing
> prince, to proclaim the law of the land, to destroy the evil and the perverse, to
> prevent the strong from oppressing the weak, so that I, like to Shamash, would
> rise above the "black heads" and would illuminate the country and insure the
> well-being of all the people. (*Código de Hammurabi* 1980:87)

Marduk, the god who was said to have divine sovereignty over humankind, had not been one of the prominent gods in the Sumerian-Acadian tradition. He had been a secondary god of the sun and vegetation. The priests altered his history in the era of Amorite splendor, in order to glorify him along with Babylon, whose patron he was, and King Hammurabi, who considered Marduk a personal god. In the literary and liturgical works of the time of this legislator, Marduk was the hero who had defeated the monsters Tiamat and Kingu, in order to form the world from the body of the first and people from the blood of the second. The glorious history of Marduk was the basis of Hammurabi's power over all people, whom, from the divine point of view, he could call "black heads." As Babylon expanded under Hammurabi, the consolidating work of law needed religious support, and the clergy were equal to the task, modifying the myth that would carry out that purpose.

The exaltation of Marduk is a good example not only of the transformation of myth for political reasons, but of its usefulness in politics. Like all social products, myth is molded by history, but it is also one of the instruments that humans—more or less consciously—use to forge their history, form their institutions, regulate their lives, and carry out their purposes. These operations of myth lead us to the topic of functions, a topic that, in turn, presents two fundamental problems: the first, what is function; and the second, to what extent is it possible and necessary, as Malinowski claimed, to explain anthropological events, among them myths, through a functional analysis of a culture? From the functionalist viewpoint, myths perform a specific, social function, and their significance can be discerned only through functional analysis.[1] Both problems are fundamental in the study of myth and difficult to solve, which makes it necessary to devote more time to them than would seem necessary at first glance.[2] In the case of both problems, the first obstacles to overcome are definitional. In elucidating the concept, it will be helpful to explain what the founders of the functionalist school considered function to be, because their opinions, and those of their critics, are valuable guides in our task. The first functionalists and their critics engaged in the most voluminous polemic about the concept of function. A brief review of their points of view will be useful, since there are many meanings of "function" and many and various functionalist schools.[3] However, this diversity, according to some anthropologists, is not sufficient reason to do away with the term.[4]

The first one to use the word *function* as a technical term for analyzing human societies was Herbert Spencer, in his essay "The Social Organism," written in 1860, so he should be considered one of the forerunners of functionalism (Mair 1970:44). Spencer says that if societies are compared with living organisms, four points of similarity exist: that they begin as small aggregates, and that little by little they increase until they reach a large size; that from possessing simple, almost nonexistent structures, they can attain great structural complexity; that their parts, at first almost mutually independent, acquire such interdependence that a separate life for any of them is impossible; and that the life and development of societies and of individual organisms continue much longer than the life and the development of any one of the elements that compose them. Starting from this analogy, Spencer correlates the functions of the biological organism and the elements of the social body, and he argues that the functional dependence on their parts by animals, plants, and societies has no counterpart in any other object. The connection is so close that there are many examples of parallel elements, processes, and functions. Spencer even says that blood is for a living organism what the consumption and circulation of merchandise is for a political body (Spencer 1972:57, 58, 65–66).

Another forerunner was Durkheim, who, after determining what is understood by function from a sociological point of view, argued that in order to understand a social phenomenon, the efficient cause that produces it and the function that it fulfills must be studied separately. Durkheim makes clear that he uses the term *function,* and not *end* or *objective,* because usually social phenomena do not exist by reason of the useful results they may produce. Function implies a correspondence between a social act and the general needs of the social organism, and it is independent of the intention of the act (Durkheim 1973:80). Durkheim (1973:78), contrary to Malinowski, also says that not all social acts have a function, because some can exist without ever relating to a vital purpose, others because they have lost their usefulness and continue to exist merely through the force of habit.

Nevertheless, functionalism—at least the name "functional school"—begins with Malinowski and his disciples (Mair 1970:46).[5] One of Malinowski's (1984:173) postulates is that culture is a hereditary tool with which human beings find the best solution to their concrete, specific problems, and that it is a system of material objects, activities, and attitudes in which each part exists as a means to an end. This idea, that all social acts have a function, is one of those that have been most strongly criticized.[6] For Malinowski (1984:98), concrete and specific problems have clear biological roots; for human physiological needs there are corresponding acts that lead to their satisfaction. Thus hunger leads to eating, which gives satisfaction, and fear leads to flight from danger, which gives relief. Basic needs have corresponding cultural consequences: for metabolism, supply; for reproduction, parenthood; for security, protection (Malinowski 1984:112); and so on, in a biologistic reduction that exaggeratedly simplifies social reality. For Malinowski (1984:194), however, functions based on individual needs should be understood as parts of the social system, the precise unit that constitutes culture, the means by which human beings satisfy their needs. He proposes that the concept of "the struggle for existence" does not imply the struggle of individual organisms nor even that of human groups, but rather that of types of cultures. Malinowski incorporates the Durkheimian idea of the general needs of the social organism, but further, when combining them into an assumed subsistence need of the cultural unit as a whole, he treats each culture as a closed system.[7]

Radcliffe-Brown emphasizes the analogy of society to a living organism, and his theory has physiological overtones. In order to understand function, he thinks of the life of the organism (social or biological) as the functioning of the structure. It is through and by the functioning of the organism that its continuity is preserved (Radcliffe-Brown 1965:179). His concept of function implies that of structure. He speaks of a "*set of relations* amongst *unit entities,* the *continuity* of the structure being maintained by a *life-process* made up of the *activities* of the constituent units" (Radcliffe-Brown 1965:180). The analogy between society and a biological organism is clear in the following:

> The term function has a very great number of different meanings in different contexts. . . . In physiology the concept of function is of fundamental impor-tance in enabling us to deal with the continuing relation of structure and process in organic life. . . . The concept of organic function is one that is used to refer to the connection between the structure of an organism and the life processes of that organism. . . .
> In reference to social systems and their theoretical understanding one way of using the concept of function is the same as its scientific use in physiology. (Radcliffe-Brown 1965:12)

For Radcliffe-Brown, function is the relationship between the structure of the social organism and the processes through which the organism itself is kept alive. He is careful, however, to avoid a possible teleological interpretation, by substituting for the Durkheimian term *need* the expression *necessary conditions of existence* (Radcliffe-Brown 1935).

One of the most influential users of the concept of function is Linton, who proposed a distinction between function and use. He uses material expressions of culture as examples to illustrate the difference, and says that an ax is used to cut, and a hoe to dig; but it would be incorrect to apply the term function to either of their uses. Another example is that medicine can be used to reduce fever; its function, however, is to restore health to the individual (Linton 1963: 390–91).

Early functionalism was strongly criticized for its synchronic view of society and for its exaggerated conservative bent. It analyzed organization and order but was not able to explain social change; it considered change as a defect in a harmonious society. Its almost metaphysical concept of a social system as closed and subject to extinction has also been criticized. How can a society be extinguished? How and when do the birth and the death of a culture take place?

> In regard to the condition of survival by a society, there is nothing comparable in this domain to the generally acknowledged "vital functions" of biology as defining attributes of living organisms. Societies do not literally die, though to be sure a society may disappear because all the human beings who constitute it die without leaving heirs or are permanently dispersed. It is therefore not easy to fix upon a criterion of social survival that can have fruitful uses and not be purely arbitrary.
>
> For example, were physical non-extinction in the manner just indicated adopted as the criterion for survival, only a relatively few societies in the history of mankind would fail to satisfy it; and, since on that criterion survival would be compatible with any form of organization characterizing the various societies that have appeared in human history, every proposed functional explanation of social survival in terms of social organization would be simply an empty tautology. (Nagel 1961:527–28)

Functionalists have been criticized for their insistence on the functionality of all elements in society. This criticism does not apply to Merton, who makes an interesting distinction. According to him, it is necessary to take into account the existence of positive functions, on one hand, and on the other, of dysfunctions or negative functions, according to their contribution to or hindrance of the adaptation of a given system. Thus the same institution can be functional and dysfunctional at the same time, but one of these characteristics predominates (Merton 1972:61). This idea leads to another question. What does Merton mean by the adaptation of the system? Kaplan and Manners (1981:110) say that adaptation is a relative term and that a theoretical standard by which adaptation can be measured is needed for empirical validity. Finally, all functionalists have been criticized, very interestingly for our purposes, on the basis that "the attribution of functions to particular institutions is always a *post hoc* question," and that "functional explanations have an air of rationality about them and seem to explain more than they do" (Kaplan and Manners 1981:108).

Much more would be needed to deal adequately with the concept of function in the functionalist school, which has such different trends and is so important today in various areas of social theory. But a more extensive coverage would take us too far afield. The ideas of the founders of functionalism and their critics will be used to propose parameters for the concept of function. The term is useful, and it can be defined in a way that makes it helpful in the study of social complexity.

In the first place, the functionalists' idea that society is a closed system, subject to extinction and protected by the action of certain functions analogous to those of living systems, must be discarded. To the contrary, human action takes place in an environment where individual, group, or class interests are different and opposed to each other. Leach (1965:277), speaking of the functions of myth, says, "Since any social system, however stable and balanced it may be, contains opposing factions, there are bound to be different myths to validate the particular rights of different groups of people." Opposite interests are debated in society, and their interplay leads to constant transformation. Under "normal" conditions, the multiple channels of confrontation are governed by rules that produce apparent harmony and equilibrium in the course of daily life. Social control is exercised by imposing rules not only on conduct but also on values and attitudes as well as patterns and institutions.

In the second place, we must remember that human conduct is governed by tastes, habitual preferences, routines, laws, rules, and all kinds of values. This is usually the basis for the characterization of different societies and of the groups and individuals in them. Institutions wear out and are overturned by social conflicts, but even the historical events that overturn institutions have some rules. Human beings, someone has said, are creatures of habit, and their history must be understood in the light of repetitive actions. The repetitions, however, will never be exactly the same, because in each social act there is a modification—breach—of custom. It is the eternal clash between the actor and the act, the interplay in which both are transformed. Function should be located in the most highly institutionalized behavior, as a result of strongly regulated actions. As an interrelation, function is repeated and retained as one more regularity; but it is not an absolute regularity. It is a process of regularities in transition that also include moments of violent rupture.

Each social act is performed in a nexus of normative directives, in which one predominates. The control of this rule is one of the fundamental characteristics of the domain of social action. Each domain is the result of something specific: in the diverse areas of nature and society in which humans act; in the objectives of particular actions humans pursue in these areas; and in their forms of action. However, the domains of social action are not closed; they are tightly and mutually interwoven. They are interconnected, because social acts are always the result of combinations, and because their effects always transcend their domain.

This interdependence of the social domains can serve as the basis for a useful concept of function, one that eliminates ahistorical and metaphysical viewpoints. If function must be used to explain process in a changing society in which opposing interests contend, the bases of functionalism become irrelevant. There are no societies stranded in time. Since change is normal in society and permeates all its aspects, it must be taken into account in any explanation of society. Social harmony and equilibrium are appearances that hide a cruder reality. The bases for functionalism (its syncronicity and avoidance of social change, the analogy it makes between society and living organisms, its concept of general interest, its idea of society as a closed and perishable system, etc.) make an adequate and useful definition of function unattainable. We will follow another path through the interrelations that arise among the domains of social action.

Two causal phases can be distinguished in a social act: that of its specific, concrete effects, almost always direct, immediate, and subject to the predominance of one of the social domains; and second, that of effects that transcend the dominant domain. The phases are very different. The second is the most interesting for us, since it leads to interdependence among social domains. The reciprocal ties between the causal process at the first level (the primary effects of the social act) and the processes and institutions of different social domains are created in this phase.

Function, therefore, can be located in the transcendence to other social domains of human actions carried out in a given social domain. The social ranges of a function vary, depending on the nature and intensity of the relationship; and the same social act can result in different effects at different institutional levels. Prescribed actions can have simultaneous opposing functions; essential or auxiliary functions; primary, secondary or unimportant functions. Some social acts are characterized by their almost infinite multifunctionality.

Social acts and the institutions in which they are produced give rise to reciprocal relations with processes and institutions in other domains. The interrelated processes can be diminished, blocked, neutralized, channeled, or strengthened in symmetrical or asymmetrical ways. The values of an incident can be inverted. Leach (1965:278) says, "If ritual is sometimes a mechanism for integration, one could as well argue that it is often a mechanism of disintegration." Institutions themselves are transformed in their relationships, and their persistence will depend to a great degree upon reciprocal action.

One aspect of functionality is important: it has a history. This would be obvious were it not for two characteristics of functions that give the illusion of universality and eternity: first, their permanence as processes of very long duration; second, functions that are similar (at least in their main elements) are produced in different epochs and in societies that have never come into contact. Their historicity is not apparent, and even less so in the field of religion. Universal postulates are often found that from the start deny the historical nature of the key elements of beliefs, practices, and of religious institutions.[8] What is religious can thus be seen as the result of a creative impulse, which fixed its nature and established its functions in all kinds of societies, forever.[9] The functions and purposes of institutions seem to retain their pristine qualities until the end of time. My position is different. Human works and their interrelations are the products of a social dynamic, and time inevitably permeates them.

In the search for the definition of myth, we will continue with the question of its functions, undoubtedly one of the central issues in the theory of myth. The answers, from the most dissimilar schools of thought, have ranged from a denial of any function whatsoever to the concept of myth as one of the sustaining pillars for some kinds of societies. P. Cohen (1969), in an intelligent attempt at global understanding, notes the simultaneity of different functions of myths, and explains how their nature as agents of communication—or simply of expression—does not depend on their original causes. The same idea of multiplicity of functions brought Kirk to set up what he calls a viable schematic and simplified typology of mythic functions. He starts from one of his most important ideas: that there is no unique kind of myth, and that unitary theories of mythical function are a waste of time. Depending on their function, he gives three types of myths: the first, the myth that entertains; the second, the repetitive myth that relates a paradigmatic origin and whose functions are to reinforce beliefs, validate processes, social, or natural states, and to harmonize customs and institutions through ritual repetition or ceremony; the third, the explicatory or speculatory myth (Kirk 1973:297–306).

Kirk's classification applies to myth as narration. Aside from the increased number of possible coincidences, it is important to distinguish groups of mythic functions when nuclei of a different nature are seen in them (see chapter 8). Remember the great differences that exist between myth-belief and myth-narration and their particular ways of articulating with different domains of the social whole. The functions of mythic belief must not be confused with mythic narration. The integration typical of myth-narration contrasts with the dispersion that characterizes myth-belief. Their particular medium of expression should also be taken into account. Myth-narration has the flexibility of oral narration, and this allows a quick change of functions when needed.[10] This is not true of myth-belief, where adaptation to other functions requires more complicated processes.

Another important aspect of the function of myth is that it has a history. Neither the functions of myth as an institution nor those of particular myths are unchangeable. To understand that, in spite of the strong narrative tradition and the persistence of many of their symbols, modern myths and ancient myths have profound differences, we only have to recall the very close and unique relationship in Mesoamerica between mythic beliefs and the power of the ruling families (Kubler 1974). The function of myth should be studied with respect to its permanence, but also in its variants, its offshoots, and its dissolution, as well as its social life. When Lucien Febvre (1971:150) sees a sense of movement as the cardinal virtue of the historian, he perceives life as no more than constructions and destructions, reunions and dislocations. The history of myth and its functions is like this. The transformations produced in a myth by the institutions and processes that affect it should be included in the interrelations of the myth.

All of this is hard to apply to the Mesoamerican religious tradition. A great hiatus of information separates ancient myth from modern indigenous myth. There are few documents and studies to elucidate the long intermediate period. The possibilities for historical understanding of the function of myth—the whole myth—in the chain of tradition are seriously limited. There is always the hope that there will be increased scientific interest in the thought of colonized Indians. Recent works, such as that of Gruzinski (1988), are encouraging. There is also the hope that more documents will be found in which the thinking of indigenous peoples during that long interregnum has been recorded. Meanwhile the principal resource is comparison across the hiatus. Of course it is a poor resource.

The diversity in the functions of myth must be analyzed from different angles. For example, functions are not the same when they are established in the broad social sphere of public life as when the relationship takes place (although repeated and constant in most cases) in the specific circumstances of an individual.[11] Neither are the profoundly structural functions the same as those involved in combinations. The functions of the same myth are not the same in every social context. When narration passes from one tradition to another, the changes can be so drastic that the loss of function leads to the loss of narrative character:

> A tale told only for amusement by one group may, as it travels, take on another
> quite different function than it had in its original habitat. Thus the type of
> Negro stories known to Euroamerica as the Uncle Remus tales, derived from
> Africa and retained in almost unchanged form, are told chiefly for recreation in
> the New World. In Africa, many of them fall into the category of myth, where
> they are called on to explain some of the most important phenomena of the
> universe. (Herskovits 1951:415)

Another interesting fact in the functionality of myth is the number of functions that operate simultaneously in and from various points. There are no functions exclusive to myth, although some seem to be emphasized in it. Functionality is extremely complex with respect to the interrelationship that links different social domains, and its action results from an intricate combinatory process.

Do quasi-eternal and quasi-universal functions exist in myth? Yes. Myth is a multifunctional crystallization of thought, and many of its functions are of supreme importance in social relationships. The organization and adventures of the gods are patterns very conducive to the consolidation of institutions. Myth and power have always marched together in every current of history, and the relationships between myth and power have run along parallel paths in the different traditions of all humanity. To the extent that social organizations resemble each other, their mythical production and the functions of their myths are similar. Myths and institutions reciprocally reinforce each other and take form in the dialectical interchange. Thus the functions of mythic narration form and accent the peculiarities of the literary genre, which produces impressive formal similarities in mythic narration throughout the world. From another perspective, similar ideological resources permit similar functions. They are the two sides of the coin. What are those almost constant functions of myth? Here are some of them:

1.   Myth—and above all, mythical narration—keeps tradition alive.[12] It is the people's great encyclopedia, in which memory is preserved and transformed. Myth safeguards ancient knowledge in the most efficient way, making it a nucleus that assimilates and incorporates new knowledge. When the Quiche learned about the existence of other peoples, the population of the East (the place of origin of all humankind) was augmented with white and black people:

> Many men were made and multiplied in the darkness. The Sun and the
> light had not been born when they multiplied. They all lived together, a great
> number existed and moved about there in the East. . . .
> At that time there were a great many black men and white men, men of
> many minds, men of many languages. It was amazing to hear them. (*Popol-vuh*
> 1964:108)

2.   Myth teaches. Mythic narration binds the generations together in its transmission of values and knowledge. But this function does not make mythic narration a vehicle for maxims or moralizing examples.[13]

3.   Myth organizes knowledge by giving it structure and classifying the cosmos, and this order reinforces knowledge. Mythic belief codifies knowledge by synthesizing structures. Margaret Redfield (1935:7), a functionalist ethnologist who studied the oral tradition of Dzitas, a Mayan town in Yucatan, speaking about myth (or "example"), said that it does not really "explain" natural phenomena through objective analysis, "But instead it locates the phenomena, new and old, in the general pattern in order to establish an order in nature." Gossen (1974:246), after recognizing the functions of teaching, conserving, and reinterpreting norms that occur in Chamula oral tradition, declares that it also serves "to order past and new experiences in credible intelligible ways." This order is general. It extends to all fields. Starting from a great cosmic plan, classification came to be for some Mesoamerican peoples the basis for political and economic unity (López Austin 1983, 1985a).

4.   It has been said that myth explains, and there have been many strong debates about this function, fed by allegations by those who deny that myth explains anything [14] and those, like Lévi-Strauss, for whom it is an epistemological resource that poses and solves contradictions not accessible by other means.

Myth explains because it is a synthesis of the explanations of society and nature that people give themselves in their daily actions. It proposes ways of being that are paradigmatic, and this makes it a guide for discovery and for action. It is generated in praxis and explains and systematizes praxis. Moreover action is based on myth, particularly when it is used to aid or subdue the supernatural. Myth is mingled with ritual, festivals, and conjuring. Thus a doctor curses asthma, attacking it as the malicious wind that at the beginning of creation threatened human efforts, "Heavily, thirteen times with my fist I struck Chacal Bul Ik [Tempestuous Wind], which went over the first man of wood, the first man of stone . . ." (El ritual de los Bacabes 1987:429).

5.   Myth binds when, through the medium of belief and narration, it reaffirms the character of the common knowledge and values of the group. Whoever knows the same thing participates in the practice of what is known and in the creation of that knowledge. They are identified in the receiving, memory, and exercise of what is held in common.

Reviling and self-reviling myths are among those that have important cohesive power. Both kinds are frequent in colonial situations. Their presence is strong in Mesoamerican tradition. [15]

6.   Finally, myth legitimizes. It shows, going back to the times that shaped things, what the reasons for customs are, [16] the foundations of institutions, the origin of social divisions, the source of territorial rights, [17] the nature and behavior of things. Above all else, myth authenticates power, to the point

of confirming the power of one people to sacrifice the people of another group. The first Quiche priests asked the god Tohil what they should get from the people in Vucamag in exchange for fire. Tohil told them the surrender of their hearts: "Will they give you their breast and armpit?" (*Popol-vuh* 1964:115).

Myth legitimizes power by making the hierarchy of the system something approved supernaturally (Service 1984:111–13). There are many different ways to do this. In Mesoamerica, as we have seen, it was believed that the supreme rulers were vessels that contained the forces of the gods, and that dynastic histories were entwined with mythic ones (Rivera Dorado 1985:133–34). In the Inca area, when the power of Cuzco assumed the civilizing banner and hurled its armies to the four directions, it was believed that Manco Cápac and Mama Ocllo had been sent to earth by Father Sun to civilize mortals (Garcilazo de la Vega 1982, 1:69–70). But the political function of myth does not automatically put it in the service of power. Positions are defended and rights supported by myth, but they are multiple and contradictory positions. Myth is flexible, malleable, rich in possibilities. In order for centralized power to take advantage of myth, it has to conquer it. It does this by taking it away from its democratic sources. Groups of specialists of the central power monopolize the tradition, make it official, at times make it esoteric. When it is convenient to their conservative interests, they freeze the tradition; or they change, interpret, or adapt it in order to send people to the destiny determined by the central authority (Balandier 1969:134–40). The struggle for the control of myth is part of the history of myth, of the history of its functions.

But there are no easy generalizations of the functions of myth. Beyond the great classifying rubrics, mythic function, historical as it is, unfolds in a range of variations, of peculiarities, of incidents and accidents. It runs along multiple courses of the future. Like the meanings, the functions can only be explained in terms of their history, in the interplay of oppression and exploitation, of defense and rebellion, of faith, doubt, or incredulity, of life, death, or wisdom. To explain them we return to one of the initial questions of the chapter. Up to what point is it possible and necessary to explain myth by means of functional analysis? If we understand function by our definition, the answer must be that the study of myth must be placed in its social context, in its interrelations, and this presupposes an investigation of its meanings and of the use that, historically, different social groups have made of those meanings. The study of myth is a study of ideology.[18] Myth exists in history. Part of a living myth is a history stretching over centuries, over millennia. Part of it is also the Amorite ambition that in Babylon took Marduk to the highest spheres of divine power, violently distorting the Sumerian-Acadian tradition. The history of myth has its years, its months, and its days.

23 HOW IT TURNS OUT THAT MYTH IS TRUE

 There was never any more inception than there is now,
Nor any more youth or age than there is now,
And will never be any more perfection than there is now,
Nor any more heaven or hell than there is now.

Walt Whitman, "Song of Myself"

In the history of myth, 1925 was an important year. A trial took place in
the United States that became famous all over the world. The lawsuit was so
unusual that it became known as the "monkey trial." The dispute concerned
the validity of evolution as opposed to biblical text. Some of the participants
came from the core of religious fundamentalism, which held to a literal interpretation of the Bible; this movement had developed during the First World
War. Some time before that, from 1910 until 1912, religious pamphlets were
published in the United States promoting exegetic orthodoxy. The title of the
pamphlets, *The Fundamentals: A Testimony to the Truth*, gave its name to the
movement and united many Baptists, Presbyterians, and members of other
churches, all defenders of literalism. The principal voice for fundamentalism
at the trial was William Jennings Bryan, a prominent politician. The accused
was John T. Scopes, a teacher in the state school system, who had explained
the evolution of species in the classrooms of Dayton, Tennessee. Scopes was
charged with violating the mandate to respect all religious beliefs when teaching. According to his accusers, his talk of evolution contradicted the Old
Testament text of creation.

Some people will say that the Dayton trial is outdated, but another contest
between evolutionists and fundamentalists in another trial took place fifty-six
years later. The circumstances were quite different. In March 1981 the state
of Arkansas passed a law that there had to be a balance in schools between
the teaching of evolution and "creation science." To what science did the law
refer? "Creation science" was a thinly veiled proposal for the teaching of Genesis. The scientific veneer was an attempt to circumvent the First Amendment.
Calling it "science" was enough to insure the speedy passage of the law, but it
did not satisfy a group of citizens who on this occasion united in the defense
of science. The trial began in December 1981, in Little Rock. The scientific
nature of "creation science" did not fare well at the trial.

Sporadic announcements in the newspapers remind us that the fight between evolutionists and fundamentalists is still going on in the United States. Candidates often include it as part of their platform in a political campaign. The American dispute is a continuation of an old story, a dispute that began in Europe at least at the time of the opposition of the church at one extreme and Voltaire at the other, to the transformationist theories of Benoît de Maillet. After this came the debates on the modificationism of Etienne Geoffrey Saint-Hilaire and the essentialism, creationism, and catastrophism of Cuvier. The high point of the European dispute was the debate in 1860 between S. Wilberforce, bishop of Oxford, and Thomas Henry Huxley. In the United States there have often been violent outbursts against the teaching of evolution in biology classes. An early example was the dismissal of young professors at the American College in Beirut. That was followed by the expulsion of Winchel from Vanderbilt University and of Woodrow from the Presbyterian Seminary in Columbia, South Carolina, because of their acceptance of the theory of evolution through natural selection (A. White 1972:116). The dispute continues today.

Underlying the debate is one of the most difficult questions believers have to face—how true is myth? Literalism is intransigent in its opposition to allegorical or mystical interpretations of the sacred texts. All religions in which sacred books officially establish basic principles have undergone this kind of conflict. Let us briefly review the key moments of the polemic on the interpretation of a sacred text in the tradition with which we are most familiar, Christianity.

The roots are deep, preceding Christianity: the exegesis of Palestinian Judaism. Origen was the first theologian and Christian interpreter to apply Platonic principles to the scriptures. His system promulgated an allegorical interpretation of the sacred text, just as Philo, a Jewish Platonist from Alexandria, had done two centuries before. The Aristotelian group in Antioch, led by Diodore of Tarsus and Theodore of Mopsuestia, who defended a literal interpretation of the Bible and its historical nature, opposed the Alexandrian school. During the medieval period, the writings of Plato and Aristotle continued to polarize positions. For centuries the opinion of Saint Augustine prevailed, with its allegorical, neo-Platonic roots that based exegesis on the harmonious whole of faith. But it declined in the thirteenth century, before the Aristotelian approach of St. Thomas Aquinas, who upheld a literal meaning. These are monuments of occidental philosophy that appear in the stream of Christian writing.

A rebellion against authority followed. The humanists of the Renaissance, freed from ecclesiastical authority, sought forgotten meanings in the sources of history. Protestantism, for its part, defended the principle of the word of Scripture alone against the preeminence that Catholics claimed for tradition and apostolic authority. Philosophers wield reason as a weapon. Kant and his contemporaries defended a rational approach, in which an interpreter must examine the Bible, applying the same rules applied to other books of antiquity. This movement was strengthened by comparative historical studies and by the archeological excavations that uncovered Egyptian and Mesopotamian buildings and texts.

The dispute continues. There are two principal, explanatory positions today: one liberal, antidogmatic, rationalist, that tries to harmonize religious faith and scientific thought; the other, absolute literalism, of which fundamentalism is a clear example. It is a complex story full of terrible incidents and polemics, in which thought has reached its highest levels; but it has also reached very low levels of stubbornness and folly. The fixed, sanctified written text resists the attacks of centuries thanks to tradition, exegesis, apostolic authority, or force.

Myth has played an important part in the long history of interpreting Christianity. Theological questions abound. How to evaluate two supernatural stories in the Bible that seem to contradict each other? How to collate sacred writings with new knowledge that seems to negate it? There are many modes of adjustment. Reconciliation has been achieved with what has been labeled "ingenious manipulations of the texts," a "dextrous juggling of phrases," the "frequent use of metaphysics that tends to dilute the facts."[1] Other more precise steps have been taken, among them the balanced distinction in the sacred texts between a precise, literal meaning, on the one hand, and a metaphoric, figurative meaning, on the other. They are problematic solutions, their inadequacies apparent before the growing pressure of scientific thought. Christianity has faced and will continue to face these problems, just as will other religious traditions whose sacred texts—among them the mythic ones—have been fixed in official books.

Why bring up this history in approaching the issue of the truth of myth in an unwritten tradition? Are the problems of written traditions the same as those of traditions whose myths are preserved by word of mouth? There are both equivalent problems, and widely differing ones; but comparison, either by parallelism or by contrast, will always be useful.

There is doubtless a great difference between the thinking of believers who belong to an oral tradition and of those who base their knowledge on a sacred book. The difference does not depend exclusively upon the instrument for preserving and transmitting the message.[2] Behind every sacred book there is a history of concentration, purification, orientation, and of making the message official. Its recording establishes the limits of orthodoxy. The difference between orthodoxy and heresy is strengthened by institutional force. Aside from the great differences arising from the sacred book and its inauguration, the distinctive features of the creeds of the great written traditions must be clearly established, because they belong to a world progressively conquered by scientific thought and political secularization. Many of these religious traditions are a part of the modern age. There is a profound difference between the functions of myth in the modern world and those it has in societies—contemporary or ancient—with an unwritten tradition. However intense the polemic between religious and scientific thought, one must acknowledge the truth in Mary Douglas's (1966:92) statement: "The European history of ecclesiastical withdrawal from secular politics and from secular intellectual problems to specialized religious spheres is the history of this whole movement from primitive to modern." In this withdrawal ties are broken, functions are weakened. The division between myth and scientific thought is a question of logical incompatibility between ways of life separated by millennia.

The separation is a fact, but it is also undeniable that truth is attributed to myth in the written traditions of the modern world. The biblical myth has been so valid for Christians that intellectual feats have been performed to sustain it. The most ingenious theological labyrinths have been constructed to conciliate it; to defend it, many have turned a blind eye on reason and on the evidence. It has been used to justify intervention, destruction, exploitation, and genocide. In its name oppression has been resisted; people have died and murdered in its name.

How can truth be found in myths from unwritten traditions? The truth assigned to myth in unwritten traditions is no great problem for some writers. Something from another time is recognized in the divine narrations. "All myths, even those that seem the most irrational, have been a matter of faith," Durkheim (1968:86) says, and he adds that the irrationality derives from the perception of an outside observer. His school accepts belief in myth as normal, as long as it is social:

> Individuals can hold on to chimeras. But collective thinking can only believe
> in what can be felt, or seen, or is tangible. Magic and religion deal with beings
> and bodies. They arise from vital needs and they survive through real passion.
> Finally they are subject to control by experience. Doubtless, the believers
> always reach affirmative answers since the wish to do so is overwhelming, but
> the proof and the confirmation exist. (Hubert and Mauss 1970:79–80)

Malinowski (1954) emphasized that myth is not just an idle tale but a primordial reality, through which life, destiny, and the present activities of humankind are determined, the knowledge of which provides the motive for ritual and for moral acts. Cassirer (1951:117–18) has said that mythic thought and that of science coincide in one area: reality. This is true, according to Cassirer, in spite of the fact that, along with the theoretical element in mythic thought, there is also an element of artistic creation. Care must be taken, however, with the meaning each author gives to the word *reality*. Turner warns that in every kind of proposition—and he is referring in particular to those of Malinowski, Jung, and Eliade—there can be different concepts of the reality alluded to in mythic narration.[3]

Other specialists have serious doubts about the possibility that believers might think that the story told in myth corresponds to an actual happening. Is it credible that actions that seem to be born in fantasy are real? Does acceptance of a myth come from completely rational thinking? For some authors the meaning of a myth is not the literal one (Urban 1979:493). For others, belief in the reality of a myth is either not rational or it corresponds to an undeveloped stage of rational thinking.[4] Both answers to the problem seem to overlook the mythic nature of the Biblical myth. For centuries millions of Christians have accepted a literal interpretation of myth as being as real as the ashes of Giordano Bruno. If the reasoning is based on the difference between written and unwritten traditions, I believe that, at least as concerns an undeveloped rationality, there is an underlying colonialism that accepts the meaning ordinary people give to myth: myth as a synonym for falsehood. The *Diccionario de la lengua española* still defines the term as "fable, allegoric fiction, especially in religious matters." This refers, of course, to someone else's beliefs.

The faithful who believe in the literal reality of myth are deemed irrational. There are also opinions that deny critical capacity to that believer when faced with a religious act. Kerényi (1972:49) says that ancient man "did not base himself on the belief that the narrations of mythology with their many contradictory variations were true," and he concludes that the believer "does not even pose the question of truth." Some students of religion ask whether the truth of myth is an ill-conceived problem or a pseudoproblem, believing that skepticism is more acute under the pressure of scientific thought, a process particularly important in the modern world (Ntumba 1985).

The advance of skepticism has been achieved in the West due to progress in scientific thinking. The loss of belief in myth is quantitatively and qualitatively very different from the former crises regarding its truth. It is profound and irreversible. But this does not justify saying that before the development of science there was no critical assessment of myth. There are other paths to understanding. Rationalism can also enter philosophy and can do so without rejecting religious thought. Look at the classical world. Rationalism denied the literal truth of myth. Since antiquity, because of rationalism it has been possible to conceive of a divinity and of an origin of the world without earthly exploits. Xenophon rejected the divine stories told by Hesiod and Homer, and in his search for a single god, a principle of existence removed from the afflictions and yearnings that beset humanity, he preferred a spherical, divine substance with no resemblance to humans (Diógenes Laercio 1946:520–21). In his Ionic vision of the world, the sins attributed to the gods were gross inventions, and his rejection of them and of the anthropomorphism of the divinity was the forerunner of a thought that 750 years later would be forcibly manifested in the Hellenistic Neoplatonism of Plotinus.

Skepticism is not a modern invention. The sharp division between modern thinking and that of the rest of humanity, past or present, is full of ideology. Historical differences in thought do exist; but their recognition and identification must be backed up by the caution and thoughtfulness of science. We should not accept a priori the existence of allegorical material that frees the faithful from a literal belief in myth, nor, on the other hand, the existence of an imperfect rationalism or a lack of analysis that forces people to accept myth without regard to truth.

Boas (1968:454–55) used good judgment when he employed native belief as a basis for determining the difference between myth and story. Indigenous peoples made distinctions among their myths, since some of them told what happened in an era when the world did not exist in its present form. The best source as to beliefs must undoubtedly be the direct statement of the believers. Are there affirmations of faith in Mesoamerican tradition? A confession of faith can appear as an express statement, regardless of whether the society under study identifies a specific literary genre as the transmitting medium of mythic truths. Today there are many statements that show that the believer sees in myth the narration of something that really happened. The Huichol speak of divine history as happenings in ancient times (Furst and Myerhoff 1972). The Mocho identify one kind of story as "the true history of the ancients" (Petrich 1985:45). The Chamula call "authentic old narrations" those that tell about actual events of the remote past, among them the transition from chaos to order (Gossen 1974:140–43, 1980). The Mazatec regard myths as gifts humanity received from God to show what the world was like formerly, and they claim to live in accordance with them, because myths tell what happens in life. They also believe that the present state of things derives from what was imposed upon them at the beginning of the world. "They are not lies, they are true!" they told an ethnologist, when they were asked to distinguish myths from merely entertaining stories (Boege 1988:90). Myths, in addition to narratives, are beliefs in the acts of personalized gods; active, willful, too often cruel, loving gods. These are concepts that should keep the investigator from thinking of myth as a mere allegory for natural phenomena. In Mesoamerica believers loved and feared their gods. They entreated them and directed their gifts to them in a personal way. Human blood was not shed in merely symbolic rituals. It was used as a real means for what was considered to be a reality—the terrible demands of the gods. Narration and mythic belief are the two faces of a single complex—the myth.

Myth is believed. Is myth believed rationally? If the lives of the gods are extravagant, cruel, terrible, immoral adventures, if there is no harmonious correlation between divine histories and the experience of daily life, how can there be a rational belief in myth? Much of the strangeness is due to the viewpoint of the outside observer. The improbability of myth is greater when it is alien. Herodotus, as a faithful historian, did not guarantee the truth of the myths he recounted: "As for the stories told by the Egyptians, let whoever finds them credible use them. Throughout the entire history it is my underlying principle that it is what people severally have said to me, and what I have heard, that I must write down" (Herodotus 1987:184–85). But from an inside viewpoint, there is little that is strange. The fact that the adventures of the gods are far removed from daily experience is not important, if the reason for their existence falls within that experience and the many spheres of daily actions. The episodes and plots of myths have permeated socially accepted reality. Myth is accepted as normal in society. It is a way of looking at the world. It is the product and the producer of that vision. Belief and knowledge are confused, as illustrated by a saying from a Guajiro shaman in the Caribbean:

> Those who know believe in that.
> Those who know nothing don't believe it.
> We who know, believe . . .
>
> (Perrin 1980:29)

Belief is one of the bases for harmonious integration in society. Myth orders and holds institutions together, giving them meaning. It is link, code, and tradition. And it is not accepted blindly. The prevailing concept of the world offers the means of verification, so the reality of myth can be empirical. It suffices for dreams and ecstatic visions to be considered special forms of perception for believers to cross the barriers that separate them from mythical terrain. This transition in Mesoamerican tradition has been mentioned in previous chapters. It has been a tradition in which myth has been proven by experience.

Paradoxically the logic found in social congruency does not lead to a single unique truth. Individuals—in oral traditions—verify the rationality of myth in their varied activities. They do not find a single, uniform message, but rather that of a rich confluence of social diversity; and this includes, in the intricate forge of reason, dissimilar elements that allow individuals to believe—and to act accordingly—within a wide range of choice. The ways of accepting, interpreting, and acting according to myth have functional effects that make it the apparent focus of conflicts with deep and diverse roots. Freedom as well as reason play a role in belief, because unconventional belief, particularly if it is shared, threatens those who have based power, wealth, or prestige on orthodoxy. The interplay of reason and freedom takes many forms. Many societies lack the rule of law and of fixed dogma. W. Robertson Smith (1965:17–18), in his study of the religion of the Semites, makes ritual so important that belief in myth becomes secondary. Perhaps Smith's evaluation is exaggerated, but his observation is interesting of how practitioners appear to be free in their acceptance of belief but have no freedom in the practice of ritual. Lowie speaks of a similar liberty in describing the religion of the Crow Indians, a people with regard to whom he carried out important investigations. Their religion has no dogma, and it does not impose doctrine. It does not prescribe general norms of behavior. The religion of the Crow, Lowie (1976:45, 47) says, "resembles subjectivism carried to its highest degree." But there are social practices that compel the Crow to have a constant and individual relationship with the gods, to the point of sacrificing a fingertip in the search for ecstasy. There is no dogma for the acceptance of one or another version of a myth, but the pressure for social prestige leaves no other outlet than a personal surrender to the gods.

The interplay of reason and freedom brings about profound differences in Mesoamerican religious tradition. In ancient Mesoamerican religion, above all in the direct and indirect forms imposed by the great centers of power, myth supported political and economic structures, and the order it established was an affair of state. In today's indigenous religions, however, the functioning of myth in political and economic matters is circumscribed. Outside is the powerful structure of the national state, for whom Indians and their myths are alien. In Mesoamerican religion the power of authority constrained believers, channeling them toward orthodoxy. Ever since the Conquest, however, indigenous peoples have been attacked for retaining their religions—the ones created through Mesoamerican religions and Christianity. Their secular, heroic struggle is one in which belief is not only one of the ways of confronting colonialism, but a means of defending reason. This is a reason congruent with their social ties, their organization of labor, with their techniques of production, their rules of kinship, and their tradition. Evangelization, which for centuries had imposed itself with force—a force with many faces—is not only foreign to indigenous peoples, but irrational in their context. Villa Rojas (1978:437–38) tells us that the principal scribe of the Maya of X-Cacal told his people the origin of human beings, speaking to them about Adam, Eve, and the apple in Paradise. "This story," says Villa Rojas, "is not taken very seriously, and when the scribe Yum 'Pol' told it to me, it caused some laughter among the natives present." With rationality indigenous peoples defend themselves against foreign forms of domination. They do so against the current.

> The following is what happened in our town a long time ago, and you should
> believe it now. Only grandmother Ca'aj was living in those times. She walked
> in the sky with a pine torch, when that happened in past times, and you should
> believe it now. (Hollenbach 1977)

Myth gives order to reality for believers. Reality and myth legitimize each other reciprocally in a common conception. This does not require that the laws that regulate the mythic world be identical to those of humankind. To quote Ovid, "The gods have their laws." But testimonies of the creation remain in the world, among them the prints children made in the rocks that were still soft after the flood (Lumholtz 1970, 1:293).

It is also acceptable for myth to have tinges of fantasy. Although for most believers myth is not allegorical, a certain latitude is allowed for rhetorical turns, emotional episodes, and the humorous passages demanded by the public as part of a creative event. This is the only way the listeners, even though mute, become coauthors, submerged in the beauty of the narration and in "discovering" the unfolding of the episode. They advance sagaciously to "verify the truth" of the tale in the concurrence of two endings that are adjusted to the rules of the narrative. The metaphor will not be completely spontaneous, because there are antecedents in the tradition. The beauty of the story validates it, even more so when aesthetic emotion is added to the message that kindles anger, vents passion, or consoles in response to collective or individual conflicts. Such must be the message of a myth, if it is to be a medium for ideological expression. Instead of giving a detailed and specialized account such as that of scientific laws, myth tries to enunciate universal truths that include social and natural laws, types of organization, and classifications. It is a rich language, inclusive, beautiful, and ambiguous, unlike the formal one proposed by Leibnitz. Myth is not only the enunciator of truth but a form of understanding reality; as such, it must provide the means to assimilate new knowledge in a domination that attempts to be total. The Chol explain the origin of the monkey with a white belly, but they know that there are very different species far from their land: "This way man was transformed into a white-bellied monkey. That is what is said. This is the monkey. Perhaps faraway men were transformed into chimpanzees" (Anderson 1957).

Mythic relation, on the other hand, does not contradict moral reality—neither reality nor what ought to be. Turner (1975) says that "Myths . . . should not be considered models for secular behavior. Neither should they be understood as admonishing narrations, as negative models that should not be imitated." Only occasionally will narrators assume the role of moral apologist. They have another mission.

Written traditions have had to face the serious problem of contradiction in their texts. Discordant texts have been excluded from the canon, but even so internal disagreement causes numerous conflicts in interpretation. In traditions that lack a sacred book, the contradictions are less obvious and do not take on the significance that fixed versions cause. However, one is nevertheless faced with the problem of rationality. What is the attitude of the faithful where faced with two opposing texts? How do they reconcile two different versions? There are no sources in Mesoamerican tradition that answer those questions. We can conjecture that contradictions become evident when there is disagreement among myths where the same characters appear, when the origin of the same character differs in different versions, or when the believer finds two or more versions of a myth. But there are perplexing answers. The parentage of the gods can often be contradictory. Loo (1987:24–25) found that in a Tlapanec myth, Fire was the father of the gods of rain, while in another he was the son-in-law of the God of Rain. When he asked how this was possible, the answer was that it was the same Fire, but in different stories. Apparently the inconsistency caused no conflict in the believer. Another interesting example, although from a different tradition, is the one given by Lipkind, an ethnographer who worked in South America: "A Carajá who accompanied me from town to town listened to some of these variations [of mythic stories] and accepted all of them with almost the same assurance. It isn't that he didn't notice the contradictions. He simply wasn't interested" (cited by Lévy-Strauss 1968b:22).

How can we explain the fact that contradictions do not cause a rational conflict in the believer? It is a difficult question to answer, and that must be recognized from the beginning. In the first place, neither the conflict nor any resulting skepticism should be laid aside, but these can be mitigated for different reasons. I suggest three; there may be more.

First, myth may be more flexible and less rigorous than scientific or philosophical thought, since its logical elaboration is much less refined. We cannot expect the same rigorous logic that we are used to in science and philosophy. Recall what Linton (1963:351) says about logical consistency: "The ordinary individual can hold a series of conflicting beliefs, providing the rules for conduct related to those beliefs are not in direct conflict." Remember also that the example used by Linton was of someone from a written tradition, a North American Protestant at the beginning of the nineteenth century. Second, perhaps our determination of a lack of agreement is false. Take as an example the existence of two or more myths that give the origin of the same being. If a myth gives the birth of the Sun in one era, another of the birth of the Sun as a celestial body, and another as the daily birth of the Sun, it is possible that the believer refers to three different processes where we see only one. Third, we can confuse the unique truth of a mythic reality with the plural reality of the tales, some of which will be more appropriate, more exact, or more beautiful than others, but not exclusive. Consider this point from the perspective of an audience: the life of the Venetian adventurer Jacob Casanova was one reality; his memoires another; the many different cinematographic works derived from his autobiography are still others. How many of these are more valuable for their artistic qualities than for their faithfulness to the book? We accept movies as references to real life and real books, and, at the same time, we are aware of the liberties taken by directors in creating those works.

The gods are forces, and mythical tales are references to processes. This is basic to understanding the reality referred to by the narration. Strictly speaking, to what does myth refer? To a form of being or to the form that was? No doubt daily life insists more on understanding the reality than upon knowing its origin. Nevertheless for the believer the reality of myth is certainly a reality of what has been called the first time. This must be stressed, because some people maintain that the reality of myth corresponds only to the present earthly existence of things. This posture resembles Aristotle's (1968: 265) view of myths as leftovers from the arts and philosophy with which people discovered the essences.

> However, our ancestors in the remotest ages have handed down to their posterity traditions in mythical form that these celestial bodies are gods and that

the divine encompasses the whole of nature. And the other traditions have been added in mythical form for the persuasion of the multitude and for their legal and social uses; for they say that these gods are in the form of men or are like some of the other animals, and they give further details such as those mentioned. But if we take only the first essential point, separately from the rest, that the first primary beings are traditionally held to be gods, we may acknowledge that this has been divinely said and that, though arts and philosophies may have been often explored and perfected, but lost, these myths and others have been preserved to the present day like ancient relics. It is only in this way that we can explain and accept the opinions of our ancestors and forerunners.

Along this line of reasoning, Dardel (1954) says that what is mythic is current, because what is original does not mean previous so much as permanent: "nothing ever begins, nothing is ever new on this horizon where the foundation of established order represents, at the same time its *founding*."

What Dardel says is very suggestive. But the divine process of creation is not that residual belief of which Aristotle was speaking, and, at least in the Mesoamerican tradition, the founding process is not identical with the present process.

In conclusion, how can the truth of myth in oral traditions be understood?

1.   In the study of myth as a social fact we cannot give priority to those references to truth or interpretations of sacred narratives made by some believers, which give second place to the references or interpretations of other believers. To an investigator the truth of the layperson is as valid as that of the theologian. Further, the investigator must see the plurality of beliefs as a highly complex object of study, in which the parts (the different concepts) are found to concur. To affirm, as some theoretical positions in the study of religions have done, that myth is born, or is followed, or ought to be interpreted either symbolically or literally,[5] is to ignore the gamut of manifestations of the beliefs of all religious traditions, including the written ones.

2.   References to reality are found in different kinds of mythic subjects, but the belief in one of them does not necessarily exclude the others. The heroic is not necessarily canceled upon reaching a higher level of abstraction. Mythic subjects do not have precise limits, and the discovery of deeper meanings does not oblige the believer to discard the more superficial ones. Myth does not answer to a single law, but to many laws operating simultaneously. Myth can have multiple, simultaneous interpretations, mysteriously equivalent through the power of equality before the law, which is for the believer one more proof of the sanctity of the tale.

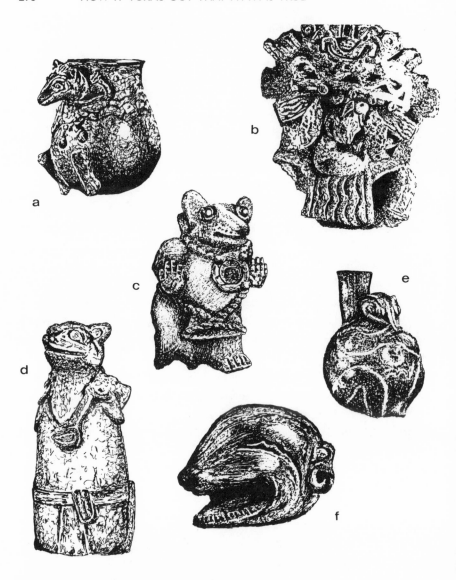

Figure 14. Opossum ceramics II

    a. Zapotec vessel with the body of an opossum, Mitla

    b. Zapotec urn of the Opossum God, Tlalixtac. The god has fragments of a helix over the nose.

    c. Zapotec opossum figure

    d. Zapotec vessel with the body of an opossum, Miahuatlán

    e. Opossum-shaped vessel, Central Highlands of Mexico

    f. Opossum head, Basin of Mexico

3.   In Mesoamerican religious tradition reference is continually made to the time of creation. It is conceived as a different reality from the present, and there is no doubt about this. Moreover there are modern explanations for the form in which the truth has been transmitted. The Chamula say:

> The ancestors saw it [what took place in myths]. And when they were old,
> they told their children how they had come to be. That is why everyone knows
> how the very first people came to be: When at last the ancestors died, they had
> already told their children how things were long ago. (Gossen 1974:140)

The time of creation is, then, a reality for the believer. And it is not strictly a reality of the past, but one with its own dimension, that of the permanent present of the other time-space, the stability of the time that only flows and works when the forces of the gods present themselves in the human world.

4.   The permanent present is the one that orders reality in the human world. However, human time cannot be identified, as Dardel proposes, with the time of origin. The human time is a mixture of the divine forces and their struggle. Each instant of human time is a combination of divine forces that circulate in cycles of different dimensions. Through myth, humans seek to know the profound reality of daily life; but they must do it through a knowledge of the origin, because the archetypes exist in the origin, and the present is the combination of a group of archetypes that can be found in the different calendric cycles.

24 MYTH IN THE TIME OF HISTORY

On windy days the wind is seen carrying the leaves
of trees, where, as you can see, there are no trees.
There were trees here sometime, because if not,
where would the leaves come from?

Juan Rulfo, *Pedro Páramo*

One of the purposes of this essay is to demonstrate the ties between modern
tales about the opossum and the old Mesoamerican beliefs. Implicit in this
supposition of ties is a fundamental problem. Does myth not change along
with the society that created it? How can the inclusion of myth in the totality
of society be defended simultaneously with the persistence of myth throughout
the history of societies that have undergone profound changes?

In order to answer this question it is necessary to examine phenomena of
long duration. According to Braudel (1974:64), there are different chronological realities by which one can measure the course of history. The topics of
traditional history, dealing with the individual and the event, correspond to a
short time frame. There is another time frame that conforms to economic and
social history. It responds to cyclic oscillations, to a slowly rhythmic history
of the movements of populations, of states, of wars, which studies the past
by means of a "recital of confluences [*conjonctures*]," dividing it into sections
of ten, twenty, or fifty years. Finally, the historian of the *Annales* points to
a much longer history, of centenary scope, that deals with a very long duration [*longue durée*]. According to Braudel (1974:74), to recognize this historical
time frame is to become cognizant of a time restrained, "at times almost to
the limit of immobility." Historical time does not flow in a single stream, but
in simultaneous layers "like the leaves of a book," so it is necessary to look
at the passage of history in a vertical way, as "parallel histories with different
velocities" (Braudel 1985).

Althusser (Althusser and Balibar 1976:110), along with other historians,
has insisted upon the different rhythms of history:

Concerning the specific structure of the Marxist whole, we can conclude at first
sight that it is not possible to think about the process of development of the
different levels of the whole in the same historical time. . . . Each level must

be assigned to its own, relatively autonomous, time, and therefore relatively independent of the times of the other levels. We should and we can say that there is a time and a history for each mode of production, with specific cadences in the development of the productive forces; a time and history proper to the relations of production, with specific cadences; a history belonging to the political superstructure . . . ; a time and a history appropriate to philosophy . . . ; a time and a history appropriate to artistic productions . . . ; a time and a history appropriate to scientific formations, etc. Each one of these histories has its own rhythms, and can be understood only on the condition that one has determined the specificity of its historical time and its cadences (continuous development, revolutions, ruptures, etc.).

Althusser (Althusser and Balibar 1976:110–11) is careful to point out the relatively autonomous character of historical times, in order to show clearly that this distinction does not make them independent of the social whole:

> The fact that each one of these times and each one of these histories is relatively independent does not mean that completely independent domains exist. The specificity of each one of these times, of each one of these histories, or expressed in another way, their autonomy and relative independence, are based upon a certain kind of dependence with respect to the whole . . .
> Therefore, it is not enough to say, as modern historians do, that there are different period classifications according to different times, that each time has its own rhythms, some slow, some long. It is also necessary to think about the basis of these differences in rhythm and cadence, in the kind of articulation, displacement, and the twisting that interlaces these different times.

How can we take into account the different concepts expressed by these writers? I believe that the long duration should be understood in relation to the difference in transformations occurring in the different domains of social action, as much because of the specific relationships between them as because of the internal differences in transformation in each one of them. It is not that human action may be slower in some social domains than in others. Social life is produced simultaneously in several domains, and these are clearly intermingled. But the same group of actions changes some social domains more rapidly than others, and within each one transforms some parts faster than others. In studying historical durations, the problems are differences in the rhythms of transformation, differences in the kinds of transformation, and the relationships that such differences produce.

It is therefore necessary to return to the topic of the domains of social action.

In chapter 22 it was stated that each social domain is the result of specific activities of humans in different areas of nature and society. Social domains arise and are altered historically. They emerge (with their rules) from the particular ends that people pursue with their actions, from the specific spheres where action is taken, from the different forms of action, and from the patterns that are created with this specialization. Human actions are not produced in limited arrays. There are generic as well as specific domains. There are confluences of different rules in each human act, and there are intersections where it is difficult to determine which is the predominant normative order.

Normative rules are one of the fundamental characteristics of each social domain, but so are the rhythms of transformation.[1] Each domain reacts with a particular tempo, and it also reacts in a different manner, according to the particular combinations occurring in different societies. The response to general changes in society is fast and widely known in some domains; in others, responses are so slow that they seem stationary. The latter may give the false impression that they are immune to social change or that they are independent. By understanding the difference in cadences and the relative independence of each historical time frame, one can place in their proper historical dimension the customs, beliefs, the oldest institutions, the artistic and literary productions of the people—among them mythic narration—and the stereotypes that have led to a persistent belief in "national characters."

Augé (1987:195) says that anthropologists became aware that the societies they were studying had a history when historians discovered the structural dimension of the long duration. No doubt he exaggerates, but there is some truth in the statement. The long duration exposes the transitory nature of the soundest structures. It shows them as processes; it makes their stability relative. And it is true that in the temporalization of everything human, the limits of traditional history (those of the individual and the event) dwindle, to be replaced by history in a broader sense. Thus the insularities of history are broken. Processes and rhythms are linked. When old boundaries are broken, the theoretical and methodological principles of the social sciences overlap. Augé is correct in saying that now the dimension of the long duration can be held in common by ethnologists and historians. We can understand why many of the historians of the *Annales* defended an idea that has long been cherished by Marxism: the development of a total historical science that studies human activity in its various aspects. Perhaps someday the unjustifiable boundaries of traditional history, ethnology, sociology, economics, archeology, and all of the other social sciences will be eliminated, and a social science will be produced in which each discipline can retain its own methods and techniques, and in which

all participate in a general methodology. Reason demands it; the bureaucra-
tization of academe, academic feuds, and the territoriality of specialization
prevent it.

Rhythms are different. What happens, then, to functions, which are the
basis for interdependence in the social domains? If the different rhythms of
different historical times maintain a correspondence among themselves and as
a whole, it is logical to suppose that in functions are to be found permanent
processes of displacement and adjustment. We live in constant conflict because
of anachronism; and we also live in a struggle to coordinate time frames.

How is the flow of functions achieved through such an adjustment? The
different elements in a domain are not homogeneous. There are nuclei and
solid structures, so resistant to change they can be altered only by revolutionary means. Others are yielding or easily substituted by equivalents, or they
have an unprepossessing appearance that conceals their importance as means of
adaptation. The possibility of adaptation depends on the relationship between
the resistant and the flexible elements. Take for example the social domain of
religion. Find an extremely solid element in that domain—a text set down in a
sacred scripture. Imagine a historical situation that involves the adaptation of
this solid element to a particular (and disputable) historical act: a sacred written text must be applied, through a typological interpretation, to a particular
evangelizing action. The interpretation is the flexible element. Any deviation
from a rigorous reading is impeded, because the text and even its vernacular
version are written down. The adaptation of the text must be sought elsewhere,
such as in the specific interpretation of the text.

The range of accommodations is so great that contradictory interpretations
can coexist. Historical examples abound. One is the parable of the impolite
guests in the Gospel of St. Luke (14:19–24), applied typologically to the
forms—violent or peaceful—of conversion of the Indians in the sixteenth century. The same parable was used to justify three different positions: that of
fray Bartolomé de las Casas, that of Juan Ginés de Sepúlveda, and that of
fray Gerónimo de Mendieta. The first one, using this parable, was opposed to
outside coercion toward nonbelievers through war, opting for their conversion
through divine inspiration. The other two, in differing degrees, defended the
use of secular weapons by the church, with legitimate authorization for the
use of force in converting the heathens (Phelan 1972:17–23). These were two
opposing interpretations, used politically, at one historical moment. The intense debate, however, did not affect the firm value of the sacred texts, which
belonged to a very long duration.

Many elements of religions persist across time, beyond the reach of revolutionary processes, still afloat in the succession of socioeconomic formations, irreducible in their strict association with one or another mode of production. They are always capable of transformation, but often their changes are imperceptible, because they take place in subterranean processes of accommodation in their functions, through their more flexible parts.

The attention of historians should be directed to two complementary sources of persistence. One is the aggregate of religious functions; the other, the relationship between the persistent, solid elements and the flexible, substitutable, weak ones. The functions may be those established in domains that are similar in their persistence. For example, a great deal of the persistence of myths is due to the fact that in spite of profound changes in society, the forms of family organization, the techniques of exploitation or possession of land, commercial practices, etc., persist. Or new functions equally favorable to their survival may exist. The changeable, substitutable, weaker parts are often the elements that reduce the conflicts due to anachronism. They safeguard the solidity of institutions, traditions, and structures, prolonging the life of the most solid nuclei indefinitely.[2] Consequently the study of religion, like that of all historical processes characterized by elements of long duration, must include its patterns of interdependence with other domains (including those characterized by elements of short duration) and the mechanisms of adaptation that operate in different epochs.

Myth, a historical fact with elements of very long duration, must be studied as an aggregate of solid nuclei, but also as one with flexible parts; as a complex of variables; as an expression of beauty; as a source of a varied gamut of possible meanings; and as a source and receiver of functions. Its time dimension moves through processes that belong to the long duration but also to the time of confluences and even to ephemeral life. The course of time slowly changes myths and ages them. It can also rejuvenate them. And it can even overcome the resistance of the changeable elements in order to penetrate and destroy even the most resistant nucleus.

What makes a myth an event of very long duration? Throughout this essay we have been answering that question without formally posing it. Myth is transformed by attacks proceeding from other social domains when serious currents of historical opposition occur in society. The solid nuclei of myth are protected by the cushioning of its ductile parts to such a degree that its life is prolonged through centuries and even millennia. When the pressure becomes too strong, or when the cushion wears thin, the nuclei are transformed or they disappear, leaving as traces of the myth disparate elements that can remain, more or less connected in some cases, to adhere to other beliefs and narratives, mythic or not. Myth remains at risk because of its ideological potential. Its ductile parts protect it. The greater the wealth of variations, of possibilities (even contrary ones) of interpretation, of vagueness in its message, the stronger the myth. Harmony and beauty may also be reasons for its stability.

Let us return to the functions of myth and its ideological nature. Daily action has a strong and multiple bond with myth. Myth is constantly reinforced from the outside by the most varied human actions. It does not matter that these actions may often oppose each other in the context of social oppositions; myth must be known and used in all the opposing foxholes. It is present in the very center of oppositions and transformations. It is impossible to attribute the persistence of myth to a natural human tendency to believe and act within traditional and institutional boundaries. This conception leads to assuming a neutral and "normal" existence of myth, endangered by the manifestations of its functions. To the contrary, the persistence of myth should always be explained in the context of its functions. Myth is born and remains in its usual niche: in its historical dimension, formed by conflicts and social disputes. Myth, affected by social disputes, is one of the products of the contest. Its particular nature derives from contention. Its persistence and its disappearance depend on the contest. It is never alien to it.

Frequent mythic anachronism should not bother us; it is a phenomenon that can give a false idea of the duration of myth through time.[3] Anachronism is a problem of the slippage of functions between spheres of different cadences. Being out of phase is not a problem between the past and the present. It is a problem of presents with different rhythms that need to be coordinated. An out-of-phase myth can be corrected at either of two extremes of the process: by means of giving it new functions (modifying or abandoning the disturbing function) or by remythification, that is, by using the solid elements of the myth, which can be changed to adapt to new requirements.[4]

The life of myth in the long duration includes everything from its vague beginning to the loss of stability leading to its disappearance as a system. The study of myth must be given its full time dimension. Sánchez Vásquez (1970) says:

> The process of development for a given, relatively stable system must be conceived not only as an accumulation of changes compatible with the quantitative limit of the system, which in a synchronic analysis can be disregarded, but as internal, structural changes, that is, qualitative changes incompatible with the nature of the system. These changes, precisely because of their incompatibility with the essence of the system, lead to a loss of its stability and finally to its disappearance.

Because of this the historical study of myth should not be limited to the dimension of the long duration.[5] The historical fact that we call myth, doubtless belonging to the very long duration, has an impact in its own social domain as well as on the domain of the functions (with the rhythms of different time frames). In its semiotic aspect, it unfolds through such a gamut of meanings that it goes from an "explanation of the event" to the significance of the eternal and the universal.

Mesoamerican religious tradition is found in the historical dimension of long duration. This tradition can be divided roughly into two important stages: the first one belongs to Mesoamerican religion; the second, to colonial indigenous religions (as they have been formed from the beginning of the colony to our time; see chapter 2). Some points need more elucidation.

1.   Mesoamerican religious tradition includes forms of thought and worship that differ widely among themselves but that belong in the same historical current.

2.   The term used to designate this tradition implies, not without arbitrariness, that its nature is Mesoamerican, a term that excludes the stages before sedentary agricultural life began. The religious tradition must have undergone great, although gradual, changes with the initiation of agriculture and the beginning of sedentariness. However, it must be noted that important preagricultural practices persisted, such as the use of hallucinogens for mystical communication; this is a very ancient custom, as is indicated by the archeological remains of psychedelic plants found in a human context dating from long before agriculture.

3.   The development of Mesoamerican religion, from the beginning of sedentary life until the time of the Conquest, proceeded in different stages, although their boundaries are not well defined. The stages are not discussed here, because the most violent transformation of this religious tradition is being emphasized, its forced integration with the Christian tradition.

4.   Beginning from this confluence, and owing as much to the colonial characteristics of indigenous life as to the tremendous conflict in the combining of the two widely differing traditions, indigenous religions became very different from either of their two original sources.

5.   However, there is such a wealth of tradition that it is possible to recognize—even in their most profound amalgamations—the lines of the two founding traditions. There is a difference in the strength of the continuity. In myth there are more Mesoamerican features than Christian ones. The same cannot be said of other components of colonial religions, such as the social organization tied to religious worship.

6.   Whatever may be the results of investigations that, like this one, include the tradition from Mesoamerican antiquity to the present day, they will
open paths to thinking about the ancient religion. For instance the vigorous
persistence of myth makes possible an examination of its forms of preservation, transformation, rupture, and disappearance under the most adverse
conditions, those that came after the Conquest. It is unlikely that myth faced
such adverse conditions in pre-Hispanic times. One must thus assume that
mythic continuity and transformations in pre-Columbian Mesoamerica must
have taken place under milder circumstances.

7.   It must be remembered that indigenous religions and myths are not
just the remains of past traditions and beliefs. They are living, contemporary
processes.

We have two very different mythical contexts. The Mesoamerican past is
the golden age of myth, when its open presence was manifested as belief and
as an accepted, even obligatory, expression. Since the Spanish Conquest, myth
has had a colonized life. In the past it flowed through a stream of homogeneous waters. During colonial times (and even today) the inclusion of alien
episodes, characters, and meanings was forced on it. In the past beliefs and
narrations were congruent within a wide context of thought. They coexisted
with their institutions, with works of art, with their legends, with their archetypes. Today indigenous people know that they are part of a world whose
nearby, powerful manifestations are alien to them. Their colonized beliefs and
practices—"customs"—are embarrassing to practice, or at least need to be
justified to strangers.

The integration of beliefs is weakened in contemporary indigenous religions; and not necessarily due to the impact of modern innovations. For instance, techniques that are truly efficient can make calling on the supernatural
unnecessary. Irrigation canals replace prayers. Wittfogel and Goldfrank (1943)
report that in the U.S. Southwest, the Havasupai, western neighbors of the
Hopi, say realistically that they have irrigation, while the Hopi, who do not,
have to resort to prayers to ask for rain. At times techniques for managing
the supernatural are replaced by others that are similar but less burdensome
and often less complex. This has happened in the Valley of Toluca. A very
simple magical technique has replaced another that required membership in a
secret society with complicated rituals. In Xalatlaco a Nahuatl ballad singer,
son and brother of *ahuizotes,*[6] explained to me that in some neighboring towns
nobody belongs to the "hail-controlling societies" nor understands their mysteries, since in order to control rain and hail, it is enough to launch fireworks
into the clouds. Complicated and burdensome complexes produce a break in

cultural bonds when they disappear. In spite of reformulations, the general transformation of indigenous societies is rapidly producing a loss of cultural congruency and cohesion.

As we have seen, myths crisscross multiple functions with organizing systems and particularly with taxonomies. It is foreseeable that the rapid growth of innovations, the difficulty of assimilation, and the introduction of outside organizing principles will weaken the bases of the indigenous world view. The systems split apart. The old character of our tales, the opossum, fond of pulque and brother to the Moon, is to this day addicted to his vice. In present-day myth he is a likable drunk. He steals pulque and gets drunk, but the story is no longer told everywhere. His tastes have changed along with those of the people, and he now also gets inebriated on *aguardiente* (raw cane alcohol). In the ancient codices, his drunkenness linked him to coldness and the Moon. Today he imbibes a drink classified by many as hot. The opossum retained his drunkenness, but inverted the values of hot/cold, and with the inversion an important part of the message is lost. The myth is damaged.

We have seen that myth is weakened when its functions go out of adjustment—such as getting out of phase—and that it is recomposed through new functions or remythification; but violent changes or rapid innovations can overwhelm the processes of refunctionalization or remythification, which are slower. The need for new kinds of functions are apparent today. They are revealed psychologically: tastes change, new requirements are created. The public asks its narrators for different topics, a different vocabulary, other plots. It applauds more enthusiastically when the narratives are connected with areas in rapid transition. Because of changing tastes, myth is transformed or disappears along many paths.

The myth of the birth of the Sun in Coatepec was one of the strongest myths during the Late Postclassic period and during the first years of the colony. Its functions worked well in the domain of the expansionist policy of the Mexica. Despite the opinion of many writers, it is improbable that the Mexica created the myth, although no doubt they changed it considerably because of its political potential for their conquests. It was the most important myth on the central high plateau at the time of the arrival of the Europeans. Today it has been replaced by the myth of the siblings who were changed into the Sun and the Moon,[7] with which it has elements in common. Why and how did the Coatepec myth die? The myth of the Sun and Moon siblings is not new. The fact that it is the most important modern indigenous myth in Mexico and Central America testifies to its antiquity, as does the fact that it exists on the continent far beyond the limits of Mesoamerica. It is likely that both myths came from a common source, and that the myth of the siblings was very much alive at the folk level at the time of the Spanish Conquest. But the Coatepec myth was part of a didactic complex with a higher ideological content and therefore, it was the one spread by the ruling class. Because of that, the myth of the siblings could have passed unnoticed by the friars who recorded the Coatepec myth. With the fall of the Postclassic states, the official myth, now without functions, yielded to the folk version.

Another form of rupture is through the separation of belief and mythic narration. There is a Totonac tale from Tajín that I have already mentioned (Williams García and García Ramos 1980:31). The Child was cold and the Virgin asked the opossum to get some fire. The opossum went to the house of the surly old woman, put his tail through the cracks in the posts and, rolling over the ground due to the blow he received from the fire's owner, he returned to the Virgin. The grateful Virgin rewarded the opossum with seven lives and with a pouch in which to keep its young. What is left of the myth of the theft of fire? The hero, the hateful old woman, the theft, the punishment, the hazardous return, the gift, and the mythic nature of the tale, since there is an inchoative action from which the life force of the marsupial and its pouch derive, have survived. But it is no longer the same myth. The central theme, the theft of fire in order to distribute it over the face of the earth, has been eliminated. The cosmogenic myth becomes a pious story that cannot be guaranteed a prolonged future.

Another case, different from that of the loss of a mythic lineage, is the breakdown of the narration through its inability to fully penetrate the realm of belief. The myth, with the same characters, acquires a completely different meaning from the original one. In this case the origin is Christian, the other half of the tradition, and the story is the birth of Christ. According to the Zinacantec (Vogt 1976:144), the Virgin Mary, nearing her time of delivery, looked for the shelter needed for the birth of her son, but she was a wanton woman, "who slept with many men, but had no husband," and the town refused to give her asylum. Only her brother Joseph allowed her to enter his stable.

A study of the processes of transformation and the loss of myth from the time of the Conquest on will be one of the solid bases for researching Mesoamerican religion. Can Mesoamerican religion be understood better by a comparison with contemporary indigenous religions? A simple yes or no is not enough. It is indispensable to study the Mesoamerican religious tradition in order to assess the possibilities. How resistant and rich are the persistent lineages? These questions make their relativity apparent; there is no abstract quantification possible. As an illustration, Eva Hunt (1977:247) tells of the reaction of two of her colleagues when she gave them the draft of her book on Zinacantec religion to read. One of them admired the persistence of Zinacantec symbolic structure. The other, to the contrary, stressed the changes that historical events had brought about on that structure.

In studying systems of thought, one can never expect to find a total congruence, an unchanged tradition, nor all the necessary information. One looks for clues. Finding the keys to indigenous thought allows the necessary hypotheses to be formulated. In some cases, starting with a hypothesis and through corresponding verifications, ethnologists have been able to make accurate reconstructions of the systems. It is the sequence of a logic revealed piecemeal. What is to be done when the pieces have lost their unity, breaking into partly disconnected subsystems? One can fall back on a comparison of the many contemporaneous indigenous religions in a search for the coherence of a Mesoamerican vision of the cosmos that was the single source of these subsystems. In fact, my work on the interpretation of beliefs and mythical narrations has occasionally included a good deal of reconstruction. Depending on the indigenous communities providing the information, I approach, to a greater or lesser degree, very complete, general pictures that allow inferences about the composition of the ancient systems. However, a global congruence based on ancient and contemporary sources corresponds to a vision of the cosmos that ceased to exist centuries ago.

25 HISTORY IN THE TIME OF MYTH

And suddenly myth was made again in the world.
Prodigious events began to happen to us city dwellers,
filling the day with an explosion of clamorous
and eager trivia.

João Guimarães Rosa,
Primeiras Estórias

Up to now—and the chapters of final adjustments and precision are still lacking—we have not reached a completely solid definition of myth. In chapter 3
myth was provisionally defined as a text that tells about the irruption of the
other time into human time, producing an origin, the beginning and foundation of something. New factors have come into play, and the promised definition seems to have gotten lost in the allegations. It is now time to discuss the
different kinds of irruption from one time to another. What kind of incursion
are we dealing with? It may be the one that established the nature of beings at
the time of creation. Or it may be that in which ritual suspends present time
and combines it with the other-time. It can also be the violence of a miracle
that momentarily destroys both divine and human paths. Others think of it as
a constant divine and terrestrial flux of the present, rather than as an irruption.
There are also those who speak, indiscriminately, about all the influences of
supernatural beings on natural ones.[1]

This is a particularly difficult matter to pin down in the Mesoamerican
tradition, since from remote eras to the present, people and gods have conversed, done business, played, and fought with great familiarity. There are
many channels of communication between people and gods, and they seem as
natural and commonplace as sleep, with its nebulous vision of an alien world;
as frequent and unexpected as finding oneself the involuntary witness to the
bath of the *chaneques*—hairy dwarfs, either very dark or very fair; or there
are those that are sought, such as the use of hallucinogenic plants, bloodlet-
ting, or petitions to the gods to manifest themselves to the faithful. Channels
are left to the ingenuity and tenacity of the supplicant. About the middle of
the fourteenth century, a Tarasca beggar named Carocomaco was sleeping in
the mountains in search of a revelation. Unsuccessful, he carried wood to the
temples in the town of Zacapu, and slept next to the wooden beam by which

the gods descended. Still without the anticipated dream, he slept on the stairs of one of the temples, climbing up farther every night, until the gods finally took notice of him and made him lord of Querécuaro (*Relación de las ceremonias* 1977:112–14).

Times fuse in ritual. The gods come down and physically fight with humans to test their valor and dexterity, and they enter their bodies in order to act from within them. The gods speak through their images and take people beyond the threshold of the world to entrust their messages to them. The miracle is always at hand, and historical traditions are filled with new births from the earth, pacts between humans and gods, of migrations along designated paths, portentous dawns and creations. Historical characters intensely experience their encounter with the sacred. In ancient Michoacan, the nobles Hiripan and Tangáxoan justify Tarasca domination by the appearance of the gods Curicaueri and Xarátanga. In the Mixtec area, 8 Deer–Tiger Claw is the warrior who goes to the underworld in search of the power needed to unite all the townships. On the Yucatan peninsula, Hunac Ceel Cauich brings the authority to rule over Chichén Itzá from the depths of the sacred well (*cenote*). On the central plateau of Mexico, Nezahualcoyotl discovers the secrets of water and fire (warfare), when the gods transport him to the top of Poyauhtecatl. An exception stands out. Tariacuri, the strong, tenacious Tarascan ruler, sought contact with the gods, but history reveals that he was unable to bring about the miracle.

It is not possible to evaluate every irruption of the divine by the same measure. There are also routine aspects of the sacred. This happened when contact with the gods became a daily affair. Rulers constantly consulted patron gods through relics or through dreams,[2] transforming the sacred into the normal, devoid of wonder. Or the wonder might cease to be unusual, even though tinged with spectacular hues. For example, the appearance of the goddess Acpaxapo was spectacular, but habitual. The goddess would emerge from the waters of Acpaxapocan as a great serpent with the face, locks, and soft scent of a woman (*Anales de Cuauhtitlán* 1945:25). The tale said that she did this in order to give advice to the Xaltocameca, her protégés, when they were fighting the Chichimec. But, at least during the war, her words of advice came too often. It is therefore necessary, in the vast complex of the marvelous, to distinguish the peculiarities of what is routine, what is outstanding, and what is really fundamental and transforming.

The ancient Nahua called a miracle *tlamahuizolli*.[3] The word connotes admiration, wonder, perhaps even fear (*mahui* means fear). Is the gods' denial of their own laws a miracle? No. It is a new impulse. It is a new creation, beginning with the marvel of a new manifestation. The new manifestation is the

Table 2. Classification of Miracles by the Nature of their Effects

1. Ritual	Revitalize the course of history without transformation
2. Private	Modify the life of individuals
3. Epic	Modify the course of historical events
4. Founding	Establish rights, institutions, or towns
5. Originators of peoples	Renew an origin myth whose effects have remained suspended during the creation of humans
6. Creating	Create new classes during historic time
7. Prophetic	Leave their effects in suspense
a. Inaugural	Prophesy important historical events
b. Messianic	Promise total transformation of human life
c. Eschatological	Announce the end of the world

presence of a purified, predominating force. The daily, normal course is more complex and balanced. There is a combination of forces in daily occurrences. The forces arrive together and mingle. A miracle, on the contrary, is the purification and intensifying of a single one of the divine forces. The emerging god imposes itself at the instant of the miracle. It is the moment of its distinctiveness, of its full and powerful expression over the other gods, similar to its expression at one instant of the time of creation. This makes the miracle a return to origins.

A miracle is an expression similar to that at the time of creation, but it takes place in historical time. And not every miracle in historical time is an origin. One of the first kinds of miracle is ritual; there are calendarized miracles. According to the ancient Maya of Izamal, the solar macaw made fire descend upon the altar precisely at noon. The Nahua of the central plateau believed that Mother Earth trembled under the feet of the faithful at the culminating moment of the ritual in her honor. Those were the days when nobody doubted the miraculous presence of the gods. Their manifestations only revitalized the already existing directions of history. They energized the calendrical cycles.

A second kind of miracle is of a private nature. There are minor miracles through which a god reveals itself to an individual and changes that person's life. A typical case is the appearance of a phantomlike being called Night Ax. The ancient Nahua believed that Tezcatlipoca appeared as a decapitated person and challenged to a duel penitent priests walking on the mountain. If the priest proved to be brave in the fight, he received a prize (Sahagún 1956, 2:18–20).

Epic miracles are the third kind. They are the miracles that produce a change in the course of historical events. Among them are military miracles. An example is the divine intervention in the Tarascan case that produced illness among the enemy troops at a critical point in the battle (*Relación de las ceremonias* 1977:83). The miracle of the god Camaxtle in Tepeticpac, when arrows were charged with marvelous potential after being bathed in milk from a maiden's breast, is also of epic importance (Muñoz Camargo 1981: fols. 111r–114v). This is also true of the miracle of Nezahualcoyotl being transported as a child to a sacred cliff to find his destiny as a conqueror (*Anales de Cuauhtitlán* 1945:40), and those of the battles told by the Cakchikel, in which the warriors traveled by earth and sky to defeat their enemies (*Memorial de Sololá* 1950: 62). These are the epic miracles.

Founding miracles make up the fourth kind. They create institutions, towns, and rights that will extend through time. They establish what is permanent, marking a milestone between two segments of the history of peoples who were poor before and glorious afterwards. Beautiful visions marked the place and moment of the foundation of Mexico-Tenochtitlan:

> The first thing they found at that spring was a very beautiful white juniper with a fountain flowing from its roots. Then they saw that the willows all around the spring, all were white, without a single green leaf; and all the reeds and stalks in that place were white; and, as they stood looking at this intently, white, showy frogs began to come out of the water. The water coming out from between two cliffs was so clear and lovely it was delightful . . .
>
> [The next day] they returned to find the fountain they had seen the day before, and they saw that the water, which before had come out beautiful and white, now flowed crimson, almost the color of blood, and was divided into two forks; and in the second stream the water was so thick and blue it was frightening. And even though they knew that this was mysterious, they continued to press on, looking for the omen of the prickly pear and the eagle, and searching for it, they at last came upon the place of the prickly pear, on top of which was the eagle. It had its wings spread toward the sun's rays gathering its warmth, and in its claws it held a splendid bird with precious, resplendent feathers. When they saw it, they humbled themselves, paying homage as to something divine, and when the eagle saw them, it humbled itself to them, bowing to them in every direction. (*Códice Ramírez* 1944:36–38)

There is a fifth kind of miracle, that of the particular origin of groups of people. Groups are "born." They have no past history. Hence there are old peoples and new peoples. The appearance of people in the world is not simultaneous. Groups of people succeed each other throughout history. Each new group arrives late in a world already populated. It is as if the myth of the creation of people were prolonged to a final installment, the particular episode of each human group, that takes place after a suspended life in a long uterine dream. The matrix is subterranean, the enclosure is the mountain. When Tollan was abandoned, many Chichimec groups had not yet emerged into the light. Within the mountain of Colhuatepec-Chicomoztoc, each group inside one of the seven caves, were the Zacatec, the Tzauctec, the Acolchichimec, the Totomihuaque, the Cuauhtinchantlaca, the Texcaltec, and the Malpantlaca. They remained there until Quetzaltehueyac and Icxicohuatl, the Toltec rulers of Cholula, brought them out miraculously to incorporate them into the now ancient history of the Toltecs (*Historia tolteca-chichimeca* 1976:fol. 16r and 160–69).

Miracles of creation are the sixth type. Unlike the inchoation of the original time, these miracles occur during the course of history. Creation miracles give rise in a definite shape to species that did not exist before in the world. An example is the creation of certain small lake animals, the *izcahuiltin,* that arrived on earth at a very late date. They will be discussed later in this chapter.

Another type is the prophesying miracle or that of a future accomplishment. Under this type is the subtype of the prediction of a historical event. Examples are the prophecies that announced to the *tlatoani* Moquihuix of Tlatelolco that his people were going to be defeated by the Tenochca-Mexica. The first portent was the dialogue of an old man and a dog; the second, the dance of some birds in a kettle of boiling water; the third, the complaints of a mask (Durán 1984, 2:257). Another subtype is the messianic, an example being the Totonac belief in the arrival of the Son of the Sun (Mendieta 1954, 3:200). A third subtype is the scatological miracle. An example is the belief of the ancient Nahua in the end of humanity: a day when the gods would descend in monstrous forms from the sky to put an end to humankind and their history.

What do the different kinds of miracles mean? Their functions vary. In the first place, it is necessary to give roots to and to legitimize everything that makes up daily life. It is possible to provide roots and legitimization through the renovation rituals of baptism and inauguration. Some rituals are minor miracles. Through them individuality is defined and becomes vigorously incorporated into the species.

Secondly, many epic myths respond to political needs. It is encouraging to believe that there are powerful gods who protect a people, and it is convenient for rulers to claim that there are miracles that place them very close to the supernatural.

In the third place, cohesion is obtained by the exactness of devotion and destiny, and this precision can be secured by means of founding myths. The adherence of the faithful is also obtained through a covenant miracle. An example is the pilgrimage of the Mexica to the place promised by their patron god. One of the important episodes is the sudden breaking of a tree, which surprised the migrants. The god Mexi spoke to his protégés, explicitly, making them unique. They would no longer be Aztec, as they had been in the Aztlan they were leaving behind. Now they would be called Mexica in his honor, and they would be distinguished from other groups by particular marks on their faces and ears. At that time the Mexica also received the instruments of their profession: the bow, the arrow, and a net they would use for fishing when they established their definitive home (Serna 1953:208). Another myth rounded out their destiny. It is told by one of the groups into which they were divided. Their god gave them two bundles. One contained a precious stone, the other two wooden sticks. Both bands wanted the precious stone, and they quarreled over its possession. The Tlatelolca won. The Tenochca took the wood; since it enabled them to light a fire, it became the most valuable gift and put its owners in the forefront of history (Torquemada 1969, bk. 2, ch. 2, 1:79–80).

There are important functions of acquisition of territorial rights and the establishment of governmental organizations, achieved through miracles of origin and foundation of towns. At times it was necessary to sanctify important places in order to give a group the right to certain benefits and the obligation to take care of them. These miracles are not found only in the Mesoamerican past. Among the Tzotzil today, each water well has a myth of an ancestral god, which links the place to the group benefited (Vogt 1976:17, 99).

Some of the miracles respond to the need to understand the world. Creation myths refer to the unchangeable nature of beings and processes; but there are processes and social beings that are modified in history and that are born and die within it. Their variable nature cannot be attributed to the great origin myths. This is especially important in the case of the role each group plays in history. Some groups emerge and dominate; others are dispersed by epidemics or by war. Some have a destiny that justifies their conquests; sovereignty ends for others. Glory comes and glory goes. The instability of history is incompatible with the fixity of the great origin. The transitory fate of peoples cannot be explained by an immutable essence. However, the explanation cannot remain outside the bounds of divine acts. Its transitory nature must be seen as a manifestation of what is sacred, but placed within history. The characteristics of groups that appear successively on the political scene are acquired with the miracle of their emergence from the depths of the mountains. Their fleeting destinies were acquired through covenants with their gods, when dawn came upon them and they founded their towns.

This leads to the conclusion that miracles of the fourth and fifth kinds share characteristics with myths of the great origin. As restorations, they are myths of the first moment that take place in historical circumstances. Moreover, they are inchoative, although their inchoation contains a different element: they are inchoative like the myths of origin, but of that which is transitory, that which has historical limits of birth and death. They are the inchoations of human societies and their activity on the surface of the earth. They can be called historical myths.

It is necessary to mention here one of the most difficult problems of Mesoamerican historiography: how to approach texts in which it is hard to distinguish history from historical myths. "This kind of text," Castellón (1987) tells us, "poses a serious problem as to the kind of analysis to be applied to written sources, that is, when these traditions are to be considered as history and when as myth." And he concludes that the historical and mythic elements are so intermingled that a method that encompasses them both must be applied. Many of us historians have dealt with the topic of the fusion of history and historical myth, sometimes in general works, sometimes in studying the history of characters with a complex nature, such as Quetzalcoatl, the priest of Tollan.[4] But our studies have not sufficed to avoid such negative judgments as that of Paz (1984:83) about Mesoamerican historiography:

> From the Mexican high plateau to the tropical lands of Central America, for more than two thousand years, various cultures and empires succeeded one another and none of them had historical consciousness. Mesoamerica did not have history but myths and, above all, rites. The fall of Tula, the Toltec penetration into Yucatan, the disappearance of the great theocracies, and the wars and wanderings of the Aztecs were events transformed into rites and lived as rites.

It is still necessary to delve deeper in order to understand the concepts that created this kind of historiography, in which not only are the passages on origins, migrations, and the founding of towns charged with a supernatural feeling, but in which the lives of some characters seem to follow the same pattern, or in which the biographies contain episodes that vividly recall the myth (see Chadwick 1971, Graulich 1987a). Not understanding this historiographic complexity makes some writers think that the source of the confusion is the divinization of the leaders. This is an unjustified position, especially since it is more than a hundred years since Brinton (1970) attacked these theories. But many keys to the understanding of Mesoamerican historiography are still missing.

Interesting questions arise when myth and history are united. Myth is often used as a pattern for history. If believers think they find in myth an ancient prophetic message for their present reality, they will apply the myth to interpret it. In the adjustment the myth may take on traces of historical elements (perhaps the name of a character or a place), acquiring a place in time it did not have before. Historians, confused, may then believe that the myth was a "corruption" of a historical event; or, on the contrary, that the mythic element was passed off as history. Leeuw (1964:401) says, "Myth, in the form of a legend, returns to enter into the time frame. Legend is a myth that has been left hanging in some place or on some historical event."

The transitions of history to myth and of myth to history are varied. There are cases of historical relations that can be purified by eliminating the strange, supernatural elements; but there are others that are meaningless if purged. If the miraculous and mythic passages in the life of the priest Quetzalcoatl of Tula are suppressed, the resulting figure will be naked. On the other hand, there are narrations where it is difficult to determine if an element is mythic in the history or historical in the myth. Let us examine an example in the light of ancient and modern texts. Today the Chinantec say that the Mother of Cotton used to live in a lake on the Ozumacin plains, where magicians took care of her. When these magicians died, the people of Ojitlan took possession of the Mother of Cotton (Krotzer 1970). So much for the mythic tale of the modern Chinantec. In the history of the Mexica, we find the memory of a conflict in which the opposing parties used both conventional and magical weapons. It was the war the Mexica waged against the Tlahuica of Cuauhnahuac. The purpose of the Mexica was to conquer the hot lands, a source of cotton. The Mexica tlatoani, Huitzilhuitl, fought both on the field of battle and that of love. By magical means he impregnated Miahuaxochitl, daughter of the ruler of Cuauhnahuac, and his armies triumphed over the Tlahuica (Alvarado Tezozómoc 1949:90–95).[5]

Let us compare today's myth with the ancient history. There is a disturbing detail in the Chinantec myth and Mexica history. It is hard to believe that the name of the Chinantec town and that of the magician governor of Cuauhnahuac would be coincidentally the same: one Ozumacin, the other Ozomatzin or Ozomatzintecuhtli.[6] In Mesoamerican history placenames often derive from rulers who were men-gods. The rulers would take the names of the gods they thought were lodged in their hearts. How can the resemblance be explained?

There is a possible explanation. It is improbable but possible that in ancient times there was a myth in which a character named Ozomatzin was the guardian of the Goddess of Cotton, who was finally abducted. From the ancient myth would come the signs that accompanied the story of the war against Cuauhnahuac, as well as the Chinantec myth. There is another, less likely, explanation: that the Chinantec of Ozumacin had attributed to themselves a deed taken from an old historical relation or mythic tale.

Traces of the insertion of history into myth are found in a well-known tale from the history of the central high plateau. According to the sources, it comes from Tetzcoco, in the Acolhua-Chichimec region. Judging by the name of the hero (Acolli), by his physical characteristics (he has only the upper part of his body), and by the name of the place where the tale is told (Acolman), the myth is Acolhua. Acolli means "shoulder" (the shoulder and arm to the elbow), Acolhua means "owner of the elbow," and Acolman is the toponym derived from Acolli. According to the myth, the first ancestor of the Acolhua was a man whose body extended only from the armpits upward. He begot his children with his mouth (Mendieta 1954, 1:87–88). A second version shows that another group took possession of the myth. There are important variations in it: the place is not Acolman, but Tezcalco; the man is not Acolli, but Tzontecomatl Tlohtli ("Head" and "Hawk"); his wife, not named in the first version, is called Tzompachtli ("Spanish-Moss [*Tillandsia usnoides*] Hair"); and the habits of Tzontecomatl are those of a hunter. In the second version the original couple and their descendants occupy Tetzcoco, where they were the first rulers. One of Tzontecomatl's sons brought the first image of the god Tezcatlipoca to Tetzcoco. This version says that the descendants of Tzontecomatl were afterwards called Otomi (*Historia de México* 1965:91–93). The changes indicate that the Chichimec of Tetzcoco took over the myth of Acolli, Acolman, and the Acolhuas.[7] The original pair were given the names of one of the first Chichimec rulers and his wife: Tlohtzin (a reverential form of Tlohtli) and Pachxochtzin ("Spanish-Moss Flower"). Why is Pachxochtzin identified with Tzompachtli? Because on the Tlotzin Map (the codex that bears the name of the husband), this woman appears several times with a glyph that shows a feminine head with tousled hair, resembling Spanish moss. Although in history her name is "Spanish-Moss Flower," the pictographic name must be read "Spanish-Moss Hair."[8] The Chichimec took possession of the myth and, afterwards, inserted historical elements, making their ruler Tlohtzin the mythic ancestor.

Not only do historical events invade myth. Through the power of magic, human beings go to the world of the gods and act there. We will refer to a case of this inverse passage later in the chapter, the expedition sent by Motecuhzoma Ilhuicamina to the Chicomoztoc Culhuacan of origin, where the messengers conversed with Coatlicue, the mother of their patron god (Durán 1984, 2:215–24).

Another kind of mythic contamination is one that makes historical events function like the myths at the time of creation. The following is a beautiful example, even if it is not Mesoamerican. Masaki Kobayashi tells us the old story of "Hoichi the Earless" in his 1965 film *Fantastic Stories*.[9] On the screen the historic combat of Dan-no-ura appears, in which the imperial house of the Minamoto completely defeated the House of Taira in 1185. The dead were transformed into crabs (*Dorippe japonica*), which bore on their backs the faces of fierce warriors. A similar tale arose in Mesoamerica. The Mexica fought the Chichimec of Poyauhtlan in a bloody battle on the banks of Lake Tetzcoco. All the banks of the lake, from Coatlinchan to Chimalhuacan, were crossed by rivulets of blood. The blood was transformed into *izcahuitin,* small, red, edible animals caught by fishermen (Muñoz Camargo 1981: fol. 99r).

In studying Mesoamerican history we must be alert to the fusion of myth and history in all these passages surrounded by miracles. None more so than the origin of peoples, tales that begin with the creation of human groups and proceed later to the pilgrimages of diverse people. Chicomoztoc, Culhuacan, Tamoanchan, Amequemecan, Wukub Pec, Wucub Siwan, Sewan Tulan, and Tollan are some of the places whose simple mention should put us on alert. Tollan, or Tulan, is the common sojourning place of all the groups and the site of the great dispersion. There each group took its gods when there was a common language. After leaving Tulan, people changed their languages and became permanently differentiated (*Popol vuh* 1964:110–111, *Título de Totoni-capán* 1983:174).[10] The texts that tell of the division of languages in Tulan are Guatemalan. Today, many miles away from the highlands of Guatemala, a group from Baja California expresses the same ideas:

> When [the first people] were in the house of God, the people filled the house.
> That is how they were, and then they departed. [Inside] everyone under-
> stood each other. After going out the door, languages changed completely
> (Mixco 1977).

Many different sources say that after leaving Tulan, the groups crossed the sea, a lake, or a body of water. They mention different ways of crossing: boats, hollow tree trunks, rafts, "rows of stepping stones, sand dunes," the backs of turtles, the stroke of a rod that dried the sea; those are the ways the Mexica, the Tarasca, the Tlaxcalteca, the Quiche, and many other groups came from the original Tulan of the Seven Caves, passing through Pánuco, Panoayan, Panco, Pantlan, or Panutla (Durán 1984, 2:16; Sahagún 1956, 3:208; *Popol vuh* 1964:118; Muñoz Camargo 1981: fol. 72v–73r, 88v; *El Título de Totonicapán* 1983:175, 177; *Lienzo de Jucutácato* n.d.). Pánuco means "the place of crossing." It is still said in the Huaxteca of Hidalgo that the Huastec came through Pánuco (Stiles, Maya, and Castillo 1985). The Paipai account from Baja California, mentioned above, tells that after the different peoples went out from the house of God and changed languages, "no one could cross [the sea]. The shaman stopped to chant. He was singing, and when [he had finished his chant] the sea receded. A canal appeared. Then everyone jumped, crossed, came" (Mixco 1977). There is no reason to allege, as some have done, that these passages derive from the biblical account of the Red Sea.[11] The variety of the tales, their dispersion throughout Mesoamerican territory and beyond, and the consistent sequence of the events are sufficient to demonstrate that there was a common myth of creation that included the event of crossing and that the myth existed prior to the arrival of Christianity.

A comprehensive study of ancient Mesoamerican migrations needs to be carried out to discover, through a comparison of passages, a group of patterns. The study should include current indigenous tales about the journeys of origin of the people. In the tales will be found (together with the ecumenical reunion in Tulan, the acquisition of patron gods, the division of languages, and passage over the stretch of sea) other pieces of the great puzzle. Here are some of the repeated passages: the placing of the migrating groups in the seven caves and their later abandonment; the stupor or drunkenness that people felt at the moment of leaving; the great fast of the travelers, when they did not find food on their journey; abandoning the place of separation of the waters of the sea;[12] the insistence that messengers or groups travel separately from east to west or from west to east; the mention of their origin as the place where the sun rises, or sets (Durán 1984, 2:17; *Título de Totonicapán* 1983:181);[13] the compact with the patron god and the people's receiving their future profession; the gift of fire; the founding miracles; the "meriting" of lands for cultivation; or perhaps even the passages in which the Chichimec are taught to eat the food suitable to sedentary people (*Historia Tolteca-chichimeca* 1976:169; *Relación de las ceremonias* 1977:27–28; *Mapa Tlotzin* 1886:310–12).[14]

Among all the mythohistorical passages, that of the dawning stands out. In spite of its importance and its repeated mention, there is no clear description. At an early point in the history of a people, the sun comes forth for them "for the first time." It is their "first dawn" on earth, recalling the other one that occurred in mythical Tulan. It is simultaneously a fundamental occurrence for the people and a ritual to be celebrated at a precise moment. An obscure comment in the *Anales de Cuauhtitlán* indicates that it took place on a date of fifty-two years or a multiple of this period after the birth of the group.[15] Dawn is the watershed. Previous history is shadowy, because the miraculous dawn is the true beginning of the group. The ritual alludes to another similar moment that happened in Tulan, and the pleas in the ceremony are directed to it (*Título de Totonicapán* 1983:184). The dark period remains behind, profoundly filled with supernatural happenings, overprotected by the first fathers (*Popol-vuh* 1964:122–23). After the miraculous dawn, there is light, legitimate owner- ship of land (*Libro de Chilam Balam de Chumayel* 1973:12), the establishment of rulers (*Memorial de Sololá* 1950:82–83), and a treaty of union among all the peoples who received the prodigious light at the same moment. It is possible that the coincidence of ritual time in various groups indicates that they left the mother mountain together.

After abandoning the mythic place of origin, dawn is awaited. In the section of the *Lienzo de Jucutácato* that depicts a human group being born into the light of day, emerging from the Precious Bowl (Chalchiuhapazco), the text says: "Now they want the dawn to come. Tezcatlipoca saw fit to say to them, 'Let us go to the new land.' Immediately they mounted the sea turtles." The drawing shows them crossing the sea mounted on turtles.

The concept of dawn is important because it supports the idea that much of Mesoamerican history is patterned by myth (López Austin 1973:159–60); by myth and by the cycles of time, as shown by the texts that tell of the calendrical determination of the historical and political events of the Postclassic period of the Maya. The most important events of their history have meaningful dates.[16] The course of events was often directed by archetypal patterns, because they had to keep in time with the rhythm that marked the arrival of the forces from the other time. Undoubtedly, as in every historiographic process, there were additions and adjustments for political reasons. But that is far from saying that historical myth was totally the product of subsequently invented historiogra- phy.[17] Remythification did occur, but at the same time, patterned history was very important.

Not all mythical history was a recomposition. Myth was also lived histori- cally. The concept of dawning is one of the indications of this patterned history. In fact the documents not only record the canonical reception of dawn, but also some failures. The sources speak of dawn as a sacred moment that estab- lished people in the promised land and initiated their political institutions. The documents also admit that the groups could fail in their attempts at harmonizing historical events with the sacred order of the calendar. Thus, time overtook the Zutuhil; they could not receive their dawn properly:

> Dawn brought light to the Quiche on Mount Tohohil; dawn broke for the Rabi-naleño in Mount Zamaneb. The Zutuhil wished to see their dawn break over Tzala, but the tribes had not yet succeeded in making fire when dawn came. They had not yet gone to Tzala when [the Sun] came forth in the sky over the Quelelat Mountain. It spread its light and it came to Xepoyom. (*Memorial de Solólá* 1950:83–84)

An analysis of the obscure text of the *Anales de Cuauhtitlán* reveals a similar failure. The Chichimec say that their wanderings lasted 364 years, at the end of which they chose a ruler; but the ruler was not important, nor could they have ended the pilgrimage at that time. History failed. The actual arrival of the Chichimec at Cuauhtitlan (in the year 5 acatl) was 368 years after leaving Chicomoztoc. The Chichimec do not accept that, since they altered the count. They allotted 364 years to the pilgrimage, when the actual count is 368. But 368 is not a multiple of 52. It is probable that at the end of 364 years they celebrated their dawn with a "beginning" they considered definitive. It was the year 1 acatl, the same year they named their ruler. If this were so, they failed in their dawn, their ruler, and their "definitive" establishment. Their final settlement in Cuauhtitlan took place on 5 acatl, with a four-year delay.

Historical myth is sensitive to political changes. There are frequent processes of remythification. A good example of such change is the history of the origin of the Mexica recorded by Fray Bernardino de Sahagún (1956, 3: 207–14). The history developed in the colonial era with pre-Hispanic mythic elements and is directed toward defending land threatened by the European invasion. It is only mentioned here, since a more complete discussion is given in López Austin (1985b).

Something similar is found in the colonial Mexica story of the expedition of the magicians to the Chicomoztoc Culhuacan of origin. There the mother of the god Huitzilopochtli reminds them of the words her son spoke upon departing. They are not words inciting a conquest, which were proper to the time of Motecuhzoma Ilhuicamina. It is a sad message, placed there retrospectively to console a people who, after a century of glory, were defeated by the Spaniards and their Indian allies:

> Mother dear, I will not delay long in returning, no more than is necessary to take these seven groups and leave them where they are to live and to populate

that land they were promised. After settling them and consoling them, I will return.

And this will be upon completing the years of my pilgrimage and the time alloted to me, during which time I will have to make war against the provinces, cities, and other places, bring them and subject them to my service. But in the same sequence in which I conquered them, they will be conquered and taken from me by foreign people, and they will banish me from that land.

Then I will come back here, to this place, because those whom I conquered with my sword and shield, those same people will turn against me, and will throw me headfirst downward, and I and my weapons will go rolling over the earth. Then, dear Mother, my time will be up and I will hasten back to your lap, and until then there must be no sorrow. (Durán 1984, 2:221)

Historical narrations, then, are made into myths. Reciprocally, for various reasons, myths acquire history. Beginning with important heroes, mythic cycles are formed, families of mythic characters come together, and the stories are arranged into periods very similar to those of historical narration. Mythic cycles are fixed in time as if they were history, and an effort is made to construct a total, general myth with them. That does not happen in all traditions. We are too accustomed to the mythic narrations systematized by a Hesiod or a Homer and with those recorded in sacred texts. We often forget that this order cannot be made general. Jiménez Nuñez (1962:33), in giving an overall picture of South American myths, notes that they are independent units. They refer to the origin of the Sun and the Moon, or to that of some plants and animals, or to that of humankind, but rarely do they give a complete account of the creation. What Jiménez Nuñez says about South America is also true of the Mesoamerican tradition. This is true in the general sense, although there are important exceptions, because the separation gives a strong narrative independence to each mythic account. Historical congruency appears to be unnecessary in many traditions.

Why is there this common independence or this lack of a need for historical congruency in myth? Because the complexity of myths makes simultaneously necessary different kinds of congruency, and one of them must predominate. Remember the distinction between heroic subjects and nodal and nomological subjects in myth. If myths develop on the congruency of nodal and nomological foundations, the adventures are displaced. The deeper aspect of myth is emphasized, the cosmic order that is manifest in each act of life. The superficial, the adventure, takes second place. There can be a congruency stemming from the most refined archetype, the fundamental myth, like the Tamoanchan myth or the formation of beings by opposing forces. But this does not guarantee "historical" congruency, that of the adventure of the gods conceived as the history of humankind.

However, there are circumstances that give historical congruency to mythic narration. One of these is the enrichment of myth: myths become extensive and complex, as in the case of the Quiche myth of Hunahpú and Ixbalanqué. The cycles accumulate the adventures of the characters until they form a macroadventure. The diverse Huichol myths, which compose the cycle of the struggle among rival deified psychotropics, approach this stage. The Huichol have rich mythical narrations in which take part the evil Kiéri-Téwiyári (jimson weed), son of the Wind, and the benevolent Káuyúmari (peyote), associated with the Sun and an ally of the people. These myths form a chain. Furst and Myerhoff (1972) say that after hearing all the myths, they believed that there was a mythic cycle that could be understood as history.

Myths must be compiled to bring about congruency. Different paths can lead to compilation: rituals that include very long tales, recreational practices with a high literary content, didactic resources, or the centralization of narrations with political aims. No doubt these are ways to generate the most important mythical epics. The narration is given greater weight by rationality. The processes of creation are united and ordered chronologically. Family ties among the gods are defined and fixed by suppressing contradictory tales. The standard versions eliminate inconvenient myths; subversive interpretations are not permitted. Thus is formed the great history of the time of origin.

It is an aesthetic triumph. But it is a triumph over the nodal and nomological depth of myth.

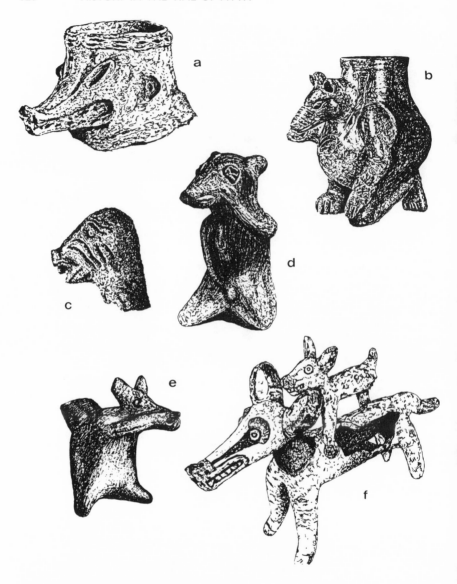

Figure 15. Opossum ceramics III
    a. Neck of a vessel shaped like an opossum head, Veracruz Huaxteca
    b. Maya vessel in the shape of an opossum porter, Progreso, Yucatan
    c. Zapotec opossum head, Tlacochahuaya
    d. Opossum from La Loma, Jalisco
    e. Opossum shaped vessel, Cuauhtemoc, Colima
    f. Opossum with her young, Tlatelolco

The fable was on hold. At the point of being written,
it lacked a theme that would bring it the respect of others,
that would give it eternal dignity.

Carlos Monsiváis,
Nuevo catecismo para indios remisos

A mythic tale is built by a large army of poet-singers. These successors of secular couriers, scattered over a vast territory, combine their present ends with
the ones proclaimed a thousand times in the tales. Purposes and acts as they
are conceived by Ibn Khaldûn (1967:335):

> If a man thinks of bringing into existence a roof to shelter him, he will progress
> in his mind [from the roof] to the wall supporting the roof, and then to the
> foundation upon which the wall stands. Here, his thinking will end, and he
> will then start to work on the foundation, then [go on to] the wall, and then to
> the roof, with which his action will end. This is what is meant by the saying:
> "The beginning of action is the end of thinking, and the beginning of thinking
> is the end of action."

Proposals and acts. Mythic narration is a project based on an overriding
purpose: to establish something in the world through a return to the initial
time. There is a development in the tale that calls for a particular closure: the
inchoation. Mythic relation is constructed starting with the need for that closure, and the validity of different statements depends on their correlation with
the exposition of this inchoation. The guide to the framework of the narration
is the inchoative purpose, and this requires a search in each interpretation of
the tale for what has been called its meaning or function: "The meaning (or the
function) of an element in the work is its possibility of correlating with other
elements of the work and with the work in its totality" (Todorov 1985). And
the meaning has been used as the basis for unity in the structural analyses of
tales: "The function is evidently, from the linguistic point of view, the unity
of its contents. It is what a declaration 'is meant to say,' what constitutes its
formal unity and not the form in which it is said" (Barthes 1985).

In the mythic tale are found an inchoative interpretation (derived from the
predominating purpose) and auxiliary explanations (some of them motivated

by weighty but secondary purposes), which, in their aggregate, link the diverse elements of the tale. The purposes achieve expression in the conjunction of very heterogeneous, normative rules,[1] sometimes contradictory, but all unified in ways characteristic of each literary genre. In other words, there is an overarching sequence of the normative rules that is typical of each form of expression. Therefore there will not be the same purposes, exactly the same norms, nor the same arrangement in the mythic tale, the story, the legend, the fable, or the jest, even though they independently share many characteristics as oral forms of popular expression. This is aside from the frequent changes of genre that take place in popular narrations.

In the complexity of normative rules, we can distinguish two important categories: one that refers to the inchoative exposition, the reason for the existence of the mythic tale; the other, that of entertainment. Public entertainment is also an end pursued in mythic narration, and it is a quite different entertainment from the one pursued by the narrator of stories, legends, fables, or jokes. The two kinds of normative rules create and correlate the different elements of the tale. Some elements will be more oriented to the nodality of the nature of the world; others, with the adventures of the characters. But all, or nearly all, of the elements of the tale are heterogeneous, because they are constructed to unite the different propositions in a congruent product. A satisfactory congruence is not always achieved. This confluence has its risks, because concessions to entertainment may modify or damage not only the nodal aspect of the mythic tale, but the belief itself.

Mythic narration is born of many purposes and normative rules. A mythic tale can simultaneously possess several messages. It is true that it is subject to literary analysis and to investigation of its deepest nodal meanings, but one must remember that abstraction as a methodology must be used cautiously. What Jakobson (1986a: 14) says about language in general is also applicable to the study of mythic narration:

> We can analyze language at the morphemic level without reference to the phenomenological level. We can examine the formal level without referring to the semantic level, and so on. But we realize that in proceeding this way, we operate in a manner similar to an acoustic filter. We can eliminate the high and the low frequencies, but we know it is only a scientific experiment.

The requirements for amusement extend to the episode itself. The public calls for daring deeds, many of them coming from other tales. It is a search for what is already known and liked, such as we find in murder mysteries. "The reader's pleasure" Eco (1985) says, speaking of Fleming's works, "consists of finding himself engaged in a game where he knows the pieces and the rules, and even the end, with minimal variation." Because of this, the characters in myths usually do not achieve their great feats in the first attempt. As in stories, they are successful after two or three failures, which increase the suspense of the tale.[2]

However, evaluating episodes is not always easy. A failure before a success may have a significant value in the nodal context. A deed common to several heroes may indicate a need to simplify these characters to a single mythic figure. Indeed there is a suspicious parallelism in the adventures of some characters. Some of the Mesoamerican heroes are abandoned at birth, some in a river, some in ant hills or in thorny plants; but they are rescued from the water, the ants respect them, or the magueys nurse them (*Popol vuh* 1964:64–65; *Leyenda de los soles* 1945:122–23; Sahagún 1956, 3:207–8; Law 1957:345–47; González Casanova 1928; González Ramos 1972:148; Hollenbach 1977). It is difficult to know if this is due to an interchange among myths or whether the episode is repeated for some deeper reason of nodal importance.

Similarly the cosmic meaning of a myth requires equivalent elements that give rise to diverse adventure stories. In the myth about the birth of the Sun and the Moon, there is an episode where two grandsons slay their grandfather. The grandfather can appear in human form or as a deer. If it is as a deer, the grandsons kill it, skin it, and blow up the skin to make his effigy. If it is as a human, a bag appears that could be a blanket or a sack inside a *petate* (woven reed mat) (W. S. Miller 1956:81, 86–97). Whichever it is, skin, blanket, or bag, it serves a purpose in the tale. It must be filled with things that have cosmic significance. The grandsons fill the blanket with bees, wasps, and other poisonous animals, or simply with lime ash. The grandmother breaks the bag and is surrounded by the furious insects or by the dust. The meaningful act is done, although the explicit meaning of it appears in only a few versions. For the Mixe, the ashes are the mist (*Ap ayuuk* 1982:112). For the Tlapanec, lime is a cloud: "That is why clouds exist, and from them come rain, thunder, and lightning, because that happened on the mountain" (Loo 1987:145).[3] Whether the meaning is explained or not, the adventure corresponds to the options of the equivalent elements utilized. The episodes change, but they need to maintain their equivalency. These elements are not arbitrary.

If the overriding purpose of the mythic tale is taken into account, it is possible to develop an outline of the structural parts of a typical myth, among which the various elements with mythic meaning are distributed. First, there is something whose existence has to be established in the world. Second, there

Table 3. Structural Parts of the Typical Myth

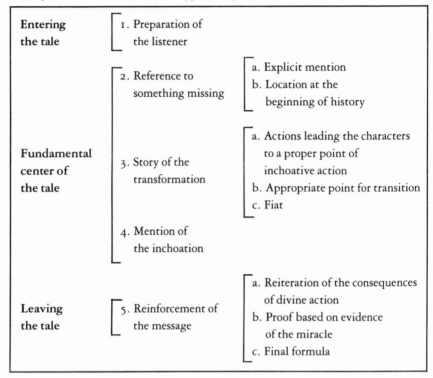

Entering the tale	1. Preparation of the listener	
Fundamental center of the tale	2. Reference to something missing	a. Explicit mention b. Location at the beginning of history
	3. Story of the transformation	a. Actions leading the characters to a proper point of inchoative action b. Appropriate point for transition c. Fiat
	4. Mention of the inchoation	
Leaving the tale	5. Reinforcement of the message	a. Reiteration of the consequences of divine action b. Proof based on evidence of the miracle c. Final formula

must be an act that produces the establishment. This presupposes a third part, a period of the absence of that thing before the establishing action. This would be the basic outline of the tale, but two complementary parts can be added. In one the narrator prepares the listeners, capturing their attention for the tale. In the other, the narrator dismisses them, after duly reinforcing the message transmitted. To summarize, and following the natural sequence of the tale, these are the different parts: 1. preparation of the listener; 2. a reference to the absence of something; 3. the story of the transformation; 4. mention of the inchoation; 5. reinforcement of the message.

1.   Preparation of the listener. In this part the elements can be a formula of an exhortational or referential nature. For instance, the "they say it was" of the Nahua (Ziehm, intro. to Preuss 1982:16–17); the "that is how it was told" of the Cora (Preuss 1912:169); "the following is what happened to our people a long time ago, and you must believe it now" of the Trique (Hollenbach 1977); or a reference to a time when the gods lived in the world, when there was not yet a sun, or when animals talked. This part is missing in many myths.

2. Reference to lacking something. This can be divided into two parts, which sometimes mingle: an explicit reference to the lack; or locating the beginning of the story, its state previous to the action of the characters. There are only a few references to the lack of something. The following are some examples:

> Well at that time there was no light.[4] They say that she was an old woman who was able to capture fire when it had scarcely detached itself from the stars or planets. She was not afraid and went to bring it from where fire fell, and she kept it for a long time. (Incháustegui 1977:67)
>
> Formerly the gods had festivals and celebrated their fiestas, but they had nothing to drink nor to smoke. They couldn't chat, because they didn't have light, they didn't have fire. But in the house of the demons, noise could be heard, dancing, a party, shouting. (Bartolomé y Barabas 1982:111)
>
> It was a cloudy day. So people lived that way, without sunlight, with absolutely nothing. They were, as you see we are right now, with only rain, full of cloudbursts.[5]

The last example is interesting, since it makes the listener participate in the circumstances of the tale.

Locating the beginning of the story is a preparation for the adventure. The indicating elements here are especially important, since in a more or less hidden way they set the framework for the action, the characters, the actions or sites of the divine sphere. These elements point out the places where the action will unfold and introduce and describe the characters of the tale. Age, kinship, trade, status, names, actions previous to the adventure, and peculiarities of the characters are, together with the mention of the places where the action begins, important data for the nodal interpretation of the myth. For example, the elderly couple who take home with them the orphans who will become the Sun and the Moon are a sterile old woman and a lazy old man who does not cultivate his fields (Parsons 1966:324). Both characteristics will be repeated significantly in other versions.

3. The story of the transformation. This is the liveliest part of the mythic tale. It includes a series of events focused on the moment of crystallization of the action of the gods. They lead to an inchoation of a being in human time. The sequence is the mediation between the state of lacking and the earthly existence of the inchoate. In the most complete sequences, each element serves as the antecedent of another in the chain, all leading up to the point of transition. It is a process of transformation, but at the same time it can be the process itself that remains fixed in the human world. The sequence

of episodes is the result of a difficult combination of a description of cosmic processes, the elements that refer to the processes and the divine beings who intervene in them, and a plot that tends to be entertaining. The preponderant purpose and the secondary aims have to come together here simultaneously in a congruent form.

This structural part of the mythic tale can be subdivided into three: the aggregate of adventures that lead the characters to the culminating point of the inchoative action; the propitious point, where the completed adventures pause so that the inchoation is produced; the transition itself, produced by a miraculous and frequently expressed fiat.

In this, as in the second structural part of the tale, the indicator elements stand out: the names, characteristics, and circumstances of the characters that relate to cosmic matters serve as contextual points.[6] The name of the priest, Yappan, and of his wife, Tlahuitzin, who in ancient mythology were converted into scorpions, signify the opposition of light and dark (Serna 1953: 228, Clavijero 1964:159). Yappan means "dark"; Tlahuitzin, "the venerable luminous one." Among the Lacandon, the maiden seduced by the small bird is the daughter of Kisin, Lord of the Underworld, and the bird is blue and wears blue clothing. Since it is blue it is the symbol of Huitzilopochtli, and the union of the bird and maiden signifies the hierogamy of the Sky and the Earth (Bruce 1974:240, 242). The same is true of places. Their names, repeated in different or in similar contexts through the centuries, are invaluable clues to understanding the cosmic meaning of myths. The Sun and the Moon hide in the mouth of the gopher, an animal of the underworld (*Ap ayuuk* 1982:112–13, Miller 1956:82). The Sun is born in the serpent's mouth or the Hill of the Serpent (Coatepec) (Sahagún 1956, 1:271–73; Croft 1957), and according to the Huichol, the Sun returns to the underworld through the serpent's mouth (Zingg 1982, 2:183, 227n6). Quetzalcoatl's brothers abandoned him in the Burned-Hill-Place (Tlachinoltepec) intending to burn him (*Historia de México* 1965:112–13), and on the Burnt Hill, according to the Huichol, the Sun, the Moon, and our ancestors were born (*Wirrakira irratsikayari* 1982:28, 54). The Grassy Place (*zacatal*) seems to have the same cosmic importance.[7] In the history of the Tohueyo, as told by Sahagún (1956, 1:283–84), Coatepec and Zacatepec ("Grass-Hill-Place") seem to be identified as the places where the hero fought against his enemies. Quetzalcoatl's Tzatzitepec, "Proclamation-Hill-Place" (Sahagún 1956, 1:278–79), is the site at which the god Xipe Totec did penitence (*Códice Vaticano Latino 3738* 1964–67: pl. 10), which leads us to look for a relationship between the two gods. The steam-bath is a place with strong significance. Brother and sister Sun and Moon receive their light from there

(*Uejkauitl nauaueueujtlajtoli* 1982:67), and it is there that their grandmother, who for the ancient Nahua was the goddess Toci,[8] meets her death. Names of mythical places occasionally bear a striking resemblance, in spite of a considerable difference in time. The resemblance cannot just be due to chance. For example, contemporary Nahua myths mention the Jail-Where-the-Living-Machetes-Are; it is a place of punishment in the underworld (González Cruz and Anguiano 1984). Its equivalent is found in another myth. The ancient Quiche speak of the Chayin-ha ("House of the Blades") in the underworld, where there are "honed cutting blades, either silent or grating against each other" (*Popol vuh* 1964:56). On the other hand, the idea that treasures (among them fire) are in the underworld, the dominion of the cold gods of water, of winds, and of death, can be made explicit in the tales. The Chatino say that corn was deposited in the Place-of-the-Bad-Airs (Bartolomé and Barabas 1982:110), a site that is obviously in the underworld. A detailed list of these indicator elements, so useful in understanding the context of myth, would be lengthy.

Next to these identifying elements can also be found explanatory elements, but less frequently. They are characterized by an interruption in the sequence of the adventure, to make clear to the audience the correlation between the characters and the actions of the tale, the gods and the cosmic processes.

4.   Mention of the inchoation. This part is an announcement of the effect on earth, of a permanent result of the action of the gods. It is usually brief and almost always a formula: "the sun is that way now," or "that was when all the dances were born" (Williams García 1972:93–94); but it can be a prolongation of the narration, as in the case of the theft of fire by the opossum: ". . . and since they [guardians of the fire], who see the world, were up there, then definitely no one could take it, and there it remained" (pers. com. Jesús Rentería; see chapter 17).

As to the nature of the effect, in some versions the results are generic; in others, specific; in others, anomalous. For example, the myth of the bitch who becomes a woman in order to make tortillas in some cases explains the origin of humankind; in others, with a biblical (Gen. 9:20–27) insertion, the origin of human races (W. S. Miller 1956:103–4); in others, that of one[9] or various ethnic groups;[10] and in still others, the origin of Indians in general, with self-denigrating overtones (Mason 1914). More noteworthy is the case of the origin of the Sun and Moon, since it explains not only the birth of the astral bodies, but the difference in their brilliance, their distance, the lunar phases, etc. Some versions say the Moon's brightness was diminished by a blow with a rabbit. There are others that explain the presence of a rabbit on the moon without mentioning the effect of a blow on the moon or its decreased brightness (Bartolomé and Barabas 1982:109). There is another myth about the flood that ends with the ascent of the rabbit to the moon (Stiles, Maya, and Castillo 1985). Finally, one version of the Sun and Moon myth has an anomalous result. In this myth all conclusions of an astral type are set aside to make the myth an account of the origin of the suffering of humankind (Hollenbach 1977).

Because of the frequent variations of specific inchoations in myths as important as that of the brothers who were the origin of the Sun and the Moon, it is plausible that the principal message of the nodal subject of the tale is not in these specific and variable endings, but in a generic consequence of the divine processes, often not explicit, from which the variants derive.

5.   Reinforcement of the message. The mythic account usually ends with a reinforcement of the different kinds of expression: a reiteration of the consequences of the divine adventures, aside from the chain of events; proof based on the traces the adventure left on earth; a formula that occasionally is an exhortation. The repetition gives vigor to the result of the divine action. After one version affirms that "man was to be the Sun and woman was to be the Moon," it ends by saying, "people say that they are still there, even today" (Hoogshagen 1971). The reiteration sometimes contains a real explanation of the result of the mythic action. The proof given sometimes involves a geographical accident, such as the presence of volcanic rocks at the place where the Sun appeared. "And, since then, there have been new pumice stones, which seem to have been boiled at the place where the Sun was born" (pers. com. Jesús Rentería 1972). The formulas are a kind of coda, as, for example: "And this is how the story ends"; or exhortations similar to those at the beginning of the tale: "This is what happened in the past, and you should believe it" (Hollenbach 1977).

The above schema applies to the structural parts of a typical, simple tale; but the tale may have complex forms. To the sequence indicated by the schema, new tales are added, with their own specific actions, transitions, and inchoations. In the complex myth it is necessary to distinguish between the *principal tale* and others with hazy outlines that can be called *subordinate, derivative,* or *accessory*. Some of these are independent myths that have been incorporated into the principal one; at times they seem to derive from it. All of them, like wedges, support the development of the main story and sometimes give great vivacity to the adventure.

Important beings of the principal tale participate in the subordinate tale, and it is hard to distinguish their deeds from the general sequence. The independent inchoation can scarcely be perceived. If it precedes that of the principal tale, it is sometimes inherent to the cosmic complex to which the principal tale belongs. A subordinate account is not indispensable, but it helps the total congruency, and it is useful in understanding the nodal subject. An example of a valuable subordinate account in the myth of the Sun and the Moon is the episode of the death of the maiden impregnated by the celestial bird. The tale is interrupted only to tell of the girl's death; but in so doing, it becomes a key element, since it identifies the young girl with Mother Earth: "The girl gave birth to two children, but she died in childbirth, and she became all that we see, everything that is the earth" (Navarrete 1966). Another example is the Mopan myth of the theft of corn. Yaluc, the eldest of the four gods of thunder and rain, cast his thunderbolt to break open the rock that concealed the corn. The wall was broken so that people could take advantage of the new food. But the tale is interrupted to talk about the origin of the colors of corn, which, when it was enclosed, had been white. The celestial fire burned some grains and smoked others, causing corn to be red, yellow, white, and black (J. Thompson 1970a:350). The colors of corn reveal that the nodal meaning of the myth goes much further than the mere provision of food to humanity.

In the derivative tale, a character, important or not, participates in an adventure whose results are directed, either directly or indirectly, toward the miraculous transition of the principal tale. But the particular inchoation of the derivative tale pertains only to the species of that character. Often this account is not essential and can easily be replaced by equivalent episodes. One example is the ant's waist in the myth of the theft of corn. Ant participates in the adventure; one of the characters catches it and squeezes the middle of its body, causing the slenderness between the thorax and the abdomen (García de León 1976:82; Petrich 1985:159–60; J. Thompson 1970a:353). Another example is the hairless tail of the opossum, who carries away or attempts to carry away fire in the myth of the origin of corn and in that of the Sun and the Moon. The animal, as in his own mythical tales, comes out with a scorched tail (Münch Galindo 1983:165–66; Técnicos bilingües 1985:21; Hollenbach 1977). In the second tale, the character may vary;[11] in the first one, the event may vary, since in another version the ant's waist becomes thinner due to the excessive weight the insects bear when they try to carry a whole ear of corn (Wagley 1957:1).

The hero of the accessory tale is not related to the principal tale. It is almost always an unimportant character, who is there more to take advantage of the mythic narration than to contribute with his adventures to reaching the climactic point of transition. The inchoation applies only to its species. Its adventure is futile and seems to exist only for entertainment, since it has no apparent cosmic value. It can be included in what some writers call "etiological myths" (S. Thompson 1965:173), which have been compared to the "Just So Stories," made popular by Rudyard Kipling (Radcliffe-Brown, cited in Lévi-Strauss 1965:128). One example is the "explanation" of why the Deer and the Rabbit have short tails. The heroes Hunahpú and Ixbalanqué wanted to catch them, and the tails remained in their hands (*Popol vuh* 1964:72). In another tale Rabbit knew the name of the Sun at the moment of his first appearance. Because of that and nothing else, its snout was broken, and it remained that way (Preuss 1982:165–67). Howler Monkey (*Aluoatta paliatta*) sailed on the stern of the ark during the flood. His testicles were underwater, and that is why his scrotum is pale, in contrast to the darker color of the rest of his body (Boremanse 1986:57). Parrot was also aboard the ark, but on the upper part, when the water rose and caused the vessel to collide with the sky. In some versions the shock fractured its skull and it was left with a red crest (Ichon 1973:53). In others, the blow deformed its legs and made it walk in a crouch (Foster 1945a:235; Münch Galindo 1983:161; Williams García 1972:79). According to others, it was not Parrot, but Dwarf Rooster who received the blow, and that is why he is short (Campos 1982:217; Genaro González Cruz, in *Seis versiones del diluvio* 1983).

"Etiological myth" is not the correct term for this kind of tale, because it is not the only type that refers to the origin of things. The others mentioned in fact deal more properly with origins. On the other hand, the accessory tale describes their nature better. But this is merely a nominal problem. A deeper and more disquieting one is: Are accessory tales myths? Jensen (1963:68, 73–74) denies this and considers them to be the work of "playful fantasy":

> We shall deal with a group of tales which we usually separate from true
> myths by calling them etiological or explanatory. Such a separation seems indicated since the resemblance of this type of tale to true myths is entirely superficial. They lack such basic characteristics as religious content and the criterion of being believed as established truths . . .
> . . . etiological myths seem mythic in form only but seem to lack foundation in religion and a belief that they state a truth . . .
> . . . we are not ready to call this tale a genuine myth. Because of its subject matter, it most definitely lacks stature. . . . Thus, the difference between etiological myth and myth proper lies, not in the form, but in the theme itself and more particularly even in the manner of its development.

Jensen takes up the problem of the separation of the two kinds of tales but concludes that "just as there is no definite division between sacred and daily objects, neither is there one between true myths and etiological ones" (Jensen 1963:77).

It is a difficult problem to solve, above all because of the implications of subjectivity on the part of the users. But even without the support of these implications and without sharing Jensen's concept of myth, one must recognize the weight of his arguments as to the lack of grandeur and the too festive nature of the tale called etiological. The minor importance of the characters and the apparent futility of the inchoations can be deceiving; but both characteristics, added to the clear separation between the direction of this tale and that of the principal one, are good grounds for seeing the accessory tale as one of entertainment, not connected to the truly nodal content, and as a side attraction, a literary ploy to please the audience. It can therefore be said that the aesthetic orientation of the accessory tale predominates to the point of not needing any reference to a cosmic process. Rather than being a mythic tale, the accessory tale is literary auxiliary to the mythic tale. I agree with Jensen that the delineation is not always precise, but an attempt to mark the boundaries is important when beginning the process of analysis.

The structural characteristics referred to in this chapter are those of the usual mythic tale (simple or complex). However, there are accounts that elude this order. Naming all of them goes beyond my purpose, but I will mention some of the forms that appear more or less frequently. In certain tales, perhaps because of the fusion of versions, the deeds of the characters are presented in different sequences, which terminate in a single inchoation. The result can be disconcerting, since it eradicates the logical reason for some episodes in the sequence. Inversely, there are also accounts in which the inchoation is multiple. The actions of the characters lead to various characteristics of the beings who establish themselves in the world. This kind of complex result is frequent. One example is the Mixe version of the origin myth of the Sun and Moon:

> Now they were near the end of the earth, and so the youth climbed first to the sky, where his grandmother could not follow him. His sister stopped at the halfway point to wash part of her face, so that the little man was already being hidden on the horizon before she could ascend into space. And the stain seen on the Moon is the mud her little brother threw at her. That is why she shines less brightly than the Sun. (P. Carrasco 1952)

There are three answers here: how the Sun and Moon were formed when they ascended to the sky; why the Moon does not march next to the Sun, but behind it; and why the Moon shines less than her brother.

Another interesting kind of tale is the chain. The episodes, almost always brief, simple, mere justifications for creation, form a long series of causes and effects. The myth of Shondá-Vee, The-Woman-of-the-Dragging-Water, is a good example. This Mazatec myth tells of a woman who makes an enemy of her father-in-law and, fearing him, runs far away. This myth could be called a "road atlas," since there is a long account in which events take place that give names to all the points along the journey. If Shondá-Vee gets stuck in the mud, the place will be called Plain-of-the-Bog; if she grinds corn, the hill will be Metate-Stone; if she sharpens a knife, Grindstone; if she lets salt fall, Plain-of-Salt; if the foxes howl, Fox-Water; and so on with the other places (Cowan 1963; Incháustegui 1977:100–104).

A similar case is the message sent by the grandmother of Hunahpú and Ixbalanqué to her grandsons. The grandmother gives the message to Louse, who travels inside Frog, who travels inside Serpent, who travels inside Hawk, who finds Hunahpú and Ixbalanqué on the ball court, where Hawk vomits Serpent, which vomits Frog, which vomits Louse, which gives the message to the youths. The chain of adventures proceeds, giving rise to the different foods of the animals and the peculiarities (salivating mouth and crooked body) of the frog (*Popol vuh* 1964:75–79).

The result of the above is that mythic tale is like Canudos, the rebellious town of northeastern Brazil, because "Canudos is not a history, but a tree full of histories" (Vargas Llosa 1981:433).

Oh, how short the day!
And even a hundred years are nothing.
The blue firmament ascends to infinity,
And time is only an unending struggle with the elements.
Maku, queen of the immortals,
Flaunts her eternal crest of ribbons,
But snowy locks abound among them.
And the king of heaven, upon seeing the virgins of jade,
Laughs heartily, a thousand, ten million times.
And I try to harness the six dragons
To a single car to ascend to the East.
I will invite the dragons to drink an exquisite wine
From the Big Dipper, the great goblet.
I do not look for riches, I do not look for honors:
Since I am mortal, I only try to live my own life
In the spirit of youthfulness.

Li Po

Poets can invite celestial beings to drink and can embrace the Moon's reflection in the lake—a delight many of us have missed. Our own mission must be to read a myth soulessly and to listen to it from outside, always outside, of the realm where it was forged. No matter how often we mingle with the chorus of the faithful, we are the outside analysts. However, the story, even if alien, even if written, allows us to discover its nodal subjects.

How does one ease the way toward the nodal subjects? We need to invent and to systematize techniques for analyzing mythic tales. While studies of Mesoamerican religious tradition progress and, in their development, provide the instruments needed for analysis, it is possible to recommend pertinent measures and to point out the problems that are the chief obstacles to the project. This part of the essay is dedicated to just that, and I begin by examining the more general aspects, touching only briefly on points already examined.

In the first place, the mythic tale should be studied and analyzed appropriately. That is, myth should not be confused with the mythic tale, since the latter is only one of its forms of expression, even though it is the most finished one. The study of the mythic tale is part of the study of myth, and the search for its significant elements should not be confined to those stated in the tale. In order to find the appropriate codes, it is absolutely necessary to understand the religious tradition that is being studied, and not to start from an imagined symbolic transparency within the reach of any analyst interested only in the identification of opposites or in universal coincidences. Analysts should have a profound knowledge of the tradition they are researching. This applies not only to whoever is interested in nodal subjects, but also to whoever is looking for the literary value of the tale.

In the second place, the study of the tale should not be confused with its analysis, which is only one of the aspects of such a study. Many of the elements of the tale, including most of its oppositions, have an origin outside of the text. These are not oppositions born in and for the tale, but expressions of oppositions relating to the cosmic order. The tale should be perceived as the product of a social interchange, and its study must be placed in this context before sifting through the text. The process of its formation (registered in the time frame of long duration as well as in the purposes present at the moment in which the myth is expounded); the context of its performance (that is, for ephemeral works, even if they may have been recorded); and the most permanent of its functions must all be taken into account. If the functions of the tale are not taken into account, for example, the reasons for particular variants of the text may pass unnoticed. We would have a flat vision of the myth, as if it were the product of a society with no internal differences, or in which these do not appear in its expressions. Even worse, the study of the myth would produce a diminished explanation: it would take into account neither the role of the myth in society, nor the way in which social relations produce the myth and its transformations.

In the third place, in an analysis of the mythic tale, considerable weight should be given to the plot. In the tale there is a significant adventure undertaken by meaningful characters that transmits knowledge of the nodal subjects. A division must be made, based on a teleological development in which the elements are valid beginning with the relationship existing between the inchoation and the transformation produced to arrive at it. Greimas (1985) is correct in stating that "the semantic theory that would claim to explain the reading of myths should operate with the sequences of declarations articulated in the tales." Accordingly, it would be inappropriate to look for the divisions in the mythic tale in a phrase or any other element of a linguistic nature, "Since the 'language' of the tale is not the language of articulated speech— although it is often supported by it—the narrative units will be substantially independent of linguistic units. They may coincide, but only occasionally, not systematically" (Barthes 1985).[1] The teleological process is completed in the tale. In principle each mythic tale is a unit capable of transmitting to the listeners a multiple message, in which both the adventure of the characters and the nodal subject are completely presented, even though an average listener is required to understand the adventure and a select listener is needed to understand the nodal subject. It is obvious that a comparison of the different myths and their versions is essential for an outside analyst as well as for a believer learned in mythic matters. But this does not prevent each story's seeking to give a complete transmission of the message.

Let us go on to the particular problems of analyzing the mythic tale. Two statements too often made by specialists should be questioned: first, that all elements in the story have equal value; second, that all versions have equal value. Regarding the first, Kirk (1973:95–99) is correct in denying that every detail of the tale is significant, and that all significant details are equally so. The division proposed in the preceding chapter of principal, subordinate, derivative, and accessory tales supports Kirk's position. The specification of the weight of each detail, which depends to a great extent on its contribution to the attainment of the primary and secondary inchoations, is fundamental to a correct analysis. It is also indispensable to know the nature of each detail in the tale. As an example, consider the case of animals seeking the old opossum to ask his advice on straightening the course of the river, and finding him getting drunk in a bar. A frivolous interpretation would stress the macho value of the story, through the hero's demonstrating his virility by ingesting alcoholic drinks. Better acquaintance with the character in the context of cosmovision would recognize this detail as one of the hero's characteristic traits.

Concerning the value of the different versions—even if limited only to the inchoative exposition—it is accurate to say that there are both complete and incomplete versions, correct and incorrect versions. Obviously all of them are important to the researcher, since a comparison of the versions gives a better understanding of the object of study. However, in mythic tales as in all literary works, there are differences in quality, and both defects and incongruencies diminish the logical and aesthetic value of the text.

Defects in the inchoative exposition can be found in various structural parts of the tale: the lack of an inchoation, the failure to determine a propitious point for the transition, or the lack of a proper sequence of actions leading to that point. The lack of inchoation is quite frequent, especially in accessory tales. Lightning tortures Ant, squeezing its middle with a cord to make it reveal where the corn is. Ant confesses and goes free, but the tale does not mention that from that time on ants have had slim waists (Taggart 1983:91). Macaw or Parrot travels in the ark, but there is no justification for its presence on the trip (Lumholtz 1970, 2:190; Taggart 1983:195). Two versions say that sugarcane torn out by the wind was repaired with mucus, and that cane has protuberances on its stalk that resemble drops of it; but another version omits the result (Taggart 1983:215–16). When Frog tells the grandmother that the meat she is eating is her own husband, the two murderous grandsons throw sand at the animal and make its haunches bumpy (*Relatos, mitos y leyendas de la Chinantla* 1981:57);[2] but sometimes no reason is given for why the gossiping creature is a frog with rough haunches; the grandsons only give the excuse with no explanation: "Oh! mother, that one is a gossiping bastard. We know our father well" (Cicco and Horcasitas 1962).

If the setting of a propitious moment for the transition is missing, it takes place precipitiously, without sufficient cause. Such is the case in the following version, which does not clarify why the brother becomes the Sun and his sister the Moon:

> Then the orphans continued on their path and came to another town where the kings and the rich were having a festival so that their children could be the Sun and the Moon. The next day they continued their journey. The man became the Sun and the woman became the Moon. (Hoogshagen 1971)

Faulty sequence in the episodes leaves some details in the tale with no possible explanation, unless the versions are compared. In the myth of the Sun and the Moon, the brother and sister tear out the eyes of a fabulous creature. The right eye, the golden one, originally in the possession of the girl and later of her brother, gave rise to solar light; the silver one became lunar light. In the Chinantec version, the brother and the sister kill the two-headed eagle and take possession of its eyes. It states that the right one was gold, but does not state that the other one was silver (Weitlaner and Castro 1973:200). The *Códice Florentino* (1979: bk. 7, ch. 2, fol. 4v–4r) version of a beautiful old myth of the birth of the Sun in Teotihuacan, states that Nanahuatzin and Tecuciztecatl cast themselves into the fire and that they were followed by an eagle and a jaguar, causing their skins to be spotted with black. However, the codex does not say why the animals jumped into the fire. The tale is missing an explanation found in the *Leyenda de los soles* (1945:122) and in Serna (1953:199): the eagle came down from the sky to lift up the Sun, and the jaguar tried to do the same with the Moon.

The principal reason for the errors in mythic tales lies in their being mixed. The tales can include foreign, prestigious episodes, and occasionally complete

Table 4. Example of the Process of Loss of Meaning of Myths

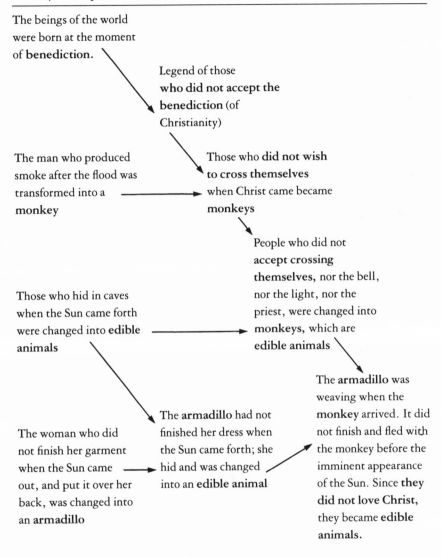

The beings of the world were born at the moment of **benediction.**

Legend of those **who did not accept the benediction** (of Christianity)

The man who produced smoke after the flood was transformed into a **monkey**

Those who **did not wish to cross themselves** when Christ came became **monkeys**

People who did not **accept crossing themselves,** nor the bell, nor the light, nor the priest, were changed into **monkeys,** which are edible animals

Those who hid in caves when the Sun came forth were changed into **edible animals**

The **armadillo** was weaving when the **monkey** arrived. It did not finish and fled with the monkey before the imminent appearance of the Sun. Since **they did not love Christ,** they became **edible animals.**

The **armadillo** had not finished her dress when the Sun came forth; she hid and was changed into an **edible animal**

The woman who did not finish her garment when the Sun came out, and put it over her back, was changed into an **armadillo**

myths are combined and thereby lose their meaning. An example is one of the myths that explains the origin of the armadillo's shell.[3] The following is one of the Chinantec versions:

> In the old days, woman was called that. The armadillo was embroidering a *huipil* [dress] to put on when the Sun came out, but she didn't finish it because it was so complicated. She was making it beautiful, and it had several panels.

When the Sun was about to come out, the paca [*tepezcuintle*] went to see the armadillo. She asked her:

"Haven't you finished your huipil?"

"No, I'm not through," the armadillo answered.

"I have already finished mine," the paca said, "It has very pretty flowers."

Hearing this, the armadillo said, "I don't think I am going to finish mine, because the Sun is about to come out."

When the Sun had risen, the armadillo's blouse was not yet finished, and she didn't know what to do. Finally she put it on, half-finished, with all the shuttles she was using to weave it still on it. That is why the armadillo has a shell.

The paca put on her finished blouse; she had completed it. That is why the paca is spotted. Even today, she still wears those pretty flowers on her skin. (Weitlaner and Castro 1973: 203)

The myth of the man changed into a monkey because he produced smoke after the flood; the one of the people who, when the sun arose, hid in caves and were transformed into animals; and the generalized motif that the origin of the world was marked with a blessing; all of these have produced combinations in the Chinantla that detract from the etiological idea that parts of the loom formed the horny plates of the armadillo shell. A fusion of the concept of the world's original blessing and the beginning of Christianity, which banished primitive pagan beings, is also involved.[4] The myth of the people who were changed into monkeys because they refused to cross themselves derives from the original blessing (confused with the beginning of Christianity) and the myth of the man who was changed into a monkey because he produced smoke. When the Sun appeared, they fled to the mountain, and there they remained (*Relatos, mitos y leyendas de la Chinantla* 1981:224). By combining this myth with that of the people who hid themselves when the Sun appeared and who were changed into edible animals, the idea is added that the people who did not accept seeing the light, nor hearing the bell, nor acknowledging the priest, nor crossing themselves, went to the mountain and were changed into shameless monkeys, to be used as food (*Relatos, mitos y leyendas de la Chinantla* 1981:226). The myth of the animals that hid in caves is also combined with the myth of the Armadillo and her loom, but in this combination there is no mention of the shell. The Armadillo with the unfinished huipil takes refuge in the cave and is transformed into edible flesh (*Relatos, mitos y leyendas de la Chinantla* 1981:224–25). As if that were not enough, this myth is combined with those of not accepting the light, the bell, the priest, and the sign of the cross, to produce the following tale, in which there is no plausible explanation for the half-finished huipil:

An armadillo was working and people came to ask her,

"What are you doing?"

"I am making a huipil!"

And she showed them how she was weaving the blouse with shuttles.

"This is how I do it."

The people wanted to have a huipil also, and the armadillo began to weave one. When she was half-finished, a monkey came.

"What are you making here?" he asked.

"I am making a blouse for the people."

The monkey didn't want to wait and he said, "Let's go to the mountain. The Sun is coming!" And he put the huipil over his shoulders.

Then the rooster crowed.

"Now Jesus Christ (the Sun) is coming," the monkey said to the armadillo.

"We are going to enter the cave, because our enemy (Jesus Christ) is coming."

They entered the forest and the bells began to ring. The cock crowed, "Jesus Christ is coming now."

Because of that, God said those animals were going to be used to make soup, because they did not want to accept Jesus Christ. (*Relatos, mitos y leyendas de la Chinantla* 1981:223–24)

The tale of Armadillo and her loom is an extreme case. The intrusion of other tales produces an aberrant product where the characters and their actions are superfluous. Investigators must be aware of these mixtures of myths in order to correctly evaluate and place each element in the text. And they must remember that these elements come from many sources: complete or partial accounts, native or foreign, mythic or not. Legends, fables, and biblical stories are included to add to the liveliness and prestige of the episodes.

The change of genre is serious. A mythic tale can completely change its nature to become simply a story,[5] or it can be contaminated by a story that distorts much of the text.[6] A parallel process is the inclusion in the Mesoamerican tradition of tales that appear to be myths but that begin with alien narrations, including fables and stories from the Bible.[7] When Samaniego's fable "The Grasshopper and the Ant" is told in Chinantla, the ant is chided as selfish, because it does not feed the grasshopper. In compensation, the grasshopper (cicada) is given the long proboscis that lets it suck the juice of plants (*Relatos, mitos y leyendas de la Chinantla* 1981:63–64, 75–76). It is necessary to distinguish all these kinds of materials in studying oral narrative; but the analyst must be aware of parallel elements, held in common by the Mesoamerican tradition and other remote traditions of the world.

One of the most frequent and difficult problems in reading and analyzing mythic tales is the separation of myths that make up complex narrations. As an illustration, take one of medium complexity, that of the flood. In it we return to the recurring theme of the opossum, thief of fire, since the inchoation of the opossum occurs in it, and the tales of the flood and fire have certain elements in common. The tale of the flood is one of the richest and most interesting and demands detailed study. Here we will mention only some of the points that directly involve the myth of the theft of fire.

The tale of the flood has many variations. In synthesis, it tells the story of a farmer who cuts down the forest and the next morning finds that the trees are standing in place again. A character, frequently a god, tells him that the earth will be flooded, and teaches him how to build a boat. The farmer builds the ark, climbs aboard (sometimes with a bitch), and waits out the flood. When the water recedes, he descends to the earth. In some versions he builds a fire, gathers the remains of fish that have remained on the dry ground, and roasts them. The smoke from the fire annoys the celestial gods, and, in punishment, they change him into an animal. In other versions the farmer lives with the bitch after the flood and finds out that when he is away from the house the bitch changes into a woman. The man prevents the bitch from changing back to its first form, and the bitch becomes a woman permanently. Together they beget the new inhabitants of the earth.

The tale of the flood contains at least two myths. This is nothing new. Fernando Horcasitas (1962) studied the two myths separately and found that the myth of the bitch changing into a woman can be found in other parts of the New World. Métraux (1948) tells of the existence of similar myths in Brazil, Ecuador, and the Guyanas. In them the animals transformed into a woman are a dog or some parrots. Recently some stories in the Mesoamerican tradition have been published, in which the myth of the bitch does not have the part about the flood (Boremanse 1986:224–26; Alejos García 1988:67).

One question comes to mind immediately. If they are different myths, to what inchoation does the first one lead? Apparently nothing becomes established with the receding of the water, but contrary to what one might suppose, it is here that the flood myth and that of the opossum come together, mutually reinforcing each other. The proposition is that this myth established the five pillars that hold up the sky. The outer four serve to transmit to earth the hot and cold forces that form time.

What is the basis for this supposition? First, that the ark did not float aimlessly, but toward definite points, the four extremes of the world and its center. Wakátame, the Huichol Noah, sailed to each of the four regions of the world and ended at the center after a journey of five days or five years (Lumholtz

1970, 2:190; McIntosh 1949; Anguiano and Furst 1987:31). At the beginning of this century, the Tepecano told of the sailor's voyage:

> He floated over the water. The first time he touched ground was to the east, then he went to the north, and from the north to the west, and then from the west to the south. Then he went to the east again, then climbed to the sky again on his return. Thus he arranged the five blows that he gave to the sky. (Mason 1914)

In the second place, the proposition is based on the shape of the ark and what Wakátame had to put inside it. The ark was a cylinder, the hollowed trunk of a fig tree [*Ficus*], to which Mother Earth glued the top.[8] Wakátame carried on board five kernels of corn, five beans, and five squash shoots, and it is said that the shoots were "to feed the fire" (Lumholtz 1970, 2:190).[9] The corn and beans are related as complementary opposites representing hot and cold (a study of this opposition will be the subject of a forthcoming work). The symbolic affinity of fire, corn, the Sun, and flowers has already been mentioned (see chapter 18). To indicate the significance of beans, it can be said that for the Chorti, Corn and Bean are brother and sister, with the same name (Hauailiká). Corn is male, and Bean is female (Fought 1972:415). As we have seen, the opposition hot/cold corresponds to the opposition masculine/feminine. There are other references to this opposition in a comparative study by Lévy-Strauss (1986:241–52). He includes examples from the Mesoamerican tradition in his study. The five squash shoots that are to "feed the fire" represent, with their spiral-shaped tendrils, the twisted paths through which the forces of the gods flow. Is all of this not similar to some of the tales of the opossum's theft of fire?

> The opossum returned to the people, who had arranged four stacks of wood. The opossum gave fire to the people, and then lighted the four piles. All the men joined together with their squash, beans, and corn, and they put everything there to cook (Loo 1987:157–58).

The above explains how grains of corn and beans can be symbols. When Mother Earth instructs Wakátame to prepare for the flood, she says, "Take with you five kernels of corn of each color and five beans, also of each color" (Lumholtz 1970, 2:190). And this also explains how equivalents are used in other stories of the flood. For example, in the above-mentioned Tepecano account, instead of five kernels of corn and five beans, the voyager is told to take "half a bushel [*fanega*] *that will not get used up* and a well of water *that will not get used up*" (Mason 1914; emphasis added), a requirement in which is found not only the fire/water opposition, but in which there is an allusion to the inexhaustible nature of the currents of the forces of the sky and the underworld.[10] The Mixe have a version in which the opposites are earth and fire. It is a tale that approximates more closely the adventures of the opossum. The ancient Noah of the Mixe climbed aboard his ark with three animals: a crow, a fox, and a dove. When the water went down, the dove flew down and plunged its feet into the mud, thus finding out that the earth was not yet habitable. In order to put the world back together, the little old man sent the crow to Hell. It was to take earth from there to harden the earth's surface. The "judgment" had not yet reached Hell, and it was dry: "There the earth is always eternal, and will not end, even if judgment comes." The crow carried out its mission of bringing soil from the underworld, but what was to be the complement of earth in the dwelling of humans was lacking:

> Then the old man was pleased. And so again they were happy that they had everything, that all was arranged. The only thing lacking was fire. But a fox also was successful here. The fox said, "I am going to bring fire." Then he went there where the crow had gone to bring earth. The fox returned there to bring fire. Because there was fire there. Then the fox went there, asking for permission to warm himself a little. The fox sat there a while, and just as he was leaving, he put his tail into the fire and then ran away. They say that is why the end of the animal's tail is now half black. That is how that gentleman found fire and made everybody happy. (Miller 1956:100–104)

The setting up of the four pillars at the extremes of the earth after the flood is documented in the sources that tell us of the beliefs of the ancient Yucatec Maya. Landa (1982:62) says:

> Among the host of gods these people worshipped, they adored four of them called bacabs. They say they were four brothers that God placed, when he created the world, at the four places holding up the sky [so that] it would not fall. They also said about these bacabs that they escaped when the earth was destroyed by the flood.

And from the *Libro de Chilam Balam de Chumayel* (1973:63):

> And then, in a single rush, the waters came. And when the Great Serpent was stolen, the firmament came down and the earth sank. Then the four gods, the four bacabs, leveled everything. At the moment they did this, they installed themselves in their places in order to organize the yellow men.[11]

Ancient Nahua sources are similar to these. The message is transmitted surreptitiously in the hidden meaning of the dates, a frequent occurrence in ancient texts. The *Leyenda de los soles* (1945:119–20) places the flood between the names of two days: the first is the name of the food that was eaten when the world was flooded; the second, the name of the day the flood began and the hills disappeared. The names are significant. Both have the number four and also the opposition hot/cold: *nahui xochitl* (4 Flower) and *nahui atl* (4 Water). The *Historia de los mexicanos por sus pinturas* (1965:32) is even more precise. When the world was flooded and the heavens fell, order was reestablished with "four paths, to enter through them and to raise the sky."

Another part of this tale presents a different problem to be taken into account: the specification of the inchoation. It is the tale in which, after the flood, one or more human beings eat the dead fish that lie on the surface. The celestial gods, displeased with the smoke that rises from where the fish are being roasted, cut off the heads of those responsible, place them on their buttocks, and so, in some versions, give rise to monkeys (Williams García 1972:79–80; Horcasitas 1962; Foster 1945a:236; Münch Galindo 1983:161); in other versions this gives rise to dogs (P. Carrasco 1960:112–13). The cause for the punishment varies in some cases, but not the form it takes: conversion to monkeys (Anderson 1957; Ichon 1973:55–56; Gossen 1974:323); or to dogs (Anderson 1957; Gossen 1974:300–301). In others there is a transformation, but not to these forms (Stiles, Maya, and Castillo 1985; Holland 1963: 71; Hollenbach 1980; Merrifield 1967). In still another myth, the guilty one is beheaded, the head put on his buttocks, and he is changed into a buzzard (Hermitte 1970:27); in another version this is not the form of transformation (Dyk 1959:6–9).

The problem of whether in times past the inchoation of the inverted head was that of monkeys, dogs, or buzzards is easily settled by ancient writings. In the *Leyenda de los soles* (1945:120), Tata and Nene left the vessel when the waters receded, roasted the fish, irritated the celestial gods with smoke from the fire, were punished by beheading, their heads were placed on their behinds, and they were turned into dogs. On the other hand, the myth of the suns says that when the winds lashed against the beings of the Sun (era) of the Wind, the survivors took refuge in the trees and were changed into monkeys (*Anales de Cuauhtitlán* 1945:5; Alva Ixlilxochitl 1975–77a:7, 1975–77b:529; Muñoz Camargo 1981: fol. 152r–152v). It is this myth, and not another about the creation of monkeys or dogs, that should guide us.[12] We can accept that the myth of the Sun of Water, in which the people's heads were inverted, was in antiquity the beginning of dogs and that of the Sun of Wind ended with the inchoation of monkeys. The mixture of these two myths is the cause of the present variety. Also, after the Conquest the influence of the missionaries contributed to the predominance of one of the cataclysms, that of the flood.

This is the evidence from documental testimony, and it is strong. However, if we listen to a Mixe observation, a shadow of doubt remains that, from ancient times, both possibilities of inchoation existed. The Mixe say about the monkey, "God turned him over. His buttocks were placed where his face was, and his head where his buttocks were. There He pulled out a tail and He threw him into a tree. Don't you see that he hangs upside down, with his buttocks above and his head below?" (W. S. Miller 1956:209–10).

Once the problem of inchoation is solved—even with that shadow of a doubt—another great problem arises. Is the inchoation of dogs enough in such a complex and important myth? A terrible inundation of the world served only to produce dogs? It is not conceivable. The myth ought to institute something of cosmic dimensions. We notice that the part of the *Leyenda de los soles* referring to the Sun of Water makes a very rapid transition from the embarking of the couple to the roasting of the fish:

> Titlacahuan called the one named Tata and his wife who was called Nene, and he said to them, "Don't ask for anything else. Hollow out a very large *ahuehuete* [Mexican bald cypress, *Taxodium mucronatum*], and then you will enter it when the vigil begins and the sky sends the flood." Then they entered it. He covered them and he said, "You will eat only an ear of corn and your wife, one, as well." When they had eaten the kernels, they saw that the water was down. The trunk no longer moved.
>
> Then they removed the top and saw a fish. They started a fire and roasted it. The gods Citlalinicue and Citlallatonac looked down and said, "Gods, who has made a fire? Who has smoked up the sky?" At this point, Titlacahuan, Tezcatlipoca, came down, scolded them and said, "What are you doing, Tata? What are both of you doing?" Then he cut their throats and put their heads on their buttocks, turning them into dogs. (*Leyenda de los soles* 1945:120)

Where is the critical point for an installation equivalent to that of the pillars or the theft of the opossum? Precisely in this offense. What is produced on earth after the flood is the union of cold and subterranean (the fish) with the celestial and hot (the fire). The myth refers to the inception on earth of the combat between opposing divine forces. The inchoation of dogs is secondary.

Between the uniting of fire and fish on the one hand and the conversion of Tata and Nene into dogs on the other, certain acts of the characters make one believe that although they are bound together, there are two inchoations in the tale. The first, the fundamental one, is barely expressed; the second one receives the entire weight of the mentioned inchoation. Today myths give dogs and monkeys to the world. However, traces remain in today's myths of the ancient inchoation of the union of the superior and the inferior. The anger of the gods is aroused by the use of a celestial element, fire, in cooking. Today the Nahua of Mecayapan say:

> When they built the fire our God was immediately aware of what was happening on earth. He smelled that now his angel was burning. Well, we believe that fire is the angel of God, and because of that, he realized that those first men in the first times at the beginning of the world were burning his angel. (*Seis versiones del diluvio* 1983:12)

The problem of the single inchoation that has more than one value is different, and the investigator should also take this into account. Jensen, as mentioned in the preceding chapter, does not find a true division between what he defines as real myths and etiological myths. One of the reasons for the blurring of the boundaries is the real uncertainty about the degree of futility of the inchoation. It is not that the inchoation of cosmic processes is masked by minor processes. It is not a question of symbolism. The problem lies in the fact that different processes of different degrees of importance have the same value for the believer. What is said about some is understood to be the same for others.

In contemporary indigenous mythology there are several accounts that include the motif of the cutting of the tongue of a *lagarto*[13] or a lizard. The reasons for the cutting vary, as does the way the cutting is done. If the tongue is chopped off, the animal species is characterized by a shortened tongue. If the tongue is split, the species will forever have a forked tongue (Foster 1945a:199; Münch Galindo 1983:167–68; Law 1957; González Cruz and Anguiano 1984). In modern indigenous classifications, the form of the tongue seems to be very important. The tongues of reptiles are noteworthy and at times impressive, above all if they are associated with a poisonous bite; it is enough to recall the long, forked tongue of the beaded lizard [*Heloderma horridum*]. It is not unusual, then, that the peculiarities of the tongues of reptiles are frequently mentioned in oral literature.[14] But we also know, as mentioned in chapter 18, and by what is clearly demonstrated in Totonac and Tlapanec versions, that the caiman's tongue is the lightning brandished by the gods of rain (Loo 1987:160–61; Ichon 1973:75, 79–80).[15] In accordance with the pattern, what will cutting the lagarto's tongue establish? It would establish its zoological characteristic, as well as the nature of lightning. The short tongue of the caiman and lightning are inchoated at the same point in the tale. One is not the symbol of the other. Tongue and lightning have the same nature.

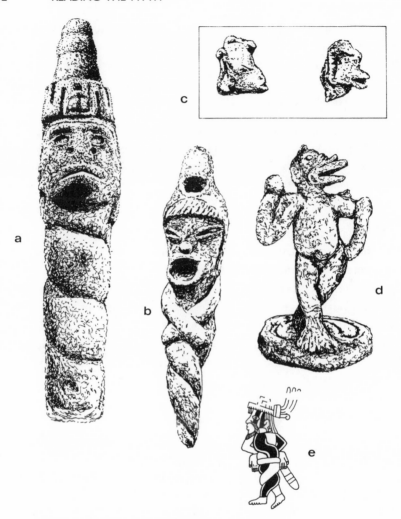

Figure 16. Helical Quetzalcoatl representations
    a. Andesite sculpture (195 cm. high) representing the god Quetzalcoatl-
       Ehecatl, possibly from Castillo de Teayo, Veracruz, Rautenstrauch-Joest
       Museum, Cologne
    b. Clay whistle from Tlapacoya (14 cm. high), National University of Mexico,
       Museum of Arts and Sciences
    c. Small Preclassic period ceramic heads, Tlapacoya-Zoapilco, Valley of
       Mexico. Niederberger Betton compares their profile with that of the Ehecatl-
       Ozomatli found in the subway excavation in *Paleopaysages et Archeologie pré-*
       urbane du Bassin de Mexico, 2:433.
    d. Ehecatl-Ozomatli (63 cm. high) found in the subway excavation, Mexican
       National Museum of Anthropology. The body of the monkey with the mask
       of the Wind God is twisted and rises over a spiral serpent.
    e. The God 9 Wind with a helical body, *Códice Vindobonensis,* plate 5-48

It is true that many of us have lost the joy of inviting celestial beings to drink wine from the immense goblet of the Big Dipper. We are the outside analysts of the tales about gods that are alien to us. But at least there remains for us the pleasure of facing the challenge of texts that promise discoveries of ever more profound meanings. But aside from the direct dialogue of the poet with the gods, and also aside from our investigation, there is the aesthetic pleasure of the adventures in the time of origin, a pleasure that unites unknown singers with their indeterminate audience. Aristotle, a profoundly wise man, confessed emotionally in his last writings, "The more isolated and solitary I am, the more I have come to love myths" (Jaeger 1946:367–68).

The inhabitants of Paradise were unchanging,
and because of that, they had no need
to reproduce themselves.

Roger Bartra,
La jaula de la melancolía

The time has come to explain two points that have been pending in this essay. The first one, a proposed definition of myth applicable to the Mesoamerican religious tradition. It will not be a definition claiming to have universal applicability. The second is an opinion about the value of inferences from antiquity in the study of this tradition. In addition to these two points, a very brief evaluation of the general contents of the book will be given, an evaluation made with the awareness that scientific works are never definite—new formulations are always latent. This is the great difference in dealing with myth, because myth creates the imperfection of the unchangeable.

Definition of Myth

Myth is a historic act [1] of production of social [2] thought,[3] immersed in currents of long duration. It is a complex act,[4] and its elements adhere to, and are organized chiefly around two mutually dependent nuclei. The first is a causal and taxonomic concept with holistic aspirations, which attributes the origin and nature of individual beings, classes,[5] and processes to strong conjunctions of personalized forces. This concept that coincides with the actions and thoughts of human beings about themselves and their surroundings, and which is manifested in expressions, behaviors, and other heterogeneous actions, distributed in the different domains of social action. The second nucleus is the construction of tales that refer to the conjunctions of personalized forces with respect to sequences of events of a social nature; this product is expressed in narrations, principally in the form of oral tales.

The Value of Inferences

The concept of a religious act as a historical act immersed in currents of long duration allows the investigator to make use of constant comparisons and inferences during the whole span of the religious tradition. This has been a deeply rooted practice in Mesoamerican studies and in ethnological investigations of Mexican and Central American peoples. It is a practice that has regularly led to the solution of difficult problems in the study of the whole of this religious tradition. However, the use of inferences has been criticized from two different viewpoints.

From the historical point of view, there is the question of explaining the enormous persistence of religious acts across such an eventful history, in which very different socioeconomic arrangements have succeeded each other. It is a fundamental problem. Chapter 24, "Myth in the Time of History," gives one answer.

From a methodological perspective, there is also an interesting criticism due to the aversion many investigators feel toward the use of inferences by analogy. Where does this methodological criticism come from? In part from the erroneous or feeble results that a careless application of analogical inference has produced in some fields of knowledge. It is perhaps also due, in part, to an unjustifiable mapping of criteria from the field of pure logic onto the field of applied logic.

Some philosophers make a fundamental distinction in the field of pure logic, allowing deduction and excluding induction. Bertrand Russell called induction "a distorted deduction or a more or less methodical conjecturing, inadequate to formulate a correct inference." [6] It is up to philosophers to determine whether this distinction in the field of pure logic is justifiable. But that does not mean that this limitation must be transferred to the field of methodology (M. R. Cohen 1957:34). Both daily life and the strict exercise of science are nourished by analogy. To ignore the value of analogical reasoning in science is to forget the great scientific triumphs that have been achieved through it. There are thousands of examples, of which one will suffice: starting from the knowledge of how sound is propagated, it was possible to discover the wavelike propagation of light.

In the study of humankind, the rejection of inference through analogy comes chiefly from some archeological schools, among them the one called "new archeology." Allison Wylie (1985), in a brilliant study, gives a historical summary of the problem and refutes the charges made by archeology of methodological distortion and uncertainty due to analogical reasoning. The greatest argument for the rejection of analogy is based on the incorrect use made of it in the comparison of vestiges from a distant past with the presence of similar material objects—and concomitant ways of life—in societies studied by ethnologists. From experiences of its inadequate use and, above all, of its failures, the disrepute of this kind of reasoning has been generalized. However, it must be acknowledged, the criticism has also produced more scientific attitudes than just one of rejection, among them those that search for criteria to distinguish between different kinds of analogy (Hodder 1982:16–24) and that suggest dependable bases for their application (Ascher 1961), so that archeology will continue to have this powerful methodological instrument at its disposal.

The disrepute of analogy also applies to studies of religion. The value of analogical inference has been categorically rejected for religious history, and specifically with regard to the possibility of comparing different epochs of the Mesoamerican religious tradition (Kubler 1972). This kind of denial leads nowhere. A valid debate on analogical inference is not so much about its acceptance or rejection, as the strictness of its application and the imagination that must be developed—in each specific field of study—to create paths along which this inference, combined with many diverse methodological and technical resources, can achieve greater levels of plausibility. Copi (1986:411) tells us that "although no argument through analogy is deductively valid, in the sense of having conclusions derived from premises by logical necessity, some are more persuasive than others." It is a problem of degree of attainable probability.

For what kind of problem must we refine analogical induction when we study myth? In the tradition we are studying, the strong persistence of mythic elements is not debatable. The great number of characters, motifs, plots, sequences, and meanings that appear, both in the older accounts of the myths of Mesoamerica and in those collected in our own time, prove in a more than sufficient manner the magnitude of the persistence. Investigation by means of analogical inference must be directed, on the one hand, to the search for very particular elements in the myth, such as structures, meanings, the lack of something in historical or ethnological accounts that disturbs the investigator. On the other hand, and in investigations where analogical inference is only one of the components of study, research should look for historical laws that explain the processes of conservation, substitution, or loss of mythic elements.

How can the most plausible conclusions be reached in the investigation of mythic acts? Historians face a complex task. First they have to record similarities and differences in the most apparent level of the myth in order to pose, on the basis of comparisons, possible inferences. But to stop at this first step is to accept results that are too weak. Among the analogous relationships compared for their logical transferability at this stage, coincidences can exist that do not result from a common causal basis. The similarity applies only to a superficial level. Inversely, elements of dissimilar appearance may be differing manifestations of the same underlying reality. Myth is a polyvalent act. Historians must continue in their search for an explanation of the historical act. This search forces them to go from one level to another, following the causal relationships that link the entire aggregate of systematizations, normativities, governing principles, primary functions, and taxonomies. They must find the concepts and relationships that are formed in daily social behavior (in which tradition, reason, congruence, opposition, and conflicts play a part) and that generate, conserve, modify, or lose the myth. Because the resemblances are fundamental and not just apparent, establishing inferences is more certain on this level. The transfer is not done blindly, but based on what is pertinent. Along with an explanation of resemblances, there should be an explanation of differences, because the course of history is a river of variables. Historians must account for the unity of what underlies and what is apparent in myth and the historical processes by which the myth is created, preserved, transformed, or lost.

Looking Ahead

This essay proposes the study of myth in its historical dimension. It avoids recommending precise techniques that would allow the student to discover the meanings of the text through quasi-mathematical operations. On the contrary, it recommends the use of as many diverse techniques as researchers might wish,[7] in as much variety as their own imaginations allow, including of course the so-called "hard" technologies, because history is, as Braudel (1974:107) states, a complex science. It will not be the kind of techniques, but the rigor with which the method is developed and the techniques applied, that will determine the scientific quality of the investigation. When Raymundo Mier (1984:10) evaluates the deconstructionist approach of Greimas (a model well accepted for the analysis of literary texts, means of communication, popular tales, and the structure of fantasies dealt with by psychoanalysis), he thinks its unusual success is due to several factors, among them the possibility of applying the model without the need to know the antecedents and theoretical bases that went into the construction of the text. In this essay the opposite is proposed: that investigators penetrate into the global complexity of the historical act under study. The path to understanding myth is complicated, since myth is an ideological act.

The proposal is not completely original. These are old practices used by Mesoamericanists when studying myth in its historical dimension. The Mesoamerican religious tradition has been explored with these approaches in order to compare and draw inferences analogically, to look for underlying meanings in the texts, and to go deeper into the functions of myth. What is original in this essay is the intention of opening the entire problem for discussion and also the rejection of that fragmentation in vogue in studying myth that allows everyone to "do their own thing" without a prior global vision. For a good investigation it is necessary to find the correct dimension of the object of study.

Does this imply that the study of myth in smaller spatial and time dimensions is not recommended? On the contrary; it is highly recommended, as long as the studies are placed in the global context of the Mesoamerican religious tradition. The nature of this essay has required a hasty run through a long time and a vast territory. This breadth allows for an understanding of the creation; but it does so to the detriment of understanding the creators. Accurately situated, myth should also be studied in the short time frame, in which those who gave it life and use it can be appreciated, people of flesh and blood who live in a condition of colonialization, seeing others established on their territory who destroy the environment in the name of the national economy, people who destroy their ways of life and thought in the name of civilization and salvation.

Looking ahead, will it be worth the time and trouble to test the proposals in this essay beyond the spatial and temporal limits of Mesoamerica? I believe that even more surprises await us when we compare more carefully the myths of the different American territories. As to the traditions of other continents, no doubt some things will be useful, but that is beyond my competence.

My task will be to continue the study of Mesoamerican ideology in visual representations. There someday will be found, among many other old acquaintances, my friend the opossum, gyrating to cast fire on the surface of the earth.

NOTES

Chapter 1 The Comings and Goings of a Marsupial

1. As Matieyka (1976:197) summarizes the point, "for Voloshinov the study of signs is a study of ideology, and the philosophy of language is the philosophy of signs."

2. *Chironectes minimus.* In Chiapas this little animal has the names water opossum and water fox. It can be found in the municipalities of Juárez, Reforma, Catazajá, and Ocosingo (Alvarez del Toro 1977:13).

3. Some say, however, that the meat is acceptable, providing the disagreeable odor is eliminated by proper cooking (Alvarez del Toro 1977:11).

4. In the Maya region it has been called fox since the sixteenth century. It should be understood that Abreu Gómez's myth *"El zorro"* really refers to the opossum. When the animal begs the creator Tamaychi to give him a way to deceive his enemies, the god tells him that when he is trapped, he is not to move, let his ears droop, and to simulate death (Abreu Gómez 1985:109). The same is true of the *"Historia de Don Zorro y el hombre,"* in which the protagonist is characterized by his ability to feign death (Incháustegui 1987:331–33). In Tabasco a distinction is drawn between the fox, with a hairy tail, and the opossum, or naked-tail fox.

5. There is a Mopan myth about the *zorra* [fox] that steals maize with the help of ants and the gods of thunder (J. Thompson 1975:418–19). As we will see later on, the honor of that theft belongs to the opossum.

6. In Zohapilco, a lake region in the southwest of the Valley of Mexico, Manantial phase (Niederberger 1976:31, pl. II-2; and see fig. 13 e, below).

7. As a guide consult Seler (1961:506–13). There are interesting references to figures in Brambila Paz et al. (1980:51–53).

8. The name *Ch'amacil* in fact corresponds to "foxes," since fox in Yucatecan Maya is *chamac, ch'amak,* and *ch'umak* (Barrera Vásquez et al. 1980:94, 292, 360). Below in chapters 18 and 19, note the opposition of coyote/opossum among the Quiche.

9. For representations of these helical noses in Zapotec depictions of the opossums, see Caso and Bernal (1952:267–68, 271–72).

10. For example in the Huichol myth told by Renteria. See the beginning of chapter 17, below.

11. Among the Totonac (Williams García and García Ramos 1980:31; Ichon 1973:95–96); among the Nahua (Taggart 1983:103–4); and among the Tepehua (Williams García 1972:67).

12. Among the Cuicatec (*Relatos, mitos y leyendas de la Chinantla* 1981:56–57). It must be taken into account that some myths are about the opossum himself, under the names of *zorro* or *zorra.*

13.   Jacques Galinier, pers. com., March 23, 1987, referring to the Otomi in the south of the Huaxteca.

14.   María Montoliu was told the tale in Chan Kom, Yucatan, in 1973.

15.   In the northwestern part of the state of Morelos (Ingrid Rosenblueth, pers. com., August 5, 1985).

16.   Of the physical features of the opossum, "the pouch of the females, as well as the anterior scrotum of the penis of the males, are peculiar characteristics of these creatures" (Ceballos González and Galindo Leal 1984:47).

17.   Three examples will suffice: Rendón 1970; the Tzeltal story, "*El tlacuache y los leones*," published in the magazine *México Indigena*; and the Nahua tale published by Pury (1982:71, 86–92).

Chapter 2   Home of the Gods

1.   It is useful to recall the relationship of myth, ideology, and history as it is set forth by Marx and Engels (1987:676): "We recognize only one science, the science of history. History, considered from two points of view can be divided into the history of nature and the history of mankind. . . . Ideology itself is one of the aspects of this history [the history of humanity]."

2.   I do this briefly, since there are summaries of the polemic in the history of the studies of myth in Mexico (Campos 1982:11–17, 51–76; Moedano Navarro 1975).

3.   According to Edmonson (1967:366), the limits of Mesoamerican influence in folkloric narrative are virtually impossible to determine.

4.   Horcasitas (1953) gives a general survey. Metraux (1948) provides interesting variations. Boas (1968:438) refers to a myth widely spread from the American Arctic to Vancouver Island.

5.   This solar myth has many versions in Mexico (Law 1957).

6.   See, for example, Hunt (1977:46), who based her judgment on the knowledgeable opinions of Jiménez Moreno, Kirchhoff, and Caso.

7.   Among these, Brinton ([1882] 1970) and Spence ([1914] 1977). Although the form of the myths cited is too free, Spence offers interesting opinions on Mesoamerican mythology.

8.   In reality the outlook is not good. There is far less recording of native oral literature than its importance warrants. Regarding this consult Edmonson (1967) and Horcasitas (1978), who is not so optimistic in his study of the oral narrative of the Nahua: "According to the 1970 census, the language is still spoken by some 750,000 people and we have only 200 printed pages to learn about oral Nahuatl narrative!" Neither is there an abundance of anthologies for the diffusion of contemporary indigenous myths, although we can cite a few good published works, such as Scheffler (1983).

9.   Horcasitas (1978) is discouraging when he refers in particular to the oral narrative of the Nahua: "Only 15 of the 105 narrations [mentioned in his book] have commentary or interpretation (some fifteen printed pages in all)."

Chapter 3   Point of Departure

1. Poincaré's (1952:143) teachings are relevant here:

It is often said that experiments should be made without preconceived ideas. That is impossible. Not only would it make every experiment fruitless, but even if we wished to do so, it could not be done. Every man has his own concept of the world, and this he cannot easily lay aside. We must, for example, use language, and our language is necessarily steeped in preconceived ideas. But they are unconscious preconceived ideas, which are the most dangerous of all.

2. That is, polythetic groups will form. See Sneath and Sokal (1973:20–23) concerning the difference between monothetic groups (possession of a unique set of features is both sufficient and necessary for membership in the group) and polythetic groups (members share the greatest possible number of traits but no single one is necessary or sufficient).

3. Neither did it exist among the ancient Maya (Rivera Dorado 1986b:33).

4. There is relevance in Marx's remarks on being able to understand history through the complexity of bourgeois society:

Bourgeois society is the most complex and developed historical organization for production. The categories that express its conditions and an understanding of its organization allow one, at the same time, to understand the organization and the relations of production in all its forms in past societies, over whose ruins and elements this society was erected and whose vestiges, still not overcome, it continues to carry, while, at the same time, what formerly was merely an indication, developed into full significance. . . . The Christian religion was able to help us understand previous mythologies in an objective way only when it accepted up to a certain point—its own self criticism. (1977:64–66)

5. Marx (1977:64–66) emphatically denied the relevance of applying the same concepts to different historical realities, when he criticized the method of economists who erased all historical differences, seeing the bourgeois form in all kinds of societies.

6. Wheelwright (1965) divides the focuses into three types: as a kind of concept (primary myth); as a narration of deliberate literary production (romantic myth); and as a complex product of a more developed cultural state (consummatory myth), although he recognizes the difficulty of distinguishing between the last two types.

Chapter 4   The Other Time

1. Among the Nahua (González Cruz and Anguiano 1984). Among many others, the Totonac speak clearly of the division of the great time of the ancestors and the present one as being the appearance of the Sun (Kelly 1966:395–96).

2. Among the Ixil, the rooster's crowing is so important that although their ritual day begins at midnight, they do not consider that a day has begun until the cock crows (Colby and Colby 1986:58).

3. Among the Huichol, he is also Teakata, the sick one, a youth covered with pustules (McIntosh 1949:20).

NOTES TO PAGES 36 TO 55

4. I use here Needham's definition of class: "A conceptual group of things due to the particular characteristics which in one way or another associate them" (Needham 1979:3).

5. Although this does not mean that one must consider simplicity and plainness as the principles of the natural sciences. Simplicity is much appreciated in theories and hypotheses in the natural sciences, but one must acknowledge that in hypotheses and theories simplicity alone does not justify preference (Hempel 1984:67–74).

6. J. L. Furst (1978:56) believes that although the Genesis-like descriptions of Fray Gregorio García sound suspiciously Judeo-Christian, the traditions they describe are essentially native.

7. I translate the word *otlaneltocac* as "order was established." Literally it means "the foundation was obeyed."

8. The text is incorrect. It says *chicuhnauh nepamichan*.

9. For example, Graulich (1983a and 1987a). I have also emphasized this aspect (López Austin 1975).

10. The Marind-anim of New Guinea call the beings of original time and the creative beings among them *demas*. They possess human as well as plant and animal forms, and ceased to exist when the creation was complete.

11. Compare this version with the one mentioned by Bunzel (1952:429).

12. Two sources of Mexica tradition, even though they divide the suns into different periods, give them the same total duration, 2,028 years. All the periods given are multiples of 52 (Nicholson 1971:399).

13. As primary sources the following can be consulted: Ruiz de Alarcón (1953) and *Leyenda de los soles* (1945). The names of the gods can be found in Caso (1967:189–99).

Chapter 5   The Other Space

1. There are numerous examples. Among the recordings of Ancient Mayan customs, I will cite only Landa (1982:49–50) and García de Palacio (1983:88). The first refers to the Maya of Yucatan and the second to the Chontal of El Salvador and Honduras.

2. Among numerous works about the persistence of the calendar consult La Farge II and Byers (1931); M. Nash (1957); Neuenswander (1981); Colby and Colby (1986); Tedlock (1982).

3. One must remember the alternation of opposites: (hot/cold, light/darkness, dryness/wetness) in the flow of time. Regarding this, see Umberger (1986).

4. The magic procedure in Ruiz de Alarcón (1953:162–65); the interpretation in López Austin (1975).

5. *Códice Florentino* (1979: bk. 6, ch. 20, fol. 86v). The translation from Nahuatl is mine. In the same folio, Sahagún gives as a version of the above: "No one escapes the descents and ascents of this world, and the tempests and winds that are in it, nor the falsehoods, solaces, and the deceit and lies therein."

6. The *cantil* is a poisonous snake, *Agkeistrodon bilineatus* (see Santamaría 1974).

7.   Compare the two versions of the myth "The Sterile Woman." It is interesting that the name *moctezumas* is given to archeological remains in many parts of the country.

8.   Regarding this see López Austin (1988, 1:242–44).

9.   In the modern Lacandon version of this myth, the god *Hachäkyum*, creator of human beings and of the stars, did not wish the people to see what he did in the distance with Our Lady. He took their eyes, toasted them on the *comal* [griddle], and then returned them to their sockets. Because of this, their visual capacity was reduced (Bruce 1974:128–32).

Chapter 6   The Passage

1.   Among the investigators who have emphasized the flow of divine forces as reasons for human sacrifice are González Torres (1985) and Duverger (1983).

2.   The Quiche are among the indigenous Maya who still personify days and years (Carmack 1979:381–82). The Ixil not only believe that the days are gods, but that they transfer their attributes to the beings in the human world (Colby and Colby 1986:143).

3.   The meaning of the name *Tamoanchan* is not entirely clear. It has been suggested that it derives from other indigenous languages. For example J. Thompson (1972:104) says that the name derives from Mayan and means "the heaven of the muan bird," and Nicholson (1971), also assuming that it derives from some Mayan language, says that it may mean "place of the bird-serpent." See also López Austin (1985b).

4.   I must also add a reason that, because it is personal, is less valid. My specialization is in the study of the history of the Nahuatl-speaking peoples who inhabited the central highlands of Mexico. I have a tendency, whether I wish it or not, to interpret starting from that knowledge.

5.   *Quetzalmizquitl, quetzalpochotl, quetzalahuehuetl,* and *quetzalhuexotl,* respectively (*Códice Tudela* 1980: fols. 97r, 104r, 111r, and 118r). Other sources vary. *Historia tolteca-chichimeca* (1976:156–57) says that the ceiba is east, the precious mesquite is north, the *iczotl* palm tree is west, and to the south, the rainbow-hued century plant.

6.   The colors vary in the different Mesoamerican traditions. The Nahua frequently distributed them thus: red to the east, black to the north, white to the west, and blue to the south. See J. Thompson (1934). Soustelle's opinions (1959:79–84) are also interesting; this text was subsequently published in his book (Soustelle 1982:157–63).

7.   These colors are: red, green, yellow, and blue. They are the same colors Acosta (1962:282) associates with the four divisions of the years.

8.   In an inverse sense, the four trees can depict the characteristics of the central tree of the universe. This point is noted by Sotelo Santos (1988:75).

9.   *Códice Telleriano-Remensis* (1964–67: pt. 1, pl. 2). This same glyph appears drawn on the mantle of the god Macuilxochitl. See fig. 12 of this essay.

10.   A strange element of the tree can also tie it to Tamoanchan: there are five dots that seem to be day numerals, but they do not bear one of the twenty day names.

The number five is related to Tamoanchan. On a nameless day five, the gods broke the branches off. For that reason the expulsion of the gods was celebrated on the days with the number five (*Códice Telleriano-Remensis* 1964–67: pt. 2, pl. 7).

11. *The Slippery Earth* by Burkhart (1989) was published after the original Spanish edition was in press. In it she makes a precise distinction based on the difference between Christian and Mesoamerican concepts of sin.

12. Not only in the old tales. In the myth just mentioned, when the people expelled by their creator Nanahuatl reached the world, they did so by way of the Pánuco River.

13. Against the notion that this belief is of Biblical origin, see López Austin (1973:92–93).

14. See, for example, the house of Lisibe and Lisiya full of seeds (Portal 1986: 47).

15. For example, the belief present-day Chontal of Oaxaca hold in this respect (P. Carrasco 1960).

16. In the *Primeros memoriales* (1905: fol. 85v, 110) there is a short list of dreams.

17. It is the Chol story "The man-tiger." The Bachajontecos are the Tzeltal population of the town of Bachajón, Chiapas (Alejos García 1988: 35).

18. Concerning the ancient Nahua concept of the cave, see López Austin (1973: 61–65); Heyden (1973, 1981); Broda (1982).

Chapter 7   How Do You Measure a Myth?

1. I take the concept of totality from Kosik (1983:55, 63):

> Totality does not mean all the facts. Totality means: reality as a structured, dialectical whole in which *any fact* (classes of facts, groups of facts) can be rationally understood. . . . The dialectical concept of the whole does not mean that the parts have an internal interaction and connection with the whole, but also that the whole cannot be made into an abstraction situated above the parts, since the whole creates itself by the interaction of the parts.

2. See the *nearika,* or yarn picture, by Ramón Medina Silva, published by P. Furst (1972b: fig. 6).

3. One must start from a pseudoconcretion and search for the essential meaning; and one must agree when Kosik (1983:28) states that "reality is the unity of the phenomenon and the meaning."

4. Gramsci (1967:95) says, "An individual may participate in numerous circles, more than one thinks, and it is through these circles that the individual joins the human species."

Chapter 8   Beliefs and Narrations

1. Language, according to Williams (1980:44–45), is not a relationship *between* some and others, but of some *with* others. Voloshinov (1976:24) says that "Conscience

takes on form and life in the material created by an organized group in the process of social interchange."

2. Prediction from the tun cycle was based on fundamentally empirical procedures, while that of the tzolkin was based on the art of combining the forces of destiny.

3. See Hyman (1965). Hvidtfelt (1958) is a polemical work on the derivation of ritual from myth in Mesoamerican thought.

4. S. Thompson (1965:172) accurately points out the circularity of the argument.

5. For example the bathing ritual for the newborn among the Chatino (Bartolomé and Barabas 1982:110).

6. I have written about these processes elsewhere. This form of magical action is frequent in the tradition under discussion, and has interesting parallels elsewhere in the world. For example the spells used by the Baruyas of New Guinea to frighten away the *kulalinna* spiders, which they consider to be dangerous to their orchards (Godelier 1974:356–57).

7. Scenes like these, particularly those of God L and the five lords of the underworld, can be admired in Coe (1978:16–21, 34–39).

8. "An angel as a sign of water" (Landa 1982:64).

9. On the influence of rhythm on myth, see Pérez (1986).

10. The bibliography on these general processes is extensive. Examples include Jiménez Moreno (1971a), Madsen (1957), and Reyes García (1961).

Chapter 9   To Think That Way

1. From the magazine *Translation* (July–September 1971), published by the Summer Institute of Linguistics; quoted in Fábregas (1980).

2. Compte (1984:27–47) noted three theoretical stages in thinking: theological, metaphysical, and positivism. Frazer (1956: ch. 49, 796–98) proposed a progression from magic to religion and from religion to science.

Chapter 10   The Nature of the Gods I

1. There are important studies of the difficult problem of the fusion of Mesoamerican religion and Christianity in general, as well as those dealing with beliefs or specific cult practices. Nutini's *Todos Santos in Rural Tlaxcala* (1988) is an interesting book about the cult of the dead, based on the theory of syncretism (see particularly the Introduction, the Conclusion, and chapters 1, 2, 3, 4, and 11).

2. According to J. Thompson (1978:31).

3. On this question see also Townsend (1979), among others.

4. Regarding the problem of ethnological analogy, see an evaluation of projections in chapter 28, below.

5. See note 2 in chapter 5.

6. Among today's peninsular Maya, according to Villa Rojas (1978:298). The same thing is believed among the Zapotec (Fuente 1977:268).

7.   See Jansen (1982, 1:136) for this idea among contemporary Mixtec. According to them, when the spirit leaves the wood it becomes harder.

8.   The text is in error. It should read Uuc-Ahau, not Bolon-Ahau.

9.   *Ca oitoloc, ca oyocaloc in topan, in ilhuicac, in mictlan.* After translating these words to Spanish, García Quintana (1980) comments, "It means that it was determined in a supernatural otherworld, the world of the gods."

10.   Huizinga (1984:141) generalizes the concept of the fight between opposites: "The agonistic element in archaic philosophy is shown, it seems to me, in a particular way in the fact that there is a tendency to see in the cosmic process an eternal struggle between primary oppositions that are lodged in the nature of all things, the same as the Chinese opposition of yang and yin."

11.   It is interesting to compare the above with what Köhler (1982) says.

Chapter 11   *The Nature of the Gods II*

1.   Although he has a different concept of the Mesoamerican gods, Brundage (1979:55–56) also considers the Mexica gods to be qualities.

2.   González Ramos (1972:136); Benítez (1985:96). The Cora also say that souls who repose in the place of the dead, called Mucchita, can be seen by day in the form of flies, and at night in their own form (Dahlgren 1961).

3.   The idea that flies bear human souls is not unique, and it still appears in literary imagination today. Monterroso (1975:81), a Guatemalan speaking from a different tradition than the Quiche, says, "When you die it is probable, and sad, that a fly suffices to carry your poor errant soul who-knows-where. The flies transport, inheriting their charge through infinity, the souls of the dead, of our forefathers, so they continue to be near us, accompanying us, bent on protecting us. Our small souls transmigrate through them and they accumulate wisdom and know all that we do not dare to know. Perhaps the last to transmit our clumsy western culture will be the body of that fly that has continued to reproduce itself without improving itself through the centuries."

4.   Born officially under that sign, that is, offered that day to the gods in a ceremony comparable to baptism.

5.   For the connection existing between maize, the spiral (the shape of the ammonite shell), and the Sun, see Ichon (1973:105).

6.   The wind was conceived as a forerunner to rain.

7.   Authors such as González Torres, Graulich, and Duverger have written various works about the effect of human sacrifice on the circulation of energy. My view may be found in López Austin (1988, 1:375–80).

8.   See invocation 13, recorded by Ruiz de Alarcón, in López Austin (1972).

9.   See the interesting comment by Roys (*Ritual of the Bacabs* 1965:3n4). Roys believes that the first word (*ch'ab*, "creation") has a relationship with the masculine principle, and the second (*akab*) with the feminine principle. Abreu Gómez (1985: 58) says, "There are two kinds of shadows, one hot, that is the daughter of the Sun, and the cold one that is the daughter of the Moon. A man's life lasts as long as his body and his shadow are together. If the shadow becomes thinner or is separated or

another person steps on it, death comes. Only certain sorcerers can speak with the cold shadow. The hot shadow is mute."

10.   The verb *elehuia* (to covet) appears copiously in the invocations of the seventeenth century.

11.   Concerning the concepts of linear time and cyclical time and their supposed opposition, it is interesting to consult Ricoeur (1985), and particularly the hypothesis presented there on page 19.

12.   References to supernatural dangers are numerous; I note only the last one mentioned. It was believed that young turkeys "died" when they were contaminated by the filth of those who had committed adultery. The "filth" was the impurity of sin (*Augurios y abusiones* 1969:85).

13.   In early colonial Nahuatl, *chone* appears (Molina 1944: fol. 21v) in the composition of the words *chonequiztli*, a "delicate or tender person," and *chonecocoya*, "to be possessed." I have not been able to understand its meaning.

14.   And during the section of the annual cycle that corresponds to the twelfth twenty-day unit (August 9–28), "only after the ceremony can the farmer touch the ears of corn".

15.   See the Tlaxcalteca case recorded by Muñoz Camargo (1981: fol. 116r). Another example is the blade of Curicaueri, which the Tarasca lord Tariacuri gave to his nephews. Tariacuri said to them, "I want to give you a part of Curicaueri, which is one of the knives he has with him; and you will wrap it in cloth, you will take it there, and you will bring your wood to it; and you will build a house with an altar where you will put the knife. They departed with the knife and passed the lagoon and began to make a *cu* [temple], and a house for the priests, and a house called the Eagle house, and a sanctuary for the knife Tariacuri had given them" (*Relación de las ceremonias y ritos . . .* 1977:126).

16.   See P. Carrasco (1971) regarding the customs of today's Tarasca. For those of the Zapotec, see Fuente (1977:344).

17.   Knowing these beliefs, P. Carrasco (1971) relates the Tarasca word for "idol" (*thaRés*) to *thaRé*, "old." He may be correct, but it is also noteworthy that Sahagún (1956, 3:20) said about the people of Michoacan that, "The god they had was called Taras, from which the Michoacan people took their name; they also say Tarasca."

18.   See Tozzer (1982:120–21), concerning the making of sacred braziers by the Lacandon.

Chapter 12   The Nature of Gods III

1.   Some Maya believe that a person can have three to thirteen animal companions. One of them is the "true one." If that one dies, the person dies (Hermitte 1970: 44–45).

2.   A modern example of this belief is that of the Tzotzil, among whom the god who frees people from the pregnant mountain is called Manojel-Tojel (Guiteras Holmes 1965:237).

3.   There is an interesting and abundant literature on the rustic gods: García

de León (1969), Vogt (1966a), Holland (1963:92–98), Villa Rojas (1978), Montoya Briones (1964:158–65), Ichon (1973:123–56). For ancient Nahua concepts about hills, see López Austin (1973:61–65), Heyden (1973), and Broda (1982).

4.   The name nagual is given both to the being who can introduce one of its souls into another, and to the one who undergoes such an invasion. The idea of a nagual as a cover for a force appears in the drawing called Nahuale Tlamacazqui, "The-Priest-who-has-a-nagual" (*Historia Tolteca-chichimeca* 1976: fol 10r). His name is written above a figure with long, priestlike hair, surrounded by a radiant halo. For more about nagualism, see Villa Rojas (1947), Aguirre Beltrán (1963:223–26, Saler (1969), Musgrave-Portilla (1982), and López Austin (1988, 1:363–74, 2:283–84). Signorini and Lupo (1989: 2.3.2.1, fol. 67–69) propose an interesting modification of my idea about the animistic force upon which nagualism is based.

5.   Concerning this problem of belonging to the Tarasca gods, see *Relación de las ceremonias y ritos* (1977:20, 32–33, 102). Among the Tarasca, foreign wives were not under the protection of their husband's god, but kept their own.

6.   Hvidtfeldt (1958:65–66), with a very different view, tends to give the word *téotl* in the Nahuatl language the meaning of "mana" rather than that of "god."

7.   In the descriptions of the birds *teutzinitzcan, teuquechol,* and *teutzanatl,* and in that of the stone *teutetl,* in *Códice Florentino* (1979: book 11, fol. 20v–21r, 53v, 209). Other meanings for téotl in composition are given in Swadesh and Sancho (1966: 67–68).

8.   A parallel case among the Nahua is Nappatecuhtli.

9.   Fr. J. de Cordova (1942: fol. 140v), from whose vocabulary the names of this god come, says, "without knowing who he was, they called him Infinite God with no beginning."

10.   This is my translation of *moyocoyani,* emphasizing the sense of "acting without a motive" conveyed by the verb *yocoya* with the reflexive prefix. The same meaning is given in the *Historia de los mexicanos por sus pinturas* (1965:24): "It means that he is all powerful, or that he does all things, without anyone offering resistance." Torquemada (1969, 2:40) speaks of "Moyocoyatzin, which means 'he who does whatever he wishes because there is neither resistance nor contradiction to his will (they believed) and that no one opposed him in anything, whether in heaven or on earth." León-Portilla (1959:167–68) translates the name in a very different sense, as "Lord who thinks himself into being or invents himself," based indirectly on Mendieta (1954, 1:95). However, Mendieta also refers in the same place to the arbitrary character of Moyocoyani: "He alone, through his authority and his will, does everything."

11.   The hegemony of the so-called "Triple Alliance," formed by Tenochtitlan, Tetzcoco, and Tlacopan in the fifteenth and sixteenth centuries, was apparently linked to the idea of three persons in the fire god, who was the mother and father of all the gods (López Austin 1985a).

12.   For an interpretation of these names, see López Austin (1985a).

13.   For examples of classifications, see: Caso (1953), Nicholson (1971); Kirchhoff (1972); Brundage (1979:66–75); Barthel (1968); P. Carrasco (1979); González Torres (1987); and based on native divisions, Vogt (1966a), Bunzel (1952:266–67). This author's classification is as follows: 1. The world, 2. natural phenomena, among them the sun and the cardinal points; 3. the saints, among them the Eternal Father and the

images of Christ in churches; 4. idols, that is, the ancient stone images; 5. the forces of destiny; 6. the bearers of death; 7. the patrons of productive activities; 8. the lords of justice, including dead human officials such as mayors; 9. the souls of the dead.

14.   P. Carrasco (1979) has a differing opinion of the role of Tlaloc as a patron god.

15.   Today the word *paga*, "payment," is used literally. For examples among the Nahua, Otomi, Totonaca, Tepehua, and Chatino: Bartolomé and Barabas (1982:118); Montoya Briones (1987); Ichon (1973:148–49).

16.   Gossen explains that the term *desear*, "to want," here means to pray sufficiently.

17.   Probably the nine places are the levels of the underworld. Remember that in today's mythology, the opossum steals tobacco from a subterranean region (Bartolomé and Barabas 1982:111–12).

18.   According to Andrews and Hassig (Ruiz de Alarcón 1984:160, 220, 227, 236, 360), Cuaton and Caxxoch may be regional variations of the Nahua gods of filth, of love, and of birth.

19.   An invocation collected by Ruiz de Alarcón; see López Austin (1972, invocation 11).

Chapter 13   Order

1.   In all these works there are fruitful attempts to find the taxonomy implicit in the lexicon.

2.   The literature is abundant. One of the best examples is Madsen (1960).

3.   See Foster (1987) and López Austin (1988, 1:270–82); both cite previous authors.

4.   This is Munz's (1986:112) proposition, based on Hayek's studies in *The Sensory Order*.

5.   Vogt's (1976:58–59) observation on the house and fields as models for the universe is very interesting.

6.   The quincunx is a symbol of an old Mesoamerican tradition, and it has always been of fundamental importance (Séjourné 1975:101–9).

7.   It is interesting to compare these practices with those of the Achi, as described by Neuenswander (1981).

8.   *Ilhuicatl*, among the ancient Nahua.

9.   Specifically to Radcliffe-Brown's proposal of 1951, not the one published in 1929. The former based the importance humans give to plants and animals on utilitarian reasons. The latter modified the former and considered that their importance rested on species that were "thinkable."

Chapter 14   Classifications

1.   Concerning these pairs in particular, see Ivanov (1979).

2.   Soustelle (1959:9–20) agrees with Seler.

3.   I have referred to this duality elsewhere. See López Austin (1961:87, 93–94;

1973:143; 1988, 1:75–76). In the latter work, I refer to the *tlaquiach* and the *tlalchiac* in vol. 1, p. 164. Also see what Graulich (1983b, 1987b:261–64) and Broda (1987) have to say on the topic.

4.   See the commentary of González Rodríguez (1987:335*n*43) on a letter from Giovanni Cubedu in Chínipas to Juan Antonio Balthasar in Mexico City, dated January 26, 1757.

5.   For this preference see the history of Mixcoatl, the warrior of Huexotzinco, a virgin chosen by the Sun to be killed in war (Sahagún 1956, 2:143).

6.   This is independent of possible real connections either now or in the remote past. Neither the taxonomic opposition *male/female* nor the grammatical categories of gender have an exact correlation with the actual or attributed sex of the objects they include. See Palmer (1978:156–57).

7.   This idea is also held by the Nahua of San Francisco Tecospa, for whom ice, hail, snow, and ice cream are hot. They explain that vegetation is "burned" by sleet and thus acquires a brown color (Madsen 1955).

8.   This point is based on Hallpike (1986:216–19).

9.   For example the *Códice Florentino* (1979: bk. 10, ch. 28, fol. 97r) says, "*icocolizyo in tonacayo ihuan in patli in inanamic,*" that is, "the illnesses of our body and their opposite medicines."

10.   Even more: the *east/west* axis is marked by the virile body of the Sun; the *north/south* axis, by that of the nocturnal bodies of the stars.

11.   I prefer to call them underworld, low sky (starting from the surface of the world), and high sky.

Chapter 15   The Gods Acquire History

1.   It is interesting to read what Lotman (1979) says, referring to the dichotomy in medieval literary texts of that which has a beginning and that which does not.

2.   In 1912 Durkheim (1968:13) said, "If by origin is meant a first absolute beginning, the question has nothing scientific about it and should be discarded. There is no original time at which religion began to exist."

3.   What Voloshinov (1976) says about the ideological sign applies. "The sign is a creation among individuals, a creation within a social medium. Therefore the element must first acquire an interindividual significance, and only then can it be converted into an object for the formation of a sign. In other words, only that which acquires social value can enter the world of ideology, take form, and be established there."

4.   Berger (1971:24) says that, "the fundamental coercive character of society is not based on its mechanisms for social control, but on its power to construct itself and impose itself as a reality."

5.   Brinton (1970:21) in his study of American myths pointed out this mental process, and said its rhetorical expression was called prosopopoeia.

6.   It is very interesting that the name "war captain" (*yaotequihua*) was also given to the patron god of the Mexica, Tetzauhteotl, sent to earth by the gods who inhabit the other world (Castillo 1966:70).

7. Cassirer (1951:145) introduces this stoic maxim in his explanation of magical belief.

8. The name of the god means "he who is like a curved piece of obsidian."

Chapter 16   Telling the Tale

1. The numbers used here are mine, based on the divisions and subdivisions of León-Portilla (1983).

2. In the text that refers to the dialogues between Christian priests and natives in 1524, the term *teotlahtolli* appears more than twenty times, all of them referring to the Bible (*Coloquios y doctrina . . .* 1986:110, 114, 116, 118, 120, 146, 158, 166, 168, 174).

3. The first, third, fourth, and fifth appear as nouns or verbal forms in *Códice Matritense* (1907: fol. 162v–165r) and *Códice Florentino* (1979: bk. 7, ch. 2, fol. 2v–7r); the second term in *Leyenda de los Soles* (1945: 1).

4. See what Todorov says about the orders of the text (Ducrot and Todorov 1974: 338–39).

Chapter 17   Invention

1. Foster (1945b) finds too much freedom in the interchange of episodes in the oral literature of Mexico.

2. It is the myth classified as number A1335.1 by S. Thompson (1955–57, 1:216).

3. As an example of opposition to this elitist concept, see Ginzburg (1982:184–85).

4. "What is called 'creative individuality' is only an expression of a fundamental policy, consistently and firmly established by the social orientation of an individual person" (Voloshinov 1976:116).

5. This does not mean that collective creativity has to come from societies that do not recognize the individual expression of human activity. I agree with Jakobson (1986b:17–18) when he states that collective creation is not alien even to a culture penetrated by individualism. "One has only to think about the anecdotes that run throughout today's media, in the form of rumors and gossip, in superstitions and the formation of myths, in social usages and style."

6. Although it is not part of our study, the question of the "ownership" of myths among the Winnebago (Radin 1978:122–23) is interesting in this respect.

Chapter 18   The Character I

1. Besides species of the genera *Marmosa, Philander* and *Caluromys, Didelphis marsupialis yucatanensis* and *D. m. cozumelae* are found in Yucatan (Hall and Nelson 1959, 1:5, 7–9).

2. In the myth both brothers have a skin disease. It is important to note that

because of Christ's solar nature, the southern Maya also consider him to be a man with a skin disease (Holland 1963:283; Colby and Colby 1986:162; *Seis versiones del diluvio* 1983:37).

3. Caso gives different forms of the Quiche names.

4. Two of the bacabs are represented with them, another with a tortoise shell, and the fourth with a spider web (J. Thompson 1964:142, fig. 10(2); Rivera Dorado 1985:179).

5. See figs. 10 and 11 of the present work.

6. J. Furst's (1978:166–68) opinion about the relationship of Lord 10 Lizard and Lady 11 Serpent to pulque and decapitation is interesting. See Caso (1963) and Jansen (1982, 1:206–17) on decapitation and pulque.

7. Today Christ should be added to this group, because of his strong solar nature. Among the Nahua of the Sierra Norte of Puebla, corn is the very flesh of Christ: "The Mesoamerican man whose cosmic destiny is to cultivate corn, finds in its different colors the attributes of Christ: white corn stands for purity (thus also for the Holy Virgin); red corn, the love of Christ for all men; red-and-white corn, Christ who sheds his blood (Christ of Holy Week with the little cross on his back is the symbol of tender corn, of Centeotl); yellow corn, the flesh of men, those of the last creation; blue corn, the celestial sky, the Celestial Father" (Segre 1987:60). Graulich (1987a) says that the hero of the myths "is often the Sun . . . he can also be identified with corn and with the regulation of the seasons." Also see Ichon (1973:105).

8. In the sixteenth century, *rosa* was a synonym of "flower."

9. Translator's note: Quiroz-Rodiles (1945) demonstrated that opossum-tail extract (from both fresh and dried tails) produced contractions in pregnant women as well as in rodent uterine tissue in vitro.

10. The forces of the gods flow along the helical paths and the same paths take human beings divine space-time. See, for example, the dream of the Ixil, when he waits to be given "the delivery of Day," that is, the power of divination. "I had risen to the sky, flying, and then I gave many turns, like airplanes do, many turns in the sky. I went up and came down through the heavens as the black vultures do . . ." (Colby and Colby 1986:77).

11. On the cold nature attributed to pulque, see López Austin (1988, 1:260–63; Fuente 1977:314).

12. Loo (1987) has pointed out the similarity between this Tlapanec myth and the Totonac myth published by Ichon (1973).

13. Lévi-Strauss (1968b:194–96) has an interesting comparison of this episode with South American myths.

Chapter 19   The Character II

1. Caso and Bernal (1952:267) note the traces of age in some Zapotec clay figures of the opossum, which also have a helix over the nose, two of them in the Transitional period. They mention another example of the elderly figure of the opossum: a head of Tlacochahuaya. See fig. 13, d and fig. 15, c of the present work.

2.   Today there is a Mopan myth similar to this ancient myth, in that two ants act as guides and the gods of thunder break open the store. But the hero in this myth from Belize is not Quetzalcoatl, but the fox (J. Thompson 1975:418–19). Remember the confusion in the region about the designation of the opossum, which is often called fox.

3.   The ancient Maya called Quetzalcoatl-Kukulcan Nacxit Xuchit, derived from the Nahuatl words *nacxitl* and *xuchitl*, "four feet" and "flower" (J. Thompson 1964: 133).

4.   Núñez de la Vega (1702: pt. 1, 9), speaking of the traditions of the Indians of Chiapas at the end of the seventeenth century, says that "the ceiba is a tree found in front of the Municipal Building in the plazas of all the towns, and they hold elections for mayors under it. They burn incense there and believe that from the roots of that ceiba comes their own lineage."

5.   In his article Nicholson refers to the relationship of Lord 9 Wind to the New Fire Ceremonies.

6.   *Ehecca, ecamalacutl quichihua, tlapitza, tlamamalli*. The word *tlamamalli*, translated as "something whirling," according to Molina (1944: fol. 125v) means "something swept or a burden on the back of the *tameme*."

7.   The sculpture is probably from the Castle of Teayo (*Glanz and Untergang des Alten Mexico* 1987, 2: fig. 163). See fig. 16, a of the present work.

8.   It is an anthropomorphic whistle with very long lips, a conical cap, and the body in the form of a twisted bar. The whistle comes from Tlapacoya and is now in the University Museum of Arts and Sciences at the National University of Mexico. See fig. 16, of the present work.

9.   See fig. 15, f of the present work. The drawing is a copy of a photograph given to me by Salvador Guil'liem, the archeologist responsible for the dig.

10.   Naturally in such abundant and extensive stories, there would have to be an anomalous version in which the astute one is the coyote and the one tricked is the opossum (Fe. Hernández 1925).

Chapter 20   Subjects Worthy of Being Related

1.   Vygotsky (n.d.:26, 42–43) says, "The primary function of language is communication, social interchange." And, "Egocentric language, taken from general social language, in due time leads to inner speech, which functions for autistic as well as symbolic thought."

2.   This is Cassirer's (1951:115–16) criticism of contemporary interpretations of myth, which in his judgment are not far removed, in spite of their complexity, from those formulated in 1609 by Francis Bacon in *The Wisdom of the Ancients*.

3.   See these two axes in Ichon (1973:35) or the Zapotec version of the four directions (Fuente 1977:348), "They are these: *so? be?* (north, where the wind comes from), *yas be?* (south, where the wind goes), *zuzilé* (east, where the dawn appears), and *zuzelé* (west, where night comes from)."

Chapter 21   Subjects Worthy of Being Believed

1. It is possible that the change from a small bird to a flea may have originated in some version in which the flea intervened as a secondary character. See the myth recorded by Colby and Colby (1986:197).

2. According to the Kekchi of Baja Verapaz, Guatemala (Schumann 1988), the maiden spilled water so that the old man would slip on the path. The latter avoided rolling down the slope by changing into a tree trunk. A very similar Pocomchi version is found in Mayers (1958:3–5).

3. The book makes it clear that the jícara served as a sounding box for the musical bow.

4. My translation "his house of round blue feathers" differs from that of Primo Feliciano Velázquez, in *Anales de Cuauhtitlán* (1945:8, 74). Both read *yxiuhtapalcal*, but he thinks it should be taken as *yxiuhhuapalcal*. If we keep the original reading, the translation might be "his house of turquoise-colored neck feathers." The morpheme *tapal* may derive from *tapalcatl*, the name of the feathers on the bird's neck and back, characterized by their curved shape.

5. See chapter 18. Chalchimmichhuacan, "the place of the owners of turquoise fish," is identified as Tamoanchan.

Chapter 22   The Functions of Myth

1. According to the positions of Malinowski and Radcliffe-Brown (Munz 1986:18).

2. Readers familiar with functionalist concepts are invited to proceed to the second half of the chapter, in which a useful concept of function in the study of myth is proposed, which will then be used to deal with specific problems.

3. Timasheff (1971:276) says that the "words function and functionality have different unrelated meanings in sociology and in social anthropology."

4. "I do not believe that this [eliminating the term] is feasible or desirable, because we need that kind of a concept, and we do not have any more adequate word at our disposal" (Nadel 1955:393).

5. Radcliffe-Brown (1935) denies calling himself a functionalist, although he admits that he constantly used the concept of social function.

6. Nadel (1955:394) says, "Unless we take this as a philosophical axiom, according to which everything that exists, exists for some reason, we will consider it simply as an assertion that is supported or falls according to whether or not it is confirmed."

7. This led to Lowie's (1974:286) question: "What group should we consider to be the bearer of this closed system: the family of the chief Omarakana, his village, the district of Kiriwina, the island of Boyowa, the Trobriand archipelago, the north zone of Massin, New Guinea, or perhaps all of Melanesia?"

8. For example, Leach (1978:99) states that "the central doctrine of all religion

is to deny that death implies the automatic destruction of the individual self." This pronouncement cannot be defended empirically.

9.   Girard (1983 : 27–28) makes all ritual a form of sacrifice, and through that sacrifice, the medium par excellence for freedom from uncontrollable violence, through channeled violence. "What is religious always tends to assuage violence, to impede its unfolding. Religious and moral behavior aim toward immediate nonviolence in daily life, and frequently in the longer term in ritual life, through the paradoxical intermediary of violence."

10.   "Orality has strength . . . that allows it to change the functions of the discourses, adapting them to their new needs and situations" (Valiñas 1985).

11.   Recall the quote by Douglas (1967) on mythic narrative: "In it each listener can find the reference to his own experience, myth can illustrate, comfort, dismay . . ." That individual experience also creates particular, individual functions in daily life.

12.   When the Spanish occupied the Antilles, before they discovered the Mayan coast, a Hieronymite friar wrote of the Taino chiefs of the Isle of Hispaniola, "These people believe in their fables with more certainty than other people. Like the Moors, they have their law stored in ancient songs, by which they are governed, as the Moors are by their writings" (Pané 1974 : 33–34).

13.   However, there are exceptions. In one version the various lives and the pouch of the opossum were a reward for his kindness. According to some others, the obligation of the Sun and the Moon to provide light was the punishment for their bad conduct. Since chili is a product of the blood of Christ, stealing it will make one's cornfield dry up. The myth of the man who married a dog requires men to treat their wives well and not mistreat dogs. See respectively: Williams García and García Ramos (1980:31); Ap ayuuk (1982:113); Gossen (1974:328); Boremanse (1986).

14.   Malinowski (1954:109) denies that myth explains. Kerényi (1972:42–43, 1973) answers, saying that even if mythology was not invented to explain, it does explain in its own way, and that explanation should be understood in the sense of "making something clear."

15.   There are many myths that explain human origin and differences. The following are sources of both denigrating and self-denigrating myths: Ichon (1973:99); Cline (1944); Fought (1972:202–4); Arizpe Schlosser (1978); Burgess (1977); Mason (1914); Benítez (1985:11). I will give only three parallel South American myths, one from the Mbyá and one from the Paressi, mentioned by Jiménez Núñez (1962:47–48, 50–51), and one from the Bakaïrí, mentioned by Métraux (1948).

16.   The Chatino base their newborn ceremony in the sweat-bath on the myth of the origin of the Sun and the Moon (Bartolomé and Barabas 1982:110).

17.   For the ancient Tzeltal, Votán was the divine messenger who divided and allocated the land (Núñez de la Vega 1702:9). Outside Mesoamerica, a good Quechua example is that of the distribution of land to the men of the Concha *ayllu* (*Dioses y hombres de Huarochirí* 1975:128–29).

18.   According to Augé (1987:24), "If it is true that institutions are useful and have meaning, it is also true that the secret of their function is not limited completely to the terrain of their meaning, and vice versa."

Chapter 23   How It Turns Out That Myth Is True

1.   This is how the American historian A. D. White (1972:7–8), about a hundred years ago, characterized the way in which St. Athanasius, St. Basil, and St. Hilary reconciled the thesis that the world had been created in six days with that of creation in an instant, both found in Genesis.

2.   Some very important sacred books have been produced in the Mesoamerican religious tradition, from pre-Hispanic codices to the books of *Chilam Balam*, the *Popol Vuh*, and the "satchels" of myths mentioned by Sánchez de Aguilar (1953:325). However, there is no assertion that any of these sacred books contained the purified, unified, and official dogma that would make it an essential, central text, as is characteristic in scriptural traditions. According to J. Thompson (1970a:331), "myths were never frozen into immutable patterns of words and incidents in pre-Columbian times."

3.   Cultural reality for Malinowski, psychological for Jung, and spiritual for Eliade (Turner 1975). The epistemological reality of Cassirer can be added to these.

4.   I cite only Frankfort and Frankfort (1954:25), who believe that the "primitive had a curious form of thought *pars pro toto* [the part equals the whole], by which he integrated the symbol and the thing symbolized into a unity."

5.   Bidney (1970:322) assigns different writers on myth to these two, supposedly mutually exclusive, approaches.

Chapter 24   Myth in the Time of History

1.   One must take into account that rules, like resistance to change, are historical events and are changeable. This means that rules and a particular resistance to transformation do not depend solely on characteristics in the social domain, but on the interrelationships that are produced with other domains of social action at a given historical moment.

2.   For other considerations of the differential "solidity" of the elements that make up ideological systems in Mesoamerican thought, see López Austin (1988, 1:11–12).

3.   Perrin (1980:243–45) points out an interesting example of anachronism in the myths of the Guajiro of Colombia and Venezuela.

4.   In chapter 25 we will return to the topic of remythification. Here I wish to indicate only that the problem of being out of phase is part of the persistence of myth.

5.   "Confluences and structures are not two alien concepts; they are aspects of common phenomena" (Vilar 1981:95).

6.   In this region members of societies dedicated to the control of rain, hail, and the winds are called *ahuizotes*. This information was collected on August 15, 1987.

7.   In some versions they are brothers; in others, the male is the Sun and the female is the Moon.

Chapter 25   History in the Time of Myth

1.   For example, the following definition: "Myths are stories of anonymous origin that prevail among primitive people and are accepted by them as truth. They concern supernatural beings and events, or natural beings and happenings that are influenced by supernatural agents" (Gayley 1911:1).

2.   See an example of communication by means of a skull in Serna (1953:129), and in dreams, in *Historia de los mexicanos por sus pinturas* (1965:60–61).

3.   The description of the great visions of the foundation of Tenochtitlan in Alvarado Tezozomoc (1949:26) says: *"niman oquittaque cenca miectlamantli in tlamahuizolli,"* "afterwards they saw many miraculous things."

4.   Many different writers with different points of view have written about these characters and the historiographical problems: Nicholson (1957, 1979); P. Carrasco (1979); Davies (1979); Jiménez Moreno (1979); Zantwijk (1979); Gruzinski (1985); D. Carrasco (1982); López Austin (1973).

5.   Torquemada (1969, bk. 2, ch. 17, 2:104) says that "from that time . . . the Mexicans began to use white clothing, of cotton, much of which grows in that province, and the people who lived there dressed in it, although the Mexicans lacked it."

6.   Not all sources give the name of Ozomatzin to the Tlahuica tlatoani of Cuauhnahuac. He is called Itzcoatl in the *Historia de los mexicanos por sus pinturas* (1965:59) and Tezcacohuatl by Torquemada (1969, bk. 2, ch. 17, 2:104).

7.   The source says that the descendants of Tzontecomatl were the Otomi. The Chichimec of Tetzcoco were Otomi. That is why this same *Historia de México* (1965: 99–100) considers the Chichimec rulers of Tetzcoco to be Otomi.

8.   See the different scenes in which this lady appears on the Tlotzin Map. In the *Códice Xolotl* (1980: pl. 2, b-5, c-5), on the contrary, the flower and not the hair is shown in the glyph of that name.

9.   The work has four stories. The one about "Hoichi the Earless" tells the tale of a blind *biwa* player who served in the Buddist temple of Amidaji. The body of the young musician was protected against the attacks of phantoms by the writing of pious texts on his skin; but his ears, which were not covered by the paintings, were destroyed.

10.   Even in relations of a historical nature, mention of the disbanding of the peoples of Tollan is suspicious; see *Historia Tolteca-chichimeca* 1976:131–32).

11.   Among those referring to biblical influences is Litvak King (1972). He mentions Durán on the passage across the sea on p. 29, n. 1.

12.   For example, the history of the origin of the Mexicans says that they came "in canin ilhuicaatl ixeliuhyan . . . ca in icuac yuh mochihua, in inic necoc moxeloa in ilhuicaatl, in anoce teuatl . . . auh ca in yehuantin in ca zatepan ohualque, inic oncan hualpanoque in ilhuicaatl ixeliuhyan, in noce teuatl ixeliuhyan," which I translate as: "by the place where the celestial water [the sea] is separated . . . because that is how it is done, the celestial or divine water is separated into opposite sides . . . and those who came afterwards, passed there through the division of the celestial water, or by the division of the divine water" (Castillo 1966:57–58).

13.   The Tepecano, at the beginning of this century, said that the royal eagle of the Mexica was the owner of the water to the west and that the Mexica came from

the west (Mason 1914). The separation of the heroes to the east and to the west is also found in South American mythology (Nimuendajú 1963:724).

14.   The episode persists among the Chatino (Bartolomé and Barabas 1982:111).

15.   For the Chichimec the key year would be 1 acatl (Reed). They said they had left Chicomoztoc in the year 1 acatl and underwent a migration of 364 years. At the end of 364 years they named a ruler. Before that, everything was in darkness for them (*Anales de Cuauhtitlán* 1945:3–4).

16.   See the establishment of the Itza in Chichén Itzá and the destruction of Tayasal (*Ancient Future of the Itza* 1982:xvi, J. Thompson 1964:172).

17.   Among others, Alcina Franch (1984) has this opinion.

Chapter 26   Putting the Tale Together

1.   In this I do not refer to strictly linguistic points. Although it cannot be generalized, what Lévi-Strauss (1979b) said when he spoke of the differences between story and myth is illuminating. "Myths can be told only during one period of the year, while stories can be told anytime. Or myths can be told only at night or on certain days. Also when myths are heard, one should take a particular position, for example, to stand very straight."

2.   See the myth of origin of corn among the Mam and that of the Sun's origins among the Cakchiquel, in J. Thompson (1975:422, 437–38).

3.   P. Carrasco (1961) gives an unsupported interpretation (wasps as the anger of the grandmother and the poisonous insects as diseases).

4.   Huichol myth about the origin of fire told by Jesús Rentería; see the beginning of chapter 17.

5.   Huichol myth about the birth of the Sun told by Jesús Rentería, in San Andrés Cohamiata, August 1972.

6.   Here, as in the rest of the book, "cosmic" and "cosmovision" refer to the aggregate of beings in the universe and their processes, and not just to what is astral.

7.   Among contemporary Nahua, *Uejkauitl nauaueuejtlajtoli* 1982:70. In this same book (73–74), see the repetition of the grandmother's complaint in the song "Xochi-pitsahuac."

8.   The name Toci means "Our Grandmother." Among the Chatino, see Cicco and Horcasitas (1962), among the Tzutujil, Orellana (1975), and many other versions. There is a specific study by Moedano Navarro (1977).

9.   Jiménez Moreno (1956: fol. 43–44) makes an interesting connection between this myth and the Chichimec. He says that the Olmeca-Xicalanca threw water from the *nixtamal* [lime water for soaking corn] at the Toltec-Chichimec to signify that they were the descendants of the dog of the myth. Compare this with what is said about the Zapotec man-god Petela, in "Relación del pueblo de Ocelotepeque" (1984:89–90).

10.   According to the Huichol, the forefathers of the Huichol, Cora, Tepehuano, and the "neighbors" were born from the offspring of the dog (McIntosh 1949).

11.   Among the Cuicatec, the fox is the one who carries fire in the myth of the Sun and the Moon (*Relatos, mitos y leyendas de la Chinantla* 1981:56–57).

Chapter 27   Reading the Myth

1.   Concerning the use of the sentence as an element in the mythic tale, see Lévy-Strauss's (1968a:190–91) proposal and Douglas's (1967) criticism of it.

2.   Or the grandmother herself throws sand on the frog, with the same effect (Dyk 1959:12).

3.   Aside from the myth mentioned here, there is at least one other, inserted in the myth of the Saint and the Spirit of Corn, in which Armadillo and Opossum try to set fire to the palm tree where the old woman is hidden (*Técnicos bilingües* 1985:21–22).

4.   Compare two Chinantec myths, "The Cactus Plantation of the Rosary" and "How People Became Monkeys," in *Relatos, mitos y leyendas de la Chinantla* (1981:218–20, 224).

5.   See the myth of the Sun and the Moon changed into a dirty story among the Huave (Ramírez Castañeda 1985).

6.   Note the presence of Hansel and Gretel in the Chontal myth of the Sun and the Moon, or the story of Brer Rabbit in the Totonac myth of the flood (P. Carrasco 1960; Ichon 1973:52–53).

7.   See the Mam story of the death of Christ as the basis for explaining the ability of blind people to move about without danger (Wagley 1957:179). An interesting case, although from the Southwest of the United States, is the Zuni tale that combines the birth of Christ, a story, and the myth of the twins (Parsons 1918).

8.   See the image in the form of a tube in Lumholtz (1970, 2:191).

9.   In another version he took five squash seeds instead of five vine shoots (McIntosh 1949).

10.   See this characteristic of the tubes whose flow never ends in the conjuration for hunting deer with a lasso in Ruiz de Alarcón (1953:79, 81), translated and interpreted by López Austin (1988:60–61).

11.   The idea that there is a close connection between the pillars and the deluge is still present among the contemporary Chorti (Fought 1972:377).

12.   The Quiche myth seems to have had no influence on this story. Hunahpú and Ixbalanqué made their brothers Hunbatz and Hunchouén climb a tree and advised them to use their sashes to descend. The sashes were changed to tails and the elder brothers into monkeys (*Popol vuh* 1964:66–67). In this inchoation there seems to be a distinction between the monkeys, since the names of the two brothers refer to the howler monkey (genus *Alouatta*) and to the spider monkey (genus *Ateles*).

13.   The name *lagarto* is not precise in Mexico. It is given to species of reptiles of the order Sauria as well as to crocodilians. In the tales the character can be either a small lizard or an alligator.

14.   The families of Mexican lizards having forked tongues are the Teiidae, Xantusiidae, Scincidae, Helodermatidae, Dibamidae, Anguidae, and Xenosauridae. Those having simple tongues are the Gekkonidae and the Iguanidae, although there is a slight division in the last ones (pers. com. Francisco Soberón Mobarak, February 1988).

15.   After transcribing the Tlapanec myth, Loo compares it to the figure on plate 4-41 of the *Códice Fejérváry Mayer* (1964–67).

Chapter 28   Ye Ixquich

1.   Its historic nature implies its dialectical tie to the social whole and therefore its perennial transformation.

2.   In Vilar's (1981:43) classification, it would be a historic act of the masses and particularly of their thoughts and beliefs.

3.   That is, a belief created and shared by wide social sectors.

4.   It is formed by social relations, acts, internal thought processes, institutions, expressions, creations, etc.

5.   I use Needham's (1979:3) definition of class, "a conceptual group of things due to particular characteristics which relate them in one form or another." This definition thus includes human groups as well as animal and plant species.

6.   M. R. Cohen (1957:33–37), citing Russell, is among those who defend this demarcation.

7.   See M. Bloch's (1965:57) proposal in the epigraph to chapter 2.

BIBLIOGRAPHY

Abbreviations

CEC	Centro de Estudios Clásicos
CEM	Centro de Estudios Mayas
CIESAS	Centro de Investigaciones y Estudios Superiores en Antropología Social
CISINAH	Centro de Investigaciones Superiores del Instituto Nacional de Antropología e Historia
FCE	Fondo de Cultura Económica
IH	Instituto de Historia
IIA	Instituto de Investigaciones Antropológicas
IIE	Instituto de Investigaciones Estéticas
IIF	Instituto de Investigaciones Filológicas
IIH	Instituto de Investigaciones Históricas
III	Instituto Indigenista Interamericano
INAH	Instituto Nacional de Antropología e Historia
INI	Instituto Nacional Indigenista
SCN	Seminario de Cultura Náhuatl
SEP	Secretaría de Educación Pública
UACH	Universidad Autónoma de Chiapas
UAM	Universidad Autónoma Metropolitana
UNAM	Universidad Nacional Autónoma de México

Abreu Gómez, E. 1985. *Leyendas y consejas del antiguo Yucatán, México.* CREA/Biblioteca Joven 39. Mexico City: FCE.

Acosta, J. de. 1962. *Historia natural y moral de las Indias* . . . 2d ed. Ed. by E. O'Gorman. Mexico City: FCE.

Aguirre Beltrán, G. 1963. *Medicina y magia. El proceso de aculturación en la estructura colonial.* Mexico City: INI.

Alcina Franch, J. 1984. El nacimiento de Huitzilopochtli. Análisis de un mito del México prehispánico. In *El mito ante la antropología y la historia*, ed. by J. Alcina Franch, 99–126. Madrid: Centro de Investigaciones Sociológicas/Siglo Veintiuno de España Editores.

Alejos García, J. 1988. *Wajalix bA t'an. Narrativa tradicional ch'ol de Tumbalá, Chiapas.* Mexico City: UNAM-IIF-CEM.

Althusser, L., and E. Balibar. 1968. *Lire le Capital*, vol. 1. Paris: François Maspero.

————. 1976. *Para leer El capital.* 12th ed. Trans. by M. Harnecker. Mexico City: Siglo Veintiuno Editores.

Alva Ixtlilxóchitl, F. de. 1975–77a. *Historia de la nación chichimeca*. In vol. 2 of *Obras históricas*, ed. by E. O'Gorman, 5–560. Mexico City: UNAM-IIH.

———. 1975–77b. *Sumaria relación de la Historia general de esta Nueva España* . . . In vol. 1 of *Obras históricas*, ed. by E. O'Gorman, 523–49. Mexico City: UNAM-IIH.

———. 1975–77c. *Sumaria relación de todas las cosas que han sucedido en la Nueva España* . . . In vol. 1 of *Obras históricas*, ed. by E. O'Gorman, 261–395. Mexico City: UNAM-IIH.

Alvarado Tezozómoc, H. 1944. *Crónica mexicana*. Mexico City: Editorial Leyenda.

———. 1949. *Crónica mexicáyotl*. Trans. by A. León. Mexico City: UNAM-IH/INAH.

Alvarez, C. 1980–84. *Diccionario etnolingüístico del idioma maya yucateco colonial*. 2 vols. Mexico City: UNAM-IIF-CEM.

Alvarez del Toro, M. 1977. *Los mamíferos de Chiapas*. Tuxtla Gutiérrez and Mexico City: UACH.

Anales de Cuauhtitlán. 1945. In *Códice Chimalpopoca*, trans. by P. F. Velázquez, 1–118, 145–64. Mexico City: UNAM-IH.

Ancient Future of the Itza: The Book of Chilam Balam of Tizimin. 1982. Trans. by M. S. Edmonson. Austin: University of Texas Press.

Anderson, A. 1957. Two Chol texts. *Tlalocan* 3(4):313–16.

Anguiano, M., and P. T. Furst. 1987. *La endoculturación entre los huicholes*. Mexico City: INI.

Ap ayuuk. Cuentos mixes. Tradición oral indígena. 1982. Mexico City: Cultura-SEP.

Apuleo. 1946. El demonio de Sócrates. In *La metamorfosis o El asno de oro*, trans. by D. López de Cortegana, 293–312. Barcelona: Joaquín, Gil.

Aristotle. 1968. *Metaphysics*. Trans. by R. Hope. Ann Arbor: University of Michigan Press.

Arizpe Schlosser, L. 1978. Un cuento y una canción náhuatl de la Sierra de Puebla. *Estudios de Cultura Náhuatl* 13:290–99.

Ascher, R. 1961. Analogy in archaeological interpretation. *Southwestern Journal of Anthropology* 17:317–25.

Augé, M. 1987. *Símbolo, función e historia. Interrogantes de la antropología*. Trans. by B. Ruiz de la Concha. Mexico City: Editorial Grijalbo.

Augurios y abusiones [texts of Sahagún's informants]. 1969. Trans., intro., and notes by A. López Austin. Mexico City: UNAM-IIH.

Balandier, G. 1969. *Antropología política*. Trans. by M. Bustamante. Barcelona: Ediciones Península.

Balsalobre, G. de. 1953. *Relación auténtica de las idolatrías* . . . In *Tratado de las idolatrías* . . . , by Serna et al., ed. by F. del Paso y Troncoso, 2:337–90. Mexico City: Ediciones Fuente Cultural.

Barlow, R. H., and V. Ramírez. 1962. Tonatiw iwan meetstli. *Tlalocan* 4(1):55–61.

Barrera Marín, A., A. Barrera Vásquez, and R. M. López Franco. 1976. *Nomenclatura etnobotánica maya. Una interpretación taxonómica*. Mexico City: INAH–Centro Regional del Sureste.

Barrera Vásquez, A. (director); J. R. Bastarrachea Manzano, W. Brito Sansores (compilers); R. Vermont Salas, D. Dzul Góngora, and D. Dzul Poot (collaborators). 1980. *Diccionario maya Cordemex*. Mérida, Yucatán: Ediciones Cordemex.

Barthel, T. S. 1968. Algunos principios de ordenación en el panteón azteca (Acerca del análisis de las listas de dioses de Sahagún). Trans. by J. Brom O. *Traducciones mesoamericanistas* 2:45–78.

————. 1968. El complejo 'emblema.' *Estudios de Cultura Maya* 7:159–93.

Barthes, R. 1972. *Mythologies*. Trans. by A. Lovers. New York: Hill & Wang.

————. 1985 Introducción al análisis estructural de los relatos. In *Análisis estructural del relato*, 4th ed., trans. by B. Dorriots and A. N. Vaisse, 7–38. Tlahuapan, Puebla: Premiá Editora de Libros.

Bartolomé, M. A. 1979. *Narrativa y etnicidad entre los chatinos de Oaxaca*. Mexico City: SEP-INAH.

Bartolomé, M. A., and A. M. Barabas. 1982. *Tierra de la palabra. Historia y etnografía de los chatinos de Oaxaca*. Mexico City: INAH–Centro Regional de Oaxaca.

Bastide, R. 1947. *Éléments de sociologie religieuse*. 2d ed. Paris: Librairie Armand Colin.

Baus de Czitrom, C. El tlacuache en el mundo mesoamericano. In *Flora y fauna de México*, ed. by D. Heyden and A. M. Velasco. In press.

Baynes, Ken. 1976. *Arte y sociedad*. with Kate Baynes and A. Robinson. Trans. by E. Riambau. Barcelona: Editorial Blume.

Beals, R. L. 1943. Problems of Mexican Indian folklore. *Journal of American Folklore* 56(219):8–16.

Benítez, F. 1985. *Historia de un chamán cora*. Mexico City: Ediciones Era.

Berger, P. L. 1971. *El dosel sagrado. Elementos para una sociología de la religión*. Trans. by N. Míguez. Buenos Aires: Amorrortu Editores.

Berger, P. L., and T. Luckmann. 1979. *La construcción social de la realidad*. Trans. by S. Zuleta. Buenos Aires: Amorrortu Editores.

Berlin, B., D. E. Breedlove, and P. H. Raven. 1974. *Principles of Tzeltal Plant Classification. An Introduction to the Botanical Ethnography of a Mayan-speaking People of Highland Chiapas*. New York: Academic Press.

Bernal, J. D. 1969. *Science in History*. 4 vols. London: C. A. Watts.

Beyer, H. 1979. Relaciones entre la civilización teotihuacana y la azteca. In *La población del Valle de Teotihuacán*, ed. by M. Gamio, 2:273–93. Mexico City: INI.

Bidney, D. 1970. *Theoretical Anthropology*. 2d ed. New York: Schocken Books.

Bloch, M. 1965. *Introducción a la historia*. 4th ed. Breviarios 64. Mexico City: FCE.

Bloch, O. 1976. Materialismo y crítica de la religión en la antigüedad. In *Filosofía y religión*, ed. by Centro de Estudios y de Investigaciones Marxistas, trans. by C. Castro, 9–31. Mexico City: Editorial Grijalbo.

Boas, F. 1912. Notes on Mexican folk-lore. *Journal of American Folklore* 25(97):204–60.

————. 1968. *Race, Language and Culture*. New York: Free Press.

Boege, E. 1988. *Los mazatecos ante la nación. Contradicciones de la identidad étnica en el México actual*. Mexico City: Siglo Veintiuno Editores.

Book of Chilam Balam of Chumayel. 1967. 2d ed. Trans. by R. L. Roys. Norman: University of Oklahoma Press.

Boremanse, D. 1986. *Contes et mythologie des indiens lacandons. Contribution à l'étude de la tradition orale maya*. Paris: Editions L'Harmattan.

Borges, J. L. 1983. *Nueva antología personal*. 13th ed. Mexico City: Siglo Veintiuno Editores.

Brambila Paz, R., et al. 1980. *El animal en la vida prehispánica*. Mexico City: SEP-INAH.

Braudel, F. 1974. *La historia y las ciencia sociales*. 3d ed. Trans. by J. Gómez Mendoza. Madrid: Alianza Editorial.

———. 1985. Interview by J.-J. Brochier and F. Ewald, Mares y tiempos de la historia. Trans. by M. de Orellana. *Vuelta* 103:42–46.

Bremond, C. 1985. La lógica de los posibles narrativos. In *Análisis estructural del relato*, ed. by R. Barthes, 4th ed., trans. by B. Dorriots and A. N. Vaisse, 99–121. Tlahuapan, Puebla: Premiá Editora de Libros.

Bricker, V. R. 1966. El hombre, la carga y el camino: antiguos conceptos mayas sobre tiempo y espacio, y el sistema zinacanteco de cargos. In *Los zinacantecos. Un pueblo tzotzil de los Altos de Chiapas*, ed. by E. Z. Vogt, 355–70. Mexico City: INI.

———. 1981. *The Indian Christ, the Indian King: The Historical Substrate of Maya Myth and Ritual*. Austin: University of Texas Press.

Brinton, D. G. [1882] 1970. *American Hero-Myths: A Study in the Native Religions of the Western Continent*. New York: Johnson Reprint Corporation.

Broda, J. 1982. El culto mexica de los cerros y del agua. *Multidisciplina, revista de la Escuela Nacional de Estudios Profesionales de Acatlán* 3(7):45–56.

———. 1987. Templo Mayor as ritual space. In *The Great Temple of Tenochtitlan: Center and Periphery in the Aztec World*, by J. Broda, D. Carrasco, and E. Matos Moctezuma, 61–123. Berkeley: University of California Press.

Bronowski, J. 1978. *El sentido común en la ciencia*. Trans. by M. Carbonell. Barcelona: Ediciones Península.

Bruce, R. D. 1974. *El libro de Chan K'in*. Mexico City: INAH.

———. 1978. The Popol vuh and the book of Chan K'in. *Estudios de Cultura Maya* 10:173–208.

Brundage, B. C. 1979. *The Fifth Sun: Aztec Gods, Aztec World*. Austin: University of Texas Press.

Bunzel, R. 1952. *Chichicastenango: A Guatemalan Village*. Locust Valley, N.Y.: J. J. Augustin Publisher.

Burgess, D. 1977. El origen del marrano en tarahumara. *Tlalocan* 7:199–201.

Burkhart, L. M. 1989. *The Slippery Earth: Nahua-Christian Moral Dialogue in Sixteenth-Century Mexico*. Tucson: University of Arizona Press.

Burland, C. A. 1967. *The Gods of Mexico*. London: Eyre & Spottiswoode.

Campbell, R. J. 1985. *A Morphological Dictionary of Classical Nahuatl*. Madison: Hispanic Seminary of Medieval Studies.

Campos, J. 1982. *La herencia obstinada. Análisis de cuentos nahuas*. Mexico City: FCE.

Cardoso, M. L. 1977. *La construcción de conocimientos. Cuestiones de teoría y método*. Trans. by A. M. Palos. Mexico City: Ediciones Era.

Carmack, R. M. 1979. *Historia social de los quichés*. Guatemala: Ministerio de Educación.

Carpentier, A. 1980. *Ecue-Yamba-O*. Barcelona: Editorial Bruguera.

Carrasco, D. 1982. *Quetzalcóatl and the Irony of Empire: Myths and Prophecies in the Aztec Tradition*. Chicago: University of Chicago Press.

Carrasco, P. 1952. El Sol y la Luna. Versión mixe. *Tlalocan* 3(2):168–69.

———. 1960. Pagan rituals and beliefs among the Chontal Indians of Oaxaca, Mexico. *Anthropological Records* 20(3):87–115. Berkeley: University of California.

———. 1961 Un mito y una ceremonia entre los chatinos de Oaxaca. In *A. William Cameron Townsend en el vigésimo aniversario del Instituto Lingüístico de Verano*, 43–48. Mexico City: n.p.

———. 1963. La reina de la sal. *Tlalocan* 4(3):225–26.

———. 1971. La importancia de las sobrevivencias prehispánicas en la religión tarasca: la lluvia. *Verhandlungen des XXXVIII. Internationalen Amerikanistenkongresses, Stuttgart-München* 3:265–75.

———. 1976a. *El catolicismo popular de los tarascos*. Trans. by A. Benavides. Setentas 298. Mexico City: SEP.

———. 1976b. La sociedad mexicana antes de la conquista. In *Historia general de México*, ed. by D. Cosío Villegas, 1:165–288. Mexico City: Colegio de México.

———. 1978. Las fiestas de los meses mexicanos. In *Mesoamérica. Homenaje al doctor Paul Kirchhoff*, ed. by B. Dahlgren, 52–60. Mexico City: SEP-INAH.

———. 1979. Las bases sociales del politeísmo mexicano: los dioses tutelares. *Actes du XLIIe Congrès International des Américanistes*, 6:11–17. Paris: Société des Américanistes.

Caso, A. 1953. *El pueblo del Sol*. Mexico City: FCE.

———. 1963. Representaciones de hongos en los códices. *Estudios de Cultura Náhuatl* 4:27–36.

———. 1967. *Los calendarios prehispánicos*. Mexico City: UNAM-IIH.

———. 1969. *El tesoro de Monte Albán*. 2d ed. Mexico City: SEP-INAH.

———. 1971. ¿Religión o religiones mesoamericanas? *Verhandlungen des XXXVIII. Internationalen Amerikanistenkongresses, Stuttgart-München* 3:189–200.

———. 1977–79. *Reyes y reinos de la Mixteca*. 2 vols. Mexico City: FCE.

Caso, A., and I. Bernal. 1952. *Urnas de Oaxaca*. Mexico City: SEP-INAH.

Cassirer, E. 1951. *Antropología filosófica. Introducción a una filosofía de la cultura*. 3d ed. Trans. by E. Imaz. Mexico City: FCE.

———. 1955. *The Philosophy of Symbolic Forms*. 3 vols. Trans. by R. Manheim. New Haven: Yale University Press.

Castellón, B. R. 1987. La subestimación del parentesco en la migración mexica como un caso de transformación mítica. In *Historia de la religión en Mesoamérica y áreas afines. I Coloquio*, ed. by B. Dahlgren de Jordán, 123–36. Mexico City: UNAM-IIA.

Castiglioni, A. 1972. *Encantamiento y magia*. 2d ed. Trans. by G. Pérez Enciso. Mexico City: FCE.

Castillo, C. del. 1966. *Fragmentos de la obra general sobre historia de los mexicanos*. Trans. by F. del Paso y Troncoso. Ciudad Juárez: Editorial Erandi.

Castro, C. A. 1963. Libro de nuestro abuelo Tlacuatzin. *La palabra y el hombre* 36:643–61.

Ceballos González, G., and C. Galindo Leal. 1984. *Mamíferos silvestres de la Cuenca de México*. Mexico City: Programme on Man and the Biosphere (UNESCO)/Instituto de Ecología y Museo de Historia Natural de la Ciudad de México/Editorial Limusa.

Cervantes de Salazar, F. 1914–36. *Crónica de Nueva España*. 3 vols. Madrid and Mexico City: Est. Fot. de Hauser y Menet/Talleres Gráficos del Museo Nacional de Arqueología, Historia y Etnografía.

Chadwick, R. 1971. Native Pre-Aztec history of Central Mexico. In *Handbook of Middle American Indians*, vol. 11, *Archaeology of Northern Mesoamerica, part 2*, ed by G. F. Ekholm and I. Bernal, 474–504. Austin: University of Texas Press.

Chapman, A. 1978. *Les enfants de la mort. Univers mythique des indiens tolupan (jicaque)*. Mexico City: Mission Archeologique et Ethnologique Française au Mexique.

———. 1985–86. *Los hijos del copal y la candela. Ritos agrarios y tradición oral de los lencas de Honduras*. 2 vols. Mexico City: UNAM-IIA.

Chávez, G. de. 1985–86. Relación de Meztitlán. In *Relaciones geográficas del siglo XVI: México*, ed. by R. Acuña, 2:49–75. Mexico City: UNAM-IIA.

Chesterton, G. K. 1952. *Orthodoxy*. New York: Mead and Co.

Chimalpahin, D. 1965. *Relaciones originales de Chalco Amaquemecan*. Trans. by S. Rendón. Mexico City: FCE.

Christiansen, R. Th. 1965. Myth, metaphor, and simile. In *Myth. A symposium*, ed. by T. A. Sebeok, 64–80. Bloomington: Indiana University Press.

Cicco, G. de, and F. Horcasitas. 1962. Los cuates: un mito chatino. *Tlalocan* 4(1):74–79.

Clavijero, F. J. 1964. *Historia antigua de México*. Ed. by M. Cuevas. Mexico City: Editorial Porrúa.

Cline, H. 1944. Lore and deities of the Lacandon Indians, Chiapas, Mexico. *Journal of American Folklore* 57(224):107–15.

Codex Magliabechiano. 1983. [Facsimile]. 2 vols. Intro. by Z. Nuttall. Ed. by E. H. Boone. Berkeley: University of California Press.

Codex Nuttall: A picture manuscript from Ancient Mexico. 1973. Ed. by Z. Nuttall. New York: Dover Publications.

Codex Vaticanus 3773 (Codex Vaticanus B). 1972. [Facsimile]. Graz, Austria: Akademische Druck- und Verlagsanstalt.

Códice Aubin. Manuscrito azteca de la Biblioteca Real de Berlín. Anales en mexicano y jeroglíficos desde la salida de Aztlán hasta la muerte de Cuauhtémoc (Códice de 1576). 1979. [Facsimile of 1902 ed.]. Ed. by A. Peñafiel. Trans. by B. de J. Quiroz. Mexico City: Editorial Innovación.

Códice Borbónico. Manuscrito mexicano de la Biblioteca del Palais Bourbon (Libro adivinatorio y ritual ilustrado). 1979. [Facsimile of 1899 ed., Paris]. Ed. by E. Leroux. Mexico City: Siglo Veintiuno Editores.

Códice Borgia. 1963. [Facsimile]. Mexico City: FCE.

Códice Boturini o Tira de la peregrinación o Tira del Museo. 1964–67. In *Antigüedades de México*, by Lord Kingsborough, ed. by J. Corona Núñez, 2:7–29. Mexico City: Secretaría de Hacienda y Crédito Público.

Códice de Dresden. 1972. [Facsimile]. In *A Commentary of the Dresden Codex: A Maya hieroglyphic book*, by J. E. S. Thompson. Philadelphia: American Philosophical Society.

Códice Fejérváry Mayer. 1964–67. [Facsimile]. In *Antigüedades de México*, by Lord Kingsborough, ed. by J. Corona Núñez, 4:185–276. Mexico City: Secretaría de Hacienda y Crédito Público.

Códice Florentino. Manuscrito 218-20 de la Colección Palatina de la Biblioteca Medicea Laurenziana. 1979. [Facsimile]. 3 vols. Mexico City: Secretaría de Gobernación, Archivo General de la Nación.

Códice Madrid. 1985. [Facsimile]. In *Los códices mayas*, ed. by T. A. Lee, 81–140. Tuxtla Gutiérrez, Chiapas: UACH.

Códice Matritense del Real Palacio [textos en náhuatl de los informantes de Sahagún]. 1907. [Facsimile]. Vol. 8. Ed. by F. del Paso y Troncoso. Madrid: Fototipia de Hauser y Menet.

Códice Pérez (Chilam Balam de Maní). 1949. Trans. by E. Solís Alcalá. Mérida, Yucatán: Ediciones de la Liga de Acción Social.

Códice Ramírez, Relación del origen de los indios que habitan esta Nueva España, según sus historias. 1944. Ed. by M. Orozco y Berra. Mexico City: Editorial Leyenda.

Códice Selden I o Rollo Selden. 1964–67. [Facsimile]. In *Antigüedades de México*, by Lord Kingsborough, ed. by J. Corona Núñez, 2:101–14. Mexico City: Secretaría de Hacienda y Crédito Público.

Códice Telleriano-Remensis. 1964–67. [Facsimile]. In *Antigüedades de México*, by Lord Kingsborough, ed. by J. Corona Núñez, 1:151–338. Mexico City: Secretaría de Hacienda y Crédito Público.

Códice Tudela o Códice del Museo de América. 1980. [Facsimile]. Ed. by J. Tudela de la Orden. Madrid: Ediciones Cultura Hispánica del Instituto de Cooperación Iberoamericana.

Códice Vaticano Latino 3738 o Códice Vaticano Ríos o Códice Ríos. 1964–67. [Facsimile]. In *Antigüedades de México*, by Lord Kingsborough, ed. by J. Corona Nuñez, 3:7–314. Mexico City: Secretaría de Hacienda y Crédito Público.

Códice Vindobonensis o Códice de Viena o Mexicanus 1. 1964–67. [Facsimile]. In *Antigüedades de México*, by Lord Kingsborough, ed. by J. Corona Núñez, 4:51–184. Mexico City: Secretaría de Hacienda y Crédito Público.

Códice Xólotl. 1980. [Facsimile]. 2 vols. 2d ed. Ed. by C. E. Dibble. Mexico City: UNAM-IIH.

Código de Hammurabi. 1980. Trans. by F. Lara Peinado. Madrid: Editora Nacional.

Coe, M. D. 1965. A model of ancient community structure in the Maya Lowlands. *Southwestern Journal of Anthropology* 21:97–114.

———. 1978. *Lords of the Underworld: Masterpieces of Classic Maya Ceramics*. Princeton: Princeton University Art Museum.

Cohen, M. R. 1957. *Introducción a la lógica*. Trans. by E. de Gortari. Mexico City: FCE.

Cohen, P. S. 1969. Theories of myth. *Man* 4(3):337–53.

Colby, B. N., and L. M. Colby. 1986. *El contador de los días. Vida y discurso de un adivino ixil*. Trans. by J. J. Utrilla. Mexico City: FCE.

Coloquios y doctrina cristiana . . . 1986. [Facsimile]. Ed. by M. León-Portilla. Mexico City: UNAM/Fundación de Investigaciones Sociales.

Compte, A. 1984. *Discurso sobre el espíritu positivo.* Trans. by C. Berges. Madrid: SARPE.

Copi, I. M. 1986. *Introduction to Logic.* 7th ed. New York: Macmillan Publishing Company.

Córdova, Fr. J. de. 1942. [Facsimile of 1578 original]. *Vocabulario castellano-zapoteco.* Ed. by W. Jiménez Moreno. Mexico City: SEP-INAH.

Costumbres, fiestas, enterramientos y diversas formas de proceder de los indios de Nueva España. 1945. *Tlalocan* 2(1):36–63.

Count, E. W. 1973. *Being and Becoming Human: Essays on the Biogram.* New York: Van Nostrand Reinhold Company.

———. 1976. On myth, method, and madness. *Current Anthropology* 17:168–69.

Covarrubias, G. de. 1986. Relación de las minas de Temazcaltepeque. In *Relaciones geográficas del siglo XVI: México,* Ed. by R. Acuña, 2:138–54. Mexico City: UNAM-IIA.

Cowan, F. M. 1963. La mujer del agua arrastradora: un texto mazateco. *Tlalocan* 4(2):144–47.

Croft, K. 1957. Nahuatl texts from Matlapa, S. L. P. *Tlalocan* 3(4):317–33.

Cruz, M. de la. 1964. [Facsimile of 1552 original]. *Libellus de medicinalibus Indorum herbis.* Mexico City: Instituto Mexicano del Seguro Social.

Dahlgren, B. 1961. Grupo cora, Sierra del Nayar, Jesús María, Nayarit, proyecto para diorama. Planeación e Instalación del Museo Nacional de Antropología, México, SEP-INAH-CAPFCE. Manuscript.

Dakin, K. 1977. Pedro Cuaresma and other Nahuatl stories. *Tlalocan* 7:47–66.

Dardel, E. 1954. Lo mítico. *Diógenes* 2(7):43–65.

Davies, N. 1979. Mixcoatl: Man and god. *Actes du XLIIe Congrès International des Américanistes,* 6:19–26. Paris: Société des Américanistes.

Davis, M. 1963. Cuicatec tales about witchcraft. *Tlalocan* 4(3):197–203.

Delibes, M. 1980. *Viejas historias de Castilla la Vieja.* 7th ed. Madrid: Alianza Editorial.

Detienne, M. 1985. *La invención de la mitología.* Trans. by M.-A. Galmarini. Barcelona: Ediciones Península.

Díaz, J. L. 1984. Plantas mágicas y sagradas de la medicina indígena de México. In *Historia general de la medicina en México,* vol. 1, *México antiguo,* ed. by A. López Austin and C. Viesca Treviño, 231–50. Mexico City: UNAM–Facultad de Medicina/Academia Nacional de Medicina.

Díaz Hernández, V. 1945. Nanahuatzin. *Tlalocan* 2(1):64.

Diccionario de la lengua española. 1984. 2 vols. 20th ed. Madrid: Real Academia Española.

Diógenes Laercio. 1946. *Vidas, opiniones y sentencias de los filósofos más ilustres.* Trans. by J. Ortiz y Sanz. Madrid: M. Aguilar Editor.

Dioses y hombres de Huarochirí. 1975. 2d ed. Trans. by J. M. Arguedas. Mexico City: Siglo Veintiuno Editores.

Domínguez Martínez, I. 1970. Moctezuma (cuento folklórico). In *Un pueblo popoloca,* by Klaus Jäcklein, 293–94. Mexico City: INI.

Douglas, M. 1966. *Purity and Danger.* New York: Praeger.

———. 1967. The meaning of myth, with special reference to "La geste d'Asdiwal."

In *The Structural Study of Myth and Totemism*, ed. by E. Leach, 49–69. London: Tavistock Pub.

Ducrot, O., and T. Todorov. 1974. *Diccionario enciclopédico de las ciencias del lenguaje*. Trans. by E. Pezzoni. Buenos Aires: Siglo Veintiuno Argentina Editores.

Dumézil, G. 1969. *The Destiny of the Warrior*. Trans. by A. Hiltebeitel. Chicago: University of Chicago Press.

Durán, Fr. D. 1984. *Historia de las Indias de Nueva España e islas de Tierra Firme*. 2 vols. 2d ed. Ed. by A. M. Garibay. Mexico City: Editorial Porrúa.

Durkheim, E. 1968. *Las formas elementales de la vida religiosa*. Trans. by I. J. Ludmer. Buenos Aires: Editorial Schapire.

————. 1973. *Las reglas del método sociológico*. Trans. by P. Wajsman. Buenos Aires: Schapire Editor.

Durkheim, E., and M. Mauss. 1971. De ciertas formas primitivas de clasificación. Contribución al estudio de las representaciones colectivas. In *Obras*, by M. Mauss, vol. 2, *Institución y culto. Representaciones colectivas y diversidad de civilizaciones*, 13–73. Barcelona: Barral Editores.

Duverger, C. 1983. *La flor letal. Economía del sacrificio azteca*. Trans. by J. J. Utrilla. Mexico City: FCE.

Dyk, A. 1959. *Mixteco texts*. Ed. by B. Elson. Norman: Summer Institute of Linguistics, University of Oklahoma.

Eco, U. 1985. James Bond: una combinatoria narrativa. In *Análisis estructural del relato*, by Roland Barthes et al., 4th ed., trans. by B. Dorriots and A. N. Vaisse, 77–98. Tlahuapan, Puebla: Premiá Editora de Libros.

Edmonson, M. S. 1965. *Quiche-English Dictionary*. New Orleans: Middle American Research Institute–Tulane University.

————. 1967. Narrative folklore. In *Handbook of Middle American Indians*, ed. by R. Wauchope, vol. 6, *Social Anthropology*, ed. by M. Nash, 357–68. Austin: University of Texas Press.

Eliade, M. 1968. *Mito y realidad*. Trans. by L. Gil. Madrid: Ediciones Guadarrama.

————. 1972. *Tratado de historia de las religiones*. Trans. by T. Segovia. Mexico City: Ediciones Era.

Elson, B. 1947. The Homshuk: a Sierra Popoluca text. *Tlalocan* 2(3):193–214.

Espinosa, A. M. 1914a. New-Mexican Spanish folklore. *Journal of American Folklore* 27(104):105–47.

————. 1914b. Comparative notes on New-Mexican and Mexican Spanish folk-tales. *Journal of American Folklore* 27(104):211–31.

Evans-Pritchard, E. E. 1965. *Theories of Primitive Religion*. Oxford: Oxford University Press.

————. 1974. *Nuer Religion*. Oxford: Oxford University Press.

Fábregas, A. 1980. El Instituto Lingüistico de Verano y la penetración ideológica. In *Indigenismo y lingüistica*, Documentos del foro 'La politica del lenguaje en México,' 153–58. Mexico City: UNAM-IIA.

Farriss, N. M. 1987. Remembering the future, anticipating the past: History, time and cosmogony among the Maya of Yucatan. *Comparative Studies in Society and History* 29:566–93.

Febvre, L. 1971. *Combates por la historia*. 2d ed. Trans. by F. J. Fernández Buey and E. Argullol. Barcelona: Ediciones Ariel.

Fernández de Oviedo y Valdés, G. 1944–45. *Historia general y natural de las Indias, islas y Tierra-Firme del Mar Océano*. 14 vols. Ed. by J. Amador de los Rios. Asunción, Paraguay: Editorial Guaranía.

——. 1950. *Sumario de la natural historia de las Indias*. Ed. by J. Miranda. Mexico City: FCE.

Feuchtwang, S. 1977. La investigación de la religión. In *Análisis marxistas y antropología social*, ed. by M. Bloch. Barcelona: Editorial Anagrama.

Florescano, E. 1987. *Memoria mexicana. Ensayo sobre la reconstrucción del pasado: época prehispánica–1821*. Mexico City: Contrapuntos.

Foster, G. M. 1945a. *Sierra Popoluca Folklore and Beliefs*. University of California Publications in American Archaeology and Ethnology 42(2):177–250. Berkeley: University of California Press.

——. 1945b. Some characteristics of Mexican Indian folklore. *Journal of American Folklore* 58(229):225–35.

——. 1951. Some wider implications of soul-loss illness among the Sierra Popoluca. In *Homenaje al Dr. Alfonso Caso*, 167–74. Mexico City: Imprenta Nuevo Mundo.

——. 1987. On the origin of humoral medicine in Latin America. *Medical Anthropology Quarterly* 1:355–93.

Fought, J. G. 1972. *Chorti (Mayan) Texts. 1*. Ed. by S. S. Fought. Philadelphia: University of Pennsylvania Press.

Frankfort, H., and H. A. Frankfort. 1954. Mito y realidad. In *El pensamiento prefilosófico*, by H. A. Frankfort et al., trans. by E. de Gortari, 1:11–44. Mexico City: FCE.

Frazer, Sir J. G. 1956. *La rama dorada. Magia y religión*. 3d ed. Trans. by E. and T. I. Campuzano. Mexico City: FCE.

——. 1981. *El folklore en el Antiguo Testamento*. Trans. by G. Novás. Mexico City: FCE.

Freud, S. 1953. El porvenir de una ilusión. In *El porvenir de las religiones*, trans. by L. López-Ballesteros y de Torres. Mexico City: Editorial Iztaccihuatl.

Fuente, J. de la. 1977. *Yalálag. Una villa zapoteca serrana*. Mexico City: INI.

Furst, J. L. 1978. *Codex Vindobonensis Mexicanus I: A Commentary*. Albany, N.Y.: Institute for Mesoamerican Studies–State University of New York at Albany.

Furst, P. T. 1972a. El concepto huichol del alma. In *Mitos y arte huicholes*, by P. T. Furst and S. Nahmad, 7–113. Setentas 50. Mexico City: SEP.

——. 1972b. El mito en el arte: un huichol pinta su realidad. In *Mitos y arte huicholes*, by P. T. Furst and S. Nahmad, 114–25. Setentas 50. Mexico City: SEP.

——. 1972c. Para encontrar nuestra vida: el peyote entre los huicholes. In *El peyote y los huicholes*, by S. Nahmad, O. Klineberg, P. T. Furst, and B. G. Myerhoff, 109–91. Setentas 29. Mexico City: SEP.

——. 1976. *Hallucinogens and Culture*. San Francisco: Chandler, Sharp.

——. 1980. *Los alucinógenos y la cultura*. Trans. by J. Agustin. Mexico City: FCE.

Furst, P. T., and B. G. Myerhoff. 1972. El mito como historia: el ciclo del peyote y la datura entre los huicholes. Trans. by C. Joseph de Hernández. In *El peyote y los huicholes*, by S. Nahmad, O. Klineberg, P. T. Furst, and B. G. Myerhoff, 53–108. Setentas 29. Mexico City: SEP.

Fustel de Coulanges [Numa Denis]. 1984. *La ciudad antigua*. Ed. by J. F. Yvars. Barcelona: Ediciones Peninsula.

Galinier, J. 1987. *Pueblos de la Sierra Madre. Etnografía de la comunidad otomi*. Trans. by M. Sánchez Ventura and P. Chéron. Mexico City: INI/Centre D'Etudes Mexicaines et Centramericaines.

Gamio, M. 1960. *Forjando patria*. 2d ed. Mexico City: Editorial Porrúa.

García, G. 1981. *Origen de los indios del Nuevo Mundo*. Mexico City: FCE.

García de León, A. 1969. El universo de lo sobrenatural entre los nahuas de Pajapan, Veracruz. *Estudios de Cultura Náhuatl* 8:279–311.

———. 1976. *Pajapan. Un dialecto mexicano del Golfo*. Mexico City: INAH–Departamento de Lingüistica.

García de Palacio, D. 1983. *Carta-relación/Relación y forma*. Ed. by M. del C. León Cázares, M. I. Nájera C., and T. Figueroa. Mexico City: UNAM-IIF-CEM.

García Gual, C. 1984. La interpretación de los mitos antiguos en el siglo XX. In *El mito ante la antropología y la historia*, ed. by J. Alcina Franch, 23–47. Madrid: Centro de Investigaciones Sociológicas–Siglo Veintiuno de España Editores.

García Quintana, J. 1980. Salutación y súplica que hacía un principal al tlatoani recién electo. *Estudios de Cultura Náhuatl* 14:65–94.

García-Ruiz, J. F. 1982. El defensor y el defendido. Dialéctica de la agresión entre los mochó: Mototzintla-Chiapas. *Cuicuilco* 2(8):12–21.

Garcilaso de la Vega "El Inca." 1982. *Comentarios reales*. 2 vols. Ed. by M. D. Bravo Arriaga. Mexico City: SEP/UNAM.

Garibay K., A. M. 1953–54. *Historia de la literatura náhuatl*. 2 vols. Mexico City: Editorial Porrúa.

———. 1964–68. *Poesía náhuatl*. 3 vols. Mexico City: UNAM-IIH.

Garza, M. de la. 1983. Análisis comparativo de la Historia de los mexicanos por sus pinturas y la Leyenda de los soles. *Estudios de Cultura Náhuatl* 16:123–34.

Gayley, C. M. 1911. *The Classic Myths in English Literature and in Art*. Boston: Ginn and Company.

Gewalt, W., and B. Grzimek. 1968. Opossums. In *Grzimek's Animal Life Encyclopedia*, ed. by B. Grzimek, 10:57–69. New York: Van Nostrand Reinhold.

Giddings, R. W. 1959. *Yaqui Myths and Legends*. Tucson: University of Arizona Press.

Ginzburg, C. 1982. *El queso y los gusanos. El cosmos, según un molinero del siglo XVI*. 2d ed. Trans. by F. Martin and F. Cuartero. Barcelona: Muchnik.

Girard, R. 1983. *La violencia y lo sagrado*. Trans. by J. Jordá. Barcelona: Editorial Anagrama.

Glanz und Untergang des Alten Mexico. Die Azteken und ihre Vorläufer. 1987. 2 vols. Mainz am Rhein: Verlag Philipp von Zabern.

Godelier, M. 1974. *Economía, fetichismo y religión en las sociedades primitivas*. Trans. by C. Amoros and I. Romero de Solís. Mexico City: Siglo Veintiuno Editores.

———. 1984. *L'idéel et le matériel. Pensée, économies, sociétés*. Paris: Fayard.

González Casanova, P. 1928. El ciclo legendario del Tepoztécatl. *Revista Mexicana de Estudios Históricos* 2(1–2):18–63.

———. 1946. El origen de los cuentos del México indigena. In *Cuentos indigenas*. Mexico City: UNAM.

———. 1979. [Facsimile of 1922 ed.]. El mexicano de Teotihuacán. In *La población del Valle de Teotihuacán*, by M. Gamio et al., 5:595–648. Mexico City: INI.

González Cruz, G., and M. Anguiano. 1984. La historia de Tamakastsiin. *Estudios de Cultura Náhuatl* 17:205–25.

González Ramos, G. 1972. *Los coras*. Mexico City: INI.

González Rodríguez, L. 1987. *Crónicas de la Sierra Tarahumara*. Mexico City: SEP.

González Torres, Y. 1975. *El culto a los astros entre los mexicas*. Setentas 217. Mexico City: SEP.

———. 1985. *El sacrificio humano entre los mexicas*. Mexico City: INAH/FCE.

———. 1987. Taxonomía religiosa mesoamericana. In *Historia de la religión en Mesoamérica y áreas afines. I Coloquio*, ed. by B. Dahlgren, 45–57. Mexico City: UNAM-IIA.

Gossen, G. H. 1974. *Chamulas in the World of the Sun*. Cambridge: Harvard University Press.

———. 1978. The Popol-vuh revisited: A comparison with modern Chamula narrative tradition. *Estudios de Cultura Maya* 11:267–83.

———. 1980. Two Creation Myths from Chamula, Chiapas. *Tlalocan* 8:131–65.

Gramsci, A. 1967. *La formación de los intelectuales*. Trans. by A. González Vega. Mexico City: Editorial Grijalbo.

Graulich, M. 1981. The metaphor of the day in ancient Mexican myth and ritual. *Current Anthropology* 22:45–50.

———. 1983a. Myths of paradise lost in Pre-Hispanic Central Mexico. *Current Anthropology* 24:575–88.

———. 1983b. Templo Mayor, Coyolxauhqui und Cacaxtla. *Mexicon* 5(5):91–94.

———. 1987a. Los mitos mexicanos y mayas-quichés de la creación del Sol. Manuscript.

———. 1987b. *Mythes et rituels du Mexique ancien préhispanique*. Bruxelles: Académie Royale de Belgique, Palais des Académies.

Greenfield, P. M., and J. S. Bruner. 1986. Cultura y desarrollo cognitivo. Trans. by K. Alvarez Tolcheff and A. Cañellas Haurie. In *Acción, pensamiento y lenguaje*, by J. Bruner, 23d ed., ed. by J. L. Linaza. Mexico City: Alianza Editorial Mexicana.

Greimas, A. J. 1985. Elementos para una teoría de la interpretación del relato mitico. In *Análisis estructural del relato*, by R. Barthes et al., 4th ed., trans. by B. Dorriots and A. N. Vaisse, 39–76. Tlahuapan, Puebla: Premiá Editora de Libros.

Gruzinski, S. 1985. *Les hommes-dieux du Mexique. Pouvoir indien et société coloniale. XVIe–XVIIIe siècles*. Paris: Editions des Archives Contemporaines.

———. 1988. *La colonisation de l'imaginaire. Sociétés indigènes et occidentalisation dans le Mexique espagnol. XVIe–XVIIIe siècles*. Paris: Gallimard.

Guiteras Holmes, C. 1965. *Los peligros del alma. Visión del mundo de un tzotzil*. Trans. by C. A. Castro. Mexico City: FCE.

Hall, E. R., and K. R. Nelson. 1959. *The Mammals of North America*. 2 vols. New York: The Ronald Press Company.

Hallpike, C. R. 1986. *Los fundamentos del pensamiento primitivo*. Trans. by F. Patán. Mexico City: FCE.

Hartman, C. 1921. Traditional belief concerning the generation of the opossum. *Journal of American Folklore* 34:321–23.

Heinemann, D., and E. Thenius. 1968. The Marsupials. In *Grzimek's Animal Life Encyclopedia*, ed. by B. Grzimek, 10:50–56. New York: Van Nostrand Reinhold.

Heller, A. 1985. *Historia y vida cotidiana. Aportación a la sociología socialista*. Trans. by M. Sacristán. Mexico City: Editorial Grijalbo.

Hempel, C. G. 1984. *Filosofía de la ciencia natural*. 10th ed. Trans. by A. Deaño. Madrid: Alianza Editorial.

Hermitte, M. E. 1970. *Poder sobrenatural y control social*. Trans. by C. Viqueira. Mexico City: III.

Hernández, Fe. 1925. El tlacuache y el coyote. *Mexican Folkways* 1(2):12.

Hernández, Fr. 1959. *Historia natural de Nueva España*. 2 vols. Trans. by J. Rojo Navarro. In *Obras completas*, vols. 2–3. Mexico City: UNAM.

Herodotus, 1987. *The History*. Trans. by D. Grene. Chicago: University of Chicago Press.

Herskovits, M. J. 1951. *Man and His Works*. New York: Alfred A. Knopf.

Hertz, R. 1973. The pre-eminence of the right hand: A study in religious polarity. In *Right and Left: Essays on Dual Symbolic Classification*, ed. by R. Needham, 3–31. Chicago: University of Chicago Press.

Hesiod. 1983. *Theogony. Works and Days. Shield*. Trans. by A. N. Athanassakis. Baltimore: The Johns Hopkins University Press.

———. 1986. *Los trabajos y los días*. Trans. by P. Vianello de Cordova. Mexico City: UNAM-IIF-CEC.

Heyden, D. 1973. ¿Un Chicomóztoc en Teotihuacan? La cueva bajo la Pirámide del Sol. *Boletin INAH* época 2(6):3–18.

———. 1981. Caves, gods, and myths: World-view and planning in Teotihuacan. In *Mesoamerican sites and World-views*, ed. by E. P. Benson, 1–35. Washington, D.C.: Dumbarton Oaks Research Library.

Historia de los mexicanos por sus pinturas. 1965. In *Teogonía e historia de los mexicanos. Tres opúsculos del siglo XVI*, ed. by A. M. Garibay K., 21–90. Mexico City: Editorial Porrúa.

Historia de México (Histoire du Mechique). 1965. Trans. by R. Rosales Munguía. In *Teogonía e historia de los mexicanos. Tres opúsculos del siglo XVI*, ed. by A. M. Garibay K., 91–120. Mexico City: Editorial Porrúa.

Historia tolteca-chichimeca. 1976. [Facsimile]. Ed. by P. Kirchhoff, L. Odena Güemes, and L. Reyes García. Trans. by L. Reyes García. Mexico City: INAH-CISINAH.

Hocart, A. M. 1970. *Kings and Councillors: An Essay in the Comparative Anatomy of Human Society*. 2d ed. Ed. by R. Needham. Chicago: University of Chicago Press.

Hodder, I. 1982. *The Present Past: An Introduction to Anthropology for Archaeologists*. London: B. T. Batsford Ltd.

Hogben, L. 1944. *Las matemáticas al alcance de todos*. 2d ed. Trans. by E. Condeminas Abós. Buenos Aires: Joaquin Gil.

Holland, Wm. R. 1963. *Medicina maya en los Altos de Chiapas. Un estudio del cambio socio-cultural*. Trans. by D. Cazés. Mexico City: INI.

Hollenbach, E. E. de. 1977. El origen del Sol y de la Luna. Cuatro versiones en el trique de Copala. *Tlalocan* 7:123–70.

————. 1980. El mundo animal en el folklore de los triques de Copala. *Tlalocan* 8: 437–90.

Hoogshagen, S. 1971. La creación del Sol y de la Luna según los mixes de Coatlán, Oaxaca. *Tlalocan* 6:337–46.

Horcasitas, F. 1953. An Analysis of the Deluge Myth in Mesoamerica. MA thesis, Mexico City College.

————. 1962. Dos versiones totonacas del mito del diluvio. *Tlalocan* 4:53–54.

————. 1978. La narrativa oral náhuatl (1920–1975). *Estudios de Cultura Náhuatl* 13:177–209.

————. 1982. La prosa náhuatl. In *Esplendor del México antiguo*, 4th ed., Ed. by R. Noriega, C. Cook de Leonard, and J. R. Moctezuma, 1:199–210. Mexico City: Centro de Investigaciones Antropológicas de México, Editorial del Valle de México.

Hubert, H., and M. Mauss. 1970. Introducción al análisis de algunos fenómenos religiosos. In *Obras*, by M. Mauss, vol. 1, *Lo sagrado y lo profano*, 57–91. Barcelona: Barral Editores.

Huizinga, J. 1984. *Homo ludens*. Trans. by E. Imaz. Madrid: Alianza Editorial, Emecé Editores.

Hume, D. 1957. *Natural History of Religion*. Ed. by H. E. Root. Stanford: Stanford University Press.

Hunt, E. 1977. *The Transformation of the Hummingbird: Cultural Roots of a Zinacantecan Mythical Poem*. Ithaca: Cornell University Press.

Hvidtfeldt, A. 1958. *Teotl and *ixiptlatli. Some Central Conceptions in Ancient Mexican Religion, with a General Introduction on Cult and Myth*. Copenhagen: Munksgaard.

Hyman, S. E. 1965. The ritual view of myth and the mythic. In *Myth. A Symposium*, ed. by T. A. Sebeok, 136–53. Bloomington: Indiana University Press.

Ibn Battuta. 1981. *A través del Islam*. Ed. and trans. by S. Fanjul and F. Arbós. Madrid: Editora Nacional.

Ibn Hudayl. 1977. *Gala de caballeros, blasón de paladines*. Ed. by M. J. Viguera. Madrid: Editora Nacional.

Ibn Khaldûn. 1967. *An Introduction to History*. Ed. by N. J. D. Awad. Trans. by F. Rosenthal. London: Rutledge and Kegan Paul.

Ichon, A. 1973. *La religión de los totonacas de la sierra*. Trans. by J. Arenas. Mexico City: INI.

Incháustegui, C. 1977. *Relatos del mundo mágico mazateco*. Mexico City: SEP-INAH–Centro Regional Puebla-Tlaxcala.

————. 1984. *Figuras en la niebla (Relatos y creencias de los mazatecos)*. 2d ed. Tlahuapan, Puebla: Premiá Editora de Libros.

————. 1987. *Las márgenes del Tabasco chontal*. Villahermosa: Gobierno del Estado de Tabasco.

Ivanov, V. V. 1979. La semiótica de las oposiciones mitológicas de varios pueblos. In *Semiótica de la cultura*, by J. Lotman and School of Tartu, ed. by J. Lozano, trans. by N. Méndez, 149–72. Madrid: Ediciones Cátedra.

Jäcklein, K. 1970. *Un pueblo popoloca*. Trans. by M. Martinez Peñaloza. Mexico City: INI.

Jaeger, W. 1946. *Aristóteles. Bases para la historia de su desarrollo intelectual*. Trans. by J. Gaos. Mexico City: FCE.

Jakobson, R. 1986a. *Ensayos de lingüística general*. Trans. by J. M. Pujol and J. Cabanes. Mexico City: Origen/Planeta.

————. 1986b. *Ensayos de poética*. Trans. by J. Almela. Mexico City: FCE.

Jansen, M. E. R. G. N. 1982. *Huisi tacu. Estudio interpretativo de un libro mixteco antiguo. Codex Vindobonensis Mexicanus I*. 2 vols. Amsterdam: Centro de Estudios y Documentación Latinoamericanos.

Jensen, A. E. 1963. *Myth and Cult among Primitive Peoples*. Chicago: University of Chicago Press.

Jiménez Moreno, W. 1956. *Notas sobre historia antigua de México*. [Mimeographic ed.]. Mexico City: Ediciones de la Sociedad de Alumnos de la Escuela Nacional de Antropología e Historia.

————. 1971a. Las religiones mesoamericanas y el cristianismo. *Verhandlungen des XXXVIII. Internationalen Amerikanistenkongresses, Stuttgart-München* 3:241–45.

————. 1971b. ¿Religión o religiones mesoamericanas? *Verhandlungen des XXXVIII. Internationalen Amerikanistenkongresses, Stuttgart-München* 3:201–6.

————. 1979. De Tezcatlipoca a Huitzilopochtli. *Actes du XLIIe Congrès International des Américanistes*, 6:27–34. Paris: Société des Américanistes.

Jiménez Núñez, A. 1962. *Mitos de creación en Sudamérica*. Sevilla: Facultad de Filosofía y Letras–Universidad de Sevilla.

Jung, C. C. 1956. *Symbols of Transformation: An Analysis of the Prelude to a Case of Schizophrenia*. Trans. by R. F. C. Hull. New York: Pantheon Books.

————. 1977. Acercamiento al inconsciente. In *El hombre y sus simbolos*, by C. G. Jung et al., trans. by L. Escolar Bareño, 15–102. Barcelona: Caralt.

Kaplan, D. and R. A. Manners. 1981. *Introducción crítica a la teoría antropológica*. 2d ed. Trans. by M. Arana. Mexico City: Editorial Nueva Imagen.

Karremans, J. A. J. 1987. Irrigation and space in a Mexican town. Reflections of a Pre-Spanish past. In *The Leiden Tradition in Structural Anthropology: Essays in Honour of P. E. de Josselin de Jong*, ed. by R. de Ridder and J. A. J. Karremans, 224–35. Leiden: E. J. Brill.

Kelly, I. 1966. World view of a Highland-Totonac pueblo. In *Summa anthropologica en homenaje a Roberto J. Weitlaner*, 395–411. Mexico City: SEP-INAH.

Kerényi, K. 1972. *La religión antigua*. Trans. by M. P. Lorenzo and M. L. Rodriguez. Madrid: Revista de Occidente.

————. 1973. Prolegomena. In *Essays on a Science of Mythology. The Myth of the Divine Child and the Mysteries of Eleusis*, by C. G. Jung and C. Kerényi, trans. by F. C. Hull. Princeton: Princeton University Press.

Kirchhoff, P. 1943. Mesoamerica. *Acta Americana* 1:92–107.

————. 1960. Mesoamérica. Sus limites geográficos, composición étnica y caracteres culturales. 2d ed. *Revista Tlatoani* (Mexico), Supplement 3. [Revision of the 1943 essay].

————. 1971. Las 18 fiestas anuales en Mesoamérica: 6 fiestas sencillas y 6 fiestas dobles. *Verhandlungen des XXXVIII. Internationalen Amerikanistenkongresses, Stuttgart-München* 3:207–21.

————. 1972. Dioses y fiestas de los nahuas centrales. In *Religión en Mesoamérica, XII Mesa Redonda*, ed. by J. Litvak King and N. Castillo Tejero, 199–204. Mexico City: Sociedad Mexicana de Antropología.

————. 1985. El imperio tolteca y su caída. Trans. by J. Monjarás-Ruiz. In *Mesoamérica y el centro de México*, ed. by J. Monjarás-Ruiz, R. Brambila, and E. Pérez-Rocha, 249–72. Mexico City: INAH.

Kirk, G. S. 1970. *Myth: Its Meaning and Functions in Ancient and Other Cultures*. Cambridge: Cambridge University Press.

————. 1973. *El mito: su significado y funciones en las distintas culturas*. Trans. by A. Pigrau Rodríguez. Barcelona: Barral Editores.

Knab, T. 1979. Talocan Talmanic: Supernatural beings of the Sierra de Puebla. *Actes du XLIIe Congrès International des Américanistes*, 6:127–36. Paris: Société des Américanistes.

Köhler, U. 1982. On the significance of the Aztec day sign "olin." In *Space and Time in the Cosmovision of Mesoamerica*, ed. by F. Tichy, 11–127. Munich: Wilhelm Fink Verlag.

Kosik, K. 1983. *Dialéctica de lo concreto*. Trans. by A. Sánchez Vázquez. Mexico City: Grijalbo.

Krickeberg, W. 1966. El juego de pelota mesoamericano y su simbolismo religioso. Trans. by Ju. Brom O. *Traducciones mesoamericanistas* 1:191–313.

————. [1928] 1985. *Mitos y leyendas de los aztecas, incas, mayas y muiscas*. Trans. and ed. by J. Faulhaber and B. von Mentz. Mexico City: FCE.

Krotzer, E. 1970. How the Mother of Cotton was stolen. *Tlalocan* 4:213–15.

Kubler, G. 1972. La evidencia intrínseca y la analogía etnológica en el estudio de las religiones mesoamericanas. In *Religión en Mesoamérica. XII Mesa Redonda*, ed. by J. Litvak King and N. Castillo Tejero, 1–24. Mexico City: Sociedad Mexicana de Antropología.

————. 1974. Mythological ancestries in Classic Maya inscriptions. *Primera Mesa Redonda de Palenque*, Part II, ed. by M. G. Robertson, 23–24. Pebble Beach, Cal.: Robert Louis Stevenson School/Pre-Columbian Art Research.

————. 1983. Portales con columnas-serpiente en Yucatán y el Altiplano. *Anales del Instituto de Investigaciones Estéticas* 52:21–45.

————. 1984. 'Renascence' y disyunción en el arte mesoamericano. *Cuadernos de Arquitectura Mesoamericana* 2:75–87.

Kundera, M. 1986. *La insoportable levedad del ser*. Trans. by F. Valenzuela. Barcelona: Tusquets Editores.

La Farge II, O., and D. Byers. 1931. *The Year Bearer's People*. New Orleans: Tulane University, Department of Middle American Research.

Landa, Fr. D. de. 1982. *Relación de las cosas de Yucatán*. 12th ed. Mexico City: Editorial Porrúa.

Las Casas, Fr. B. de. 1967. *Apologética historia sumaria*. 2 vols. Ed. by E. O'Gorman. Mexico City: UNAM-IIH.

Lastra, Y. 1970. El conejo y el coyote. Cuento chichimeco. *Tlalocan* 6(2):115–18.

Law, H. W. 1957. Tamakasti: A Gulf Nahuat text. *Tlalocan* 3(4):344–67.

Leach, E. R. 1965. *Political Systems of Highland Burma*. Boston: Beacon Press.

———. 1967. Genesis as myth. In *Myth and Cosmos: Readings in Mythology and Symbolism*, ed. by J. Middleton, 1–13. Austin: University of Texas Press.

———. 1970. *Lévi-Strauss, antropólogo y filósofo*. Published with *El oso y el barbero*, by C. Lévi-Strauss, 5–43. Barcelona: Editorial Anagrama.

———. 1978. *Cultura y comunicación. La lógica de la conexión de los símbolos. Una introducción al uso del análisis estructuralista en la antropología social*. Trans. by J. O. Sánchez Fernández. Mexico City: Siglo Veintiuno Editores.

Leeuw, G. van der. 1964. *Fenomenología de la religión*. Trans. by E. de la Peña. Mexico City: FCE.

León-Portilla, M. 1959. *La filosofía náhuatl estudiada en sus fuentes*. 2d ed. Mexico City: UNAM-IIH-SCN.

———. 1968. *Tiempo y realidad en el pensamiento maya. Ensayo de acercamiento*. Mexico City: UNAM-IIH.

———. 1983. Cuícatl y tlahtolli. Las formas de expresión en náhuatl. *Estudios de Cultura Náhuatl* 16:13–108.

Leopold, A. S. 1982. *Fauna silvestre en México. Aves y mamíferos de caza*. Trans. by L. Macías Arellano. Mexico City: Instituto Mexicano de Recursos Naturales Renovables.

Lévi-Strauss, C. 1964. *El pensamiento salvaje*. Trans. by F. González Aramburo. Mexico City: FCE.

———. 1965. *El totemismo en la actualidad*. Trans. by F. Gonzáles Aramburo. Mexico City: FCE.

———. 1966. *The Savage Mind*. Chicago: Univ. of Chicago Press.

———. 1968a. *Antropología estructural (I)*. Trans. by E. Verón. Buenos Aires: Editorial Universitaria de Buenos Aires.

———. 1968b. *Lo crudo y lo cocido*. Vol. 1 of *Mitológicas*. Trans. by J. Almela. Mexico City: FCE.

———. 1970. *El oso y el barbero*. Published with *Lévi-Strauss, antropólogo y filósofo*, by E. Leach, 45–73. Barcelona: Editorial Anagrama.

———. 1972. La estructura y la forma. Reflexiones sobre una obra de Vladimir J. Propp. In *Polémica Lévi-Strauss–Propp*, by Lévi-Strauss and V. Propp, trans. by J. M. Arancibia, 7–45. Madrid: Editorial Fundamentos.

———. 1979a. *Estructuralismo y ecología*. 2d ed. Trans. by A. Cardín. Barcelona: Editorial Anagrama.

———. 1979b. El mito y el cuento (Conferencia de Claude Lévi-Strauss en la UNAM, 14 de febrero de 1979). Trans. by N. Pasternak. *Sábado, Unomásuno* Feb. 24.

————. 1981. *The Naked Man*. Trans. by J. Weightman and D. Weightman. London: Jonathan Cape.

————. 1983. *El hombre desnudo*. 3d ed. Vol. 4 of *Mitológicas*. Trans. by J. Almela. Mexico City: Siglo Veintiuno Editores.

————. 1984. *El origen de las maneras de mesa*. 5th ed. Vol. 3 of *Mitológicas*. Trans. by J. Almela. Mexico City: Siglo Veintiuno Editores.

————. 1985. *Las estructuras elementales del parentesco*. 2 vols. Trans. by M. T. Cevasco. Mexico City: Origen/Planeta.

————. 1986. *Mirando a lo lejos*. Buenos Aires: Emecé Editores.

Lévy-Bruhl, L. 1975. *La mentalidad primitiva*. Trans. by G. Weinberg. Buenos Aires: Ediciones Leviatán.

Lewis, O. 1968. *Tepoztlán. Un pueblo de México*. Mexico City: Editorial Joaquín Mortiz.

Leyenda de los soles. 1945. In *Códice Chimalpopoca*, trans. by P. F. Velázquez, 119–64. Mexico City: UNAM-IH.

Libro de Chilam Balam de Chumayel. 1973. Trans. by A. Mediz Bolio. México, UNAM.

Libro de los cantares de Dzitbalché, El. 1965. Trans. by A. Barrera Vásquez. Mexico City: INAH.

Libro de los libros de Chilam Balam, El. 1949. Trans. by A. Barrera Vásquez and S. Rendón. Mexico City: FCE.

Lienzo de Jucutácato. n.d. Held by Sociedad Mexicana de Geografía y Estadística.

Linton, R. 1963. *Estudio del hombre*. 6th ed. Trans. by D. F. Rubín de la Borbolla. Mexico City: FCE.

Lisón Tolosana, C. 1971. *Antropología social en España*. Madrid: Siglo Veintiuno de España Editores.

Litvak King, J. 1972. La introducción posthispánica de elementos a las religiones prehispánicas: un problema de aculturación retroactiva. In *Religión en Meso-américa, XII Mesa Redonda*, ed. by J. Litvak King and N. Castillo Tejero, 25–29. Mexico City: Sociedad Mexicana de Antropología.

Lok, R. 1987. The house as a microcosm. In *The Leiden Tradition in Structural Anthro-pology: Essays in Honour of P. E. de Josselin de Jong*, ed. by R. de Ridder and J. A. J. Karremans, 211–23. Leiden: E. J. Brill.

Loo, P. L. van der. 1987. Códices, costumbres, continuidad. Un estudio de la religión mesoamericana. Ph.D. diss., Rijksuniversiteit te Leiden, Faculteit der Letteren.

López Austin, A. 1961. *La constitución real de México-Tenochtitlan*. Mexico City: UNAM-IH-SCN.

————. 1965. Los temacpalitotique. Profanadores, brujos, ladrones y violadores. *Estudios de Cultura Náhuatl* 6:97–117.

————. 1970. Religión y magia en el ciclo de las fiestas aztecas. *Religión, mitología y magia* 2:3–29. Mexico City: Museo Nacional de Antropología.

————. 1972. Conjuros médicos de los nahuas. *Revista de la Universidad de México* 27(4):i–xvi.

————. 1973. *Hombre-dios. Religión y política en el mundo náhuatl*. Mexico City: UNAM-IIH.

————. 1975. Algunas ideas acerca del tiempo mítico entre los antiguos nahuas. In

Historia, religión, escuelas, XIII Mesa Redonda, 289–98. Mexico City: Sociedad Mexicana de Antropología.

―――. 1979. Iconografía mexica. El monolito verde del Templo Mayor. *Anales de Antropología* 16:133–53.

―――. 1980. *Cuerpo humano e ideología. Las concepciones de los antiguos nahuas*. 2 vols. Mexico City: UNAM-IIA.

―――. 1983. Nota sobre la fusión y la fisión de los dioses en el panteón mexica. *Anales de Antropología* 20 (vol. 2):75–87.

―――. 1985a. El dios enmascarado del fuego. *Anales de Antropología* 22:251–85.

―――. 1985b. El texto sahaguntino sobre los mexicas. *Anales de Antropología* 22: 287–335.

―――. 1986. The Masked God of Fire. In *The Aztec Templo Mayor*, ed. by E. H. Boone, 257–91. Washington, D.C.: Dumbarton Oaks.

―――. 1988. *Human Body and Ideology: Concepts of the Ancient Nahuas*. 2 vols. Trans. by T. Ortiz de Montellano and B. R. Ortiz de Montellano. Salt Lake City: Univ. Utah Press.

López Cogolludo, Fr. D. 1957. *Historia de Yucatán*. 2 vols. 5th ed. Ed. by I. Rubio Mañé. Mexico City: Editorial Academia Literaria.

López de Gómara, F. 1954. *Historia general de las Indias*. 2 vols. Ed. by P. Guibelalde. Barcelona: Editorial Iberia.

Lotman, J. M. 1979. Valor modelizante de los conceptos de "fin" y "principio". In *Semiótica de la cultura*, by J. M. Lotman and School of Tartu, ed. by J. Lozano, trans. by N. Méndez, 199–203. Madrid: Ediciones Cátedra.

Lotman, J. M., and B. A. Uspenskij. 1979. Mito, nombre, cultura. In *Semiótica de la cultura*, by J. M. Lotman and School of Tartu, ed. by J. Lozano, trans. by N. Méndez, 111–35. Madrid: Ediciones Cátedra.

Lowie, R. H. 1974. *Historia de la etnología*. Trans. by P. Kirchhoff. Mexico City: FCE.

―――. 1976. *Religiones primitivas*. Trans. by J. Palao. Madrid: Alianza Editorial.

Lumholtz, C. 1970. *El México desconocido*. 2 vols. Trans. by B. Dávalos. Mexico City: Editora Nacional.

Madsen, Wm. 1955. Hot and cold in the universe of San Francisco Tecospa, Valley of Mexico. *Journal of American Folklore* 68:123–39.

―――. 1957. *Christo-Paganism: A study of Mexican Religious Syncretism*. New Orleans: Tulane University–Middle American Research Institute.

―――. 1960. *The Virgin's Children: Life in an Aztec Village Today*. Austin: University of Texas Press.

Maimonides. 1956. *Guide to the Perplexed*. New York: Hebrew Publishing Company.

Mair, L. 1970. *Introducción a la antropología social*. Trans. by C. M. Ramírez. Madrid: Alianza Editorial.

Mak, C. 1977. Maguey tapping in the Highland Mixteco. *Tlalocan* 7:115–19.

Malinowski, B. 1954. Myth in Primitive Psychology. In *Magic, Science, and Religion*, 93–148. New York: Doubleday Anchor.

―――. 1984. *Una teoría científica de la cultura*. Trans. by A. R. Cortázar. Madrid: Sarpe.

Mapa Tlotzin. Historia de los reyes y de los estados soberanos de Acolhuacan. 1886. In *Memoire sur la peinture didactique et l'escriture figurative des anciens mexicaines,* by M. Aubin, *Anales del Museo Nacional de México* 3:304–20.

Marcus, J. 1976. *Emblem and State in the Classic Maya Lowlands.* Washington, D.C.: Dumbarton Oaks.

————. 1979. Los orígenes de la escritura mesoamericana. *Ciencia y desarrollo* 24: 35–52.

————. 1980. La escritura zapoteca. *Investigación y ciencia* 43:28–44.

Martín del Campo, R. 1940. Ensayo de interpretación del Libro Undécimo de la Historia general de las cosas de Nueva España de Fray Bernardino de Sahagún. Las aves. *Anales del Instituto de Biología* 11(1):385–408.

Martínez, J. M. 1985. El Conejo Juan y otros relatos (Una contribución al estudio de lo cómico en la narrativa popular mesoamericana. In *Literatura, relato popular y religiosidad en el Sureste de México,* by A. Díez-Canedo, J. M. Martínez, and J. E. Tappam, 33–94. Mexico City: CIESAS-CIESAS del Sureste.

Marx, K. 1966. *Tesis sobre Feuerbach.* In *Obras escogidas en dos tomos,* by K. Marx and F. Engels, 2:404–6. Moscow: Editorial Progreso.

————. 1967. Introducción a 'En torno a la crítica de la Filosofía del derecho de Hegel. In *La sagrada familia y otros escritos filosóficos de la primera época,* by K. Marx and F. Engels, 2d ed., trans. by W. Roces, 3–15. Mexico City: Editorial Grijalbo.

————. 1977. *Introducción general a la crítica de la economía política.* 11th ed. Trans. by M. Murmis, P. Scaron and J. Aricó. Mexico City: Ediciones Pasado y Presente.

Marx, K., and F. Engels. 1987. *La ideología alemana.* Trans. by W. Roces. Mexico City: Editorial Grijalbo.

Mason, J. A. 1914. Folk-tales of the Tepecanos. *Journal of American Folklore* 27(104): 148–210.

Matieyka, L. 1976. Acerca de los primeros prolegómenos de la semiótica en Rusia. In *El signo ideológico y la filosofía del lenguaje,* by V. N. Voloshinov, 195–211. Buenos Aires: Ediciones Nueva Visión.

Matos Moctezuma, E. 1987. The Templo Mayor of Tenochtitlan. History and interpretation. In *The Great Temple of Tenochtitlan: Center and Periphery in the Aztec World,* by J. Broda, D. Carrasco, and E. Matos Moctezuma, 15–60. Berkeley: University of California Press.

————. 1988. Excavaciones recientes en Tlatelolco. Museo del Templo Mayor. (Exhibition Catalog). Mexico City: Secretaría de Turismo.

Mauss, M. 1968. *Les Fonctions Sociales du Sacré.* Vol. 1 of *Oevres.* Paris: Les Editions de Minuit.

————. 1971. Introducción a los mitos. In *Obras,* vol. 2, *Institución y culto. Representaciones colectivas y diversidad de civilizaciones,* 147–49. Barcelona: Barral Editores.

Mayers, M. 1958. *Pocomchi texts with grammatical notes.* Ed. by B. Elson. Norman: Summer Institute of Linguistics, University of Oklahoma.

McIntosh, J. 1949. Cosmogonía huichol. *Tlalocan* 3(3):14–21.

Memorial de Solalá. Anales de los cakchiqueles. 1950. Trans. by A. Recinos, 45–208. Mexico City: FCE.

Mendelson, E. M. 1967. Ritual and mythology. In *Handbook of Middle American Indi-*

ans, vol. 6, *Social anthropology*, ed. by M. Nash, 392–415. Austin: University of Texas Press.

Mendieta, Fr. G. de. 1954. *Historia eclesiástica indiana*. 4 vols. Mexico City: Salvador Chávez Hayhoe.

Merrifield, Wm. R. 1967. When de Sun rose for the first time. A Chinantec creation myth. *Tlalocan* 5(3):193–97.

Merton, R. K. 1972. *Teoría y estructura sociales*. Trans. by F. M. Torner. Mexico City: FCE.

Métraux, A. 1948. Esayos de mitología comparada sudamericana. *América indígena* 8(1):9–30.

Mier, R. 1984. *Introducción al análisis de textos*. Mexico City: UAM Xochimilco/ Terra Nova.

Miller, A. G. 1974. West and East in Maya Thought: Dead and rebirth at Palenque and Tulum. In *Primera Mesa Redonda de Palenque*, Part II, ed. by M. G. Robertson, 45–49. Pebble Beach, Cal.: Robert Louis Stevenson School/Pre-Columbian Art Research.

Miller, W. S. 1956. *Cuentos mixes*. Mexico City: INI.

Mitos cosmogónicos del México indígena. 1987. Ed. by J. Monjarás-Ruiz. Mexico City: INAH.

Mixco, M. J. 1977. Textos para la etnohistoria en la frontera dominicana de Baja California. *Tlalocan* 7:205–26.

Moedano Navarro, G. 1975. Los estudios de folklore literario en prosa. *Boletín del Departamento de Investigación de las Tradiciones Populares* 2:5–33.

———. 1977. El temazcal y su deidad protectora en la tradición oral. *Boletín del Departamento de Investigación de las Tradiciones Populares* 4:5–32.

Molina, Fr. A. de. 1944. *Vocabulario en lengua castellana y mexicana*. Madrid: Ediciones Cultura Hispánica.

Monterroso, A. 1975. *Antología personal*. Mexico City: FCE.

Montoliu Villar, M. 1980. Los dioses de los cuatro sectores cósmicos y su vínculo con la salud y enfermedad en Yucatán. *Anales de Antropología* 17(2):47–65.

———. 1981. El dios solar en la religión y mitología mayas. *Anales de Antropología* 18(2):29–57.

———. 1988. Utilidad de la tradición oral maya contemporánea en la reconstrucción de las historias sagradas del Sol y la Luna según los sistemas de ideas religiosas y míticas de este pueblo. In *La etnología: temas y tendencias, I Coloquio Paul Kirchhoff*, 177–88. Mexico City: UNAM-IIA.

Montoya Briones, J. de J. 1964. *Atla: Etnografía de un pueblo náhuatl*. Mexico City: INAH.

———. 1987. Persistencia de un sistema religioso mesoamericano entre indios huastecos y serranos. In *Historia de la religión en Mesoamérica y áreas afines, I Coloquio*, ed. by B. Dahlgren, 145–52. Mexico City: UNAM-IIA.

Monzón, A. 1949. *El calpulli en la organización social de los tenochca*. Mexico City: UNAM-IH/INAH.

Morales Bermúdez, J. 1984. *On o t'ian. Narrativa indígena chol*. Mexico City: UAM Azcapotzalco.

Moreno de los Arcos, R. 1967. Los cinco soles cosmogónicos. *Estudios de Cultura Náhuatl* 7:183–210.

Morley, S. G., and G. W. Brainerd. 1965. *The Ancient Maya*. 3d ed. Stanford: Stanford University Press.

Münch Galindo, G. 1983. *Etnología del Istmo Veracruzano*. Mexico City: UNAM-IIA.

Munn, H. 1984. The opossum in Mesoamerican mythology. *Journal of Latin American Lore* 10(1):23–62.

Muñoz Camargo, D. 1981. *Descripción de la ciudad y provincia de Tlaxcala . . . gobierno y ennoblecimiento dellas*. Mexico City: UNAM-IIF. [Facsimile of the Glasgow ed.].

Munz, P. 1986. *Cuando se quiebra la rama dorada. ¿Estructuralismo o tipología?*. Trans. by F. Patán. Mexico City: FCE.

Musgrave-Portilla, M. 1982. The nahualli or transforming wizard in Pre- and Post-conquest Mesoamerica. *Journal of Latin American Lore* 8(1):3–62.

Nadel, S. F. 1955. *Fundamentos de la antropología social*. Trans. by F. M. Torner. Mexico City: FCE.

Nagel, E. 1961. *The Structure of Science*. New York: Harcourt, Brace & World.

Nash, J. 1970. *In the Eyes of the Ancestors: Belief and Behavior in a Mayan Community*. Prospect Heights, Ill.: Waveland Press.

Nash, M. 1957. Cultural persistences and social structures: The Mesoamerican calendar survivals. *Southwestern Journal of Anthropology* 13:144–55.

Navarrete, C. 1966. Cuentos del Soconusco, Chiapas. In *Summa anthropologica en homenaje a Roberto J. Weitlaner*, 421–28. Mexico City: SEP-INAH.

———. 1982. *San Pascualito Rey y el culto a la Muerte en Chiapas*. Mexico City: UNAM-IIA.

Needham, R. 1979. *Symbolic Classification*. Santa Monica, Cal.: Goodyear Publishing Company.

Neuenswander, H. 1981. Vestiges of early Maya time concepts in a contemporary Maya (Cubulco Achi) community: Implications for epigraphy. *Estudios de Cultura Maya* 13:125–63.

Nicholson, H. B. 1957. Topiltzin Quetzalcoatl of Tollan: A Problem in Mesoamerican Ethnohistory. Ph.D. diss., Harvard University.

———. 1971. Religion in Pre-Hispanic Central Mexico. In *Handbook of Middle American Indians*, vol. 10, *Archaeology of Northern Mesoamerica*, Part one, ed. by G. F. Ekholm and I. Bernal, 395–446. Austin: University of Texas Press.

———. 1976. Preclassic Mesoamerican iconography from the perspective of the Postclassic: Problems in interpretational analysis. In *Origins of Religious Art and Iconography in Preclassic Mesoamerica*, ed. by H. B. Nicholson, 157–75. Los Angeles: UCLA Latin American Center Publications.

———. 1978. The deity 9 Wind "Ehecatl-Quetzalcoatl" in the Mixteca pictorials. *Journal of Latin American Lore* 4(1):61–92.

———. 1979. Ehecatl Quetzalcoatl vs. Topiltzin Quetzalcoatl of Tollan: A problem in Mesoamerican religion and history. *Actes du XLIIe Congrès International des Américanistes*, 6:35–47. Paris: Société des Américanistes.

Niederberger, C. 1976. *Zohapilco. Cinco milenios de ocupación humana en un sitio lacustre de la Cuenca de México*. Mexico City: INAH-Departamento de Prehistoria.

————. 1987. *Paleopaysages et Archeologie pré-urbaine du Bassin de Mexico*. 2 vols. Mexico City: Centre d'Etudes Mexicaines et Centraméricaines.

Nimuendajú, C. 1963. The Tucuna. In *Handbook of South American Indians*, vol. 3, *The Tropical Forest Tribes*, ed. by J. H. Steward, 713–25. New York: Cooper Square Publishers.

Ntumba, T. 1985. ¿Existe un mito del mito?. *Diógenes* 132:113–35.

Núñez de la Vega, Fr. F. 1702. *Constituciones dioecesanas del Obispado de Chiapas*. Rome: Nueva Imprenta y Formación de Caracteres de Caietano Zenob.

Nutini, H. G. 1988. *Todos Santos in Rural Tlaxcala. A Syncretic, Expressive, and Symbolic Analysis of the Cult of the Dead*. Princeton: Princeton University Press.

Obregón Rodríguez, M. C. 1985. El atavío de los tlatoque mexicas. lic. thesis in history, UNAM.

Orellana, S. L. 1975. Folk literature of the Tzutujil Maya. *Anthropos* 70:839–76.

Ortega y Gasset, J. 1964. *Ideas y creencias*. 7th ed. Madrid: Espasa-Calpe.

————. 1984. *Historia como sistema y otros ensayos filosóficos*. Madrid: SARPE.

Ortiz, A. 1985. Entrevista con un narrador purépecha. Los cuentos salen de un vivir. *México indígena* 5:58–63.

Ortiz de Montellano, B. R. 1976. ¿Una clasificación botánica entre los nahoas? In *Estado actual del conocimiento en plantas medicinales mexicanas*, 27–49. Mexico City: Instituto Mexicano para el Estudio de las Plantas Medicinales.

————. 1984. El conocimiento de la naturaleza entre los mexicas. Taxonomía. In *Historia general de la medicina en México*, vol. 1, *México antiguo*, ed. by A. López Austin and C. Viesca Treviño, 115–32. Mexico City: UNAM-Facultad de Medicina/Academia Nacional de Medicina.

Ovidio. 1985. *Metamorfosis*. 2 vols. Ed. by R. Bonifaz Nuño. Mexico City: SEP-Cultura.

Palmer, F. R. 1978. *La semántica. Una nueva introducción*. Trans. by A. Poniato. Mexico City: Siglo Veintiuno Editores.

Pané, Fr. R. 1974. *Relación acerca de las antigüedades de los indios: el primer tratado escrito en América*. Ed. by J. J. Arrom. Mexico City: Siglo Veintiuno Editores.

Parsons, E. C. 1918. Nativity myth at Laguna and Zuñi. *Journal of American Folklore* 31(120):256–63.

————. 1966. *Mitla, Town of the Souls and Other Zapoteco-Speaking Pueblos of Oaxaca, Mexico*. Chicago: University of Chicago Press.

Paso y Troncoso, F. del. 1886. Estudios sobre la historia de la medicina en México. *Anales del Museo Nacional de México* 3:137–235.

————. 1979. [Facsimile]. *Descripción, historia y exposición del Códice Borbónico*. Mexico City: Siglo Veintiuno.

Paz, O. 1984. *Claude Lévi-Strauss o el nuevo festín de Edipo*. 5th ed. Mexico City: Editorial Joaquín Mortiz.

Pérez, S. 1986. Oralidad: estructura y reproducción del mito. In *Palabras devueltas. Homenaje a Claude Lévi-Strauss*, ed. by J. J. and Y. -M. Gourio, 61–69. Mexico City: INAH/Instituto Francés de América Latina/Centre d'Etudes Mexicaines et Centramericaines.

Pérez Castro, A. B. 1978. Mitos, leyendas y relatos de hechos y sucedidos en Hidalgo-titlán, Ver. Manuscript.

Perrin, M. 1980. *El camino de los indios muertos. Mitos y símbolos guajiros.* Trans. by F. Núñez. Caracas: Monte Avila Editores.

Petrich, P. 1985. *La alimentación mochó: acto y palabra (Estudio etnolingüístico).* San Cristóbal de Las Casas: Centro de Estudios Indígenas, UACH.

———. 1986. Los mochós cuentan de dónde vino el fuego. *Estudios de Cultura Maya* 16:271–94.

Phelan, J. L. 1972. *El reino milenario de los franciscanos en el Nuevo Mundo.* Trans. by J. Vázquez de Knauth. Mexico City: UNAM-IIH.

Piña Chan, R. 1968. *Jaina. La casa en el agua.* Mexico City: INAH.

Poincaré, H. 1952. *Science and Hypothesis.* Trans. by G. B. Halstead. New York: Dover.

Pomar, J. B. de, 1985–86. *Relación de la ciudad y provincia de Tetzcoco.* In *Relaciones geográficas del siglo XVI: México,* ed. by R. Acuña, 3:21–113. Mexico City: UNAM-IIA.

Ponce, P. 1953. *Breve relación de los dioses y ritos de la gentilidad.* In *Tratado de las idolatrías . . . ,* by Serna et al., ed. by F. del Paso y Troncoso, 1:369–80. Mexico City: Ediciones Fuente Cultural.

Popol Vuh: The Sacred Book of the Ancient Quiche Maya. 1950. Trans. by A. Recinos. English trans. by D. Goetz and S. G. Morley. Norman: Univ. Oklahoma Press.

Popol vuh. Las antiguas historias del Quiché. 1964. 7th ed. Trans. by A. Recinos. Mexico City: FCE.

Portal, M. A. 1986. *Cuentos y mitos en una zona mazateca.* Mexico City: INAH.

Preuss, K. T. 1912. *Die Nayarit-Expedition. Textaufnahmen und Beobachtungen unter Mexikanischen Indianern.* Vol. 1, *Die Religion der Cora-Indianer in Texten nebst Wörtebuch.* Leipzig: B. C. Teubner.

———. 1982. *Mitos y cuentos nahuas de la Sierra Madre Occidental.* Ed. by E. Ziehm, trans. by M. Frenk-Westheim. Mexico City: INI.

Primeros memoriales. 1905. [Facsimile of Nahuatl texts of Sahagún's informants]. Ed. by F. del Paso y Troncoso. Vol. 6. Madrid: Fototipia de Hauser y Menet.

Propp, V. J. 1972. Estructura e historia en el estudio de los cuentos. In *Polémica Lévi-Strauss–Propp,* by C. Lévi-Strauss and V. Propp, trans. by J. M. Arancibia. Madrid: Editorial Fundamentos.

———. 1977. *Morfología del cuento.* 3d ed. Trans. by L. Ortiz. Madrid: Editorial Fundamentos.

Pury, S. de, 1982. Cuentos y cantos de Tlaxcalancingo, Puebla. *Tlalocan* 9:71–105.

Questions of King Milinda (Milindapañha). 1963. 2 vols. Trans. by T. W. Rhys Davids. New York: Dover Publications.

Quiroz-Rodiles, A. 1945. Breve historia de la obstetricia en Mexico. *Obstetricia y Ginecologia Latino-Americanas* 3:77–92.

Radcliffe-Brown, A. R. 1935. On the concept of function in social science. *American Anthropologist* 37:394–402.

———. 1965. *Structure and Function in Primitive Society.* New York: Free Press.

Radin, P. 1943–44. Cuentos y leyendas de los zapotecos. *Tlalocan* 1(1–3):3–30, 134–54, 194–226.

————. 1944. The nature and problems of Mexican Indian mythology. *Journal of American Folklore* 57(223):26–36.

————. 1978. *The Trickster: A Study in American Indian Mythology.* New York: Schocken Books.

Radin, S., and A. M. Espinosa. 1917. *El folklore de Oaxaca, recogido por Paul Radin y publicado por Aurelio M. Espinosa.* New York: Escuela Internacional de Arqueología y Etnología Americanas/The Hispanic Society of America.

Raglan, Lord. 1965. Myth and ritual. In *Myth: A Symposium*, ed. by T. A. Sebeok, 122–35. Bloomington: Indiana University Press.

Ramírez Castañeda, E. 1985. Así contaban los antiguos. *México indígena* 5:14–17.

————. 1987. *El fin de los montiocs. Tradición oral de los huaves de San Mateo del Mar, Oaxaca.* Mexico City: INAH.

Ramírez-Pulido, J. and C. Müdespacher. 1987. Estado actual y perspectivas del conocimiento de los mamíferos de México. *Ciencia. Revista de la Academia de la Investigación Científica* 38(1):49–67.

Ramón, A. 1972. *Dioses zapotecos.* Mexico City: SEP-INAH-Museo Nacional de Antropología–Servicios Educativos.

Rank, O. n.d. El sueño y el mito. In *La interpretación de los sueños*, by S. Freud, trans. by L. López-Ballesteros y de Torres, 2:285–306.

Redfield, M. P. 1935. *The Folk Literature of a Yucatecan Town.* Washington: Carnegie Institution.

Redfield, R. 1942. *The Folk Culture of Yucatan.* Chicago: University of Chicago Press.

Redfield, R., and A. Villa Rojas. 1934. *Chan Kom: A Maya Village.* Washington, D.C.: Carnegie Institution of Washington.

Relación de las ceremonias . . . 1977. [Facsimile of 1541 ed.]. Ed. by J. Tudela. Morelia, Michoacan: Balsal Editores.

Relación del pueblo de Ocelotepeque. 1984. In *Relaciones geográficas del siglo XVI: Antequera*, ed. by R. Acuña, 1:87–93. Mexico City: UNAM-IIA.

Relaciones de Xonotla y Tetela. 1985. In *Relaciones geográficas del siglo XVI: Tlaxcala*, ed. by R. Acuña, 2:375–436. Mexico City: UNAM-IIA.

Relaciones histórico-geográficas de la Gobernación de Yucatán (Mérida, Valladolid y Tabasco). 1983. 2 vols. Ed. by M. de la Garza, A. L. Izquierdo, M. del C. León and T. Figueroa. Mexico City: UNAM-IIF-CEM.

Relatos, mitos y leyendas de la Chinantla. 1981. 2d ed. Ed. by R. L. Weitlaner. Compiled by Roberto J. Weitlaner. Mexico City: INI.

Rendón, J. J. 1970. El tlacuache y el coyote en zapoteco. *Tlalocan* 6:119–23.

Reyes García, L. 1961. *Pasión y muerte del Cristo Sol.* Xalapa: Universidad Veracruzana.

————. 1978. La visión cosmológica y la organización del imperio mexica. In *Mesoamérica. Homenaje al doctor Paul Kirchhoff*, ed. by B. Dahlgren, 34–40. Mexico City: SEP-INAH.

Reyes Gómez, L. 1988. Introducción a la medicina zoque. Una aproximación etnolingüística. In *Estudios Recientes en el Area Zoque*, ed. by S. Villasana Bénitez and L. Reyes Gómez, 158–383. Chiapas: UACH.

Ricard, R. 1947. *La conquista espiritual de México.* Trans. by A. M. Garibay K. Mexico City: Editorial Jus/Editorial Polis.

Ricoeur, P. 1985. The history of religions and the phenomenology of time consciousness. In *The History of Religions: Retrospect and Prospect*, ed. by J. M. Kitagawa, 13–30. New York: Macmillan.

Ritual de los Bacabes. 1987. Ed. by R. Arzápalo Marín. México UNAM-IIF-CEM.

Ritual of the Bacabs. 1965. Trans. by R. L. Roys. Norman: University of Oklahoma Press.

Rivera Dorado, M. 1985. *Los mayas de la antigüedad*. Madrid: Editorial Alhambra.

———. 1986a. Cambios en la religión maya, desde el período clásico a los tiempos de Hernán Cortés. In *Los mayas de los tiempos tardíos*, ed. by M. Rivera and A. Ciudad, 147–65. Madrid: Sociedad Española de Estudios Mayas/Instituto de Cooperación Iberoamericana.

———. 1986b. *La religión maya*. Madrid: Alianza Editorial.

———. 1987. Una interpretación del mito Hunahpú e Ixbalanqué. In *Memorias del Primer Coloquio Internacional de Mayistas*, (August 5–10, 1985) 1115–32. Mexico City: UNAM-IIF-CEM.

Robinson, D. F. 1961. Textos de medicina náhuat. *América Indígena* 21(4):345–54.

Rodríguez Adrados, F. 1984. El mito griego y la vida en Grecia. In *El mito ante la antropología y la historia*, ed. by J. Alcina Franch, 49–73. Madrid: Centro de Investigaciones Sociológicas/Siglo Veintiuno de España Editores.

Rojas Rabiela, T., ed. 1983. *Paul Kirchhoff: principios estructurales en el México antiguo*. Mexico City: CIESAS/SEP-Cultura.

Roys, R. L. 1931. *The ethno-botany of the Maya*. New Orleans: Department of Middle American Research, Tulane University.

Rubel, A. J. 1985. Dos cuentos tzotziles de San Bartolomé de los Llanos (Venustiano Carranza), Chiapas. Trans. by V. M. Esponda. *Revista de la UNACH, Tuxtla Gutiérrez, Chiapas* (2a época) 1:77–83.

Ruiz de Alarcón, H. 1953. *Tratado de las supersticiones . . .* In *Tratado de las idolatrías . . .* by Serna et al., ed. by F. del Paso y Troncoso, 2:17–130. Mexico City: Ediciones Fuente Cultural.

———. 1984. *Treatise on the heathen superstitions that today live among the Indians native to this New Spain, 1629*. Trans. by J. R. Andrews and R. Hassig. Norman: University of Oklahoma Press.

Ryesky, D. 1976. *Conceptos tradicionales de la medicina en un pueblo mexicano. Un análisis antropológico*. Trans. by Y. Sassoon. Setentas 309. Mexico City: SEP.

Sahagún, Fr. B. de. 1956. *Historia general de las cosas de Nueva España*. 4 vols. Ed. by A. M. Garibay K. Mexico City: Editorial Porrúa.

Saint Augustine. 1907. *Confessions*. Trans. by E. B. Pusey. London: J. M. Dent.

Saler, B. 1969. *Nagual, brujo y hechicero en un pueblo quiché*. Guatemala: Ministerio de Educación.

Salustio. 1956. *De los dioses y del mundo*. Trans. by G. Murray. In *La religión griega. Cinco ensayos sobre la evolución de las divinidades clásicas*, by G. Murray, trans. by S. Ferrari and V. D. Bouilly, 202–26. Buenos Aires: Editorial Nova.

Sánchez Azuará, G. 1985. Los indígenas abandonados por sus dioses. *México indígena* 5:17–21.

Sánchez de Aguilar, P. 1953. *Informe contra idolorum cvltores . . .* In *Tratado de las idola-*

trías . . . by Serna et al., ed. by F. del Paso y Troncoso, 2:181–336. Mexico City: Ediciones Fuente Cultural.

Sánchez Vázquez, A. 1970. Estructuralismo e historia. In *Estructuralismo y marxismo*, by H. Lefevbre et al., 41–79. Mexico City: Editorial Grijalbo.

———. 1985. *Filosofía de la praxis*. 4th ed. Mexico City: Editorial Grijalbo.

Santamaría, F. J. 1974. *Diccionario de mejicanismos*. 2d ed. Mexico City: Editorial Porrúa.

Saussure, F. de. 1982. *Curso de lingüística general*. Ed. by C. Bally and A. Sechehaye. Trans. by M. Armiño. Mexico City: Ediciones Nuevomar.

Scheffler, L. 1983. *La literatura oral tradicional de los indígenas de México. Antología*. Mexico City: Dirección General de Culturas Populares de la SEP/Premiá Editora de Libros.

Schökel, L. A. 1984. Lenguaje mítico y simbólico en el Antiguo Testamento. In *El mito ante la antropología y la historia*, ed. by J. Alcina Franch, 75–97. Madrid: Centro de Investigaciones Sociológicas/Siglo Veintiuno de España Editores.

Schultze Jena, L. 1946. *La vida y las creencias de los indígenas quichés de Guatemala*. Trans. by A. Goubaud Carrera and H. D. Sapper. Guatemala: Sociedad de Geografía e Historia de Guatemala.

———. 1977. *Mitos y leyendas de los pipiles de Izalco*. Trans. by G. Menjivar Rieken and A. Parada Fortín. San Salvador, El Salvador: Ediciones Cuscatlán.

Schumann, O. 1988. El origen del maíz (versión k'ekchi'). In *La etnología: temas y tendencias. I Coloquio Paul Kirchhoff*, 213–18. Mexico City: UNAM-IIA.

Sedat S., G. 1955. *Nuevo diccionario de las lenguas k'ekchi' y española*. 2d ed. Chamelco, Alta Verapaz, Guatemala: Casa Editorial Antonio Goubaud Carrera.

Sedeño, L., and M. E. Becerril. 1985. *Dos culturas y una infancia: psicoanálisis de una etnia en peligro*. Mexico City: FCE.

Segre, E. 1987. *Las máscaras de lo sagrado*. Trans. by R. Solís Vicarte. Mexico City: INAH.

Seis versiones del diluvio. 1983. Mexico City: SEP–Dirección General de Culturas Populares.

Séjourné, L. 1975. *Pensamiento y religión en el México antiguo*. Trans. by A. Orfila Reynal. Mexico City: FCE.

Seler, E. 1904. Wall paintings of Mitla. In *Mexican and Central American Antiquities, Calendar Systems, and History*, by E. Seler et al., trans. by C. P. Bowditch, 243–324. Washington, D.C.: Smithsonian Institution.

———. 1961. Die Tierbilder der mexikanischen und der Maya-Handshriften. In *Gesammelte Abhandlungen zur Amerikanischen Sprach- und Altertumskunde*, 4:453–758. Graz, Austria: Akademische Druck- und Verlagsanstalt.

———. 1963. *Comentarios al Códice Borgia*. 2 vols. Trans. by M. Frenk. Mexico City: FCE.

Serna, J. de la. 1953. *Manual de ministros de indios* . . . In *Tratado de las idolatrías* . . . by Serna et al., ed. by F. del Paso y Troncoso, 1:47–368. Mexico City: Ediciones Fuente Cultural.

Service, E. R. 1984. *Los orígenes del estado y de la civilización. El proceso de la evolución cultural*. Trans. by M.-C. Ruiz de Elvira Hidalgo. Madrid: Alianza Editorial.

Shaw, M. 1971. *According to Our Ancestors: Folk Texts from Guatemala and Honduras*. Norman: Summer Institute of Linguistics.

Signorini, I., and A. Lupo. 1988. Las fuerzas anímicas en el pensamiento nahua. *México indígena* 4(20):13–21.

————. 1989. *Los tres pilares de la vida. Almas, cuerpo, enfermedad entre los nahuas de la Sierra de Puebla*. Trans. by A. Cortés. Xalapa: Editorial UV.

Siméon, R. 1977. *Diccionario de la lengua náhuatl o mexicana*. Trans. by J. Oliva de Coll. Mexico City: Siglo Veintiuno Editores.

Slocum, M. C. 1965. The origin of corn and other Tzeltal myths. *Tlalocan* 5(1):1–45.

Smith, W. R. 1965. *The Religion of the Semites: The Fundamental Institutions*. New York: Meridian Books.

Sneath, P. H. A., and R. R. Sokal. 1973. *Numerical Taxonomy: The Principles and Practice of Classification*. San Francisco: W. H. Freeman and Company.

Solís Olguín, F. R. 1976. *Catálogo de la escultura mexica en el Museo de Santa Cecilia Acatitlan*. Santa Cecilia Acatitlan, México: INAH.

Sorel, G. n.d. *Reflexiones sobre la violencia*. Trans. by L. A. Ruiz. Buenos Aires: Editorial La Pleyade.

Sotelo Santos, L. E. 1988. *Las ideas cosmológicas mayas en el siglo XVI*. Mexico City: UNAM-IIF-CEM.

Soustelle, J. 1959. *Pensamiento cosmológico de los antiguos mexicanos (Representación del mundo y del espacio)*. Trans. by M. E. Landa A. Puebla, Mexico City: Federación Estudiantil Poblana.

————. 1982. *El universo de los aztecas*. Trans. by J. L. Martínez and J. J. Utrilla. Mexico City: FCE.

Spence, L. 1923. *The Gods of Mexico*. London: Adelphi Terrace/T. Fisher Unwin Ltd.

————. [1914] 1977. *The Myths of Mexico and Peru*. Boston: Longwood Press.

Spencer, H. 1972. *On social evolution*. Ed. by J. D. Y. Peel. Chicago: University of Chicago Press.

Spranz, B. 1982. *Los dioses en los códices mexicanos del grupo Borgia. Una investigación iconográfica*. Trans. by M. Martínez Peñaloza. Mexico City: FCE.

Stiles, N., I. Maya, and M. Castillo. 1985. El diluvio y otros relatos nahuas de la Huasteca Hidalguense. *Tlalocan* 10:15–32.

Stresser-Pean, G. 1952–53. Les indiens huasteques. *Revista Mexicana de Estudios Antropológicos* 13(2–3):213–34.

Suárez de Cepeda, J. 1983. *Relación de los indios colimas de la Nueva Granada. 1581*. Mexico City: Editorial Innovación.

Sullivan, T. D. 1980. Tlatoani and tlatocayotl in the Sahagun manuscripts. *Estudios de Cultura Náhuatl* 14:225–38.

Swadesh, M., and M. Sancho. 1966. *Los mil elementos del mexicano clásico. Base analítica de la lengua nahua*. Mexico City: UNAM-IIH.

Taggart, J. M. 1983. *Nahuat Myth and Social Structure*. Austin: University of Texas Press.

Taylor, F. S. 1957. *Los alquimistas. Fundadores de la química moderna*. Trans. by A. and F. Giral. Mexico City: FCE.

Técnicos bilingües de la Unidad Regional de Acayucan. 1985. *Agua, mundo, montaña*.

Narrativa nahua, mixe y popoluca del Sur de Veracruz. Tlahuapan, Puebla: Premiá Editora de Libros.

Tedlock, B. 1982. *Time and the Highland Maya.* Albuquerque: University of New Mexico Press.

Thompson, J. E. S. 1934. Skybearers, colors and directions in Maya and Mexican religion. *Contributions to American Archaeology* (Washington, Carnegie Institution; contribution 10) 2:209–42.

———. 1962. *A Catalog of Maya Hieroglyphs.* Norman: University of Oklahoma Press.

———. 1963. *The Rise and Fall of Maya Civilization.* Norman: University of Oklahoma Press.

———. 1964. *Grandeza y decadencia de los mayas.* 2d ed. Trans. by F. Blanco. Mexico City: Siglo Veintiuno Editores.

———. 1965–67. Maya creation myths. *Estudios de Cultura Maya* 5:13–32, 6:15–43.

———. 1970a. *Maya History and Religion.* Norman: University of Oklahoma Press.

———. 1970b. The Bacabs: Their portraits and their glyphs. *Papers of Peabody Museum, Cambridge, Harvard University* 61:471–87.

———. 1972. [Facsimile]. *A Commentary on the Dresden Codex: A Maya Hieroglyphic Book.* Philadelphia: American Philosophical Society.

———. 1975. *Historia y religión de los mayas.* Trans. by F. Blanco. Mexico City: Siglo Veintiuno Editores.

———. 1978. *Maya Hieroglyphic Writing: An Introduction.* 3d ed. Norman: University of Oklahoma Press.

Thompson, S. 1955–57. *Motif-index of folk-literature.* 5 vols. Rev. ed. Copenhagen: Rosenkilde and Bagger.

———. 1965. Myth and folktales. In *Myth: A Symposium,* ed. by T. A. Sebeok. Bloomington: Indiana University Press.

Timasheff, N. S. 1971. *La teoría sociológica. Su naturaleza y desarrollo.* Trans. by F. M. Torner. Mexico City: FCE.

Titulo de Totonicapán. 1983. Trans. by R. M. Carmack and J. L. Mondloch. Mexico City: UNAM-IIF-CEM.

Tlacuache y los leones, el. 1985. *México Indígena* 4:61–62.

Tocqueville, A. de. 1945. *Democracy in America.* 2 vols. Ed. by P. Bradley. Trans. by H. Reeve. New York: Alfred A. Knopf.

Todorov, T. 1981. *Introducción a la literatura fantástica.* 2d ed. Mexico City: Premiá Editora de Libros.

———. 1985. Las categorías del relato literario. In *Análisis estructural del relato,* by Roland Barthes, et al., 4th ed., trans. by B. D. and A. N. Vaisse, 159–95. Tlahuapan, Puebla: Premiá Editora de Libros.

Tonalámatl de Aubin. 1981. (Manuscrits Mexicains nos. 18–19). Ed. by C. Aguilera. Tlaxcala: Estado de Tlaxcala.

Torquemada, Fr. J. de. 1969. *Monarquía indiana.* 3 vols. 4th ed. Mexico City: Editorial Porrúa.

Toscano, S. 1952. *Arte precolombino de México y de la América Central.* 2d ed. Mexico City: UNAM-IIE.

Townsend, R. F. 1979. *State and Cosmos in the Art of Tenochtitlan*. Washington, D.C.: Dumbarton Oaks.

Tozzer, A. M. 1982. *Mayas y lacandones. Un estudio comparativo*. Mexico City: INI.

Trías, E. 1970. *Metodología del pensamiento mágico*. Barcelona: Edhasa.

Trujillo Maldonado, J. 1980. Ja' cuento yu' un conejo soc coyote. El conejo y el coyote. Relato en tzeltal de Ocosingo, Chiapas. *Tlalocan* 8:167–77.

Turner, V. W. 1967. *The Forest of Symbols: Aspects of Ndembu Ritual*. Ithaca: Cornell University Press.

—————. 1975. Mito y símbolo. In *Enciclopedia internacional de las ciencias sociales*, ed. by D. L. Sills, 7:150–54. Madrid: Aguilar.

Turok, M. 1976. Diseño y símbolo en el huipil ceremonial de Magdalenas, Chiapas. *Boletín del Departamento de Investigación de las Tradiciones Populares* 3:123–36.

Tylor, E. B. 1977. *Los orígenes de la cultura*. Trans. by M. Suárez. Madrid: Editorial Ayuso.

Uejkauitl nauaueuejtlajtoli. Cuentos nahuas. Tradición oral indígena. 1982. Mexico City: SEP, CONAFE.

Umberger, E. 1986. Events commemorated by date plaques at the Templo Mayor: Further thoughts on the solar metaphor. In *The Aztec Templo Mayor*, ed. by E. H. Boone, 411–49. Washington, D.C.: Dumbarton Oaks.

Urban. 1979. *Lenguaje y realidad. La filosofía del lenguaje y los principios del simbolismo*. Trans. by C. Villegas and J. Portilla. Mexico City: FCE.

Vaillant, G. C. 1960. *La civilización azteca*. 2d ed. Trans. by S. Vasconcelos. Mexico City: FCE.

Valiñas, L. 1985. El diluvio y la tradición oral. *México Indígena* 4:22–24.

Vansina, J. 1968. *La tradición oral*. 2d ed. Trans. by M. M. Llongueras. Barcelona: Editorial Labor.

Vargas Llosa, M. 1981. *La guerra del fin del mundo*. Barcelona: Editorial Seix Barral.

Veinte himnos sacros de los nahuas [text of Sahagún's informants]. 1958. Ed. by A. M. Garibay K. Mexico City: UNAM-IIH-SCE.

Vilar, P. 1981. *Iniciación al vocabulario del análisis histórico*. 3d ed. Trans. by M. D. Folch. Barcelona: Editorial Crítica, Grupo Editorial Grijalbo.

Villacorta C., J. Antonio, and C. A. Villacorta. 1976. *Códices mayas reproducidos y desarrollados*. 2d ed. Guatemala: n.p.

Villa Rojas, A. 1947. Kinship and nagualism in a Tzeltal community, Southeastern Mexico. *American Anthropologist* 49:578–87.

—————. 1978. *Los elegidos de Dios. Etnografía de los mayas de Quintana Roo*. Mexico City: INI.

Vogt, E. Z. 1966a. Conceptos de los antiguos mayas en la religión zinacanteca contemporánea. In *Los zinacantecos. Un pueblo tzotzil de los Altos de Chiapas*, ed. by E. Z. Vogt, 88–96. Mexico City: INI.

—————. 1966b. Réplica estructural y réplica conceptual en la cultura zinacanteca. In *Los zinacantecos. Un pueblo tzotzil de los Altos de Chiapas*, ed. by E. Z. Vogt, 129–41. Mexico City: INI.

—————. 1971. The genetic model and Maya cultural development. In *Desarrollo cultural de los mayas*, ed. by E. Z. Vogt and A. Ruz L., 9–48. Mexico City: UNAM–Coordinación de Humanidades–CEM.

————. 1973. *Los zinacantecos: un grupo maya en el siglo XX*. Trans. by C. Viqueira. Setentas 69. Mexico City: SEP.

————. 1976. *Tortillas for the Gods*. Cambridge: Harvard University Press.

Voloshinov, V. N. 1976. *El signo ideológico y la filosofía del lenguaje*. Trans. by L. Matieyka, I. R. Titunik, and R. M. Russovich. Buenos Aires: Ediciones Nueva Visión.

Vygotsky, L. S. n.d. *Pensamiento y lenguaje. Teoría del desarrollo cultural de las funciones psíquicas*. Mexico City: Editorial Alfa y Omega, Ediciones Quinto Sol.

Wagley, C. 1949. *The Social and Religious Life of a Guatemalan Village*. Memoirs of the American Anthropological Society 71. [New York].

————. 1957. *Santiago Chimaltenango. Estudio antropológico-social de una comunidad indígena de Huehuetenango*. Trans. by J. Noval. Guatemala: Seminario de Integración Social Guatemalteca.

Walker, E. P., et al. 1975. *Mammals of the World*. 2 vols. 3d ed. Baltimore: Johns Hopkins University Press.

Wasson, R. G. 1980. *The Wondrous Mushroom: Mycolatry in Mesoamerica*. New York: McGraw-Hill.

Watts, A. W. 1954. *Myth and Ritual in Christianity*. London: Thames and Hudson.

Weitlaner, R. J., and C. A. Castro. 1973. *Usila (morada de colibríes)*. Mexico City: Museo Nacional de Antropología.

Wellek, R., and A. Warren. 1949. *Theory of Literature*. New York: Harcourt, Brace & Co.

Wheelwright, P. 1965. The semantic approach to myth. In *Myth: A Symposium*, ed. by T. A. Sebeok, 154–68. Bloomington: Indiana University Press.

White, A. D. 1972. *La lucha entre el dogmatismo y la ciencia en el seno de la cristianidad*. Trans. by R. Rivero Castro. Mexico City: Siglo Veintiuno Editores.

White, L. A. 1949. *The Science of Culture*. New York: Farrar, Strauss and Co.

Whitecotton, J. W. 1985. *Los zapotecos. Príncipes, sacerdotes y campesinos*. Trans. by S. Mastrangelo. Mexico City: FCE.

Williams, R. 1980. *Marxismo y literatura*. Trans. by P. di Masso. Barcelona: Ediciones Península.

Williams García, R. 1972. *Mitos tepehuas*. Setentas 27. Mexico City: SEP.

Williams García, R., and C. García Ramos. 1980. *Tradición oral en Tajín*. Jalapa: SEP–Universidad Veracruzana.

Wirrarika irratsikayari. Canciones, mitos y fiestas huicholes. Tradición oral indígena. 1982. Mexico City: SEP, CONAFE.

Wittfogel, K. A., and E. S. Goldfrank. 1943. Some aspects of Pueblo mythology and society. *Journal of American Folklore* 56(219):17–30.

Wittgenstein, L. 1985. *Comentarios sobre La rama dorada*. Ed. by R. Rhees. Trans. by J. Esquivel. Mexico City: UNAM–Instituto de Investigaciones Filosóficas.

Wright, N. P. 1983. *A Guide to Mexican Mammals and Reptiles*. 4th ed. Mexico City: Minutiae Mexicana.

Wylie, A. 1985. The reaction against analogy. In *Advances in Archaeological Method and Theory*, ed. by M. B. Schiffer, 8:63–111. New York: Academic Press.

Ximénez, Fr. F. 1985. *Primera parte del tesoro de las tres lenguas* . . . Ed. by C. Sáenz de Santa María. Guatemala: Academia de Geografía e Historia de Guatemala.

Zantwijk, R. van. 1979. El parentesco y la afiliación étnica de Huitzilopochtli. *Actes du XLIIe Congrès International des Américanistes*, 6:63–68. Paris: Société des Américanistes.

————. 1985. *The Aztec Arrangement: The Social History of Pre-Spanish Mexico*. Norman: University of Oklahoma Press.

Ziehm, E. 1982. Introduction. In *Mitos y cuentos nahuas*, by K. T. Preuss, ed. by E. Ziehm, trans. by M. Frenk-Westheim. Mexico City: INI.

Zimmer, D. E. 1985. *Dormir y soñar. La mitad nocturna de nuestras vidas*. Trans. by Diorki traductores. Barcelona: Salvat.

Zingg, R. M. 1982. *Los huicholes. Una tribu de artistas*. 2 vols. Trans. by C. Paschero. Mexico City: INI.

INDEX

Abortion, 226
Adam and Eve, 65, 67, 123, 141
Adaptation of system, 278
Adultery, 66
African myth, 214
Agave: god, 68; plant, 115. *See also* Maguey
Alexandrian school, 287
Allegorical concept of myth, 49
Althusser, Louis, 300–301
Anachronism, mythic, 305
Analogy, 356
Ancestors, the: 36, 41, 57, 58, 141, 298
Andean myth, 18
Annales school, 302. *See also* Braudel
Anthropomorphism, 144, 291
Arabian myth, 208
Aristotle, 296–297
Armadillo, 69, 344–345
Arrival of Spanish, 8, 97, 107, 323. *See also* Spanish Conquest
Art, Mesoamerican, 15, 152
Assimilation of myth, 215
Astral: forces, 176; ideas, 254, 259; symbolism, 164
Aztlan, 316

Ball game, 88, 225
Belief: accumulation of, 80–81; and myth, 78; as pretext for aggression, 97–98
Believers, behavior of, 151–152
Biblical: interpretation: literal, 287; Platonic, 287; mythic nature, 290. *See also* Christian references
Binary opposites, 170, 178
Blindness, 65

Bloch, Marc, 181. *See also Annales* school
Boas, Franz: classification, 163; defines myth, 26; Hispanic American folk narrative, 16; myth vs. belief, 92; native belief, 291; rabbit-coyote tales, 244; stories, 245; U.S. narrative, 197
Braudel, Fernand, 11, 300–301, 357. *See also Annales* school
Buddhist reincarnation, 73–74
Buzzard, 237

Calendar, 19, 43, 85. *See also* Calendric System
Calendric: flow, 59; names of gods, 56; succession, 45
Calendric system: and agriculture, 189; disappearance of, 110, 164; divine and human time-space, 86; effects of Conquest, 108; geometry of the universe, 257; Mayan, 46–47, 61–62; miracles, 313; modern Mixtec, 269; mythic origins, 239; Nahua, 48, 52, 64, 147; offerings, 134; pre-Conquest, 50. *See also* Time
Capitalist society, 2
Cardinal directions, 271–272
Carpentier, Alejo, 77–78
Catholic tradition, 288
Central theme of myth, 213, 253
Central themes of book, 21, 23
Chain of adventures, 338
Chaneque, 113, 311
Childbirth, 154, 191, 225, 226, 238
Chili, 191
Christ: the Dead, 136; origin of name, 215; and the Sun, 35
Christian references: animals, 34; ant-